D0072147

LANGUAGE, RELIGION AND POLITICS IN NORTH INDIA

PAUL R. BRASS

Professor of Political Science and Asian Studies
University of Washington

CAMBRIDGE UNIVERSITY PRESS

Published by the Syndics of the Cambridge University Press
Bentley House, 200 Euston Road, London NW1 2DB
American Branch: 32 East 57th Street, New York, N.Y. 10022

© Cambridge University Press 1974

First published 1974

Library of Congress Catalogue Card Number: 73–82453

ISBN: 0 521 20324 4

Typeset in Great Britain
by William Clowes & Sons, Limited
London, Beccles and Colchester
Printed in the United States of America

409.54
B823L

173704

CONTENTS

List of figures and tables

Abbreviations

Acknowledgements

Preface

PART I INTRODUCTION

1 Language, religion and group identities   3

PART II THE POLITICS OF LANGUAGE

2 The Maithili movement in north Bihar   51

PART III THE POLITICS OF LANGUAGE AND RELIGION: URDU AND THE MUSLIM MINORITY IN UTTAR PRADESH AND BIHAR

3 Muslim separatism in the United Provinces: the social context and political strategy of the Muslim minority before partition   119

4 Urdu and Muslim grievances in north India, 1947–71   182

5 Contemporary Muslim politics and political organization in north India   235

PART IV THE POLITICS OF LANGUAGE AND RELIGION IN THE PUNJAB: SIKHS, HINDUS, AND THE PUNJABI LANGUAGE

6 Sikhs and Hindus in the Punjab: the development of social and political differentiation   277

7 Government policy and party politics   337

8 Electoral politics and communal cleavage in the Punjabi Suba   367

PART V CONCLUSION

9 The process of nationality-formation in north India   403

Bibliography   435

Index   451

FIGURES AND TABLES

Figures

1   Political map of India   *page*   xvi
2   Map of the Maithili-speaking areas of Bihar and Nepal, according to
    Grierson; divisions and districts of Bihar, 1972   50
3   Linguistic distribution of Bihar districts according to Grierson and
    according to the census of 1961   85
4   Distribution of Bihar districts according to levels of literacy, urban-
    ization, and industrialization, 1961   89
5   Voting turnout by district in Bihar Legislative Assembly elections,
    1952–69   94
6   Distribution of the top nine support districts for the Congress,
    measured by percentage of valid votes polled in Bihar Legislative
    Assembly elections, 1952–69   96
7   Political divisions of the Punjab, 1956–66   276
8   Punjabi Suba, 1966   324

Tables

2.1   Major languages of Bihar, according to *Census of India*, 1911–61   65
2.2   Estimated speakers of Maithili, Magahi, and Bhojpuri in Bihar,
      1891–1961, using Gait's computation   66
2.3   Percent rural–urban distribution of speakers of Hindi, Maithili,
      Magahi, and Bhojpuri mother tongues in north and south Bihar
      districts, 1961   87
2.4   Selected indices of social mobilization and assimilation to Hindi in
      Bihar districts, 1961   88
2.5   English bilingualism in Bihar state, 1961   92
2.6   Male literacy in English in Bihar by natural divisions, 1901–31 (in
      percentages)   93
3.1   Urban and rural populations in Uttar Pradesh by religion, 1881–
      1961 (in percentages)   143
3.2   Number and percentage of Muslims in the total population and in
      the population at school in the major provinces of India, 1871–2   146
3.3   Male literacy by religion in the United Provinces, 1881–1931 (in
      percentages)   147
3.4   Male English literacy by religion in the United Provinces, 1891–
      1931 (in percentages)   148

Figures and Tables

3.5 Male literate and illiterate populations of the United Provinces by religion, 1872–1931   149

3.6 Occupation by religion (for selected occupations) in the United Provinces, 1921   152

3.7 Occupation by religion (for selected occupations) in the United Provinces, 1911   154

3.8 Hindi, Urdu, and English newspapers and periodicals in Uttar Pradesh, 1873–1960   159

4.1 Hindustani, Hindi, and Urdu in Uttar Pradesh, 1881–1961   190

4.2 Hindustani, Hindi, and Urdu in Bihar, 1881–1961   192

4.3 Ratio of Urdu-speakers to the Muslim populations of Uttar Pradesh and Bihar, 1951 and 1961   196

4.4 Facilities for instruction in Urdu at the primary and secondary stages of education in Uttar Pradesh   208

4.5 Facilities for instruction in Urdu at the primary and secondary stages of education in Bihar   209

4.6 Representation of Muslims in government and administration in Uttar Pradesh, 1 July 1964   231

6.1 Speakers of most important languages in the Punjab, 1911–61   295

6.2 Changes in the proportions of Hindus, Hindi-speakers, Sikhs, and Punjabi-speakers in the Punjab, 1921 and 1961   297

6.3 Total and urban population by religion in the undivided Punjab, 1881–1941 (in percentages)   299

6.4 Urban and rural populations in the Punjab (post-partition boundaries) by religion, 1901–61 (in percentages)   301

6.5 Urban and rural populations of Hindus and Sikhs in the Punjab by division, 1961 census (in percentages)   302

6.6 Male literacy by religion in the Punjab, 1901–31 (in percentages)   302

6.7 Male English literacy by religion in the Punjab, 1901–31 (in percentages)   303

6.8 Male literacy in the most important vernaculars (scripts) of the Punjab by religion, 1901 and 1931   304

6.9 Number and percentage of male literates in important vernaculars of the Punjab as a proportion of the total literates of the major religious groups, 1901 and 1931   305

6.10 Newspapers and periodicals published in the Punjab by script, 1891–1931   307

6.11 Newspapers and periodicals published in the Punjab (pre- and post-reorganization) by language   307

6.12 Books published in the Punjab by language, 1891–1931   308

7.1 Punjab Legislative Assembly election results by party and community, 1946   358

7.2 Composition of the Punjab Legislative Assembly by party and community, 1962–7   359

Figures and Tables

7.3   Composition of the Punjab Legislative Assembly by party and community, 1967 general elections   360

7.4   Composition of the Punjab Legislative Assembly by party and community, 1969 mid-term elections   361

7.5   Party constituents of Punjab ministries, 1967–71   363

8.1   Percentage of votes polled by political parties in the Punjab, 1952–1972   371

8.2   Number and percentage of seats won by political parties in Punjab Legislative Assembly elections, 1952–72   372

8.3   Correlation matrix of cultural variables and Congress vote shares for Punjab grouped constituencies, 1952–69   381

8.4   Correlation matrix of cultural variables and Akali votes for Punjab grouped constituencies, 1952–69   385

8.5   Correlation matrix of cultural variables and Jan Sangh votes for Punjab grouped constituencies, 1952–69   388

8.6   Correlation matrix of cultural variables and Communist votes for Punjab grouped constituencies, 1952–69   391

8.7   Correlation matrix of cultural variables and votes for the SCF and RPI for Punjab grouped constituencies, 1952–69   392

8.8   Correlation matrix of cultural variables and independent votes for Punjab grouped constituencies, 1952–69   394

8.9   Summary of positive and negative correlations for communal variables and party votes for Punjab grouped constituencies, 1952–69   396

ABBREVIATIONS

AD	Akali Dal
ADM	Akali Dal (Master)
ADS	Akali Dal (Sant)
AICC	All-India Congress Committee
AMU	Aligarh Muslim University
BKD	Bharatiya Kranti Dal
CLM	Commissioner for Linguistic Minorities
CPI	Communist Party of India
CP(L)	Lal Communist Party
CPM	Communist Party of India (Marxist)
DMK	Dravida Munnetra Kazagham
HLS	Haryana Lok Samiti
IAS	Indian Administrative Service
ISC	Indian Statutory Commission
KMPP	Kisan Mazdoor Praja Party
MLA	Member of the Legislative Assembly
MMM	Muslim Majlis-e-Mushawarat
MP	Member of Parliament
NAP	National Agriculturalist Party
PEN	Poets, Playwrights, Essayists, Editors, Novelists Club
PEPSU	Patiala and East Punjab States Union
PSP	Praja Socialist Party
RPI	Republican Party of India
RSS	Rashtriya Swayamsevak Sangh
SCF	Scheduled Castes Federation
SDPS	Sanatan Dharam Pratinidhi Sabha
SGPC	Shiromani Gurudwara Parbandhak Committee
SP	Socialist Party
SRC	States Reorganization Commission
SSP	Samyukta Socialist Party
SVD	Samyukta Vidhayak Dal (United Legislature Party)
U.P.	United Provinces (Uttar Pradesh)

This book is dedicated to the memory of my mother
EVA BAVLEY BRASS
who left me, among other things I cherish, that ironic sense of humor
which she herself kept until the last day of her life

ACKNOWLEDGEMENTS

Thanks are due to the authors of the *Economic and Political Weekly* for permission to incorporate in Chapter 3 'Muslim Separatism in United Provinces: Social Context and Political Strategy before Partition', *Economic and Political Weekly*, v (January 1970), 167–86, and to Harry W. Blair for permission to adapt Fig. 2b from 'Caste, Politics and Democracy in Bihar State, India: The Elections of 1967', unpublished Ph.D. dissertation, Duke University, 1969.

PREFACE

This book has been six years in the making. In the original design for the research with which it began in my field work in north India in 1966–7, a study of the language policies of the three north Indian states was to be part of a more general analysis of their policies on several issues of political and economic development. Some of the other questions which concerned me then have since been written up and published in articles and contributions to other books, but my interest in the study of language policies and the politics of language and their association with religious identity in north India continued and grew.

My specific interest in the issues with which this book is concerned began with simple curiosity to pursue a reference in a Patna newspaper to demands made on behalf of the Maithili language in the Bihar legislature. In following up the initial newspaper reference, I talked with Maithili spokesmen in Patna and then moved on to the center of the Maithili language area in Darbhanga, north Bihar, where I met the leading persons involved in the movement and collected some pamphlet and newspaper material, mainly in Maithili. What began as simple curiosity soon developed into a theoretical question, namely, how does one explain why it is that some language movements in India and elsewhere develop into powerful political movements whereas others, such as the Maithili movement, do not?

The analysis of the Maithili movement also left me with a sense of discovery and a broader interest in the symbolic uses of language in relation to other symbols of identity in nationality movements. My sense of discovery had two elements. One concerned simply the satisfying of the initial curiosity concerning the Maithili movement and its failure to develop. The other concerned my new awareness of the fact that the Hindi movement has been enormously successful in north India in absorbing speakers of minority languages and dialects during the past century and that this was an historic process of assimilation of great intrinsic and theoretical interest. Theoretically, it raised the question of how minority language speakers resist an historic tide of assimilation by a standardizing, modernizing, and politically powerful language movement. To answer this question, I turned toward two other, more successful movements in north India in which language was involved along with religion, namely, the Muslim movement on behalf of Urdu and the Sikh movement in relation to the Punjabi language. When these two movements were brought into the comparison, however, it became clear that language was actually a secondary line of cleavage everywhere in north India, in contrast to the situation in other parts of the subcontinent and other parts of the world, and that the priority given to religious conflict in the north had profoundly affected processes of language change. Out of this comparative interest in language- and religion-based movements there emerged the final design of the study, namely, an explicit comparison of the conditions under which such movements succeed or fail, the ways in which these two powerful symbols of group identity are manipulated, and the interrelationships between the two great processes of religious differentiation and linguistic assimilation which have been occurring in the north for over a century. And, ultimately, out of these concerns, I developed an interest in the process of nationality-formation in general and a descriptive model of that process which I believe is applicable to other kinds of nationality movements using symbols other than language and religion.

In the years during which the research for and the writing of this book have been done, I have acquired a long list of debts to people and agencies who have contributed to its completion. The American Institute of Indian Studies provided me a Faculty Research Fellowship for field research in north India in 1966–7 to pursue research on the comparative study of politics and policy making in Bihar, Uttar Pradesh, and Punjab. Simultaneously, I held a research grant from the American Council of Learned Societies and Social Science Research Council. At that time, the language portion of the study was a small part of my work on the politics of the north Indian states. In 1968–9, I was awarded a Ford Foundation Fellowship in Political Science to continue my research on north Indian politics. It was during this year that the project, instead of being completed, took on its final shape. I also received support for this research in the form of summer salary and research assistance from the University of Washington Graduate School Research Fund Committee and from the South Asia Committee of the Institute for Comparative and Foreign Area Studies, University of Washington.

My research on the Maithili movement could not have been completed without the assistance of Sri Ganganath Thakur, who travelled with me to Darbhanga in 1967 and during another visit in 1969 and who translated mountains of Maithili pamphlets and newspaper articles for me over the years. Others who assisted me by translating Maithili, Urdu, or Punjabi pamphlets were: Sri Govind Misra, Dr Hori Lal Saksena, and Mr S. P. Nirash. Surjit Singh Sandhu accompanied me on a trip from Chandigarth to Amritsar in February 1967 and helped me to meet some Akali Dal personalities, including Master Tara Singh. Several people provided me with special kindness or hospitality during my research and visits. They include the late Professor Ramanath Jha and Dr Laksman Jha of Darbhanga, both of whom gave me valuable research materials and personal hospitality. Dr Ram Rajya Prasad Singh provided friendship and good humor in Patna. Dr Chetkar Jha gave me his own sharp insights into Bihar politics. Mr P. R. Mehendiratta did so much for me and my family in New Delhi in 1966–7 that it would take several paragraphs to recount. Several of my colleagues have read and made helpful suggestions for the improvement of parts of this manuscript. I especially want to acknowledge the criticisms of Harry Blair, Frank Conlon, Richard Flathman, Michael Hechter, Ruth Horowitz, Ramanath Jha, W. H. Morris-Jones, Peter Reeves, Francis Robinson, Ralph Russell, and Michael Shapiro; and I particularly want to thank Susanne Rudolph for her careful and constructive criticism of the entire manuscript, which materially assisted me in making final revisions.

The views expressed in this book, however, and the responsibility for all statements of fact and for any errors they may contain are entirely my own.

The completion of this book has also been made possible by research assistance provided by Thomas M. Brownlee, Frances Svensson, and Keith Kleinhen. The bulk of the typing of the original manuscript was done by Roberta Nelson and of the final revisions by Norma Howard.

My work on this book took too much time away from my family, who also had to put up with my frequent changes of mood, depending upon how the writing went. My wife, Linda, also did some concrete things like clipping newspapers in India and, more important, reading various versions of the manuscript, criticizing them, and saying the right things about them to keep me going. It is impossible to acknowledge adequately or repay my debt to her. As for David Michael and Leah Sarah, I can only say that this book is what I was doing all those mornings downstairs.

Seattle, Washington   Paul R. Brass
23 February 1973

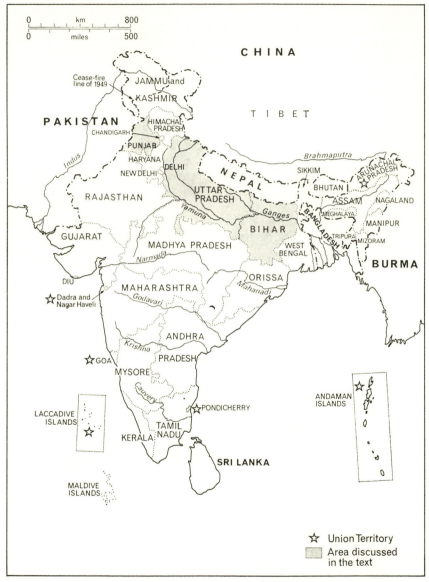

Fig. 1   Political map of India

SOURCE. Adapted from B. L. Sukhwal, *India: A Political Geography* (Bombay, Allied, 1971), facing p. 24.

PART I

INTRODUCTION

1

LANGUAGE, RELIGION, AND GROUP IDENTITIES

Language and religion have been among the major symbols of group identity in South Asia during the past century. They have competed with each other for the loyalties of the hundreds of millions of peoples of the Indian subcontinent and Sri Lanka, with the narrower loyalties of caste, kinship, and locality, and with the broader loyalties to the developing states of the South Asian region. Language and religion have been used both to broaden men's identities in the South Asian countries and to undermine the sovereignties of existing political units. The evocation of Islamic unity in the pre-independence period in India led to the development of a powerful mass movement behind the demand for the creation of Pakistan, causing the formation of two successor states to the British empire instead of one. The unity created in the state of Pakistan by the bond of Islam was in turn broken by the movement of the Bengali linguistic-cultural group toward regional autonomy and ultimately toward sovereignty. India too has experienced since independence a succession of regional linguistic and religious movements which have sometimes seemed to be on the point of breaking the unity of the country.

How is it that these two symbols have now and again been able to move millions of people in South Asia to make political demands, which have sometimes led to violent confrontations between opposing groups? How is it that language and religion have both provided the motive power for nationalism in the South Asian states and also constituted the chief threat to national unity in those states? How is it that, at one time language, at another time religion, at other times neither of these symbols is used as a basis for political mobilization? What are the dynamic processes by which people come to identify their interests with their language or their religion, to build associations to pursue those interests, and to form bonds strong enough to build or destroy states?

Questions such as these have not been commonly asked about Asian nationalisms. Numerous studies have been done of the political movements which have used language or religion to appeal to the sentiments of people. Studies have been written which describe

3

inter-group conflicts and their consequences for national unity in developing societies. There have been studies which describe the ideological influence of language and religion on Asian nationalisms. There have also been analyses of the policies pursued by some Asian states on such questions as official language, the medium of instruction in public schools, and on state policies towards religion.[1] However, much less has been done to relate sociological concepts of nationalism and nationality-formation to the changes taking place in contemporary Asian societies. Most studies of Asian national groups concentrate on the demands made on behalf of a group by its political elites and on the consequences of political movements launched to achieve group demands. However, rarely are questions asked about how group identity was formed in the first place, how one set of elites rather than another came to be the carrier of the group's demands, how processes of social change have affected the relations among different groups, and what role party and government actions and policies play not only in satisfying or failing to satisfy particular demands, but in affecting the solidarity and cohesion of groups. Another question which is almost never asked concerns why some language or religious groups either do not make political demands or do not do so successfully. This book has been written to find answers to questions such as these by applying to the rich historical mosaic of inter-group relations in north India concepts and hypotheses derived from the literature on nationalism, national integration, and nationality-formation.

NATIONALISM, NATIONAL INTEGRATION, AND NATIONALITY-FORMATION

The central questions in sociologically oriented theories of nationalism concern how and why ethnic group cohesion grows and develops at particular times among some people and not others to a sufficient degree of intensity to become politically significant. Theories of 'national integration' begin with the examination of the state and ask how loyalties transcending those to primary groups are built and

---

[1] Among the important recent studies of the politics of language and religion in the South Asian states are Jyotirindra Das Gupta, *Language Conflict and National Development: Group Politics and National Language Policy in India* (Berkeley: University of California Press, 1970); Robert N. Kearney, *Communalism and Language in the Politics of Ceylon* (Durham, N.C.: Duke University Press, 1967); Baldev Raj Nayar, *Minority Politics in the Punjab* (Princeton, N.J.: Princeton University Press, 1966) and *National Communication and Language Policy in India* (New York: Frederick A. Praeger, 1969); and Donald Eugene Smith (ed.), *South Asian Politics and Religion* (Princeton, N.J.: Princeton University Press, 1966).

how attachments to the institutions of state authority are developed among diverse peoples. Unfortunately, the two kinds of theories are rarely considered together. Competing ideologies of the state and of the nation, which have permeated the scholarly as well as the polemical literature on these subjects, and terminological inconsistencies have caused confusion in an area of social science research which is otherwise relatively well-developed in theoretical sophistication.

The tendency in the literature on political development and modernization of late has been to focus upon 'national integration' as a process of state-building and to treat all other loyalties except those to the state as 'parochial' or 'primordial' loyalties, divisive in their impact and detrimental to 'national integration'. This focus upon 'national integration' has had both ideological and analytical implications and consequences. Ideologically, it has fostered an exaltation of the contemporary nation-state and a downgrading of ethnic values, Western ethnocentrism, and anti-democratic and pro-authoritarian tendencies. The nation-state has been exalted as the inevitable companion and instrument of the world-historic processes of modernization, including 'industrialization, rationalization, secularization, and bureaucratization'[1] and as the repository of the values of civility in societies threatened by the divisive antagonisms of 'primordial' groups.[2] Ethnocentrism has entered the conceptual framework in the emphasis on the Western origins of both the processes of modernization and nation-state formation. Both modernization and nationalism in contemporary Asia and Africa are then seen as responses to and consequences of 'the imperial spread of Western European civilization over the face of the earth'.[3] Having begun with the Western-derived teleology of modernization and the nation-state, theories concerning both processes soon reach the conclusion that authoritarian means to these two ends, rather than democratic ones, are necessary because the values and skills associated with the drive toward modernization in Asia and Africa are concentrated in the minds and hands of a tiny, Westernized elite and because the nation-state does not yet exist in fact in these regions of the world. It is here, therefore, that the concept of 'national integration' becomes articulated as the process by which the 'gap' between the modernizing

---

[1] Dankwart A. Rustow, *A World of Nations: Problems of Political Modernization* (Washington, D.C.: Brookings Institution, 1967), pp. 1–6; citation from p. 6.

[2] Clifford Geertz, 'The Integrative Revolution: Primordial Sentiments and Civil Politics in the New States', in Clifford Geertz (ed.), *Old Societies and New States: The Quest for Modernity in Asia and Africa* (New York: The Free Press, 1967), pp. 105–57.

[3] Rupert Emerson, *From Empire to Nation: The Rise to Self-Assertion of Asian and African Peoples* (Boston: Beacon Press, 1962), p. vii.

elite, holding in its hands the instruments of the modern state, and the traditional mass of the people is reduced or overcome by the communication to the mass of the goals of the elite and the transformation of mass values to make them compatible with the aspirations of the elite. The primary instruments of the elite in bringing about this transformation have been seen as the charismatic leader and the single, mass party.[1]

Some of the analytical consequences of this approach should by now be apparent. 'National integration', seen as a process of reducing the elite–mass gap and transforming loyalties from parochial to national orientations, is a simplistic concept to apply to the predominantly multi-ethnic states of Asia and Africa. It is not only that inter-ethnic relations become more important to the integrative process than elite–mass relations in such states, but that the processes by which intermediary loyalties are developed are largely ignored in this approach. There is no doubt that vast movements of change have been taking place throughout Asia and Africa in the broadening of identities of local populations, but the transformation rarely involves a quantum leap from family, kin group, or village to the modern state. In between, many old social categories have frequently intervened and been adapted as new forms of identity and as new vehicles of participation in the modern state. Tribes become nationalities, local caste groups join broader caste associations, language becomes a symbol of group identification, and religion becomes a basis for community. How the leaders of the modern developing state relate to these new formations is usually more important for the future of the state than the ability of a charismatic leader or a mobilizing party to appeal to the sentiments of the people. In fact, as these new loyalties develop, the appeals of parties and leaders may be mediated, even diluted, through them.

A second analytical consequence of the emphasis on national integration has been a loss of touch with reality as the Westernizing elites and the charismatic leaders gradually disappear from view, along with the single, mobilizing party. Political understanding of Asian and African political processes has suffered from an overemphasis on particular, ephemeral institutions and from a neglect of historic, dynamic processes of identity formation. In much of Asia and Africa, charismatic leaders and mobilizing single parties have proved to be ephemeral. Where they existed, they have more often

---

[1] This formulation of the concept of national integration and its authoritarian implications are most explicit in Claude Ake, *A Theory of Political Integration* (Homewood, Ill.: The Dorsey Press, 1967).

than not been overturned and replaced as governing instruments by the military and civilian bureaucracies left behind by the imperial powers. In other places, such as Nigeria and Pakistan, the instruments of state authority have been completely rejected by entire peoples striving for self-determination and new sovereignties. Political continuity seems to have been maintained in post-independence developing countries chiefly in multi-ethnic societies characterized, on the one hand, by non-mobilizing political party-dominated regimes and, on the other hand, by a vigorous indigenous group life. These conditions have obtained, among Asian states, particularly in Malaysia, Sri Lanka, and India.

A third analytical consequence of the national integration approach has been the failure to consider alternative models of state–nation relations other than either nation–state integration or secession. Yet both the history of Europe and contemporary developments in Asia and Africa reveal a wide range of pluralistic solutions to problems of state–nation relations in multi-ethnic societies. Switzerland, Canada, and South Africa are commonly cited examples of societies in which culturally distinct groups have been either granted or denied political rights. A moment's thought, however, brings to mind a much larger range of European and American examples, including such vastly different societies as the Soviet Union, Yugoslavia, Belgium, and Guyana. These are all societies which vary in their degree of political integration, but in which the accommodations that have been reached among diverse linguistic, religious, and racial groups have not involved either cultural amalgamation or political secession. The experiences of these countries are more relevant to the multi-ethnic societies of much of Asia and Africa than are the nation–state models built upon the experiences of the United States, Great Britain, France, or Germany.

An alternative to the 'national integration' approach lies in sociological theories of nationalism, viewed as a process of nationality-formation rather than state-building.[1] Sociological theories of nationalism are comparative rather than teleological. They do not begin with the nation-state and the process of modernization and ask only how does each and every territorial group of people reach these goals. They begin first with ethnic groups and ask: under what conditions do ethnic groups develop into nations; how does the process

---

[1] The pre-eminent theorist of this approach to nationalism is, of course, Karl Deutsch, whose book *Nationalism and Social Communication: An Inquiry into the Foundations of Nationality*, 2nd ed. (Cambridge, Mass.: M.I.T. Press, 1966), is the conceptual beginning point for this study. My ideas have also been influenced strongly by Benjamin Akzin's book, *State and Nation* (London: Hutchinson University Library, 1964).

7

unfold; how are decisions made to include and exclude categories of people; what are the patterns of relationship between included and excluded categories, between one ethnic group or nation and another; what are the relations between the institutions and policies of the state and the developing nationalities; and how can the state influence the processes of nationality-formation? Such questions do not assume the superiority of state over nation or nation over state. They are not ethnocentrically biased since they concern processes of change which may occur in any society with or without Western intervention. They also leave open the question of what kinds of political regimes can function best in the midst of ethnic group transformations.

Problems of definition and classification

Before such questions as these can even be approached it is necessary to introduce some definitions and some terminological consistency. The term 'ethnic group' will be used synonymously with the term 'people' to refer broadly to any 'group of individuals who have some objective characteristics in common'[1] which go beyond their mere place in a societal division of labor. That is, factory workers are not an ethnic group. Ethnic characteristics refer more to language, culture, territory, diet, and dress than to a role in the division of labor, although such ethnic characteristics may sometimes be reinforced by common work roles. In this study, the examination of the attributes of ethnic groups is the starting point in the analysis. The notion of identity has been left out of the concept of ethnicity here deliberately. An ethnic group is a group which is objectively distinct, but whose members do not *necessarily* attach subjective importance or political significance to that fact. The central analytical concern of this book is with the process by which objectively distinct ethnic groups become transformed into subjectively conscious and politically oriented communities. The term 'community' will be used to refer to ethnic groups whose members have developed an awareness of a common identity and have attempted to define the boundaries of the group.[2] A community becomes a nationality or a nation when it mobilizes for political action and becomes politically significant,[3]

---

[1] Deutsch, *Nationalism and Social Communication*, p. 17; Akzin, p. 30.

[2] For a useful discussion of the 'concept of community', see C. W. Cassinelli, 'The National Community', *Polity*, II, No. 1 (September 1969), 16–19.

[3] This definition follows Akzin, *State and Nation*, who also stresses that a nation must have 'exceeded purely local dimensions' (p. 31). The size criterion distinguishes isolated

that is, when it makes political demands and achieves a significant measure of success by its own efforts. Some examples of significant political successes would be the achievement of political sovereignty,[1] or a separate political status within a sovereign state, or a system of communal political representation, or control over the educational process in the public schools attended by the members of the group.[2] It must be stressed, however, that it is not these political indicators which define a nationality or nation but the fact of having achieved one or more of these political results through group action. The nation-state is a state in which either there is only one nation or nationality or in which one nation or nationality is overwhelmingly dominant and in which political rights are either not granted or are granted only exceptionally to ethnic minorities. There are not many such nation-states in the contemporary world. A few of the Western European countries, Japan, and some other Asian societies fit this description. Most other states in the world are either multi-ethnic or multi-national.

It is also essential to define the processes by which these different forms of group consciousness are attained. The movement toward communal consciousness in an ethnic group is accompanied by processes of assimilation and inclusion, as well as differentiation or exclusion. Assimilation involves both the definition and standardization of attributes assumed to be shared by members of an ethnic group and the definition of the terms of entry into the group where such entry is permitted. Differentiation is simply the other side of the coin, defining the grounds for exclusion from the group. 'Separatism' will be used synonymously with the more common South Asian term, 'communalism', to describe all movements which attempt to build a differentiated group consciousness and identity among a defined population. The term 'nationalism' in this study will be used in two senses. For the most part, it will be used to refer to the process by which ethnic groups and communities are mobilized for action to

villages or kinship groups whose separateness arises from an absence of communication with other groups rather than out of a self-conscious awareness of differences from other groups.

[1] It is common to associate this particular achievement or at least the demand for it as the only kind of political demand that distinguishes a nation from other kinds of communities. I prefer the term 'nation-state' for a nation which achieves political independence and 'nationality' or 'nation' for ethnic groups whose political goals do not necessarily include separate sovereignty. For an emphatic statement of the view 'that the nation is a community that believes it ought to be politically independent', see Cassinelli, 'The National Community', pp. 26–7.

[2] On the importance of control over the public schools in multi-ethnic societies generally, see Akzin, *State and Nation*, p. 133, and Geertz, 'The Integrative Resolution', p. 125.

attain political ends. Another common use of the term 'nationalism', which will also be adopted in this book, refers to the process by which loyalties are developed to the state. Some scholars have suggested using other terms such as 'patriotism'[1] or 'nationism'[2] to describe loyalties to the state, but the former term has other associations and the latter term is artificial and too easily read as nationalism, on the printed page in any case. Moreover, since there do exist significant segments of elite opinion in developing countries who do not acknowledge other loyalties of nationality than those to the state, its territory, and its entire population, the term 'nationalism' will also be used to refer to the sentiments of such people. An even more important reason for retaining this dual use of the term is that the two types of processes to which the term refers are subtypes of a more general process. That more general process is sometimes referred to as identity formation. In this study, it will be referred to as the process of striving to achieve multi-symbol congruence among a group of people defined initially by a single central symbol, whether that symbol is an ethnic attribute or loyalty to a particular state.

Finally, two broad kinds of state policy and institutional arrangements to accommodate the demands of separatist groups and nationalities will be distinguished – integrative and pluralistic. A policy of 'national integration' is one which seeks assimilation of the entire population of a state to a common identity and which recognizes only individual rights, privileges, and duties.[3] Such a policy is to be distinguished from one of political integration, which seeks only to maintain the cohesion and territorial integrity of a political unit but does not necessarily demand the cultural assimilation of diverse groups to either a dominant or composite culture.[4] A policy of pluralism recognizes the existence of differentiated groups in a

---

[1] See Akzin, *State and Nation*, p. 44.

[2] Joshua A. Fishman, 'Nationality-Nationalism and Nation-Nationism', in Joshua A. Fishman *et al.* (eds.), *Language Problems of Developing Nations* (New York: John Wiley, 1968), pp. 39–51. See also Walker Conner, 'Nation-Building or Nation-Destroying?' *World Politics*, XXIV, No. 3 (April 1972), 332–6. Connor argues that, since 'ethnic identity' constitutes the only 'true nationalism' and since the process of building state loyalties often involves overcoming ethnic indentities, the proper term for the development of state loyalties is 'nation-destroying' rather than 'nation-building'.

[3] This use of the term 'national integration' as a synonym for assimilation to the nation state follows both Akzin, *State and Nation*, pp. 44 and 76–111, and the general thrust of theorists of political modernization who associate the latter process with nation-state formation. Difficulties in the use of the term 'national integration' arise when it is assumed that this process is the only feasible alternative to disintegration or secession.

[4] Cf. Myron Weiner, 'Political Integration and Political Development', in Jason L. Finkle and Richard W. Gable (eds.), *Political Development and Social Change* (New York: John Wiley, 1966), p. 555, and Jyotirindra Das Gupta, 'Language Diversity and National Development', in Fishman, *Language Problems*, pp. 21–4.

population and concedes to such groups as well as to individuals' rights, privileges, and obligations.[1] Both policies – of national integration and pluralism – may be promoted in more or less accommodating and equalitarian ways. Integrationist policies may be liberal and equalitarian or they may amount to forced assimilation of minorities into a common mold. Pluralist policies may recognize all differentiated groups as equal or they may discriminate among groups, treating the members of some groups as superior or full citizens and others as inferior or not entitled to full citizenship rights. While the predominant policies of most states can usually be identified as either integrationist or pluralist, the more complex multi-ethnic states may follow mixed strategies.

Most contemporary states are multi-ethnic. The range of ethnic diversity among states and the number of dimensions along which populations may be divided are very large, however. Moreover, the state of group consciousness among different ethnic groups in different countries also varies.

Clifford Geertz has identified five types of multi-ethnic situations, based primarily on the number, size, and gradation of the groups.[2] They include asymmetrical and symmetrical duality, asymmetrical multiplicity (one large and several smaller groups), multiple ethnic fragmentation, and the most complex situation of all and the category to which India belongs, characterized by 'a relatively even gradation of groups in importance, from several large ones through several medium-sized ones to a number of small ones, with no clearly dominant ones and no sharp cut-off points'.

An article by Donald Horowitz suggests two other differences of importance in distinguishing types of ethnic politics.[3] One is 'the structure of group differentiation'; that is, whether ethnic group relations are characterized by hierarchical relationships in which one group is 'superordinate' and another is 'subordinate' or whether 'parallel ethnic structures exist, each with its own criteria of stratification'.[4] The first type of system is characteristic of caste societies or the system of Negro slavery in the West. Myron Weiner, applying a similar distinction among types of social systems, has argued that India does not fit either of these two models but rather constitutes a

---

[1] Four broad state-nation patterns are distinguished in Akzin, *State and Nation*, in ch. 6–9: 'the integrationist pattern'; 'pluralism on the basis of inequality'; 'pluralism on the basis of equality'; and 'secession'.

[2] Geertz, 'The Integrative Resolution', pp. 117–18.

[3] Donald L. Horowitz, 'Three Dimensions of Ethnic Politics', *World Politics*, XXIII, No. 2 (January 1971), 232–44.

[4] *Ibid.*, pp. 232 and 236.

third case.[1] India contains a series of 'parallel ethnic structures' each of which is characterized by internal hierarchical ethnic group relations. That is, the predominant pattern in India is one of segmentation in which each language, tribal, or religious group contains within itself a complete societal division of labor and also contains internal caste groups which may or may not be successfully assimilated into the broader ethnic structure. Thus, there are in India ethnic groups within ethnic groups so that, for example, processes of assimilation and differentiation may be going on at one level between competing language groups, while within each language group similar processes may be affecting the relations between different castes in the same language group.

Horowitz presents another useful distinction, based upon 'the locus of political interaction', that is, 'whether the primary focal point of political activity among the [ethnic] groups is parochial or national'.[2] One pattern, often characterized by 'constant tension' and severe conflict, exists in centralized political systems when 'one group confronts another directly'.[3] The second pattern is characterized by the existence of a large number of dispersed ethnic groups that compete with each other for local power rather than for dominance in the system as a whole. While there is no lack of conflict and tension in such systems, the pressures on the central government are somewhat less because conflicts may be handled singly and separately and the center may even play a mediating role in resolving them. Both types of patterns have existed in India at different times. As independence approached, Indian politics was dominated by a fundamental cleavage between two mammoth groupings of Hindus and Muslims, who competed for power in the central government. The consequence of the conflict was the partition of India into two states in 1947. Since 1947, however, the predominant patterns of ethnic politics have been based upon conflict among large, but dispersed regional linguistic, religious, and caste groups.

A sixth distinction – in addition to the number, size, gradation, structure of differentiation, and locus of interaction of ethnic groups – which is suggested by the general theoretical literature in social science on social cleavage relates to whether or not ethnic bases for cleavage in a society are cumulative. That is, do religious, language, and territorial bases for group differentiation reinforce each other or

---

[1] Myron Weiner, *Party Building in a New Nation: The Indian National Congress* (Chicago: University of Chicago Press, 1967), pp. 114–17.
[2] Horowitz, 'Three Dimensions in Ethnic Politics', p. 237.
[3] *Ibid.*, p. 239.

not? Examples of situations where cleavages have reinforced each other are abundant: Tamil Hindus and Sinhalese Buddhists in Sri Lanka; Greek Christian and Turkish Muslims in Cyprus; Malays and Chinese in Malaysia, and so forth. It is generally argued that societies characterized by cumulated cleavages are potentially subject to the most severe conflicts. Where does India fit on this dimension? India is characterized by an extraordinary abundance of ethnic dimensions – caste, tribe, language, religious, and cultural differences of which some are cumulative and some are not. More often than not, one dimension is considered crucial by an ethnic group in India and efforts are then made to bring other dimensions into congruence with the central unifying symbol. Indeed, this theme is central to this book. For example, a caste group self-consciously oriented towards changing its social status will change its religion, if necessary, to achieve the result.[1] A religious group seeking political dominance will change its language for political ends.

A final point of distinction concerns the extent of communal and national consciousness among the ethnic groups in a multi-ethnic state. The range of variation on this dimension would be from societies in which linguists and anthropologists might observe cultural differences among diverse peoples, but in which the peoples concerned themselves are not aware of such differences, to societies in which group consciousness is self-evident in literature and cultural artifacts and takes organized political form. At one end of limited group consciousness of difference would be many of the multi-lingual and multi-tribal African states. At the other end of the spectrum would be the contemporary cleavage between English and French in Canada. India is characterized not only by multiplicity of ethnic dimensions but by differential group consciousness within and between groups concerning the symbolic importance of ethnic differences. There are large numbers of people in India today who do not care that they speak a language different from that taught in the schools to which they send their children. There are groups which are far advanced toward national consciousness, aware of the differences between themselves and other groups and eager to preserve and protect those differences.

If we take these features of ethnic politics together and apply them to India, the following general description emerges. India is a

---

[1] This strategy has been followed by the Chamar caste category in the shift of large numbers of its members from Hinduism to Buddhism; see Owen M. Lynch, *The Politics of Untouchability: Social Mobility and Social Change in a City of India* (New York: Columbia University Press, 1969).

multi-ethnic society in which there are a large number of ethnic groups which vary in size from highly localized caste and tribal groups to great language and religious groups, in which no single group is clearly dominant, and in which the boundaries between groups are not entirely fixed. These groups also vary enormously in the extent to which a self-conscious awareness of a common identity different from other groups exists among them. There is a multiplicity not only of groups, but of ethnic features, which are not always congruent or cumulative. The system as a whole is a segmented one characterized by the existence of parallel ethnic structures, which are in turn divided hierarchically within themselves. Competition among ethnic groups in the recent past has been regionalized and has not involved a confrontation between polarized communities for dominance of the entire system.

INDIA AS A MULTI-NATIONAL STATE

Dual nationalism: problems of regionalism and national unity in India

Problems of political integration in India exist both at the center and in the several states. Although central and state policies toward regional, linguistic, religious, and cultural demands for political self-expression by minority groups are closely interconnected, it is essential to distinguish between the two levels for two reasons. One reason for doing so is simply to clarify the problems of national unity in India which, though very great, have sometimes been both exaggerated and misinterpreted. Exaggeration of the problems has occurred through the tendency on the part of both scholars and policy-makers in India to interpret the persistent demands of all ethnic and community groups as threats to the unity and integrity of the Indian Union when, in fact, the vast majority of such demands have involved local or regional inter-ethnic conflicts in which the center has been not the target of the demands, but the source for the redress of legitimate grievances and the arbiter and mediator of group conflicts. Misinterpretation has occurred through a failure to appreciate the nature of the nationality problem in India and its duality. One source of misinterpretation lies in the deficiencies in the theoretical approach to state–nation relations, which are shared by scholars of political modernization and many of India's own intellectual elite, because they arise from the same intellectual sources. That is, both the most Westernized of India's intellectuals and the leading theorists of political modernization in the west have shared the notion that national integration must involve the creation of modern nation-states in which loyalties to national community and to political structure ultimately merge, so that nationalism and patriotism become one. In fact, however, it was pointed out above that this is merely one type of solution to the state–nation relationship, achieved primarily in the countries of Western Europe, the English-speaking world, and Japan. This model is simply not relevant to the Indian subcontinent and attempts to emulate it in India can only lead to disaster and disintegration. More relevant to India is the model of the multi-national state, of which the leading examples are the Soviet Union, Yugoslavia, and Switzerland, countries which comprise many nations bound together in a single political and territorial unit by feelings of patriotism derived from ideology, memories of a common struggle against external or alien powers, and rational calculations of common advantage in the sharing of a single political structure, but not by a common nationality. It goes without saying that the problems of state–nation relations are vastly different and vastly more complex in such countries than they are in the nation-states of Western Europe, the English-speaking countries, and Japan. It can only confuse our understanding of the processes of state–nation relations to place these two different kinds of situations in the same theoretical framework by continuing to use such terms as 'national integration' or 'nation-building' and identifying them with the general processes of political modernization in those developing countries, such as India, which are not developing nation-states, but developing multi-national states. In such countries, the problem is not to bring about an identity between state and nation, but to learn to recognize the existence and to cope with the development of regional-national sentiments while simultaneously promoting and developing patriotic ties among diverse nationalities to a common political and territorial unit. In India this may ultimately lead to what Paul Shoup has described in the case of Yugoslavia as the development of dual national personalities.[1]

A second source of misinterpretation is more specific to India, namely, the notion that there exists in India a dominant nationality – a Hindu nation or a Hindi-speaking heartland – and a number of smaller, minority religious, linguistic, and cultural groups. The idea of a dominant nation appears in contemporary political dialogue in India.[2] It is fostered by Hindu revivalist political organizations and

[1] Paul Shoup, *Communism and the Yugoslav National Question* (New York: Columbia University Press, 1968), pp. 262–3.
[2] See Selig S. Harrison, 'Hindu Society and the State: The Indian Union', in K. H.

by interest associations devoted to the spread of Hindi and its adoption as the sole official language of India, which in turn elicit charges of northern domination and imperialism from the southern language groups. The attempts to create a Hindu nation and to promote Hindi as the sole official language of India are very real and important political forces in India, but neither have yet achieved success. In fact, Hindu nationalism and Hindi sentiment are largely concentrated in the northern states of Uttar Pradesh, Madhya Pradesh, Haryana, and Bihar. Hindi sentiment and Hindu nationalism are, therefore, as regionally based as are other linguistic-cultural attachments in the Indian Union. Nor is there any meaningful sense in which the Hindi-speaking states dominate at the center or over other states in the Union, despite frequent assertions to the contrary.

India is, in fact, a developing multi-national state or a state containing a number of dualized nationalities without a dominant nationality, in which the central leadership of the country seeks to accommodate the political demands of diverse language, religious, and cultural groups in ways which do not detract from the unity and integrity of the country. By far the most important of such demands in the past decades have been those made on behalf of the major religious and language groups of the subcontinent. The attitudes of central government leaders toward religious and linguistic demands have been conditioned by their persistent fear of the political disintegration of the country. Nor has this fear been imaginary or misplaced. Freedom was bought at the price of partition of the subcontinent and civil war between Hindus and Muslims. Moreover, there has never been a time since independence when secessionist demands have not been voiced by one or more segments of the population of the subcontinent – in Kashmir, in Madras, in Nagaland, and in Assam.

One consequence of this persistent fear was the reluctance of the central leadership to accept demands for linguistic reorganization of states, which were conceded only reluctantly and only in the aftermath of public agitations in nearly every case. Yet, over the past two decades, the central leaders seem to have been developing a more realistic attitude toward expressions of regional identifications. The central leaders continue to use euphemisms to describe India's diversity and refer to regions and regionalism or to subnational loyalties, but an implicit awareness seems to be spreading among them that India is, in fact, a developing multi-national state. Along

Silvert (ed.), *Expectant Peoples: Nationalism and Development* (New York: Random House, 1963), for an explicit discussion of the prospects for the development of 'a pan-Indian Hindu consciousness', citation from p. 275.

with this awareness has come both an increasing willingness to accommodate regional demands and a recognition that regional diversity must be respected in the central government itself. This means, for example, that not only is Hindi not to be imposed upon the non-Hindi areas of the country as the official language of India but that the regional languages of the subcontinent are to be recognized by the central government as media of examination for entry into the public services of the country.[1]

There are four rules which have increasingly come to regulate the attitude of the central government towards regional demands. One rule, since 1963 written into the constitution of the country, is that regional demands must stop short of secession.[2] All demands short of secession will be allowed full expression, but secessionist demands will be suppressed, if necessary, by armed force. Thus the central government has been willing to grant a separate state to Nagaland and to talk about greater regional autonomy in the tribal areas and it has as yet not revoked the special status of Kashmir. However, the Government of India has suppressed by force demands for secession in Nagaland and in Assam and has demonstrated in 1965 that it is prepared to go to war with Pakistan to prevent the secession of Kashmir. On the other hand, once secessionist demands have been dropped, regional movements are permitted full expression. Thus, in Tamil Nadu, the DMK gave up its demand for secession after 1963 and is now the governing party in that state.

The second rule is that regional demands based on language and culture will be accommodated, but that regional demands which are explicitly based on religious differences will not be accepted. This rule is the heritage of partition and Hindu–Muslim conflict, but it has been applied as well to the demands of the Sikhs for a separate Sikh-majority state. The Sikhs now have a separate majority state in the Punjab, but they achieved it only after a transfer of leadership in the Akali movement from Master Tara Singh to Sant Fateh Singh, who explicitly rejected the religious basis of the demand and insisted that the demand was only for the creation of a separate Punjabi-speaking state.[3] Although it remained obvious to everyone that the new demand was the same as the old one, only in a different garb, the emphasis on language rather than religion gave the demand legitimacy and made it possible for non-Sikhs to support it and for the central government to concede it.

[1] Nayar, *National Communication*, p. 137.
[2] For details of the anti-secession amendments, see *Indian Affairs Record*, IX, No. 6 (June 1963), 193–5.
[3] This development is discussed in detail in ch. 6 below.

The third rule is that regional demands will not be conceded capriciously. That is, a regional movement must not only have a legitimate case, but it must have broad popular support in the region. For example, in March 1954, 97 members out of 100 from among all parties in the western districts of the Legislative Assembly of Uttar Pradesh supported a demand for the formation of a new state out of the western districts of Uttar Pradesh and portions of the Haryana region of Punjab.[1] The demand was couched in terms of linguistic and cultural affinities, historical precedent, and administrative convenience. However, it was a demand entirely of politicians which would also have been of immediate benefit to the politicians by creating new opportunities in a smaller state to achieve political power. The demand was neither preceded nor followed by any attempts to build popular support and it has never been considered seriously. Similarly, in north Bihar, the demand has been expressed from time to time for the creation of a separate state of Mithila out of the Maithili-speaking districts of the state. This demand has even more justification from a linguistic point of view, since Maithili is a distinct language, different from both Bengali and Hindi. However, for a variety of reasons, no significant popularly based movement has ever developed on the demand, which has consequently been ignored. In contrast, those demands which have been conceded have been preceded by agitations often leading to violence: by political mobilization which transcends most other political divisions in the region, cutting across party lines and frequently social and economic divisions; and by confrontations between opposing linguistic and cultural groups. Thus, not only has the Government of India been willing to accommodate regional demands which stop short of secession, but it has in practice made it necessary for regional movements to demonstrate their strength. In other words, the Government of India has not encouraged, but neither has it resisted the strengthening of regional identifications which, in most other developing societies, have either been suppressed or have been so feared for their disruptive potential that they have provided an excuse for eliminating political competition entirely.

The fourth rule is that demands for the division of multi-lingual states must have some support from different linguistic groups. This rule actually operates in such a way as to promote regional identifications. Thus, the division of the old Bombay state into Marathi-speaking and Gujarati-speaking states was first demanded by the

[1] *Memorandum of Members of the U.P. Legislative Assembly (Western Districts) to the Indian Central Commission for Reorganisation of States* (Saharanpur: Malhipur Branch Press, 1954).

Marathi-speaking peoples and opposed by Gujarati businessmen and others in Gujarat who had a stake in an undivided Bombay, supported by the Gujarat Congress organization. Consequently, the States Reorganization Commission rejected the demand for division of Bombay state on the grounds that the Gujarati-speaking people were 'content to remain in the composite State of Bombay' and that 'influential sections amongst the Gujaratis would prefer to stay in a composite State'.[1] The decision to maintain a bilingual state not only antagonized the Maharashtrians, but it provided the necessary catalyst to popular sentiment in Gujarat. The relatively weak Maha Gujarat Parishad now began to gather strength in certain areas of Gujarat, acquiring support in the Gujarati press, among students, and among different groups and parties opposed to the Congress. In 1957, the Parishad took five parliamentary and 29 Assembly seats from the Congress.[2] With this evidence of popular sentiment for division now apparent in both regions and with Congress power threatened in both regions by the increasing strength of the two linguistic movements, the decision was taken to divide the state. The course of events leading up to the division of Punjab in 1966 was similar, with the development of increasing sentiment in the Haryana region for separation from the Punjabi-speaking, Sikh-dominated areas of the old Punjab state.

Thus, Indian democracy has functioned with a set of written and unwritten rules which limit the form in which regional demands can be made but not the right of regional groups to assert their separate identities, which define those demands which are legitimate and which can be accommodated and those which are illegitimate and will not be accommodated, and which sometimes work in such a way as to promote the strengthening of regional identifications. There is no evidence that this strategy has either weakened Indian unity or prevented economic growth. The strategy of accommodation of regional demands seems to have had three main consequences – reduction of conflicts directed against the central government; regionalization of politics; and increased political participation and, in some cases, increased political organization in several states.[3]

The satisfaction of the major demands for linguistic reorganization

---

[1] Government of India, Home Department, *Report of the States Reorganisation Commission, 1955* (New Delhi: Government of India Press, 1955), pp. 113 and 120.

[2] Devavrat N. Pathak, 'State Politics in Gujarat: Some Determinants', in Iqbal Narain (ed.), *State Politics in India* (Meerut Meenakshi Prakashan, 1967), p. 126.

[3] On the last point, see Myron Weiner, 'Political Development in the Indian States', in Myron Weiner (ed.), *State Politics in India* (Princeton, N.J.: Princeton University Press, 1968), pp. 35–6.

has transformed situations of confrontation between regional groups and the central government into problems of inter-provincial relations in which the center plays the role of mediator. In a sense, the center has played a mediating role throughout the entire process of linguistic reorganization of states. In the old multi-lingual provinces of Madras, Bombay, and Punjab, the movements for division followed a regular pattern of, first, initiation of a demand for reorganization by the most regionally conscious linguistic group and mobilization of articulate segments of the group in political organizations such as the DMK, the Akali Dal, or the Sampurna Maharashtra Samiti; second, opposition and resistance to the demand from the provincial Congress organization and others who stand to lose by division; third, initiation of parallel movements for reorganization from other linguistic groups in the province, the Gujaratis in Bombay and Haryana Hindus in the Punjab; fourth, the crumbling of opposition to the demands in the face of growing popular sentiment for reorganization; fifth, the intervention of the central government directly or through a commission and the decision to divide and reorganize. Although central political leaders may play mediating or arbitrating roles at any stage in the development of linguistic movements, a decision to divide or reorganize has never been taken until stage four has been passed.

Unresolved problems and issues

It is widely believed in India and by scholars of India abroad that the major problems of linguistic reorganization of states have been solved. The last serious crisis in linguistic reorganization was the agitation for a separate Punjabi-speaking state or Punjabi Suba, which was partly resolved by the decision to reorganize the state of Punjab in 1966 and by an award made in 1971 after mediation by the central government in connection with disputes concerning areas claimed by the two new states of Punjab and Haryana. Two recent studies of the official language policy of the Government of India have suggested that an accommodation on this divisive issue also is gradually, though often delicately, being reached.[1]

Three great problems and issues concerning language and religion, however, remain unresolved and presently indeterminate. One concerns the consequences of the linguistic reorganizations of the Indian provinces for the future of Indian unity. Part of the initial resistance to linguistic reorganization arose out of the fear that such a clear

[1] Nayar, *National Communication*, and Das Gupta, *Language Conflict and National Development*.

20

demarcation of linguistic and cultural boundaries in India would foster the growth of subnationalisms in the reorganized states and to secessionist demands as new subnations were created.[1] This concern serves to emphasize the importance both from the point of view of the future of Indian unity and from the point of view of theories of nationalism of directing research towards the study of the processes of formation and the content of India's regional and cultural identities. In recent years, increasing attention has been devoted, especially by students of Indian history, to the regional aspects of Indian nationalism and to the development of regional nationalism.[2] It is time for political and other social scientists also to enter this area of inquiry, to examine on a comparative basis in India the processes of nationality-formation in different parts of the subcontinent and to relate their findings to theories of nationalism and national integration.

A second major question concerns the nature of group identity formation in the north Indian states, which are characterized as Hindi-speaking states. Most studies of contemporary language problems in India have concentrated their attention on the demands of the non-Hindi-speaking states. The entire Hindi-speaking region is often looked upon by non-Hindi-speakers in India as a vast, backward region which, by its sheer size, threatens to dominate the Indian Union and to impose Hindi as the official language of India upon the non-Hindi-speaking states. Yet very little is known about historic processes of social and political change in this region. Histories of the development of Indian nationalism have concentrated on processes of change in the three great presidency provinces of Bengal, Bombay, and Madras. It is often noted that, from the 1920s onwards, the center of all-India nationalist political activity moved to north India. Yet very little work has been done on the development of group identities and political movements in the two huge states of Uttar Pradesh and Bihar.

[1] Constituent Assembly of India, *Report of the Linguistic Provinces Commission* (New Delhi: Government of India Press, 1949), pp. 1–3, 27–35; reprinted in Myron Weiner (ed.), *Introduction to the Civilization of India: Developing India* (Chicago: University of Chicago Press, 1961), pp. 1–20.

[2] See especially J. H. Broomfield, 'The Non-Cooperation Decision of 1920: A Crisis in Bengal Politics', in D. A. Low (ed.), *Soundings in Modern South Asian History* (Berkeley: University of California Press, 1968), pp. 225–60; Eugene F. Irschick, *Politics and Social Conflict in South India: The Non-Brahman Movement and Tamil Separatism, 1916–1929* (Berkeley: University of California Press, 1969); John G. Leonard, 'Politics and Social Change in South India: A Study of the Andhra Movement', *Journal of Commonwealth Political Studies*, v, No. 1 (March 1967), 60–77; Anil Seal, *The Emergence of Indian Nationalism: Competition and Collaboration in the Later Nineteenth Century* (Cambridge: Cambridge University Press, 1968).

Three aspects of the religions and languages of the states of north India (including the Punjab, Uttar Pradesh, and Bihar in north India) stand out. One is that this area, especially the Punjab and Uttar Pradesh, has been the primary arena in India of religious cleavage – between Hindus and Muslims in Uttar Pradesh and among Hindus, Muslims, and Sikhs in the Punjab. The Pakistan movement received its primary impetus after 1937 in Uttar Pradesh, was moved forward when Punjab Muslim politics were captured by the Muslim League in the 1940s, and culminated in the communal violence and mass migrations in the Punjab in 1947. Since independence, Hindus and Sikhs have contested for political power in the Punjab and Hindus and Muslims for political and cultural rights in Uttar Pradesh. The great questions raised by these events concern why religion has been such a powerful force behind regional and national movements in north India and why conflict between religious groups in the north has been more bitter and prolonged here than elsewhere in India.

The second aspect of religion and language in the north, which is of special interest, is that the two types of cleavages have been non-congruent. This point will be elaborated in this work. It needs to be noted at the outset, however, that language has *not* been a barrier in fact to communication between religious groups, but has been turned into a symbolic barrier by political elites seeking to advance the interests of their religious communities. This aspect of the relation between linguistic and religious cleavage in the north raises an important theoretical question concerning the general relation between social cleavages and political conflict. Is it the case, as the political science literature on this subject generally argues, that political conflict between different groups tends to arise when the social cleavages between them are cumulative and congruent, or can political activity affect social processes in such a way as to create congruence and cumulative cleavages which otherwise did not exist between ethnic groups?

A third aspect of the language situation in north India is the enormous dialectal diversity. The states called Hindi-speaking contain nearly two dozen regional and tribal dialects, some of which can and do lay claim to status as languages distinct and separate from Hindi. Yet the only languages in the 'Hindi-speaking' region which have so far made good on such a claim are Punjabi and Urdu. How is it that the other languages and dialects of the north have not become effective symbols of group identity? This question requires that attention be turned to processes of assimilation of language and ethnic groups to each other as well as to processes of differentiation. The north Indian states provide examples of both types of processes.

A study of the relationships among language, religion, and politics in the north Indian states also must pay attention to a third unresolved problem left in the wake of linguistic reorganization of states, namely, the status and rights of minority language speakers and minority religions. The demarcation of the boundaries of the Indian states on linguistic lines has nowhere neatly divided and compartmentalized the segmented groups of Indian society. Every state has both linguistic and religious minority groups. In 1960, the range in the size of linguistic minorities in eleven of the 'linguistic states' was from 5.7% in Kerala to 45.0% in Assam; of religious minorities, the range was from 2.4% in Orissa to 39.2% in Kerala.[1] All the Hindi-speaking states contain significant linguistic and religious minorities, whose numbers are themselves in dispute. What kinds of policies do the state governments in the north pursue towards linguistic and religious minorities and what effects do they have on patterns of inter-group relations and on processes of assimilation and differentiation among groups?

This discussion of the unresolved problems and issues of language and religion in India and of the special features of the north Indian states in this regard should make it apparent that a comparative study of the processes of nationality-formation and of assimilation and differentiation among north Indian ethnic groups is of consequence both for an understanding of problems of national integration in India and for its potential contribution to theories of nationalism. There is a broad agreement among students of nationalism on the central focus for research on the question of nationality-formation, namely, the point at which objective differences among ethnic groups become translated into the subjective consciousness of peoples and become symbolic referents for political demands. There is also broad agreement concerning the important questions which must be asked about how this transformation takes place. The remainder of this introduction will be devoted to framing those questions and to presenting the north Indian cases which will be examined for the answers.

THE PROCESS OF NATIONALITY-FORMATION

Four categories of questions recur in the literature on nationalism concerning the conditions under which the transformation from

---

[1] Weiner, 'Political Development', pp. 26–7.

ethnic group to nation takes place. One category concerns the importance of objective differences between peoples. A second set of questions emphasizes the internal values and the internal processes of social change which exist or are taking place within a group of people. A third set of questions relates to inter-group relations and emphasizes the frequency and character of inter-ethnic contacts and the differential rates of social mobilization among different ethnic groups. Finally, a fourth set of questions concerns the importance of political organization and suggests the relevance of differing government policies and the relationships between state and nation.

Objective differences between peoples

There is a general recognition among students of nationalism, which contrasts with nineteenth-century beliefs on the subject, that, while certain objective characteristics of peoples (such as language and territory) are more important than others in the development of national consciousness, the mere existence of one or more such characteristics among a group of people is not at all sufficient to guarantee the eventual emergence of a nation.[1] It is less commonly recognized that there is a wide range of variation in the structure and characteristics of many objective criteria, which are too often accepted as 'givens', and that a group's language, religion, and even its territory may be altered as group consciousness develops.[2]

Recent research in sociolinguistics has emphasized the enormous variation in the linguistic composition of states, in the development of different languages, and in the capacities of individuals and groups to command different linguistic codes. States differ in the number of languages spoken within their territories, in the relative size of different language groups, in the development of their languages, and in the use of indigenous and foreign tongues.[3] India may be described, in terms of the use of its most important languages, as a country in which one indigenous language, Hindi, is spoken by a large minority

---

[1] Cf. Akzin, *State and Nation*, p. 34: 'It is in vain that we shall search in the nature or in the extent of objective similarities and dissimilarities for a clue to the riddle why some ethnic groups have become, or are showing signs of developing into, nationalities, while others have not crystallized into nations or have ceased to appear as such.' See also Deutsch, *Nationalism and Social Communication*, p. 97; Emerson, *From Empire to Nation*, Pt. II; Rustow, *A World of Nations*, ch. 2.

[2] Cf. Robert Melson and Howard Wolpe, 'Modernization and the Politics of Communalism: A Theoretical Perspective', *American Political Science Review*, LXIV, No. 4 (December 1970), 1123.

[3] See the elaborate scheme of classification of Heinz Kloss, 'Notes Concerning a Language–Nation Typology', in Fishman, *Language Problems*, pp. 69–85.

of the people of the country and is an official language of the country, but where a foreign language, English, is also used for official purposes, and where a dozen other languages are spoken by large numbers of people and used regionally for official purposes also.[1]

The languages of India differ widely in the extent to which they have been standardized and modernized for contemporary use and in the existence (or not) of competing standards for the same group of dialects.[2] Among the languages of north India which will be discussed in this book, Maithili is characterized by great variation in dialect and mode of address according to position in the social structure. Hindi and Urdu represent competing standards for the spoken varieties of north Indian Hindustani. Punjabi, Hindi, and Urdu are all undergoing both standardization and modernization.

Contemporary research in sociolinguistics has also revealed considerable variation in the capacities of individuals and groups to command more than one linguistic code. Joshua Fishman has pointed out that there is a 'principle of co-territoriality' with regard to language use such that 'one and the same population usually controls several fully systematic varieties (whether registers, dialects, or languages) and these varieties may come to influence *each other* quite systematically as well'.[3] Specifically in north India, John Gumperz has shown that an ordinary villager may have command of two or three forms of speech, including his village dialect; a dialect of the region which he uses in town or in the bazaar and which may or may not have a standardized literary form; and, if he has had formal education, the regional language taught in the schools.[4] An educated town dweller may know several other codes. Throughout India, the regional standard languages have been 'superimposed' on a 'chain of local dialects'.[5] The transition from one dialect area to another will generally be very gradual so that communication barriers do not exist among adjacent groups of people in their spoken language, but become sharp between the regional standard languages. Moreover, there is frequently great discontinuity within a region between the

[1] *Ibid.*, p. 78.
[2] Standardization, restandardization, and modernization as aspects of language change are discussed in Charles A. Ferguson, 'Language Development', in Fishman, *Language Problems*, pp. 31–3.
[3] Joshua A. Fishman, 'Sociolinguistics and the Language Problems of the Developing Countries', in Fishman, *Language Problems*, p. 3.
[4] John J. Gumperz, 'Some Remarks on Regional and Social Language Differences in India' and 'Language Problems in the Rural Development of North India', in University of Chicago, The College, *Introduction to the Civilization of India: Changing Dimensions of Indian Society and Culture* (Chicago: University of Chicago Press, 1957), pp. 31–47.
[5] Gumperz, 'Language Problems', p. 42.

spoken and the written language so that there is a gap between the language of the educated elites and the language of the mass of the people within a region. Where there are competing regional standards, such as Hindi and Urdu in Uttar Pradesh and Bihar or Punjabi and Hindi in the Punjab, the choice of the regional standard to be used in schools and in government offices will depend on factors other than the actual form of speech prevalent in the region, such as a religious group's preference for one literary form or another.

Another significant type of language variation relates to script. Most Indian languages are associated with particular scripts. Some languages are associated with more than one script. The contemporary processes of language standardization and modernization have also affected the adoption of scripts, but cultural preferences have been more important. Hindi and Urdu can be written in either Devanagari or Persian-Arabic script. Hindi and Punjabi can be written in either Devanagari, Persian-Arabic, or Gurumukhi script. The selection of a common script for each language would facilitate written communication between their speakers, but each of these scripts is a powerful symbol for the different religious communities of north India. Choice of script then may affect elite communication. A common script or scripts for the same or similar languages clearly facilitates literary communication; the choice of different scripts impedes such communication.

Religion, like language, is another objective criterion which is usually treated as a 'given'. Static approaches to the linguistic composition of societies can no longer be accepted thanks to the new research in sociolinguistics. Unfortunately, the comparative sociology of religious organization and communication has not begun. Western notions of religious organization and communication, including popular and academic ideas on the subject, reflect conceptualizations based upon Christian patterns of hierarchical bureaucratic organization, compartmentalization of sects, congregational worship, and division between spiritual and temporal spheres of life. In contrast, South Asian religions lack some or all of these features. Hierarchical bureaucratic organizations do not exist in Hinduism, Islam, or Sikhism. Christian-syle congregational worship exists in Islam but not in Hinduism or Sikhism. Sectarian compartmentalization has been growing in South Asian religions during the past century, but pre-modern religious communication in South Asia not only crossed sectarian lines, but it crossed the lines of the great religions as well. It continues to do so at popular levels of religious belief and practice. Individuals and families might be eclectic in their forms of worship and in their visits to shrines of different sects and religions and a single family might contain followers of different religious sects. Hindu–Muslim marriages were probably never common, but Hindu–Sikh marriages certainly were. Indeed, the British census authorities in the nineteenth century found, to their dismay, and could not comprehend the fact, that many people in the Punjab returned their religion as 'Hindu Sikh' or 'Sikh Hindu'. Since the British saw the two religions as distinct, they expected the believers to see things the same way and they ultimately enforced their conceptions in the census by refusing to record such ambiguities. Finally, the notion of a sharp distinction between spiritual and temporal spheres is alien to Islam and Sikhism. It exists in Hinduism in the *varna* distinction between priestly and warrior or ruling orders of society, but such distinctions have been more theoretical than real and have certainly not involved the Western notion of separation of church and state.

South Asian religions have revealed, in varying degrees, the following patterns, particularly in pre-modern times. At the philosophical level and between religious elites of the different religions, differences are great and recognized. At the popular level, there has been considerable fusion of religious beliefs and practices and, therefore, discontinuity in religious beliefs between religious leaders and ordinary believers. Consequently, before religion could become a basis for group differentiation in South Asia, the elite–mass gap within each religion had to be narrowed and religious consolidation had to occur. These developments were not 'givens' but dynamic processes of historical change. However, once such consolidation and differentiation between religious groups took place, few institutional or ideological obstacles existed to the merging of religious and political values, to the growth of group identities along religious lines of division, and to the infusion of nationalism with religious symbols.

In north India, then, we have two 'objective' criteria of ethnic identification which have themselves been subject to variation. Moreover, as has been pointed out above, the two criteria have not been congruent. The two types of cleavage have generally cross-cut each other, a situation which is generally considered to be conducive to stability and adjustment of group differences. In fact, one cleavage has been more important in north India than the other: religion has been the primary line of cleavage, language a secondary one. In order to differentiate themselves further from each other and to obtain political benefits, however, the political elites of the opposing religious communities have struggled to make religion and language congruent, to erect further symbolic barriers to effective communication between groups. This process suggests a theoretical argument of general significance. Whereas the theory of cumulative cleavages argues that political group conflict is likely to arise and be most intense when several cleavages between different groups coincide, the central argument of this book is that the process in north India has been entirely different. Phrased in general terms, the argument is that political elites choose the cultural symbols upon which they wish to base their claims for group rights, that they make a determination as to which symbol is decisive, and that they then work to make other cleavages congruent with the primary cleavage. Therefore, political conflict may induce cumulated cleavages just as the reverse process may occur in which cumulated cleavages produce political conflict. In the former case, members of a group may change their 'objective' marks of distinction, even such presumed 'givens' as their language or their religion.

Internal values and processes of social change

The second set of questions concerning the conditions under which the transformation from ethnic group to nation takes place emphasizes the internal values and the internal processes of social change which exist or are taking place within a group of people. The significant questions here are: do the predominant values in the group emphasize 'other-than-ethnic links' or emphasize 'the ethnic group and its characteristics'?[1] Are processes of social change and social mobilization taking place within the group, leading especially to the spread of literacy and mass communication media? Do these processes of change work in such a way as to produce a core of people, an elite, dedicated to the values of the group and willing to take the leadership to spread, protect, and defend them?

Internal values

Some groups, such as the Jewish people, have from time immemorial had a set of values which have emphasized the special role of the group as a people. Other groups, such as white Anglo-Saxon Protestants in the United States, though recognized by minority groups as separate, have hardly any sense of a common group consciousness or ethnic identity. Every group which seeks to build a sense of consciousness, however, at some point creates a myth of its origin and destiny which is designed to instill pride among its members in

[1] Akzin, *State and Nation*, p. 64.

28

its past and to create confidence in its ability to mold its own future.[1] An oppressed group, whose contemporary condition contrasts unfavorably with its golden past and its hoped-for future, may also add a myth to explain the causes of its decline which attributes its contemporary decadence to the intervention of one alien group or another.

This process of internal value creation or myth construction, so characteristic of both South Asian nationalisms and other South Asian revivalist movements, is a universal aspect of national movements under alien rule or under the domination of other ethnic groups. An identical process has been described by Oscar Jaszi in his classic account of the rise of the nationalities in the Austro-Hungarian empire in the nineteenth century. He remarks how 'the founders of nationalism [in Central and Eastern Europe] attributed a paramount importance to the reconstruction of the historical consciousness of the nation and to the achievements of its language, art, and literature';[2] how 'all the peoples began to discover the forgotten documents of their literature, art, music, and popular customs'; how 'this glorification of the past' inspired some groups among these aspiring nations 'to construct for their struggling nations a promising ideal of future achievements'; and ultimately how this turning to the past to construct a new future also led to the glorification of 'the maternal tongue' which 'became almost sacred, the mysterious vehicle of all the national endeavours'.[3] Finally, an oppressed group seeking to assert its new identity usually finds it convenient to identify one or more opposing groups who stand in its way, from whom the group wishes to separate itself or from whom it demands its rights.[4] Even if the group is not in fact oppressed or discriminated against, it is nevertheless common for a sense of grievance against another group to be cultivated. Indian nationalists asserted their identity against and demanded their rights from the British; Muslims from Hindus; low castes from Brahmans.

The general implications of this whole process of myth formation are clear. Involved, first, is the attachment of value and pride to the 'objective' markers of a group's identity. Second, however, there is a search for new symbols of group identity from the past. Third, there is also involved a process of identification of oppressors, of those who have held or do hold the advancement of the group in check.

---

[1] Cf. Emerson, *From Empire to Nation*, pp. 206–7.
[2] Oscar Jaszi, *The Dissolution of the Hapsburg Monarchy* (Chicago: University of Chicago Press, 1966), p. 249.   [3] *Ibid.*, pp. 260–2.
[4] Lynch, *The Politics of Untouchability*, in his study of the Agra Jatavs uses the term 'negative reference group' to refer to the opposing group (p. 9).

Elites

The attachment of value to symbols of group identity does not happen spontaneously. There is always a particular segment of the group which takes this task upon itself, a class or an elite.[1] Certain classes and elites have historically been considered the special carriers of national consciousness – the urban bourgeoisie in Europe, the Westernized elite in the origins and early stages of nationalism in colonial countries.[2] Other classes and elites have often been associated with other-than-national concerns or have been opposed to the growth of separatist nationalism in their ethnic group. Such classes and elites in Europe, Asia and Africa, and North America have included traditional aristocracies, upper segments of the clergy, civilian and military bureaucrats, and non-indigenous capitalists and traders.

Whether or not a nationalist movement originates within a group, its success or failure, and the form it takes depend upon the character of the elites who have economic and political influence in the society, on whether they are willing to take the lead, and on how capable they are of mobilizing broader segments of the community. Throughout colonial-dominated Asia and Africa, the imperial powers relied upon and used as collaborators in their rule traditional elite groups – chiefs, princes, and landlords.[3] Many of these traditional elites were representatives of local, regional, and ethnic cultures. Some traditional leaders extracted concessions for their groups from the imperial authorities, others were not concerned with ethnic, tribal, or community matters at all. Rarely did traditional elites mobilize their followers for political action around symbols of group identity.

In British- and French-ruled territories, the conditions of imperial rule made available educational opportunities which ultimately led to the emergence of a Western-educated and Westernized elite. This elite, whose members often were sons of the traditional elites, had supralocal cultural, economic, and political orientations. They knew the language and understood the culture of the ruling authorities and some sought access to the highest positions of governance in the colonial administration. Others took employment in modern, urban professions. A relative lack of economic opportunities and restricted access to the instruments of rule fostered discontent among these Westernized groups, who were also developing a sense of a common

[1] Deutsch, *Nationalism and Social Communication*, pp. 31–7, 101–4.
[2] The role of the Westernized elites in spreading nationalism in former colonial countries is the main theme of Emerson's study; see especially, pp. 18–20, 44, 164, 194–7, 208–9.
[3] Cf. *ibid.*, pp. 251–2, and Seal, *The Emergence of Indian Nationalism, passim.*

identity and destiny as a result of increased communication. Before long everywhere, these new elites were developing a national consciousness and mobilizing their peoples to remove the Western powers and to establish independent states.

This story is too well known to require further elaboration. It has been common in the literature which has explored this theme of the rise to national consciousness of the Westernized elite to emphasize its narrowness and alienation from the broad masses of the people and to speculate about what will happen as new aspirants to power rise to challenge the narrow Westernized elite. In most of contemporary Asia and Africa, after the nationalist elites have exhausted themselves in inter-elite competition or have been actually challenged by counter-elite groups, the military and civilian bureaucratic leaders have stepped in with the remnant instruments of colonial power to restore 'order'.

For India, however, the story is somewhat more complex and the *dénouement* different. In India, even during British rule, there were layers and layers of leading groups. The landed gentry, the princes, the 'urban landed elite',[1] and people from many upper caste groups formed the collaborative base for British rule in India. In the various regions of the country, however, certain segments of the old elites and new elites arose to develop an all-India sense of nationality and to challenge British rule – the *bhadra lok* in Bengal, the Chitpavans in Maharashtra, Tamil Brahmans in Madras, urban Hindu castes in Punjab, local rural land controllers in north India. Within each region, however, there were other elites from other groups who contested for political access and economic opportunity in their regions. Non-Brahmans contested for power against Tamil Brahmans and Chitpavans in Madras and Maharashtra;[2] Muslim and Sikh elites contested against Hindu elites in the north. If the Tamil Brahmans spoke the idiom of an all-India nationality, their local non-Brahman rivals spoke the idiom of Dravidian regional nationalism.[3]

---

[1] For a description of these and other elite groups in Indian society in the nineteenth century, see Bernard S. Cohn, 'Recruitment of Elites in India under British Rule', reprinted from Leonard Plotnicov and Arthur Tuden (eds.), *Essays in Comparative Social Stratification* (Pittsburgh: University of Pittsburgh Press, 1970), pp. 121–47; citation from p. 134.

[2] *Ibid.*, esp. pp. 135–46; see also Bernard S. Cohn, 'Regions Subjective and Objective: Their Relation to the Study of Modern Indian History and Society', in Robert I. Crane (ed.), *Regions and Regionalism in South Asian Studies: An Exploratory Study* (Duke University: Program in South Asian Studies, 1967), pp. 29–31. On the role of the *bhadra lok* in Bengal, see J. H. Broomfield, *Elite Conflict in a Plural Society: Twentieth-Century Bengal* (Berkeley: University of California Press, 1968), esp. pp. 1–41.

[3] Irschick, *Politics and Social Conflict in South India.*

If northern urban Hindu elites used symbols of all-India nationality, Muslim and Sikh elites emphasized symbols of Muslim and Sikh separatism. In this way, the symbols of regional and all-India nationalism became instruments in struggles for local and all-India power by competing groups. This multi-layered struggle, with its attendant processes of symbol manipulation, began at different times in different regions of India, but it was well under way in the major provinces in the late nineteenth century. It continues up to the present time and has become, if anything, increasingly complex as new layers of Indian society have become mobilized and still newer elites have risen to prominence.

Social change and social mobilization

Elites attach value to selected symbols of group identity. Competing elites may choose other symbols, may define the group differently, or may seek to separate one group of people from another. The outcome, in a modernizing society moving toward equality and political participation, will depend upon which elites can communicate their goals most effectively to the mobilizing groups in the society – to those segments of a group who are acquiring education, moving to towns, and seeking employment in modern sectors of the economy.

The Westernized elites who led the early phase of nationalist development in India attached value to symbols of all-India nationality and communicated with each other through the medium of English. But English education was not made available to all the mobilizing groups in Indian society. When the nationalist movement gained momentum and when leaders of the Indian National Congress wanted to communicate with broader classes in Indian society, they had to turn to the vernacular languages. On this terrain, however, there were other elites communicating different messages. In this way, competition developed between different elites, attaching value to different symbols, for the allegiance of the already 'mobilized population' of literates, town dwellers, persons employed in non-agricultural occupations, newspaper readers, and the like.[1] More than that, competition developed to mobilize the unmobilized elements of society to be receptive to particular messages. Regional elites established schools to impart education through the medium of a particular vernacular language and to communicate the values of the group. Regional caste elites formed associations to advance the economic and political interests of their groups.

[1] This use of the term 'mobilized population' follows Deutsch, *Nationalism and Social Communication*, p. 126.

32

This process of social change and social mobilization by which people become available for new and 'more intensive' kinds of communication can be measured.[1] The potential long-term prospects of a particular nationalist message can be assessed by looking at the size and composition of the mobilized population and those remaining to be mobilized and by examining rates of change. Where an elite is attempting to communicate a particular nationalist message, the important questions then become: What is the size of the mobilized population which is likely to be receptive to this message? How fast is the unmobilized population being mobilized? How effectively is the message being communicated to the mobilizing population? These questions can be approached, as Karl Deutsch has demonstrated, by collecting figures on rates of change in urbanization,[2] occupational structure, literacy and education, newspaper and book publishing, and the like. Such figures are available from the Indian census volumes, going back to 1872. They rarely have been used to answer questions such as these for any other than the presidency provinces of Bengal, Bombay, and Madras and have hardly ever been used to compare rates of change at different points in time. There are enormous problems in using the Indian provincial census volumes in this way; but, used creatively, they provide a vast fund of information on processes of change among different groups in Indian society. They provide a considerable portion of the data base for this volume.

Inter-group relations

The existence of an elite which attaches value to symbols of a group's identity and of a socially mobilized population to whom the message of group consciousness can be communicated provides the necessary but not sufficient conditions for the transformation of an ethnic group into a self-conscious community. In the absence of

[1] *Ibid.*, pp. 126ff.
[2] A recent article by David Elkins suggests that urbanization by itself is not necessarily a reliable indicator of political mobilization. He has shown, in fact, that levels of electoral turnout are often higher in rural areas than in large cities in south India. However, the more general pattern in the Indian states in post-independence elections was a spurt of urban electoral turnout ahead of rural turnout after the 1952 elections, followed by a more recent closing of the gap between the two as rural political mobilization has increased. In the three north Indian states, urban turnout has been ahead of rural turnout in all post-independence elections except that for Punjab in 1952. See David J. Elkins, 'Regional Contexts of Political Participation: Some Illustrations from South India', *Canadian Journal of Political Science*, v, No. 2 (June 1972), 167–89, and Myron Weiner and John Osgood Field, 'India's Urban Constituencies', unpublished paper presented at the Seminar on Electoral Patterns in the Indian States (Boston, 1972).

other ethnic groups with different, or potentially different, identities, the process of social change would lead only to modernization of the society. It is perception of objective differences between groups, and particularly of uneven rates of social change between them, which provides the catalyst for the development of group consciousness.[1] The important questions here are: Are inter-group relations marked by tensions arising out of frustrated expectations on the part of one group or competition for the allocation of scarce resources between two or more groups? Are there differences in the rates of social mobilization among different ethnic groups such that one group dominates and attempts to assimilate another? Or are processes of social mobilization taking place unevenly, precipitating competition for education and employment?

Assimilation and differentiation

Differential rates of social change between different ethnic groups create conditions which may lead either to the assimilation of one group to another, usually the less advanced to the more advanced, or to differentiation of one group from another. A group can be assimilated by adopting the language or religion of another group or, alternatively, divergent cultural symbols may be relegated to non-public spheres and either secular or composite cultural symbols may be adopted to unite culturally distinct groups. The relative size and levels of advancement of different groups will have a bearing on the process.

Several kinds of situations of inter-group interaction may occur. One common pattern is of a socially mobilized and economically and politically dominant minority, concentrated in urban areas, inter-acting with a less advanced but mobilizing rural hinterland, whose members move to the towns in search of jobs and find that the best jobs are already occupied by a privileged minority, whose language and behavior are also alien. The privileged minority may try to assimilate the mobilizing majority culturally and admit its members into economically and politically desirable positions or it may try to resist the demands of the majority and struggle to maintain its privileges. Even if the privileged minority attempts the method of assimilation, it may fail. There may not be enough schools to provide the desired education, enough jobs to go around, or enough political

---

[1] The importance of uneven rates of change between peoples is stressed generally by Deutsch, *Nationalism and Social Communication*, esp. pp. 29 and 76, and specifically with respect to the development of nationalism in India by Seal, *The Emergence of Indian Nationalism*, esp. p. 22.

positions to be shared. In either case, inability to assimilate or resistance to the group demands of the mobilizing majority, the conditions for group differentiation, and conflict, are created. Such failures of assimilation have occurred in the nineteenth century, between Germans and Czechs in the Sudetenland between the two world wars,[1] between English and French in Quebec in contemporary times. Attempts by privileged minorities to resist assimilation of the mobilizing majority and to maintain dominance are common in the relations between the white minorities in the South African states and the black majorities.

At the other extreme is the situation, characteristic of the relations between whites and blacks in the United States, of a more advanced majority confronted with the needs and demands of a mobilizing minority. In such a situation, especially if the minority is dispersed, either cultural assimilation of the minority or its economic and political absorption into advantaged positions, or both, may more easily occur. If there is resistance on the part of the majority to assimilation of the minority, however, or if the minority group occupies a compact geographical area, then group differentiation and conflict may be the more likely result. Resistance to the assimilation of blacks into cultural and social institutions has engendered inter-group conflict in the United States. Geographical concentration of Welshmen and Scotsmen in the United Kingdom has made possible the development of new nationalisms there among peoples whose assimilation to English or British culture and society had already been well advanced.

In between these two extreme situations, there are innumerable variations in the size, relative social mobilization, and the dimensions of social life in which particular groups are dominant or not. For example, a group may be numerically and politically dominant, but educationally and economically less advanced than other groups. Groups may also be relatively evenly balanced in size, but differ in levels of social mobilization and rates of change. Given the enormous range of variation, how can the outcomes be anticipated? Karl Deutsch has shown that rates of assimilation and rates of social mobilization between different groups can be measured and compared. The essence of his theory of nationalism, in fact, is that the conditions for group differentiation and national conflict arise when the rates of social change by which a newly mobilized group enters into economic and technological interaction with another group proceed more rapidly than the development of communicative

[1] These cases are used by Deutsch, *Nationalism and Social Communication*, pp. 130–4.

capacities between the groups. In short, assimilation progresses when it keeps ahead of the social mobilization of a newly mobilizing group or groups and differentiation occurs when social mobilization moves faster than the assimilation of such a group.[1] This theory has never been tested systematically in an Asian society. It is a central purpose of this book to show that these processes can be compared in an Asian society and that Deutsch's theory can be tested. It will be argued, however, that the theory requires two important modifications. One modification arises out of the fact that there is a difference between capacity to communicate and willingness to communicate. Assimilation may fail where the capacity to communicate exists, but where the willingness to communicate does not. In other words, where group differentiation is consciously sought for political or cultural reasons, communication barriers may be erected. The process emphasizes the centrality of communication to national differentiation, but also suggests the existence of objective and subjective dimensions to effective communication between groups. The second major modification in the theory concerns the importance of politics and political organization in the process of nationality-formation.[2] Deutsch is ambiguous in his assessment of the centrality of politics. At times, he argues that, after all, it is political activity which determines the outcome.[3] At other places, he suggests that, over time, the grand historic processes of social change and social mobilization have a more fundamental impact than political activities.[4] It will be argued in this book that political organization and party and government policies are more often than not decisive in both the formation of group-consciousness and in the character of inter-group relations.

Political action

The fourth set of questions concerns the roles of political organizations and party and government policies in developing group consciousness, presenting group demands, and influencing the course of social and ethnic conflict. What roles do political organizations play in the development of group consciousness and the presentation of group demands? Do political parties exacerbate or ameliorate social and ethnic conflicts in multi-ethnic societies? Do government policies promote integration and assimilation or do they recognize and

---

[1] *Ibid.*, pp. 125–6.
[2] Deutsch himself notes that *Nationalism and Social Communication* 'lacks a discussion of the roles of leading individuals, political organization, and historical decisions' (p. vi).
[3] E.g., *ibid.*, pp. 63–4.
[4] E.g., *ibid.*, p. 133.

tolerate or foster pluralism? Are government policies discriminatory toward minorities or do they recognize equality?

Political organization

Nationalism is, by definition, a political phenomenon. It presumes the making of demands by an ethnic group either already conscious of its communal interests or in the process of being made aware of its communal interests. It requires stressing, however, that nationalism may develop as an elite phenomenon in the absence of a widespread sense of group consciousness of a common identity. In fact, it has been argued above that elite consciousness is a precondition for and, therefore, precedes the development of mass consciousness. In most former colonial countries, the gap between elite and mass consciousness has been wide. It is political organization which everywhere has been called upon to bridge that gap.

Political organizations in multi-ethnic societies vary in the extent to which they promote the aspirations of particular groups or foster an inter-group consciousness of a broader identity. At one end of the continuum are the broad-based national movements which attempted to represent all segments of the population of the colonial territory and to define the nation in all-inclusive terms coextensively with that territory. The prototypical organization of this sort was the pre-independence Indian National Congress, which sought to include all classes, castes, regions, language groups, and religions in its fold and to promote a composite national identity. However, the Congress failed to integrate significant groups in Indian society – particularly the minority religious groups, some regional groups, and low caste groups.

At the other end of the continuum are political organizations and voluntary associations which seek to promote the interests of a single ethnic group, which attempt to define the boundaries of the group, and which confine their membership to members of the group. In India, the best examples of political organizations of this type have been the Muslim League and the Akali Dal. In between the broad-based integrative movement and the restricted particularist movement are political organizations which do not restrict their membership to members of a single ethnic group and do not confine their political demands to those which are concerned primarily with group interests, but which integrate into their party programs and infuse their electoral appeals with ethnic, regional, and religious symbols. Examples of parties of this type in South Asia are the Sri Lanka

37

Freedom Party in Sri Lanka, the Awami League in Bangladesh, and the DMK in Tamil Nadu.

In a developing society, where ethnic identities have not been fully formed, it matters a great deal what kinds of political organizations come to dominate the political arena. The characteristics of political organizations will influence the kinds of appeals and demands that are made. They will also play a role in shaping group consciousness, in defining and redefining the ethnic group. Thus, in Tamil Nadu, several different kinds of organizations have existed in modern times with different definitions of Dravidian identity. Some have included all south India, others have confined their attention to Tamil Nadu, and others have wanted to include only non-Brahmans. In north India, the issues before voluntary associations and political parties have been whether to define the group and present its demands in terms of language or religion. The important point in either case, which will be demonstrated in the case studies in this volume, is that political organizations and voluntary associations do not arise spontaneously to reflect the demands of a 'natural' ethnic group. They often precede the existence of a widespread sense of group identity and they play a critical role in shaping it or failing to shape it.

Party politics and social and ethnic cleavage

The relationship between party competition and social and ethnic cleavages has been a major area for research on political parties during the past half century and one in which there exists a relatively well-developed body of theory. It has been argued that the stability of representative regimes largely depends upon the congruence or non-congruence of party political and social or ethnic cleavages. This theme has its origins in the writings of A. Lawrence Lowell and Arthur Bentley.[1] It has been formulated systematically in recent times in the works of Seymour Lipset, David Truman, and Gabriel Almond.[2] In the writings of the latter, stable democracy has been

[1] A. Lawrence Lowell, *The Government of England*, new ed. (New York: The Macmillan Co., 1931), vol. I, p. 453, and Arthur F. Bentley, *The Process of Government: A Study of Social Pressures*, 4th ed. (Evanston, Ill.: The Principia Press, 1955), p. 208. See also Arend Lijphart's reference to Bentley and his discussion of some of the same issues with which I am concerned here in *The Politics of Accommodation: Pluralism and Democracy in the Netherlands* (Berkeley: University of California Press, 1968), p. 8.

[2] See especially Seymour Martin Lipset, *Political Man: The Social Bases of Politics* (New York: Anchor Books, 1963); David B. Truman, *The Governmental Process: Political Interests and Public Opinion*, 2d. ed. (New York: Alfred A. Knopf, 1971); Gabriel A. Almond, 'Comparative Political Systems', *Journal of Politics*, xviii, No. 3 (August 1956), and 'Introduction: A Functional Approach to Comparative Politics', in Gabriel A.

associated with societies characterized by cross-cutting cleavages, overlapping group memberships, and homogeneous political cultures. In contrast, unstable democracies have been associated with mutually reinforcing cleavages, an absence of overlapping group membership, and fragmented political cultures.

The contemporary theory tends also to see political parties as reflections of societal cleavages. Although the tendency to treat the political parties as dependent variables is more pronounced among some writers than others, and although some writers whose research emphasizes the impact of social cleavages on parties explicitly concede that parties may also play independent and causative roles, the weight of theory and of research in recent years has emphasized the dependence of parties and of the political stability of parliamentary regimes upon social cleavages and the broader political culture.[1] Little room has been left in the theory for the parties and for political leadership to shape the social environment.

The emphasis of the political theory of the political party is of more than academic interest, for it is nowadays one of the favorite arguments of authoritarian political leaders and one of the primary justifications for the imposition of military-bureaucratic or single-party regimes in contemporary developing societies that regimes of competitive political parties are dangerous threats to national unity and national integration in multi-ethnic societies because the parties tend to reflect ethnic differences. Much contemporary scholarship on the relationship between political parties and social and ethnic cleavages in developing societies provides evidence to support such a view.[2]

There is another tradition of theory and research on political

Almond and James S. Coleman (eds.), *The Politics of the Developing Areas* (Princeton: Princeton University Press, 1960); and Gabriel A. Almond and G. Bingham Powell, *Comparative Politics: A Developmental Approach* (Boston: Little, Brown, 1966).

[1] See, for example, Seymour Martin Lipset and Stein Rokkan, 'Cleavage Structures, Party Systems, and Voter Alignments: An Introduction', in Seymour M. Lipset and Stein Rokkan, *Party Systems and Voter Alignments: Cross-National Perspectives* (New York: The Free Press, 1967), esp. pp. 1–6; Almond and Powell, *Comparative Politics*, esp. pp. 110–12. A notable exception is the concluding essay by Myron Weiner and Joseph La Palombara, 'The Impact of Parties on Political Development', in Joseph La Palombara and Myron Weiner (eds.), *Political Parties and Political Development* (Princeton, N.J.: Princeton University Press, 1966), in which parties are looked at as independent variables. However, several essays in that volume treat parties in the more conventional way as dependent variables.

[2] See, for example, Rupert Emerson, 'Parties and National Integration in Africa', in La Palombara and Weiner, *Political Parties*, p. 296; Kearney, esp. pp. 116ff.; Morton Grodzins, 'Political Parties and the Crisis of Succession in the United States: The Case of 1800', in La Palombara and Weiner, *Political Parties*, esp. pp. 303 and 317ff. and Melson and Wolpe, 'Modernization', p. 1122.

parties and social cleavages which is also compatible with the hypothesis about mutually reinforcing cleavages. This tradition can be traced at least as far back as to Henry Jones Ford and, to more recent times, in the work of Pendleton Herring. These writers share with Bentley, Truman, and Lipset an awareness of the importance of cross-cutting cleavages for political stability, but they stress much more the independent role of political parties and political leaders in contributing to the process. Whereas Almond sees the cross-cutting and aggregative character of American (and British) political parties as reflective of their homogeneous cultures, Ford, Lowell, and Herring saw both societies as historically divided and argued that political parties and political leadership had played decisive roles in cross-cutting the divisions in them, moderating social antagonisms, and adjusting diverse interests.[1] While both Ford and Herring agreed that unity and stability in the United States have depended upon the cross-cutting of social cleavages, they saw the primary responsibility for this task in a democracy as resting upon the parties and their leaders.

A more recent study of parliamentary democracy in the Netherlands, by Arend Lijphart, has shown that leadership may preserve unity and stability in a divided society even when the parties do in fact reflect the basic social and religious cleavages. In the Netherlands, the parties are non-aggregative. They represent 'highly distinct clienteles'[2] and reflect the deep and mutually reinforcing social cleavages of class and religion in Dutch society. Unity and stability are maintained by the leaders of the main parties who accept the fundamental character of the divisions between them as 'basic realities which cannot and should not be changed',[3] but which do not prevent negotiation between party elites to reach accommodations on vital issues, including the formation of inter-party coalitions to govern the country. In the Netherlands, the subcultural cleavages of a fragmented society have been overcome by means of deliberate action at the elite level through a strategy of inter-party coalition rather than interest aggregation by broad-based parties.

Thus, students of party politics in the past half-century have uncovered three broad patterns of relationship between party politics and social cleavages in representative systems. There is, first, the situation when a series of mutually reinforcing cleavages divide different social groups and these cleavages are also reflected in the

---

[1] Henry Jones Ford, *The Rise and Growth of American Politics: A Sketch of Constitutional Development* (New York: The Macmillan Co., 1911), pp. 302–7, and Pendleton Herring, *The Politics of Democracy: American Parties in Action* (New York: W. W. Norton, 1965).

[2] Lijphart, *The Politics of Accommodation*, p. 302.

[3] *Ibid.*, p. 124.

relations between competing political parties, making stable and effective government and national unity difficult if not impossible. There is, second, the situation described by Henry Jones Ford and Pendleton Herring where the conflicts of a deeply divided society are moderated and compromised by broadly based political parties which strive to unite different sections, ethnic groups, and classes in a common platform, making possible both national unity and stable and effective government. Third, there is the case of Dutch democracy, where social and religious cleavages are sharp, mutually reinforcing, and reflected in the organization of the political parties, but where elite consensus and leadership overcome and transcend existing social antagonisms through accommodation of differences, rather than through pragmatic solution of differences. To recognize these three patterns is to admit the importance of leadership and the independent role of political parties in determining the outcomes. If the first pattern is not inevitable in deeply divided societies, then one is tempted to conclude that when civil wars or political disintegration do occur, leadership is involved here as well. In fact, there are good grounds for believing that parties and leaders play independent roles as much or more when they seek to exploit social and ethnic differences as when they seek to compromise and accommodate them. Civil wars, revolutions, and new nationalities do not just happen. Men, communities, and parties will them and work for them.

North Indian politics provides examples of all three patterns of relationship between political parties and ethnic cleavages, but in all cases political parties and their leaders have played decisive roles in determining the outcomes. Hindus and Muslims in Uttar Pradesh and Hindus and Sikhs in the Punjab have been divided by mutually reinforcing cleavages, but it is parties and voluntary associations which have worked to reinforce the cleavages. The parties have not simply reflected pre-existing cleavages. The second pattern of an aggregative party working to moderate group conflicts has also been important in north India in the roles played by the Indian National Congress generally and by the Unionist Party in pre-independence Punjab. Finally, there have also been examples of 'the politics of accommodation' where competing party leaders, after contesting against each other on ethnic-religious issues in the electoral arena, have joined hands in forming coalition governments after the elections are over.

Government policies

Governments also are very far from being silent spectators to or victims of the pre-existing cleavages of divided societies. In the decisions and policies they make and in the general strategies they follow, they influence the development of group consciousness and the patterns of group conflict. In India, during British rule, government made crucial decisions which affected the development of language and religious groups. Some languages were used for official, administrative purposes or as media of instruction in schools, others were not. Some were encouraged earlier than others. Political mechanisms of representation were used, such as separate electorates and weightage in representation for religious minorities, which facilitated the political consolidation of the minorities. Some policies and decisions were made in response to group demands, but others were simply decisions taken for reasons of administrative convenience. Whatever the bases for the decisions, they invariably had significant consequences for group identity and for patterns of inter-group conflict.

In general, whatever the specific policies of the British toward particular language or religious groups, the predominant strategy of British rule towards ethnic diversities was to recognize such diversities and to grant them institutional expression whenever it was politically feasible to do so. In essence, the British followed a strategy of 'pluralism on the basis of equality'. Some groups were sometimes favored or given special privileges, but the British did not seek to establish one group as everywhere dominant over another and they did not encourage discriminatory policies. Their strategy was to equalize or ameliorate perceived imbalances of one group *vis-à-vis* another. With respect to the major cleavage on the subcontinent in pre-independence times, that between Hindus and Muslims, British policies failed to prevent catastrophe. Ultimately, the Muslim League leaders convinced themselves and the enfranchised Muslim electorate of the time that no amount of institutionalized pluralism would prevent domination in an independent India. They, therefore, opted for secession or partition of India.

Since independence, the Government of India and the state governments have followed a mixture of strategies, some assimilationist or integrationist, others pluralist. In general, while some government leaders have tended to speak the language of national integration and to pursue integrationist solutions in politics, the central government in practice has permitted and encouraged pluralist solutions in some areas in the schools, in official language policies, and in linguistic reorganization of states. Insofar as central government leaders have condemned the forces of caste, community, and region, as they occasionally have done, have urged citizens of India to focus their loyalties on the Indian state and the sanctity of its entire national territory, and have searched India's past for symbols to use to unite the diverse peoples of India, they have pursued an integrationist ideal. However, both the Constitution of India and the informal rules which the central government has pursued in relation to regional demands place the emphasis of the policy of the Government of India in the direction of a general strategy of 'pluralism on the basis of equality'. That strategy is indicated normatively in several articles of the Constitution, which grant to both individuals and groups the right to preserve their separate languages, scripts, cultures, religions, and educational institutions. It is also supported structurally by the existence of institutions and offices under the Government of India to protect the rights of minorities, such as the Commissioner for Linguistic Minorities and the Commissioner for Scheduled Castes and Scheduled Tribes. On the other hand, many state governments have pursued policies of assimilation of minority groups, sometimes to the point of discrimination, while others have permitted pluralist solutions to group demands.

Central and state government policies toward linguistic and religious group rights and demands in north India will be examined in detail in the case studies. At this point, it is necessary to stress only that government policies have consequences for the development of group consciousness and the articulation of group demands. Assimilationist policies may succeed when the actual imbalances in language development and social mobilization between a dominant and a non-dominant group are great. They may fail and lead to an intensification of group conflict when the non-dominant group is mobilizing rapidly or has already passed the threshold of group consciousness. Pluralist policies may ameliorate group conflicts and make accommodation possible, but this too will depend upon the relative imbalances between groups and the perceived and actual consequences of different types of pluralist solutions for the political relationships between groups.

Themes, arguments, and hypotheses

The view of nationality-formation which will be elaborated in the case studies in this book may be summarized as follows. The process of nationality-formation is one in which objective differences between peoples acquire subjective and symbolic significance, are translated into group consciousness, and become the basis for political demands. There are two stages in the development of a

43

nationality. In the first stage, a particular elite takes the leadership, attaches symbolic value to certain objective characteristics of a group, defines the boundaries of the group, creates a myth of group history and destiny, and attempts to communicate that myth to the defined population, particularly to the socially mobilizing segments of it. Four requisites are essential to the successful transformation of an objectively different group of people into a subjectively conscious community – the existence of a 'pool of symbols' of distinctiveness to draw upon; an elite willing to select, transmit, and standardize those symbols for the group;[1] a socially mobilizing population to whom the symbols of group identity can be transmitted; and the existence of one or more other groups from whom the group is to be differentiated. Of central importance at this stage is the relationship between rates of social mobilization and assimilation of an ethnic group in relation to another, dominant or competitive group. The leading hypothesis here is that the conditions for the differentiation of a culturally distinct ethnic group from a rival group with which it must interact and communicate occur when the rates of social mobilization within the group move faster than the rates of assimilation of the group to the language and culture of its rival. For example, let us assume a decennial rate of emigration of 100,000 school age children of speakers of language X from the countryside to towns in which language Y is the official language. Assume also that the schools of the towns, teaching only through the medium of language Y, are absorbing only 20,000 of these children (who receive no other competing form of language instruction) and that, of the remaining 80,000, 40,000 are not receiving instruction at all and 40,000 are receiving instruction through their own tongue in community-run schools. In this case, therefore, on this one measure of urbanization, the social mobilization of the speakers of language X is clearly proceeding faster than its assimilation to language Y. To the extent that all or most such indicators suggest the same trend, then the conditions for group differentiation and cultural separatism are being created. The elaboration of this hypothesis and the development of measures to test it will be a major concern throughout this volume.

The second stage in the formation of a nationality involves the articulation and acquisition of political rights for the group. Political demands may be articulated by an elite even before a group acquires cohesion. They may even be conceded in the absence of group cohesion. But the only proof of the existence of a nationality is the achievement and maintenance of group rights through political

---

[1] Cohn, 'Regions', pp. 22–31.

activity and political mobilization. The movement from communal consciousness to political action requires two conditions: a perception of inequality in the distribution of and competition for the allocation of scarce values and material rewards between different groups and a political organization to articulate group demands. Government policies may intensify or moderate group conflicts, but the kinds of political demands made are likely to depend more upon calculations relating to the relative power of competing elites and competing groups in a political system than to the adequacy or inadequacy of government policies in satisfying group demands. The willingness of competing communal elites to share political power is of greater importance in maintaining the political cohesion of multi-ethnic and multi-national societies than any other factor. Where that willingness to share power exists, communal conflicts between mobilized groups can be accommodated. Where it does not exist, conflict, escalation of political demands, and ultimately violence are common.

There are two levels of analysis and argument in this book. On a general level, three themes will be elaborated at some length. The first is that objective marks of group identity, such as language or religion, are not 'givens' from which group indentities naturally spring, but are themselves subject to variation. The second theme is that, in the formation of group identities, nationalist elites tend to emphasize one symbol above others and strive to bring other symbols into congruence with the primary symbol. Where it is not possible to induce such congruence of symbols, those symbols which are not subject to change or are considered too explosive may be declared illegitimate for political purposes. Thus, the Westernized elites in developing countries attach value to the modern state and seek to create a national identity coextensive with it and to declare caste, tribe, and religion as illegitimate bases for political activity. Indigenous political elites who attach value to such symbols as caste, tribe, and religion, on the other hand, seek to induce multi-symbol congruence in their groups to achieve separateness and political rights. They may ultimately seek to make the state congruent as well by demanding sovereignty for their group.

The third theme which will be stressed in this book is the centrality of politics and political organization to the formation and channeling of group identities. Political organizations do not simply reflect or transmit communal demands. They shape group consciousness by manipulating symbols of group identity to achieve power for their group. Moreover, the character of the political arena and the outcome of struggles for political power between competing

45

elites within it may determine whether a communal group is mobilized for political action or not. Institutional political mechanisms,
such as separate electorates, may promote communal political conflict. Defeated political elites who have not previously made use of
communal symbols may choose to change the rules of the game in
order to recapture power. The process may also move in the other
direction. A change in the political arena and the rules of the game
may also induce elites who have manipulated communal symbols to
cease doing so or to use other symbols. In either case, political
mechanisms and the struggle for political power may determine
whether or not a group moves from communal consciousness to
national consciousness.

The second level of analysis concerns the nature of Indian society
and politics. The view of Indian society and politics presented here is
of a multi-ethnic society containing many ethnic groups and
nationalities moving toward the development of a politically integrated but multi-national state, with workable rules for solving most
group conflicts successfully and with the power to suppress those
conflicts which are pursued against the prevailing rules and norms.
It is a society in which grand processes of both social differentiation
and assimilation between peoples are taking place. In north India,
particularly, processes of assimilation and differentiation have been
in progress which have affected the relations between religious groups
(Hindus, Muslims, and Sikhs) and language groups (Hindi-users and
users of other north Indian languages). In contrast to the rest of
India, where language has been the chief symbol of group identity
and religion a less politically salient symbol, religion has been the
more potent symbol in the north and language the secondary symbol.
Indeed, where language identification in the north has not been
reinforced by a separate religious identification, assimilation of
minority language speakers to Hindi has taken place. On the other
hand, where religion has been the chief source of separatist sentiment, the political strategy of opposing groups has been to strive to
make language and all other differences congruent with the religious
cleavage. And, in a curious political turnabout caused by the illegi-
timacy of religious demands in Indian politics, political conflicts
based on religion can be resolved only by reference to the secondary
cleavage of language. Thus, members of religious groups who speak
the same language seek to reinforce the differences between them
and other groups by changing their language identification. They
then pursue political rights on behalf of their language group, not on
behalf of their religious group. In the meantime, since language and

religion have become congruent, illegitimate demands have been made legitimate politically. In this way, political considerations have influenced dramatically the development of group identities.

THREE CASES

The themes and arguments of this book will be elaborated by examining three case studies of the relationships between language, religion, and politics in north India. The first case study, of the Maithili movement in north Bihar, in Part II of this book, describes and explains the failure of a regional linguistic movement to develop strength around the symbol of the Maithili language and the consequent absorption of Maithili-speakers into the Hindi speech community. Part III is a case study of Urdu and the Muslims in Uttar Pradesh and Bihar and is divided into three segments. The first segment, in chapter 3, describes the origin of Muslim separatism in the United Provinces before independence. The second segment, chapter 4, describes the transformation of Muslim politics in the north after independence, the focus of the Muslim minority on the linguistic symbol of Urdu, and the efforts of the dominant Hindu political leaders to assimilate Urdu-users into the Hindi speech community. The third segment, chapter 5, describes the efforts of Muslim political elites and organizations to develop a viable political strategy for the Muslim minority in both Uttar Pradesh and Bihar and their failure so far to do so. Part IV describes the most successful regional linguistic movement in north India, the movement of the Sikhs to achieve a separate Punjabi-speaking state. Chapter 6 analyzes the historical dimensions of language, religious, and political change in the Punjab. Chapter 7 describes the ways in which party and government policies have influenced and accommodated linguistic and religious demands in the Punjab. Chapter 8 analyzes the development of an electoral and party system based upon communal cleavages between Hindus and Sikhs. Part v consists of a concluding chapter 9, in which the three cases are compared systematically and generalizations are drawn from the comparisons concerning the process of nationality-formation in north India.

The three case studies provide a meaningful range of variation, from the Maithili movement, which has achieved neither communal consciousness nor significant political success; to the Muslim movement, which has developed communal consciousness but has failed (in the post-independence period) to achieve political success; to the Sikh and Punjabi Suba movement, which has achieved both

47

communal consciousness and political success. These three cases will be examined both diachronically, in order to show the historic dimensions of language, religious, and political change, and synchronically, in order to set in a comparative context the view of nationality-formation presented above.

PART II

THE POLITICS OF LANGUAGE

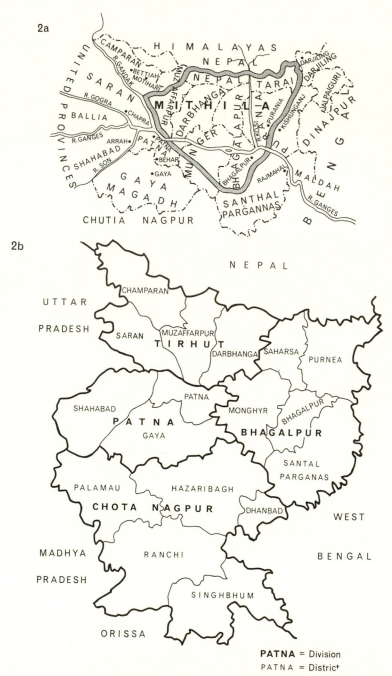

Fig. 2a   Map of the Maithili-speaking areas of Bihar and Nepal, according to Grierson

Fig. 2b   Divisions and districts of Bihar, 1972

2

THE MAITHILI MOVEMENT
IN NORTH BIHAR

One weakness in the body of literature on nationalism and regionalism is the excessive emphasis given to the great movements of history
which either have succeeded or have caused sufficient political tur-
moil to attract wide attention. We know more about the conditions
for the success of national movements than we do about the conditions
for their failure. In other words, social science theories of nationalism
have not provided controlled tests of their hypotheses. We know
more about the Irish national movement in the nineteenth century
than we do about the integration of Scotland and Wales into British
society and politics in the same period. We know more about the
Muslim and Punjabi movements or even about separatism in Nagaland than we do about the processes of integration and assimilation
which have been taking place in the north Indian states, involving
the absorption by the Hindi movement of the diverse languages and
dialects of the north.

This chapter focuses on the most distinctive of the regional
language groups in north India, that of the Maithili-speaking people
of north Bihar, and raises the question why the Maithili-speaking
people, objectively different from the other peoples of Bihar in
language, culture, and territory, have not so far transformed their
objective differences into a significant subjective consciousness. It will
be demonstrated here that while the objective conditions for a
Maithili regional identity exist in abundance, the major requisites for
subjective regional consciousness have been lacking.

With respect to the internal values and processes of change among
the Maithili-speaking people, it will be shown, first, that ethnic values
are emphasized by an elite which has failed to communicate those
values effectively to the majority of the people. Moreover, the elite
itself has been ambiguous about the priority of its identities between
Mithila and India. Second, internal processes of social mobilization
among the Maithili-speaking people have been very slow. North
Bihar is, in fact, one of the most backward areas in the entire country
on most measures of social and economic modernization. In contrast, politically, north Bihar has been in the forefront of most

modern political movements in the state. The political elites of the region have, however, chosen not to emphasize regional symbols in the state political arena.

The external relations of the Maithili-speakers with other ethnic groups have been of two sorts. On the one hand, there are the socially mobilized Maithils who have migrated to cities outside their region for employment, who have acquired a consciousness of their language and culture, and who have taken a disproportionate share in the making of political demands on behalf of Maithili. On the other hand, there have been contacts between the more backward Maithili-speaking people on the periphery of the Maithili region with the more advanced Magahi- and Hindi-speaking people, leading to the absorption of Maithils by the dominant ethnic group in the state.

Finally, political action on behalf of Maithili has been minimal. The Maithili movement has lacked dynamic leadership and strong organization and has not become a significant political constituency. There have been no great demonstrations or movements pressing the demands of the Maithili-speaking people. The government of Bihar, in the absence of serious political pressure, has followed a policy of symbolic concessions, granting sympathy and rights to Maithili-speakers, but no effective protection to the Maithili language and no effective implementation of rights conceded. The Bihar government has not opposed Maithili, but it has refused to provide state assistance to the Maithili-speakers to foster a sense of separateness among them.

The failure of the Maithili-speaking elite to promote successfully a sense of identity among the mass of Maithili-speakers has both a specific and a general explanation. The specific explanation, which will be discussed in detail in this chapter, concerns the social and political relations among speakers of different mother tongues, dialects, and languages of Bihar. The more general explanation, which will become clearer when the Sikh–Punjabi and Muslim–Urdu movements are contrasted with the Maithili movement, is that religion has been the more powerful symbol in north India during the past century. The Maithili movement not only lacks an association with religion, but has been partly overwhelmed by the broader north Indian conflicts between Hindus and Muslims, manipulating the linguistic symbols of Hindi and Urdu.

MITHILA AND MAITHILI

The demand for a Mithila state

In 1954, a memorandum was presented to the States' Reorganization

Commission by Jankinandan Singh, putting forth a reasoned statement justifying the formation of a new state of Mithila out of the districts of north Bihar.[1] The demand was considered too unimportant and non-controversial even to be mentioned in the report of the Commission.[2] Yet, the *prima facie* case made out on behalf of the Mithila state was no less reasonable on grounds of administrative convenience, linguistic homogeneity, common culture, and geography than the demands and arguments put forth by other linguistic and tribal groups in India and considered by the Commission. The history of the Mithila state demand provides some insight into the relationship between the objective factors which may form the basis for regional demands in India and the subjective conditions necessary for their success.

The demand for the formation of a Mithila state was first formally made in 1940 in a resolution passed at a meeting of the Maithil Mahasabha at Darbhanga.[3] The demand was repeated on several occasions by the Maharaja of Darbhanga during his annual speeches at the Maithil Mahasabha meetings,[4] in the pages of the *Mithila Mihir* from time to time,[5] in a series of pamphlets written by Laksman Jha of Darbhanga,[6] and was taken up by several other Maithili organizations in the years after independence.[7] In January 1954, the movement reached its high point when a series of meetings was held

[1] Jankinandan Singh, *Memorandum for the Formation of the Mithila State* (Darbhanga: Jankinandan Singh, 1954). The author of the report, a relative of the Maharaja of Darbhanga, was a prominent politician of Darbhanga district, who had been involved in a factional struggle for power in the Darbhanga District Congress Committee at the time. He later left the Congress, at first to form his own Jan Congress, then to join in the formation of the Swatantra Party in 1959–60. It is possible that the Maithili cause was being used by Jankinandan Singh as a useful symbol for a politician in search of a political base and a platform. Interview (M6:3) in Patna on 19 April 1967. See also Howard L. Erdman, *The Swatantra Party and Indian Conservatism* (Cambridge: Cambridge University Press, 1967), pp. 72, 113, 124, 161, 166–7.

[2] The 'more important and controversial issues' concerning Bihar which the Commission considered were the demand for a Jharkhand state and the Bihar–West Bengal and Bihar–Orissa border disputes. Government of India, Home Department, *Report of the States Reorganisation Commission* (Delhi: Government of India Press, 1955), pp. 168–71.

[3] *Mithila Mihir* (*MM*), January 1942.

[4] *Presidential addresses of His Highness, the Maharajadhiraja of Darbhanga, at the 37th Conference of the Maithil Mahasabha and at the 38th Conference of the Maithil Mahasabha held at Madhubani on 7 May 1949* (no publication details); translated from Maithili.

[5] *MM*, 17 July and 9 October 1947, 28 February and 20 April 1948, 19 February 1949, and 7 March 1953.

[6] Dr Laksman Jha wrote nine pamphlets in English between 1952 and 1956, which he very graciously presented to me during a visit to him in Darbhanga in April 1967. The titles are given in the bibliography and in the footnotes where relevant.

[7] The Maithil Mandal of Banaras supported the demand in 1947; *MM*, 7 November 1947. The Maithili Sahitya Parishad added its support in December 1953; *MM*, 30 January 1954.

53

in Darbhanga under the leadership of Jankinandan Singh to support the demand for a separate state and to send a delegation to the Calcutta session of the All-India Congress Committee (AICC) to present the demand. The delegation was arrested at the Asansol railway station and was not permitted to attend the session.[1] Another meeting under Jankinandan Singh was held in February 1954,[2] and his memorandum was presented to the States' Reorganization Commision around this time. Since that time, the demand has not been voiced seriously by the prominent leaders and organizations of the Maithili movement. Nor does there appear to be any significant sentiment for the revival of the demand even among the intellectual leaders of the Maithili movement at the present time.[3] There have also been charges that the original demands reflected the ambitions of the Maharaja of Darbhanga[4] and that the 1954 demands arose largely out of a factional fight in the Congress organization of Darbhanga district[5] rather than out of any heartfelt sentiment of either the leaders or the people of Mithila.

The Mithila state demand is clearly of greater theoretical than practical significance. The arguments made on behalf of the Mithila state are familiar arguments made by many nationality movements in India and elsewhere and they are objectively reasonable. Yet the demand has been of no consequence politically. The question naturally arises, what factors are present in or absent from the Mithila movement, which have prevented the demand from acquiring any force?

The objective bases for the Mithila demand

The objective arguments put forth by the sponsors of the Mithila demand are of a type familiar to students of nationalism and fall into three categories – the artificiality of the existing administrative boundaries of the state of Bihar; the distinctive characteristics which distinguish Mithila from the rest of Bihar and the rest of India; and a charge of discriminatory allocation of political power and economic resources among the regions of Bihar.

The present boundaries of the state of Bihar have arisen out of the stages in British annexation of territory westward from Bengal in the nineteenth century, out of the wars with the Gurkhas of Nepal and the treaty of Sugauli in 1816, and out of the separation of the Bengali-

[1] *MM*, 16 and 23 January 1954.
[2] *MM*, 27 February 1954.
[3] Interviews (M5:3) in Darbhanga on 17 April 1967 and (M10:3, 9–13) in Patna on 7 July 1967.
[4] Laksman Jha, *Mithila: A Union Republic* (Darbhanga: Mithila Mandal, 1952), pp. 58–9.
[5] Interview, M6:3.

and Oriya-speaking peoples from Bihar in 1912, 1936, and 1955. Consequently, in the east and south, Bihar is separated from the provinces of Bengal and Orissa largely on linguistic grounds. The treaty of Sugauli between the British and the Gurkhas, however, divided the north Bihar plain and conceded the Maithili-speaking tarai districts to Nepal.[1] On the west, there are no natural or cultural distinctions between Bihar and Uttar Pradesh. In fact, the boundary between these two states divides the Bhojpuri-speaking people.

Nor is Bihar in any significant respects at all homogeneous internally. There are major geographical distinctions, partly reinforced by linguistic and cultural distinctions, between the Maithili-speaking north Bihar plain, separated from the rest of Bihar by the Ganges river; the Magahi- and Bhojpuri-speaking plains districts south of the Ganges; and the heavily tribal hill districts of Chota Nagpur. Consequently, it is objectively quite true that the external boundaries of Bihar are largely artificial and that it is internally extremely heterogeneous.

In contrast, it is argued, a Mithila state would form a compact and homogeneous political unit. However, the distinctive features called upon to justify the formation of a Mithila state do not entirely reinforce each other. The geographical boundaries commonly given for the proposed state of Mithila are indeed sharply defined natural boundaries, consisting of the Himalayas on the north, the Ganges river on the south, and the Gandak and Kosi rivers on the west and east respectively.[2] However, these boundaries are highly impractical and, even if they could be achieved, would not conform to the linguistic and cultural boundaries of the Maithili-speaking people. The northern boundary of the Himalayas would require revision of the 1816 treaty with Nepal, the western boundary of the Gandak would include the Bhojpuri-speaking people of Champaran and north-western Muzaffarpur districts, the southern and eastern boundaries of the Ganges and the Kosi would exclude the Maithili-speaking people of Monghyr, Bhagalpur, and Purnea districts (see fig. 2).

The nonconformity of geographical and linguistic boundaries notwithstanding, the claim that the people of north Bihar speak a separate language, which has a long and glorious literary tradition, has been a central element in the Mithila state demand. The language

[1] The division of the Maithili-speaking people in this way is the subject of a pamphlet by Laksman Jha, *The Northern Border* (Darbhanga: Mithila Mandal, 1955).
[2] *MM*, 7 March 1953 and 23 January 1954; Laksman Jha, *Mithila: A Union Republic*, p. 23; Jankinandan Singh, *Memorandum*, p. 36.

issue will be discussed more extensively below, but it should be noted here that the distinctness of the Maithili language and the greatness of its literature have provided the basic underlying justification for regional demands. The literary history of Maithili also provides the central symbol of the movement in the great Maithili poet of the fifteenth century, Vidyapati.[1] All the literary and cultural organizations of the Maithili-speaking people hold annual Vidyapati week celebrations to recite the poetry and sing the songs of the master. The annual Vidyapati week celebrations are as important to the building of regional consciousness in Mithila as Tilak's Ganesh and Shivaji festivals were in Maharashtra at the turn of the century.

It is also claimed that the people of Mithila of all castes form a territorial community, called Maithils.[2] In fact, however, this identification of castes with the territory of Mithila is distinctive primarily of the Brahmans and Kayasthas, who distinguish themselves from Brahman and Kayastha castes of other regions, maintain their genealogies most carefully, and do not marry outside of the Mithila region or with castes which do not have a proper genealogical table.[3] The dominance of Maithil Brahmans, especially, in the territory both economically and culturally has been a distinctive characteristic of the area, noted by Grierson and others.[4] The Brahmans have held much of the land, have provided the last ruling dynasty of the region, and have preserved the ancient history, language, and culture of Mithila over the centuries. However, the Brahmans are not the largest caste in the region. This position is held by the Yadavs, a backward caste, who are twice as numerous as the Brahmans in north Bihar, constitute the largest caste in every district in the region except Purnea,[5] and increasingly threaten the economic and political dominance of elite castes in the region. Most important from the point of view of the unity of Maithil castes, the Yadavs do not have strong identifications with the Maithili culture and region, they intermarry with Yadavs outside Mithila, and they identify more

[1] Vidyapati celebrations, centering around the poetry, drama, and music of Vidyapati, are sponsored annually by the leading Maithili organizations in Mithila and in Maithili centers outside Mithila. E.g., see *MM*, 5 and 12 December 1965. The importance given to Vidyapati as the central symbol of the Maithili movement is explicitly noted in *MM*, 20 June 1965.

[2] Jankinandan Singh, *Memorandum*, p. 19.

[3] Ramanath Jha, 'The Panjis of Mithila', *Indian Nation*, 11 April 1971.

[4] G. A. Grierson, *Linguistic Survey of India*, vol. v, pt. II (Delhi: Motilal Banarsidass, 1968), p. 4.

[5] See Joseph E. Schwartzberg, 'The Distribution of Selected Castes in the North Indian Plain', *Geographical Review* LV, No. 4 (1965), 490–1 and map: the Yadavs are referred to in Schwartzberg by their original census designation as Ahirs.

with their caste brethren in other parts of Bihar. In fact, cross-regional caste ties seem to be far more important politically for most castes in Mithila, with the exception of the Brahmans and Kayasthas. Even the latter castes have formed political alliances with their counterparts from other regions in the state.

A third element, in addition to geography and language, commonly considered to be a building-block of regional and national identity, is a distinct and common historical tradition.[1] Mithila, it is argued, has had a long and continuous existence as a compact territorial unit always either independent or treated as a separate administrative unit.[2] However, the history of Mithila is as ambiguous on this question as its geographical and linguistic boundaries. There is historical evidence that Mithila has had a separate history from the rest of Bihar, but there is also evidence of close association between Mithila and the rest of Bihar. Much of Mithila has been independent in the past or has been at times a separate administrative unit, but its historical boundaries do not always coincide with its geographical and linguistic boundaries.

There are objective distinctions, as well as similarities, between Mithila and the rest of Bihar in culture and religion also. Mithila is a land of traditional Vedic orthodoxy, a continuing center to this day of Sanskrit learning and culture. It has a separate calendar, a special insistence on genealogical purity, a separate language and script, unique festivals, and some distinctive habits of diet and dress.[3] At the same time, there are few cultural and religious symbols which Mithila does not share with other parts of Bihar or with neighboring Bengal. Mithila may be especially orthodox, but it is Hindu; it may have more than its share of Sanskrit pandits, but no monopoly of them; it may have unique festivals, but it celebrates others jointly with the people of south Bihar and Bengal. In short, there are distinct symbols of culture and religion to be called upon to build regional consciousness, but there are also common symbols which can be used to unify Mithila with the rest of Bihar.

Finally, the supporters of a separate Mithila state have argued that not only is Mithila a distinct region, artificially bound to an artificial province, but that the tie to Bihar has been an exploitative one. It is argued that the Bihar government spends much less on Mithila than it receives in taxes, that north Bihar has fewer irrigation

---

[1] All these 'elements of nationhood' are discussed theoretically by Rupert Emerson, *From Empire to Nation: The Rise to Self-Assertion of Asian and African Peoples* (Boston: Beacon Press, 1962), ch. 6–8.

[2] *MM*, 6 February 1954, Jankinandan Singh, *Memorandum*, pp. 24–35.

[3] Jankinandan Singh, *Memorandum*, pp. 21–3.

facilities, that its industrial potential has not been explored, that unemployment is higher than in south Bihar, that there are fewer roads and fewer educational facilities available in the region than elsewhere in the state.[1] It is also argued that the economic exploitation and neglect of north Bihar is no accident, but has arisen out of the political domination of the Magahi- and Bhojpuri-speaking people in the political life of the state.[2] Many of these charges are objectively true. However, in contrast to other minority groups in north India who have been able to cultivate a sense of grievance where there was no objective basis, the people of north Bihar have remained largely indifferent to objective evidence of differential economic development and political power.

Regional identity and the Darbhanga Raj

Regional and national movements in India and elsewhere frequently select out of the past symbols which establish the continuity, distinctness, and grandeur of the historical-political traditions of the area.[3] It appears, in fact, that such movements benefit more from the full freedom to select the desired symbols from the past than from the living embodiment of an historical-political tradition in the present. The cultivation of the Shivaji myth to build a Maharashtrian regional identity has not suffered from the absence of living descendants wielding royal power. By the same token, the presence in Mithila of a living ruler with pretensions to the status of an hereditary prince, who was able to trace his origins to a dynasty established by Akbar in the sixteenth century, has provided no guarantee of the emergence of a national identity in Mithila. In fact, some have argued that the living presence of a Maharaja in Mithila has hindered the development of Maithili regional consciousness.

The Darbhanga Raj traces its origins to the grant by Akbar to the Brahman scholar, Mahesh Thakur, of the Sarkar of Tirhut, roughly corresponding to the present districts of Darbhanga and Muzaffarpur.[4] It has been argued by the contemporary Maharajas and their apologists that the rulership is an hereditary one and that the Sarkar of Tirhut was practically an independent kingdom by the eighteenth

[1] *Ibid.*, pp. 39–52; Laksman Jha, *Mithila in India* (Laheriasarai, Darbhanga: Mithila Mandal, 1953), p. 41.
[2] Laksman Jha, *Mithila: A Union Republic*, pp. 134, 155.
[3] Bernard S. Cohn, 'Regions Subjective and Objective: Their Relation to the Study of Modern Indian History and Society', in Robert I. Crane (ed.), *Regions and Regionalism in South Asian Studies: An Exploratory Study* (Duke University: Program in Comparative Studies on Southern Asia, 1967), p. 6.
[4] Jnanendra Nath Kumar, *The Genealogical History of India*, pt. II (Calcutta: Jnanendra Nath Kumar, 1933 [?]), p. 10.

century. However, after the conquest of Bengal and Bihar by the British, the Raja of Tirhut or Darbhanga was recognized in the Permanent Settlement only as a zamindar.[1] The lands of the Darbhanga Raj were spread over large portions of the region of Mithila, including estates in the districts of Muzaffarpur, Darbhanga, Bhagalpur, Purnea, and the south Bihar districts of Patna and Monghyr.[2] The Darbhanga estate was among the very largest in Bengal, the 'zamindars' of Darbhanga were called Rajas (later Maharaja and Maharajadhiraja), and most of the trappings of princely status were present in Darbhanga; but the Maharaja was never formally granted the status of a ruling prince.[3]

Leaders in the Maithili and Mithila movements looked upon the Raja of Darbhanga as the ruler of Mithila, as the living embodiment of the independent history and culture of the region. The Maharaja of Darbhanga was the pre-eminent head of the Maithil Brahman community and the hereditary leader of the Maithil Mahasabha, the caste association of the Maithil Brahmans and Kayasthas.[4] The Maharajas also favored the cause of the Maithili language, supporting the revival of Maithili literature and the introduction of Maithili in Patna University.[5]

There is no doubt that the Maharajas of Darbhanga, therefore, played a leading role in the development of interest in the culture of Mithila. However, the activities of the Maharajas on behalf of Maithili were but a small portion of their activities. Moreover, many of the causes which the Maharajas have supported have been detrimental to the development of a Mithila regional consciousness.

The Maharajas of Darbhanga were supporters of orthodox Hindu practices in both caste and religion[6] and were devoted to the Sanskrit tradition.[7] These practices and traditions partly transcend and partly hinder the development of Maithili regional consciousness because of their all-India orientation and their elitist exclusivism.

The Maharajas of Darbhanga also had political and economic interests which drew them away from the narrow interests of the Mithila region to the broader arenas of provincial and national

---

[1] *Ibid.*, pp. 11–13.
[2] *Ibid.*, pp. 16, 36.
[3] Laksman Jha, *Mithila: A Union Republic*, pp. 57–8.
[4] Kumar, *Genealogical History*, p. 78; Laksman Jha, *Mithila: A Union Republic*, p. 58; *MM*, 1 January 1942.
[5] Kumar, *Genealogical History*, pp. 56, 78; Grierson, *Linguistic Survey*, vol. v, pt. II, p. 18; *MM*, 10 February 1945 and 4 December 1948.
[6] Kumar, *Genealogical History*, pp. 28–9, 31–2, 34, 38, 61; Jankinandan Singh, *Memorandum*, p. 50.
[7] Kumar, *Genealogical History*, pp. 41, 64–5, 71, 77.

politics.[1] Throughout the nationalist period, while maintaining their loyalty to the British Raj, the Maharajas contributed financially to the Indian National Congress.[2] Finally, if the Maharajas supported Maithili, they also supported the cause of Hindi. Contemporary leaders of the Maithili movement note the national activities of the Darbhanga rulers with some regret. Thus, the secretary of the Maithil Mahasabha remarked that the last Maharaja of Darbhanga:

> was a great nationalist, one of the founders of the Indian National Congress. Now he worked for national integration. So, he removed the claims of Maithili itself and fought for Hindi. We have a script of our own, but when he established a printing press here [in Darbhanga], he established a Hindi printing press. A great contribution to national integration, but a loss for Mithila.[3]

Clearly, the existence of a contemporary ruler, with pretensions to hereditary princely status and a genuine solicitude for the language and culture of the people in his domain, does not necessarily contribute to the development of regional consciousness. The Maharajas were leaders of a closed elite group rather than popular princes of the people of Mithila and they were devoted more to all-India symbols than to the cultural symbols of their region. The Darbhanga rulers were so divorced from the concerns of the people of Mithila that the last Maharaja was unable to win election to Parliament in the first general election in Bihar in 1952.[4] The Darbhanga Raj has been heirless since the death of the last Maharaja, Kameshwar Singh. The remaining descendants of the Raj, involved in a contest over the inheritance, do not enjoy a favorable reputation among the elite of Darbhanga.[5] If the Maithili movement should ever acquire sufficient momentum to demand seriously a separate state in Mithila, the symbols of the independent political history of the region will surely be stressed, but it will not be possible to argue that the rulers of Darbhanga made a substantial contribution to the purpose either in their devotion to the ideal or in their capturing of the devotion of the people of the region.

The absence of subjective regional consciousness

Although the symbols which distinguish Mithila are not entirely unique and do not invariably reinforce each other, there can be no doubt that there is a rich and varied pool of symbols[6] to draw upon

[1] *Ibid.*, pp. 17, 18, 25–8, 38, 39, 41, 57, 77, 79.
[2] *Ibid.*, p. 19; *MM*, 12 January 1952.
[3] Interview (M4:9) in Darbhanga on 16 April 1967. See also Jayadhari Sinha, 'Claims of Maithili as Language and Literature', *Searchlight*, 5 April 1970.
[4] *MM*, 14 November 1953.
[5] See *Searchlight*, 7 and 9 July 1968.
[6] This useful phrase is Cohn's ('Regions Subjective and Objective', pp. 22ff.).

from the history, geography, language, and culture of the region for those who would wish to develop a sense of regional or national identity among the people of north Bihar.[1] The ambiguity of the symbols and their only partially reinforcing character are no less characteristic of all nationality movements in modern times and of all regional movements in modern India. Moreover, there exists in north Bihar a very distinct regional elite in the Maithil Brahmans, who have been simultaneously the carriers of the distinct culture of the region and among the leading recipients of modern education. Yet, the Maithil Brahmans have not been able to build a broad sense of regional consciousness in north Bihar either around the territorial symbol of Mithila or around the linguistic symbol of Maithili.

There are four primary reasons for the relative absence of regional consciousness in north Bihar, which will be explored in the remainder of this chapter. One is that symbols of national indentification have been given priority by the elites of the region over regional symbols. A second reason is that the regional elite has failed to extend the cultural symbols of Mithila and Maithili to the non-Brahman castes of the region and build a common Maithil identity. Third, a process of differential social mobilization has been at work in Bihar over the past half century and more by which the people of south Bihar have become mobilized more rapidly than the people of north Bihar, have adopted the language and culture of the Hindi movement centered in Banaras, and have extended the sphere of Hindi in preference to the mother tongues of the state. Consequently, an interesting process of absorption and assimilation of a diversity of mother tongues has been taking place in Bihar by a language, Hindi, which is not the mother tongue of any major group in the state. Finally, the political elites of the Mithila region have been integrated effectively into all-Bihar political movements and into the state government on the basis of nationalist, ideological, and caste symbols rather than in terms of regional linguistic and cultural symbols.

The Maithili language

Maithili

In 1880 and 1881, A. F. R. Hoernle and G. A. Grierson published

---

[1] National symbols in the Indian context can also be reinterpreted and altered to give them regional significance. In Tamil Nadu, the Ramayana has been reinterpreted to glorify the demon king Ravanna as a hero fighting Aryan invaders. In a similarly imaginative vein, Laksman Jha has argued for a reinterpretation of the Mahabharata which would glorify the Kauravas, with whom Mithila was allied, against the victorious Pandavas; see Laksman Jha *Mithila: A Union Republic*, p. 95, and *Mithila Will Rise* (Darbhanga: Mithila Mandal, 1955), pp. 26, 37.

grammars which established the grammatical distinctness of Maithili from other dialects of both Hindi and Bengali.[1] Only occasionally before that time had Maithili been considered anything other than a form of either Hindi or Bengali.[2] Grierson found sufficient similarity among the three major mother tongues of Bihar (Maithili, Magahi, and Bhojpuri) and sufficient difference between these three tongues, on the one hand, and Hindi or Bengali, on the other hand, to classify the three mother tongues as dialects of a common language, for which he coined the term Bihari.[3] However, there was no such thing as a Bihari spoken language and, when Grierson offered examples to distinguish Bihari from Hindi and Bengali, the language he used for comparative purposes was Maithili. It is hardly surprising, therefore, that the leaders of the Maithili movement have frequently found inspiration in Grierson, to whom they have turned for authoritative support for their claims that Maithili is the language of nearly the whole of north Bihar and large portions of south Bihar and Chota Nagpur as well,[4] that it is the most important distinct language of Bihar,[5] and the only one with a literary tradition.

However, the elevation by Hoernle and Grierson of the dialects of Bihar to the status of a separate language group distinct from Hindi has not gone undisputed either by other linguists or by political and social leaders dedicated to the spread of Hindi. J. H. Budden argued in 1881 against the view that Maithili or any of the other dialects of north India should be treated as anything other than 'provincial forms' of Hindi and that to do otherwise could only retard 'the process of natural unification and assimilation' of the various 'vernacular dialects of the Hindus' of the region under the rubric of

[1] Grierson refers to Hoernle's grammar and to other previous descriptions of the Maithili language in George A. Grierson, *An Introduction to the Maithili Dialect of the Bihari Language as Spoken in North Bihar*, 2d. ed., pt. 1: *Grammar* (Calcutta: Asiatic Society, 1909), pp. xv–xviii. Hoernle discusses the history of the grammatical research which led both him and Grierson to assert the separateness of the Bihari language group in A. F. Rudolf Hoernle, *Centenary Review of the Asiatic Society of Bengal From 1784–1883*, pt. II: *Archaeology, History, Literature, &c.* (Calcutta: Published by the Society and printed by Thacker, Spink, 1885), pp. 169–71.

[2] *Ibid.* This attitude toward Maithili formed the basis for British policy on the medium of instruction in the schools of Bihar. In 1871, Hindi was introduced as the medium of instruction in north Bihar schools rather than Maithili. See J. C. Jha, 'Language Controversy in Bihar', *Indian Nation*, 11 and 18 August 1968.

[3] Grierson, *Linguistic Survey*, vol. v, pt. II, 1–4. For a critical view of a similar attempt by Grierson to classify the languages and dialects of Rajasthan, see Kali C. Bahl, 'On the Present State of Modern Rajasthani Grammar', mimeo, University of Chicago, Department of South Asian Languages and Civilizations, December 1971, pp. 9–13.

[4] *MM*, 13 May 1951; Laksman Jha, *Mithila in India*, p. 4.

[5] *MM*, 1 March and 26 April 1964.

'standard Hindi'.[1] Kellogg, who published an influential Hindi grammar in 1875, took note of the work of Hoernle and Grierson on the languages of Bihar and incorporated examples of Maithili and Magadhi (Magahi) into the second edition of his grammar published in 1893, but he classed them both as 'colloquial dialects' of the eastern variety of Hindi.[2]

It should be stressed also that Grierson's distinctions were grammatical ones and that he did not raise the sociolinguistic question of how far the grammatical differences between Maithili and other dialects and between the Bihari dialects and Hindi constituted barriers to effective communication among the peoples of Bihar. It is generally recognized that Hindi/Urdu, often referred to in its popular spoken forms as Hindustani, has been widely used for inter-group communication by speakers of regional dialects throughout most of north India, especially in the cities and towns. However, the issues in dispute in Bihar today do not revolve centrally around the question of the ability to communicate, but rather concern the right of peoples with distinctive tongues and literatures to develop and use their languages for a wide variety of purposes.

While there is, therefore, much that is arbitrary and open to dispute in the linguistic definition of Maithili and the Maithili-speaking region, there are certain reasonably clear and objective characteristics of Maithili which can be pointed out and which have influenced the claims made on its behalf. Although it has been open to dispute in India whether Maithili is a distinct 'language', there has been, for over a century, agreement among linguistic scholars of India that Maithili is a grammatically distinct dialect, with a distinctive literature. The most famous literary figure in Maithili history and the central symbol of the whole Maithili movement is the great fifteenth-century poet, Vidyapati. Although Vidyapati has been claimed by both Hindi and Bengali enthusiasts as a Hindi poet and a Bengali poet, respectively, such claims presume that Maithili is a dialect of either Hindi or Bengali. Whatever the status of Maithili in relation to these two languages, there is no dispute that Vidyapati wrote in Maithili. Vidyapati was followed by a long line of poets who

[1] J. H. Budden, 'Primary Education Among Hindus in North India, with Reference Chiefly to Language', reprinted with alterations from the *Indian Evangelical Review* of January 1881 at the Medical Hall Press, Benares, in 1882 and republished in Madan Mohan Malaviya, *Court Character and Primary Education in the N.-W. Provinces & Oudh* (Allahabad: The Indian Press, 1897), app., pp. 24 and 26

[2] S. H. Kellogg, *A Grammar of the Hindi Language*, 3rd ed. (London: Routledge & Kegan Paul, 1938), pp. v–ix.

imitated his style and who maintained an unbroken literary tradition for more than five centuries.[1]

The second objective fact about the Maithili language is that it continues to be the predominant spoken language in most of north Bihar and in portions of Monghyr, Bhagalpur, and the Santal Parganas districts, but that there are considerable dialectal differences both spatially and socially. Grierson judged that Maithili and its dialects could fairly be characterized as the language of the entire population of Darbhanga and Bhagalpur districts and of a majority or a significant minority of the populations of the districts of Muzaffarpur, Monghyr, Purnea, and Santal Parganas.[2] Grierson arrived at an estimate of the total Maithili-speaking population in Bihar in 1891 of 9,389,376. Regretfully, neither Grierson's estimate and his method of arriving at it nor any other impartial criterion based on philological distinctions has ever been used since by policy-makers in the Bihar government or by the spokesmen of the Maithili movement in assessing the appropriate place for Maithili in the education and administration of the state.

There is no way short of a new linguistic survey of Bihar of knowing how many people in contemporary Bihar actually speak Maithili. It is reasonably certain that the Maithili-speakers are fewer than the number claimed by Maithili spokesmen and a good deal more than the number conceded by non-Maithili Bihar politicians or enumerated in the census. Maithili spokesmen estimate the total Maithili-speaking population in Bihar, Nepal, and in other non-Maithili areas of India at between 20 and 30 million.[3] In Bihar alone, it is claimed that the Maithili-speaking population is more than 20 million. However, this figure is arrived at by adding up the total population of all districts in which Maithili is spoken by a significant portion of the population,[4] ignoring Grierson's computations. Inflated as this figure surely is, it is nevertheless probably closer to the truth than the 1961 census figure of less than 5 million (table 2.1). If Grierson's method of calculation is applied to the total 1961 population figures, the Maithili-speaking population can be estimated at 16.5 million or roughly a third of the entire population of the state of Bihar (see table 2.2).

It must be kept in mind, however, that this figure is only an esti-

[1] Grierson, *Linguistic Survey*, vol. v, pt. ii, p. 17; Ramanath Jha, 'Maithili: Needs Popular Patronage' (reprint of article for which publication details are not known), p. 55; Laksman Jha, *Mithila in India*, p. 16.
[2] Grierson, *Linguistic Survey*, vol. v, pt. ii, pp. 13, 14, 54, 118.
[3] See, for example, *MM*, 22 March and 26 April 1964.
[4] See *Maithili: What it is and what it claims* (Patna: Chetana Samiti, 1964), p. 1.

TABLE 2.1 *Major languages of Bihar according to Census of India, 1911–61*[a]

Language	1911		1921		1931		1951		1961	
	Number	%	Number	%	Number	%	Number	%	Number	%
Hindi[b]	23,771,781	83.95	24,257,956	86.24	27,193,593	86.74	31,428,651	81.03	20,580,643	44.30
Bihari[b]	164,536	0.58	97,554	0.35	(not available)		111,767	0.29	16,442,087	35.39
Maithili	..	0.00	1,641	0.01			87,674	0.23	4,982,615	10.73
Magahi	165	0.00	..	0.00			3,728	0.01	2,818,492	6.07
Bhojpuri	7	0.00	..	0.00			1,699	0.05	7,842,722	16.88
Otherwise listed	164,364	0.58	95,913	0.34			18,666	0.05	798,258	1.72
Urdu	324,686	1.15	238,364	0.85	(counted in Hindi)		2,646,437	6.82	4,149,245	8.93
Tribal[c]	2,422,314	8.55	2,351,084	8.36	2,742,493	8.75	2,957,308	7.62	3,460,341	7.45
Other	1,798,135	6.35	1,281,804	4.56	1,415,806	4.52	1,753,788	4.52	1,823,294	3.92
Total	28,316,916	100.00	28,129,208	100.01	31,349,892	100.01	38,786,184	99.99	46,455,610	99.99

[a] *Census of India 1961*, vol. IV, pt. II–C, pp. 199–208.

[b] For 1911–51 the figures for Bihari languages were also counted in Hindi. Consequently, the Bihari figures for those years should be disregarded in adding the totals.

[c] Tribal includes all Munda languages, Oraon, and Malto. Tribal figures for 1911–51 are the original figures for those years, as figures adjusted for later boundary changes since then were available only for the three major languages – Hindu, Urdu, and Bihari – and for the total. Figures for those years are taken from the *Census of India, 1911*, vol. V, pt. III, table X; *1921*, vol. VII, pt. II, table X; *1931*, vol. VII, pt. II, table XV; *1951*, vol. V, pt. II–A, table D–I.

TABLE 2.2 *Estimated speakers of Maithili, Magahi, and Bhojpuri in Bihar, 1891–1961, using Gait's computation*[a]

	Maithili		Magahi		Bhojpuri	
Census Year	Computed estimate[b]	Census enumeration	Computed estimate[b]	Census enumeration	Computed estimate[b]	Census enumeration
1891	9,207,131	..	7,117,531	..	7,103,089	..
1901	10,387,897	964[d]	6,144,299	12,509[d]	7,181,183	246[d]
1911	10,580,838	..	6,394,795	165	7,178,329	7
1921	10,380,104	1,641	6,284,721	..	7,213,330	..
1931	11,361,011	..	7,195,065	..	7,896,326	..
1941	12,429,475[c]	..	8,273,047	..	8,990,149	..
1951	13,621,538	87,674	9,299,665	3,728	9,406,039	1,699
1961	16,565,477	4,982,615	11,073,843	2,818,492	11,629,425	7,842,722

[a] *Census of India, 1901*, vol. VI, pt. I, *The Report*, ch. X, 'Language', p. 320n. 'Maithili includes persons *born in* (1) all Darbhanga and Bhagalpur, (2) $\frac{9}{10}$ Muzaffarpur, (3) $\frac{1}{2}$ Monghyr, and (4) $\frac{3}{4}$ Purnea; and also $\frac{4}{5}$ of the Hindi speakers enumerated in the Sonthal Parganas.' 'Magahi includes persons *born in* (1) all Patna and Gaya, (2) $\frac{11}{12}$ Hazaribagh, (3) $\frac{1}{2}$ Monghyr, (4) $\frac{5}{8}$ Malda, and (5) $\frac{1}{15}$ Ranchi and Palamau; also 166,679 persons enumerated in the Sonthal Parganas, 47,949 in the Chota Nagpur States, and 286 persons in the Orissa States.' 'Bhojpuri includes persons *born in* (1) all Champaran, Saran and Shahabad, and (2) $\frac{1}{4}$ Palamau and Ranchi; also 59,937 persons enumerated in the Chota Nagpur States, and 362,571 immigrants from the United Provinces comprising immigrants from the districts of the United Provinces where Bhojpuri is spoken, viz. the whole of Gorakhpur Division, Benares, Ghazipur, Ballia, $\frac{3}{4}$ Mirzapur, $\frac{1}{6}$ Jaunpur and $\frac{2}{7}$ Fyzabad'.
[b] Using district population figures adjusted to make them correspond to present boundaries; *Census of India, 1961*, vol. IV, pt. II–A, pp. 173–5. For Maithili speakers in Santal Parganas, for which Gait computed a percentage of the Hindi-speakers enumerated, this adjustment for 1911–61 is taken from *ibid.*, pt. II–C, pp. 199ff. For Purnea it was assumed that the area taken from Purnea and placed in Bengal in 1955 included no Maithili-speakers. The adjusted figure was divided by the figure arrived at by using Gait's computation for the original district and the resulting proportion, 0.79, was used for subsequent years. It was assumed that the proportion of immigrant Bhojpuri-speakers in relation to natives was the same (0.053) in later years as in 1901. A 0.014 computation was used as the equivalent of Gait's figures for Chota Nagpur after 1901.
[c] As there are no language returns for 1941, it was necessary to estimate the number of Hindi-speakers in Santal Parganas. This calculation was done on the assumption that the number of Hindi-speakers changed at the same rate as the total population from 1931 to 1941 (+0.09).
[d] Figures include the following listed in the 1901 census volume under 'other districts of Bengal': Maithili, 84; Magahi, 116; Bhojpuri, 48.

mate and that Grierson's calculations included many border dialects and most of the Muslims in Mithila. However scientific Grierson's calculations and classifications may have been on linguistic grounds, it must always be remembered that, in a situation of linguistic and cultural diversity where processes of social mobilization are taking place at uneven rates, there is no way of predicting the ultimate linguistic composition of the population when it is fully mobilized. Whether the speakers of such dialects as Chikka-Chikki or Angika or Bajika[1] or whether the Muslims of Bihar identify with Maithili or

[1] On the relationship between the Maithili movement and dialect movements behind Angika and Bajika, see *Searchlight*, 16 February 1966, and *Indian Nation*, 3 August 1969.

become assimilated to Hindi or launch movements on behalf of their mother dialects are questions which cannot be predicted simply on the basis of grammatical distinctions. Such questions are decided by the forms taken by the processes of social mobilization, cultural inter-action, opportunities for employment, political competition, and government policies.

The third feature of the Maithili language, which has affected its spread, is the existence of sharp differences in the use among dif-ferent classes in Mithila of both the spoken and written forms of Maithili. Not only is the literary form of the language quite different from the spoken form, but the elite Brahman castes of Mithila speak a distinctive form of Maithili and use a different script from other castes, high or low. When Grierson wrote at the turn of the century, he found three scripts in use for Maithili – the Maithili or Tirhuti script, used only by Maithil Brahmans; the Kaithi script, used by educated classes in north India generally; and the Devanagari script, promoted by the Hindi literary scholars of Banaras and used by those educated people in Bihar who had been influenced by the Banaras school.[1] It is a measure not only of the more rapid progress of Hindi, but of the importance of the social structure, that Devanagari has nearly completely taken the place of both Kaithi and the Maithili script in Mithila. The contrast with the role played by the Guru-mukhi script in the development of the Punjabi movement is worth noting. It will be shown later that Gurumukhi, a symbol of the Sikh religious scriptures not tied to a particular class of Sikhs, became a reinforcing symbol of the separateness and distinctness of Punjabi from the Hindi language. The Maithili script, the exclusive property of an elite caste and not associated with a distinctive mass culture in any way, has not so far been able to perform the same role for the Maithili language.

The sharp differences between the culture of the elite castes in Mithila and in the form of the Maithili language used by them com-pared to the culture and language of the mass of the people and the fact that these same elite castes have been the primary leaders of the Maithili movement have placed them on the defensive. The leaders of the Maithili movement have tried to dispute the notion that the Maithili language is a language of Maithil Brahmans only and have eschewed any identification of language and caste, as the following quotation indicates: 'Many people have the notion that Maithili is the language of Maithil Brahmans alone. In fact, it is the language of all the people of Mithila and it has no relation to a particular caste

---

[1] Grierson, *Lingustic Survey*, vol. v, pt. ii, p. 21.

though, of course, it has been more propagated by Maithil Brahmans and Karna Kayasthas.[1]

While it is objectively indisputable that Maithili is a distinct and independent dialect, predominant in north Bihar, and not the language only of Maithil Brahmans, it is also true that the drawing of linguistic boundaries involves some arbitrariness, that there are dialects and languages in north Bihar distinguishable from each other and potentially distinguishable from Maithili as well, and that the main carriers of Maithili language identity have been Maithil Brahmans. These latter factors have affected the revival and development of the Maithili language and the ability of its supporters to instill an attachment to the language in the consciousness of the people of Mithila. They have also complicated the problems involved in standardizing the language.

Proposals have been made from time to time by Maithili supporters to standardize the Maithili language, but no significant progress has been made. The failure to standardize the Maithili language is a most serious impediment to the long-term success of the movement. Individual scholars have made efforts in this direction, but it remains true that Maithili has developed much more slowly than the other major literary languages of India,[2] that students have been afraid to study Maithili because they can never be certain if the form of the language taught to them will be the same form used by the outside examiner,[3] and that Maithili-speakers generally consider their language inferior for discourse outside the home.[4] In all these respects, Hindi has an advantage over Maithili.

Maithili, Bhojpuri, and Magahi

Grierson considered Maithili, Magahi, and Bhojpuri the three main dialects of the Bihari language. However, Grierson sometimes divided the three dialects into two groups – an eastern group, consisting of the closely related dialects of Maithili and Magahi, and a western group, consisting of Bhojpuri.[5] Maithili and Magahi are both languages primarily of Bihar, whereas the Bhojpuri-speakers are divided between Bihar and Uttar Pradesh. Hindi, the official language of the state of Bihar, does not become a spoken language in north India until west of the Bhojpuri area.

[1] *MM*, 2 June 1951.
[2] A fact recognized by Maithili supporters, e.g. *MM*, 15 November 1947.
[3] *Ibid.*, 13 May 1951.
[4] *Ibid.*, 26 April 1964 and 29 August 1965.
[5] Grierson, *Linguistic Survey*, vol. v, pt. ii, p. 41.

The politics of language in Bihar are complicated by the fact that the official language of the state is not the mother tongue of any major population group. It became the official language of the state because the predominant ethnic groups in Bihar, the Magahi and Bhojpuri peoples, lacking a standard literary language of their own, chose to adopt Hindi as the medium of education, administration, and political communication.[1] In fact, Hindi in Bihar has become pre-eminently the language of the Magahi-speaking people, who have been the most socially mobilized and politically advanced segment of the population of the state.

Thus, among Hindus in Bihar (leaving aside the question of Urdu),[2] the language issues involve a competition between two literary languages: one, Hindi, which has had the advantages of earlier standardization and official status, and is the chosen language of a politically important ethnic group; the other, Maithili, an independent literary language and the mother tongue of the largest ethnic group in the state, but an unstandardized language, lacking official status, and spoken in the economically and socially less advanced areas of the state. In this competition, Hindi has so far run far ahead of Maithili.[3]

Maithili and Hindi

Although Grierson and Hoernle asserted emphatically the distinctness of Maithili from Hindi and the existence of a separate literary heritage in the language, it has been shown that their assertions by no means settled the issues. Maithili has only gradually been recognized as a separate literary language by the universities in north India, by PEN, and by the Sahitya Akademi. It has also achieved official recognition as a mother tongue of Bihar. Yet the spokesmen

---

[1] Maithili supporters note, sometimes with regret and resentment, that Rajendra Prasad, first President of India and a Bhojpuri-speaker – I have heard somewhere that he sometimes listed his mother tongue as 'Maithili-Bhojpuri' – was a leading political supporter of Hindi from Bihar; interview, M7:12.

[2] The Urdu issue is discussed in Part II, below. Here it is important to note only that the more highly mobilized Urdu supporters are in competition with both Maithili and Hindi for the allegiances of Muslim speakers of Bihari languages. Maithili leaders naturally claim that Muslims in Bihar speak the local dialects, not Urdu, and they resent the fact that Urdu organizations have gone further than they have in presenting political demands; interviews, M4:24 and M5:4.

[3] As for Bhojpuri and Magahi, occasional demands have been made for their recognition as media of education and, in the case of Bhojpuri, there have been occasional demands for the creation of a Bhojpuri-speaking state. However, so far neither of these two languages has been given even official recognition in the state of Bihar as a mother tongue and neither can, therefore, be used as a medium of education in the schools. Interview (M2:11) in Patna on 14 April 1967; *Indian Nation*, 26 June 1967; on the Bhojpuri state demand, see *MM*, 2 March 1947.

of the Maithili movement retain to the present a lingering fear that, as one Maithili devotee put it, 'the wolf of Hindi want[s] to swallow the whole of the language of north Bihar'.[1]

Supporters of Maithili tend to have ambivalent feelings toward Hindi. On the one hand, they sincerely wish to see Hindi become the official and national language of India, but they also fear the absorption of Maithili by Hindi. Some Maithili-speakers have been more concerned with the spread of Hindi than with the development of their own language, but many have come to resent the predominant position of Hindi in Bihar, if not in India as a whole.

Most Maithili supporters, however, are sensitive to any implications that Maithili is merely a dialect of Hindi and are insistent upon asserting its separate character whenever the issue seems in doubt.[2] Maithili sensitivity on this point has been so great that supporters of Maithili have frequently refused the patronage of Hindi organizations and government agencies when such patronage has implied a subordinate relationship of Maithili to Hindi. Thus, the great spokesman for Maithili, Dr Amarnath Jha, considered it 'shameful' in 1943 that Maithili books were being published by the Hindi Sahitya Sammelan.[3] In 1947, an Indian Council of Hindi was formed at Allahabad University, which decided to publish a history of Hindi literature in three volumes. In the third volume, it was planned to include Awadhi, Marwari, Bundeli, Bhojpuri, and Maithili literature. Dr Umesh Mishra, a Maithili scholar, was asked to contribute an article for the volume. He refused, arguing that Maithili was an independent literary language, whose history might be included in a volume devoted to modern Indian languages, but not in a series devoted only to Hindi. Dr Mishra considered this invitation to him as evidence that 'the Hindi-speaking people are not willing to accept Maithili as an independent language' and urged the readers of the *Mithila Mihir* to make sure 'that Maithili is, under no circumstances, associated with Hindi and that no Maithil scholar should ever consider writing anything about Maithili in Hindi books'.[4] Similar protests have been raised at the inclusion of Maithili in the Hindi-speaking population in the decennial censuses, at the inclusion of radio programs on Maithili in which Maithili is associated with

---

[1] Interview, M7:9.
[2] Contemporary arguments demonstrating grammatical distinctions among the Maithili, Hindi, and Bengali languages can be found in Laksman Jha, *Mithila: A Union Republic*, pp. 67–78; *Maithili: What it is and what it claims*, pp. 3–4; and Jankinandan Singh, *Memorandum*, pp. 14–17. See also *MM*, 9 January 1966, and *Indian Nation*, 29 March, 2 and 6 April 1970.
[3] *MM*, 24 April 1943.   [4] *Ibid.*, 9 October 1947.

Hindi, and at an (unjustified) fear that the Sahitya Akademi in 1964 intended to grant only part recognition to Maithili.[1] Controversy between Maithili protagonists and the leaders of Hindi organizations has flared from time to time on these and other similar issues.[2]

It appears that 'the wolf of Hindi' has not been entirely unsuccessful in north Bihar. Maithili spokesmen themselves admit that the majority of the people living in north Bihar are not aware that Maithili is the name of their mother tongue. It has also been noted that many Maithili-speaking students who know very well that Maithili is their mother tongue reject it because they believe that employment is open only to those who study Hindi.[3] Moreover, some Maithili-speakers themselves argue that common spoken Hindi is closer to spoken Maithili than is literary Maithili. Several generations of Maithili-speakers have been educated through the medium of Hindi and have become more proficient in Hindi than in their own mother tongue.[4] A Communist MLA from a backward caste described the relationship he saw between Maithili and Hindi as follows:

In Bihar, there are Maithili-speaking people, Bhojpuri, Magahi, and tribal. So far as these languages are concerned, no doubt common people speak it; but, in my personal opinion, gradually [these languages] will merge into Hindi . . . There is not a single man in the Maithili-speaking area who does not understand Hindi. With respect to Maithili, the issue is whether it is a language or a dialect. In that area [Mithila], nobody can understand books written in Maithili. If you tell me to write a letter in Maithili, I can't even write a letter so simply and rapidly as in Hindi because of the practice. Secondly, the language in the villages and the language in the books is very much different. We have requested those people [Maithili writers] to write in a simple language. In a village, there are many castes. Only some upper caste people can read this pure Maithili.[5]

This quotation sums up very well the fears and problems of the leaders of the Maithili movement – the fear of absorption by Hindi and the fear that social differentiation, reflected in language differentiation, will be a bar to the development of consciousness of Maithili-speakers of their mother tongue and of an attachment to it. Social differentiation is not the only problem, however, because Maithili Brahmans have expressed similar feelings. Thus, a Maithil Brahman member of the Bihar legislative council and a patron of the Maithili movement, remarked:

[Maithili is] our home language, colloquial language . . .

[1] *Ibid.*, 13 March 1948, 22 March 1964, and 14 February 1965.
[2] *Indian Nation*, 7 and 13 November 1968.
[3] *MM*, 21 January 1950 and 12 March 1951.
[4] *Ibid.*, 17 July 1966.   [5] Interview (M9:1, 2) in Patna on 6 July 1967.

[How close is it to Hindi?]
It's very close to Hindi . . . But actually in one's home they [Maithili-speakers] do not use Hindi . . . So far as writing is concerned, we write pure and chaste Hindi. But speaking, we speak these dialects.

Yet, the respondent argued that Maithili is a literary language and supports the demand for inclusion of Maithili in the eighth schedule of the Constitution of India.[1]

It is clear from the comments of both these legislators that the problem before the leaders of the Maithili movement is whether consciousness and use of Maithili in a standardized form can be spread at a rate which will outpace the assimilation of Maithili-speakers to Hindi. The 1961 census figures suggest that assimilation to Hindi may have made more progress in Mithila than anywhere else in Bihar, if the figures can be trusted. If we compare the number of people who were reported to have declared Maithili as their mother tongue in 1961 with the total potential underlying population of Maithili-speakers in Bihar (see table 2.2), then only a third of the underlying population are aware that their mother tongue is Maithili and fully two-thirds have been swallowed by the wolf of Hindi. Of course, this kind of assimilation of an illiterate and unmobilized population to a dominant language (even assuming that more than 11 million Maithili-speakers actually declared Hindi as their mother tongue) is not necessarily permanent. The struggle between Maithili and Hindi could be materially altered both by the general processes of social mobilization and by changes in educational policy towards the medium of instruction at the primary and secondary stages of education in Bihar.

Despite the real fears of Maithili supporters over Hindi domination, their devotion to Hindi as a national language should not be underestimated. The feelings of the Maithils are quite different from those of the Tamil-speaking people who have come to oppose the adoption of Hindi as the official language of India, or even of many Sikhs who have been thoroughly embittered by the conflict between Punjabi and Hindi supporters. The difference can be seen in the fact that there are Maithili supporters who consider the issue of Hindi as the national language of greater importance than the issue of regional languages.[2] Whether or not this common devotion to both Maithili

[1] Interview (BG14a:18–21) in Patna on 5 December 1966.
[2] Interview, M10:16. Several different kinds of terms are used in India to refer to the various languages and dialects of the country. Some terms refer to the relationship between the language and its speakers, others have a symbolic meaning, and still others refer to the official status of a language. A mother tongue is the speech learned by a person at home and spoken in his own household. A regional language is a standardized

and Hindi will be sustained depends very much upon the future language policy of the Bihar government.

Maithili and the census

The fears of Maithili supporters over Hindi domination are reinforced every ten years during the census operations. It has been charged by Maithili scholars and organizations that the language of the majority of the Maithili-speaking people has been entered as Hindi by the census enumerators against the wishes of the people in the past three censuses.[1] The census superintendent of Bihar acknowledged in the 1961 *General Report* volume that there is some basis for this charge, as far as the 1951 and 1961 censuses were concerned:

> The great and unusual interest aroused in local languages and dialects at the 1961 census . . . has been alluded to. Although it resulted, expectedly, in an unprecedented increase in the numbers of those speaking Bhojpuri, Maithili and Magahi, it cannot be said that the figures even now are truly representative of the real position. As in 1951, the bulk of the population in 1961 also has preferred to return Hindi as its mother-tongue. It is possible that the enumerator's own predilections and preferences in the matter might have worked to some extent in producing the results as they are.[2]

In order to counteract this process of absorption by allegedly incorrect enumeration, the Maithili leaders and organizations urge the people of Mithila before each census operation to see to it that

version of the speech and writing common to a geographical region of India and taught in its standardized form in the schools of one or more of the states. Most of India's regional languages are listed in the eighth schedule of the Constitution of India. They include such languages as Bengali, Hindi, Kannada, and Tamil. Maithili supporters refer to Maithili as a regional language, but it is so only in the geographical sense. It is not yet adequately standardized for contemporary use or recognized in the eighth schedule.

An official language of a state or of India is simply any language recognized by law as an appropriate or required medium of communication for specified administrative and legal purposes. Hindi is the official language of India and English is an associate official language. The term national language is used by Indians in two ways. It is used by supporters of Hindi as a synonym for the official language of India. It is also sometimes used to distinguish the indigenous regional languages of the country from languages, particularly English, considered to be alien or non-national languages.

Thus, in the present context, Maithili is a mother tongue whose supporters aspire to achieve for it status as a regional language. Hindi is the official language of both Bihar and India. Maithili supporters deny that Hindi is a regional language of Bihar at all, but they do award to Hindi symbolic status as the national language of India and favor its continued use as a link language of India and Bihar.

[1] *MM*, 6 and 13 March 1948, 2 June 1951, and 14 February 1965; *Indian Nation* 7 January 1971.

[2] *Census of India*, 1961, vol. IV: *Bihar*, pt. I-A (i), by S. D. Prasad (Delhi: Manager of Publications, 1968), p. 460.

73

Maithili is recorded as their language.[1] At the end of each census operation, the Maithili supporters are dissatisfied with the results.

Maithili supporters sometimes attribute the underenumeration of Maithili to the conspiratorial designs of the census officials and the government of Bihar in collaboration with the Hindi Sahitya Sammelan.[2] In fact, it appears that the problem is more complex. After Grierson completed his linguistic survey of Bihar, he and Gait, the census superintendent, divided the districts of Bihar according to the number of speakers of the three Bihari mother tongues of Maithili, Magahi, and Bhojpuri and arrived at estimates of the total Maithili-, Magahi-, and Bhojpuri-speaking populations in the state.[3] The Grierson–Gait computations are the only impartial and objective estimates available on the populations of speakers of the Bihari languages. Those computations have been projected forward in table 2.2, but several points of caution must be made about reading the figures and comparing them with the census enumerations. First, although the computations have been altered to adjust for changes in administrative boundaries, no account has been taken of migration patterns, patterns of assimilation to Hindi via public school education, and the like. Second, the figures are estimates for *all* census years. There has never been a scientific census count, based on philological distinctions, in any census of India.[4] Third, in comparing the 1961 projections with actual census enumerations, it should not be assumed that the much lower enumerated figures necessarily support the charges of conspiracy made by Maithili supporters. There are at least two other contributing factors which may explain the large gaps between the projected estimates and the enumerations. These include the well-known fact that the majority of the people of India either do not know the names given to their mother tongues by linguists or for other reasons give the names incorrectly. In fact, the problem of Hindi 'domination' in Bihar may arise largely out of lack of knowledge, which was recognized clearly by Gait in the 1901 census report, where he commented as follows:

A ... serious difficulty [in correct census enumeration of mother tongue] lay in the fact that the philological distinctions between languages and dialects are not

[1] *MM*, 14 February 1965; also 4 September 1948 and 13 January 1951.
[2] *Ibid.*, 14 February 1965; Jankinandan Singh, *Memorandum*, p. 13.
[3] See table 2.2, n. a.
[4] It was reported in the *Indian Nation*, 29 July 1967, that the Bihar government had allocated Rs. 100,000 to the Bihar Rashtrabhasha Parishad to carry out a new linguistic survey of Bihar. However, the Parishad and its chairman, Dr L. N. Sudhanshu, are dedicated to the spread and promotion of Hindi.

always reflected in the names by which they are known to the people. This was especially the case in respect of the dialects spoken in Bihar.

These dialects, taken together, constitute a language which is now recognized as being entirely distinct from Hindi properly so-called, and are now known collectively to grammarians as Bihari. But to the ordinary native they are all alike called Hindi . . . So far therefore, as the Bihari dialects are concerned, the census returns are not of much use.[1]

In addition to lack of knowledge, however, there is another factor which has been at work during the past half-century and more, namely, the efforts of Hindi organizations by persuasion to confirm the speakers of Bihari dialects in their philological ignorance and the natural process of assimilation to Hindi in two or three generations of public school education through the medium of Hindi.

Clearly, then, there are severe limitations upon the utility of the census as an objective measure of the distribution of languages in Bihar (and other parts of India). However, the census is an extremely useful political document which reveals at least two important kinds of political information in the counting process – the policy of the government and the relative success of competing cultural-political organizations in their decennial census drives. The policy of the government and changes in it are revealed in the method of linguistic classification. In Bihar, policy decisions relating to the enumeration and classification of languages and dialects have gone through three phases. In the first phase, in the censuses of 1881 and 1891, such decisions were influenced primarily by the Hindi–Urdu controversy and lacked any rational philological underpinnings. From 1901 until 1931, the census authorities in Bihar showed a greater awareness of dialectal diversity as a result of the completion of Grierson's work, but the primary consideration in enumeration and classification continued to concern the Hindi–Urdu question. Thus, in 1911 and 1921, when Hindi and Urdu were recorded separately, the Bihari dialects were also. However, in 1931, the Bihar census superintendent, presumably in order to avoid renewed Hindi–Urdu agitation on the language issue, recorded Hindi, Urdu, and the Bihari languages all under the head of 'Hindustani'. In the third phase, in the post-independence censuses of 1951 and 1961, the Bihar census superintendents have attempted to combine faithfulness to the returns given by respondents with adherence to the classification system of Grierson.[2] This decision had little impact on the number of speakers

[1] *Census of India, 1901*, vol. VI, pt. I, *The Report*, p. 311.
[2] See the chapter, 'Language Classification and Grammar Project', in *Census of India, 1961, A Guide to the 1961 Census Publication Programme* (Delhi: Manager of Publications, 1965), pp. 57–8.

of Bihari dialects returned in the 1951 census. However, in the 1961 census, after a decade of public discussion and controversy on language issues in Bihar, the Bihari dialects – Maithili, Magahi, and Bhojpuri – were returned by large numbers of people for the first time in the history of the census operations. More significantly, the way in which the figures were recorded, showing only 44% of Hindi-speakers in the state, seemed to challenge the assumption behind the language policy of the Bihar government that Bihar is primarily a Hindi-speaking state, and thereby gave new encouragement to language groups in Bihar demanding official recognition for their mother tongues.

The second category of political information contained in the census is the extent of language-consciousness of different language groups and the relative degree of absorption of the mother tongues by Hindi. Thus, if we compare the census enumeration of 1961 with the projected estimates of actual mother-tongue populations (keeping in mind the limitations of the figures), it appears that approximately two-thirds of Bhojpuri-speakers are aware that their mother tongue is Bhojpuri, whereas less than a third of Maithili-speakers and only a quarter of Magahi speakers know the names of their mother tongues. Or, to put the matter differently, one-third of the Bhojpuri-speakers, more than two-thirds of the Maithili-speakers, and three-quarters of the Magahi-speakers have been swallowed by the 'wolf of Hindi'. The 1971 census will show whether these speakers of the Bihari dialects have been fully digested or whether the language agitations of the past decade will cause further regurgitation from the Hindi wolf.

Although the census classifications and enumerations of 1951 and 1961 represent a considerable advance for the minority language groups of Bihar, they remain unsatisfactory to the Maithili supporters, who have reacted to them with a mixture of despair, sarcasm, and contempt. Thus, the *Mithila Mihir* thought that efforts of Maithils to get Maithili enumerated properly in the 1961 census had proved 'futile' and that 'a strange language known as Bihari' had become an 'important language of Bihar'.[1] Moreover, although the census authorities followed the broad classificatory scheme of Grierson, they deviated from it in the classification of sub-dialects. For example, Grierson clearly stated that Chikka-Chikki Boli was definitely a local variation of Maithili, whereas the 1961 census lists Chikka-Chikki (among other sub-dialects) as a separate dialect of the Bihari language.[2] The inclusion of a variety of dialects and village place

---

[1] *MM*, 14 February 1965.
[2] The problems faced by the census authorities in classifying and presenting the figures on

names in the Maithili area as separate dialects of Bihari brought forth derisive comments from the *Mithila Mihir*, whose editor discovered that, according to the 1961 census, 'a language named "Chero" is spoken only by one man. It appears that that man's mother died after leaving behind the "Chero" language and now he is the only man who survives in the vast universe who speaks that language'.[1]

There is some evidence that the census is a political document in a third sense also, in that the count itself can be influenced by persuasion of the census officials. Sri Adya Charan Jha in the *Mithila Mihir* tells of his success in influencing the census officials during 1951 when a census enumerator came to him and asked him all appropriate questions, except those related to language, which he entered on his own as Hindi for mother tongue and English for other languages. The author, a Maithili-speaker, reports that, 'Fortunately, the census enumerator was Maithili-speaking. He spoke a little in Maithili. After entertaining him at breakfast, I convinced him of the issue . . . The gentleman left my place assuring me that he would record Maithili as a mother language from now on.' The author went further and reported the matter to the district census official, a Maithil Brahman, who in turn reported the matter to the District Magistrate who, being a Bengali, 'had a soft corner for the cause of Maithili', and issued appropriate instructions that the mother-tongue column was to be filled only after personal inquiry. The matter was also raised by Harinath Misra in the Legislative Assembly. The author meanwhile 'helped' the census officials by getting 5,000 pamphlets printed and distributed by an airplane belonging to the Darbhanga estate.[2]

There are three aspects of this story which bear stressing. The first is that the census enumerator was Maithili-speaking and yet assumed that Hindi was the mother tongue of the Maithili-speaking people (or assumed that it was expected of him to enter Hindi as the mother tongue of the Maithili-speakers). Second, it appears that the census enumeration can be influenced by persuading the enumerators and those officials who have appropriate sympathies to take necessary action – in this case necessary corrective action. Third, the final count is a mixture which depends upon the attitudes of the census enumerators, the success of pamphlet distributors, and the beliefs of the people about the names of the languages they speak. The only

dialects of Bihar are discussed in *Census of India, 1961*, vol. IV: *Bihar*, pt. I-A (i) (Delhi: Manager of Publications, 1968), pp. 458–71.

[1] *MM*, 28 February 1965.   [2] *Ibid.*, 9 January 1966.

point in the census enumeration at which philological considerations arise is in the classification of the languages and dialects for enumeration and presentation. From a sociological point of view, the census is even more interesting in this form than it would be if it were based upon scientific considerations because the processes of differentiation and assimilation can be estimated directly through the census count. However, the census enumeration provides a totally inadequate basis for policy formation on issues relating to the media of education and administration.[1]

THE MAITHILI MOVEMENT:
PROBLEMS OF SOCIAL AND POLITICAL MOBILIZATION

Weakness of the Maithili movement

Language and community

The Maithili movement is an elite movement whose leaders claim to represent more than 20 million people, but are themselves aware of the low degree of political consciousness which exists among the Maithili-speaking people on the language issue.[2] In fact, nowhere in north India has language yet provided a sufficient basis for the creation of community. The Sikhs and Muslims would be separate and distinguishable communities even without the Punjabi and Urdu languges. For both Muslims and Sikhs, it will be argued later that language is not a necessary mark of community. For the Maithils, the situation is quite different. Language is a necessary, but not a sufficient mark of the existence of a community. Moreover, the absence of community feeling may also affect the linguistic identification of different social groups. In north Bihar, the Maithili language movement has been an instrument for the broadening of community identifications, but it has had to contend against social and religious differences, which would narrow the definition of the Maithil community and, thereby, the scope of the language.

It is not that the objective differences are not sufficient to distinguish the Maithili-speaking people from the people of other parts of Bihar.[3] It has been demonstrated above that the ancient history of

---

[1] *Indian Nation*, 30 July 1967, makes this point.
[2] Comparisons are frequently made in the *MM* between the weakness of the Maithili movement and the strength and successes of less developed languages, such as Assamese; e.g. 3 July 1966.
[3] Grierson, *Linguistic Survey*, vol. v, pt. II, pp. 4–5, characterized the language groups of Bihar as 'nationalities', among whom the 'ethnic differences' were 'great'. He stressed

Mithila provides a sufficiently vast symbol pool – rich in symbols of political history, literary excellence, and religious and philosophical contributions – for community builders to draw upon. There are also objective contemporary differences of geography, economy, dress, and bearing. Finally, the area has produced a Western-educated elite in the Maithil Brahman community, which maintains and desires to transmit the traditions of Mithila to the present generation through the medium of the Maithili language.

In their efforts to build a broad Maithil community, however, the leaders of the Maithili movement have run up against an obstacle, distinctive of the Maithili area, but detrimental to the building of community consciousness. That obstacle has been the continued hold of caste sentiments among the elite Brahman and Kayastha castes of Mithila, which in turn has contributed to the growth of caste movements among the middle or backward castes of the area. The issue has turned upon the definition or the criteria for recognition of a Maithil. The conservative leaders of the Maithil Mahasabha continue to resist the inclusion in the membership of the organization of any castes other than Brahmans or Karna-Kayasthas, who can demonstrate by their genealogical table and by the maintenance of Maithil traditions that they are truly Maithils.[1]

Sentiment within the Mahasabha and to a much greater extent outside the organization has increasingly been in favor of a much broader definition of the term Maithil. Increasingly, students from Mithila studying in the universities and the leaders of the Maithili Sahitya Parishad and other Maithili interest associations have insisted that the term Maithil cannot be restricted to Brahmans and Kayasthas,[2] but should apply to all the inhabitants of Mithila of whatever caste or religion[3] who speak the Maithili language. The reasons for the shift in definition are not difficult to understand. As the movement for the recognition of the Maithili language has acquired momentum, it has been increasingly evident that the restriction of the movement to the Maithil Brahmans and Kayasthas has

---

in particular, in rich prose, Brahman-dominance, pride, and conservatism among the Maithili-speaking people; lack of education, lack of enterprise, and uncouthness among the Magahi people; and alertness, activeness, ability, fighting skill, and lack of scruples among the Bhojpuri-speaking people.

[1] Raghunath Prasad Misra, 'Touchstone of a Maithil or the Criterion of being a Maithil', *Mithila Bandhu*, XVII, Nos. 1 and 2 (January–February 1956), translated from Maithili; *MM*, January 1942 and 15 April 1950.

[2] *MM*, 10 February 1945.

[3] *MM*, 6 January 1951, 6 and 27 February 1954, 12 January, 22 March and 1 November 1964; *Searchlight*, 10 January 1966 and 5 December 1969; *Indian Nation*, 4 December 1969; interviews (M1:11) in Patna on 7 December 1966, and M10:1, 17.

been a liability – first because the movement has been open to the charge of caste parochialism and second because it has become increasingly clear that the leaders of the Maithili movement must demonstrate that their demands for recognition of Maithili have broad popular support if they are to be successful.[1]

The broadening of the definition of a Maithil to conform to the needs of the Maithili movement has not been sufficient to create a sense of community among all or most Maithils. In the first place, consciousness of, pride in, and knowledge of the special traditions, customs, and history of Mithila continue to be most pronounced among the Brahmans and Kayasthas.[2] Second, internal differentiation in Mithila along caste and religious lines has moved faster than the Maithili movement. That is, the political mobilization of the middle or backward classes in north Bihar has developed as a movement toward increased economic and political power for these castes,[3] but it has not – unlike the non-Brahman movement in Tamil Nadu – been associated with symbols of regional identification. Moreover, the Urdu movement, which appeals primarily to Muslims in all parts of the state, including north Bihar, has moved ahead of the Maithili movement in its demands for recognition and in the mobilization of its underlying population. Nearly 75% of the Muslim population of Bihar declared Urdu as their mother tongue in the 1961 census, whereas less than a third of the underlying Maithili-speaking population did so for Maithili.

The consequences of an exclusive definition of the term Maithil have been, therefore, to retard the development of community consciousness and to threaten the hold of the Maithili language itself. Not only the Muslims, but Hindu speakers of dialects of Maithili (as defined by Grierson) have been declaring their mother tongue by the name of the dialect, rather than Maithili.[4]

It seems clear, therefore, from the Maithili case that language is not a sufficient condition for community identification. In the Maithili case, the Maithili language movement has created the basis

[1] In fact, it is sometimes argued that these elite castes of Mithila are not qualified to lead the Maithili movement because they have been more devoted to Sanskrit than to the regional vernacular; interview, M7:15; Laksman Jha, *Mithila Will Rise*, pp. 22–3.
[2] Interview, M5:9.
[3] For discussions of the caste basis of political mobilization in Bihar, see especially Harry Blair, 'Caste, Politics and Democracy in Bihar State, India: The Elections of 1967', unpublished Ph.D. dissertation, Duke University, 1969; and Ramashray Roy, 'Dynamics of One-Party Dominance in an Indian State', *Asian Survey*, VIII, No. 7 (July 1968), 553–75.
[4] Interview, M7:2. See also *Searchlight*, 16 February 1966, and *Indian Nation*, 3 August 1969.

for new community identification, but it has not been sufficiently appealing by itself to overcome caste exclusiveness and other forces of differentiation.

Political mobilization

The absence of a strong bond of community among Maithili-speakers in north Bihar is reflected in the lack of mass support for the movement. Attempts at mass contact have been sporadic and have lacked utterly the drama and militancy of similar language movements elsewhere in India. In 1948, Sri Adya Charan Jha regretted in the pages of the *Mithila Mihir* that the 'movement for a Mithila state is restricted to a selected few and the remaining populace is unaffected'.[1] Speakers at the annual meetings of the Maithili Mahasabha have commented on the small attendance.[2] Other Maithil leaders have remarked that the Maithili movement has revolved around the activities of individual devotees, but collective action has not been organized.[3] In despair, the *Mithila Mihir* has noted that, though Maithili is spoken by more people than is Assamese or Oriya, 'we lack utterly the spirit and enthusiasm with which they served the cause of their languages. We also lack the feeling of pride for our mother language which they do not lack.'[4] In fact, it has been admitted that most of the people in Mithila do not even know the word 'Maithili'.[5]

In 1951, the *Mithila Mihir* called upon the people of Mithila to take a series of steps to intensify the Maithili movement, including making sure that children in primary schools are taught through the medium of Maithili and that Maithili students in secondary schools and colleges offer Maithili as one of their subjects; use of Maithili outside the home, in work and other public activities; financial contributions to the movement; purchase of books and magazines in Maithili; and formal participation in the Maithili Sahitya Parishad, including the establishment of new branches in villages and towns throughout Mithila.[6] Occasionally, there have been calls to go beyond methods of persuasion and launch an agitation.[7] These appeals have not been entirely unsuccessful. Some credit must go to the Maithili movement for the fact that nearly 5 million Maithils declared Maithili as their mother tongue in the 1961 census.

However, if 5 million represents the potentially mobilizable constituency of the Maithili movement at this time, the weakness of the

[1] *MM*, 29 May 1948.   [2] *Ibid.*, 3 July 1948.   [3] *Ibid.*, 31 July 1948.
[4] *Ibid.*, 21 January 1950; see also 16 December 1950 and 20 November 1966.
[5] *Ibid.*   [6] *Ibid.*, 6 January 1951.   [7] *Ibid.*, 24 October 1953.

movement is all the more evident. Complaints are still made, fifteen years and more after the 1951 call, that parents in Mithila do not have sufficient interest to see that their children are educated through the medium of Maithili and that no collective actions are taken by the Maithili-speaking people to secure their rights;[1] Maithils are still being urged to speak their mother tongue;[2] and the thin attendance at meetings is still noticed.[3] The secretary of the Maithil Mahasabha felt in 1967 that the time had come to launch a movement in Mithila 'to arouse consciousness among the people about their language, which will bring a sense of unity among the people'. To this end, the Mahasabha was sending out its workers to tour the Maithili-speaking areas and make the people 'language-conscious'.[4] A Maithili Prachar Sena was formed for a similar purpose in July 1969.[5] Clearly, the Maithili movement is still at the stage of developing a feeling of common identity among the Maithili-speaking people. How far the movement must travel to achieve its ends is clear when it is considered that less than one-third of the potential underlying population of more than 16 million Maithili-speakers know the name of their mother tongue; fewer than 5,000 people read Maithili magazines and papers; the same number were mobilized into the political act of sending a postcard to the Sahitya Akademi to demand recognition for Maithili;[6] and fewer than 500 active workers were found to launch a signature campaign to support the demand for a Mithila university.[7] In short, as the secretary of the Maithil Mahasabha put it, 'the movement' has so far been 'confined only to the intellectuals'.[8]

Communications, social mobilization, and assimilation

Books and publications in Maithili

Supporters of the Maithili language base many of their claims for increased recognition of Maithili on the fact that Maithili is not only the mother tongue of a large portion of the population of Bihar but is also one of the important literary languages of India. However, the literary claims of Maithili lie primarily in the past. As a medium of

---

[1] *Ibid.*, 25 April, 20 and 27 June, 11 and 18 July 1965, and 9 May 1966.
[2] *Ibid.*, 5 December 1965.   [3] *Ibid.*, 12 December 1965.   [4] Interview, M5:1.
[5] *Searchlight*, 10 and 11 July 1969. Maithili Prachar Sena means, literally, Maithili Promotion Army.
[6] 5,000 also is the figure given for attendance at the 34th session of the Maithil Mahasabha in 1945; *MM*, 10 February 1945.
[7] *MM*, 1 November 1964.   [8] Interview, M5:5.

social communication in contemporary India through textbooks, prose works, and newspapers, Maithili is a language of negligible importance.

The quantity and quality of publications are the surest indicators of the spread of a written language. By these standards, Maithili is presently virtually an underdeveloped language. There are no textbooks in Maithili for the schoolchildren whose parents wish them to be instructed through the medium of their mother tongue. There are few prose works of any substance either in modern or more traditional subjects of inquiry. There is not a single daily newspaper in a language spoken by more than fifteen million people.

The leaders of the Maithili movement are fully aware of these deficiencies in the development of the Maithili language and have urged that steps be taken to promote both increased publication in Maithili and changes in the content of publication. To this end, they have demanded state patronage for the publication of textbooks and popular patronage for the publication of books and newspapers.[1] In neither respect has significant success been achieved.

Part of the problem of Maithili publication relates to the particular literary tradition of Maithili, which has been predominantly poetical. Such prose works as have been written have been predominantly 'about fairies and things of that calibre', as one respondent put it.[2] In short, Maithili has not been converted into a vehicle for the communication of modern knowledge. Such serious prose works as have been written in recent years have been either revivalist in character (such as histories of Maithili literature) or have been on traditional subjects such as religion and philosophy. In order to demonstrate that progress was being made in the publication of Maithili literature, a Maithili book exhibition was held in Delhi in 1964, which Pandit Nehru was asked to inaugurate. However, Nehru's response to the exhibition was to point out that only languages which produce modern, scientific literature could flourish in contemporary India and that the mere writing of books about songs or stories and novels would not be sufficient.[3]

A second aspect of the problem of developing Maithili prose and promoting newspaper and periodical publications has been the failure of publication to keep pace with education and literacy in Mithila. That is, educated Maithils have been assimilated either to English or to Hindi and have preferred to read and write serious

[1] See, for example, *MM*, 12 February 1967.
[2] Interview, M7:5; also *MM*, 3 July 1943.　　　[3] *Ibid.*, 22 March 1964.

works in those languages, rather than in Maithili.[1] The *Mithila Mihir* complained in 1942 that whenever it was proposed to publish a magazine or paper to promote the cause of Maithili, not even 500 people could be found to subscribe to such a paper, though there were more than 500 Maithil subscribers to English, Hindi, and Bengali magazines.[2] In other words, as the *Mithila Mihir* later put it, 'Among the Maithili-speaking populace, the hunger for literature is satisfied by the taste of other languages.'[3]

The consequence has been that there have been many attempts to publish magazines and journals in Maithili, but few have survived very long. From 1905 to 1962, twenty-five magazines and papers were started in Maithili, of which only ten were listed as current in 1962.[4] Five Maithili papers were listed by the registrar of newspapers in 1965, seven in 1968, and nine in 1969.[5] The two most important papers in 1969 were the *Mithila Mihir*, a primarily literary weekly (with some news on the Maithili movement) with a circulation of 1,578, and *Vaidehi*, a purely literary monthly, with a circulation of 1,100.[6] The total circulation of Maithili papers in 1969 was only 5,000, a figure higher than those for Bhojpuri or Magahi, but lower than that for the 'non-literary' tribal language of Santali.[7] The pre-eminent Maithili paper, the *Mithila Mihir*, has survived since 1908, but only because of the patronage of the Maharaja of Darbhanga, who made provision in his will for the continued publication of this paper. Even more revealing of the state of the development of the Maithili language in Mithila itself is the fact that there were four Hindi papers and two Urdu papers published from Darbhanga in 1969 with a combined circulation of 5,000, compared to only two Maithili papers with a circulation of 1,100.[8] In other words, although the absolute circulation figures for Maithili papers have increased since *Mithila Mihir* complained in 1942 that no paper could obtain even 500 subscribers, the relative position of Maithili papers remains behind Hindi and Urdu even in the Maithili-speaking centers. Consequently, in this respect, as in other respects, the evidence indicates that assimilation of Maithili-speakers to Hindi and Urdu (for Muslims) is keeping ahead of Maithili differentiation and that the

[1] *Ibid.*, 7 December 1946.   [2] *Ibid.*, January 1942.   [3] *Ibid.*, 21 January 1950.
[4] *What They Say About Maithili* (Allahabad: All-India Maithili Sahitya Samiti, 1963), pp. i–ii.
[5] Government of India, Ministry of Information and Broadcasting, *Press in India 1965*, pt. 1 (Delhi: Manager of Publications, 1965), p. 172; *Press in India 1970*, pt. 1 (Delhi: Manager of Publications, 1970), p. 262.
[6] *Press in India 1969*, pt. II (Delhi: Manager of Publications, 1970), pp. 75 and 84.
[7] *Press in India 1970*, pt. I, pp. 262–3.   [8] *Press in India 1969*, pt. II, pp. 68–89.

social mobilization of Maithils is proceeding at a rate which permits the absorption of most educated Maithils into occupations and activities involving the use of Hindi or English.

Hindi and Maithili: social mobilization, assimilation, and differentiation

Fig. 3 compares the distribution of the languages and predominant mother tongues in the districts of Bihar according to Grierson and according to the census of 1961. The figure reveals much about the varying levels of language-consciousness in the districts of Bihar and among the various mother tongues. First, it is clear that the 'Hindi' of Bihar is really primarily the language of the Magahi-speaking

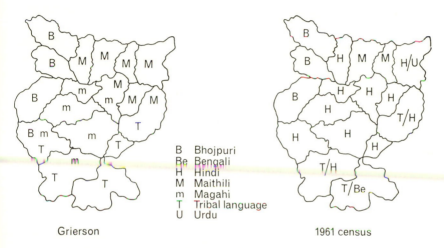

B   Bhojpuri
Be Bengali
H   Hindi
M   Maithili
m   Magahi
T   Tribal language
U   Urdu

Grierson   1961 census

Fig. 3   Linguistic distribution of Bihar districts according to Grierson and according to the census of 1961

people of the state. Second, however, it is also evident that Hindi dominates as the declared mother tongue of the people in other districts than the Magahi language area. Third, the districts in which the tribal languages and Bhojpuri predominate show a much higher degree of language-consciousness than do the Maithili-speaking districts. According to Grierson, Maithili was the language of the people of *all* Darbhanga and Bhagalpur districts (including the present district of Saharsa), nearly all of Muzaffarpur district, half of Monghyr, nearly all of the present district of Purnea, and much of Santal Parganas. According to the 1961 census, Maithili is the dominant language only in the districts of Darbhanga and Saharsa. The name Maithili is hardly known to the people of Bhagalpur,

Monghyr, and Santal Parganas districts. In Muzaffarpur, 8.61% of the population declared Maithili as their mother tongue, but 77.48% declared Hindi (see table 2.3). In Purnea, more than 10% declared Maithili as their mother tongue, but Maithili takes third place in the district after Hindi and Urdu.

Moreover, Maithili, along with the other Bihari dialects, is primarily a language of the countryside, even in the predominantly Maithili-speaking districts of Darbhanga and Saharsa (table 2.3). In all four districts which have significant numbers of Maithili-speakers – Darbhanga, Saharsa, Purnea, and Muzaffarpur – the proportion of Maithili-speakers to the total urban population is much less than their proportion to the total rural population. In contrast, the proportion of Hindi-speakers is generally higher in urban than in rural areas. Only in Saharsa – the least urbanized district in the whole of Bihar – is the proportion of Maithili-speakers in urban areas higher than that of Hindi-speakers. Thus, Hindi dominates as the declared mother tongue in most of the Maithili-speaking country and is especially important as a language of urban communication. The distribution of the Hindi and Bihari dialect groups in many of the Bihar districts conforms to the classic European pattern described by Deutsch in which a minority language dominates as the language of urban and elite communication for the mobilized population, whereas the vast unmobilized, rural population speaks a different language.[1] What is not clear is the direction of change, whether the trend is toward assimilation to Hindi or toward dialect differentiation. It is possible that Hindi has, in fact, assimilated Maithili in several districts, but it is also possible that a process of linguistic differentiation is taking place among Maithili-speakers in which the districts of Darbhanga and Saharsa have taken the lead so far and which will be accelerated as the rates of social mobilization increase in these and other Maithili-speaking districts.

While it is, therefore, not possible to assess the direction of change, it is possible to relate the present level of language-consciousness among the peoples of Bihar to other processes of social change which have been taking place in the province over the last half century or more. An examination of trends and present levels of social mobilization in the districts of Bihar may suggest the existing patterns of association between rates of social mobilization and linguistic assimilation and differentiation, which will hopefully be further clarified in the 1971 census. Table 2.4 and fig. 4 show the levels of moderniza-

[1] Karl Deutsch, *Nationalism and Social Communication: An Inquiry into the Foundations of Nationality*, 2d. ed. (Cambridge, Mass: M.I.T. Press, 1966), pp. 130ff.

TABLE 2.3 *Percent rural–urban distribution of speakers of Hindi, Maithili, Magahi, and Bhojpuri mother tongues in north and south Bihar districts, 1961*

District	Hindi			Maithili			Magahi			Bhojpuri		
	Total	Rural	Urban	Total	Rural	Urban	Total	Rural	Urban	Total	Rural	Urban
1. Patna	63.33	62.38	67.10	0.27	0.07	1.04	26.76	31.31	8.70	1.87	2.00	1.36
2. Gaya	57.24	56.01	72.86	0.03	0.01	0.31	34.92	37.29	4.64	0.14	0.13	0.30
3. Shahabad	9.74	8.53	25.33	0.04	0.02	0.28	0.55	0.48	1.48	85.49	88.07	52.28
4. Saran	14.19	12.69	48.52	0.08	0.06	0.40	..	..	..	79.34	81.40	32.17
5. Champaran	26.52	26.10	34.74	0.42	0.42	0.43	..	..	..	61.86	62.79	43.70
6. Muzaffarpur	77.48	77.49	77.41	8.61	8.97	1.18	..	..	..	4.56	4.74	0.69
7. Darbhanga	18.17	17.35	36.22	69.85	71.37	36.03	0.03	0.02	0.23	0.09	0.05	0.98
8. Monghyr	79.77	80.13	76.87	1.47	1.20	3.62	9.99	10.69	4.35	0.08	0.07	0.13
9. Bhagalpur	85.34	87.54	67.39	0.19	0.12	0.77	..	..	..	0.72	0.78	0.26
10. Saharsa	25.25	24.83	35.72	65.93	66.71	46.60	..	..	..	0.30	0.26	1.25
11. Purnea	47.45	47.19	51.64	10.19	10.37	7.34	..	..	..	0.55	0.50	1.39

SOURCE. Compiled from *Census of India, 1961, Bihar, District Census Handbooks*, from the sections numbered '11. Language' in the introduction to each district handbook.

TABLE 2.4 *Selected indices of social mobilization and assimilation to Hindi in Bihar districts, 1961*

District	Literacy		Urbanization		Workers in registered factories		Predominant mother tongues		
							1961 census		Grierson
	%	Rank	%	Rank	%	Rank	Language	%	Language
1. Patna	28.7	1	20.1	3	1.46	4	Hindi	63.33	Magahi
2. Dhanbad	25.5	2	25.0	1	4.77	2	Hindi	54.63	N.A.
3. Singhbum	22.9	3	21.5	2	5.28	1	Tribal	44.84	Tribal
4. Shahabad	21.8	4	7.2	9	0.91	6	Bhojpuri	85.49	Bhojpuri
5. Bhagalpur	20.3	5	10.9	5	0.59	10	Hindi	85.34	Maithili
6. Gaya	19.2	6	7.3	8	0.32	15	Hindi	57.24	Magahi
7. Ranchi	19.1	7	9.5	6	0.50	13	Tribal	44.33	Tribal
8. Monghyr	19.0	8	11.1	4	1.33	5	Hindi	79.77	Maithili, Magahi
9. Saran	18.2	9	4.2	16	0.52	12	Bhojpuri	79.34	Bhojpuri
10. Muzaffarpur	17.2	10	4.6	14	0.36	14	Hindi	77.48	Maithili
11. Darbhanga	16.8	11	4.3	15	0.60	9	Maithili	69.85	Maithili
12. Purnea	16.1	12	6.0	10	0.71	7	Hindi	47.45	Maithili
13. Santal Parganas	14.6	13	5.3	11	0.21	16	Tribal	37.44	Tribal
14. Hazaribagh	14.5	14	8.4	7	1.94	3	Hindi	71.80	Magahi
15. Saharsa	14.0	15	3.9	17	0.13	17	Maithili	65.93	Maithili
16. Palamau	13.6	16	4.7	13	0.67	8	Hindi	75.88	Tribal
17. Champaran	13.2	17	4.8	12	0.56	11	Bhojpuri	61.86	Bhojpuri
Bihar	18.40		8.43		N.A.				

SOURCES. Literacy and urbanization figures from *Census of India, 1961, Paper No. 1 of 1962, Final Population Totals* (New Delhi, Government of India Press, 1962), p. 333; workers in registered factories from *ibid.*, vol. I India, pt. I-A(ii): *tables*, table IV.2.

tion in Bihar districts on three major indices – literacy, urbanization, and industrialization. It is clear from the figure that there is a fundamental division in levels of modernization between the south Bihar districts and the districts of Chota Nagpur, on the one hand, and north Bihar on the other hand. This geographical division only

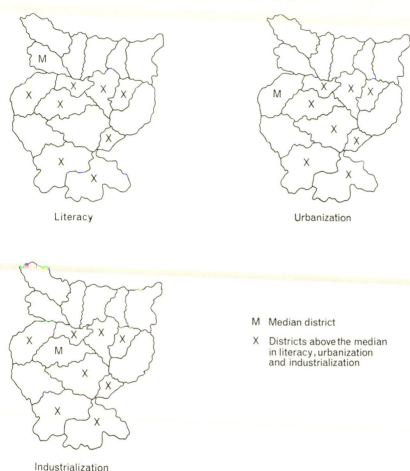

Literacy

Urbanization

Industrialization

M   Median district

X   Districts above the median
    in literacy, urbanization
    and industrialization

Fig. 4   Distribution of Bihar districts according to levels of literacy, urbanization, and industrialization, 1961

partly reinforces the linguistic divisions, but it does clearly show most of the Magahi-Hindi and the tribal districts as more literate, more urbanized, and more industrialized and the north Bihar Maithili- and Bhojpuri-speaking districts as less literate, urban, and industrial.

89

The clear association between high levels of modernization and Hindi dominance, on the one hand, and the low levels of modernization and Maithili predominance suggests the possibility that the more rapid social mobilization of the Magahi-Hindi districts has meant also the dominance and spread of Hindi to Maithili districts. Even within the predominantly Maithili-speaking districts of Darbhanga and Saharsa, the proportion of Maithili-speakers correlates negatively with indices of social change, whereas the percentage of Hindi-speakers correlates positively with such indices. For example, in the forty-four anchals (development blocks) of Darbhanga district and the twenty-one anchals of Saharsa district, the correlation coefficients for percent literacy with percent Maithili-speakers are -0.54 and -0.25, respectively.[1] These correlations hold even when the anchals with urban places are removed from the calculations. They are -0.53 for Darbhanga and -0.24 for Saharsa district for rural anchals only. Conversely, the correlations between percent Hindi-speakers and percent literacy (including anchals with urban places) are 0.47 for Darbhanga and 0.16 for Saharsa. The negative correlations between literacy and Maithili-speakers are reduced somewhat when the more elite category of 'matriculation and above' is used instead of general literacy. The correlations for matriculates and Maithili-speakers are -0.36 for Darbhanga district and -0.009 for Saharsa district, less strongly negative than for general literacy, but still negative. Thus, whether one looks at rates of change at the district level or at the distribution of rural and urban speakers of Hindi and Maithili or at literacy rates within the predominantly Maithili-speaking districts, it is Hindi which seems favored by association with the process of social mobilization and Maithili which lags behind.

Although it is not possible on the basis of existing census data to make a definite statement on the process of assimilation of Maithili-speakers to Hindi and the relationship between the two processes of assimilation and social mobilization, the available data do support the following hypotheses. The data suggest that differential rates of social mobilization between speakers of two language groups may favor the absorption of the less mobilized language speakers by the more mobilized, particularly *in the peripheral areas of the competing languages*. That is, Maithili and its dialects (as defined by Grierson) appear to have been absorbed by Hindi in the districts peripheral to

[1] The anchal figures are available in *Census of India, 1961, Bihar, District Census Handbook 7, Darbhanga* (Patna: Government of Bihar, 1968) and *10, Saharsa* (Patna: Government of Bihar, 1966), both by S. D. Prasad.

the central core of the Maithili language and culture and where it has come into contact with the more mobilized Magahi people. In the core culture and political areas of Maithili, the encroachments of Hindi have been more effectively resisted; but, even in those areas, Maithili-speakers tend to be less prominent in the more urbanized and more literate zones. Thus, Magahi, a language which Grierson considered little more than a sub-dialect of Maithili, has attached itself to standardized Hindi, which in turn has absorbed the fringe dialects of Maithili, but has had somewhat less success in affecting the linguistic identifications of speakers of the elite forms of Maithili in its core culture areas.

Maithili consciousness has been strongest, however, outside both the core cultural and peripheral areas. In fact, the development of the Maithili movement supports the hypothesis that ethnic consciousness tends to develop as strongly, if not more strongly, among socially mobilized members of the group who come into contact with members of other ethnic groups in urban contexts outside the home territory.[1] In the history of the Maithili movement, initial successes were achieved outside Mithila in the universities of Calcutta and Banaras. Moreover, a disproportionate number of Maithili organizations and periodicals have been founded outside Mithila and outside Bihar. A list of thirteen Maithili organizations in 1963 showed eight outside of the Maithili-speaking area, including six outside the state of Bihar.[2] Similarly, a list of thirty Maithili journals published during the twentieth century shows fifteen published outside Mithila, including twelve outside Bihar.[3] The evident enthusiasm of Maithili organizations outside Mithila for Maithili caused Sri Adya Charan Jha to remark in the *Mithila Mihir* that if Maithils living in Mithila had the same enthusiasm as those living in such places as Bombay, Calcutta, Delhi, and other cities, then the problems of Maithili would be more easily resolved.[4]

Social mobilization and English education

The history of Indian politics during the past century suggests that the most significant aspect of social mobilization for political change has been English education. The leaders of the Maithili movement themselves consider their failure to adopt Western education as rapidly as other regions in Bihar and their attachment to Sanskrit

---

[1] Benjamin Akzin, *State and Nation* (London: Hutchinson University Library, 1964), ch. 5.
[2] *What They Say About Maithili*, p. 40.
[3] Jankinandan Singh, *Memorandum*, pp. 8–10.
[4] *MM*, 9 January 1966.

education as primary causes of their political backwardness and of their failure to gain due recognition for Maithili.[1] The importance of English education for Maithili revival has been stated succinctly in a pamphlet of the Maithili Sahitya Samiti:

> As long as the Maithili speaking people themselves were not educated in 'English' Schools and Colleges, they did not care much for what was being propagated about Maithili in the 'English' educated circles. But when they also began to receive 'English' education, they asserted themselves and by now they have succeeded in freeing it from the clutches of Bengali, Hindi or the so-called Behari.[2]

While other indices are more ambiguous, the extent of knowledge of English among the major language groups of Bihar reflects exactly the relative political weight of those groups. Table 2.5 shows that

TABLE 2.5. *English bilingualism in Bihar state, 1961*[a]

Mother tongue	All males bilingual in English
	%
Maithili	1.73
Magahi	2.20
Bhojpuri	2.02
Urdu	2.52
Hindi	3.94

[a] This census enumeration does not include all English-speakers in Bihar because the census shows only the first language given by respondents after their mother tongue. Thus there may have been speakers of Maithili or Magahi who gave Hindi as their second language and English as a third language. In such cases, these speakers would not be shown as bilingual in English. Consequently, the figures cannot be considered to reflect accurately the English-speaking population of the state and they should be considered with this reservation.

SOURCE. *Census of India, 1961*, vol. IV, pt. II-C, pp. 212–23.

those who declared Hindi as their mother tongue, the dominant linguistic-political group in Bihar, also had the largest proportion of people bilingual in English. Urdu-speakers, whose linguistic demands have the greatest contemporary political saliency in Bihar politics, rank second. Among those who declared one of the Bihari dialects as their mother tongue, Magahi-speakers, the dominant group, rank first in English bilinguals; Bhojpuri-speakers rank second; and Maithili-speakers rank last. The backwardness of the Maithili region in English education is reflected also in the census

[1] *Ibid.*, 22 May 1948, 13 January 1951, and 13 November 1954; *Inaugural Address by the Maharajadhiraja of Darbhanga at the XIV all-India Oriental Conference, Darbhanga, 1948* (no publication details), p. 5.
[2] *What They Say About Maithili*, p. 6.

returns for male literacy in English between 1901 and 1931, shown in table 2.6. Thus, it appears that the backwardness of Maithili-speakers with respect to English and Western education has contributed to a lower level of political consciousness of cultural differences among them, which in turn has made possible the dominance of Magahi-Hindi speakers over Maithils in Bihar. This statement of the process of political-cultural change in Bihar has a curious ring to it, but it repeats exactly the historic role of English education as a factor in inter-group relations and political change throughout India during the past century.

TABLE 2.6   *Male literacy in English in Bihar by natural divisions, 1901–1931 (in percentages)*

Natural division	1901	1911	1921	1931
North Bihar[a]	0.32	0.38	0.61	0.70
South Bihar	0.57	0.64	1.02	1.19
Chota Nagpur	0.34	0.43	0.75	0.91

[a] Includes the Maithili-speaking districts of Muzaffarpur, Darbhanga, Bhagalpur, (including Saharsa), and Purnea and the Bhojpuri-speaking districts of Saran and Champaran

SOURCE. *Census of India, 1931,* vol.VII; *Bihar and Orissa,* pt. 1, *Report,* p. 225 (Patna 1932–3).

Political participation and integration

Although Maithili-speakers lack a political consciousness of their separateness from other ethnic groups in Bihar, there is no lack of political consciousness in the Maithili-speaking region generally, in comparison with other regions of the state. The north Bihar and Maithili-speaking districts, which rank low on indices of social mobilization and modernization, appear consistently in the upper half of Bihar districts in voting turnout (fig. 5). It is, therefore, not because of a low level of political mobilization in the region that the Maithili movement has failed to generate support. On the contrary, political consciousness is relatively high in the region, but the population has been mobilized politically on other-than-linguistic bases.

In fact, most available evidence from the political history of the state suggests a high degree of political integration of the north Bihar and Maithili-speaking districts into all-Bihar politics. Gandhi launched his first major *satyagraha* in India, after his return from South Africa, in the north Bihar district of Champaran in 1917. The *satyagraha* in Champaran drew the attention and participation of Congressmen from other parts of north Bihar as well. From this point on, the north

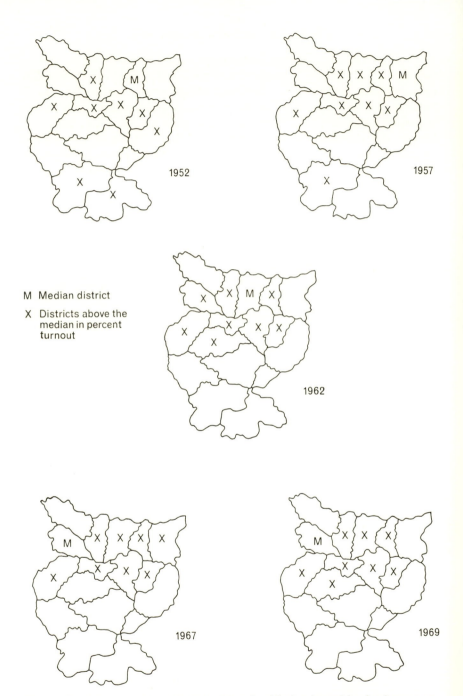

Fig. 5   Voting turnout by district in Bihar Legislative Assembly elections, 1952–1969

Bihar districts remained at the center of all the major nationalist agitations which occurred in the state. In the post-independence period, the Congress has consistently won comparatively high vote percentages in several north Bihar and Maithili-speaking districts (fig. 6). All the other leading parties of Bihar, including the leftist parties – the SSP, PSP, and CPI – and the Jan Sangh have had strong support in north Bihar and Maithili districts. Darbhanga district, the central Maithili-speaking district, has been a particularly strong district in providing leadership for and electoral support to parties of the radical left.[1] Moreover, the political elite from the north Bihar and Maithili-speaking districts has been fully integrated into the structure of political power in Bihar. Of twenty-six ministers for whom information was available[2] and who held portfolios in the Congress government in Bihar from 1962 to 1967, thirteen came from the Maithili region – four from Darbhanga, four from Muzaffarpur, three from Purnea, and one each from Monghyr and Bhagalpur.

Politically, then, the historic tendency in north Bihar and Mithila has been overwhelmingly toward political integration of the region into all-Bihar politics. This does not mean, however, that alternative bases of political mobilization could not be developed in the future. Although rates of voting turnout have been relatively high in north Bihar compared to other parts of the state, they have been relatively low compared to other regions of India.[3] And, although the leading parties of Bihar are relatively well-entrenched in Mithila in comparison to their position in other parts of the state, political parties and the party system as a whole are less institutionalized and more fractionalized in Bihar than in most other Indian states.[4] A counter-elite or a political party which sought to intensify political mobilization in the Maithili-speaking region on the basis of language would not face insurmountable odds against its success.

THE MAITHILI MOVEMENT AND THE LANGUAGE POLICY OF THE BIHAR GOVERNMENT

Maithili organizations

The oldest Maithil organization concerned with the language and

[1] On the distribution of left party support in Bihar, see Paul R. Brass, 'Radical Parties of the Left in Bihar: A Comparison of the SSP and the CPI', in Paul R. Brass and Marcus F. Franda (eds.), *Radical Politics in South Asia* (Cambridge, Mass.: M.I.T. Press, 1973).

[2] From *Bihar Vidhan-Sabha ke SadasyoN ka Sankshipt Jivan-Parichay* (Patna: Bihar Vidhan-Sabha Press, 1966).

[3] See Paul R. Brass, 'Political Participation, Institutionalization and Stability in India', *Government and Opposition*, IV, No. 1 (Winter 1969), 26.   [4] *Ibid.*, pp. 40–2.

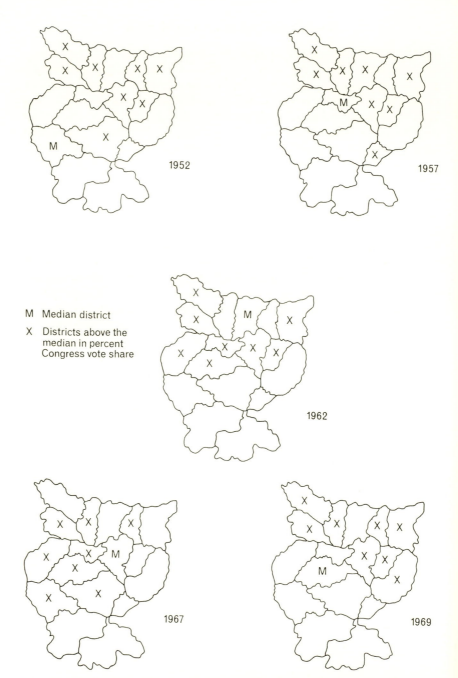

M Median district

X Districts above the
  median in percent
  Congress vote share

Fig. 6   Distribution of the top nine support districts for the Congress, measured
by percentage of valid votes polled in Bihar Legislative Assembly elections,
1952–69

96

culture of the Maithili-speaking people in Mithila is the All-India Maithil Mahasabha founded in 1910 with the patronage of the Maharaja of Darbhanga. The Maithil Mahasabha is a caste federation of the elite Brahman and Kayastha castes of north Bihar. Like many other caste associations in India, the Maithil Mahasabha has functioned as a 'paracommunity' based upon *both* birth and voluntary association and oriented towards uniting related castes into a larger association.[1]

Some leaders of the Mahasabha, especially the Maharaja Kameshwar Singh, argued that the Mahasabha was fulfilling the needs of the whole of Mithila in its devotion to the language and culture of the Maithili people.[2] However, there have been others in the Mahasabha who have for decades advocated opening the organization to all castes in Mithila[3] and thereby broadening the meaning of the term Maithil and identifying all the people of the region with the cause of the Maithili language and literature. In fact, however, the organization to this day remains open only to Brahmans and Kayasthas.

The Mahasabha has played the typical role in Mithila which other and earlier social reform and caste organizations played in Bengal in the nineteenth century, that of working for the elimination of social practices considered to be undesirable, such as child marriages, marriages of old men to young women, the dowry system, and polygamy.[4] However, unlike many of the early reform organizations in Bengal and the other presidency provinces, the Mahasabha has not suggested any reform of caste or religious practices. In fact, the Mahasabha has promoted the maintenance and extension of orthodox caste practices relating to food and marriage and has opposed any proposals to abolish the caste system or to reform Hinduism or to enact a uniform civil code for Hindus. The Mahasabha has also been a supporter of the cow protection movement.[5] Many of the

[1] Lloyd I. and Susanne Hoeber Rudolph, *The Modernity of Tradition: Political Development in India* (Chicago: University of Chicago Press, 1967), pp. 33–6.

[2] *Presidential Address of His Highness, the Maharajadhiraja of Darbhanga, Dr Sir Kameshwar Singh, D.Litt., LL.D., K.C.I.E., at the 44th Conference of the Maithil Mahasabha* (no publication details), 5 November 1955. Translated from Maithili.

[3] *MM*, January 1942 and 17 March 1945.

[4] *Address by the Chairman, Reception Committee, Pandit Sri Amar Choudhry, B.A., LL.B., at the 27th Conference of the Maithil Mahasabha at Sitamarhi; Address by the Chairman, Reception Committee, Babu Sri Chandradhari Singh, at the 38th Conference of the Maithil Mahasabha* (no publication details); *MM*, 17 July 1943, 10 February 1945, 3 July 1948, 15 April 1950, and 18 July 1965.

[5] *Address of Chandradhari Singh; Address by His Highness, the Maharajdhiraja of Darbhanga at the 40th Conference of the Maithil Mahasabha* (no publication details), 20 January 1951; *MM*, 10 February 1945, 10 July 1943, 3 July and 18 September 1948, 15 April 1950, and 15 December 1951.

modernizing religious and social reform movements in India from the Brahmo Samaj through the Arya Samaj have adopted similar attitudes on some of these issues, but it is important to stress that the reform proposals of the Maithil Mahasabha have been confined only to the most obvious social evils. In all other respects, the Mahasabha has defended Hindu orthodoxy of the most conservative sort.

A third area of activity for the Mahasabha has been the development of educational institutions in the region and the awarding of scholarships to Maithil students. Here also the Mahasabha has played a conservative role. Although the organization has supported modern education in Mithila, it has also given a disproportionately large share of aid to educational institutions and scholarships to students in areas of traditional knowledge, particularly Sanskrit education. For example, it was reported in 1942 that the Mahasabha had over the years awarded scholarships to more than 500 students, of whom 200 had received a Sanskrit education.[1] The Mahasabha has supported modern education in Mithila, including aiding in the establishment of technical colleges and the modern C. M. College at Darbhanga, but the predominant emphasis has been towards traditional, Sanskrit education.[2]

Finally, with respect to the promotion of the Maithili language and Maithil culture, the Mahasabha has acted as a pressure group, demanding state and university patronage for the Maithili language. However, the direct contribution of the Mahasabha to the spread and development of the Maithili language has been minimal, since its primary orientations have been toward traditional Sanskrit education, on the one hand, and modern English education, on the other hand. The Mahasabha did make an annual contribution to the Maithili Sahitya Parishad, but a contribution of only Rs. 200.[3]

The aims and character of the Maithil Mahasabha have changed very little since its founding in 1910. The secretary of the Mahasabha listed the primary objectives of the organization in 1967 as, first, uniting the Maithil Brahman and Kayastha castes spread all over the country; second, promoting the cause of Maithili language and literature; third, advancing Sanskrit teaching and research. The secretary considered that the primary achievements of the Mahasabha

---

[1] *MM*, January 1942.

[2] In the year 1943, it was reported that the Mahasabha had awarded scholarships to 51 students, out of which 26 were given to students entering Sanskrit institutions. *MM*, 17 July 1943. In 1945, there were 69 scholarship awards, of which 33 were for Sanskrit students; *ibid.*, 10 February 1945. In 1948, the figures were 35 Sanskrit scholarships out of 92; *ibid.*, 3 July 1948, see also Jankinandan Singh, *Memorandum*, p. 50.

[3] *MM*, January 1942.

in the past had been the removal from the region of social evils in marriage practices, the spread of education, and the achievement of recognition by Patna University of Maithili as a subject of study in the curriculum. The leadership of the Mahasabha remains with the Darbhanga Raj family, but the constitution has been altered so that the head of the Darbhanga royal family is no longer life president, but is elected every year.

After the Maithil Mahasabha, the oldest organization in Mithila concerned with the language and culture of the region is the Maithili Sahitya Parishad, founded in 1931.[1] The composition and functions of the Parishad contrast significantly with those of the Mahasabha in that its membership is open to all castes in Mithila and its functions are more specific. The primary concern of the Parishad has always been the spread and development of the Maithili language and literature. To this end, it publishes books and conducts examinations in Maithili, holds annual Vidyapati week celebrations, and engages in political representation on issues concerned with the use of the Maithili language in education and administration in Bihar. However, it was said in 1966 that the organization had been in decline in recent years and had not held an annual meeting in the previous seven or eight years.[2]

The association has quite consciously and explicitly welcomed all castes into the organization, has insisted that the term 'Maithil' should not be confined to Brahmans and Kayasthas, and has objected to the tendency on the part of Brahman and Kayastha writers to overemphasize their role and achievements in the history and literature of Mithila. The Parishad is only somewhat less than the Mahasabha in fact an organization of the elite castes of Mithila, but its orientation is both more modern, more specific, and more inclusive.

At present, the most effective organization of the Maithili community is the Chetna Samiti, a literary and cultural organization of the Maithili-speaking people, formed in Patna in 1955. The political importance of the Chetna Samiti derives from the fact that many prominent politicians from the Maithili area of all political parties are members.[3] Most recently, the Chetna Samiti has been used as a vehicle for bringing together the MLAs and MPs of Mithila to discuss the grievances of the Maithili-speakers and to decide the political strategy to be followed in presenting demands on behalf of Maithili.[4]

[1] Jankinandan Singh, *Memorandum*, pp. 7–8.
[2] *MM*, 2 January and 26 June 1966.
[3] Interview, M6:1–2.
[4] Interview, M10:2, 5–6; *Indian Nation*, 19 June and 18 July 1967.

In addition to these organizations, there are many other Maithili literary and cultural organizations in Patna, in Bihar, and in the large cities of north India outside Bihar which have significant Maithili populations. None of the Maithili organizations, however, has a large membership, a significant mobilizable constituency, or any financial resources. There is no Maithili organization which carries any political weight in Bihar politics.

Political action on behalf of Maithili

Most of the major language movements in India have found it necessary to enter the political arena directly, either through the formation of specific organizations to contest elections and seek power, or through such effective mobilization of the population on the issue that linguistic politics come to dominate the political process, or both. The Maithili movement, however, has not gone beyond the stage of representation and interest group politics[1] and the Maithili issue has never become politically salient. The activities of Maithili interest associations receive coverage in the leading Bihar newspapers, the *Searchlight*, the *Indian Nation*, and *Arya Varta*. Three or four items per month, on the average, appear in these papers, describing the meetings of the Maithili associations, their demands and grievances. The editorial policies of these papers are favorable to the demands of the Maithili spokesmen. In fact, the *Indian Nation* press, which also publishes the Hindi daily, *Arya Varta*, and the Maithili monthly, *Mithila Mihir*, was founded by the Maharaja of Darbhanga and has many Maithili Brahman supporters of the Maithili movement on its staff.

However, over the past two decades, the primary forms of political action reported in these newspapers have been of the most innocuous sort – resolutions passed by the Maithili interest associations, such as the Maithil Mahasabha, the Maithili Sahitya Parishad, and others; postcard campaigns, such as the one launched in connection with the effort to gain recognition for Maithili in the Sahitya Akademi (see below); delegations to state government ministers and to the governor to request specific actions on behalf of the Maithili language and its speakers;[2] and efforts to win the support of prominent Bihar politicians, particularly those from Mithila.

In recent years, supporters of Maithili have attempted to make

---

[1] Threats to launch mass agitations have been made from time to time by some Maithili interest associations. See, for example, the report on the meeting in Darbhanga of the All-India Maithili Mahasangh in *Indian Nation*, 4 December 1969.

[2] See especially the eleven-point demand presented to the governor of Bihar by the All-India Maithili Mahasangh; *Indian Nation*, 4 and 11 August 1968.

more effective use of representational devices to press their claims at both the center and state levels. These efforts were partly prompted by a growing discontent on the part of Maithili supporters over the inaction and disinterest of MPs and MLAs from Mithila with respect to the interests of Maithili. The supporters of Maithili have, therefore, been pressing legislators from Mithila to represent the cause of Maithili more effectively in the legislatures.[1] In addition, attempts have been made to coordinate the actions of legislators from Mithila through informal caucuses of MPs and MLAs at Vidyapati celebrations and meetings of Maithili cultural organizations.

These efforts at more effective representation notwithstanding, it is clear that the Maithili movement continues to lack explicit, formal political organization and that it does not constitute a mobilized political constituency. Neither in the 1967 general elections nor in the 1969 mid-term elections was the Maithili issue a significant one for the major political parties.

Before the mid-term elections in Bihar, twenty-four party leaders and candidates of the CPI, CPM, SSP, PSP, Loktantric Congress, Jan Sangh, and the Congress were interviewed in Patna and in Darbhanga districts. Each respondent was asked to give the name of his mother tongue and the names of other languages he spoke and to say whether or not he favored granting Urdu and Maithili official status as second languages of Bihar. Three features of the responses are worth summarizing. First, there were no substantial differences from party to party in attitudes towards Maithili. The significant differences in responses related more to the respondent's place of origin, mother tongue, and caste status. Hindi- and Bengali-speakers interviewed in Patna tended to consider Maithili only a dialect. However, most low-caste and some non-Maithil Brahman high castes in Darbhanga itself also characterized Maithili as a dialect and some even gave Hindi as their mother tongue. Sentiment is most favorable to Maithili among politicians from Darbhanga, but particularly among Maithil Brahmans. Second, there is little strong anti-Maithili feeling, in contrast to the attitudes towards Urdu. Nearly all respondents opposed the granting of official status to Maithili as a second language, but the general sentiment regarding Maithili was favorable towards its development and encouragement in other ways short of official status. Third, the general character of the responses suggested that the Maithili issue was not a major concern for the leading parties of Bihar.

There was, however, one curious political party, known as the

[1] *MM*, 18 September and 25 December 1966.

Proutist Bloc of India, which contested 63 seats to the legislative assembly in the Bihar mid-term elections of 1969, and which focused its campaign on issues concerning the regional languages of Bihar. This party is sponsored by a Hindu religious sect, known as the Anand Marg. Its platform favors greater encouragement to all the regional languages of Bihar and north India, including Maithili, Magahi, Bhojpuri, and Angika in Bihar. Little is known about this party. It was of no consequence in the 1969 elections, in which it polled only 0.3% of the total popular vote. Its candidates lost their security deposits in all 63 seats contested.

Maithili and the language policy of the Bihar government

Status of the Maithili language

Formal recognition of the Maithili language was first achieved outside Mithila and outside Bihar in the University of Calcutta where, in 1919,[1] Maithili was accepted as a modern Indian language subject for study up to the M.A. stage. In 1933, Banaras Hindu University followed suit. It was not until 1939, however, that Maithili received recognition in the major university of Bihar, Patna University.[2] By 1948, Maithili was recognized as a subject of study in Patna University for both the B.A. and M.A. examinations[3] and four Maithil students passed their M.A. examinations in Maithili in 1950. In 1964, a Vidyapati chair was established at the Bihar University.[4] Thus, Maithili has become well-established as a literary language worthy of study and serious scholarship at the university level.

Of much greater political significance, however, was the achievement of national and international recognition for the Maithili language by the inclusion of Maithili as a modern Indian language by both PEN and the All-India Sahitya Akademi. Recognition by the Indian branch of PEN was achieved as early as 1947 without difficulty.[5] However, recognition by the Sahitya Akademi proved more difficult to achieve and was not granted until 1965.[6]

---

[1] *Ibid.*, 4 December 1948; interview, M7:3; Laksman Jha, *Mithila in India*, p. 30, gives the date 1919.

[2] *Ibid.*; interview, M4:10.

[3] *Presidential Address at the 38th Conference of the Maithil Mahasabha*, translated from Maithili; *MM*, 4 December 1948.

[4] *MM*, 9 February 1964.

[5] *MM*, 11 September 1947; interview (M7:3) in Patna on 3 July 1967.

[6] Recognition by the Sahitya Akademi was considered essential for the progress of Maithili as early as 1947; see *MM*, 15 November 1947 and 17 January 1948.

Recognition by the Sahitya Akademi carries with it both literary and political significance. From a literary point of view, recognition brings the financial patronage of central government funds for publications and translations of Maithili literature and prizes for literary achievement. From a political point of view, recognition carried a dual significance for Maithili – formal recognition by a quasi-governmental agency (chaired at the time by Pandit Nehru himself) of the Government of India for the Maithili language which, in turn, gave national recognition to Maithili as an independent language distinct from Hindi.[1]

Politics were involved in the recognition of the Maithili language in another respect also, namely, in the use of techniques of political pressure by the leaders of the Maithili movement to persuade the members of the Akademi to admit Maithili. The various Maithili organizations met throughout 1964 to pass resolutions demanding the inclusion of Maithili in the Sahitya Akademi and to launch a postcard campaign for the same purpose. It was reported that some 5,000 postcards were sent to Pandit Nehru, the chairman of the Sahitya Akademi. The services of politicians were also enlisted in the cause. A meeting of the MLAs and MPs from Mithila met in Patna in March to pass a resolution supporting the inclusion of Maithili in the Akademi.[2]

The most important issue for the advocates of Maithili was not simply recognition by the Akademi, but recognition of the distinctness of Maithili from Hindi. When the Akademi did ultimately grant full recognition to Maithili, the decision was hailed in the *Mithila Mihir* as a complete vindication of the independent status of Maithili and a rebuff to those who sought to diminish its stature by treating it as a dialect of Hindi.[3]

Recognition by the Sahitya Akademi in 1964 brought to a successful conclusion the literary demands of the Maithili spokesmen. However, while recognition by the Akademi carries political significance, its importance in the political arena is largely symbolic and useful as a referent for making other demands. Far more important for the long-term progress of Maithili is the successful introduction of Maithili in the public schools of Mithila as the medium of instruction for students whose mother tongue is Maithili.

There are a number of steps and several obstacles to be overcome before a minority language can achieve such a position of importance in a multi-lingual province. These steps include recognition of the

---

[1] *MM*, 3 January 1965.   [2] *Ibid.*, 12 January, 1 and 22 March 1964.
[3] *Ibid.*, 3 January 1965.

minority language as a mother tongue, to be used as the medium of instruction in both the primary and secondary stages; implementation of recognition by the educational authorities and the parents of the children; and provision of teachers and textbooks in the minority language on non-language subjects. In the state of Bihar, Maithili received recognition as the mother tongue of a minority as early as 1949,[1] which entitled Maithili-speaking students to be instructed through the medium of Maithili. However, as late as 1960–1, there were only 54,674 students at the primary level and only 3,006 students at the secondary level receiving instruction in Maithili. Moreover, for these 57,680 students, Maithili was not the medium of instruction, but only a subject of study.[2]

The leaders of the Maithili movement attribute the slow progress of Maithili in the public schools of Bihar both to the hostility of the officers of the education department[3] and to the apathy of the parents of the Maithil students.[4] As evidence of hostility, they cite the failure to provide textbooks[5] and the placing of the onus of responsibility for requesting instruction through the Maithili medium upon the parents.

At the secondary stage, Maithili is recognized only as an optional language subject and not as a medium of education. The latter status has been granted in Bihar to other minority languages, including Urdu, Bengali, Santali, and Nepalese. The inferior status of Maithili at the secondary level has been a source of resentment for Maithili leaders.[6]

While complete victory in the area of public school education is still far off, this has not prevented many spokesmen of the Maithili movement from making more directly political demands, including that for acceptance of Maithili as a subject of examination for admission into the Bihar Public Service,[7] recognition of Maithili as a

---

[1] *Ibid.*, 9 July, 1949, and letter of Jayakant Mishra to *Indian Nation*, 7 February 1970.

[2] Government of India, Ministry of Home Affairs, *Report of the Commissioner for Linguistic Minorities (Sixth Report)* (Delhi: Manager of Publications, 1965), pp. 127, 196. (Hereafter referred to as *CLM*.)

[3] *MM*, 26 September 1953, 13 December 1964, 7 February and 13 June 1965, 24 July and 18 September 1966; interview, M4:20.

[4] *MM*, 25 April, 20 June and 11 July 1965, and 18 September 1966.

[5] *Ibid.*, 3 April 1954, 9 February and 13 December 1964, 7 February and 13 June 1965, 30 January and 24 July 1966. The following comment by Sri Bacha Thakur in *MM*, 30 January 1966, is representative: 'More than sixteen years have passed since Maithili was accepted as the medium of instruction up to the middle standard. But not even a single book has been published in Maithili so far by the Text Book Committee.' See also the letter of Jayakant Mishra to *Indian Nation*, 7 February 1970.

[6] *MM*, 21 June 1952.

[7] *Ibid.*, 12 January and 22 March 1964, 28 February, 21 March and 12 December 1965,

provincial or second official language of Bihar,[1] inclusion of Maithili in the eighth schedule of the Constitution of India,[2] and the presently dormant demand for the creation of a separate province of Mithila.[3] Whereas progress is being made in the educational arena, no specifically political demand of the Maithili organizations has so far been accepted.

The political demand which has been pressed most strongly in recent years is that for the inclusion of Maithili in the eighth schedule of the Constitution.[4] Inclusion of Maithili in the eighth schedule would have an impact on the use of Maithili in the public schools as well as on the entire future course of the movement. In the public school question, while the mother tongue is considered an appropriate medium of instruction for any linguistic minority at the primary stage, only the fourteen major languages of India have so far been considered as media of instruction at the secondary stage. The Government of India also accords representation on language development committees to languages listed in the eighth schedule and has denied Maithili such representation because it is not so listed.[5] For the long term, the inclusion of Maithili in the eighth schedule is even more significant, since all languages listed in the eighth schedule that have significant regional concentrations have spawned movements which have ultimately led to the creation of new linguistic states. Punjabi was the last language in the eighth schedule to form the basis for such a movement and one of the more effective arguments of the Akali Dal was to point to the discrimination involved against the Punjabi language as the only regional language listed in the schedule without a state of its own. It is apparent that that argument will be available to the leaders of the Maithili movement if their demand for inclusion is accepted.

The demand for inclusion of Maithili in the eighth schedule became especially insistent at the end of 1966 and in the early months of 1967, when it became clear that Sindhi, a language of refugees

and 31 July 1966; Ramanath Jha, 'The Panjis of Mithila', p. 55; *Maithili: What it is and what it claims*, p. 6; *Indian Nation*, 20 March 1967.

[1] *MM*, 11 September 1948; *Indian Nation*, 24 March 1967; *Searchlight*, 12 August 1967; interview, M5:1.

[2] *MM*, 26 September 1953, 27 February and 13 November 1954, 1 January and 1 and 22 March 1964, 21 March, 18 July, and 12 December 1965; interviews M8:1, M10:4, BG14a:15, 22; Ramanath Jha 'The Panjis of Mithila', p. 54; Laksman Jha, *Mithila: A Union Republic*, p. 65.

[3] A Union minister of state surprised a gathering of Maithils in Madhubani in June 1969 by referring favorably to this demand in a public speech there; *Searchlight*, 10 June 1969.

[4] *MM*, 24 July and 20 November 1966; *Searchlight*, 18 August 1967.

[5] *Indian Nation*, 1 July 1968.

from the Sindh area of Pakistan, was to be included as the fifteenth language in the schedule. Maithili leaders expressed some resentment that Sindhi, a language spoken only by a million people in India and without a regional concentration, should have received recognition before Maithili. At the same time, it was argued that now that Sindhi had been recognized, there could be no excuse for denying Maithili a place as the sixteenth language in the eighth schedule.[1] However, it was not until April 1969 that a Constitution (Amendment) Bill to include Maithili in the eighth schedule was introduced into the Lok Sabha by an SSP MP from Madhubani constituency of Darbhanga district,[2] but without the support necessary for success. Another non-official bill was introduced for the same purpose on 27 February 1970.[3] In December 1970, a delegation of MPs from Mithila and other spokesmen for Maithili waited upon prime minister Gandhi and claimed to have received assurances from her 'that she would try her best to get a place for Maithili in the eighth schedule of the constitution'.[4] However, in May 1971, the central minister of state for home affairs, in reply to a question in the Lok Sabha, said that no additional languages should be included in the eighth schedule.[5]

Much stronger feelings of resentment were expressed by Maithili spokesmen, also at the end of 1966 and early 1967, when it appeared that Urdu was going to receive recognition as the second official language of Bihar. This resentment was reinforced by the knowledge that the proportion of Urdu-speakers in the state was smaller than that of Maithili-speakers and by the feeling that, although the demand for recognition of Urdu was seen as a Muslim demand, most Muslims in Bihar did not actually speak Urdu, but spoke the regional languages of the state – Maithili, Magahi, and Bhojpuri. Consequently, it was argued that, if any language of Bihar was to be given the status of second official language, that language should be Maithili, not Urdu.[6] However, the demand to make Maithili a second official language of Bihar was explicitly rejected by the first united front government of Bihar in July 1967.[7] In both the cases

[1] See *MM*, 6 and 11 December 1966, 8 January and 9 April 1967.
[2] *Searchlight*, 5 April 1969.
[3] *Indian Nation*, 27 February 1970.
[4] *Indian Nation*, 24 December 1970.
[5] *Ibid.*, 28 May 1971.
[6] See *MM*, 18 December 1966, 12 and 26 March, 2, 9, and 23 April 1967. This argument was supported by the Jan Sangh alone among the major parties of Bihar, but Jan Sangh support reflected more anti-Urdu than pro-Maithili sentiment.
[7] *Searchlight*, 11 July 1967; see also the statement of the Revenue Minister in the United Front government in *ibid.*, 12 June 1968.

of Sindhi and Urdu, where prior recognition was given to languages whose *prima facie* case for special status was seen as less worthy than that of Maithili, it was brought home to the spokesmen for the movement that the demands for Maithili would not be successful without more rigorous political action and mobilization of public opinion.[1]

Maithili and the language policy of the Bihar government

Bihar is presently the most linguistically diverse state in India. Mounting conflict over the various language issues in the state is a virtual certainty in the foreseeable future. Demands for official recognition of Urdu and Maithili have already been made. If the Maithili and Jharkhand forces were to join together and revive seriously demands for separate states for the Maithili-speaking people and for the tribal population, the dismemberment of the state of Bihar would become a real possibility in the long term.

The Bihar government has failed to consider the language issues with any seriousness. The policy of the government has been based upon simplification of complexity, misinformation on the extent of linguistic diversity in the state, and a symbolic adherence to all-India policies for the protection of linguistic minorities combined with a refusal to inform itself or anyone else of the actual state of implementation of such policies. It is not clear to what extent the approach of the Bihar government towards the language issues has been deliberate or has simply reflected an unwillingness to open the Pandora's box until demands are pressed more vigorously by the linguistic groups concerned. The latter explanation seems the more likely one, since the Bihar government has not adopted the stance of the Uttar Pradesh government of open defiance of all-India policy and deliberate refusal to provide satisfaction to linguistic minority demands.

The basic simplification upon which the policy of the Bihar government is based is the notion that Bihar is overwhelmingly a Hindi-speaking state. Until 1951, the census figures supported that notion, but those figures had for half a century been based upon an extremely broad definition of Hindi, which ignored the linguistic distinctions of Grierson and the claims of minority language speakers. If Grierson's classifications were accepted, there would in fact be no Hindi-speakers at all in Bihar, except for migrants. When the census finally did adopt the classification of Grierson in 1961, after more than half

---

[1] See, for example, the comments in *MM*, 25 December 1966, 1 and 8 January, 12 February, and 12 March 1967.

a century of Hindi promotion and fifteen years in which Hindi was used as the official language of the state, much less than half of the total population of the state (44.30%) declared (or were reported as declaring) their mother tongue as Hindi.[1] However, the policies of the Bihar government have so far been based upon an acceptance of the 1951 census figures, which show more than 81% of the population as Hindi-speaking.

The reasons for the adoption of the view that Bihar is a Hindi-speaking state are reasonably clear. The predominant mother tongues of Bihar are Magahi and Bhojpuri, neither of which are literary languages and both of which owe much to both Maithili and Hindi. Magahi and Bhojpuri could be classified as dialects either of Hindi or of Maithili. However, the movement for the standardization and spread of Hindi, which originated in Banaras in the late nineteenth century, extended its influence over educated and socially mobilized Magahi- and Bhojpuri-speakers, who accepted the view that their mother tongues were dialects of Hindi.[2] The Maithili movement was never in a position to exercise this kind of influence since the language has yet to be standardized and spread in Mithila itself, the population has been relatively unmobilized, and physical communication between Banaras and south Bihar has been more convenient than between north and south Bihar. Thus, Bihar has been a Hindi-speaking state by choice, in which recognition as linguistic minorities has been conceded primarily to the tribal languages and languages recognized in the eighth schedule of the Constitution, secondarily and only gradually to Maithili, and not at all to the mother tongues of Magahi and Bhojpuri.

There are two principal areas of government policy-making with respect to the use of minority languages in an Indian state – education at both the primary and secondary stages and administration. In its attitude toward Maithili, the government of Bihar in both areas has maintained the view that Hindi is the predominant language of Bihar and that Maithili is a minority mother tongue with a small and indeterminate number of speakers. The government has granted full rights to Maithili-speakers in theory at the primary stage, but not entirely in practice; it has resisted the demands of

---

[1] *Census of India, 1961*, vol. IV, pt. II-C, p. 199.

[2] The more easy acceptance of this view on the part of Magahi-speakers may have something to do with the fact that Magahi not only lacks a literature of its own, but is generally considered to be an inferior form of speech, used only by country bumpkins and uneducated people. Consequently, Magahi speakers would naturally be inclined to adopt the more prestigious Hindi speech once they step out of their local environment. I am indebted to Harry Blair for this point.

Maithili spokesmen at the secondary stage; and it has refused to grant official recognition to Maithili for purposes of administration.

At the primary stage, Maithili-speakers have had the right to have their children instructed through the medium of their mother tongue since 1949, in cases where such a request is made by 40 pupils in a school or 10 in a class.[1] While the right has been conceded, the Bihar government has either refused or delayed measures to make implementation easier and has failed to provide evidence of the progress being made. Only in 1960–1 were figures first made available on the number of pupils receiving instruction through the medium of Maithili and then only for Darbhanga district.[2] Since 1960–1, no figures have been provided by the state government.[3]

At the secondary stage, government policy has been far more resistant to the claims of Maithili. The official policy of the state government for a time diverged from the safeguards provided in all-India policy in recognizing only Hindi as the medium of instruction in secondary schools. Under pressure from the Commissioner for Linguistic Minorities, the Bihar government claimed that it was willing to provide, and had in fact provided in the past, for instruction through the medium of minority languages when a large number of students so requested, but the government refused to accept the all-India policy that such instruction must of necessity be provided when at least one-third of the students are minority language speakers (later changed to 60 in a school, 15 in a class).[4] Despite annual reminders from the Commissioner for Linguistic Minorities of this divergence between Bihar and all-India policy, no other language but Hindi could be used as the medium of instruction in secondary schools in the state as late as 1967.[5] Instruction was given in minority languages as subjects of study, but not as instructional media for non-language subjects. Even as a subject of study, however, Maithili was sorely neglected. Only 4,479 students were reported to be studying Maithili at the secondary stage in Bihar in 1961–2.[6] No figures have been available after that date.[7] In March 1967, the new united front government in Bihar announced that a decision had been made to permit minority language students to be instructed through the medium of their mother tongue where there

---

[1] *CLM* v: 19, 20.   [2] *CLM* v: 169; *CLM* vi: 127.

[3] The failure of the state government to provide these figures to the Commissioner for Linguistic Minorities is noted in *CLM* vi:12; *CLM* vii:15; *CLM* viii:12.

[4] *CLM* vi:21, 23; *CLM* vii:30, 31, 92, 93; *CLM* viii:38–39.

[5] Interview, M2:8.   [6] *CLM* vii:197.

[7] For the complaints of the Commissioner for Linguistic Minorities in this connection, see *CLM* vi:32; *CLM* vii:15, 44.

were 15 or more students of a minority language in a class. It was announced that the scheme had been introduced in the schools and would be fully in force by 1969.[1]

If the policy of the Bihar government toward the use of Maithili as a medium at the secondary stage of education was one of opposition to such use and divergence from all-India policy in this respect, its policy toward the use of Maithili as an official language at the district level or below was to claim that the issue did not exist. According to the all-India policy, a minority language is entitled to recognition as an official language at the district level if 60% of the population of the district speaks or uses it. Where, in a district or a smaller area, 15 to 20% of the population speaks a minority language, important government notices and rules are supposed to be published in the minority language. If this policy were to be strictly followed in Bihar, Maithili should be given either official or semi-official status in the districts of Darbhanga, Bhagalpur, Muzaffarpur, Monghyr, Purnea and Santal Parganas. No such recognition has been given because policy has so far been based on the 1951 census,[2] in which only 87,674 Maithili speakers were enumerated in the whole of Bihar.

Lest the policy of the Bihar government be construed as an oppressive one, it should be noted that the leaders of the Maithili movement have not made use of all the means at their disposal to achieve due recognition of the rights of Maithili-speakers. Although a full range of demands has been made in the pages of the *Mithila Mihir*, those demands have apparently not been forwarded to the Commissioner for Linguistic Minorities. In the Commissioner's most recent reports listing the complaints received from linguistic minorities in the states, specific complaints were made about the treatment of Urdu, Bengali, Oriya, Ho, and Punjabi, but none about Maithili.[3]

In effect, then, the language policy of the Government of Bihar has so far not been effectively challenged by the Maithili-speaking language group in the state. An interview with the previous Congress Minister of Education in Bihar in 1967 revealed that the minister had never felt significant political pressure on the Maithili question, that he nevertheless was aware that there were more Maithili-speakers than indicated in the census, but that he did not believe the Maithili movement would 'catch fire', and that he considered that the Maithils should be satisfied that their language has been recognized as a mother tongue by the Bihar government.[4] In short, if the

[1] *Searchlight*, 21 March 1967.   [2] See *CLM* v:81, 82.
[3] *CLM* vii: apps. ix and xiii; *CLM* viii:272-4.
[4] Interview (BG27:34-7, 42, 43) in Patna on 24 March 1967.

Bihar government has not fulfilled the demands of the most devoted spokesmen for the Maithili movement, it is at least partly because the politicians of the state have not been made aware that their demands reflect the wishes of the majority of the people of Mithila.

Two regional-linguistic demands

In addition to specific demands for the recognition of the Maithili language as a medium of education and administration in Bihar, demands have been made which combine linguistic and regional interests. Two such demands (in addition to the Mithila state demand) have been those for a Mithila university and for a radio station in Mithila.

Mithila university

Of the regional demands which have been raised on behalf of Mithila, that for a Mithila university has been pressed most consistently and has come closest to being achieved. The history of the demand and the response to it by the Bihar government reflect the relative lack of political influence of the leaders of the Mithila-Maithili movement.

Before independence, there was only one university in the state of Bihar, Patna University, founded in 1917. Since independence, five new universities have been created in Bihar – the Bihar University at Muzaffarpur in 1952; the Bhagalpur and Ranchi universities in 1960; the K.S. Darbhanga Sanskrit Vishvavidyalaya in 1961; and Magadh University at Gaya in 1962.[1] The establishment of each new university has taken precedence over the demand for a Mithila university at Darbhanga.

The Mithila university demand has been raised more or less continuously since 1945 by the Maithili social and cultural organizations. A Mithila university committee was established in 1947.[2] The demand had two primary justifications when it was first proposed. One was simply that there was no modern university in the entire Mithila region and that the people of south Bihar, therefore, had had greater educational opportunities than the people of north Bihar.[3] The second justification was that a university was needed which would be named after and reflect the particular culture of the Maithili region.[4] Thus, the demand has been for a modern Mithila

---

[1] Government of India, Ministry of Education, *Report of the Education Commission, 1964–66: Education and National Development* (Delhi: Manager of Publications, 1966), p. 298.
[2] *MM*, 18 February 1947 and 28 February 1948.
[3] *Ibid.*, 22 May 1948.   [4] *Ibid.*, 8 July 1950.

university, to be located in Darbhanga, the central town of the Maithili-speaking region.

Unlike the Mithila state demand, which has not been pursued, the Mithila university issue has remained alive over the years. The demand was pressed very vigorously upon the first non-Congress ministry in Bihar in March and April 1967. In those months, the Education Minister of Bihar accepted the demand in principle, and placed the proposal before the Union Education Minister and the chairman of the University Grants Commission.[1] The Bihar government agreed to place the proposal for a Mithila university at Darbhanga before the University Grants Commission in July 1967.[2] A committee of the University Grants Commission visited Darbhanga and submitted a favorable report on the proposal to the Commission in January 1968.[3] The Commission recommended the conversion of the Sanskrit University at Darbhanga into the desired Mithila university and gave its recommendations to the Bihar government. In June 1971, a state minister announced in the assembly that the Bihar government had accepted the recommendations in principle.[4] It appears likely that the next university to be established in the state of Bihar will be the long-awaited Mithila university at Darbhanga, but the long delay in the achievement of the demand reflects both the internal weakness of the Maithili-Mithila movement and the relative lack of political influence of the Maithili constituency in the Bihar government.

The demand for a radio station at Darbhanga

The demand for a radio station at Darbhanga has been primarily a linguistic issue, rather than a regional issue. While it has sometimes been argued that a radio station at Darbhanga would better reach more remote areas of north Bihar than the present Patna Radio Station,[5] the primary justification for the demand has been the need to service the Maithili-speaking people with programs in the medium of Maithili and concerning the culture of Mithila. The demand is of long standing, is another example of a Maithili demand as yet unfulfilled, and reflects the latent tensions between Maithili and Hindi.

The demand arose initially out of the failure of the Patna Radio

---

[1] *Ibid.*, 9 and 16 April 1967; *Indian Nation*, 24 April and 1 June 1967.
[2] *Searchlight*, 4 July 1967.
[3] *Ibid.*, 23 and 24 January 1968.
[4] *Indian Nation*, 16 June 1971.
[5] Jayakanta Mishra, *A Case for a Radio Station in the Maithili Area at Darbhanga* (Allahabad, Tirabhukti Publications, 1956), p. 29.

Station authorities to satisfy the desires of Maithili cultural organizations for more programs on Maithili culture and through the Maithili medium. In July 1948, Dr Umesh Misra, acting on behalf of the Maithili Sahitya Samiti of Allahabad, began a correspondence with the director of the Patna Radio Station requesting increased facilities for Maithili. This correspondence began politely, but became increasingly harsh as it became clear that the station authorities considered the demands on behalf of Maithili out of proportion to the status of the language, which in turn elicited the fears of Maithili-speakers of Hindi imperialism.[1]

Dr Misra then took his case to the Information and Broadcasting Ministry of the Government of India, from which he received greater sympathy, but no significant action. The Information and Broadcasting Ministry requested information on the areas in which Maithili is spoken and the number of speakers of the language and whether speakers of Maithili can understand Hindi. Apparently, the ministry was quite ignorant of the Maithili language and referred to it as a dialect rather than a language with a script and literature.[2] Dr Misra replied that Maithili is not a dialect, but a separate literary language, and that 'it is insulting its speakers if you refer to it as a dialect' and that ordinary rural speakers of the language cannot understand Hindi.[3] Nothing further came of this correspondence.

Another attempt to appeal to the director of the Patna Radio Station was made in 1952, but it became clear that the director remained unwilling to go beyond provision of the existing facilities for Maithili, which by his own admission amounted to no more than an average of 'a little over an hour of Maithili items per week'.[4]

The entire affair left a bad feeling toward the Patna Radio Station on the part of Maithili supporters, who saw these responses by the radio station authorities as further evidence of the existence of a 'Hindi atmosphere' and an 'anti-Maithili feeling' in Bihar. It was felt that there was now no alternative but to demand a separate radio station for the Maithili area in Darbhanga.[5] In recent years, especially after the installation of a Maithili-speaker as Union Minister for Information and Broadcasting, the demand has been again renewed. The Chetna Samiti has taken up the demand and has complained of the continuing policy of the Patna station of treating Maithili as nothing more than a dialect.[6] In July 1966, the Information Minister visited Darbhanga and expressed his complete agreement with the Maithili demands and agreed that the policy of

[1] *Ibid.*   [2] *Ibid.*, pp. 17–18.   [3] *Ibid.*, p. 19.
[4] *Ibid.*, p. 28.   [5] *Ibid.*, p. 29.   [6] *MM*, 5 September 1965 and 17 July 1966.

the Patna Radio Station was unsatisfactory for Maithili and that it was necessary to establish a radio station at Darbhanga. However, the minister gave no indication as to when the station would be established.[1]

Consequently, the basic demands of the Maithili leaders remain unsatisfied. There is no radio station at Darbhanga and the transmission of Maithili programs from Patna continues not only to be unsatisfactory from the point of view of the Maithili leaders, but to reflect in their eyes 'the dirty policy of the radio authorities against Maithili'.[2]

CONCLUSION

The history of the Maithili movement confirms by its failure and weakness many elements in the description of the process of nationality-formation outlined in chapter 1. It confirms by the extent of the objective differences between the language, culture, and geography of Mithila and other ethnic groups in Bihar the futility of finding in such differences any 'clue to the riddle why some ethnic groups have become, or are showing signs of developing into, nationalities, while others have not crystallized into nations'.[3]

It points also to the importance of the internal values, social structure, and processes of change taking place within a group in determining whether and when the transformation from ethnic group to nation will take place. Maithil Brahmans and Kayasthas in north Bihar form an elite, similar to the *bhadra lok* of Bengal,[4] devoted to the language, culture, and traditions of Mithila and concerned with the maintenance of the distinctiveness of their Maithil character and genealogical purity. However, the elite Maithil castes have been ineffective in transmitting their sense of regional identity to the mass of the Maithili-speaking people, largely for three reasons. First, their orientation toward the distinctiveness of Maithili culture has placed less emphasis on the separateness of Maithili culture from other cultures in India than on its distinctive purity and devotion to all-India culture, particularly to Sanskrit education and orthodox Hinduism.

[1] *Ibid.*, 24 July 1966; *Searchlight*, 13 July 1966. In January 1968, the minister, Satya Narain Sinha, who had by then moved to Health and Family Planning, announced in Darbhanga that Darbhanga would soon have its radio station. *Ibid.*, 4 January 1968; see also *ibid.*, 16 February 1968.

[2] *MM*, 24 July 1966.

[3] Akzin, *State and Nation*, p. 34.

[4] On the *bhadra lok*, see J. H. Broomfield, 'The Non-Cooperation Decision of 1920: A Crisis in Bengal Politics', in D. A. Low (ed.), *Soundings in Modern South Asian History* (Berkeley: University of California Press, 1968), pp. 231ff.

Second, and partly for this very reason, the cultural gap between the elite castes and the rest of the population of Mithila has been very sharp. Third, the elite castes of the region have maintained the cultural gap by pursuing a policy of caste exclusiveness and adherence to principles of caste hierarchy and orthodoxy. These differences in social structure do not alter the objective facts that Maithils of all castes speak Maithili, but they do prevent the forging of the bonds of community necessary to the building of a common Maithili consciousness.[1]

Also absent in Mithila have been the social prerequisites of regional consciousness.[2] Publication of books and magazines in Maithili has not only not kept pace with publication in Hindi, but it has not kept pace with the development of literacy and education in the Maithili-speaking region itself. Maithils prefer to read and write in Hindi and to use their mother tongue only in the home and among friends. Second, voluntary associations have been weak, for the most part organizations of narrow groups or of castes or of individuals. Nor have there been any specifically regional political organizations in Mithila comparable to the Akali Dal in the Punjab or the DMK in Tamil Nadu. On the contrary, the leading all-Bihar political parties have been stronger in several districts of Mithila than they have been in other parts of Bihar. Third, social mobilization among Maithili-speakers has been slow both in absolute and in relative terms. Both absolute levels and rates of change over time in literacy, urbanization, industrialization and English education have been among the lowest in the entire subcontinent.

The character of inter-ethnic contacts between Maithils and non-Maithils also supports the view suggested in chapter 1 of their importance in the development of identity. Outside the Maithili-speaking area, socially mobilized Maithils have retained their separate identities and formed associations and established publications in far greater numbers than have their compatriots at home. However, within the Maithili region itself, Maithili identity is stronger in the more backward districts of the region, where the language and cultural traditions exist in a purer form. In the more modernized districts where subdialects of Maithili are spoken, in areas peripheral to the core culture area of Mithila and adjacent to the more advanced Magahi/Hindi-speaking districts, Maithili identity is insignificant and Hindi continues to be dominant.

[1] On the relationship in general between social structure and ethnic group cohesion, see Akzin, *State and Nation*, p. 31.
[2] See Cohn, 'Regions Subjective and Objective', for a general discussion of 'the structural and cultural prerequisites of Indian regionalism', pp. 22ff.

Government policy in Bihar towards the demands of the Maithili leaders has deviated somewhat from central government policy. The Government of India favors a policy of linguistic pluralism, of granting equal rights to the use of minority languages in public life, including education and administration. The Government of Bihar has never disagreed with the central government on the fundamental principle of linguistic pluralism and equality, but it has followed a policy of assimilation in practice by ignoring or minimizing the extent of linguistic diversity in the state and by granting only symbolic concessions to Maithili.

The history of the Maithili movement contrasts very sharply with both the Punjabi and the Urdu language movements, not only in the degree of success achieved but in the intensity of the passions aroused. Two features of the Punjabi and Urdu movements not present in the Maithili movement are, first, the association between language and religion and, second, intense inter-ethnic antagonism. Maithili-speakers and Magahi-speakers are distinguishable ethnic groups, competitive in some respects with each other, but by no means hostile to each other. Nor do the politics of language inspire great hostility between the two groups, for the conflict is between Maithili and Hindi and Hindi is not the mother tongue of any ethnic group in Bihar. The situation with respect to Urdu and Hindi, however, is quite different. The Urdu movement, discussed in the next part, differs from both the Punjabi and Maithili movements in that it lacks a territorial base. However, the association of the Urdu movement with Muslims and with communal antagonisms in north India makes the politics of Urdu far more salient than the politics of the Maithili movement. These contrasts between the Maithili movement and the Muslim, Urdu, and Punjabi movements will be developed in the remainder of this book.

PART III

THE POLITICS OF LANGUAGE
AND RELIGION:
URDU AND THE MUSLIM MINORITY IN
UTTAR PRADESH AND BIHAR

3

MUSLIM SEPARATISM IN THE UNITED PROVINCES:[1] THE SOCIAL CONTEXT AND POLITICAL STRATEGY OF THE MUSLIM MINORITY BEFORE PARTITION

The association of the Muslim and Urdu movements in India with a universal religion may seem to some to place the development of Muslim identities in India in an entirely different category from the Maithili movement. Indeed, there is a school of historical scholarship on the Hindu–Muslim question in India which argues that the development of separate Hindu and Muslim nations on the subcontinent was pre-ordained from pre-modern times because of the fundamental differences between Islamic religion and civilization and Hindu religion and civilization. Others, including both scholars and Indian nationalists, have disputed this view and have pointed to the objective similarities of race, language, and culture – even religion – among the common mass of Muslims and Hindus, to the development in India of a composite culture and nationality embracing both Hindus and Muslims from medieval times, and to the very late and seemingly fortuitous acceptance by the Muslims of the idea that they formed a separate nation in India.[2]

This chapter will not support either of these polar views. There have been, in fact, both objective similarities and dissimilarities in language, religion, culture, diet, and dress between Hindus and Muslims in India, upon which either two separate nations or a single composite nation might have been built. It will be argued here that, even accepting the predominant historical view that religious and cultural separatism had become the standard at the elite level in

---

[1] Before 1902, the province now known as Uttar Pradesh, was called the North-Western Provinces and Oudh. From 1902 until 1947, the name was changed to the United Provinces of Agra and Oudh. Since 1947, the official name is Uttar Pradesh, which means simply 'Northern Province'.

[2] A useful collection of different viewpoints on the origins of Muslim separatism in India is in T. Walter Wallbank (ed.), *The Partition of India: Causes and Responsibilities* (Boston: D. C. Heath and Co., 1966).

pre-modern times, the translation of this separatism into politics was not pre-ordained, but that the political differentiation of Muslims in the United Provinces at least has been related to processes of political and social change which have occurred only during the past century. The ideology of Muslim separateness did not flow necessarily and inexorably out of the objective differences between Hindus and Muslims, but out of the uses which were made of those differences through the manipulation of symbols of Muslim unity and Hindu–Muslim separateness by an elite concerned to preserve its political privileges.

The overwhelmingly predominant scholarly interpretation of the history of Hindu–Muslim relations and the rise of Muslim separatism in the Indian subcontinent in the late nineteenth and early twentieth centuries adds to the notion that there existed fundamental differences between Hindus and Muslims four assumptions and arguments, which stress the backwardness of the Muslims compared to the Hindus with respect to the new forms of education introduced during British rule, the Muslim perception of their backwardness, and their efforts to rectify their backwardness through education and political mobilization. The first argument is that the introduction of British rule in India and its consolidation after the Mutiny (for which the British allegedly blamed the Muslim aristocracy especially) led to the displacement of the former Muslim ruling classes, their dejection, and their consequent failure to compete with the Hindus for English education and government jobs. The second argument is that the Muslim masses, because of their poverty and backwardness, also failed to take advantage of the new opportunities for education and employment and were encouraged to do so by the opposition of the orthodox ulama (Muslim clerics) to modern secular education. The third argument is that the Hindus, who did not suffer from the same disabilities, took advantage of the new opportunities and moved ahead of the Muslims. Finally, the Aligarh movement arose and was followed by the political mobilization of the Muslims in an effort to overcome their backwardness and their disadvantaged position in relation to the Hindus. To achieve their ends, the Muslims felt obliged, because of their backwardness in relation to Hindus, to demand special privileges for themselves in education, administration, and politics. Hindu and Congress resistance to these Muslim demands caused estrangement between the two communities, which led to increased Hindu–Muslim tension and ultimately to the partition of the subcontinent.[1]

[1] The general argument originated with W. W. Hunter's, *The Indian Mussalmans*, pub-

It will be demonstrated in this chapter that this entire argument and its assumptions do not apply to the United Provinces and that the objective situation in the late nineteenth and early twentieth centuries in the United Provinces was in most respects exactly the opposite of that described above. If the assumptions and arguments described above were true, the Muslim separatist movement in India would stand as a pre-eminent exception to theories of nationalism. A backward people, unable to overcome its backwardness, would have succeeded in promoting a successful nationalist movement in the absence of the underlying social prerequisites for the development of nationalist sentiment.

In fact, however, the history of the Muslim nationalist movement does not support such a view. The Aligarh movement, the ideology of Muslim separatism, and the political organization of the Muslim community began, not in the backward areas of Muslim Bengal, but in north India and particularly in the United Provinces, where, far from being a backward people, the Muslim elite constituted a dominant elite bent upon preserving its dominance and preventing the rise to self-assertion of the backward Hindus and the achievement by the Hindus of a share proportionate to their numbers in education and government employment. It was the ideology of this dominant Muslim upper-class elite which ultimately spread throughout eastern and western India from its base in the United Provinces and which led to the formulation of a set of political demands by Muslim political leaders for political concessions warranted not by their numbers, but by their desire to retain, if not dominance, at least equality with the much larger Hindu population of the country.

The history of Muslim separatism demonstrates two important general features in the development of nationalist movements – the primacy of political choice and the ways in which a people creates its own history through a conscious process of symbol selection. The social scientist who wishes both to understand the development of a

lished in 1871, which was based primarily on his analysis of the condition of the Bengal Muslims. The argument, or elements of it, generalized for the whole of India, has appeared in most works on Indian Muslims published since then, including such classic accounts as Wilfred C. Smith, *Modern Islam in India* (London: Victor Gollancz, 1946), and Murray T. Titus, *Islam in India and Pakistan* (Calcutta: Y.M.C.A. Publishing House, 1959), pp. 199–214. For a more recent reiteration of the argument by a political scientist, see Khalid B. Sayeed, *The Political System of Pakistan* (Boston: Houghton Mifflin, 1967), pp. 4, 10, 12, 32. (Sayeed, however, is aware that the Muslims occupied a different position in U.P. where, he notes, 'they occupied a favored position in the provincial services' [p. 32].) The entire argument has become enshrined in the mythology of the origins of the Pakistan movement in Mahmud Husain *et al.* (eds.), *A History of the Freedom Movement* (Karachi: Pakistan Historical Society, 1961), esp. vol. II, pt. II, ch. 13 and *passim*.

nationalist ideology and to explain its success must attempt to recon-
struct both the objective circumstances of the times and the process
of symbol manipulation by which a myth is constructed to achieve
political objectives. However, it would be a mistake to believe that
historical myths are less real or important than the objective circumstances. The creation of an historical myth is itself an objective
fact of history in the development of a nation. To say simply that a
myth is not true history leads neither to true history nor to social
scientific explanation. The success of Muslim separatism in north
India can be understood and explained only if the processes of symbol
manipulation and the objective processes of change which have
taken place in the Muslim community in the north are juxtaposed.
The difficulty with the predominant interpretation of the development of Muslim nationalism is that it accepts the Muslim historical
myth not simply as one aspect of historical truth – as created history
which became a mainspring for action – but as a self-sufficient
explanation, itself the whole historical truth.

SYMBOLS

Religion and the impact of revivalism

There is very little difference between the famous statement of
Jinnah in his presidential address at the Lahore session of the All-
India Muslim League in 1940 and the predominant scholarly
explanation of Muslim separatism. In that speech, Jinnah has been
quoted as follows:

It is extremely difficult to appreciate why our Hindu friends fail to understand the
real nature of Islam and Hinduism. They are not religions in the strict sense of the
word, but are in fact different and distinct social orders, and it is a dream that the
Hindus and Muslims can ever evolve a common nationality . . . They neither
inter-marry, nor inter-dine together and, indeed they belong to two different
civilisations which are based mainly on conflicting ideas and conceptions. Their
aspects on life and of life are different. It is quite clear that Hindus and Mussalmans derive their inspirations from different sources of history. They have different epics, their heroes are different, and different episodes. Very often, the Hero
of one is a foe of the other and likewise their victories and defeats overlap. To yoke
together two such nations under a single state, one as a numerical minority and the
other as a majority, must lead to growing discontent and final destruction of any
fabric that may be so built up for the government of such a state.[1]

Contrast this statement with the following quotations from two
historians and a political scientist concerned with India.

[1] Cited in Sayeed, *The Political System of Pakistan*, p. 40.

The standpoint taken here is that the treatment of Muslims by Hindus as merely another caste; the interpenetration of Hindu customary law among Muslims in the villages; the creation of a Hindu–Muslim ruling class by the Mughal emperors with a system of rank in the imperial service and common interest in polo, elephant fighting, and common modes of dress; the development of a lingua franca, Urdu, combining Hindi grammar with a largely Arabic and Persian vocabulary; the study of Hindu thought by Muslims like al-Biruni or Abu'l Fazl; the composition of histories in Persian by Hindus; the syncretist religions of Kabir and Guru Nanak – all of these notwithstanding – neither educated Muslims nor educated Hindus accepted cultural coexistence as a natural prelude to cultural assimilation. Thus long before British rule and long before modern political notions of Muslim nationhood, the consensus of the Muslim community in India had rejected the eclecticism of Akbar and Dara Shikoh for the purified Islamic teachings of Shaikh Ahmad of Sirhind and Shah Wali-Ullah. Cultural apartheid was the dominant ideal in medieval Muslim India, in default of cultural victory.[1]

* * *

They [the Muslims] are sufficiently different to consider themselves a separate nation; they differ from the Hindus not only in belief, but also in culture, traditions, and, above all, in their sense of values. A Methodist may feel at home with a Roman Catholic on almost everything except theology and worship, but a Muslim must make an effort to feel at home with a Hindu on anything outside business. Dress, customs, food, codes of conduct, and ideals are all different, and it is only when these have been successfully relegated to the background that the average Muslim can be at ease with the average Hindu.[2]

* * *

Perhaps the principal reason for the existence of Pakistan is that there has never been a confluence of the two civilizations in India – the Hindu and the Muslim. They may have meandered towards each other here and there, but on the whole the two have flowed their separate courses – sometimes parallel and sometimes contrary to one another.[3]

There seems to be a natural and logical progression in the three quotations from the first which simply notes that, despite areas of Hindu–Muslim interaction before British rule and before modern nationalism, the dominant pre-modern tendency in Hindu–Muslim relations was towards separatism; to the second, which notes that the differences between Hindus and Muslims have been sufficiently great for the Muslims 'to consider themselves a separate nation'; to the third, which imparts historically determinative force from the pre-existing cultural differences between Hindus and Muslims to the formation of a separate Muslim nation-state and which is identical in meaning with the quotation of Jinnah. It would seem from these quotations that there is nothing for the social scientist to explain. Hindus and Muslims are, so it seems, as objectively distinct from

---

[1] Theodore de Bary *et al.* (eds.), *Sources of Indian Tradition* (New York: Columbia University Press, 1960), pp. 369–70.

[2] Percival Spear, *India, Pakistan and the West* (London, 1949), cited in Wallbank, *The Partition of India*, p. 1.

[3] Sayeed, *The Political System of Pakistan*, p. 8.

each other as any two groups of people on the face of the earth and it is but natural that they have developed into two nations. Nationalism, from this point of view, naturally arises through the historical process out of the objective differences between peoples. The difficulty in accepting this point of view is twofold. There is first the general consideration that the historical record of mankind provides sufficient evidence of the amalgamation of diverse peoples and religions into composite racial and national groups to cast doubt on any argument which assumes ineradicable differences between peoples. Second, it is evident from the historical record in India itself that there have been significant areas of religious and cultural sharing between Hindus and Muslims, that there have been and are now in India Muslim elites (religious and otherwise) who believe in a composite Indian nationality, and that the two-nation theory itself did not become articulated into a demand for separate national sovereignties until the late 1930s in India.

In the late nineteenth and early twentieth centuries, men in India – Hindus, Muslims, and British – made choices which ultimately led to the partition of India. No responsible Muslim political leader of any consequence conceived such an idea before the late 1930s, no political organization adopted it as its goal until the Muslim League did so in 1940, and the idea had no chance of success until the Muslim League demonstrated its persuasive power in the elections of 1946. It is not the purpose here to deny the importance of pre-modern Hindu and Muslim religio-cultural differentiation as a factor in Muslim separatism. The purpose here is more limited, namely, to reveal the process by which the pre-existing differences separating Muslims from Hindus were emphasized, communicated, and translated into a political movement; the groups which took the lead in that process; and the kinds of choices which they made.

Historians of Islam in India have noted the existence in pre-modern times of tendencies toward both religious differentiation and integration between Islam and Hinduism, between Muslims and Hindus. Titus noted that, despite large numbers of conversions to Islam in the north-west and in eastern India, India remained an historical failure in terms of the spread of Islam and that Hindu civilization in its core areas presented 'stubborn resistance to the Muslim propaganda'.[1] It nevertheless remains true that Islam did become the religion of tens of millions of Indians over the centuries and that, if most converts came from low caste groups, many came from high Hindu castes as well. Historically, according to Titus, Muslim rulers for the most

---

[1] Titus, *Islam*, p. 71.

124

part displayed 'intolerance or indifference'[1] to both Hindus and Hinduism, but Akbar employed Hindus in high positions, had Hindu wives, and promoted eclecticism in religion. The importance of Mecca and of the Haj to pious Muslims oriented Muslim religious belief towards a source external to India, but ordinary, low caste Hindus have long worshipped at the shrines of Muslim saints, saint worship among Muslims in the villages is itself a common heresy, Muslims in the countryside are as idolatrous as Hindus, and Muslim *pirs* often had Hindu disciples and Hindu yogis had Muslim chelas.[2]

The theoretical contrast between the unity of Islam and the brotherhood of all believers with the diversity of Hinduism and caste hierarchy has been modified substantially in India in practice. Internal religious and social differentiation among Muslims in India has always been great. The sectarian differences between Sunnis and Shi'as in India are well known and have been frequently bitter and violent, but there have been many other sects in Indian Islam, some of them hardly distinguishable from Hindu religious groups.[3] Caste differentiation among Muslims was in the nineteenth century and continues in the present to be great – between the high caste Saiyyid, Shaikh, Mughul, Pathan, and Rajput and the low caste Nau Muslim, Julaha, Teli, and others. Moreover, the sectarian and social differences among Muslims, as among Hindus, had different regional distributions in India.

It is a matter of perspective, inevitably influenced by hindsight, whether one chooses to emphasize the processes of differentiation or the processes of assimilation in Hindu and Muslim religious practices. From the point of view of social science theories of nationalism, what matters is that it cannot be maintained that either Hindus or Muslims constituted sufficiently solidary groups in the nineteenth century, bound together by conscious communal identifications uniting all classes, regions, and sects, with a common view of their past and that recognition of a common destiny which characterizes the modern nation. The two religious communities did not constitute two nations in the nineteenth century, if only because the idea of nationalism had not yet entered the minds of the educated elites.[4]

[1] *Ibid.*, p. 16.   [2] *Ibid.*, pp. 83, 161.   [3] *Ibid.*, p. 161.
[4] On these points, see the excellent book by Anil Seal, *The Emergence of Indian Nationalism: Competition and Collaboration in the Later Nineteenth Century* (Cambridge: Cambridge University Press, 1968), pp. 338–9 and his statement on p. 339, referring to late nineteenth-century India: 'In so shapeless, so jumbled a bundle of societies, there were not two nations, there was not one nation, there was no nation at all. What was India? – a graveyard of old nationalities and the mother of new nationalisms struggling to be born.'

Up through the nineteenth century in India, both communities were characterized more by their internal differentiation than their internal religious unity. At the mass level, religious communication between and common worship among Hindu and Muslim believers were common; but, at the elite level, religious differences were emphasized. It was, however, during the late nineteenth century that the religious differences between Hindus and Muslims were reinforced by the movements of religious revivalism which became the precursors of political organization among both Hindus and Muslims alike. Although there were objective bases either for Hindu–Muslim differentiation or for the development of a composite Hindu–Muslim culture and nationality in nineteenth-century India, the impact of Hindu and Muslim revivalist movements turned both communities away from shared symbols to ancient and exclusive symbols and from religious interaction to increasing religious opposition through competitive proselytization.[1] Movements such as the Arya Samaj and the early writings of Hindu nationalists such as Bankim Chandra turned Hindus back to the glories of Hindu civilization and culture before the arrival of the Muslims in the subcontinent. Muslim revivalist movements, seeking reasons for the decline of Muslim power in India and elsewhere, found the explanation in the decline of Islamic religion and ideology (among believers especially in India) from the pristine purity of Islam in its formative period. For many Muslim revivalists, this emphasis on the ancient values turned Muslims to a non-Indian heritage and ultimately to pan-Islamism. A return to the pristine practices of Islam naturally meant eliminating all heretical ceremonies and rituals derived from Hindu–Muslim religious interactions.[2]

It was in the Muslim and Hindu revivalist movements of the nineteenth century, therefore, that the first important choices were made by the religious elites to emphasize differences rather than similarities between Hindus and Muslims. That this was a process of explicit choice rather than an ineluctable historical movement ought to be stressed, for all revivalisms are distinguished by their lack of historiographical method, by an approach to history which sweeps 'the past into the present, selecting ideals from any stage, real or imaginary, of the past'. The two revivalisms initially were not necessarily in competition with each other. Each sought to find solace and inspiration

---

[1] Beni Prasad, *India's Hindu–Muslim Questions* (London: George Allen and Unwin, 1946), pp. 20, 27–8; see also Louis Dumont, 'Nationalism and Communalism', *Contributions to Indian Sociology*, VII (March 1964), 59–61, and Ziya-ul-Hasan Faruqi, *The Deoband School and the Demand for Pakistan* (Bombay: Asia Publishing House, 1963), p. 85.

[2] Beni Prasad, *India's Hindu–Muslim Questions*, p. 31.

from the past as a 'recompense for the present degradation'[1] felt by the religious leaders of both communities, in consequence of the British conquest of India and the introduction of Western ideas. In practice, however, this meant a bifurcation between Hindu and Muslim revivalisms, which ultimately brought them into competition with each other.[2]

Even the development of revivalist movements among the Hindus and Muslims, which intensified the existing bases of religious differentiation, would not necessarily in themselves have made inevitable the development of separate national movements. The importance of the two streams of religious revivalism lies in the degree to which they infused the nationalist organizations which came after them with different religious symbols. The nationalism of Bengalis influenced by Bankim Chandra became infused with Hindu symbols. Men like Lajpat Rai in the Punjab moved from the Arya Samaj to the Congress directly, while Tilak in Maharashtra promoted patriotism by creating and enlarging Hindu religious festivals. Gandhi himself was, in a sense, the most successful of the Hindu revivalist politicians, but his great success in bringing the Hindu masses into participation in the nationalist movement, by infusing Indian nationalism with the symbols of the Gita, the ethics of non-violence, and the promise of Ram Rajya, was also his greatest failure, for his revivalism had no appeal to Muslims.[3] For their part, when the Muslims entered nationalist politics on a mass scale for the first time in 1921, it was the revivalist pan-Islamic symbol of the khalifa of Turkey which provided the motive force and neither before then nor since have Muslims in India ever found a symbol sufficiently compelling for them to join forces with Hindus in mass political action.

Language

The sharp differences between the core values of Islam and Hinduism were, in pre-modern times, qualified by significant interactions between the two great religions in practice, and by considerable internal differentiation within both religious systems. Interaction and internal differentiation were even more characteristic of the two religious communities in language. Although Urdu was the *lingua franca* of the Muslim elites in those areas of India which were under their direct rule both before and after the British established their rule in India,

---

[1] *Ibid.*, p. 30.   [2] *Ibid.*, p. 31.
[3] *Ibid.*, p. 51, and, for a Muslim view, K. Sarwar Hasan, *The Genesis of Pakistan* (Karachi, 1950), cited in Martin Deming Lewis (ed.), *Gandhi: Maker of Modern India?* (Boston: D. C. Heath, 1968), pp. 43–5.

for the mass of Muslims, language divided them from their religious brethren in other parts of the subcontinent and united them with Hindus in the localities and the regions of India. Most Muslims everywhere spoke the language of the region, as did the Hindus.[1]

Yet, in north India, the controversy between Urdu and Hindi has been one of the most divisive issues between educated Muslims and Hindus for more than a century. The Hindu–Urdu controversy by its very bitterness demonstrates how little the objective similarities between language groups matter when peoples attach subjective significance to their languages. Willingness to communicate through the same language is quite a different thing from the mere ability to communicate. It is essential, therefore, to disentangle the objective similarities and dissimilarities in the origin, development, and present characteristics of Urdu from the subjective observations of Urdu and Hindi supporters.

Linguists and literary specialists have differed on some aspects of the origins of the Urdu language and on the character of its early development, but there is a general agreement on the main features of its modern development as a vernacular language of the north.[2] Urdu is a Turkish word meaning camp; it came to be the name of the language because it was spoken in the camps or courts of the Muslim invaders, who entered India from the eighth century onwards. In its original form, it was nothing more grammatically than the spoken Hindustani of north India, particularly the Khari Boli of the Delhi area, with an infusion of Persian, Arabic, and Turkish vocabulary. As Muslim rule spread over north India, especially after the eleventh century, Urdu went with it as the court language and interacted with local dialects, introducing Persian words into them and adopting indigenous vocabulary from them, but gradually developing a more or less standard spoken, urban form distinct from the local dialects.

The development of Hindi as a standard spoken language of the north cannot be separated from the development of Urdu. Both were essentially derived from the Khari Boli of the Delhi area, infused in varying degrees in different regions of the north with Persian, Arabic and Turkish words, on the one hand, and words of local origin, on the other hand. In effect, until the development of modern Urdu and Hindi literature and until the rise of the movements for the spread of

[1] Cf. Beni Prasad, *India's Hindu–Muslim Questions*, pp. 15–16, and Titus, *Islam*, p. 281.
[2] See, among other sources, Suniti Kumar Chatterji, *Indo-Aryan and Hindi*, 2nd ed. (Calcutta: Firma K. L. Mukhopadhyay, 1960), pt. II; Ram Babu Saksena, *A History of Urdu Literature* (Allahabad: Ram Narain Lal, 1927), pp. 1–7; N. S. Gorekar, *Glimpses of Urdu Literature* (Bombay: Jaico Publishing House, 1961); Hafeez Malik, *Moslem Nationalism in India and Pakistan* (Washington: Public Affairs Press, 1963), pp 28–30.

Hindi in the nineteenth century, the terms Urdu, Hindi, and Hindu-stani equally described the standard, spoken, urban language of the north. Even today, as a spoken language, Hindi and Urdu cannot be distinguished for purposes of ordinary discourse.

Three factors have contributed to an increasing divergence be-tween Urdu and Hindi both linguistically and emotionally. The first was the fact that the Muslim rulers of north India chose to write Urdu in the Persian script with which they were familiar, rather than the indigenous Devanagari script. In time, the Persian script came into wide use not only for administrative purposes, but for literary purposes as well. In the eighteenth and nineteenth centuries espe-cially, a large and vital body of literature was written in Urdu in Persian script, frequently drawing heavily on Persian also for vocabulary and literary symbols.[1] It is important to recognize that both Muslims and Hindus contributed to this literature.[2] Although a division gradually developed between Hindus who preferred to write Hindi–Urdu in Devanagari, on the one hand, and Hindus and Muslims who wrote Hindi–Urdu in Persian script, this division was not initially entirely a communal one. Only Hindus used the Devanagari, but both Hindus and Muslims used the Persian script.

The second factor contributing to divergence between Hindi and Urdu was the development of the Hindi movement in north India in the late nineteenth century, which promoted both the use of the Devanagari script in administration and education and the Sanskritization of Hindi by drawing vocabulary from Sanskrit rather than Persian. In 1837, Persian had been replaced by English and the vernacular languages of the various provinces of British-ruled India as official and court languages. In north India, however, the verna-cular language chosen was not Hindi in the Devanagari script, but Urdu in the Persian script.[3] Between 1868 and 1900, Hindus of the North-Western Provinces and Oudh agitated through pamphlets and deputations to the government for the replacement of Urdu in Persian script with Hindi in the Devanagari script as the official court language.

The Hindi movement had its origins among educated Hindus in

---

[1] On the Persianization of Urdu, see Gorekar, *Glimpses of Urdu Literature*, pp. 6–14.

[2] See, for example, the list of prominent Muslim and Hindu Urdu writers of the middle nineteenth century in K. Sajun Lal, *A Short History of Urdu Newspapers* (Hyderabad, A. P.: Institute of Indo-Middle East Culture Studies, 1964), p. 25.

[3] The relevant government orders on these changes in official language are collected in an appendix to a very large pamphlet and collection of government documents, attributed in the British Museum catalogue to Madan Mohan Malaviya and titled *Court Character and Primary Education in the N.-W. Provinces and Oudh* (Allahabad: The Indian Press, 1897), appendix II, pp. 49–54.

Banaras in the 1860s and achieved its first significant public notice with the publication in 1868 of a 'Memorandum on Court Characters' by Babu Shiva Prasad, in which it was argued that the official encouragement given to the study of Urdu and Persian in the North-Western Provinces and Oudh was impeding both the study of Hindi and the development of primary education. In this pamphlet, the term Hindi was used synonymously with the Devanagari script. Thus, Babu Shiva Prasad concluded his memorandum with an appeal that 'the Persian letters may be driven out of the Courts as the language has been, and that Hindi may be substituted for them'.[1] In 1873, a memorial was presented to Sir William Muir, the Lieutenant-Governor of the provinces, making a similar appeal.[2] In this memorial, it was argued that 'the Persian characters are foreign to this country'; that they could not be read by ordinary people in the courts; and that their continued use encouraged the use of 'generally unintelligible Arabic and Persian words'. It was urged instead that 'Hindi or Nagri characters' should replace the Persian because 'Hindi being national with us is more easily learnt and read than Persian' and 'is in general use among the people of this country'. The memorialists recognized that the Muslim population would not like the change, but argued that the advantage to the much larger Hindu majority outweighed the disadvantages to the Muslim minority, among whom some in the villages were alleged to use Hindi also.

The Hindi movement in the North-Western Provinces received significant encouragement in 1881 when Hindi in Devanagari script replaced Urdu in Persian script as the official language of the neighboring province of Bihar.[3] In 1882, the supporters of Hindi submitted to the Education Commission 118 memorials from cities and towns all over the provinces and signed by some 67,000 persons.[4] In these memorials, the main lines of argument pursued in the earlier pamphlets were continued, namely, that official recognition of Urdu led to its use in the schools rather than Hindi, which was the proper

[1] 'Memorandum by the Late Raja then Babu Sivaprasad. (1868.) Court Characters in the Upper Provinces of India', in Malaviya, *Court Character*, appendix, pp. 72–4; citations from p. 73.

[2] 'Memorial Presented to Government in 1873 Praying for the Restoration of Nagri Characters in Courts and Public Offices. To the Honorable Sir William Muir, LL.D.K.C., S.I., Lieut.-Governor of the North-Western Provinces', in Malaviya, *Court Character*, appendix, pp. 74–5.

[3] For the official orders, see *ibid.*, app. II, pp. 54–6.

[4] These figures are from Von Jürgen Lütt, *Hindu-Nationalismus in Uttar Prades, 1867–1900* (Stuttgart: Ernst Klett Verlag, 1970), p. 50.

vernacular of the provinces; and that the progress of primary education in the provinces was, therefore, being retarded by the use of an
essentially foreign tongue. The Persian script was described in one
such memorial as 'uncouth and outlandish' and the Urdu language
was described as 'surcharged with Arabic, Persian and Turki terms',
which 'make it an altogether foreign tongue to the Hindu population
of villages and hamlets'. In contrast, it was argued that Hindi was
'written in characters ancient, well known, and regarded with feelings akin to reverence'.[1] Therefore, the Education Commission was
urged 'to declare that, at best, for mass education in the . . . N.-W.P.
and Oudh, Hindi written in Devanagari character is the proper and
fittest language, and that it should be introduced in all vernacular
primary schools in them, exceptions being made only of those
schools which are entirely composed of Mahomedan boys, or the
majority of whose pupils are Mahomedans, who object to read
Hindi'.[2]

The polemical *coup de grâce* in the Hindi–Urdu pamphlet controversy of the late nineteenth century was delivered in 1897 by Madan
Mohan Malaviya in a massive collection of documents and statements, entitled *Court Character and Primary Education in the N.-W.
Provinces & Oudh*.[3] In the main narrative portion of this collection,
Malaviya pursued the theme that primary education in the pro-
vinces was being hindered by the official encouragement given to
Urdu.[4] Moreover, he argued that the Urdu in use as the official
language of the courts was only slightly different from the Persian it
was supposed to have replaced in 1837. The court officers, who were
mostly Muslims and Kayasthas, allegedly used a highly Persianized
Urdu jargon which was as unintelligible as English to the rural
Hindu and Muslim masses alike.[5] It was claimed that this highly
Persianized Urdu not only separated the urban, educated elite, brought
up in an atmosphere of Indo-Persian culture, from the rural masses,
but it served to perpetuate the dominance of a narrow class of people
trained in the official jargon in the positions of employment open to
Indians in the courts and government offices of the time.[6] Thus, by

---

[1] These remarks come from a memorial sent from Allahabad, dated 13 August 1882 and
reprinted in Malaviya, *Court Character*, appendix pp. 85–93; citations from pp. 86–7.
[2] *Ibid.*, p. 92.
[3] Publication details given on p. 129, n. 3.
[4] Malaviya, *Court Character*, esp. pp. 24–63.
[5] *Ibid.*, pp. 3–9, 12–13.
[6] These views were expressed most vehemently by British observers of the time, cited in
Malaviya, *Court Character*. Two examples, among many in the volume, are worth citing.
In some excerpts from S. W. Fallon's preface to *A Hindustani-English Law and Commercial*

the turn of the century, the argument on behalf of Hindi, which began as a movement to replace Persian characters by Devanagari characters in the courts and schools of the provinces, had been transmuted by Hindu memorialists into a conflict between Hindus and Muslims over the use of a 'national' versus a 'foreign' language and, implicitly if not always explicitly, into a competition for government jobs. In this conflict, the Hindi memorialists appealed on behalf of the overwhelming majority of the rural Hindu masses, whose interests, which they claimed to serve, were seen as outweighing the interests of a small minority of urban Muslims.

The response of the supporters of the Urdu language in the North-Western Provinces and Oudh to the Hindi movement came too slowly and too late to prevent the admission of Hindi in Devanagari script to an equal position with Urdu in Persian script as an official language of the provinces, which took place in 1900. However, the response of the leaders of the Urdu movement has an important bearing on the issue of linguistic divergence at this time. The weightiest response to the arguments of the Hindi protagonists came in the form of a direct reply and rebuttal of the 1897 Malaviya pamphlet, published anonymously in 1900 under the title, *A Defence of the Urdu Language and Character*.[1] In this pamphlet, long, detailed, and tedious arguments were presented to demonstrate the technical superiority of the Persian over the Nagari script as a form of writing and to rebut the charge that the official recognition given to Urdu in Persian script had a deleterious effect on the growth of

Dictionary (1879), reprinted in the volume, there are such statements as these: 'The language of the Law Courts of the Provinces in which Hindustani is spoken is made up almost entirely of foreign Arabic phrases. In a great many instances the Hindi equivalents . . . clearly show that Arabic has been drawn upon without the slightest excuse, simply because Arabic is esteemed a learned language while Hindi is only the vulgar vernacular of the people of the country. And then it serves to keep up that mystification which is the nefarious advantage of the few, and a wrongful injury to the many.' And, further on, 'A small section only of the people are able to learn the foreign language of their rulers or the highly Persianized and Arabic-ridden Urdu of the Courts of law, and so to stand between the governing class, and the great body of the people.' (Citations from pp. 37 and 39 of the appendix.) In an excerpt from Mr Fink's *General Report on Public Instruction in the N.-W. P.* for 1844–5, it is remarked that the Persian and Persianized Urdu languages were studied mainly by Muslims and Kayasthas; that the Urdu then in use in the courts was 'nearly as foreign to the mass of the people as the Persian'; and that the education imparted through Persian schools and the continued use of Urdu in the courts led to 'the barbarous application of Persian idiom to the Urdu language, to be observed in the papers prepared in the Courts, and the difference between the style of the written composition and that of the conversation of a native' (citations from pp. 61–2 of the appendix).

[1] *A Defence of the Urdu Language and Character* (being a reply to the pamphlet called *Court Character and Primary Education in the N.-W. Provinces and Oudh*), (Allahabad: Liddell's N.-W. P. Printing Works, 1900).

primary education in the provinces. More important, it was argued that, aside from the question of the script, Urdu was not a distinct language separate from Hindi; that Urdu was, in fact, 'nothing more than a highly developed Hindi' or the prevalent standard for the variety of Hindi dialects of north India; and that it was a mistake to confuse the two issues of language and script. Far from Urdu being a language of Muslims only, it was pointed out that Urdu had been the *lingua franca* of the north for several hundred years, used equally by Hindus and Muslims, and it was lamented 'that attempts have been made to excite racial feeling by identifying the advocates of Nagri with the Hindu population and the advocates of Urdu with the Muhammedans'.[1] If there was a distinction to be made on the basis of language and speech, rather than script only, the distinction was not between Muslims and Hindus, but between the educated and the uneducated. Urdu was seen as the language of the educated in the cities and towns, whereas Hindi was described as nothing more than a collection of non-standardized dialects spoken by illiterate villagers. As for the Nagari character, it was claimed that its use was 'confined to a small minority among the educated classes',[2] whose interests alone would be served by its official use. While the Hindi movement was, thus, accused of being a vehicle for the advancement of a small elite, the elite bias of the Urdu movement was self-evident in the very arguments presented on its behalf. Urdu was described as 'the language of refinement and of upper and civilized classes of people'. It was 'the duty of Government ... to encourage learning ... and not to consult the whim of the peasantry'. Otherwise, 'it may as well be said that every scheme of Government should be regulated according to the taste and inclination of the Indian vulgarity and not according to the demand of civilization and advancement'.[3] Moreover, in response to the argument of the protagonists of Hindi that the introduction of the Nagari character was a measure to benefit the overwhelming majority of Hindus, the Urdu reply was that numbers alone should not prevail:

Though the Hindus, including of course all classes of them, constitute the majority; but it cannot be said that the entire body of them can claim the same political and social importance as the Mohammadans . . . Are these two classes [Hindus and Muslims] then merely to be judged by their quantity and not quality, by their size, and not by their importance, by their bare numbers and not their influence?[4]

Thus, the Urdu response in this and other pamphlets of the time,[5]

[1] *Ibid.*, p. i.   [2] *Ibid.*, p. 35.   [3] *Ibid.*, p. 69.   [4] *Ibid.*, pp. 38–9.
[5] Similar arguments were presented in Hamid Ali Khan, *The Vernacular Controversy: An Account and Criticism of the Equalisation of Nagri and Urdu, as the character for the Court of the*

which was presented as a defence of the Urdu script against the Devanagari, revealed itself also as a defence of Muslim privilege in the public life of the North-Western Provinces and Oudh.

Consequently, behind the dispute between the supporters of Hindi in Devanagari script and Urdu in Persian script, which was frequently presented in technical terms as a controversy over which script was most suited to write a common language, there lay a cleavage between the aspirations and interests of educated Hindus and Muslims. Educated Hindus wanted to secure official recognition for Devanagari so that the cultural aspirations and employment opportunities for Hindus might be better served thereby. Educated Muslims wanted to preserve the official dominance of Urdu because Indo-Persian culture, which they favored, and their employment opportunities would also be enhanced thereby. Though the Hindi appeal was couched in terms of the interests of the broad masses of the majority Hindu population and the Urdu appeal in terms of the interests of educated Hindus and Muslims alike, the two movements were led primarily by educated members of the two communities and they fostered both linguistic and cultural divergence between them. Linguistically, Hindi, written in Devanagari script, was becoming a vehicle for the Sanskritization of the language, whereas Urdu in Persian script continued to draw heavily from the Persian language. Culturally, Hindi began to be seen as the culture language of Hindus and Urdu as the culture language of Muslims.

In addition to a cultural-communal divergence, the Hindi–Urdu controversy of the late nineteenth century widened the divergence between the languages of the educated urban elites and the rural masses, who, Hindus and Muslims alike, spoke a variety of dialects, generically referred to as 'Hindi'. Even in the cities, the literary forms of the two languages were quite different from the spoken language of ordinary people. This process of dual divergence has been confirmed by sociolinguistic studies of language change in Hindi and Urdu in north India, particularly in the work of Das Gupta and Gumperz, who note:

Each of these groups ['the predominantly westernized Muslim elite' and the 'rival group of Hindi intellectuals'] identified language with their community, invoking and glorifying the history of their respective religious and cultural background, and in this way each tended to drift away from the other. As the Hindu–Muslim conflict grew, literary Hindi and Urdu began to grow more and more distinct, not only from each other but also from the spoken everyday idiom of the

North-West Provinces and Oudh, under the Resolution No. 5885 of Sir A. P. Macdonnell, The Lieutenant-Governor, N.-W. P., and Chief Commissioner, Oudh, dated 18th April 1900 (no publication details, but apparently published in 1900).

urban middle classes. Rising social mobilization and political consciousness were thus accompanied by a widening rift between these two groups and, within each group, between the elite and the yet unmobilized masses.[1]

By the time the mass politics of the nationalist era came to the United Provinces in the 1920s, this dual divergence was well advanced and was particularly deplored by Gandhi, whose political goals were contrary to both historic tendencies. In the face of Hindu–Muslim divergence, Gandhi favored communal unity; in the face of elite–mass divergence, Gandhi favored mass mobilization. In his writings on language,[2] Gandhi showed an acute awareness of both kinds of divergence and proposed their resolution through the re-merging of the two languages, Hindi and Urdu, into the common, everyday language of the masses, which he called Hindustani and which he thought could be written in either script. Gandhi worked through Hindi and Hindustani voluntary associations for the spread of the spoken language, with its fusion of Persian-Arabic, Sanskritic, and indigenous vernacular elements, in the educational institutions of north India and the rest of the country.

Thus, in contemporary times, the people of the United Provinces have been presented with competing forms of both political and educational mobilization. Moreover, the two processes of mobilization have been intimately connected for the past century. Throughout this period, education in the United Provinces has been a political issue of great importance and has been profoundly influenced by the competing aspirations of politico-literary elites. In the process, language and education in the United Provinces, which once united elite segments of Hindus and Muslims, came to be used for purposes of competitive mobilization between elite Hindus and elite Muslims, offering to the rural masses alternative standards for the same language and reinforcing religious divisions thereby. Gandhi and the mass politics of the Congress after the 1920s offered still a third alternative – political and educational mobilization of the mass of the people, Hindus and Muslims alike, with Hindustani as the medium of mass education and the vehicle of intercommunal discourse.

These divisions also took organizational form through the development of voluntary associations promoting the spread of the different forms of Hindi, Urdu, and Hindustani.[3] The leading organization

[1] Jyotirindra Das Gupta and John J. Gumperz, 'Language, Communication and Control in North India', in Joshua A. Fishman *et al.* (eds.), *Language Problems of Developing Nations* (New York: John Wiley, 1968), p. 157.
[2] M. K. Gandhi, *Our Language Problem* (Bombay: Bharatiya Vidya Bhavan, 1965).
[3] See Jyotirindra Das Gupta, *Language Conflict and National Development: Group Politics and National Language Policy in India* (Berkeley: University of California Press, 1970), esp. ch. 3, 4, and 7 for an account of these associations.

of the Hindi movement in the late nineteenth century was the Nagari Pracharini Sabha, formed in Banaras in 1893.[1] In 1910, the Hindi Sahitya Sammelan was formed in Allahabad and has since become the leading organization promoting the spread of Sanskritized Hindi.[2] On the Urdu side, the Anjuman Taraqqi-e-Urdu was formed to promote Urdu in 1903 and has remained the leading Urdu voluntary association in north India ever since.[3] Associations promoting the fusion of the two languages were also formed from time to time, of which the most prominent was the Hindustani Prachar Sabha, formed by Gandhi in 1942.[4] However, in the United Provinces, it was not the Hindustani associations which held the field but the Hindi associations promoting their Sanskritized version of Hindi and the Urdu associations struggling to preserve, first, the dominance of Urdu in the public life of the United Provinces and, later, its survival. These Hindi and Urdu voluntary associations, through their own activities, and through their close connections with the prominent political leaders and organizations in the United Provinces, including the Congress, the Aligarh movement, and the Muslim League, contributed to the growth of separatist sentiment among Hindus and Muslims alike.

The third force leading to divergence between Hindi and Urdu was the parallel and associated development of Hindu and Muslim revivalisms and communal antagonism, which had the consequence for the Hindi–Urdu conflict of reinforcing the tendency to identify Urdu as the language of Muslims and Hindi as the language of Hindus.[5] Although objectively this is not entirely true even today, it is undeniable that the historical tendency has been in this direction. To this day, it remains a fact that colloquial Hindi and Urdu are nearly identical languages, which diverge in fact only in script and in the vocabulary of the educated elite. Many Hindus also continue to write in Urdu, both in literature and in the mass media. However, Hindu writers in Urdu are a dying generation and Hindi and Urdu have increasingly become subjectively separate languages identified with different religious communities. For Muslims in the north, the Urdu language has become second only to Islam itself as a symbol of Muslim cultural identity.

---

[1] Das Gupta and Gumperz, 'Language, Communication and Control', pp. 157–8.
[2] *Ibid.*, p. 158; Das Gupta, *Language Conflict*, pp. 113 and 118–26.
[3] Das Gupta, *Language Conflict*, p. 11.
[4] Gandhi, *Our Language Problem*, pp. 76–86.
[5] Beni Prasad, *India's Hindu–Muslim Questions*, p. 105; Beni Prasad also noted that this tendency, pursued to its logical end, would 'constitute a gigantic stride towards a double nationality in India' (p. 113).

The Hindi–Urdu conflict and Hindu–Muslim differences

It has been argued that the Hindi–Urdu controversy of the late nineteenth century was the critical factor in the development of Muslim separatism and Hindu–Muslim conflict from that time forward. It is frequently asserted particularly that the Hindi–Urdu controversy was responsible for a fundamental change in the attitudes of Syed Ahmad Khan and his followers towards Hindu–Muslim unity, of which they despaired when the movement to replace Urdu by Hindi as the court language of the northern provinces began.[1] It is known that Syed Ahmad and his followers played the key role in the defense of Urdu during this period.[2]

Some historians and political scientists have challenged this view. Jyotirindra Das Gupta has pointed out that Muslim separatism developed also in Bengal where Urdu was not spoken. Moreover, he has argued that 'religion was the overriding criterion' in Syed Ahmad's conception of nationality, not language.[3] M. S. Jain has argued further that Syed Ahmad had expressed separatist views and views concerning Hindu–Muslim antagonisms long before the Hindi–Urdu controversy developed.[4]

The point of view taken here is rather different. It is one which emphasizes the political differences between elite groups of Hindus and Muslims, who were in competition for administrative and political power and for employment, and for whom the symbols of religion and language were both subjectively meaningful and politically useful. The Muslim elites in the United Provinces sought to maintain their privileged positions both by appealing to the special needs and historic importance of the Muslim community and also by defending the exclusive use of Urdu as the official vernacular language of those provinces. They themselves found it politically useful to accuse the Hindu protagonists of Hindi of promoting Hindi and opposing Urdu because of their hostility to Muslims.[5] However, it was not the Hindi–Urdu controversy which precipitated the

---

[1] E.g., see Choudhry Khaliquzzaman, *Pathway to Pakistan* (Lahore: Longmans, 1961), p. x; Aziz Ahmad, *Islamic Modernism in India and Pakistan, 1857–1964* (London: Oxford University Press, 1967), pp. 33–4; *Pakistan Freedom Movement*, vol. II, pt. II. pp. 517–20; Malik, *Moslem Nationalism*, p. 210; Rafiq Zakaria, *Rise of Muslims in Indian Politics: An Analysis of Developments from 1885 to 1906* (Bombay: Somaiya Publications, 1970), p. 294.

[2] *Pakistan Freedom Movement*, vol. II, pt. II, pp. 517–20; Khaliquzzaman, *Pathway to Pakistan*, p. 8; Faruqi, *The Deoband School*, p. 47; M. S. Jain, *The Aligarh Movement: Its Origin and Development, 1858–1906* (Agra: Sri Ram Mehra, 1965), pp. 66–7, 76–7.

[3] Das Gupta, *Language Conflict*, pp. 91–3.

[4] Jain, *The Aligarh Movement*, pp. 138–9; 143–4.

[5] See, for example, *Defense*, appendix, pp. 12, 14–15, and 17.

political differences between Hindus and Muslims. Rather, it was the imbalance between elite Muslims and elite Hindu groups in the public life of the provinces which made the Hindi–Urdu controversy so politically salient. 'Hindu–Muslim unity' among these elite groups of Hindus and Muslims is a description of an emotional relationship between them which is devoid of any political sense or content relevant to those times. Hindu elites sought official recognition of their cultural aspirations and an enhanced position in the public life of the provinces. Muslim elites feared the consequences of such recognition of Hindu demands for their own privileged cultural and political positions. Religion and language were the symbolic instruments in this essentially political conflict.

Historical symbols and the myth of Muslim backwardness

Bernard Cohn has argued that the development of regional and national loyalties in India may be viewed as a process of 'selection, standardization, and transmission of symbols' by elites who select out of a vast 'pool of symbols' available in all parts of India those which may best serve to unite the people of a particular region or of India as a whole and which may serve to create regionalism or nationalism. These symbols tend to be religious, literary, and political-historical in character. He urges social scientists concerned with India not to forget that, while there are innumerable symbols which may be used to build regional identities, there is also 'a pool of traditional Indian symbols, certainly Hindu symbols, which have been standardized through the nationalist movement and the emergence of an Indian state'. Among the all-India symbols Cohn lists are 'a distinctive world view'; 'a rhetoric and style'; 'languages, Sanskrit, Persian, Urdu, and English, which have been used or are used throughout India'; 'definitive life styles which cut across regional life styles, the Brahmanic, the courtly-Persian, the modern or cosmopolitan'; 'a national administrative service'; 'subcontinent-wide educational institutions'; 'the international identity of India among Bengalis, Tamils, and others who have traveled abroad'; 'and the mass culture of the movies and popular magazines'.[1]

The difficulty with this formulation is the assumption that such symbols have already been standardized and have already led to the emergence of an Indian nation-state. In fact, however, while it is

[1] Bernard S. Cohn, 'Regions Subjective and Objective: Their Relation to the Study of Modern Indian History and Society', in Robert I. Crane (ed.), *Regions and Regionalism in South Asian Studies: An Exploratory Study* (Duke University: Program in Comparative Studies on Southern Asia, 1967), pp. 22 and 32.

necessary to recognize that there are 'countervailing processes to regional identity and regionalism' and that there are all-India symbols as well as regional symbols, it is also important to note that regional and national symbols are frequently in conflict and that many all-India symbols are competitive. Shivaji, the regional hero of Maharashtra, has been adopted also as a Hindu national hero, but to the Muslims he is a predator, who obstructed the unification of India under the Mughal Empire. Sanskrit, Urdu, and English have all served in the past as all-India languages, but today no Muslim would urge the adoption of Sanskrit as a link language and few Hindus would accept Urdu for the purpose. All-India symbols can also be subverted to serve regional purposes, as when the Ramayana in Tamil Nadu is turned into a saga of southern resistance to northern domination, or the Mahabharata becomes in the hands of a Maithili pamphleteer a saga of resistance by the eastern Kauravas to the dominance of the Kurukshetra-based Pandavas.

When the Muslims are brought into the efforts at national integration through symbol manipulation, a two-dimensional problem becomes three-dimensional. It is relatively easy for Hindu nationalists to adopt regional heroes, especially since many of these regional heroes fought against the Muslim powers in India, and sometimes easy for regional nationalists to integrate all-India symbols, such as Ashoka, into the regional-national folklore, but Muslim symbols tend to compete with both. Some Muslim leaders insist that Muslims in India 'are an inseparable part of Indian nationality, Indian culture, and Indian civilisation'.[1] Most Hindus of the composite culture school would agree; but defining Indian nationality, culture, and civilization in ways which would integrate both Hindus and Muslims is a task easier to conceive than to accomplish. Clearly, for Jinnah by 1940, the task was viewed as hopeless. He considered the fact 'that Hindus and Mussalmans derive their inspirations from different sources of history' another among the numerous unbridgeable barriers of communication and understanding between the two communities.

Yet, again, it is not objective history which is the unbridgeable barrier, but the historical orientation itself and the conscious selection of separatist symbols which constitute the barrier. Given the will, it was not and is not impossible to select unifying symbols rather than separatist symbols from the Indian past, to appoint Akbar rather than Aurangzeb as a Muslim hero, to consider Ashoka an

---

[1] Maulana Syed Abul Hasan Ali Nadwi, *Welcome Address* (Lucknow: All-India Muslim Consultative Convention, 8–9 August 1964), p. 11.

Indian rather than a Hindu hero. Revivalism, however, turned the Hindus in their historical orientation either to the great empires and Hindu civilization of the pre-Muslim period or to the regional Hindu kingdoms of the Mahrattas and the Sikhs, who fought against the Muslim power. Muslims, for their part, found their inspiration in history from the period of Muslim dominance in India and, before that, from Muslim achievements in Arabia.[1] Still, there is no intrinsic reason why men who wish to build new nations must search the past for symbols of either unity or disunity if once they recognize that it is not their past that matters but their common destiny. Muslim leaders in north India in the late nineteenth century did not recognize a common destiny with the Hindus, because they saw themselves in danger of losing their privileges as a dominant community as the Hindus rose to self-assertion, and so they searched their past to find inspiration and a justification for retaining their privileges. Out of this search arose a special sense of history incompatible with Hindu aspirations and a myth of Muslim decline into backwardness.

This special sense of Muslim history and the myth of Muslim backwardness were articulated by the Muslim aristocracy of north India, in an effort to retain their dominance in the area of the sub-continent where Muslims generally were most advanced by making use of evidence from regions of the subcontinent, particularly Bengal, where the Muslim aristocracy had declined and the Muslim masses were indeed backward.[2] Thus a myth which originated in yearnings by an upper class for the maintenance of aristocratic privilege, entirely anti-democratic in content, became later, when attached to the theory of Muslim backwardness, a means of uniting elites and mass in the Muslim community by exploiting fears of Hindu dominance. As Khalid Sayeed has put it, 'Memories of Muslim rule in India not only remained alive [in the late nineteenth century], particularly among the upper-class Muslims, but were constantly used by them to impress upon the Muslim masses that having ruled India, Muslims should not allow themselves to be ruled by the Hindu majority.'[3] The second part of the myth, which made the bridge to the masses, was provided initially by the publication of W. W. Hunter's *The Indian Mussalmans*, in 1871. In this little book, which was based primarily on Hunter's analysis of the condition of the Bengal Muslims under British rule, Hunter argued in phrases which

---

[1] Beni Prasad, *India's Hindu–Muslim Questions*, pp. 32–3; I. H. Qureshi, 'The Muslim Revival', in de Bary, *Sources of Indian Tradition*, p. 739.
[2] Seal, *The Emergence of Indian Nationalism*, p. 336.
[3] Sayeed, *The Political System of Pakistan*, p. 6.

have echoed and re-echoed for a century that the Muslims were shunning Western education, that they were being eliminated from government employment, that prominent Muslim families and Muslim traders had been economically ruined and replaced by Hindu landlords and traders, and that, in a nutshell, the Muslims of Bengal at least constituted 'a race ruined under British rule'.[1] Hunter's arguments, generalized for the whole of India,[2] soon became integrated, with embellishments, into the minds of Muslim elites, who used them to appeal to British policy-makers and later to the Muslim masses to separate Muslim from Hindu interests. These arguments were used in the famous memorial of the National Muhammadan Association presented to Ripon in 1882 to demonstrate 'the depressed and desperate condition of the Muhammadans' in India and their need for state patronage to restore the balance between them and the Hindus.[3] They were used by Syed Ahmad Khan to urge Muslims to concentrate on adopting modern education because, if they did not do so, 'they will not only remain a backward community but will sink lower and lower'.[4] They were still being used as late as 1937 by Muhammad Ali Jinnah in a Muslim League presidential address, in which he remarked that 'Mussalmans all over India are numerically in a minority and weak, educationally backward, and economically nowhere'.[5]

It will be demonstrated below that the arguments and assumptions of Muslim backwardness do not apply to the United Provinces, where the objective situation in the late nineteenth and early twentieth centuries was exactly the opposite of that described above in most respects. The Muslims in the United Provinces from 1859 up through 1931 at least were not significantly behind the Hindus and in many important respects were more advantaged than the Hindus in urbanization, literacy, English education, social communications, and employment, especially government employment.[6]

---

[1] W. W. Hunter, *The Indian Mussalmans*, 2nd ed. (London: Trubner, 1872), citation from p. 146.

[2] See also Seal, *The Emergence of Indian Nationalism*, on this point (p. 307).

[3] Selections from the Records of the Government of India, Home Department, *Correspondence on the Subject of the Education of the Muhammadan Community in British India and Their Employment in the Public Service Generally* (Calcutta: Superintendent of Government Printing, India, 1886), p. 237. Hereafter referred to as *Correspondence on the Subject of the Muhammadan Community*. I am indebted to my colleague, Frank Conlon, for bringing this volume to my attention.   [4] Cited in de Bary, *Sources of Indian Tradition*, p. 744.

[5] Cited in Smith, *Modern Islam in India*, p. 264.

[6] The point of view and the data presented below will support the similar conclusions reached earlier by Ram Gopal concerning the position of U.P. Muslims in his *Indian Muslims: A Political History (1858–1947)* (Bombay: Asia Publishing House, 1959), esp. pp. 26, 32–5, 57, 83.

HINDUS AND MUSLIMS IN THE UNITED PROVINCES, 1859–1931:
SOCIAL MOBILIZATION AND COMMUNICATIONS

Urbanization

Table 3.1 gives the distribution of the population of the United Provinces from 1881 to 1961 by religion for urban and rural areas and shows the percentage of Hindus and Muslims living in towns from 1881 to 1951. It is possible, from these figures, both to compare the relative proportions of Hindus and Muslims living in the cities and towns of the province and to show the difference in the degree and rate of urbanization among Hindus and Muslims over a considerable period.[1] The table demonstrates that the Muslim population of U.P. has been far more urbanized than the Hindu population from 1881 up to the present. As late as 1931, 29% of the Muslim population of U.P. lived in cities and towns, compared to less than 8% of the Hindu population, and more than 38% of the total urban population of the province was Muslim. Moreover, there were twenty-one towns in U.P. in 1931 in which the Muslims comprised more than 50% of the population and another thirty-one towns, including such important cities as Lucknow and Agra, in which they comprised between a third and a half of the total population.[2]

The most striking feature of the figures on urbanization in U.P. from the point of view of differential rates of change between the two communities is that, in the period between 1881 and 1931, the proportion of Muslims in the urban population of the province increased from 34.6% in 1881 and 33.85% in 1891 to 38.23% in 1931, while the proportion of Hindus declined in the same period from 64.5% and 64.27% in 1881 and 1891 respectively to 59.52% in 1931.[3] Some of this change seems to reflect a higher rate of urbanization among Muslims than among Hindus, but most of the Muslim increase probably reflects the greater rate of increase in the Muslim population of the province as a whole, in urban and rural areas alike. It is only after 1931 that the rural–urban population ratio begins to shift in favor of the Hindus, until by 1961 the proportion of Muslims in the urban population of the state is reduced to less than 30%. Nevertheless, the much higher degree of urbanization among Muslims in

---

[1] However, see table 3.1, n. a (p. 143, below).

[2] *Census of India, 1931*, vol. XVIII, *United Provinces of Agra and Oudh*, pt. 1: *Report*, by A. C. Turner (Allahabad: Superintendent, Printing and Stationery, 133), p. 138.

[3] The increase in the proportion of urban Muslims seems to have been a persistent feature of the period, not simply dependent on the changes in the number of census towns.

TABLE 3.1 *Urban and rural populations in Uttar Pradesh by religion, 1881–1961 (in percentages)*[a]

	Total population		Urban population[b]		Rural population		Living in towns		
	Hindu[c]	Muslim	Hindu[c]	Muslim	Hindu[c]	Muslim	Total[a]	Hindu[c]	Muslim
1	2	3	4	5	6	7	8	9	10
1961	84.67	14.63	68.05	29.16	87.12	12.48	12.85	N.A.	N.A.
1951			(68.1)	(28.6)					
	85.05	14.28	66.02	31.30	88.05	11.60	13.64	10.5	29.9
1941			(59.1)	(38.1)					
	83.67	15.43	59.49	38.06	86.52	12.20	12.4	9.0	30.6
1931			(57.9)	(39.3)					
	84.36	14.98	59.52	38.23	87.65	11.88	11.2	7.7	29.0
1921			(59.8)	(37.5)					
	84.92	14.46	59.41	37.41	87.45	11.74	10.6	7.4	27.4
1911			(58.4)	(38.5)					
	85.05	14.38			N.A.	N.A.	10.2	7.2[d]	26.9[d]
1901			(64.2)	(33.9)					
	85.20	14.38			N.A.	N.A.	11.1	N.A.	N.A.
1891	85.86	13.82	64.27	33.85	N.A.	N.A.	11.4	8.46	28.34
1881	85.97	13.74	64.5	34.6	88.2	11.1	11.7	7.25	25.02

It must be stressed that the relative proportions of urban and rural population in different census years are not strictly comparable. The following *caveat* from the *Census of India, 1951*, vol. II, pt. I–A, p. 162, should be kept in mind in reading the table: 'It is to be remembered that the number of towns [has] varied from census to census and due to administrative changes the villages of one census were regarded as towns and even certain towns of a particular census which had lost their urban characteristics were regarded as villages at the other subsequent censuses.' Such changes would naturally also affect the relative proportions of Hindus and Muslims in urban and rural areas. Moreover, the changes have sometimes been considerable, for example, between 1951 and 1961 when the number of census towns was reduced from 486 to 244. (The numbers of census towns for other census years were as follows: 1941, 456; 1931, 450; 1921, 446; 1911, 435; 1901, 453; 1891, 484; 1881, 288.) Consequently, the table can be used to show the relative urban–rural balance for the population as a whole and by religion at each census for a variable number of census towns, but it can suggest only approximately the general and relative rates of urbanization over time.

Other factors than census redefinition have also sometimes affected the results in an arbitrary or capricious manner, as in 1911 when, at the time of census enumeration, bubonic plague was raging in many towns of the province and many urban residents had been evacuated temporarily to rural areas.

Wherever possible, figures in each column have been taken from retrospective tables in census volumes for later years, in which adjustments have been made to include the former princely states and in other ways make the figures more comparable.

Figures in parentheses in columns 4 and 5 refer to the city population for 30 cities. They were taken from a 1951 retrospective table.

The figures for 'Brahmanic Hindus' and 'Hindu Aryas', sometimes listed separately in the old census reports, have been combined in this table.

Figures in columns 9 and 10 for 1911 and earlier are for British territory only, excluding the princely states. All other figures include both. The differences were usually slight, but the inclusion of Rampur state increases the Muslim proportions in the total population and in the urban population.

SOURCES. Compiled from *Census of India Paper No. 1 of 1962, 1961 Census, Final Population Totals*, 325, and *Census of India, 1961*, vol. XV, pt. I–C (iii), p. 64, and pt II–C (ii), pp. 516–17; *1951*, vol. II, pt. I–A, pp. 162, 419–22; *1941*, vol. V, pp. 56, 81; *1931*, vol. XVIII, pt. I, pp. 154, 526; *1921*, vol. XVI, pt. I, pp. 39, 64; *1911*, vol. XV, pt. I, pp. 23, 36; *1901*, vol. XVI, pt. I, p. 100; *1891*, vol. XVI, pt. I, p. 191; *1881*, *Report on the Census of the N.-W. P. and Oudh and of the Native States of Rampur and Native Garhwal*, pp. 59–60, 96.

U.P. remains a fact up to the present. In 1951, nearly one out of every three Muslims in the province lived in a city or town whereas only one Hindu in ten was a town-dweller.

The second important feature of the differential rates in Hindu–Muslim urbanization in U.P. is the shift in urban–rural population ratios between 1931 and 1951. The most important factors in this shift were clearly the migration of urban Muslims to Pakistan in the post-partition period, and the influx to the U.P. towns of Hindu refugees from Pakistan, reflected in the very sharp drop in the Muslim proportion of the urban population between 1941 and 1951. However, the increase in the percentage of Hindus living in towns from 7.7% in 1931 to 10.5% in 1951 seems larger than could conceivably have been produced by immigration from outside the province, suggesting that in the crucial years of Hindu–Muslim political conflict in the 1930s and 1940s, the urban Hindu–Muslim population ratio was beginning to shift against the Muslims. It is doubtful, however, that this shift was sufficiently pronounced in this period to influence Muslim political attitudes, that is, to make Muslims conscious and fearful of increased Hindu movement to cities and towns of the province.

More important for understanding the context in which the Muslim separatist movement flourished are the simple facts that the Muslim urban population of the province was very large relative to the Muslim proportion in the total population and that their urban proportion was increasing until some time in the 1930s. It was in the cities that the Muslim League acquired its initial strength and urban Muslims supported the Muslim League more heavily than did rural Muslims. Even in the 1937 elections, more than 50% of the urban Muslim vote went to the League, compared to less than 30% of the rural Muslim vote. The League won nine out of the thirteen urban Muslim seats in 1937, but only twenty (out of twenty-seven contested) of the fifty-one rural Muslim seats. In 1946, more than 71% of the urban Muslim vote was won by League candidates, compared to 62% of the rural Muslim vote.[1]

Literacy and English education

In the early 1870s and again in the early 1880s, the Government of India solicited the views of the provincial governments on the status

---

[1] These figures come from P. D. Reeves, 'Changing Patterns of Political Alignment in the General Elections to the United Provinces Legislative Assembly, 1937 and 1946', *Modern Asian Studies*, v, No. 2 (April 1971), 113–14 and 135.

of Muslim education in the provinces, in response to the charges being made at the time that Muslims were not receiving the benefits of
modern education to the extent that Hindus were. The governments
of the North-Western Provinces and Oudh on both occasions vigorously insisted that the allegations had no substance as far as those
provinces were concerned. The figures on the proportions of Muslims at school in 1871–2 provided by the major British provinces at
the time showed that, in fact, Muslims were proportionately over-
represented in comparison to Hindus in schools and colleges in both
the North-Western Provinces and in Oudh and that Muslims in those
provinces were better represented in this respect than in any other
province in British India (table 3.2). The Muslim advantage was
especially pronounced in Oudh, where the Director of Public Instruction reported that the percentage of Muslim boys of school-going age
in school was 8.1%, compared to only 3.3% of Hindu boys in school.[1]
In 1883, the government of the North-Western Provinces and Oudh
reported again that, in the combined provinces, Muslims were
taking greater advantage of the new educational opportunities than
the Hindus. It was reported then that the proportion of Muslim
boys in school to the total Muslim population was 2.18% compared
to only 1.33% for Hindus.[2] Thus, by the time of the publication of
Hunter's *Indian Mussalmans* and before the memorial of the National
Muhammadan Association, Muslims in the North-Western Provinces
and Oudh were taking greater advantage of the new system of
education than the Hindus.

The Muslim educational drive persisted up through 1931, the
latest date for which comparative figures for Hindus and Muslims
are available. Tables 3.3, 3.4, and 3.5, showing male literacy and
male English literacy rates broken up by religion and rural–urban
population divisions, demonstrate dramatically the persistent force
of educational change among Muslims. Although Muslims were behind the Hindus in general male literacy in 1881 (table 3.3),[3] they
gradually closed the gap until they were ahead of the Hindus by 1911
and significantly ahead by 1931. More important politically is the
fact that male English literacy among Muslims was consistently

[1] *Correspondence on the Subject of the Muhammadan Community*, p. 212.
[2] *Ibid.*, p. 287.
[3] However, it must be stressed that literacy figures before 1911 are not comparable with
the figures after that date. The 1881 and 1891 censuses distinguished between 'scholars',
that is, children in school, and 'literates', who were enumerated separately. As the
previous paragraphs point out, there were proportionately more Muslim than Hindu
boys in school in the 1870s in the provinces, which would not be reflected in the literacy
figure. See table 3.3, n. d (p. 147, below).

TABLE 3.2 *Number and percentage of Muslims in the total population and in the population at school in the major provinces of India, 1871–2*

Provinces	Total population	Muslims	Percentage	At school		
				Total	Muslims	Percentage
Madras	31,281,177	1,872,214	6.0	123,689	5,531	4.4
Bombay	16,349,206	2,528,344	15.4	190,153	15,684	8.2
Bengal and Assam	60,467,724	19,553,420	32.3	196,086	28,411	14.4
North-Western Provinces	30,781,204	4,188,751	13.5	162,619	28,990	17.8
Oudh	11,220,232	1,111,290	9.9	48,926	12,417	25.3
Punjab	17,611,498	9,102,488	51.6	68,144	23,783	34.9
Total	167,711,041	38,356,507	22.8	789,617	114,816	14.5

SOURCE. Selections from the records of the Government of India, Home Department, *Correspondence on the Subject of the Education of the Muhammadan Community in British India and Their Employment in the Public Service Generally* (Calcutta, Superintendent, Government Printing, India, 1886), p. 355.

TABLE 3.3   *Male literacy by religion in the United Provinces, 1881–1931*[a]
(*in percentages*)

	1931	1921	1911	1901	1891	1881
Total population	(9.4)	(7.4)				(5.14)
	8.0	6.5	6.1	5.78	5.15	4.5
All Hindus[b]	(8.9)	(7.0)				(5.05)[d]
		6.7	5.8	5.61	5.06[d]	
All Muslims	(9.7)	(7.4)				(4.41)[d]
		6.5	5.9	5.26	4.52[d]	
Total urban[c]	(29.6)	(23.6)				
		21.3	17.9	17.60	N.A.	N.A.
Urban Hindu	(32.1)	(24.4)				
		22.1	19.4	19.76	N.A.	N.A.
Urban Muslim	(22.1)	(17.2)				
		15.4	13.0	10.99	N.A.	N.A.

[a] Figures in parentheses are for males aged five and over; other figures are for all males. Urban figures include the princely states. Other figures refer to British territory only.
As with other *Census of India* historical statistics, a *caveat* must be entered here against interpreting the figures too literally to show changes over the entire time period. The criteria for determining literacy and the categories for classifying literates and illiterates varied from census to census until 1911, when they were fixed. The 1881 and 1891 figures distinguished between those 'learning' and the 'literate'. Some in the 'learning' category would have been classed as literate in later census years. The 1901 figures eliminated this distinction, but used a loose criterion for determining literacy.
[b] 'Brahmanic' Hindus only.
[c] Urban here refers to the population of the cities. The number of cities included in these tabulations in the respective census years were: 1931, 23; 1921, 24; 1911, 24; 1901, 19.
[d] The combined figures for scholars and literates eliminate the imbalance in favor of the Hindus in 1881 and 1891. They are: 5.80% learning and literate among Hindus and 5.87% learning and literate among Muslims in 1881, and 5.92% and 6.06% respectively for Hindus and Muslims in 1891.

SOURCES. Compiled from *Census of India, 1951*, vol. II, pt. I–A, pp. 385, 390, 393; *1931* vol. XVIII, pt. I, pp. 453, 457, 465–7, 475–9, 481–2; *1921*, vol. XVI, pt. I, pp. 115, 118–23, 127; *1911*, vol. XV, pt. I, pp. 252, 264–9; *1901*, vol. XVI, pt. I, pp. 156, 164–70; *1891*, vol. XVI, pt. I, p. 258; *1881, Report on the Census of the North-Western Provinces and Oudh and of the Native States of Rampur and Native Garhwal*, pp. 91–2.

higher than among Hindus throughout the period 1891 to 1931 and that the gap in their favor increased during this period (table 3.4).

In the urban areas of the province, the situation was somewhat different. Urban Hindus had higher rates of both male literacy and male English literacy in the period between 1901 and 1931. In this respect, it can be said that the urban Muslims were more 'backward' than the urban Hindus. However, from another point of view, comparing the proportion of the Muslim urban literate and English educated population to the proportion of Muslims in the total

TABLE 3.4   *Male English literacy by religion in the United Provinces, 1891–1931*[a] *(in percentages)*

	1931	1921	1911	1901	1891
Total population	(1.10)	(0.75)			
	0.94	0.66	0.49	0.36	0.17
All Hindus[b]	(0.84)	(0.53)			
	0.47	0.29	0.22	0.08	
All Muslims	(1.48)	(0.92)			
	0.81	0.65	0.38	0.13	
Total urban	(9.59)[c]	N.A.	N.A.	3.69	N.A.
Urban Hindu	(9.66)[d]	N.A.	N.A.	3.74	N.A.
Urban Muslim	(5.94)[d]	N.A.	N.A.	1.97	N.A.
Rural Hindu	(0.48)	N.A.	N.A.	N.A.	N.A.
Rural Muslim	(0.78)	N.A.	N.A.	N.A.	N.A.

[a] Figures in parentheses are for males aged five and over; other figures are for all males. Unless otherwise noted, figures are for British territory only.
[b] 'Brahmanic' Hindus only.
[c] Figures are for 23 cities for the entire province, including the princely states.
[d] Figures are for 22 cities in British territory.

SOURCES. *Census of India, 1931*, vol. XVIII, pt. I, pp. 463, 465–7, 479; *1921*, vol. XVI, pt. I pp. 119, 123; *1901*, vol. XVI, pt. I, pp. 156, 164–70; *1891*, vol. XVI, pt. I, p. 261.

population of the state, the Muslims were in advance of the Hindus in both respects, at least from 1901 onwards (table 3.5). Moreover, in the period between 1901 and 1931, Muslims were closing the gap in the urban areas also with respect to both male literacy and male English literacy.

The figures in table 3.5, which show the proportions of Hindus and Muslims in the total literate and English-educated populations in the rural and urban areas of the province demonstrate most dramatically the more rapid rate of change among Muslims in this period. Among all the literate categories of the population, Muslims increased their proportion in the population steadily every ten years until, by 1931, Muslims comprised more than 15% of the literate population of the province, nearly 20% of the English-educated population, more than 28% of the urban literate population, and more than 22% of that tiny but politically crucial population segment, the urban English-educated class.

Thus, up to 1931 at least, in education as in urbanization, Muslims in U.P. were mobilizing more rapidly than Hindus. From the Muslim political point of view, however, this could be little consolation, for, even with a somewhat slower rate of urbanization and education, the

TABLE 3.5 *Male literate and illiterate populations of the United Provinces by religion, 1872–1931*[a]

	Literate			Literate in English			Urban literate			Urban literate in English			Illiterate		
	Total	Hindu	Muslim	Total	Hindu	Muslim	Total	Hindu	Muslim	Total	Hindu	Muslim	Total	Hindu	Muslim
1931															
No.	2,043,410	1,631,640	311,569	240,140	153,031	47,740	364,801	230,542	103,589	118,377	68,838	26,375	23,401,596	19,680,691	3,468,884
%		79.85	15.25		63.73	19.88		63.20	28.40		58.15	22.28		84.10	14.82
1921															
No.	1,556,626	1,248,545	221,503	156,900	95,039	27,384	258,519	160,502	68,180	87,498	49,370	16,121	22,231,119	18,882,269	3,166,648
%		80.21	14.23		60.57	17.45		61.98	26.33		56.42	18.42		84.94	14.24
1911															
No.	1,505,945	1,213,997	205,212	121,529	63,782	20,966	221,018	131,974	52,239	65,304	31,210	11,701	23,135,886	19,735,664	3,261,075
%		80.61	13.63		52.48	17.25		59.71	23.64		47.79	17.92		85.30	14.10
1901															
No.	1,422,924	1,178,622	181,125	87,641	47,739	12,919	174,735	127,426	35,882	36,504	24,104	6,421	23,194,018	19,847,621	3,258,772
%		82.83	12.73		54.47	14.74		73.11	20.59		66.03	17.59		85.57	14.05
1891															
No.	1,257,149	1,060,471	146,777	43,364	17,465	4,189	N.A.	N.A.	N.A.	N.A.	N.A.	N.A.	22,808,011	19,715,647	3,047,084
%		84.36	11.68		40.27	9.66								86.44	13.36
1881															
No.	1,033,458	879,182	116,763	N.A.	N.A.	N.A.	N.A.	N.A.	N.A.	N.A.	N.A.	N.A.	N.A.	N.A.	N.A.
%		85.07	11.30												
1872[b]															
No.	531,608	469,248	59,578	N.A.	N.A.	N.A.	N.A.	N.A.	N.A.	N.A.	N.A.	N.A.	N.A.	N.A.	N.A.
%		88.27	11.21												

a Figures for Hindus exclude Aryas and other small Hindu sects where they were listed separately in the census volumes, which was frequently, but not consistently, the case. Their exclusion does not significantly affect the percentages in the table. Where the combined percentages for Hindus and Muslims in any category fall significantly short of 100, the bulk of the difference is invariably made up by Christians.

b North-Western Provinces only.

SOURCES. *Census of India: 1931*, vol. I, pt. II, p. 434, and vol. XVIII, pt. II, pp. 448–9, 470; *1921*, vol. XVI, pt. II, pp. 108, 128–32; *1911*, vol. XV, pt. II, pp. 106–107, 146–50; *1901*, vol. XVI–A, pt. II, pp. 82–3, 114–19; *1891*, vol. XVI, pt. I, p. 261, vol. XVIII, pt. II, pp. 1–13; *1881*, *Report on the Census of the North-Western Provinces and Oudh, 1881 and of the Native States of Rampur and Native Garhwal*, p. 92; *1872*, *Census of the N.-W. Provinces, 1872*, vol. I, p. 30.

Hindus continued to comprise a majority in the cities, among the literate, and among the English-educated. Both the differences in the rates of change among Hindus and Muslims as well as the impossibility of the Muslims overcoming the numerical preponderance of the Hindus, no matter how much faster they changed, can be illustrated by comparing the absolute numbers of Hindus and Muslims among the urban English-educated classes in 1901 and 1931. Between 1901 and 1931, Muslims multiplied themselves in this key category more than four times, whereas the Hindus multiplied themselves by slightly less than three times. Whereas in 1901 Hindus outnumbered Muslims in this category in the ratio 4:1, their advantage in 1931 was considerably less than 3:1. Yet the overwhelming political fact of 1931 remained that there were 68,838 Hindus in the class which provided the lawyers, politicians, and government servants, but only 26,375 Muslims. The Muslims were not backward in U.P. compared to the Hindus, but they could not hope to overcome their minority status in all walks of life, no matter how slowly the overwhelmingly larger Hindu majority mobilized itself.

Employment

W. W. Hunter had tried to show that, in Bengal, the Muslim aristocracy had been economically ruined, that Muslims were practically eliminated from positions of government which they had previously dominated, and that Muslim traders and businessmen had also suffered eclipse. The memorial of the National Muhammadan Association generalized Hunter's comments for the whole of India. Although the memorialists themselves were aware that, 'in the North-Western Provinces the disproportion between the two races is probably not so great', they nevertheless complained that 'the Hindus outnumber the Muhammadans in the Government offices'.[1] The comments of the government of the North-Western Provinces and Oudh on the position of Muslims in government employment in the provinces at the time revealed that, in fact, not only were the Muslims not under-represented in government offices, but they held positions, in the words of the officiating secretary to the government, 'out of all proportion to the population figures'.[2] It was reported then that 'out of the 54,130 native officials holding appointments under this Government 35,302 are Hindus and 18,828 Muhammadans, being 65.22 per cent Hindus and 34.78 per cent Muhammadans, as against 86.75 and 13.25 in the general population'.[3] In the highest-

---

[1] *Correspondence on the Subject of the Muhammadan Community*, p. 240.
[2] *Ibid.*, p. 289.   [3] *Ibid.*, p. 286.

paid and most prestigious positions, such as deputy collectors and tahsildars, Muslims in many years outnumbered Hindus during the period from 1859 to 1882.[1] The imbalance in favor of the Muslims in the provinces was so great at this time that the Secretary to the Government of India, in summarizing the reports of the provinces on this question, remarked:

In the North-Western Provinces and Oudh and in the Punjab the enquiries which have been instituted prove that the allegations of the memorialists as to the exclusion of their community from a fair share of Government patronage do not apply. The figures submitted indicate that in respect of offices in the Subordinate Executive and Judicial services, including all the higher and better paid appointments, the Muhammadans have secured not only a fair proportion, but almost an unduly liberal share of patronage.[2]

The available figures for later years show that the original advantage of the Muslims in government employment in these provinces was not only maintained, but was increased significantly. In 1886–7, 45.1% or 235 out of 521 positions in the executive and judicial branches of the uncovenanted service in the province were held by Muslims.[3] In 1867, 1877, and 1887, Muslims held 32.5, 27.4, and 29.6% respectively of the appointments open to Hindus and Muslims in the salary scale of Rs. 75 per month and above in the government of the province.[4] Most striking, however, is the fact that, as late as 1911 and 1921, Muslims held 41.94 and 47.67% of government positions (tables 3.6 and 3.7), compared to their proportion of 34.78% in 1882.

The census figures for 1911 and 1921 on employment by religion in U.P., which are the latest available comprehensive figures, demonstrate clearly that up to that time Muslims were either over-represented or proportionately well represented in comparison to the Hindus not only in government employment, but in every major category of employment both in the modern urban sectors of the economy and in elite sectors of the traditional rural economy. In many key categories, Muslims approached equality in numbers with and even surpassed the number of Hindus.

The figures for 1921 and 1911 for occupation by religion in U.P. must be treated cautiously and cannot be used without discrimination to show changes in occupational distribution between 1911 and 1921, because of significant alterations in the bases of enumeration in the two censuses and because of the peculiar circumstances under which the census of 1911 was taken.[5] Nevertheless, the figures taken

---

[1] *Ibid.* [2] *Ibid.*, p. 389.
[3] Seal, *The Emergence of Indian Nationalism*, p. 118. [4] *Ibid.*, p. 305.
[5] See table 3.1, n. a (p. 143, above).

TABLE 3.6   *Occupation by religion (for selected occupations) in the United Provinces, 1921*[a]

Occupation	Total	Hindus[b]		Muslims	
		No.	%	No.	%
Total population	46,510,668	39,292,926	84.48	6,724,967	14.28
1. Agriculture, forestry, and fishing	35,716,334	33,371,748	93.44	2,144,973	6.01
(a) Ordinary cultivators	29,849,821	28,709,783	96.18	999,111	3.35
(b) Income from rent of land	818,437	569,677	69.61	225,734	27.58
(c) Agents, managers of landed estates, clerks, rent collectors, etc.	136,201	111,707	82.02	21,171	15.54
(d) Other	4,911,875	3,980,581	81.04	898,957	18.30
2. Exploitation of minerals	8,208	4,230	51.54	3,622	44.13
3. Industry	5,113,564	2,765,144	54.07	2,224,166	43.50
4. Transport	401,870	206,657	51.42	187,261	46.60
5. Trade[a]	2,060,338	1,147,735	55.71	832,339	40.40
(a) Bank managers, money lenders, exchange and insurance agents, money changers, and brokers and their employees	113,960	49,832	43.73	51,690	45.36
(b) Brokers, commission agents, commercial travellers, warehouse owners and employees	31,454	14,037	44.63	15,544	49.42
(c) Trade in piece goods	145,706	65,980	45.28	69,671	47.82
(d) Grain and pulse dealers	549,830	319,287	58.07	194,936	35.45
6. Public force	253,503	127,782	50.41	116,616	46.00
(a) Army	78,821	41,392	52.51	30,238	38.36
(b) Police	85,706	41,983	48.98	42,670	49.79
(c) Village watchmen	88,493	44,318	50.08	43,394	49.04
7. Public administration	245,862	142,586	57.99	92,167	37.49
(a) Service of the state	121,147	57,382	47.37	57,747	47.67
(b) Municipal and other local (not village) service	20,252	10,555	52.12	8,752	43.22
8. Professions and liberal arts	488,424	374,284	76.63	89,965	18.42
(a) Lawyers	15,948	10,126	63.49	4,476	28.07
(b) Medical practitioners	33,087	16,932	51.17	13,178	39.83
(c) Instruction	74,608	50,467	67.64	16,768	22.47
(d) Letters and arts and sciences	61,293	29,703	48.46	30,176	49.23

[a] Tables 3.6 and 3.7 are not meant to show and should not be used to demonstrate shifts between 1911 and 1921 in occupational categories. Although the categories in 1911 and 1921 are the same, the bases of enumeration changed. In agricultural occupations, the basis of enumeration was entirely different in 1921 from 1911. Moreover, there was a change in 1921 in the basis of enumerating principal and subsidiary occupations, which may have had a considerable impact on the results in some categories of employment, e.g. money lenders and brokers (5a and 5b) in the table. All 1911 urban statistics must be treated with caution because of the peculiar conditions under which the census was taken (see n. a to table 3.1).

[b] 'Brahmanic' Hindus only; excludes Aryas.

SOURCE. *Census of India, 1921*, vol. XVI, pt. II, pp. 396–407.

together in tables 3.6 and 3.7 do reveal certain consistent and persistent features. Muslims were under-represented compared to Hindus
among ordinary cultivators in the province, but were over-represented
in both census years among the rent-receiving and rent-collecting
categories of the population. Moreover, the urban rentier class of
Muslims in 1911 was larger, in absolute terms, than the class of
Hindu urban rent receivers and rent collectors. In the industrial and
commercial life of the province, Muslims were also well represented.
There are some very sharp differences between 1911 and 1921 in
some of these categories, probably because of changes in the instructions to the census enumerators, but here also there are some consistent features. Muslims were clearly over-represented (in proportion to their numbers in the total population) in the industrial life
of the province both in 1911 and in 1921, in the province as a whole
and in the cities. They were over-represented in transport and trade
in the province as a whole in both census years and only slightly
under-represented in these categories in the cities. (Some of the
sub-categories under trade, however, show major inconsistencies
between 1911 and 1921, indicating heavy over-representation of
Muslims in 1921 and under-representation in 1911.)

In the politically crucial occupations in government service and
the liberal professions, Muslim representation was very high in both
1911 and 1921. Muslims were over-represented in the army in
both years in the province as a whole; they outnumbered Hindus in
both years in urban and rural sectors alike in the police departments;
and they were over-represented even in the category of village watch-
men both in 1911 and 1921. In the all-important category of public
administration, especially in state employment, it has already been
noted above that Muslims were heavily over-represented. Nor was
Muslim employment confined to the lower levels of government
administration. Figures on the castes of gazetted officers in U.P. in
1921 reveal that Brahmans provided the largest contingent of 1,019
officers, but that Shaikhs (707) and Saiyids (265) came next, followed by the Hindu Jats (259) and Kayasthas (198).[1] In the professions and liberal arts, which were the classes that provided the
urban and district town politicians, Muslims were well represented
or heavily over-represented as lawyers in the province as a whole in
1911 and 1921 and only slightly under-represented in this respect in
the twenty-four cities. Muslim doctors outnumbered Hindus in the

[1] *Census of India, 1921*, vol. XVI: *United Provinces of Agra and Oudh*, pt. II: *Imperial Tables*,
by E. H. H. Edye and W. R. Tennant (Allahabad: Superintendent, Government Press,
United Provinces, 1923), p. 413.

TABLE 3.7 *Occupation by religion (for selected occupations) in the United Provinces, 1911*[a]

Occupation	Whole province					24 cities				
	Total	Hindus[b] No.	%	Muslims No.	%	Total	Hindus[b] No.	%	Muslims No.	%
Total population	48,014,080	40,705,353	84.78	6,904,731	14.11	2,148,858	1,240,471	57.73	832,619	38.75
1. Agriculture, forestry, and fishing	35,267,372	31,633,423	89.70	3,481,886	9.87	247,907	163,743	66.05	79,445	32.05
(a) Ordinary cultivators	28,712,015	25,756,942	89.71	2,846,778	9.91	110,987	80,470	72.50	28,765	25.92
(b) Income from rent of land	866,419	671,534	77.51	175,797	20.29	53,821	25,230	46.88	27,186	50.51
(c) Agents, managers of landed estates, clerks, rent collectors, etc.	196,722	124,579	63.33	68,736	34.94	19,593	9,193	46.92	9,833	50.19
(d) Other	5,492,216	5,080,368	92.50	390,575	7.11	63,506	48,850	76.92	13,661	21.51
2. Exploitation of minerals	8,868	7,943	90.18	826	9.38	545	456	83.67	82	15.05
3. Industry	5,834,384	4,021,696	68.93	1,741,716	29.85	670,467	354,479	52.87	304,156	45.36
4. Transport	449,610	296,919	66.04	138,197	30.74	138,406	79,081	57.14	51,050	36.88
5. Trade[a]	2,140,395	1,602,422	74.87	464,478	21.70	344,487	214,268	62.20	117,389	34.08
(a) Bank managers, money lenders, exchange and insurance agents, money changers and brokers and their employees	144,283	120,191	83.30	9,993	6.93	26,214	20,928	79.84	2,801	10.69
(b) Brokers, commission agents, commercial travellers, warehouse owners and employees	29,411	24,925	84.75	3,328	11.32	8,569	6,967	81.30	1,132	13.21
(c) Trade in piece goods	133,429	95,216	71.36	30,137	22.59	25,091	17,519	69.82	6,195	24.69
(d) Grain and pulse dealers	686,906	602,925	87.77	60,609	8.82	67,593	54,327	80.37	9,677	14.32
6. Public force	336,627	214,780	63.80	92,523	27.49	65,559	25,710	39.22	22,450	34.24
(a) Army	61,180	24,757	40.47	14,472	23.65	31,508	7,778	24.69	7,349	23.32
(b) Police	85,623	38,279	44.71	43,090	50.33	26,154	11,960	45.73	13,468	51.49
(c) Village watchmen	189,807	151,749	79.95	34,957	18.42	7,891	5,972	75.68	1,629	20.64

Occupation	Whole province					24 cities				
	Total	Hindus[b] No.	%	Muslims No.	%	Total	Hindus[b] No.	%	Muslims No.	%
7. Public administration	269,593	181,363	67.27	78,090	28.97	64,771	29,999	46.32	31,720	48.97
(a) Service of the state	123,022	65,224	53.02	51,598	41.94	41,929	21,794	51.98	17,717	42.25
(b) Municipal and other local (not village) service	20,897	11,389	54.50	8,507	40.71	9,037	4,478	49.55	4,241	46.93
8. Professions and liberal arts	534,027	387,293	72.52	123,612	23.15	121,691	74,771	61.44	38,717	31.82
(a) Lawyers	16,867	10,115	59.97	5,497	32.59	8,441	4,857	57.54	2,936	34.78
(b) Medical practitioners	30,050	15,246	50.74	12,510	41.63	10,696	4,486	41.94	5,437	50.83
(c) Instruction	66,906	37,306	55.76	22,675	33.89	17,937	7,778	43.63	7,653	42.67
(d) Letters and arts and sciences	96,313	42,638	44.27	51,694	53.67	21,859	7,852	35.92	13,170	60.25

[a] See n. a to table 3.6.

[b] 'Brahmanic' Hindus only; excludes Aryas.

SOURCE. *Census of India, 1911*, vol. XV, pt. II, pp. 550–63, 588–9, 614–15, 640–1, 666–7.

cities and were over-represented in the province as a whole in both years. Muslims were also over-represented in the teaching profession and in other miscellaneous occupations included under letters and arts and sciences.

The proportionate over-representation of Muslims in the non-agricultural sectors of the economy of U.P. in 1911 and 1921 is apparent. Although the imbalance in 1921 in favor of the Muslims in comparison to 1911 seems almost impossible to believe, it is nevertheless clear that both in 1911 and in 1921 Muslims were considerably over-represented (in terms of their proportion to the total population) both in industry and in the service sectors of the economy of the state. In contrast, the proportion of Muslims engaged in agricultural occupations was very small in both 1911 and 1921, much smaller than their proportion even in the rural population of the state. Thus, in employment as in urbanization and education, it is clear that the Muslims were already more advanced than the Hindus in the nineteenth century and that they increased their advantage up through 1921. The figures on the employment of Muslims in government service between 1859 and 1921 suggest, in fact, that the advantaged Muslims constituted a privileged community, nearly a dominant administrative elite, and that it was the Hindus in this region who were denied a share of government posts in a proportion reflecting their numbers.

Communications

It has been noted above that Urdu alone was the court language in the North-Western Provinces and Oudh from 1837 until 1900, when the lieutenant-governor, Sir A. P. MacDonnell, issued a circular giving Hindi equal status with Urdu in the provinces. Until that time, Urdu was the pre-eminent symbol of the continued dominance of the Muslim elite in the administrative and cultural life of the province.

Studies of the origins of nationalism in India have emphasized the importance of English education as a unifying element in the spread of communications, which made possible nationalist organization.[1] But the trends which were of greater importance in the long run and which have not been given the attention due them by historians of nationalism were those taking place in vernacular education in the provinces. English education was providing a medium of communication and a precondition for all-India nationalist organization for

---

[1] The classic account is Bruce Tiebout McCully, *English Education and the Origins of Indian Nationalism* (Gloucester, Mass.: Peter Smith, 1966).

that tiny elite which dominated all-India politics in the period between 1885 and 1920, but the more important issue in the U.P. in this period was not the spread of English education but whether Hindi or Urdu would be the predominant medium of primary education.

The two issues of court language and medium of primary education were closely connected in the late nineteenth century, for as long as Urdu was the sole official (vernacular) language in use in the province, Hindu children whose parents wished their sons to have access to government positions would be compelled to have them educated in Urdu-medium schools. Many Hindus did study Urdu in preference to Hindi in the period when Urdu was the official court language. Pandit Madan Mohan Malaviya's pamphlet, *Court Character and Primary Education in the N.-W. Provinces and Oudh*, published in 1897, cited government figures to show that, in the government schools in the North-Western Provinces between 1860–1 and 1873–4, the proportion of Urdu-learners was far in excess of the proportion of Muslims in the schools at that time.[1] In 1873–4, 16.2% of the boys in the middle and lower vernacular schools of the provinces were Muslim, but nearly 35% of the boys in government schools of all kinds were studying Urdu.[2] In Oudh, the situation was even more favorable to Urdu and the Muslims. In 1872, the secretary to the chief commissioner of Oudh revealed that, 'although the Hindu so largely out-numbers the Mahomedan population of the province, the course of instruction is practically a course of Urdu-Persian, rather than a course of Hindi-Sanscrit; and is thus . . . more suited for Mahomedan than for Hindu scholars'. The secretary reported at the time that, in government schools, 22,074 students were learning Urdu, Persian, or Arabic, whereas only 4,959 students were taking up Hindi or Sanskrit.[3] The most recent figures which distinguished between Hindi- and Urdu-learners in the provinces before the change in court language are for 1896, and they show that there were 50,316 boys studying Urdu and 100,404 studying Hindi in the vernacular elementary schools in the combined North-Western Provinces and Oudh.[4]

[1] *Court Character and Primary Education*, pp. 20, 28.
[2] *Ibid.*, app., p. 77, where the figures are shown as an extract from a government order of 1874. The populations compared, boys in the middle and lower vernacular schools studying Urdu and Muslim boys in government schools of all kinds, are not identical, but the discrepancy between Urdu-learners and Muslims in school is consistent with other information presented in this chapter.
[3] *Correspondence on the Subject of the Muhammadan Community*, p. 212.
[4] *Court Character and Primary Education*, p. 28, where it is reported that 'it has been ascertained that on the 31st March, 1896, 50,316 boys were reading Urdu and 100,404,

Moreover, the trend in the middle and late nineteenth century was toward increasing displacement of Hindi by Urdu in the schools. In 1860–74, the number of Urdu- and Persian-learners had multiplied by more than four times to 48,229, whereas the number of Hindi-learners had increased by less than a third to 85,820.[1] In the middle vernacular examinations, figures for the period 1873–4 to 1895–6 show that, during this time, Urdu displaced Hindi as the dominant language for this purpose. Whereas only 434 candidates took this examination in Urdu in 1873–4 and 1,315 students took it in Hindi, by 1895–6 the proportions were reversed, with 2,814 candidates taking the examination in Urdu compared to only 785 taking it in Hindi.[2]

In effect, large numbers of Hindus, primarily because of the continued official importance given to Urdu in the provinces, were adopting the cultural language and script of the Muslims in the late nineteenth century. It was this process of linguistic assimilation to which the leaders of the Hindi movement were opposed in the late nineteenth century and which Muslims of the Aligarh school wanted to continue. However, even though the North-Western Provinces were the most educationally backward of the British Indian provinces during this period and relatively small proportions of Hindus were entering the government schools, the size of the Hindu majority and the growing sense of self-consciousness being fostered by Hindu revivalists and Hindi protagonists was too great to permit the absorption of most Hindus into Urdu-medium schools. Although Hindus who went up to the middle and secondary examinations opted for Urdu for the sake of employment, Hindus learning Hindi were still more than twice the number of Urdu-learners at the primary stages in 1896. In this situation, where the social mobilization of the Hindus (however slow it was at this time) and the development of a sense of identity based upon religion were proceeding faster than the process of assimilation to the Urdu language and Indo-Persian culture, lay the basic condition for Hindu–Muslim conflict in the late nineteenth century.

Although figures are not available to demonstrate it, it can be presumed that the process of assimilation to Urdu was reversed by the government order of 1900. However, it was not until much later that Hindi overtook Urdu as the predominant vernacular language of public communications in the U.P. Data on the number of Hindi

Hindi, in the vernacular primary schools in these Provinces'. How the information was 'ascertained' is not stated, but there is no reason to doubt the accuracy of the figures.
[1] *Ibid.*   [2] *Ibid.*, p. 31.

and Urdu papers between 1873 and 1964 (table 3.8) demonstrate the earlier predominance of Urdu as the elite vernacular language of the province and reveal that it was not until 1920 that the number of Hindi papers in U.P. exceeded the number of Urdu papers. Until 1930, the number of both the Hindi and Urdu papers continued to increase, but the rate of increase in the number of Hindi papers was greater than that of the Urdu papers. As in other aspects of the process of social mobilization of the two communities, the problem of the Muslims was not so much their backwardness but that no matter how fast they ran, the Hindus either ran faster or, even when they walked, nearly always outnumbered the Muslims in the end.

TABLE 3.8   *Hindi, Urdu, and English newspapers and periodicals in Uttar Pradesh, 1873–1960*

	1970	1960	1950	1940	1930	1920	1910	1900	1890	1873
Hindi	604	594	435	367	253	175	86	34	24	9
Urdu	114	161	140	268	225	151	116	69	68	25
English	79	88	62	109	84	71	56	34	N.A.	N.A.

SOURCES. *Court Character and Primary Education in the N.-W. Provinces and Oudh* (Allahabad Indian Press, 1897), p. 78; *Census of India, 1951*, vol. II, pt. I–A, p. 409; *Census of India, 1931*, vol. XVIII, pt. I, p. 474; Government of India, Ministry of Information and Broadcasting, *Annual Report of the Registrar of Newspapers for India, 1961* (Delhi, Manager of Publications, 1961), pt. I, p. 309; and *Press in India 1971* (Delhi, Manager of Publications, 1971), pt. I, p. 327.

Taken together, the available data on vernacular education and newspaper publication suggest that it was not the Muslims but both Hindi and the Hindus who were backward compared to Urdu and the Muslims, and Hindus who were struggling for self-assertion and for their linguistic expression in the public life of the northern provinces against the dominance of Urdu and the educated Muslim elite.[1] Moreover, in their resistance to the claims of Hindi, as in their later demands for weightage in political representation and for separate electorates, the Muslim elites of U.P. made it clear from the beginning that they intended to fight to maintain their privileges.

MUSLIM ELITES

The Muslim aristocracy

Although the Muslim community was more advanced in most respects than the Hindus in nineteenth- and twentieth-century U.P.,

[1] On this point, see also D. A. Low, 'Introduction', in D. A. Low (ed.), *Soundings in Modern South Asian History* (Berkeley: University of California Press, 1968), pp. 13 and 17.

its political leadership was more narrow. Congress nationalism (which reflected Hindu aspirations) in U.P. was a movement led by the middle-class professionals in the cities and towns and the petty zamindars and bigger peasants in the countryside, supported financially by the textile- and sugar-mill owners and the big cloth traders.[1] Muslim separatism in U.P. had a quite different class basis, reflecting differences in both the socio-economic conditions of the Muslims and their religious organization.

The Muslim community in U.P. was not primarily a peasant community and Muslim separatism, therefore, did not have the peasant base which Congress nationalism had. The leaders of the nineteenth-century Muslim educational and political movements in U.P. were largely Muslim aristocrats and government servants. All the prominent leaders and financial backers of the Aligarh movement belonged to these groups.[2] Syed Ahmad Khan was a descendant of a noble Muslim family of prominence in the Mughal court. Members of his family served in both the Mughal and British administrations and he himself entered government service under the British in 1838, from which he retired as a judge in 1876. In 1878, he was appointed to the Imperial Council by the viceroy. His closest associate in the Aligarh movement, Sami' ullah Khan, 'belonged to a well-to-do family' and also served in the judicial service from 1858 until 1892, when he retired from his post of district judge. Syed Ahmad's successor in the Aligarh movement, Mohsin-ul-Mulk, whose 'father was not a literate person', nevertheless also became a government servant, reaching the highest position available to Indians in government service in 1867, that of deputy collector. After his retirement from the British administrative service, he served as Political and Financial Secretary of the Hyderabad state before settling in Aligarh and taking over the leadership of the Aligarh movement.[3] The Aligarh College was originally funded and its board of trustees controlled by the Muslim landlords of U.P.[4] The Raja of Mahmudabad, the second largest talukdar of Oudh, was for a time vice-chancellor of the college.[5]

---

[1] Smith, *Modern Islam in India*, p. 217, and Paul R. Brass, *Factional Politics in an Indian State: The Congress Party in Uttar Pradesh* (Berkeley: University of California Press, 1965), pp. 229ff.

[2] Faruqi, *The Deoband School*, p. 39; Jain, *The Aligarh Movement*, pp. 55–9, 65, 74–5; Khaliquzzaman, *Pathway to Pakistan*, pp. 8, 35, 114; *Pakistan Freedom Movement*, vol. II, pt. II, ch. 18 and 21.

[3] *Pakistan Freedom Movement*, vol. II, pt. II, ch. 18 and 21, pp. 451, 453–8, 463, 533–6, 538–9.

[4] Faruqi, *The Deoband School*, p. 39; Khaliquzzaman, *Pathway to Pakistan*, p. 114.

[5] *Ibid.*, p. 35.

The Muslim League, itself an offshoot of the Aligarh movement, was dominated by Muslim landlords from the beginning.[1] The delegation of 1906, which won for Muslims the right of separate electorates, was led by the Aga Khan, and the petition to Lord Minto was signed by 'nobles, ministers of various states, great landowners, lawyers, merchants, and . . . many other of His Majesty's Mahommedan subjects'.[2] The Raja of Mahmudabad was one of the leading figures in the U.P. League and a financial backer of the League from the beginning.[3] He was president of the all-India Muslim League in 1913 and again in 1928.[4] His son continued to support the League after his father's death in 1931.[5] The Raja of Salempur, another Oudh talukdar, played a prominent role in Muslim and Muslim League politics in the 1920s and 1930s – as president of the Muslim Unity Board in 1933–4 and as a member of the parliamentary board of the League in 1936.[6] The seven members of the League central parliamentary board from U.P. in 1937 included the Rajas of Mahmudabad and Salempur, the Nawabzada Liaquat Ali Khan, and the (honorary) Nawab Ismail Khan.[7] As late as 1942, the Muslim League Council contained 163 landlords (in a total membership of 503), most of them from the Punjab and U.P.[8] The Committee for the Demands of U.P. Muslims, which submitted a lengthy representation to the Simon Commission in 1928, had a membership of thirty, including sixteen persons whose names included the titles of Khan Bahadur, Nawab and Khan Saheb.[9]

Upper middle class

The statistics given above on Muslim literacy and employment demonstrated that there was in late nineteenth- and early twentieth-century U.P. no dearth of Muslims among the urban, English-educated professional classes. It was these classes among the Hindus who took the leadership in the Indian National Congress. In the Muslim League, leadership positions were divided between the Muslim aristocracy and the upper middle class professionals. In the early

[1] *Ibid.*, p. 137.
[2] Cited in Sayeed, *The Political System of Pakistan*, p. 13.
[3] Khaliquzzaman, *Pathway to Pakistan*, p. 137.
[4] *Ibid.*, pp. 18, 97.
[5] *Ibid.*, pp. 145, 159, 214, 233.
[6] *Ibid.*, pp. 102, 144.
[7] *Ibid.*, p. 416.
[8] Sayeed, *The Political System of Pakistan*, p. 55.
[9] *Representation of the Muslims of the United Provinces (India) to the Indian Statutory Commission (July 1928)* (no publication details), pp. xiii–xiv.

period of the nationalist movement in India, class background was more important than community ties. The Muslim lawyers of Bombay and Madras were initially attracted to the Indian National Congress, in which Jinnah was an early member and a disciple of Gokhale. In U.P. also, Chaudhury Khaliquzzaman was a lawyer and a member of the Congress until his break with it during the 1937 elections. Sayeed notes that, for a time, 'middle-class, English-educated Muslims and Hindus' were able to cooperate effectively with each other, as they did during the negotiations over the Lucknow Pact.[1] However, this cooperation broke down when the struggle for power intensified after the passing of the Government of India Act of 1935, which opened the provincial governments to control by Indians.[2] The Congress was unable or unwilling in U.P. to accommodate both the 'nationalist' Muslims in its own ranks and the Muslim aristocrats and lawyers whose political bases lay in the Muslim constituencies. The memoirs of both Maulana Azad and Chaudhury Khaliquzzaman suggest that it was competition for political power, as much as communal issues, which led to the final break between the Congress and the Muslim League over the composition of the provincial government in U.P. in 1937.[3]

In 1937, the Muslim leadership was divided between the National Agriculturalist Party (NAP), a party of landlords, and the Muslim League, which combined the landlords and the Muslim professional classes. The final breakdown between the Hindu and Muslim middle-class leaders in the competition for political power in 1937, combined with the split between the Hindu and Muslim landlords in the NAP, polarized U.P. politics between Hindus and Muslims on a wholly communal basis, eliminating previous elements of class cooperation. It was this alliance of the two leading elite groups among Muslims in U.P. which swept the Muslim constituencies in the 1946 elections (see below).

Sayeed's data on the membership of the Muslim League Council in 1942 reveal that, after the landlords, Muslim lawyers constituted the second largest group, comprising 145 out of 503 members, compared to 163 landlords.[4] The significance of this alliance between landlords and lawyers for understanding the bases of Muslim separatism lies in the fact that these were the classes who were the most modern, the most secular, and the most oriented to political

[1] Sayeed, *The Political System of Pakistan*, p. 22.
[2] *Ibid.*, p. 31.
[3] These points are discussed in detail below.
[4] Sayeed, *The Political System of Pakistan*, p. 55.

power among the Muslim leadership. It was these classes who stood to benefit most from separate electorates and from weightage in representation and government service. The bases of Muslim League leadership in U.P. and elsewhere lay not among the religious elites, but among the political elites, with the landlords bent upon maintaining aristocratic privilege and upper middle-class Muslim lawyers competing for political power with the Hindu leadership of the Congress.

Ulama

The main opposition to the Pakistan demand and to the Muslim League among Muslims came from that segment of the Muslim elite most concerned with the protection of Islam and Muslim culture, from the ulama. The ulama differed from the two other leading segments of the Muslim elite in class background, in religious and cultural orientation, and in numbers. Those ulama who were not simply sons of ulama tended to come from a petit-bourgeois background. They operated in an environment far removed from that in which the great Muslim landlords and lawyers lived and worked – in the villages and small towns, in the Muslim elementary schools teaching through the vernacular, and among the lower middle class of a pre-industrial society, printers, lithographers, booksellers, teachers, retail shopkeepers, skilled craftsmen and petty *zamindars*.[1] Their religious orientation tended towards traditionalism and revivalism, rather than rationalism and modernism. Through their leading madrasahs in U.P., especially in Deoband, they opposed the modernist tendencies of the Aligarh school. Their primary religio-political concern was to protect the *shari'a* from the attacks of secularists, whether they were Hindus or Muslims, and they found little comfort in the secularist program of the Muslim League under Jinnah. Culturally, they were oriented toward traditional education through the medium of Urdu, rather than toward modern education through the medium of English. Politically, they operated through two organizations, the Jamiyyat-ul-Ulama, founded in 1919, and the Jamaat-e-Islami, founded in 1941.

Some scholars have found it curious that the Pakistan demand, which was ostensibly based on an appeal to the religious sentiment of Muslims, found so little favor among the religious elite, and have wondered how the demand could have prevailed against their oppo-

[1] P. Hardy, *The Muslims of British India* (Cambridge: University Press, 1972), p. 169.

sition. Two explanations have been offered. One is that the ulama were themselves divided and that some ulama and some League politicians masquerading as ulama supported the Muslim League through a directly religious appeal to the masses in 1946.[1] The second explanation is that the Muslim masses, with whom the ulama had their greatest appeal, were simply not part of the enfranchised electorate before independence.[2] Both explanations are probably partly correct, but both tend to overemphasize the actual and potential influence of the ulama. For one thing, there does not seem to be any *prima facie* reason for believing that the religious appeal of the ulama was capable of transcending and surpassing the economic and political influence of the Muslim landlords in relation to rural Muslims, the Muslim lawyers in relation to their clients, or the Muslim politicians in relation to their followers. Moreover, the number of ulama was small, smaller in fact than the number of their rivals for leadership of the Muslim community among the aristocratic and professional classes. In 1921, there were only 10,647 Muslims in U.P. who made their living by religion, compared to 11,404 Muslims dependent on the law, 20,096 working in medicine, 17,642 in instruction, and 30,176 in other professional occupations.[3] Table 3.7 also shows that the landowning and government employee segments of the economy had larger numbers of Muslims by far than there were ulama. Even if one assumes, as is probably not the case, that a single *alim* could mobilize a larger segment of the Muslim population than a single landlord or lawyer, there simply were not enough ulama available to compete politically with the more modern segments of the Muslim elite.

There is a final consideration which helps to explain the inability of the ulama to compete with the Muslim League, namely, that their program was an archaic one, which lacked appeal to the modernizing Muslim elites. The program of the ulama envisioned that the Muslims in an independent India would constitute an internally autonomous community – governed by the *shari'a*, guided by the ulama, and 'headed by an Amir-i Hind'.[4] Although the demands of the League and the Jamiyyat on specific questions of Muslim rights and representation were often similar, there was a basic incompatibility

[1] Sayeed, *The Political System of Pakistan*, p. 52.
[2] Faruqi, *The Deoband School*, p. 96.
[3] The source for these figures is the same as for the figures in table 3.7, but they differ from the figures in the table because they include both the professional classes proper and others employed in related occupations.
[4] Peter Hardy, *Partners in Freedom – and True Muslims: The Political Thought of Some Muslim Scholars in British India (1912–1946)* (Lund: Studentlitteratur, 1971), p. 32.

in their goals. The League leaders were oriented towards achieving secular political power in a modern constitutional-bureaucratic state structure, in which the *shari'a* would be respected but would not prevent legislatures from acting in a sovereign manner and in which secular political leaders would be dominant in a representative regime. In both their goals and their political skills, the Muslim League leaders were more oriented towards and ultimately more successful in the secular political arena in which the political choices had to be made.

POLITICAL DIFFERENTIATION: THE ALIGARH MOVEMENT
AND THE MUSLIM LEAGUE

The Aligarh movement

Despite the overwhelming evidence to the contrary, which was readily available at the time, the myth was promoted in the late nineteenth century and has continued to exist in contemporary polemical and scholarly literature that 'Sayed Ahmad Khan, the father of the Muslim people in India, rescued them from ignorance, lethargy and hopelessness'[1] through the founding of the Muhammadan Anglo-Oriental College in 1877 and the Aligarh movement. The Aligarh movement has so far been seen by most politicians and scholars as a movement which led the Muslims of India out of their educational and political backwardness and united the Muslims of the entire subcontinent into a cohesive community and ultimately into a political nation. In fact, it is now beginning to become clear that the Muslims of India outside Bengal were not in most respects more backward than the Hindus, that the Muslims of U.P. were relatively a more advanced community than the Hindus, and that the Aligarh movement, out of which the Muslim League and Muslim separatist ideology developed, was a movement of the Muslim aristocracy of the U.P. and was oriented towards maintaining the political predominance of that Muslim aristocracy.

It has already been noted that U.P. Muslims held nearly half of the senior government posts in the province and nearly half of the senior government posts held by Muslims in British India in 1886–1887. M. S. Jain has shown, citing government documents of the period, that, in 1871 and in 1884–5, 'Muslims took advantage of the educational facilities in a much greater measure than what would be

---

[1] Khaliquzzaman, *Pathway to Pakistan*, p. 109.

justifiable [*sic*] on the basis of population'[1] and that they were heavily over-represented in private and secondary schools.[2] At the university stage, Muslims were not over-represented in U.P. in 1884–1885, but they did constitute 12.5% of the combined Hindu and Muslim enrollment.[3] Even before the founding of the Muhammadan Anglo-Oriental College, Muslims were not seriously under-represented in the colleges of the North-Western Provinces. In 1869–70, 169 of the 1,423 students in colleges in the North-Western Provinces were Muslims.[4] Nor did the Muhammadan Anglo-Oriental College in its early period make the greatest contribution to the university education of Muslims in the province. In the period 1882–1902, 'the M.A.O. College produced only 220 Muslim graduates', whereas the Allahabad University produced 410.[5]

It is nevertheless true that the Muslims even in north India were not taking advantage of university education to the extent that Hindus of the time were doing and that the Muslim weight in public life would be reduced in time if this state of affairs continued. Syed Ahmad Khan believed that the failure of the Muslims to take advantage of university education to a greater extent was because religious education was not provided in the government institutions. Consequently, Syed Ahmad hit upon the plan of founding a college which would provide both a Western education and instruction in Islamic religion. To this end, the Muhammadan Anglo-Oriental College was founded in 1877. M. S. Jain has argued that the college, in addition to its stated aims of combining Western and Islamic education, had three other educational objectives from the beginning. First, the high tuition fees and the residential character of the university both ensured that it would provide education primarily for the aristocratic and upper classes of Muslims. Second the education given at Aligarh was designed to create 'a feeling of Muslim solidarity' and to 'train a class of future leaders of the Muhammadan community'. Third, the education at Aligarh, in which British educators participated prominently, was meant also to develop cordial relations between Muslims and the British people in India to overcome the distrust which the British were supposed to have nourished against the Muslims since the mutiny.[6]

In all respects, the Aligarh movement succeeded in its aims. The

---

[1] Jain, *The Aligarh Movement*, p. 31, fn. 1.
[2] *Ibid.*, p. 41.
[3] *Ibid.*
[4] *Correspondence on the Subject of the Education of the Muhammadan Community*, p. 191.
[5] Jain, *The Aligarh Movement*, p. 71.
[6] *Ibid.*, ch. 4.

College (and the University which it became in 1920) was funded and run by the Muslim Nawabs of north India and it was to Aligarh that the Nawabs and Muslim zamindars sent their children.[1] The graduates of Aligarh became the leaders of an increasingly cohesive Muslim community and they increasingly supported a separatist ideology.[2] How important Aligarh was from this point of view is evident from the list of graduates, among whom were numerous presidents of the Muslim League, the Ali brothers, and two prime ministers of Pakistan. While it is also true that Aligarh produced men like Rafi Ahmad Kidwai, Zakir Husain, and others who became prominent anti-separatist Congress leaders, Aligarh influenced many of its graduates in the direction of a belief in the importance of Muslim solidarity. Although Jinnah was not himself a graduate, he left a sum of money in his will for the Aligarh University.[3] Finally, the third subsidiary objective of the Aligarh movement, of fostering better relations between Muslims and the English in India, bore fruit in government patronage for the University and its leaders,[4] but more important in British acquiescence in the major political demands of the Aligarh movement.

The Aligarh movement had a political orientation from the beginning, which expressed itself in two ways. First, its leaders favored working with the British authorities in India to win government patronage and concessions for the university and for Muslims rather than joining forces with the Indian National Congress in loyal opposition to the government. Second, it favored separate Muslim organizations to work for Muslim causes and political rights. In 1886, Syed Ahmad founded the Muhammadan Educational Conference in order to promote more broadly the educational objectives of the Aligarh movement.[5] However, the Conference also took up political issues such as the defence of Urdu and later became the Muslim counterpart of the Indian National Congress, holding annual conferences in different cities on the subcontinent.[6] In 1893, a more

---

[1] Khaliquzzaman, *Pathway to Pakistan*, ch. 3.
[2] The *Pakistan Freedom Movement* gives pride of place to both Syed Ahmad Khan, who 'laid the foundations' of the structure completed by Jinnah and to the Aligarh College, which became 'much more than a seat of learning, . . . the centre of the political, cultural and literary life of the Indian Muslims', retaining this position until partition and producing 'leaders who contributed to the strength and progress of the community'; citations from vol. II, pt. II, pp. 478, 491.
[3] Hector Bolitho, *Jinnah: Creator of Pakistan* (London: John Murray, 1954), p. 43.
[4] Jain, *The Aligarh Movement*, ch. 10.
[5] *Ibid.*, ch. 6; *Pakistan Freedom Movement*, vol. II, pt. II, pp. 499ff.
[6] During the time of Syed Ahmad's leadership, from 1886 to 1896, the Conference met ten times, only once outside U.P. During the next ten years, under Mohsin-ul-Mulk's leadership, the conference met five times outside U.P. – in Lahore, Calcutta, Madras,

directly political association called the Muhammadan Anglo-
Oriental Defence Association was formed in Aligarh at the annual
session of the Conference.[1] At the 1906 session of the Conference at
Dacca, the Muslim League itself was formed.[2]

Throughout this period, Aligarh was the center of Muslim educational and political activity and the leaders of the Aligarh institution
were leaders in Muslim political activities. Nawab Mohsin-ul-Mulk,
Syed Ahmad's successor as secretary of the Aligarh institution, also
took over the leadership of the Muhammadan Education Conference
after Syed Ahmad's death.[3] It was Nawab Mohsin-ul-Mulk also who
led the opposition in U.P. to the MacDonnell circular of 1900, which
gave Hindi equal status with Urdu as a court and official language
of the province.[4] And it was Mohsin-ul-Mulk who prepared the
famous 1906 representation of the Muslim League, which won the
right of separate electorates for Muslims under the Morley–Minto
reforms.[5] Mohsin-ul-Mulk's close colleague and the driving force in
the founding of the Muslim League was Nawab Viqar-ul-Mulk, who
succeeded Mohsin-ul-Mulk as secretary of the Aligarh institution.[6]
Moreover, Aligarh itself was the early seat of most meetings of the
early Muslim organizations, and was the headquarters of the Muslim
League until 1910.

M. S. Jain and others have traced the origins of the two-nation
theory to Syed Ahmad and the Aligarh movement.[7] Although
there are grounds for disputing this argument concerning the origins
of the two-nation theory as such, there is no doubt that the early
political demands and the justification for them first articulated by
the Aligarh movement in the 1890s reappeared persistently in the
Muslim League representation of 1906, in a representation of the
Muslims of U.P. to the Simon Commission in 1928, and in Jinnah's
fourteen points. The Muhammadan Anglo-Oriental Defence Association at Aligarh was the first Muslim political organization to put
forth the demands which became the hallmark of Muslim politics in
India henceforth, namely, separate electorates for Muslims and

Bombay, and Dacca in 1906 when the Muslim League was founded. *Pakistan Freedom Movement*, vol. II, pt. II, p. 542.
[1] Jain, *The Aligarh Movement*, p. 125.
[2] Khaliquzzaman, *Pathway to Pakistan*, p. 12.
[3] Jain, *The Aligarh Movement*, p. 78.
[4] *Ibid.*, p. 66; Faruqi, *The Deoband School*, p. 47.
[5] Khaliquzzaman, *Pathway to Pakistan*, pp. 11–12; *Pakistan Freedom Movement*, vol. II, pt. II, p. 543.
[6] Khaliquzzaman, *Pathway to Pakistan*, p. 12; Jain, *The Aligarh Movement*, pp. 146–51.
[7] Jain, *The Aligarh Movement*, pp. 140ff.; *Pakistan Freedom Movement*, vol. II, pt. II, pp. 521, 523, 531–2.

weightage for Muslims in any representative system, justified in terms of the past historical and political importance of Muslims in India rather than in terms of their numbers. These demands were first articulated in 1896 through the *MAO College Magazine*[1] and they remained the bedrock of Muslim politics in north India from that time forward.

The political strategy of a privileged elite: Muslim politics and the growth of the Muslim League in the United Provinces

It is no doubt true, as Wilfred Cantwell Smith has pointed out, that the Muslim League in the end succeeded in winning the support of 'the bulk of the middle classes', as well as the lower middle classes, in U.P. as elsewhere.[2] However, Muslim separatism in U.P. was, in origin, the ideology of an upper class and upper middle class elite attempting to preserve its privileged position in society through political means.[3] The leadership of the movement remained in the hands of the landlords and the lawyer-politicians until the end. The ideology of the movement, not so much anti-secular as anti-democratic, reflected its class leadership. Its consistent political purpose was to prevent the introduction into India of a representative system based on Western democratic principles of territorial representation and one man–one vote in which the Muslims as a community and the Muslim elites as a class would be an ineffective minority. In the pursuit of this purpose, the Muslim political leaders of U.P. and the other minority provinces adopted a notably consistent political strategy, which they succeeded in imposing on the rest of the country, sometimes to the detriment of the interests of the Muslims in the majority provinces.

Muslim political leaders in U.P., from the nineteenth century up to the Lahore resolution ('Pakistan resolution') of 1940, adopted two broad kinds of measures in U.P. to preserve the privileged status of the Muslim minority – measures to enhance the effectiveness of the Muslim minority and measures to decrease the effectiveness of the Hindu majority. To justify their demands, which will be noted presently, Muslim politicians in U.P. used two mutually contradictory arguments. One was that the Muslims were backward in education and in economic condition compared to the Hindus, who were seen as determined to capitalize on their advantage by

---

[1] Jain, *The Aligarh Movement*, pp. 128–9.
[2] Smith, *Modern Islam in India*, pp. 257 and 269ff.
[3] Cf. Smith, *Modern Islam in India*, pp. 246–69.

establishing their political dominance and 'crushing the minority community'.[1] From this point of view, special political rights for Muslims were needed to defend a weak and impoverished minority from a ruthless and bigoted majority.[2] The other argument, which more accurately reflected the objective condition of the Muslim elites and their ideology, was that the Muslims were historically and currently more important and influential in the social and economic life of the province and that rights should be granted to them on this basis rather than according to their numbers:

The Mohammedans form only 14.28 p.c. of the population of these Provinces, but it cannot be denied that they have played a glorious part for centuries past in the material, social and cultural progress of these Provinces. A major portion of these Provinces is considered to be the heart of the Muslims of India. They were the rulers and the landed magnates of the country in the last century, and they still hold a prominent place in these Provinces. Their civic rights should be judged more on these considerations than on their numerical strength.[3]

The two arguments were used alternately, depending on their suitability to the purpose at hand, in justifying measures to increase Muslim minority effectiveness and decrease Hindu majority effectiveness. In the first category of measures may be included efforts to promote Muslim solidarity generally, through such institutions as the Muhammadan Anglo-Oriental College and through such symbols as the defense of Urdu. Specific political demands which grew out of this strategy were those for separate electorates (which made possible the effective political organization of a scattered Muslim minority in U.P.), for weightage in all forms of representation in politics and administration, and for a veto to political representatives of the Muslim community over legislation affecting the interests of Muslims.

In the second category of measures to decrease Hindu effectiveness were efforts to split the Hindu community into caste Hindus and depressed classes. In U.P. the class orientation of the Muslim elites prevented Muslim political leaders from seriously attempting to join forces politically with the middle and lower Hindu castes. Instead, Muslim leaders demanded that caste Hindus should not benefit from the numbers of the depressed Hindu groups in the representative system, but that those groups should either be given separate electorates also, or, failing separate electorates, the representation to which the Hindu depressed classes would be entitled by their numbers should be divided equally between caste Hindus and Muslims until such time as the Hindu depressed classes were capable of effectively represent-

[1] *Representation of the Muslims of United Provinces*, pp. 2 and 6.
[2] *Ibid.*, p. 58.   [3] *Ibid.*, p. 55.

ing themselves.[1] The second major tactic adopted by Muslim leaders to decrease Hindu effectiveness was to oppose measures of democratization. Syed Ahmad Khan warned the Muslims against accepting the Western representative system in India, by which they would be reduced to a permanent minority. Muhammad Ali, who saw the Muslim community in the 1920s as 'small in numbers, ignorant, and poor', noted that Muslims found it painful to learn that, in a representative system, 'wisdom consisted in lung-power multiplied by the millions and political strength lay in the counting of heads'.[2] And, in 1928, Muslim political leaders in U.P. praised the extension of local self-government powers to the towns, where Muslims were concentrated and given weightage, but regretted the extension of similar powers to the district boards, where the principle of weightage could not overcome the overwhelming Hindu preponderance in the rural areas. The Muslims argued that 'the District Boards Act was precipitate; it conferred power on an ignorant and illiterate peasantry, and this power was, and has been utilised, by members of the majority community for the organisation and consolidation of their party, community, or caste, in the rural areas'.[3] In this way, the Muslim aristocracy who would naturally be opposed to representative democracy by their class interests alone could use an elitist argument to stir in the minds of the Muslim masses a fear of permanent backwardness and a permanent minority status under a representative system inevitably dominated by Hindus.

The explanation offered above for the leading role of the U.P. Muslims in the development of Muslim separatism in India seems reasonable until 1940. Until that time, Muslim separatism was a movement for minority privileges within India. U.P. Muslims took the lead because they were already a privileged minority and were determined to maintain their privileges. Moreover, until 1936, their strategy was eminently successful in U.P. Separate electorates were conceded in 1909 with respect to provincial and central legislative bodies. They were extended to municipalities and district boards in U.P. in 1916 and 1922 respectively. Under the terms of the Lucknow Pact between the Congress and the Muslim League in 1916,

---

[1] *Ibid.*, p. 8: 'The depressed classes both touchable and non-touchable who outnumber in these provinces the Hindus proper as well as the Moslems will take [a] long time to come on a par either with the Hindus or the Moslems . . . It will be impolitic to let the caste Hindus alone monopolize the advantages that should have gone to the depressed classes had they been in a position to take advantage of the reformed constitution. In fairness to the Moslem, these advantages should be apportioned equally between the caste Hindu and the Moslem.'

[2] Cited in de Bary, *Sources of Indian Tradition*, p. 775.

[3] *Representation of the Muslims of United Provinces*, p. 28.

Muslim representation in the U.P. legislative council was fixed at 30%. The Communal Award of 1932 provided for Muslim representation of 28.9% (66 out of 228 seats) in the U.P. Legislative Assembly. The available figures on the political representation of the Muslims in elected local self-governing bodies in U.P. in the 1920s show that the Muslims were over-represented in these bodies as well. In 1923, 25.2% and in 1925–6, 33.7% of the elected members of the forty-eight district boards in U.P. were Muslims. In March 1928, the U.P. government revealed that 66 out of 240 members of Notified Area Committees (small town governments), or 27.5%, and 391 out of 935 members of municipal boards, or 41.8%, were Muslims.[1] Most important, until 1936, the great Muslim zamindars and talukdars, such as the Nawab of Chhatari and the Raja of Salempur, among others, were trusted allies and advisors of the British governors in U.P. and were ministers in the provincial government.[2]

After 1936, however, with the election of a Congress majority in the U.P. Legislative Assembly and the installation of a Congress government, the privileged position of the Muslim elites in the province was seriously threatened. Within a few years of this great change in provincial politics, the strategy of Muslim political leaders in the U.P. Muslim League had changed from demanding minority rights only to demanding in addition a separate sovereign homeland for Muslims in areas where Muslims were a majority. How the Muslim League leaders in north India could have arrived at such a position has been a vexing historical question.

Several published and unpublished papers by Peter Reeves on the politics of the period between 1937 and 1946 in U.P. suggest that the explanation lies in the struggle for political power between three sets of political leaders in the province at the time – the alliance between the Hindu Congress leaders with the Jamiyyat-ul-Ulama, the lawyer-landlord combination in the Muslim League, and the Hindu and Muslim landlord combination in the National Agriculturalist Party (NAP).[3] At the time when the reforms under the Government of India Act came into force and preparations began for the 1937 elections in U.P., there existed neither a communal polarization between Hindus and Muslims nor any significant political solidarity

[1] Calculated from *ibid.*, apps. A, B, C.
[2] Khaliquzzaman, *Pathway to Pakistan*, p. 155.
[3] I am greatly indebted to Peter Reeves for making available to me an unpublished paper, '"Class or the Communal Platform": Muslim Political Strategy in the United Provinces, 1936'. The account in the next few pages is based heavily on this and two other published papers of Reeves, cited below. However, Reeves is not responsible for the interpretation I have given to the events described below.

in the Muslim community. The Muslim League had been practically a defunct organization in the province since the 1920s.[1] The three major elite groups in the Muslim community were internally divided. The political ulama in 1937 were not at first entirely committed to alliance with the Congress. The most prominent Muslim lawyer politician of the province, Chaudhury Khaliquzzaman, had been an active member of the Congress since the Khilafat movement. The Muslim aristocracy was torn between its communal interests, represented by the Muslim League, and its class interests, represented by the NAP.

It was only after, and as a result of, a complicated struggle for power both among the competing Muslim elites, on the one side, and between the Muslim leadership which emerged the strongest and the Congress, on the other side, that a nearly complete communal polarization and the mobilization of the Muslim electorate behind a single set of leaders emerged to contest the 1946 elections and sweep the Muslim constituencies for the Muslim League.

In 1936, efforts to reorganize the Muslim League to fight the elections of the following year were complicated by a struggle for leadership between Chaudhury Khaliquzzaman and the Oudh Muslim talukdars, on one side, and the Nawab of Chhatari, backed by the Agra Muslim zamindars, on the other side.[2] In this struggle, which centered around the composition of the Muslim League provincial parliamentary board, the Khaliquzzaman–Oudh talukdar faction prevailed, with the backing of Jinnah. The consequence was that the two competing sets of leaders split in the election of 1937, fighting the elections and each other in the constituencies, through both the Muslim League and the NAP.

In contrast to the divisions within the Muslim leadership, relations between the League and Congress leadership were relatively cordial. Although the League fought the elections separately from the Congress, there was an informal electoral understanding between the two organizations. At any rate, the Congress did not contest against the League candidates in the Muslim constituencies, except in one case, and the League refrained from opposing the important Congress Muslim leader, Rafi Ahmad Kidwai. Both the League and the Congress did contest against the NAP candidates, however, in a complementary pattern.[3] The ulama in this election worked for both League and Congress candidates.[4]

---

[1] Khaliquzzaman, *Pathway to Pakistan*, p. 137.
[2] Reeves, '"Class or the Communal Platform"'.
[3] Reeves, 'Changing Patterns', pp. 111–42.
[4] Khaliquzzaman, *Pathway to Pakistan*, pp. 142, 152.

For its part, the NAP coalition of Hindu and Muslim landlords, though it was the third major organized force in the 1937 elections, had begun to divide on communal lines even before those elections. The great Oudh Muslim talukdars, the Rajas of Mahmudabad and Salempur, opted for the Muslim League in 1937. The Nawab of Chhatari, defeated in the struggle for power in the Muslim League, remained in the NAP, but found himself locked in a struggle for leadership there also with a Hindu industrialist, leading the Hindu talukdars.[1] This struggle led to the defeat of Chhatari in this arena also and to the defection of some of the Hindu talukdars to form a separate Hindu landlord organization. Within the NAP, the contest for leadership polarized the Hindu and Muslim landlords on a clear communal basis. Nevertheless, the NAP, divided though it was, entered the 1937 elections with a slate of candidates drawn from both the Hindu and Muslim landlord classes.

In the 1937 elections, the Congress swept the general seats, winning 125 out of 134, won also nine special constituencies, but carried only one out of the twelve Muslim constituencies which it contested.[2] Thus the Congress emerged clearly as the only significant force in the Hindu constituencies, but was unable to gather any significant support even in the few Muslim constituencies where the party chose to contest. In the Muslim constituencies, no such solidary pattern emerged. However, the results were significant from the point of view of the League, which carried the largest bloc of seats, twenty-nine out of the thirty-nine seats it contested, demonstrating its superior organizational strength against the NAP, which won only ten seats out of twenty-one contested. The remainder of the seats in the Muslim constituencies went to independent candidates.

In general, it can be said that the seeds of a communal political polarization in the province were laid before and during the 1937 elections in the pattern of Congress strength, in the communal conflict within the NAP, and in the emergence of the Muslim League as the strongest organized force in the Muslim constituencies; but communal political polarization did not in fact occur during those elections and did not have to follow from them. The decisive change came after the elections in the formation of the provincial governments in U.P. and in the five other provinces where the Congress emerged from the elections with a majority. It was politics and the

[1] P. D. Reeves, 'Landlords and Party Politics in the United Provinces, 1934–7', in D. A. Low (ed.), *Soundings in Modern South Asian History* (Berkeley: University of California Press, 1968), pp. 272ff.
[2] Reeves, 'Changing Patterns'.

competition for political power which ultimately led to the complete communal split in the province and the country and which made it possible for the Muslim League to mobilize the Muslim electorate in the 1946 elections as effectively as the Congress had done in the general constituencies in 1937.

Four great changes in political alignments occurred in U.P. in the period between 1937 and 1946, which produced the total communal polarization of 1946. The first, and the most important, was the failure of Congress and League leaders to reach agreement on a Congress–League coalition government for the province. The details of the negotiations have been provided in the autobiographies of Maulana Azad and Chaudhury Khaliquzzaman, which differ on some points of interpretation, but which together provide a reasonably clear understanding of the reasons for the failure of the negotiations.[1] The Congress, safely in power with a clear majority of seats in the assembly, was under no political compulsion to reach agreement with the League. Moreover, the Congress leaders were determined to demonstrate the secular character of the party by including in their ministry the Muslim Congressman, Rafi Ahmad Kidwai, and a defector from the Muslim League, Hafiz Mohammad Ibrahim. By including Hafiz Mohammad Ibrahim, the Congress demonstrated that it believed it could outmanoeuver the League politically and, incidentally, established in its first period in power the principle of political defection as a means of undercutting the political support of its opponents. Finally, the Congress insisted as a condition for coalition with the League upon terms which were organizationally unacceptable to it, namely, disbandment and complete merger into the Congress. The League, for its part, attempted to negotiate with the Congress as the representative of the entire Muslim community, rather than as a party which had won twenty-nine seats, and demanded that the principle of weightage be observed so that one-third of the members of the cabinet would be nominated by the League. Given the insistence of the Congress upon negotiating from strength and the refusal of the League leaders to negotiate by recognizing their political weakness, it is hardly surprising that the negotiations failed and the League decided to sit in opposition.

The second change in political alignments at this time was the transfer of allegiance of the political ulama overwhelmingly to the Congress. Again, the evidence suggests that politics, as much as religion, were decisive in the shift of the ulama. The ulama,

[1] Maulana Abul Kalam Azad, *India Wins Freedom: An Autobiographical Narrative* (Bombay: Orient Longmans, 1959), pp. 160–2, and Khaliquzzaman, *Pathway to Pakistan*, ch. 17.

175

dissatisfied with the dominance of the lawyer-landlord leadership of the League and with the Congress–League negotiations in which they had no importance, allowed themselves to be persuaded by one of their own, Maulana Azad, and resigned in a body from the Muslim League Parliamentary Board in May 1937 to join forces with the Congress.[1]

The Congress thus demonstrated great political skill, but little foresight, in so undercutting the political support of the Muslim League in the province. With the breakdown of negotiations between the Congress and the League by this process came the third great change in political patterns, namely, the decision of the two organizations to compete with each other directly for the support of the Muslim masses. The Congress, imbued with the spirit of Jawaharlal Nehru's belief that the economic problems of the Muslim masses were more important to them than communal issues and that the Congress could appeal to them on such a basis, and reinforced by the support of the majority of the ulama, launched a Muslim mass contact campaign. The League, for its part, determined to organize itself more effectively and went to the masses with an increasingly strident communal appeal, charging the Congress governments of U.P. and other provinces with numerous atrocities against Muslims, Islam, and Urdu and with imposing a Hindu Raj upon the country.[2] The Congress drive for power in all the provinces of British India brought the Muslim leaders of different parties from the different provinces increasingly to work in concert and increasingly under the direction of Jinnah. The Muslim League in U.P., defeated in the struggle for power in the province, looked to the Muslims of Punjab and Bengal for support. At the 1937 session of the Muslim League, held in Lucknow, the agreement of the Punjab Unionist party to work in concert with the League in that province, and of Fazlul Haq to do the same in Bengal, gave the League leaders in U.P. the necessary impetus to continue their struggle.[3] In turn, the U.P. leaders at Lahore in 1940 supported the Pakistan resolution. Although some expressed concern over the prospects for the Muslim minorities in U.P. after partition, Khaliquzzaman himself gave this question only secondary attention.[4] After 1940, and in the elections of 1946, the

[1] Khaliquzzaman, *Pathway to Pakistan*, pp. 155–8.
[2] The charges, elaborated in the famous Pirpur and Shareef reports, and the replies to them by the Congress governments, are discussed in R. Coupland, *Indian Politics, 1936–1942* (London: Oxford University Press, 1943), pp. 184–94.
[3] Khaliquzzaman, *Pathway to Pakistan*, p. 171.
[4] Khaliquzzaman apparently had no hesitation in supporting wholeheartedly the Pakistan resolution. In fact, he claims credit for the whole idea. However, he notes the fears of

provincial League organizations in the minority provinces were committed to partition.

The fourth great change in political alignments in U.P. was the disintegration of the NAP and the absorption by the League in the 1946 elections of seven of the 1937 NAP candidates, six of whom had been successful in that election.[1] In addition, the League absorbed ten other independent candidates who had contested in 1937. In this way, the fragmentation of Muslim leadership in the Muslim constituencies which had been so marked in 1937 was appreciably reduced and the stage was set for a direct confrontation between the Muslim League and the Congress–ulama combination.

The character and the results of the 1946 elections were entirely different from 1937. The Congress and its nationalist Muslim allies challenged the Muslim League directly, contesting fifty-seven of the sixty-six Muslim seats. The political ulama, who had worked for both the Congress and the League in 1937, worked predominantly with the Congress in 1946. The Muslim landlords, who had been divided between the League and the NAP in 1937, were now overwhelmingly with the League. Moreover, most interest in this election turned on the Muslim seats, for competition against the Congress declined significantly in 1946 in the general seats and the Congress, therefore, was assured of overwhelming success once again in its own domain. Despite the continued division among the Muslim elite groups, with the ulama arraigned against the League, the result of the election was a total communal political polarization. The League contested sixty-three seats and won fifty-three, polling 71.34% of the vote in urban constituencies and 62.39% in rural. The Nationalist Muslims contested twenty-nine seats, but won only six, with 11.45 and 14.23% of the votes respectively in urban and rural seats. The Congress failed utterly in the Muslim seats, winning only three out of twenty-eight contested and only 0.75% of the votes in urban and 18.90% of the votes in rural seats.

The League success in U.P. in 1946 was mirrored throughout the country in majority and minority provinces alike. In all provinces, the League won 425 out of 492 Muslim seats. In the other great northern Muslim minority province of Bihar, the League won thirty-

the Nawab of Chhatari, among others, about the absence of 'sufficient safeguards for the minority provinces Muslims' (p. 235). One simple piece of information of the greatest importance, which I have not been able to find, is the method of voting for the Lahore resolution. All accounts I have seen simply note that it was 'passed'. Was it passed by voice vote or by a count, recorded by the names of delegates? If so, how did the U.P. and Bihar delegates vote?

[1] Reeves, 'Changing Patterns'.

four out of forty seats. The stage was now set for the partition of the country.

The partition of India in 1947, which the Muslims of U.P. and Bihar had brought about as much as any other Muslims by their votes for the Muslim League in 1946, was a catastrophe for them. The grievances, real or alleged, which had been enumerated in such detail in the 1928 U.P. Muslim representation to the Simon Commission and the atrocities alleged in the famous Pirpur and Shareef reports prepared by committees of the Muslim League in 1938 and 1939 referred to the specific problems of the Muslim minorities in the minority provinces, none of which could be resolved through Pakistan. Moreover, the Muslim minorities no longer could depend upon the support of the great Muslim populations of the Punjab and Bengal. Instead of belonging to a Muslim nation 100 million strong, they found themselves reduced to provincial minorities in a predominantly Hindu country in which all provinces but one were also predominantly Hindu. Nor were their demands in any way satisfied by the partition. Instead, separate electorates were abolished, no provisions were made in independent India for special representation for Muslims in services and education, and Hindi in Devanagari script was declared the official language of the Union and of the north Indian provinces. Finally, their most prominent leaders deserted them for Pakistan.

CONCLUSION

The course of Muslim separatism in north India suggests the importance of four factors in determining the success of a nationalist movement – the ability of a people to draw upon cultural and historical symbols to create a myth and to cultivate a sense of grievance capable of appealing to the sentiments of the entire community; the importance of a socially mobilized population to whom the sense of communal identification can be communicated; the existence of one or more elite groups in positions of economic and political power willing to take the lead in promoting communal identity; and the need for political organization. The history of Muslim separatism in the U.P. suggests several additional conclusions. The first is that the objective differences between Muslims and Hindus and the objective circumstances of the Muslims in the north were less important in creating Muslim solidarity than the subjective process of symbol manipulation and myth creation. It cannot be denied that Islam and Hinduism constitute wholly different religious systems at the elite level.

However, it was only through the social mobilization of the Muslim population that these differences could be communicated and stressed to the mass of Muslims, whose religious practices and language did not differ as significantly from the mass of Hindus as did the religious practices and language of the elite Muslim groups from the Hindu.

The second conclusion is that, from the point of view of social science, what stands out in the history of Muslim separatism is not the ineluctable movement of events on an historically predetermined course, but the process of conscious choice by which men decide, because it suits their interests to do so, to emphasize the differences, rather than the similarities between peoples. It was in the interests of the Muslim elites, in order to preserve their special privileges in the north, to argue that Muslims had a different history from Hindus both before and during British rule and that the Muslims were backward compared to the Hindus and needed special protection. It also served the interests of the Muslim elites occasionally to use a different and somewhat contradictory argument which stressed that not their numbers, but both their historical and contemporary political and economic importance, should be considered in schemes of political and administrative representation. It served the interests (as well as the sentiments) of the Muslim elites to defend the continued use of Persianized Urdu in the courts, offices, and schools of the northern provinces, because it was through Persianized Urdu that the Muslim elites maintained their dominance and limited the access of others to positions of dominance in the ruling institutions of the provinces. For all these reasons, among others, it served the interests of the Muslim elites in the Aligarh movement to advise Muslims to cooperate with the British rather than the Hindus, whose own interests, as Syed Ahmad Khan well foresaw, would inevitably be in conflict with those of the dominant Muslim elites.

The third conclusion which should be stressed is that, although there was considerable internal differentiation among the Muslim elites (as well as between elite and mass), which expressed itself in a competition for leadership within the Muslim community and in political differentiation among the elite groups, the three major Muslim elite groups did not differ significantly in their determination to defend and protect the separate rights and interests of the Muslim community. The lawyer-politicians and landlords in the Muslim community competed with each other for political leadership both within and between the Muslim League and the NAP, but they did not differ on the need for separate electorates and weightage for Muslims (among other Muslim interests). The ulama, who did adopt a

different ideological position from the Muslim League, did not oppose Pakistan because they differed with the lawyer-politicians and
landlords on the need to protect Muslim interests, but because they
could not find in the League and in the Pakistan idea an appropriate
leadership position for themselves as the true protectors of Islam and
the *shari'a*.

Finally, the importance of politics and political choice as an independent variable must be stressed. If history does not exclusively
determine the relations between peoples, neither is it inevitable that
objectively different peoples must choose to separate when they
reach a certain stage of social mobilization. There must be, ultimately, political organization – and not only political organization,
but political polarization. In the north, the Muslims, however
emotionally united at the elite levels, were politically divided and
without strong and united political leadership or organization in the
period between the 1920s and the 1937 elections. It was the antici-
pation of increased political opportunities under the 1935 reforms
which restimulated political organization among Muslims and the
revival of the Muslim League. Nor were the choices available to the
Muslim elites confined only to separate political organization. Some
worked in the Muslim League, others in the NAP, others with the
Congress. Communal political polarization occurred only in 1946
after a political struggle for leadership within the Muslim community
and for political power with the Congress. The group which won the
struggle for leadership within the Muslim community lost in the
struggle for political power with the Congress in the 1937 elections
and in the formation of the government afterwards. It then served the
interests of the dominant Muslim political elite in the U.P. to call in
the aid of the Muslims of Punjab and Bengal, to join forces with
them, and to transform the terms of political competition to demonstrate to the Congress that its failure to accommodate the Muslims
on their own terms in positions of political power was a dangerous
course. The Congress and the League attempted to bargain for
power with each other in 1937, but the Congress chose instead the
methods of political manoeuver and of undercutting the support of
the Muslim League. The League leaders, outmanoeuvered in political tactics by the Congress, then changed their strategy and concentrated on political mobilization of the Muslim community around
the symbols of Muslim identification – Islam, Urdu, and the new
slogan of Pakistan.

The new League strategy was overwhelmingly successful in terms
of political mobilization, but promised no success in the relevant

political arenas in the northern Muslim minority provinces. The League leaders who won this massive Pyrrhic victory for the Muslim community moved to the new political arena in Pakistan, some of them to achieve positions of political power which they could not dream of in U.P. or Bihar. Their followers and the Muslim community in general found themselves after independence operating in a new political structure and in a new political game with different rules, which are the subject of the next chapter.

4

URDU AND MUSLIM GRIEVANCES
IN NORTH INDIA, 1947–71

In the post-independence period, the condition of the Muslims in north India and the nature of Muslim demands underwent a profound change. The condition of the Muslims changed radically in two respects – in politics and political leadership and in their objective circumstances as a minority community. In 1946, Muslim League leaders of the north, including such prominent personalities as Chaudhury Khaliquzzaman and the Nawabzada Liaquat Ali Khan in U.P., mobilized the Muslims of north India behind the Pakistan demand and succeeded in demonstrating their overwhelming hold on the enfranchised Muslim electorate. After independence, Liaquat Ali Khan became the first prime minister of Pakistan, Chaudhury Khaliquzzaman found himself torn between the protection of Indian Muslims and his loyalty to the new Pakistan state and also left India,[1] and many other prominent Muslim League leaders of north India did the same. The Muslim League, deprived of its leadership; of its mechanism of demonstrating its hold over Muslims, with the abolition of separate electorates; and of the powerful support of the Muslim zamindars and talukdars, with the abolition of zamindari in 1951, disappeared from the north Indian political scene. The Congress, which had always had the support of a few 'nationalist' Muslim leaders in the north and of the Jamiyyat-ul-Ulama, renewed its pledges of secularism and protection of minority rights and provided a haven for Muslim politicians and the Muslim electorate for the next two decades.

Although the Congress, therefore, became the primary vehicle for Muslim political aspirations in the post-independence period, Muslims in the Congress have had neither the power nor the will to prevent a deterioration in the objective circumstances of the Muslim minority. Muslims lost their position as a privileged minority in the representative system, their economic influence and their political opportunities in government service declined precipitately, their language and culture were in danger of being absorbed by the dominant Hindi language and Hindu culture of the north, and recurring

---

[1] Chaudhury Khaliquzzaman, *Pathway to Pakistan* (Lahore: Longmans, 1961), pp. 410–13.

communal riots in the cities and towns of north India threatened the lives and property of the urban Muslim middle and lower classes.

Moreover, the political context and the rules of the political game changed. The Muslim minority became a minority nearly everywhere in independent India, without the support of the great Muslim populations of the Punjab and Bengal, and certain kinds of demands were no longer acceptable. Muslim leaders could still legitimately demand proper representation for Muslims in politics and government service, but not weightage and separate electorates. They could make linguistic demands, but the informal rules of post-independence Indian political behavior prohibited the association of linguistic with religious or communal demands. Finally, Muslim political leaders who wished to demand protection for Muslim minority rights were now on the defensive, forced to defend not only their rights but their loyalties, which were called into question by Hindu communalist leaders whenever Muslim demands became assertive.

Consequently, in the post-independence period, the nature of Muslim demands also underwent a considerable change. In the pre-independence period, the basic demands were political ones, justified in terms of the historical importance of the Muslim community in India and the separateness of their religion and culture. In the post-independence period, the basic initial demands have been cultural ones, particularly the demand for the preservation and protection of Urdu, and politics have been used as the means rather than the end. Only in recent years has a Muslim political organization re-emerged in the north with an inclusive list of political demands.

This chapter will be concerned with describing Muslim grievances in the post-independence period and with analyzing the changes which have taken place in the position of Muslims in Uttar Pradesh and Bihar. The following chapter will describe the attempts of Muslim political leaders to re-enter the political arena directly and to bargain for their rights in the political and electoral process.

URDU AND GOVERNMENT LANGUAGE POLICIES

The status of Urdu

In his discussion of the radically changed position of Muslims in post-independence India, Wilfred Cantwell Smith observed in 1956 that the Muslim 'community is in danger of being deprived of its language, than which only religious faith is a deeper possession. Nine years of gradual adjustment in other fields have brought no improvement in this, and little prospect of improvement.'[1] Smith's observation echoes the fears of Muslim leaders in north India, who have charged that Urdu, once the dominant language of the north, is being displaced and eliminated in Uttar Pradesh and Bihar as a language of education and administration. The Urdu issue has been the most persistent and the most clearly and consistently articulated issue concerning Muslims in north India during the past two decades. In recent years, the demand to declare Urdu the second official language of the states of Uttar Pradesh and Bihar has become a bitter and divisive issue in the politics of the two north Indian states. This section will examine the relationship of the Urdu language to the Muslim community in the north, its status, and government policies with regard to Urdu in the post-independence period.

The Urdu language and Muslim cultural identity

In the case of no other language in India is there such a mixture of fact and fancy as surrounds the simple description of the nature and characteristics of the Urdu language and the Urdu speech-community. All the languages of the north have had to struggle against the attempts of Hindi supporters to absorb them and declare them as mere forms of Hindi. The efforts of the leaders of both the Punjabi and Maithili language movements have been oriented toward demonstrating that their languages are separate and distinct from Hindi. The issues between Urdu and Hindi, however, are further complicated by the fact that the two languages are, at the spoken level, and in grammatic structure, essentially identical. They diverge at the literary level and in speech among the educated elite in vocabulary and in the script. Consequently, there is some ambivalence among the leaders of the Urdu movement about the proper approach to be adopted to preserve and develop the Urdu language. In order to preserve the separate identity of Urdu, it is necessary to stress its unique characteristics. In order more effectively to advance its claims and to keep the Hindi–Urdu dispute separate from Hindu–Muslim communalism, it is desirable to claim the maximum number of Urdu-speakers and to suggest that Urdu is the spoken language of both Hindus and Muslims throughout north India. In its most extreme form, the latter assertion directly challenges the claim of Hindi to be the predominant language of north India, for, it is argued, the real language of the people of the north is Urdu.[2]

---

[1] Wilfred Cantwell Smith, *Islam in Modern History* (New York: New American Library, 1959), p. 267.

[2] 'The honest truth is that a majority of the people of the Punjab, Delhi and Uttar

It was pointed out in the previous chapter that the objective similarities between Hindi and Urdu have been overshadowed during the past century by the subjective attachments of Muslims to Urdu and Hindus to Hindi as the languages of their respective communities. If this separation could be accepted and conceded by both sides, the controversy might be confronted directly and an accommodation might be reached. There are two major obstacles to such an accommodation. One is the informal rule of Indian politics, discussed earlier, which prohibits the association of religious with linguistic demands. The second obstacle is the fact that Hindi in the Devanagari script and Urdu in the Persian script are in direct competition for the capturing of the unmobilized and still illiterate Muslim masses, whom the state governments in Bihar and Uttar Pradesh wish to bring into the Hindi fold, and whom the Muslim leaders of north India wish to bring into the Urdu fold and, thereby to bring more firmly into an identification with the separate cultural identity of Muslims.[1] Herein lies the essence of the competition between Hindi and Urdu, in its most fundamental aspect a conflict between the leadership of the dominant Hindu majority of north India and the leadership of the Muslim minority over the terms on which the Muslims of the north will participate in the public life of their provinces.

The consequence of the objectively close identity between spoken Hindi and Urdu, on the one hand, and the vital importance of cultural differences between Hindi and Urdu in the consciousness of the Hindu and Muslim elites is that this conflict, which plays upon the deepest religious emotions of the people of north India, has both a superficial and a deeply serious aspect. Superficially, the conflict between Hindi and Urdu frequently appears as nothing more than a technical dispute over which script to use for the same language. Thus, Acharya Kripalani, the chairman of the Uttar Pradesh Language Committee, whose charge it was to report on the status of

Pradesh, and a large population of Bihar have Urdu as their mother-tongue'; *Two Words with Well-Wishers of Urdu*, pt. II (Patna: Bihar State Anjuman Taraqqi Urdu, n.d.), translated from Urdu.

[1] The conflict is almost never stated openly in this way. Dr A. J. Faridi, however, goes to the heart of the matter in his proscribed pamphlet, *Tashkent Declaration and the Problem of Indo-Pak Minorities* (Lucknow, 1966), where he argues that India is a multi-national state, that the Muslims are a national minority in India, and that Urdu is the religious and cultural language of Indian Muslims. One may or may not accept this view in its entirety, but there is no doubt that Dr Faridi is not alone among Indian Muslims in this view and that his statement that 'the new generation, i.e., Muslim children below the age of 20 years, hardly know any Urdu' is an expression of fear widely shared among Muslim leaders that they may lose the allegiance of the new generations to the Muslim community. Citation from p. 32.

Urdu in Uttar Pradesh, expressed the pious thought that 'if the contending [Hindi and Urdu] parties could reconcile themselves to the use of one script, it would be a very great advantage'.[1] How far this hope is from the reality of Muslim attachment to the Persian script and the reasons for this attachment are revealed in the following quotation:

In the same way in which an army, before starting on its march, fires some bombs and, behind the dust raised thereby, collects material for the destruction of the enemy, in the same way Urdu . . . was deceived by being told that even though Urdu was accepted as a language, the Urdu people were asked to write Urdu in the Devanagari script. This was the iron claw with the help of which it was planned to send Urdu to eternal sleep by piercing it in the back. But, even this sleeping pill [*sic*] was not swallowed by the Urdu people. They maintained that behind a language and its script, there was always a chain of traditions and a culture of its own and, when any language or script was attacked, it could not help affecting adversely the civilization and culture behind it.[2]

In the eyes of the more militant Hindu supporters of Hindi as the sole official language of India and the north Indian states, this attachment of Muslims to Urdu and its script is an attachment to a 'foreign' script and an alien culture by a communal minority whose loyalties to India are suspect.[3] Urdu supporters deny this charge and argue that Urdu is as indigenous as Hindi itself, that it was born in India and is understood throughout the subcontinent. Moreover, it is argued that Urdu is not the language of Muslims only, but of Hindus and Muslims alike, and that it reflects a heritage 'of brotherhood between the two big communities of the country'. From this point of view, to oppose Urdu is to oppose 'Hindu–Muslim unity' and to go 'against the people of the past generations, who made efforts to develop a composite Hindu–Muslim culture'.[4]

[1] *Report of the Uttar Pradesh Language Committee* (Lucknow: Superintendent, Printing and Stationery, 1963), p. 7. Hereafter referred to as the *Kripalani Committee Report*.

[2] *Two Words from Well-Wishers of Urdu*, translated from Urdu. Of course, the attachment to the Nagari script is equally profound and has the same basis for Hindus. S. K. Chatterji has pointed out that the first society established to spread Hindi in north India was called the Nagari Pracharini Sabha (Society for the Propagation of the Nagari Script) because 'the Hindi thought-leaders in Northern India realised the importance of the Nagari script for the maintenance or preservation of Hindu culture'; *Indo-Aryan and Hindi*, 2nd ed. (Calcutta: Firma K. S. Mukhopadhyay, 1960), p. 241.

[3] See the report in the *National Herald*, 2 July 1961, of the debate in the U.P. Assembly on a Jan Sangh-sponsored resolution to censure the U.P. government for appointing the U.P. Language Committee.

[4] *Presidential Address by Mr Shiva Prasad Sinha, Senior Advocate, Supreme Court, Delhi, at the Bihar Urdu Convention, held at Patna, on 10 and 11 September 1966* (translated from Urdu); for similar statements on Urdu as an expression of a composite culture and a link between Hindus and Muslims, see the remarks of Maulana Sayed Fakhruddin, president of the Jamiyyat-ul-Ulama Hind as reported in the *Leader*, 11 December 1960, and the report on the memorandum submitted to the Uttar Pradesh chief minister by the

The official position of the state governments and of the Uttar Pradesh Language Committee has tended to fall between these two views. During the period of Congress rule in the 1950s and 1960s, it was the official view that Urdu was not a foreign language, and it was 'wrong to suppose that the Urdu script had come from abroad and is not indigenous', and that it was dangerous for Hindu–Muslim unity and self-defeating for Muslims to identify the Urdu language as 'the language of a particular minority community or religious group'.[1] This view has much truth in it and, in part, represents an attempt to prevent the Hindi–Urdu controversy from reviving Hindu–Muslim antagonism. In fact, however, the conflict cannot be properly understood unless it is recognized that while Urdu 'is spoken by tens of millions of Non-Muslims, . . . it is a special heritage of the Indian Muslims' and that 'the religious literature as well as the cultural achievements of Indian Muslims are mostly in Urdu'.[2] In other words, it is not Hindu–Muslim unity which is threatened by the decline of Urdu, but the cultural vitality and sense of identity of the Muslim community, which the Muslim elites of north India wish to preserve and strengthen.[3] That sense of a separate identity

Anjuman Taraqqi Urdu in the *Statesman*, 19 August 1961; also the *Manifesto on the Position of Urdu in India* (New Delhi, 1966), p. 1.

[1] *Kripalani Committee Report*, p. 7; in a more ominous vein, Dr Sampurnanand warned in 1961 in connection with the appointment of the Kripalani Committee that 'unless steps are taken to set right in the very beginning the mischief created by the unfortunate use of the term linguistic minority language in connection with Urdu, we may plunge the state into serious trouble', *National Herald*, 21 July 1961. See also the editorial in the Bihar paper, *Searchlight*, 11 September 1961.

[2] Faridi, *Tashkent Declaration and the Problem of Indo-Pak Minorities*, p. 32; see also p. 52. (This pamphlet, which contains even stronger stuff from the point of view of Indian nationalists, has been proscribed in India.) In contrast to Dr Faridi's point about the connection between Urdu and Muslim culture, there is the flat statement of Dr Sampurnanand that 'Urdu is not the language of people professing a common religion or inheriting a culture different from that of the majority in which they live', *National Herald*, 21 July 1961; see also the report in the *National Herald*, 5 August 1961, of the debate in the U.P. Assembly on a Jan Sangh-sponsored resolution to censure the U.P. government for appointing the U.P. Language Committee and the statement of chief minister C. B. Gupta in the *Statesman*, 19 August 1961, in which he is reported as deprecating 'the widespread tendency to regard Urdu as the language of a particular religious minority'. This tendency is also usually deprecated by Urdu supporters, despite Dr Faridi's outspoken statement; see *Manifesto on the Position of Urdu in India*, p. 3.

[3] This feeling is not confined only to upper-class Muslims and those who share the ideology of the Jamaat-i-Islami. A leader of the Muslim weavers in Bihar made the following remarks relating Urdu to Muslims and to Islam: 'Non-acceptance of this [Urdu] language will be entirely ruinous and disastrous for Muslims in coming generation and they may not be able to follow their own religion. And, therefore, establishment of this language is essential for the Muslims of India . . . I feel that majority people are denying to give privilege to Urdu due to jealousy, hatred, and bringing the Muslims in such condition that they may be converted to other religion. This is my personal view'; interview document L5:12 (untaped interview).

derives not from the spoken Urdu of everyday speech, which is the same as the spoken Hindi or Hindustani, but from the more Persianized Urdu written in the Persian script and frequently deriving its literary symbols and forms of cultural expression from Islamic ideology and history.[1]

In short, the demand for the preservation of Urdu is a demand for the preservation and extension of the language and culture of the Muslims of north India. Urdu supporters have chosen to de-emphasize this underlying basis for their demands and to stress instead the cosmopolitan character of Urdu and its supposed contributions to Hindu–Muslim unity. This approach has three self-defeating elements in it, however. It goes against the historical tendency in north India towards divergence between the two languages, Hindi and Urdu. It does not unequivocally identify the linguistic minority whose interests are sought to be protected, leaving it open to governments to deny that Urdu is the language of any well-defined group in the population. Finally, it poses a direct challenge to the dominance of Sanskritized Hindi in the north, by claiming to be the true *lingua franca* of the north.

An alternative strategy for Urdu supporters, which more accurately reflects contemporary objective circumstances, has been suggested by Gopal Mittal, the Hindu editor of a Delhi Urdu newspaper, who argues that, while Hindus may not be generally hostile to Urdu, they have 'no special stake in its preservation'. The necessary enthusiasm to preserve Urdu can be provided only by the Muslims 'because, more than any other language, Urdu expresses their peculiar genius and is a symbol of their culture'. Consequently, Gopal Mittal argues, Hindus should be asked to extend their support to Urdu 'as the language of the Muslim community' and Muslims should demand protection for Urdu, not because of its contribution to 'secularism or composite culture', but because it is a 'fundamental right' in the Constitution of India.[2] The difficulty with this proposal and the dilemma of Muslims who would follow it is the refusal of either the Government of India or the state governments to entertain any proposals which associate both religion and language in a direct manner.

Urdu and the census

As was the case in the Maithili movement, leaders of the Urdu move-

---

[1] See Chatterji, *Indo-Aryan and Hindi*, pp. 162, 208–10, 218, 220, 243.
[2] The article by Gopal Mittal appears in *Radiance*, 8 January 1967. Article 29 of the Constitution of India says: 'Any section of the citizens residing in the territory of India or any part thereof having a distinct language, script or culture of its own shall have the right to conserve the same.'

ment charge that the census figures do not accurately reflect the numbers of Urdu-speakers in U.P. and Bihar. The *Manifesto on the Position of Urdu in India* claims 'that even in census operations efforts were made [after Independence] to minimise as much as possible the numbers of those who claimed Urdu as their mother tongue, thus artificially bringing down the importance and status of Urdu'.[1] Dr A. J. Faridi, president of the U.P. Muslim Majlis-e-Mushawarat, has been more blunt. He has charged that the 1961 'census [in U.P.] was absolutely incorrect, absolutely bogus'. His belief that the 1961 census of Urdu-speakers is 'bogus' is based on the notion that all Muslims and many millions of Hindus speak Urdu, but that the census recorded approximately two million fewer Urdu-speakers than Muslims in Uttar Pradesh.[2] In response to such charges and doubts concerning the accuracy of the census returns for Urdu, the 1961 census superintendent for Uttar Pradesh remarked that the belief that there should be at least as many Urdu-speakers as there are Muslims arises from the 'fallacy' of 'confusing language with religion and presupposing that the language of Hindus is Hindi, of Muslims Urdu, and of Christians English. If this were so, there would be no point in enumerating language separately from religion.' Rather, he said that the ordinary people of Uttar Pradesh spoke 'the common local dialects irrespective of the religion they profess'. The census enumerators, moreover, had 'done their job in the best possible manner with a high degree of impartiality'.[3] This question of the reliability of the census is a matter of the utmost importance to the leaders of the Urdu movement, because decisions made by the U.P. and Bihar governments on the facilities to be provided for Urdu-speakers in education and administration are frequently based on the census figures and opponents of Urdu and government policy-makers frequently refer to the small percentages of Urdu-speakers in the two states as justification for providing fewer facilities than Urdu supporters demand.[4]

[1] *Manifesto on the Position of Urdu in India,* p. 2.
[2] Interview document L1: 19. Similar charges have been made specifically about the 1951 Bihar census, in *Two Words with Well-Wishers of Urdu,* which claims that 'due to the mischief and dishonesty of the Census enumerators, the number of the Urdu people was deliberately reduced' (translated from Urdu).
[3] *Census of India, 1961,* vol. xv: *Uttar Pradesh,* pt. 1-A (ii), by P. P. Bhatnagar (Delhi: Manager of Publications, 1967), p. 83.
[4] For example, the Jan Sangh leader, Yadavendra Dutt Dube, has remarked that according to the 1951 census figures, only 6% of the people of the state spoke Urdu and that it would be an injustice to impose the language of such a small minority on the people of the state for any official purposes. *National Herald,* 5 August 1961. *The Kripalani Committee Report* itself accepted the 1951 figures without comment, at p. 20.

In fact, however, no census of Hindi- and Urdu-speakers in either Uttar Pradesh or Bihar has ever in any way accurately reflected the number and relative proportion of Hindi- or Urdu-speakers, partly because the tasks set by the census directors have been impractical and self-contradictory and partly because the census operations have not since 1891 been free from political considerations and pressures (see tables 4.1 and 4.2). It has been suggested in chapter 2, and it is confirmed by the history of the Hindi–Urdu controversy recorded in the decennial reports of the census directors, that the language censuses in north India are political, not philological, documents.

TABLE 4.1 *Hindustani, Hindi and Urdu in Uttar Pradesh, 1881–1961*[a]

	1961[b]	1951[c]	1941[d]	1931[e]	1921[f]	1911[g]	1901[h]	1891[i]	1881[j]
	%	%	%	%	%	%	%	%	%
Hindustani	00.1	10.67	N.A.	99.68	99.75	..	..	98.01	98.08
Hindi	85.39	79.82	N.A.	..	..	91.16	89.36	..	..
Urdu	10.70	6.80	N.A.	..	..	8.53	10.36	..	..
Muslim	14.63	14.28	15.43	14.98	14.46	14.38	14.38	13.82	13.74

[a] Bases of enumeration from 1881 to 1961 varied as follows: 1881: 'mother-tongue'; 1891: 'parent-tongue'; 1901: 'language ordinarily used'; 1911: 'language ordinarily spoken in the household'; 1921: 'language ordinarily used'; 1931–61: 'mother-tongue'.

[b] Sri Bhatnagar remarks in the 1961 report volume that the instructions to the enumerators have remained the same since 1941, namely, 'to record the mother-tongue as returned without any attempt to impose a formula for recording the language of the State as a whole or any parts thereof'. He also noted that, in several districts, 'a sustained propaganda was made exhorting a section of the population to return its mother-tongue as Urdu . . . Some complaints to the effect that Urdu was not being recorded as mother-tongue were forwarded by the Anjuman Taraqqi-e-Urdu. They were investigated and the fears turned out to be unfounded.' *Census of India, 1961*, vol. xv, pt. I–A (ii), pp. 82–3.

[c] The report volume notes: 'The name of the mother-tongue was to be recorded *as given out by the respondents*. [Italics in original.] Thus the citizen was free to give out the name of his mother-tongue as Hindi or Urdu or Hindustani and the enumerator had to record it as such in the census slip . . . The Hindi–Urdu–Hindustani controversy . . . was not allowed to raise its head in this census. The citizen was free to describe his mother tongue by any means he pleased and the enumerator was bound to record it in the census slip. The instructions were thoroughly understood at this census and the statistics may be taken as presenting an accurate account of the language distribution of the state.' *Census of India, 1951*, vol. II, pt. I–A, pp. 412–3.

[d] No language returns in 1941.

[e] The instructions to enumerators were: 'Enter the ordinary language of the province as Hindustani. Do not write "Urdu" or "Hindi".' The report notes: 'At this census . . . no attempt was made . . . to distinguish between Urdu and Hindi because the information so collected would be of no material use, and secondly in order to avoid a revival of the former bitter controversy referred to by Mr Blunt in the 1911 report.' *Census of India, 1931, United Provinces of Agra and Oudh*, vol. XVIII, pt. I, pp. 485–8.

f Mr Edye, the census superintendent, notes in the report volume: 'The rules for filling up the language column directed that for people using the ordinary speech of the province "Hindustani" was to be entered.' He also says: 'I made, with the approval of government, no attempt to distinguish between Urdu and Hindi.' *Census of India, 1921,* vol. XVI, pt. I, pp. 129–31.

g Mr Blunt notes in his report: 'The figures relating to language are given in imperial table x, but it is necessary at once to explain that as they stand they are extremely inaccurate. The rule for filling up this column in the schedule laid stress on the points that the language to be entered was that which the person enumerated *himself* [italics in original] returned, and was to be the language he spoke in his own home, i.e., his mother-tongue. The rule was perfectly clear: but for various reasons it was so much more honoured in the breach than the observance, that the figures relating to the provincial vernaculars are totally vitiated. . . .

'. . . The average inhabitant of the United Provinces if asked what his language is will reply either Hindi or Urdu. He may not always clearly comprehend the difference between the two, and his vagueness of thought on the subject is not made any clearer by the fact that as like as not he will speak both at different times. He often has, too, reasons for answering in a particular way that are not linguistic in nature. And as a result, the totals of "Hindi" speakers and of "Urdu" speakers are not necessarily accurate. . .

'. . . it was hopeless to expect a correct return of all Hindi dialects, and it was also certain that the return would as a matter of fact be of Hindi or of Urdu. In such circumstances Hindi was taken to mean all vernaculars which were not Urdu. . .

'In 1901 a controversy had raged over the merits and demerits of Hindi (i.e. High Hindi) and Urdu as languages. The immediate cause was certain orders issued by the government in 1900 directing that court documents might be written in either script . . . There was a good deal of excitement, and it is probable that the figures were to some extent vitiated thereby. At this census the controversy broke out again with far more violence. The cause on this occasion seems to have been a discussion, which aroused a good deal of government attention, about the nature of primary school textbooks . . . As in 1901, the census schedule was dragged into [this controversy], and the question, which was really one of the style of textbooks, was misinterpreted as applying to the spoken language. . . .

'. . . As in 1901, there were undoubtedly steps taken to cause the returns to be falsified: complaints were common that Hindi enumerators were recording Hindi whether the persons enumerated returned Hindi or not, and on the other side that Muhammadan enumerators were acting in the same way with regard to Urdu. I have no doubt whatever that such events did occur . . . As a consequence (of the intense and usually bitter feeling) though the total of one language (Hindi) is not much affected, the total of Urdu is less by one-fifth than in 1901 . . . Simply because they refused to define their terms before they argued, or rather because they would not take the trouble to understand the terms as used by the census authorities, the controversialists, who were really quarrelling about the respective merits of certain styles as vehicles of instruction succeeded in utterly falsifying a set of important statistics related to something entirely different.' *Census of India, 1911,* vol. XV, pt. I, pp. 279–91.

h Burn, apparently less ruffled than Blunt by the Hindi–Urdu controversy, simply noted in 1901: 'There is . . . one great distinction which is universally made, viz. that between Urdu and the variety of language spoken by the mass of the people in each district. At the present census advantage was taken of this distinction, and the instruction directed that Urdu should be separately recorded, and all other indigenous languages and dialects should be shown as Hindi.' *Census of India, 1901,* vol. XVI, pt. I, p. 174.

i Bailie noted in his report that the instructions to enumerators were: 'The languages ordinarily spoken throughout these provinces except in the Himalayan districts will be entered as Hindustani.' He went on to remark: 'The word Hindustani was selected in its widest sense, the language of Hindustan including both the Urdu of the towns and the Hindi of the villages.' *Census of India, 1891,* vol. XVI, pt. I, p. 264.

^j Edmund White noted that the enumerators were told: 'The name to be applied to the common vernacular of these provinces is Hindustani, whatever the dialect be, whether Purbia, Urdu, etc.' *Census of India, 1881, Report on the Census of the North-Western Provinces and Oudh*, p. 88.

SOURCES. Compiled from the following *Census of India* reports: *1961*, vol. XV, *Uttar Pradesh*, pt. II–C (ii), by P. P. Bhatnagar; *1951*, vol. II, *Uttar Pradesh*, pt. I–A, by Rajeshwari Prasad; *1931*, vol. XVIII, *United Provinces of Agra and Oudh*, pt. I, by A. C. Turner; *1921*, vol. XVI, *United Provinces of Agra and Oudh*, pt. I, by E. H. H. Edye; *1911*, vol. XV, *United Provinces of Agra and Oudh*, pt. I, by E. A. H. Blunt; *1901*, vol. XVI, *N.-W. Provinces and Oudh*, pt. I, by R. Burn; *1891*, vol. XVI, *The North-Western Provinces and Oudh*, pt. I, by D. C. Baillie; *1881*, *Report on the Census of the North-western Provinces and Oudh*, by Edmund White.

TABLE 4.2 *Hindustani, Hindi, and Urdu in Bihar, 1881–1961*^a

	1961^b	1951^c	1941^d	1931^e	1921^f	1911^g	1901^h	1891ⁱ	1881^j
	%	%	%	%	%	%	%	%	%
Hindustani	..	..	N.A.	86.73	..	..	..	..	89.49
Hindi	44.30	81.03	N.A.	..	86.22	83.93	88.26	89.13	..
Urdu	9.83	6.82	N.A.	..	0.85	1.15	0.07	..	..
Muslim	12.45	11.58	12.91	12.72	12.25	12.03	12.05	13.33	13.69

^a Bases of enumeration from 1881 to 1961 varied as follows: 1881 and 1891: 'parent-tongue'; 1901: 'language ordinarily used'; 1911 and 1921: 'language ordinarily spoken in the home'; 1931–61: 'mother-tongue'.

^b 1961 instructions to enumerators: 'Write the mother-tongue in full including dialect as returned by the person enumerated.' The low figure for Hindi is because Bihari languages were listed separately in this census. *Census of India, 1916*, vol. IV, pt. II–C, p. 181.

^c Report volume not presently available to the writer.

^d No language returns in 1941.

^e W. G. Lacey reported: 'The term "Hindustani" has been used in the present report to cover both Hindi and Urdu, both western Hindi and Bihari, and no attempt has been made to tabulate separate statistics for the various sub-divisions of these languages ... In previous occasions an effort has indeed been made to distinguish "Hindi" from "Urdu", but the resultant figures are of little value. In 1911, when there was considerable agitation among the Muslim population on the subject, 387,621 persons were returned as speaking Urdu. Ten years later the agitation had died down, and the number dropped to 293,638 ... Very little interest was manifest in the matter at the present census.' *Census of India, 1931*, vol. VII, pt. I, p. 232.

^f No discussion of the Hindi–Urdu controversy was found in the 1921 report, which says only: 'The enumerators were directed to enter the language which each person ordinarily speaks in his own home.' *Census of India, 1921*, vol. VII, pt. I, pp. 207–8.

^g L. S. S. O'Malley noted: 'The Musalmans were strongly adverse to their language being entered as Hindi, and were anxious to have it returned as Urdu. The Hindus were opposed to the entry of Urdu and complaints were received that, in some cases, Hindu supervisors or enumerators changed or tried to change entries of Urdu into Hindi. It was assumed that Hindus must speak Hindi and Musalmans Urdu, though the great majority speak neither one or the other, but Bihari ... The result of the agitation on the subject is that the number of persons recorded as speaking Urdu has jumped up from 89,677 to 542,059.' *Census of India, 1911*, vol. V, pt. I, pp. 382–3. The reason for the discrepancy between the figure 542,059 here and 387,621 noted in n. e for Urdu-speakers in 1911 is not known to the writer.

ʰ E. A. Gait wrote in 1901: 'Excluding the districts dealt with in the Patna Office, where the details were not tabulated separately, Urdu has been returned as the language of 89,677 persons. These figures, however, are worth very little. Urdu or the literary Persianized form of Hindi is spoken by the upper ranks of Muhammadan society and is generally looked on as the proper language for a Muhammadan to speak. In Patna there was a general agitation amongst the Muhammadans to have their language shown as Urdu, and there can be no doubt that it was thus described by many who in reality speak the local form of Bihari.' Bihari, of course, was not listed separately either because, as Gait noted, the Bihari dialects 'are all alike called Hindi' by 'the ordinary native'. *Census of India, 1901*, vol. VI–A, pt. II, pp. 311 and 322.

ⁱ No discussion found relating to the change in classification from Hindustani to Hindi. Possibly the earlier change in Bihar than in U.P. came about because of the earlier development of the Hindi–Urdu controversy in Bihar and the adoption of Hindi as the official court language in 1881. A similar change did not take place in U.P. until 1900.

ʲ The actual listing in the census is 'Hindi, Hindustani, and Urdu', but referred to in discussion as Hindustani. *Report on the Census of Bengal*, vol. I, by J. A. Bourdillon, pp. 148–66.

SOURCES. Language figures from 1961 to 1911 from *Census of India, 1961*, vol. IV, *Bihar*, by S. D. Prasad, pt. II–C, *Social and Cultural Tables*, pp. 199–208; figures for Muslims from 1901 to 1961 from *ibid.*, pt. I–A (i), p. 480; other figures from *Census of India, 1891*, vol. III, *The Lower Provinces of Bengal and Their Feudatories*, by C. J. O'Donnell (Calcutta: Bengal Secretariat Press, 1893), p. 234; *Census of India, 1881, Report on the Census of Bengal*, by J. A. Bourdillon (Calcutta; Bengal Secretariat Press, 1883), vol. I, pp. 75 and 165. Language figures before 1911 and figures for Muslims before 1901 were calculated from relevant census volumes, for all north and south Bihar and all Chota Nagpur, ignoring later boundary adjustments. Hence the figures before and after 1911 for language and 1901 for religion are not strictly comparable.

It has been the stated purpose of the census directors from 1881 to the present to provide an accurate enumeration of the 'mother-tongues' of the provinces of U.P. and Bihar. The precise instructions to the enumerators on how to phrase their questions to respondents have varied somewhat from time to time: from 'mother-tongue' in 1881, to 'parent-tongue' in 1891, to 'language ordinarily used' in 1901 and 1921, to 'language ordinarily spoken in the household' in 1911 and back again to 'mother-tongue' from 1931 to 1961, in the case of U.P. However, the intention has always been to enumerate the languages actually spoken by the people of the two provinces in ordinary discourse as opposed to the literary forms of the languages. This goal has been impractical from the beginning because there has never been a satisfactory definition of the term 'mother-tongue'; because the variety of dialects and languages actually spoken is too great and because, in many areas, they shade off imperceptibly into one another; and because the mass of the people do not know the names given to their mother tongues by philologists. The goal has been contradicted in practice because the enumerators in most censuses before 1951 were instructed to record as mother tongue something different from what they were told by the people.

In 1881 and 1891, enumerators in U.P. were instructed to ask for 'mother-tongue' and 'parent-tongue' respectively, but they were also instructed to record 'Hindustani' for all 'the languages ordinarily spoken throughout these provinces except in the Himalayan districts'.[1] In 1901, however, two major efforts coincided to compound the difficulties of the census directors and enumerators. One was the completion of Grierson's linguistic survey, which revealed the variety of languages and dialects 'ordinarily spoken' in both U.P. and Bihar and identified with greater precision than ever before the areas where these languages and dialects were spoken. The results of Grierson's efforts were taken note of in succeeding census volumes, but no attempts were made to use Grierson's distinctions as a basis for enumeration and recording, although the census directors in some reports did attempt to estimate the proportions of the population who spoke these dialects and languages.

The second difficulty which arose in 1901 was the growth in intensity of the Hindi–Urdu controversy and of sentiment among elite Hindus and Muslims to distinguish between Hindi and Urdu and to have that distinction recorded in the census. Before 1891 in Bihar and before 1901 in U.P., the census directors had chosen to characterize Hindustani as the ordinary spoken language of the north, Hindi as the elite and literary language of Hindus who drew vocabulary from Sanskrit and used the Devanagari script in writing, and Urdu as the elite and literary language of those who drew vocabulary from Persian and used the Persian script in writing. Grierson himself continued to use the three terms in this way,[2] although he identified four major dialects of Hindustani in U.P. and a new language group which he called Bihari in Bihar.

Nevertheless, as a result of the political pressures from both Hindi and Urdu supporters, two changes were made in the 1891 and 1901 censuses in both U.P. and Bihar. First, Hindustani was to be replaced by Hindi (in Bihar in 1891, in U.P. in 1901) as the generic term to be recorded for the languages ordinarily spoken in the two provinces, but second a distinction was to be made for Urdu (in both provinces in 1901), which was to be recorded separately. However, the Hindi–Urdu controversy had by this time become so intense that the census enumerators could not be relied upon to record truthfully the languages reported to them. Possibly for this reason, the census supervisor in Bihar did not tabulate separately the figures for dis-

---

[1] See table 4.1, n. i and j (pp. 191–2, above).
[2] G. A. Grierson, *Linguistic Survey of India*, vol. I, pt. I, *Introductory*, p. 167. See also *Census of India, 1911*, vol. xv, *United Provinces of Agra and Oudh*, pt. I, by A. E. H. Blunt, pp. 279–91.

tricts 'dealt with in the Patna Office' in 1901.[1] The census supervisor in Uttar Pradesh, after noting the difficulties of enumerating Hindi- and Urdu-speakers accurately in both the 1901 and 1911 censuses, remarked: 'It is not too much to say that the [1911] figures as they stand are evidence only of the strength or weakness of the [Hindi–Urdu] agitation in particular districts.'[2] It is a matter for regret that the census authorities in U.P. in 1921 and in Bihar in 1931 reverted to the previous census classification of Hindustani and decided not to attempt to record Hindi and Urdu separately. Even if it is true that the census returns of 1901 and 1911 recorded only the strength or weakness of the language agitations and were subject to false enumeration, they are at least useful as indicators of political and social change. For the sake of 'accuracy', the census authorities returned to a classification which was entirely useless. The result was that, in Uttar Pradesh, the census reported the absurdity that 99.75% and 99.68% of the population in 1921 and 1931 respectively spoke the same mother tongue, arbitrarily defined as Hindustani.

In 1951, the census authorities once again reverted to enumerating and recording Hindi and Urdu separately.[3] In Uttar Pradesh, the consequence of this decision in 1951 was that there was a three-way division in the census returns, with 79.82% reported as returning Hindi, 6.80% returning Urdu, and 10.67% returning Hindustani (table 4.1). If one assumes that, on this occasion, there was no or very little falsification of the returns by the enumerators,[4] these returns would at most reflect accurately the names given to their mother tongues by the people of U.P. and the minimum number of people who are conscious that Urdu is the preferred name for their mother tongue. In 1961, when the instructions to the enumerators were the same as in 1951, the 'Hindustani'-speakers practically disappeared, only 0.1% of the population being so recorded. Clearly, somewhat less than 6% of the 10.67% of 1951 Hindustani-speakers were added to the Hindi column and somewhat less than 4% were added to the Urdu column, reflecting the intensified consciousness produced by the Hindi and Urdu movements in the 1950s.[5]

Given the vagaries of census enumeration and record over the past

[1] *Census of India, 1901*, vol. VI, *Bengal*, pt. I, by E. A. Gait, p. 332.
[2] *Census of India, 1911*, vol. XV, *United Provinces of Agra and Oudh*, pt. I, by E. A. H. Blunt, pp. 285–91.
[3] See table 4.1, n. c (p. 190, above).
[4] Unlike earlier census reports, the 1951 and 1961 reports do not acknowledge any substantial falsification. Charges of falsification, however, have been made, as noted above.
[5] *Census of India, 1961*, vol. XV, *Uttar Pradesh*, pt. I–A (ii), by P. P. Bhatnagar, pp. 83, 90, 92.

80 years, it is risky to attempt to use the census figures for Urdu as an accurate measure of the degree to which the Muslim masses have acquired a consciousness that their mother tongue should be called Urdu. Nevertheless, there are some suggestions that can be made about Urdu-speakers and about Muslim consciousness of Urdu in U.P. and Bihar. First, in no census year in either state has the recorded number of Urdu-speakers equalled the Muslim population. This suggests two conclusions, namely, that it is highly unlikely that many Hindus are giving Urdu as their mother tongue and that, even allowing for some falsification by some Hindu enumerators, the potential underlying population of Urdu-speakers has not yet been fully mobilized to identify with Urdu. Second, in both U.P. and Bihar the percentages of people recorded as Urdu-speakers increased from 1951 to 1961, suggesting at least that political action on behalf of Urdu has reduced falsification and possibly increased Urdu-consciousness among Muslims. Third, at the minimum, more than 70% of the Muslim population in both states now identify with Urdu (assuming that few Hindus declare their mother tongue as Urdu and that Muslim enumerators have not in this census falsified the returns to a greater extent than Hindu enumerators). Fourth, assuming that falsification of the census returns is no greater in the rural areas than in urban areas, Urdu-consciousness among Muslims is much higher in the cities and towns than in the villages. Table 4.3 shows that the

TABLE 4.3   *Ratio of Urdu-speakers to the Muslim populations of Uttar Pradesh and Bihar, 1951 and 1961*

	1961			1951		
	Whole province	Rural	Urban	Whole province	Rural	Urban
Bihar	71.20	69.20	91.76	59.96	N.A.	N.A.
U.P.	73.29	66.40	92.12	47.62	32.79	80.86

SOURCE. Figures computed from *Census of India, 1961*, vol. xv, pt, I–C (iii), pp. 62–3, 64–7; vol. IV, pt. I–C, pp. 594–5, 596–7; and *Census of India, 1951*, vol. VI, pt. I–B, p. 206; vol. II, pt. II–C, pp. 358, 560–2; vol. V, pt. II–A, pp. 285, 310–11.

ratio of Urdu-speakers to Muslims was higher than 90% in the urban areas of both U.P. and Bihar in 1961. Finally, despite objections of leaders of the Urdu movement to the 1961 census, it is clear that the 1961 census has been more favorable to their cause than any previous census. In both U.P. and Bihar, a higher proportion of Urdu-speakers were recorded in 1961 than ever before in the history of the census. This in itself represents a considerable achievement in the history of the Urdu movement and one that, in the context of the high degree of language-consciousness which exists presently in north India, cannot easily be taken away. If the census cannot be taken as an accurate reflection of the spoken mother tongues of the people of north India from a philological point of view, there is good reason to believe that it more than ever before (relatively and increasingly) accurately reflects the state of language consciousness among the speech-communities of north India.

The problem of the status of the Urdu language

The problems of achieving and maintaining an appropriate status for Urdu as a language of literature, education, and administration in north India have been substantially different from those related to the status of either Punjabi or Maithili. All three language groups have had to confront the competing demands of the leaders of the Hindi movement, of the dominant language of the north. The leaders of the Maithili movement have struggled to prevent the complete absorption of their language by Hindi and to achieve recognition for Maithili as a separate and independent language. The leaders of the Punjabi movement went further and demanded successfully the displacement of Hindi from the Punjabi region and its replacement by Punjabi as the language of the people of Punjab for all purposes, except inter-state and inter-governmental communication. Both languages have had to struggle against the pre-existing official dominance of Hindi in their regions. Urdu, in contrast, was not long ago the dominant language of north India and the *lingua franca* of the entire subcontinent. Moreover, the vitality of Urdu as a language of both *belles-lettres* and modern communications surpassed until recently (and even now surpasses in many respects) all other languages of the north, including Hindi. Thus, it has been the Hindi movement which has challenged the dominance of Urdu, rather than the Urdu movement which has challenged Hindi. The struggle for the protection of Urdu, therefore, has been one to prevent the downfall of the Urdu language from dominance to neglect and to preserve for Urdu and for Urdu-speakers at least the rights achieved by all other major modern Indian languages.

In the struggle to preserve Urdu, two major obstacles have stood in the way. One, already discussed above, has been the association of the Hindi–Urdu competition with Hindu–Muslim communal

antagonism and the partition of the subcontinent. The second obstacle, relevant here, is the dispersion of Urdu-speakers throughout
the north and the consequent absence of a large and compact
regional concentration of Urdu speakers. Consequently, Urdu supporters cannot hope to carve out a regional niche or a separate state
for Urdu, but must strive for recognition in areas where Hindi is now
the dominant language and cannot be displaced.[1]

The steps by which Urdu was displaced from dominance as the
official language of north India by both English and Hindi in the
pre-independence period have been discussed in the preceding chapter. In the post-independence period, Hindi acquired the position of
pre-eminence in U.P. and Bihar which Urdu had in the nineteenth
century. Hindi in Devanagari script was adopted as the official
language of India in the Constitution and the official language of
Uttar Pradesh and Bihar in the Bihar Official Language Act, 1950,
and the Uttar Pradesh Official Language Act, 1951. The Uttar
Pradesh and Bihar acts and related administrative orders established
Hindi alone as the official state language, but did not exclude the
continued use of either English or Urdu for certain purposes for
those people who were 'not familiar' with Hindi in the Devanagari
script.[2] Thus, the legal position of Urdu in Uttar Pradesh and Bihar
is that it has no official status in those states, but that Urdu-speakers
are not necessarily to be denied the right to use Urdu for official
purposes. In addition, Urdu does have official status in the eighth
schedule of the Constitution of India as one of the fifteen languages
of the country and, therefore, is entitled to the privileges of a minority
language and the protection of the President of India on the advice
of the Commissioner for Linguistic Minorities. In other words, the
rights and privileges of Urdu are matters for policy decision, administrative implementation, and constitutional interpretation.

During the past two decades, Urdu supporters have claimed that
Urdu has not been given the status due to it according to the Constitution, that government policy and implementation have not
adequately protected the rights of Urdu-speakers, that facilities
enjoyed by Urdu-speakers before independence have been with-

---

[1] In a characteristically ironic way, Dr Faridi, president of the U.P. Muslim Majlis-e-
Mushawarat, remarked on this point 'about Urdu, although it has been recognized as
one of the fourteen national languages, it was not given its proper place because Urdu
is the only language which has no region. Other languages – Bengali has got a region,
Tamil has got a region, Telugu has got a region, Punjabi has got a region, Kannari has
got a region. Urdu, poor thing, has got no region. And it is spoken mostly in the northern
parts of India, which are called Hindi-speaking areas.' Interview, L1:3 (taped).
[2] *Kripalani Committee Report*, p. 51.

drawn since independence by the governments of Uttar Pradesh and Bihar, and that the orders of the U.P. government in particular have virtually 'banished the [Urdu] language from its place of birth'.[1] Specifically, Urdu organizations and their leaders have claimed that the rights of Urdu-speakers to have their children educated through the medium of Urdu at the primary stage, to have facilities for learning Urdu at the secondary and university stages, to present petitions to courts and state offices in Urdu, to have the right to speak in the legislatures and have their speeches recorded in Urdu, and to have all important government notices, laws, publications, and sign boards published in Urdu as well as Hindi[2] have either not been granted at all or have not been granted to the full extent warranted by the desires and numbers of the Urdu-speaking population.

It is the contention of the Bihar Anjuman Taraqqi Urdu that these deficiencies in the facilities provided to Urdu-speakers in Bihar reflect the fact that:

a policy of continued injustice to Urdu has been followed, its rights and interests have been coolly and contemptuously disregarded, impediments have been put in the way of the enforcement of its constitutional rights and no steps have been taken to prevent the precipitate proceedings for wiping out Urdu in all the offices and departments of the Government and other public bodies.[3]

Similarly, Dr A. J. Faridi, commenting on the status of Urdu in U.P., insisted in 1965 that:

The Government is very sweet, eulogises and pays lip service to the beauty and the popularity of Urdu. Even our present Prime Minister, like his predecessor, wants Urdu to be given its due share in all the provinces where it is extensively used. But in spite of assurances, Urdu remains at the same place where it was pushed back 17 years ago.[4]

It has been the argument of the leading Muslim and Urdu organizations of north India for the past two decades that the injustices done to Urdu will not be set right and the assurances given will not be

---

[1] *Times of India*, 30 May 1961. See also *Manifesto on the Position of Urdu in India*, pp. 1–2.

[2] These are the basic, specific demands frequently reiterated on behalf of Urdu in most petitions and memoranda.

[3] *Memorandum* submitted to the chief minister of Bihar by Bihar Urdu deputation on behalf of Bihar Reyasati Anjuman Taraqqui-e-Urdu, Patna, for recognition of Urdu as regional language of Bihar on 14 June 1966 (Patna: Bihar Reyasati Anjuman Taraqqui-e-Urdu, 1966), p. 14. Hereafter referred to as *Bihar Urdu Memorandum, 1966*.

[4] *Presidential Address of Dr A. J. Faridi* delivered at the district conference, Dini Talimi Council, held on 21 March 1965 at Shahjahanpur (pamphlet), p. 8. Some statements in the pro-Urdu press go further. For example, an article (by a Hindu) in *Radiance*, 8 January 1967, states simply that the 'dirty truth is that Urdu language is gradually dying in India'.

fully implemented until Urdu is given official status by presidential order as a regional or second official language in the states of Bihar and Uttar Pradesh. This demand has been pressed over the past two decades through deputations, petitions and memoranda to the state and central governments and to the President of India.[1] During and after the 1967 elections, the demand for recognition of Urdu as the second official language of Uttar Pradesh and Bihar became a major political issue in the politics of the two states. In effect, Urdu supporters have sought to rectify the disadvantages which they face because of the dispersion of Urdu-speakers by having the Hindi states admit Urdu to a position of near-equality as a language of those states.

Urdu and government language policies

Urdu and the Government of India

Central government and all-India policies towards Urdu and other linguistic minorities in India have evolved over the past twenty years through a series of resolutions, memoranda, and statements published by the central government itself or by meetings of central and state ministers, beginning with the Provincial Education Ministers Conference in 1949 and including the most recent meeting of the Committee of Vice-Chairmen of Zonal Councils held in August 1964. The constitutional power to enforce central government and all-India policy decisions on language is divided between the center and the states. Education is primarily a state subject. Article 345 of the Constitution also gives the states the power to adopt whatever language or languages they choose for official purposes within their states. However, state powers with regard to language policies are not unlimited. The Constitution guarantees certain rights to linguistic minorities, which the states are obliged to provide. Article 29 guarantees the right of citizens in any part of India to preserve their 'distinct language, script or culture'. Article 30 guarantees minorities, 'whether based on religion or language . . . the right to establish

---

[1] The history of these deputations and memoranda in U.P. and at the center has been described from press reports by Jyotirindra Das Gupta, *Language Conflict and National Development: Group Politics and National Language Policy in India* (Berkeley: University of California Press, 1970), pp. 142ff., but the Bihar memoranda and deputations are not noted. There were two important memoranda submitted by Bihar Urdu deputations, one to the President of India on 24 February 1956: *Memorandum*, submitted to the President of India by Bihar Urdu Deputation on behalf of Urdu-speaking people of Bihar for recognition of Urdu as regional language of Bihar, on 24 February 1956 (Patna: Ghulam Sarwar, 1956), p. 2, hereafter referred to as *Bihar Urdu Memorandum, 1956*; the other to the chief minister of Bihar, cited on p. 199, n. 3, above.

and administer educational institutions of their choice' and to receive state aid for such institutions without discrimination. Article 350 gives every citizen of India the right to submit representations for redress of grievances to any central or state authority in any language 'used in the Union or in the State'. Article 350A obliges every state and local authority 'to provide adequate facilities for instruction in the mother-tongue at the primary stage of education to children belonging to linguistic minority groups'.

State powers are also limited by three constitutional provisions which permit the President of India to intervene in the formation of state language policy and in its implementation and which provide him with a special officer to report on state language policies directly to him. Article 347 empowers the President if a demand is made to him, to direct a state government to grant official recognition throughout a state or any part of a state for purposes which he may specify to any language spoken by 'a substantial proportion of the population of a State'. Article 350A empowers the President to 'issue such directions to any State as he considers necessary' to ensure adequate facilities to linguistic minorities for instruction in their mother tongue at the primary stage of education. Finally, article 350B establishes a 'Special Officer for linguistic minorities' to be appointed by the President and to report to him on 'all matters relating to the safeguards provided for linguistic minorities' under the Constitution.[1] These reports are then placed before parliament and sent to the state governments.

In the various meetings of state and central ministers and in the policy statements of the central government over the past twenty years, specific all-India policy guidelines have been laid down to ensure the enforcement of the constitutional rights of minorities. The Commissioner for Linguistic Minorities maintains a careful compilation of both the constitutional safeguards and the all-India policy guidelines, which he uses in his annual reports to assess the progress of their implementation in each state of the union.

The Commissioner for Linguistic Minorities is the key to the whole system of safeguards. He not only reports on the progress of implementation in the states, but he receives complaints from linguistic minority interest groups and associations against state government policies. These complaints are then sent to the state governments for comment and reply. The commissioner cannot force a state government which fails to reply or to satisfy legitimate grievances to do so,

---

[1] All citations in the previous two paragraphs were taken verbatim from the relevant articles of *The Constitution of India* (as modified up to 1 April 1966).

but he maintains the record which can then be brought before the parliament, the press of the country, and the president, each of whom may apply different kinds of pressure upon a state government to demand that justice is done. The commissioner also sometimes visits the state capitals and places where grievances have been reported and frequently points out to the state governments where their policies or the implementation of them have not met the minimum agreed safeguards. Finally, the reports of the commissioners provide statistics on primary and secondary enrollment figures of linguistic minority pupils by which the policies of the state governments may be judged and compared.

The Constitution and the all-India policy guidelines which have been established clearly recognize the enormous linguistic diversity of India. The safeguards for linguistic minorities are invariably liberal, if not generous, and they promote a broad policy not simply of toleration for minorities but of protecting and promoting linguistic pluralism. However, this broad policy has been subjected to modifications in practice because many of the states actually promote integration and assimilation of minorities rather than pluralism and because the center has been reluctant to invoke the presidential powers to force such states to implement linguistic minority rights.

These difficulties in implementing all-India policies on language have been particularly evident in the case of Urdu. Deputations of Urdu supporters have from time to time in the past twenty years appealed to the central government to invoke article 347 of the Constitution to protect the rights of Urdu-speakers, especially in the states of U.P. and Bihar, where serious charges of discrimination against the Urdu-speaking minorities have been made and frequently confirmed by the reports of the Commissioner for Linguistic Minorities. In a press note issued on 14 July 1958, the Government of India itself acknowledged that: 'While the policy of Government in regard to various languages and in particular Urdu, has been repeatedly stated and is clear, there appears to be some justification for the complaint that it has not always been fully implemented.' That the Government of India was referring to the policies of the states of U.P., Bihar, and Punjab in particular in this respect is clear from the note. Yet the central government refused to invoke article 347 and instead simply reiterated and listed the facilities which the state governments are constitutionally obliged to provide to Urdu-speakers as a recognized linguistic minority group. Despite recurring complaints by Urdu supporters since 1958 and persistent demands by Urdu interest associations to invoke article 347, the Government of India has never deviated from its policy as stated in the press note of 14 July 1958. Although the Government of India has refused to enforce its policy towards Urdu, that policy is generous and pluralistic in phraseology and intent and provides a standard by which the policies of the U.P. and Bihar governments may be judged. The press note says: 'It is desirable to encourage and facilitate the use of Urdu by those who have been in the habit of using it and those who consider it as their mother-tongue. This would apply especially to Uttar Pradesh and Bihar.' Five specific points were also emphasized in that note:

In areas where the Urdu language is prevalent, the following facilities should be especially provided:

(1) Facilities should be provided for instruction and examination in the Urdu language at the primary stage to all children whose mother-tongue is declared by the parent or guardian to be Urdu.

(2) Arrangements should be made for the training of teachers and for providing suitable text-books in Urdu.

(3) Facilities for instruction in Urdu should also be provided in the secondary stage of education.

(4) Documents in Urdu should be accepted by all courts and offices without the necessity of translation or transliteration in any other language or script, and petitions and representations in Urdu should also be accepted.

(5) Important laws, rules and regulations and notifications should be issued in the Urdu language also in areas where this language is prevalent and which may be specified for this purpose.[1]

Urdu and the Uttar Pradesh government

It is the contention of Urdu supporters that the policy of the Uttar Pradesh government in the post-independence period has been unsympathetic to Urdu and has been leading toward the elimination of the language from the province of its birth.[2] The Uttar Pradesh government has repudiated this accusation and has insisted to the contrary that it has 'throughout been following a policy of sympathetic and liberal attitude towards the minorities and for the development of the Urdu language'.[3] At most, the Uttar Pradesh government has conceded that there have been occasional deficiencies in the implementation of government policies and directives, but it has never accepted the view either that the policies themselves require

[1] *Kripalani Committee Report*, p. 80.
[2] See the *Memorandum Submitted by Dr H. N. Kunzru, President, Anjuman Taraqqi Urdu (Hind) to Shri Lal Bahadur Shastri, Prime Minister of India on 7th April, 1965*, p. 8: 'We have with great regret come to the conclusion that, owing to the present unsympathetic attitude of the State Government of the U.P. towards Urdu and the continued inaction of the Central Government in the matter, this language is being ousted in the U.P.'
[3] *National Herald*, 9 June 1961.

change or that any intervention from the center is necessary to secure the rights of Urdu-speakers.[1] In fact, the stated policy of the U.P. government and the administration of that policy have been consistently marked by three features – minimization of the size and importance of the Urdu-speaking minority, deliberate deviation from the policy guidelines set by Government of India and inter-state committees, and persistent and recurring deficiencies in providing the facilities for Urdu-speakers which the state government itself has conceded in principle. Moreover, in elaborating and implementing its policy towards Urdu, the Uttar Pradesh government has tended to act as if it had a special responsibility to preserve the unity and national integration of the country as a whole and to see to it that no impediments come in the way of Hindi as the official language of the state and the country.

The broad policy of the U.P. government towards Urdu has been based upon a remarkable sophistry. It has been the stated position of the U.P. government and of the U.P. Language Committee that 'a certain percentage of persons' in the state retain Urdu as their mother tongue[2] and that 'Urdu is the language of a minority of people' living in the state, but that the speakers of that language do not constitute either 'a particular minority community or religious group'.[3] In other words, there is an Urdu-speaking minority in Uttar Pradesh, but no Urdu-speaking community. Nor is there any culture particularly associated with the Urdu language.[4]

This statement of the position of Urdu-speakers in Uttar Pradesh goes considerably beyond an attempt to separate the language issue from religion. Rather it reflects a view of the nature of Indian society as not only a 'composite culture', but as essentially a homogeneous culture, in which there may be differences of language or script or religion, but no differences of culture.[5] A language or a script or a religion may be entitled to protection, but no group of people is

[1] Chief minister Gupta justified the appointment of the Kripalani Committee in 1961 and gave it as its charge 'to find out exactly what were the difficulties in implementation of the policies of the Government and to suggest suitable measures for their removal'; *National Herald*, 5 August 1961.

[2] See the statement of chief minister C. B. Gupta in the *National Herald*, 22 July 1961.

[3] *Kripalani Committee Report*, p. 7.

[4] *Ibid.*, p. 6. There is no difference on this point between secularists and believers in the composite culture of India, such as Kripalani and C. B. Gupta, on the one hand, and outspoken Hindu revivalists, such as former chief minister Sampurnanand, on the other hand. Compare the remarks of Dr Sampurnanand: 'Urdu is not the language of [a] people professing a common religion or inheriting a culture different from that of the majority in the midst of which they live' and chief minister Gupta's complete agreement with this statement in the *National Herald*, 22 July 1961.

[5] *Kripalani Committee Report*, p. 6.

entitled to consider itself a minority cultural group and to demand protection for its cultural expressions on behalf of the group. This point of view was made clear in the inaugural address of Acharya Kripalani to the U.P. Language Committee and in the conclusion of the committee's report. The U.P. Language Committee, which was ostensibly appointed to inquire into the grievances of Urdu-speakers in Uttar Pradesh, began its deliberations with an emphasis on the homogeneity of Indian society and culture and concluded by arguing that minorities have no 'special rights of their own' and that Hindi must be developed into 'a fit vehicle' of Indian culture in the interests of 'the unity and integration of the people of the whole country and more particularly in Uttar Pradesh'. Minorities were advised 'to refrain from being cantankerous' and the government was urged not 'to create special vested interests, which may be difficult to dislodge afterwards and which may create discontents, harmful to the country as a whole'.[1] It bears stressing that, although the view that Indian culture is a composite one is common, the view that Indian culture is homogeneous is much less common. Moreover, the attitude of the Kripalani Committee report towards minorities and minority cultures stands in direct contradiction to articles 29 and 30 of the Constitution of India, which expressly concede to minorities the fundamental rights to preserve their distinct languages, scripts, or cultures and to 'establish and administer educational institutions of their choice'. The views of the Kripalani Committee are in no way different from the official views expressed by most government spokesmen in Uttar Pradesh and in official policy statements over the past two decades.[2]

Thus, the underlying basis of government policy towards Urdu in Uttar Pradesh contains three elements which limit the rights of Urdu-speakers in that state. That policy assumes that Uttar Pradesh is a homogeneous society in which demands cannot be made which contradict its homogeneity. Urdu is not to be identified with any

---

[1] *Ibid.*, pp. 68–69.

[2] Acharya Kripalani's views on minorities and national integration were well known before he was appointed to chair the U.P. Language Committee (see J. B. Kripalani, *Minorities in India* (Calcutta: Vigil Office, n.d.); his report nowhere departed significantly from official government policy; and the recommendations of the committee were, therefore, naturally accepted by the government without difficulty. For a criticism of the Kripalani Committee and the government from this point of view, see the *Presidential Address by Mr Shiva Prasad Sinha*, where he says: 'Doubts were created in the minds of people from the very time when this committee was appointed, because the appointment of a person as the chairman of the committee, who had had no connection with Urdu, and who was opposed to the provision of protection to minorities on grounds of national interests, was sufficient for the people to understand the evil intentions of the Government.' Translated from Urdu.

well-defined group in the population, but is to be considered a mother tongue only of 'a certain percentage of persons'.[1] Finally, Urdu will not be permitted to come in the way of the advancement of Hindi and its acceptance as the sole official language of the state.[2]

It is not surprising, therefore, that the specific actions of the Uttar Pradesh government to 'safeguard' Urdu in all relevant policy areas have fallen short of the demands of Urdu supporters and have consistently failed to satisfy the Commissioner for Linguistic Minorities. In the area of primary education, article 350A of the Constitution provides that it is the duty of 'every State and of every local authority within the State to provide adequate facilities for instruction in the mother-tongue at the primary stage of education to children belonging to linguistic minority groups'. It is here that the distinction between a 'linguistic minority group' and 'a certain percentage of persons' becomes significant, for the U.P. government has never conceded that there is a 'linguistic minority group' in the state. Consequently, the U.P. government and its local authorities have placed the burden upon Urdu-speakers of requesting facilities for instruction through the medium of their mother tongue and have placed various obstacles in the way of their doing so. Among the burdens and obstacles repeatedly noted in the reports of the Commissioner for Linguistic Minorities are the following: limiting facilities for Urdu-speakers only to classes where there are ten such students or schools where there are forty Urdu-speaking students; failure to provide such facilities in some schools even where the requisite number of pupils existed; failure to issue orders 'that there will be no reduction of facilities existing earlier for education through the media of minority languages except under specific orders of the State Government and that additional facilities will be provided wherever necessary'; withdrawal of such facilities by the Varanasi municipal authorities and decrease in such facilities in certain districts of the

---

[1] At times, it is implicitly denied in official government documents that Urdu is a language and implied that it is only a script for Hindi, a blatant oversimplification of the differences between Hindi and Urdu. See, e.g., Government of India, Ministry of Home Affairs, *Report of the Commissioner for Linguistic Minorities (Sixth Report)* (Delhi: Manager of Publications, 1965), p. 48. Hereafter referred to as *CLM* VI.

[2] The appointment of the Kripalani Committee in 1961 was greeted with criticism and apprehension on this score by former chief minister Dr Sampurnanand and by the Jan Sangh. Chief minister Gupta, however, hastened to assure the critics on behalf of the state government 'that there is no occasion for entertaining any apprehension . . . that any section of the people of U.P. could claim that this state could be made a bilingual state'. Moreover, he insisted, 'the acceptance of the principle of safeguards for and encouragement to Urdu, should in no way be taken to imply the acceptance of the wholly untenable proposition that Urdu should be equated with the language of the state of Uttar Pradesh'; *National Herald*, 22 July 1961.

state and in the state as a whole; failure to make 'arrangements for advance registration of linguistic minority pupils' in all primary schools in the state; and failure to implement a decision, previously agreed to in discussions with the commissioner, to introduce a mother tongue column in the school admission form.[1] On investigation by the commissioner and by state authorities, some of these burdens and obstacles have from time to time been removed and others have been found not to exist in fact. The report of the Kripalani Committee has especially emphasized this point.[2] On the other hand, many of these impediments have been recurring, most reflect at the least persistent delay, and some reflect misinformation provided by the state government itself.[3] Moreover, the performance of the state government in safeguarding the rights of Urdu-speakers can be assessed by comparing the proportion of Urdu-speakers in Urdu-medium schools and classes to the total primary school enrollment in the state. Table 4.4 demonstrates clearly that, even according to the standards of the 1961 census, the proportion of Urdu-speakers in Urdu-medium classes is far below their proportion in the population of the state as a whole. Although the absolute numbers of students enrolled in Urdu classes at the primary stage more than doubled between 1956–7 and 1963–4, the proportion of students enrolled in Urdu classes has not kept pace with the increase in total primary school enrollment. Moreover, the proportionate Urdu enrollment at the primary stage in Bihar has been much higher than in Uttar Pradesh, even though the Urdu-speaking population is smaller in Bihar (see table 4.5).

In regard to the area of secondary education, the Constitution does not oblige the state governments to provide facilities for minority languages. However, there have been numerous Government of India policy statements and several meetings of the education ministers and chief ministers of the states to evolve policy guidelines for secondary education. The all-India policy on instruction in minority languages at this stage is that facilities should generally be provided for the study of minority languages at the secondary stage where

---

[1] *CLM* v, 12–13; *CLM* vi, 9–10, 135; *CLM* vii, 12–15, 41, 153–4.

[2] *Kripalani Committee Report*, p. 33.

[3] A not untypical example was the information provided to the CLM that there were no Urdu-medium schools in the district of Etah in 1959–60, 1960–1, and 1961–2 when, in fact, there were 13, 13, and 17 such schools in the respective years. The state government informed the CLM 'that a "nil" report was rendered by the local authorities under a wrong impression'; *CLM* vi, 10. One cannot help wondering what sort of 'wrong impression' the local authorities might have had. Similarly, one must wonder at the exclusion by the deputy inspector of schools of Gorakhpur district of 45 Islamia schools and Makhtabs 'inadvertently'; *CLM* vii, 14.

TABLE 4.4 *Facilities for instruction in Urdu at the primary and secondary stages of education in Uttar Pradesh*[a]

Year	Primary stage					Secondary stage				
	Total enroll-ment	Change	Urdu enroll-ment	Change	Percentage of Urdu to total enroll-ment	Total enroll-ment	Change	Urdu enroll-ment	Change	Percentage of Urdu to total enroll-ment
		%		%	%		%		%	%
1955–6	N.A.		73,704			N.A.		5,432		
1956–7	2,915,286		77,827	+5.59	2.67	1,103,254		5,308	−2.28	0.48
1957–8	3,257,050	+11.72	65,324	−16.07	2.01	1,179,937	+6.95	5,393	+1.60	0.46
1958–9	3,523,562	+8.18	55,067	−15.70	1.56	1,286,824	+9.04	5,591	+3.67	0.43
1959–60	3,762,713	+6.79	100,465	+82.44	2.67	1,377,694	+6.91	14,699	+162.90	1.07
1960–1	3,958,828	+5.21	111,779	+11.26	2.82	1,461,904	+6.54	14,827	+1.55	1.01
1961–2	4,723,419	+19.31	121,570	+8.76	2.57	1,622,721	+11.00	20,599	+38.93	1.27
1962–3	5,281,694	+11.82	153,699	+26.40	2.91	1,786,645	+10.10	26,491	+23.69	1.48
1963–4	5,804,526	+9.90	159,794	+3.83	2.75	1,983,807	+11.04	33,227	+25.43	1.67
1964–5	7,915,259	+36.36	182,396	[incomplete]		2,244,500	+13.14	37,682	[incomplete]	
1965–6	N.A.		231,383			N.A.		37,699	[incomplete]	
1966–7	N.A.		225,922	[incomplete]		N.A.		43,248	[incomplete]	

a Figures for instruction in the Urdu language and for instruction through the medium of Urdu, which are listed separately in the *CLM* reports, have been combined in this table.

SOURCES (for both tables 4.4 and 4.5). Government of India, Ministry of Education, *Education in India*, *1957–8*, vol. I, pp. 52, 116, 138; *ibid.*, *1958–9*, vol. I, pp. 52, 113, 132; *ibid.*, *1959–60*, vol. I, pp. 50, 109, 124; *ibid.*, *1960–1*, vol. I, pp. 49, 111, 126; *ibid.*, *1961–2*, vol. I, pp. 51, 120, 139; *ibid.*, *1962–3*, vol. I, pp. 43, 86, 100; *ibid.*, *1963–4*, vol. I, pp. 43, 98, 118; *ibid.*, *1964–5*, vol. I, pp. 46, 96, 124, 126; Government of India, Ministry of Home Affairs, *Report[s] of the Commissioner for Linguistic Minorities* (*CLM*): *CLM* IV, pp. 108–9; *CLM* V, pp. 197–8, 238; *CLM* VI, p. 194; *CLM* VIII, pp. 194, 259, *CLM* IX, pp. 145, 212; *CLM* X, pp. 143, 189; *CLM* XI, pp. 134, 142.

TABLE 4.5 *Facilities for instruction in Urdu at the primary and secondary stages of education in Bihar*[a]

	Primary stage					Secondary stage				
Year	Total enroll-ment	Change	Urdu enroll-ment	Change	Percentage of Urdu to total enrollment	Total enroll-ment	Change	Urdu enroll-ment	Change	Percentage of Urdu to total enrollment
		%		%	%		%		%	%
1955–6	N.A.		130,771			N.A.		28,255		
1956–7	1,653,992		137,773	+5.35	8.34	740,991		30,453	+7.78	4.11
1957–8	1,693,314	+2.38	144,492	+4.88	8.53	797,161	+7.58	31,639	+3.89	3.97
1958–9	2,180,607	+28.78	160,142	+9.77	7.34	1,054,325	+32.26	35,214	+11.30	3.34
1959–60	2,499,591	+14.63	196,296	+22.58	7.85	1,199,974	+13.81	32,159	−8.68	2.68
1960–1	2,711,991	+8.50	216,330	+10.21	7.98	1,335,644	+11.31	37,377	+16.23	2.80
1961–2	2,854,805	+5.27	213,936	[incomplete]		1,476,389	+10.54	39,226	+5.05	2.66
1962–3	2,842,835	−0.42	285,176		10.03	1,667,766	+12.96	41,243	+5.14	2.47
1963–4	3,005,932	+5.74	294,845	+3.39	9.81	1,802,613	+8.09	37,169	−9.88	2.06

[a] Figures for instruction in the Urdu language and for instruction through the medium of Urdu, which are listed separately in the *CLM* reports, have been combined in this table.

SOURCES. The references given in table 4.4 and *Education in India, 1963–4*, vol. I, pp. 42, 97; *CLM* IV, pp. 110, 114; *CLM* V, pp. 199–200; *CLM* VII, p. 197; *CLM* VIII, pp. 196, 260. The Bihar government has not furnished any figures on Urdu enrollments to the *CLM* since 1963–4.

there is a minimum number of students desiring it and that facilities should also be provided for instruction through the medium of minority languages where there is a sufficiently large demand for it.[1] Although these guidelines are not binding on the individual states, it is clear that the Uttar Pradesh government has declined to work even according to their spirit. The state government has categorically refused to provide instruction through the medium of Urdu in secondary schools in the state and it has placed obstacles in the way of those students who wish to study Urdu as an optional language subject.[2] In contradiction both to the all-India policy guidelines on safeguards for minority languages, and to the purpose of the three language formula, the state government has provided for Sanskrit as one of the alternatives in that formula in place of a modern Indian language and has made the choice of the third language dependent on the majority wish of the students. In Uttar Pradesh, the effective choice is between Urdu and Sanskrit, which means that in most secondary schools in Uttar Pradesh, Hindus and Muslims alike are practically required to learn Sanskrit as their third language.[3] Although the figures on enrollment in Urdu classes at the secondary stage show an increase both in the absolute numbers and in the percentage to the total enrollment, both figures were very low in 1963–4 and were again lower than the corresponding figures for Bihar (compare tables 4.4 and 4.5). In this case, however, the Uttar Pradesh percentages have been moving up over the years while the Bihar figures have shown a downward trend.

With regard to the language of administration, the state government has accepted in principle that important government notices and rules should be published in Urdu where there is an Urdu-speaking minority of 15 to 20% or more in a district. However, it has refused, despite a provision to that effect in the report of the chief ministers' conference and despite repeated complaints by the Commissioner for Linguistic Minorities, to extend this right to administrative units below the district. Petitions and representations to government offices are accepted in Urdu, but replies are given in Hindi.[4] Finally, the policy of the state government with regard to

---

[1] Sixty pupils in the last four classes of the higher secondary stage and 15 pupils per class.
[2] The deficiencies of the U.P. government's policies towards Urdu in the area of secondary education, as perceived by Urdu supporters and by the CLM, are noted in *CLM* v, 13–15, 149; *CLM* vi, 21, 23, 25–6, 29, 31, 205–6, 230–2; *CLM* vii, 30, 36, 38, 44, 92, 93, 119, 120, 203–7.
[3] The Deeni Talimi Council has pointed out that, in effect, 'Sanskrit has come to assume the position of a compulsory subject in U.P. instead of an optional one'; *Brief Scrutiny of Prescribed Books in U.P.* (Lucknow: Deeni Taleemi Council, 1966), p. 20.
[4] *CLM* v, 79–80, 120, 150; *CLM* vi, 44, 46, 48; *CLM* vii, 61–2, 64.

recruitment to the public services in the state has also diverged from the agreed principles of the chief ministers' conference in refusing to permit Urdu to be used as a language of examinations.[1]

This survey of the policy of the U.P. government towards Urdu during the past two decades does not support the charge that Urdu is being ousted from Uttar Pradesh. However, it does indicate clearly that the state government is following a deliberate policy of linguistic and cultural integration through both Hindi and Sanskrit for Hindus and Muslims[2] alike and that it has departed from that general policy only reluctantly, under pressure, and with procrastination. Most important, the figures on primary and secondary education suggest that the state government is succeeding in diverting large numbers of Urdu-speakers and even larger numbers of Muslims from a path of education which would reinforce their separate cultural identity.

Urdu and the Bihar government

Table 4.5 demonstrates that the facilities provided to Urdu-speakers in Bihar have been proportionately greater than those provided in U.P. Although the facilities provided in Bihar fall short of the demands of Urdu-supporters in the state and are considerably below what they claim to be their right in proportion to their population in Bihar, government policy has been somewhat more favorable to Urdu in principle than in U.P.[3] For example, in the area of primary education, the U.P. government had not issued orders as late as 1965 for the implementation of the decision of the chief ministers' conference of 1961 that each state would determine the facilities available for instruction through the mother tongue of minority pupils as of 1 November 1956, and see to it that no reductions in those facilities were made without specific orders from the state government, whereas the Bihar government did issue the necessary orders. In the area of secondary education, the Bihar government has not agreed to specify 'the minimum strength of linguistic minority pupils which would make it imperative to provide mother-tongues as media of instruction', but it has not taken the position of the U.P.

---

[1] *CLM* v, 105, 150–1; *CLM* vi, 51–2, 61; *CLM* vii, 82, 96, 119.

[2] Any doubts that this intention is deliberate should be dispelled by knowledge of the fact that Uttar Pradesh is the only state in the Indian Union where even secondary 'schools established and run by linguistic minorities cannot use their languages as media of instruction'; *CLM* vii, 30.

[3] The differences in government policy toward Urdu in these two states have been noted by Urdu supporters themselves, e.g. in the *Memorandum* submitted by H. N. Kunzru, pp. 4–5, and in the *Presidential Address* by Shiva Prasad Sinha at the Bihar Urdu convention held at Patna on 10 and 11 September 1966, p. 14 of my typescript translation from Urdu.

government that no other medium of instruction but Hindi will be allowed at the secondary stage. In fact, the Bihar government does provide some facilities for instruction through the media of Urdu, Bengali, Oriya and Santali as well as Hindi, at the secondary stage. The Bihar government has also agreed to make arrangements for maintaining advance registers of pupils who wish to receive secondary education through the medium of their mother tongue. Finally, with regard to the examination for entrance to the public service, Bihar, in contrast to U.P., has abolished the compulsory paper in Hindi.[1]

There are several possible explanations for the somewhat more liberal policy followed by the Bihar government in contrast to U.P. One is that the pre-independence antagonism and competition between Hindus and Muslims, Hindi and Urdu, was somewhat less intense in Bihar than in U.P., where the Muslim League was stronger and where Muslim and Urdu culture were more deeply entrenched. The second, and probably more important, is the fact that Bihar is linguistically far more heterogeneous than Uttar Pradesh. Practically speaking, the issue of facilities for minority languages in Uttar Pradesh is almost entirely an Urdu issue. In Bihar, government must contend as well with the demands of Maithili, of the tribal languages, and of the Bengali- and Oriya-speaking minorities. The existence of small Bengali- and Oriya-speaking minorities in Bihar is of greater importance to the other minority language groups in Bihar. Bengali and Oriya cannot be ignored because discrimination against these minorities would offend the Bengal and Orissa governments. Policies of necessity adopted to provide facilities for these languages then indirectly benefit the speakers of tribal languages, Maithili, and Urdu. Third, as will be shown below, Muslims have been better represented in the Bihar government since independence than in the U.P. government. Finally, and perhaps most important, the Director of Public Instruction in Bihar from 1958 to 1968 was a Muslim.[2]

Although Bihar government policy in theory and practice has been more favorable to Urdu than that of U.P., table 4.5 reveals two disquieting features from the Muslim point of view. While the proportion of primary students receiving instruction in or through the medium of Urdu to the total primary school enrollment in the period between 1956–7 and 1963–4 exceeded the proportion of Urdu-speakers enumerated in the 1951 census, and the Urdu primary school enrollment in 1962–3 and 1963–4 exceeded the proportion of Urdu-speakers enumerated in the 1961 census, the Urdu primary

---

[1] *CLM* v, p. 258, and *CLM* vii, pp. 82, 122–4, 172–9.
[2] The Director of Public Instruction in Bihar in this period was Mr Kalimuddin Ahmad.

school enrollments for all years listed are far short of the proportion of Muslims enumerated in both censuses (see table 4.2). Second, at the secondary stages of education in Bihar, the proportion of Urdu students enrolled has shown a decline from 1956–7. It is not clear from the available evidence whether the relative decline at the secondary stage reflects a failure of the educational authorities to provide the necessary facilities for Urdu-speakers or an adjustment on the part of Urdu-speakers themselves to the need to acquire sufficient mastery of Hindi to secure employment in a state where Hindi is the sole official language.

Urdu and the three-language formula in Uttar Pradesh and Bihar

The three-language formula, evolved by the Government of India in consultation with all the state governments in a meeting of the chief ministers of states and central ministers held in August 1961,[1] provides one example among many of a complete failure to develop realistic all-India policies to promote consistency on subjects which fall primarily within the constitutional domain of the states.[2] The formula had three aims: first, to promote all-India unity and inter-state communication by requiring students at the secondary stage of education to learn, in addition to their regional language, a modern Indian language of another region of the country. It was hoped and assumed that most south Indian students would learn Hindi and most north Indian students would study a south Indian language. In this way, the second, implicit aim of the formula, of 'equalizing the burden of language learning among the different linguistic regions'[3] and avoiding thereby giving advantage to Hindi-speakers who had no need to learn languages of other regions of the country unless compelled to do so, would also be realized. Third, to maintain India's ability to function effectively in international bodies and to absorb modern technological knowledge, English or another modern European language also was to be taught.

The proposal was unrealistic and impractical from the very beginning. It contradicted the language policy of the center toward protection of linguistic minorities in the provinces, it ignored the nearly total absence of teachers in the north Indian states qualified to teach south Indian languages, and it ignored the predictable pressures from

[1] See the statement issued after this conference published in the annual *CLM* reports.
[2] For other examples, see Michael Brecher, *Nehru's Mantle: The Politics of Succession in India* (New York: Frederick A. Praeger, 1966), ch. 6 and Marcus F. Franda, *West Bengal and the Federalizing Process in India* (Princeton: Princeton University Press, 1968).
[3] Baldev Raj Nayar, *National Communication and Language Policy in India* (New York: Frederick A. Praeger, 1969), p. 152.

linguistic minorities and supporters of Sanskrit education within the northern states for instruction in their mother tongues and in Sanskrit.

The formula not only contradicted central policy for protection of linguistic minorities, but it discriminated against such minorities. Although the meeting of chief ministers of the states and central ministers in 1961 explicitly recognized that 'no State is completely unilingual' and that arrangements must be made for minority languages, it agreed on a formula which would require linguistic minority students to learn four languages instead of three; '(a) the regional language *and* mother tongue when the latter is different from the regional language; (b) Hindi or, in Hindi-speaking areas, another Indian language; and (c) English or any other modern European language.'[1] Urdu supporters immediately saw the implications of this formula and protested against it, as did linguistic minority groups in other states. In Uttar Pradesh and Bihar, the formulae ultimately adopted eliminated this discrimination as it affected Urdu speakers in U.P. and Urdu and other minority languages in Bihar. The U.P. formula became: '(i) Hindi; (ii) an Indian language other than Hindi as given in the Eighth Schedule of the Constitution [which includes Urdu]; and (iii) English or any other modern European language.'[2] The Bihar formula is more complicated, but it has the same effect.[3] Although the U.P. and Bihar formulae eliminated the discrimination against Urdu, they also effectively eliminated the prospect that minority language speakers in the north would learn a south Indian language.

However, it soon became clear that Hindi-speaking students would not be learning south Indian languages either, because there were hardly any qualified teachers and because Sanskrit was included as an alternative. It was pointed out in the *Pioneer* of 29 June 1962 that serious implementation of the teaching of south Indian languages in U.P. would require more than 6,000 teachers who knew both Hindi and a south Indian language, a patent impossibility. Both the U.P. and Bihar governments solved this dilemma and satisfied Sanskrit supporters as well by including Sanskrit as an alternative Indian language. The inclusion of Sanskrit was utterly opposed to the

---

[1] *CLM* VI, p. 81; emphasis supplied.
[2] *CLM* VII, p. 176.
[3] '(a) (i) Mother-tongue; or (ii) regional language; or (iii) a composite course of mother-tongue and a regional language; or (iv) a composite course of mother-tongue and a classical language; or (v) a composite course of a regional language and classical language. (b) English or a modern European language. (c) Hindi for non-Hindi-speaking students and another Indian language for Hindi-speaking students provided it is not any one of the languages offered under group (a) above'; *CLM* VII, p. 176.

spirit and purpose of the original formula,[1] but the central government ultimately accepted its inclusion and, thereby, admitted that
the original formula could not work.[2]

In practice, then, the three-language formula as applied to the
north Indian states provides two main streams of education – Hindi,
Sanskrit, and English for the vast majority of secondary students;
and Hindi, Urdu (or Maithili or other minority languages in Bihar),
and English for the linguistic minority students. The failure of the
three-language formula in the north has commonly been attributed
to Hindi chauvinism and the pressures for Sanskrit education and
Sanskritization of Hindi. However, the pressures of linguistic
minority speakers for education in their mother tongue also stand
in the way of a serious effort to teach south Indian languages, which
suggests that all-India policies designed to promote interstate integration, which do not at the same time take into account intrastate
problems of integration, are bound to fail.

Urdu, national integration, and cultural pluralism

Running through the controversies surrounding the status of Urdu
and of the Muslim minorities in north India are two distinct views
of the nature of the Indian Union and of the proper role of the Muslim and other minorities in the Union. There is, first, the predominant Congress ideology of secular nationalism, which assumes that
there is a single composite culture in India and a single nation.
Linguistic and cultural minorities are entitled to protection, and all
individuals are entitled to live in India without discrimination on the
grounds of race, creed, language, or religion, but no concessions are
to be granted which would imply that a minority constitutes a distinct national group. In fact, however, there is a basic contradiction
between the ideology of secular, composite nationalism and the
policies of the central government. In principle, most relevant provisions of the Constitution of India and the ideology of the central
leaders promote what Akzin would describe as a non-discriminatory
integrationist policy, which promotes individual equality regardless
of ethnic origin, but discourages demands for group rights. However,
article 350A of the Constitution and central government policies
urged upon the states in various conferences on 'national integration' and by the Commissioner for Linguistic Minorities promote a
policy of 'pluralism on the basis of equality', in which the various
minority ethnic and linguistic groups are to be granted privileges

---

[1] See, e.g., *CLM* vii, pp. 36–7.
[2] See the *Times of India*, 15 August 1966.

which in other historical contexts have been given only to nationalities in multi-national states, most especially the privilege of being educated in the public schools through the media of their mother tongues.[1]

If one takes the view that the actual policies of the central government are those best designed to achieve national unity, then the policies of the U.P. and Bihar governments work against that goal. If, however, one takes seriously the ideology of secular nationalism, composite culture, and national integration, then it is *only* the U.P. and Bihar governments which have been pursuing this goal by resisting the efforts of Muslims and other minorities to be educated through the media of their mother tongues. In other words, whereas the center has been promoting a policy of linguistic pluralism, the states of U.P. and Bihar have been promoting policies of integration.

What complicates matters and contributes to this difference between central and state policies on language and culture is the refusal of the central government to recognize the logical implications of its policies, which may be leading to the development of a multi-national state in India. The view that India is, in fact, a multi-national state is a second view that appears in the controversy over Urdu and Muslim culture in north India. This view has been adopted explicitly and openly only by Dr Faridi among Muslim leaders. Dr Faridi has expressed this view especially in two pamphlets, of which one has been proscribed by government. He has argued that every state in India is multi-lingual and should be declared as such, that there is presently no such thing as a common Indian culture, and that India (and Pakistan as well) is a multi-national country. He goes on to demand that it is high time for the government to 'acknowledge the existence of National minorities' in India, to stop propagating the 'unmitigated nonsense' that the 450 million people of India belong to one nation, and to give to the racial, linguistic, and religious minorities of India 'the official status of National Minorities . . . eligible for every kind of protection according to . . . internationally recognised principles'.[2]

At this time the informal rules of the political game in India prohibit the phrasing of the issues in this way. It is apparent, however, that central and state policies toward linguistic minorities are contradictory. Central government policies are designed to promote

[1] Benjamin Akzin, *State and Nation* (London: Hutchinson University Library, 1964), ch. 6 and 7.
[2] A. J. Faridi, *Communal Riots and National Integration* (Lucknow, 1962), pp. 37, 49, 50, 53, and *Tashkent Declaration and the Problem of Indo-Pak Minorities*, pp. 3–4, 7–8, 26, 44.

national unity while accepting linguistic-cultural pluralism. State government policies seek in fact to promote intrastate integration and avoid the implications of linguistic and cultural pluralism and the political demands of linguistic and religious minorities for privileges which foster separate cultural identities.

The contradiction pointed out here between the principle of integration and a policy of linguistic pluralism would not be admitted by central leaders. Most would agree with the Commissioner for Linguistic Minorities that the goal of national integration can be achieved only if linguistic minority rights are protected and only if 'not merely justice but generosity in dealing with the problems affecting minorities' becomes the rule.[1] It may be that, for some minorities, the satisfaction of their linguistic aspirations will in fact promote a sense of oneness with an Indian nation in which national loyalties transcend linguistic loyalties. In the case of the Muslims, however, it has been amply demonstrated that language is not the heart of the matter, for there are no strictly linguistic difficulties facing Muslim minorities in north India. Urdu is, in fact, an instrument for strengthening religious-cultural differences between two groups of people speaking the same language, but some of whose political leaders hold contrary views on the nature of Indian society and culture and on the proper means to achieve a cohesive basis for a transcendent nationalism, and some of whom do not even concede that such a transcendent nationalism is a practical goal.

OTHER MUSLIM GRIEVANCES

The protection of the Muslim minority, culture, and institutions

The Urdu issue is the most politically salient issue concerning Muslims in north India, around which specific political demands have been made and through which Muslim discontent has become a major political factor in party and electoral politics in Uttar Pradesh and Bihar. However, it is not the only source of Muslim discontent. The Urdu issue itself must be seen primarily as a reflection of the desire of a major section of the Muslim community to maintain the security and preserve the cultural identity of Muslims in India. The perceived threats to Muslim security and identity are diverse and touch all areas of public life, including law and order, politics, economics, education, and religion.[2]

[1] *CLM* vi, p. 62.
[2] Cf. Theodore P. Wright, Jr., 'The Effectiveness of Muslim Representation in India', in

Communal riots

Among the sources of Muslim discontent in the north, the major grievance, in addition to the status of Urdu, and the one which most clearly affects the Muslim urban masses, is the persistence of communal riots in the cities and towns of north India, to such an extent that hardly a month passes without a communal outbreak of violence in one place or another and hardly a year passes without a serious riot, in which large numbers of Muslims lose their lives. In recent years, Muslim leaders have given a direct political interpretation to these recurring riots, which has taken them out of the broader social context of generalized Hindu–Muslim antagonisms and has had the effect of channeling Muslim grievances over their security to governmental and political agencies. That interpretation contains the following elements: that Muslim misdemeanours, individually or collectively, are never responsible for the riots; that only Muslims are killed in these riots; that Hindu communal parties, organizations, and individuals purposefully and willfully organize such riots with the intent of harassing and killing Muslims; that the police and army not only stand aside while Muslims are killed, but frequently participate themselves in attacks on Muslims; that the senior administrative officers in the districts where riots break out ignore the actions of the police because they are themselves often 'communal-minded'; and that government itself is directly responsible because it almost never appoints inquiry committees after communal riots to investigate their causes and to punish and discipline the guilty and negligent elements in the population and in the administration.[1]

Information is not presently available to provide an objective assessment of all elements in this interpretation of the causes and consequences of communal riots in north India. There have been several accounts of individual riots published by the political parties and by such organizations as the Sampradayikta Virodhi Committee which tend to support the Muslim charges.[2] However, the *Raghubar Dayal Commission Report* on the communal riots of 1967–8,

Donald E. Smith (ed.), *South Asian Politics and Religion* (Princeton, N.J.: Princeton University Press, 1966), pp. 105–8.

[1] For some examples of the conservative Muslim interpretation of the riots, see the pamphlets of A. J. Faridi, *Communalism: Its Causes and Cures*, p. 4; *Communal Riots and National Integration*; the resolutions and the *Welcome Address* of Maulana Syed Abul Hasan Ali Nadwi at the All-India Muslim Consultative Convention, Lucknow, 8–9 August 1964, available in pamphlets; various issues of *Radiance*, e.g. 9 October, 13 and 20 November, 4 and 18 December 1966, and 1 and 8 January 1967; and interviews, L1:3–7, L2:2, L4:51.

[2] See, e.g., Aswini K. Ray and Subhash Chakravarti, *Meerut Riots: A Case Study* (New Delhi: Sampradayikta Virodhi Committee (1968 or 1969)).

which focused especially on the Ranchi-Hatia riots of August 1967, does not entirely support the Muslim point of view. The report did not support the view either that Hindu communal parties and groups willfully organize such riots or that Muslims are never at fault,[1] but such conclusions are, in any case, not likely to alter the Muslim perceptions of the causes and consequences of communal riots.

It is sufficient for purposes of this chapter to note that communal riots are a persistent feature of the public life of the provinces of Uttar Pradesh and Bihar, that the available evidence does lend support to some of the charges (e.g. that it is mostly Muslims who are killed), and that these riots are often directly related to contemporary political events. In Uttar Pradesh and Bihar, there have been a series of major communal riots during the past decade – in Aligarh in 1961, in Jamshedpur in 1964, in Ranchi in 1967, and in Meerut in 1968. Three of these riots were directly associated with communal politics and political issues. The Aligarh riot of 1961 grew out of student politics at the Aligarh Muslim University. It was the Aligarh riot which produced the beginning of a major change in Muslim politics in U.P., when Muslims of the university and city allied with the Republican party, representing the low-caste Chamars, and with discontented factional groups in the Congress to administer a crushing defeat to the Congress in the 1962 elections in that district.[2] The extremely severe Ranchi riot of August, 1967, in which it is estimated that 184 persons, mostly Muslims,[3] lost their lives, was preceded by and associated in the public mind with demonstrations for and against the declaration of Urdu as the second official language of the state of Bihar. The Meerut riot of January 1968 was occasioned by a visit of Sheikh Abdullah to a meeting sponsored by the Jamiyyat-ul-Ulama in Meerut city, which was opposed by Hindu communal groups.

Figures on communal riots and deaths occasioned thereby are not easily available. The annual reports of the home department of the Government of India for the three years 1965–6 to 1967–8 mention only that there were 173 'communal incidents' in India as a whole in 1965, 133 in 1966, and 209 in 1967.[4] In reply to a question in the Lok

---

[1] Government of India, Home Department, *Report of the Commission of Inquiry on Communal Disturbances, Ranchi-Hatia (August 22–29, 1967)* (New Delhi: Government of India Press, 1968), pp. 15, 62, and *passim*. [Hereafter referred to as *Raghubar Dayal Commission Report*.]

[2] Paul R. Brass, *Factional Politics in an Indian State: The Congress Party in Uttar Pradesh* (Berkeley: University of California Press, 1965), pp. 98–111.

[3] *Raghubar Dayal Commission Report*, p. 48.

[4] Government of India, Ministry of Home Affairs, *Report, 1966–67*, p. 51, and *Report, 1967–68*, p. 40.

Sabha on 13 December 1968, the home ministry revealed that there had been 5, 17, and 20 communal riots in U.P. in 1966, 1967, and 1968 respectively, and that 31 persons had been killed in such riots in 1967 and 36 in 1968.[1] Comparable figures for Bihar are not available, but the death toll in Ranchi-Hatia alone in 1967 was 184 by official reckoning. It is, at any rate, clear from the patterns of the major riots in Aligarh, Meerut, and Ranchi that political action involving communal issues represents a serious threat to public order and to the personal security of Muslims in the cities and towns of north India.[2]

Muslim culture: Personal Law and school textbooks
The view of the world held by many Muslim leaders includes the fear that the secularist leaders of the country and the Hindu revivalists wish to undermine Muslim culture and religion in India by tampering with their Personal Law (*shari'a*)[3] and by providing school textbooks which glorify Hindu religion and culture and disparage Islam and Muslim culture. Article 44 of the Constitution of India, in the part on directive principles of state policy, says that 'the State shall endeavour to secure for the citizens a uniform civil code throughout the territory of India'. Although the directive principles are not binding and no governmental proposal has yet been brought forward to change the Muslim Personal Law, the conservative Muslim leaders have warned that no change whatsoever will be tolerated nor will any government attempts to pass laws contradicting the Personal Law (such as a ban on polygamy). The Jamaat-e-Islami, which takes the most militant position on the issue of change in the Personal Law, argues that even a ban on polygamy cannot be accepted, because Muslims are sure it will be only 'the first step in the direction of erasing every symbol of a separate Muslim culture in India'.[4] Instead, the Jamaat leaders have proposed that article 44 of the Constitution should be deleted.[5]

Some Muslims have found confirmation of their view that the dominant Hindu majority is attempting to assimilate Muslims and

---

[1] *Radiance*, 22 December 1968.
[2] It is known that the overwhelming majority of persons killed in these riots are Muslims. For example, 16 of the 17 persons killed in the January 1968 Meerut riots were Muslims (Ray and Chakravarti, *Meerut Riots*, p. 11), most of the 36 persons killed in the Aligarh–Meerut–Moradabad riots of October 1961 were officially acknowledged to be Muslim by the home minister of U.P. (*National Herald*, 15 November 1961), and 164 of the 184 persons killed in Ranchi-Hatia were Muslims (*Raghubar Dayal Commission Report*, p. 48).
[3] See Theodore P. Wright, Jr., 'The Muslim Personal Law Issue in India: An Outsider's view', *Indian Journal of Politics*, IV (1970), 69–77.
[4] *Radiance*, 4 December 1966.   [5] *Ibid.*, 11 December 1966.

'erase' Muslim culture from the textbooks prescribed in the schools in Uttar Pradesh. The Deeni Talimi Council of U.P. has provided documentary evidence from the prescribed textbooks to support its charge that 'the books prescribed in the schools and colleges' have been designed 'to suit the religious beliefs, rituals and mythology of [the] majority community' by narrating Hindu mythological stories which 'tend to teach idolatry and superstition in an indirect manner and offend against the basic principles of Islam'. In addition, it is argued, the textbooks disparage the role played by Muslim conquerors and rulers in India. These grievances against the general educational policy in Uttar Pradesh relate directly to the Urdu issue, for it is pointed out that Muslims are not only forced to learn Hindu religion and culture, but they are denied the opprtunity to learn of their own culture and religion through Urdu books.[1]

The controversy over the U.P. textbooks led to an exchange of letters between Dr Sampurnanand, former chief minister of U.P., and Dr Faridi, which deserve some analysis because of the light they shed upon the differing perceptions of the meaning of national integration to a Congress Hindu revivalist and a Muslim political leader. The exchange reveals some of the perceptual differences involved when Hindus and Muslims look at all-India symbols.[2] Both Dr Faridi and Dr Sampurnanand claimed to accept the view that India has a composite culture and that cultural integration between Hindus and Muslims was a goal to be worked toward in the educational process. However, Dr Faridi claimed that the U.P. textbooks were not promoting cultural integration or composite culture, but Hindu ideals and composite religion through material 'opposed to the basic tenets of Islam and derogatory to the personality of the Prophet'; lessons 'unjust to Muslims [and] likely to produce anti-Muslim feelings'; and 'lessons . . . which would help the propagation of Hindu mythology'. Dr Sampurnanand recognized that some of the examples cited might have such effects and proposed that truly offensive passages be eliminated, but he insisted that it was legitimate to teach Hindu mythology as part and parcel of Indian culture and to teach the truth about the anti-Hindu actions of Muslim conquerors in India.

On the first point of a common culture, Dr Sampurnanand remarked: We have not only a common culture but a common ancestry. This fact is often lost sight of.

[1] *Brief Scrutiny of Prescribed Books in U.P.*, references to pp. ii, iv–v, 17.
[2] The letters are contained in A. J. Faridi, *Communal Riots and National Integration*, pp. 13–35. There are four letters in all, two from Dr Sampurnanand to Dr Faridi, dated 27 June and 31 August 1961, and two from Dr Faridi to Dr Sampurnanand, dated 6 July and 6 October 1961.

The people of Iran, for example, are Muslims today but they are proud of their Dara, Kaikhusro, Nausherwan and Rustam who were all Parsis by religion. But whatever their religion, they were the great heroes of Iran and the common ancestors of Parsis and Muslims. Unfortunately, the Indian Muslim does not share with his Hindu fellow countrymen admiration for Rama and Krishna, Arjun and Bhim, Ashoka and Harsh Vardhan. These men were Hindus by religion [*sic*] but they were Indian heroes and the common ancestors of both Hindus and Muslims . . . The pity of it is that the Indian Muslim also speaks with pride of those heroes of another land. He speaks with reverence about Plato, Socrates and Aristotle, all non-Muslims by religion and Greek by race, but he knows nothing about Vyas and Vashishtha, Gautam and Shankarcharya and Budha, Hindus [*sic*] no doubt but his great ancestors, nevertheless.[1]

Dr Sampurnanand went on to argue the necessity of including in school textbooks stories from the Ramayana and the Mahabharata, for if these great epics are not included in Indian composite culture, 'the result would be that Indians, both Hindus and Muslims, instead of belonging to a great nation with a noble history extending over thousands of years, in no way less distinguished than that of China and Egypt, would appear before the world as descendants of savages with no history of their own'. Finally Dr Sampurnanand saw nothing improper in teaching the truth about Muslim conquerors such as Mahmood Ghaznavi, who demolished Hindu temples, and Aurangzeb, who imposed a head-tax on Hindus.[2]

In his reply, Dr Faridi did not point out the logical deficiencies in Dr Sampurnanand's comparison of the adoption by a majority in Iran of the ancient symbols of a minority with his proposal for the adoption by a minority of the ancient symbols of identity of a majority group in India. However, it did not escape his attention that Dr Sampurnanand had integrated Ashoka and the Buddha into Hindu culture. Dr Faridi refused to accept the appropriateness of including Hindu religio-mythological stories in the school textbooks, even if similar stories were included from Islamic, Judaic, and Christian mythology. To treat such accounts as 'the immaculate birth of Christ, the origin of Ganges through the braided hair of Lord Vishnu, the birth of Sita or the story of Abraham's sacrifice' as mere stories would be blasphemous. As for the teaching of true history, Dr Faridi claimed to have no objection to the narration of stories of Muslim conquerors destroying Hindu temples if it was also taught how Hindu rulers destroyed Buddhist temples. He accepted the view that Hindus and Muslims alike in India shared a common racial ancestry, but he objected to the view that that common ancestry was a Hindu one.[3]

[1] *Ibid.*, pp. 26–7.   [2] *Ibid.*, p. 29.   [3] *Ibid.*, pp. 31–5.

In short, Dr Faridi's argument was that integration should not be confused with 'assimilation by the majority'.[1] It was desirable to select symbols of a composite culture and to appoint national heroes of different religions from the past, but this must be done with great care. If Aurangzeb did not meet the qualifications for a national hero, neither did Shivaji or Rana Pratap. If true history must be taught, it must be taught in full, and it must reveal that the conquerors of the past 'massacred irrespective of religion, caste, or creed'.[2] Finally, Dr Faridi expressed his willingness to accept the Buddha, Ashoka, and Harsh Vardhan as great Indians, but not as great Hindus.

The exchange between Dr Sampurnanand and Dr Faridi is instructive from two points of view. First, it reveals that two Indians, sharply opposed in religion and politics, shared the view that it is possible to create out of the symbols of Indian history a common Indian national identity. Second, however, it reveals that the automatic standardization of such symbols and the emergence of an Indian nation-state out of such standardization cannot be assumed. One of the great untouched areas of social science research on Indian national integration is the study of the process of symbol selection and transmission in the schools in the different regions of India. The controversy over the U.P. textbooks suggests that it is by no means clear that the content of such textbooks promotes symbols of common nationality acceptable to all Indians. Dr Faridi's charge essentially is that U.P. textbooks promote Hindu nationalism, not Indian nationalism. It is an open question how far the textbooks in the Punjab, in Tamil Nadu, or in Maharashtra promote a synthesis between regional and national, Hindu and Muslim symbols or how far their weight is on regional or Hindu symbols.

The Aligarh Muslim University

In April 1965 a student agitation at the Aligarh Muslim University (AMU), involving a student–police confrontation and student-inflicted personal injury to the vice-chancellor of the university, became the occasion for the Government of India to introduce fundamental changes in the governing of the university. These changes added further intensity to Muslim discontent, particularly in north India, and became a new source of Muslim grievance and political agitation against government policy.

The AMU has for nearly a century been a central symbol both for Muslim identity in modern India and for Hindu hostility to the separate cultural identity of Muslims. The AMU was the fruit of the

---

[1] This quote is not in the letters, but is in *ibid.*, p. 49.   [2] *Ibid.*, p. 32.

Aligarh movement of Syed Ahmed Khan. Founded as the Muhammedan Anglo-Oriental College in 1877, it soon became the center 'of the Muslim educational movement in India' and was transformed into the Aligarh Muslim University by a Government of India Act of 1920.[1]

Three features of the university and of the Act of 1920 have been seen by some of its defenders as important in maintaining the university as the pre-eminent center of modern education for Muslims in India.[2] One was the combination of modern secular education with Islamic religious education, which was compulsory for Muslim students at the university. The second was the residential character of the university, which made it possible for the university to draw Muslim students from all parts of India to an area where Muslims are in a minority. The third feature was that the university was to be administered by Muslims, who alone could be members of the governing bodies of the university.

The growth of Hindu–Muslim communal antagonism in India and the consequent partition of India, combined with the fact that the university became identified before independence with the Muslim League (providing both a sympathetic environment for Muslim League ideology and the major source of educated leadership for the League) brought the university increasingly under attack from both Hindu communalists and secular leaders from the Hindu and Muslim communities. Over the past two decades, demands have been made both from within and from outside the university to give it a more secular orientation. These demands have been interpreted by the conservative Muslim leadership as attempts to undermine the basic Muslim character of the university. In 1951, the Government of India passed amendments to the Act of 1920, abolishing compulsory religious education, opening the university court (the governing body) to non-Muslims, and empowering the university to affiliate to it colleges within a radius of fifteen miles.[3] Demands to alter the residential character of the university by actually affiliating to it the three predominantly Hindu colleges in Aligarh town have so far been successfully resisted, however,[4] as have demands to eliminate the term Muslim from the name of the university.

[1] A brief history of the AMU and of the Government of India legislation regulating the functioning of the university is given in *Estimates Committee (1965–66) Hundred and First Report (Third Lok Sabha) : Ministry of Education, Aligarh Muslim University* (New Delhi: Lok Sabha Secretariat, 1966), ch. 1.

[2] N. Y. Nuri, *Presidential Address* (Lucknow: All-India Aligarh Muslim University Old Boys' Convention, 1965), p. 25.

[3] *Ibid.*, pp. 25–7; *Estimates Committee*, pp. 4–5.

[4] A proposal to start evening classes at the AMU for the benefit of university employees

In April 1965 the vice-chancellor of the university took a decision which affected the students in residence directly and was interpreted by many as a further step in de-emphasizing the Muslim character of the university, namely, a decision to reduce the percentage of places reserved in the technical and professional colleges of the university for AMU graduates to 50% from 75%.[1] Since the student body is estimated to be approximately 65% Muslim, the 75% reservation served effectively to preserve Muslim student predominance in the technical schools as well.[2] The student agitation of 25 April 1965 was concerned with this issue. When the agitation led to violence, the education minister of the Government of India took this opportunity to make further changes in the administration of the university. By an ordinance,[3] the substance of which was later enacted into law by parliament, the Government of India reduced the powers of the university authorities and arrogated to itself greater powers to intervene in university affairs.[4]

The policies adopted by the Government of India towards the AMU have probably not been taken only or primarily to appease Hindu communal sentiment. Rather, they have been formulated with the advice and consent of that small minority of the Muslim leadership which considers itself nationalist, secular, and progressive. The vice-chancellors of the AMU appointed by the Government of India since independence have been from this category, as was Mr Chagla, the education minister who promulgated the Aligarh ordinance. Moreover, there is an influential group of Muslim Communists and other 'progressive' faculty members in the university itself which supports such changes and is at loggerheads with the dominant conservative leadership and alumni of the university in university politics.[5]

It is this latter segment of Muslim leadership, however, which appeals most effectively to Muslim sentiment in north India. Through

and for the people of Aligarh town has also been opposed by the Old Boys as a design 'to destroy the basic residential character of the University'. Resolution passed at the All-India Aligarh Muslim University Old Boys' Convention Council of 10 and 11 September 1966, *Radiance*, 18 September 1966.

[1] M. Y. Nuri, *Presidential Address*, p. 34.

[2] It is claimed that non-Muslim students at AMU also supported the 75% reservation (M. Y. Nuri, *Presidential Address*, p. 35), which is understandable, but does not alter the fact that the Muslim students would be proportionately better served by it.

[3] The Aligarth Muslim University (Amendment) Ordinance, 1965, *Gazette of India Extraordinary*, pt. II, 20 May 1965.

[4] *Estimates Committee*, pp. 5–6.

[5] On this conflict in the university, see Brass, *Factional Politics in an Indian State*, pp. 99–100; M. Y. Nuri, *Presidential Address*, pp. 29–30; *Radiance*, 6 November and 18 December 1966.

their efforts, the struggle over the secularization of the AMU has become laden with the symbols of Muslim identity embattled with Hindu communal forces who would destroy the AMU as a source of inspiration for Muslims in India. Thus, the Old Boys of the AMU rushed to the defence of the university which, to them, 'is much more than a teaching establishment. It is a symbol of the movement for the educational and cultural re-generation of Muslims.' For the Old Boy leaders, 'the Aligarh question' was, therefore, not simply a question of the rules regulating the governance of the university, but a 'question of the survival of the Muslims in India'.[1] The efforts of the Government of India to secularize the university are seen as efforts 'to de-Muslimise it'.[2] The All-India Muslim Majlis-e-Mushawarat also saw the issue in the same terms and added its support to defend 'the proudest priceless possession of the sixty million Muslims of India, and their greatest single monument of community enterprise and the citadel of their culture and genius'.[3]

The Old Boys and the Muslim Majlis held public meetings, agitated the issue in Muslim press organs, and supported a writ petition to the Supreme Court of India against the Aligarh ordinance and for the reinstatement of the original Act of 1920 on the grounds that the AMU was a minority institution entitled to govern itself without interference according to article 30 of the Constitution.[4] Ultimately, the Supreme Court ruled that the AMU was not a minority institution, but a national institution and the new Aligarh Act, consequently, continued in force. While the agitation, therefore, failed in its objectives, it succeeded in mobilizing Muslim sentiment in north India against the government and the Congress party, particularly in Uttar Pradesh, where the AMU is located and from which nearly 90% of the student body of the university comes.[5] Thus, the AMU controversy provided an additional unifying symbol of Muslim discontent, along with the Urdu issue and the communal riots, in the months preceding the general elections of 1967.

[1] *The Aligarh Muslim University: Its Past, Present and Future* (Lucknow: All-India Aligarh Muslim University Old Boys' Convention, 1965), p. 12; see also Md. Ehtram Ali Alvi, *Address of Welcome* (Lucknow: All-India Aligarh Muslim University Old Boys' Convention, 1965), p. 1, and M. Y. Nuri, *Presidential Address*, pp. 39–40.

[2] M. Y. Nuri, *Presidential Address*, p. 39.

[3] Resolution passed by the All-India Muslim Majlis-e-Mushawarat at its meetings in Delhi on 19 and 20 June 1965; quotation from typescript in my possession.

[4] *Resolution* passed by the All-India Aligarh Muslim University Old Boys' Convention, Lucknow, held on 7 and 8 August 1965, pp. 3–4; *The Aligarh Muslim University: Its Past, Present, and Future*, pp. 8–9; resolution of the All-India Muslim Majlis-e-Mushawarat passed at its meetings in Delhi on 19 and 20 July 1965, typescript in my possession; *Radiance*, 9 October 1966 and 8 January 1967.

[5] *Estimates Committee*, p. 13.

It was generally argued by Muslim leaders that the AMU issue was one of the major factors in contributing to the withdrawal of Muslim support from the Congress in the 1967 elections and in other elections in north India until the 1971 parliamentary elections. As part of its strategy of appeal to the minorities, the Congress of Mrs Gandhi included in its 1971 election manifesto the statement that, if brought to power, 'the Congress will strive to ensure that all minorities have full freedom to establish, manage and run educational and other institutions'.[1] Many Muslim political leaders interpreted this statement as a direct reference to the AMU,[2] an interpretation which was encouraged by Mrs Gandhi herself in a press conference.[3] After the election, Muslim defenders of the minority status of the AMU demanded that Mrs Gandhi fulfill the Congress campaign pledge by passing a new Aligarh Muslim University Bill which would explicitly declare AMU to be a Muslim minority institution, provide that all the executive officers and a majority of the members of the university court would be Muslims, and repeal the provision of the 1951 Act which gave the university the power to affiliate local colleges to it.[4] When the Aligarh Muslim University (Amendment) Act, 1972, was finally introduced into the Lok Sabha and passed in June, it failed to satisfy leaders of conservative Muslim opinion in the north. Although the Muslim designation in the name of the university and its residential character were maintained, it was not explicitly designated a minority institution and no specific measures were written into the Act to ensure Muslim dominance. Moreover, the self-governing character of the university was fundamentally altered in certain features of the Act which gave great powers of appointment of the vice-chancellor and of 45 out of 104 members of the University Court to the President of India, that is, in effect to the minister of education and the cabinet. These provisions were particularly ominous to the conservative defenders of AMU because of the fact that the current minister of education, Dr Nurul Hasan, had been for many years a professor at the university and a leading force in the progressive group which favored its modernization and secularization.[5] Consequently, opposition to the new AMU Act has been voiced and demonstrations against it have been held by Muslim political parties and voluntary associations in the north.

[1] *Handbook of Election Manifestos, 1971* (Bombay: Commerce Ltd., 1971), p. 21.
[2] *Radiance*, 27 June 1971, p. 6.   [3] *Ibid.*, 29 August 1971, p. 7.
[4] *Ibid.*, 26 September 1971, p. 5; 10 October 1971, p. 1; 31 October 1971, p. 8; 7 November 1971, p. 10; 2 April 1972, p. 1; 9 April 1972, p. 4.
[5] For conservative Muslim reactions to the AMU (Amendment) Act, 1972, see the issues of *Radiance* for June, July, August, and September 1972.

*Muslims in the political parties and in government service in Uttar Pradesh
and Bihar*

Muslims and party politics

The view of the contemporary political arena in India held by discontented Muslim elites involves two perceptions. The first is that
the political arena contains powerful overt and covert elements hostile to Muslims. Muslims complain of the general role of Hindu communal parties and organizations and of Hindu revivalism in political
affairs. It is the contention of many Muslim leaders that Hindu communal organizations organize communal riots and create the soil for
them in the minds of the Hindu masses through 'constant vicious
propaganda of the basest type'[1] designed to instill hostility towards
Muslims and to brand them as agents of Pakistan. Some feel that
Hindu communal sentiment is even more deeply rooted in Indian
political life, that it has permeated the ranks of all the major political
parties, with the possible exception of the Communists, that 'there
are Secularist leaders who have been speaking a language danger-
ously similar to the language of the communalists',[2] and that 'sometimes it seems that it is actually these Hindu communal organisations
that are ruling the country behind the Congress smoke-screen'.[3]

Combined with this perception of the political arena as a hostile
one is a feeling that Muslims are politically under-represented in the
political system. Not only are there far fewer Muslim candidates set
up by the major parties and far fewer Muslim legislators in the state
assemblies and in parliament than are warranted by the size of the
Muslim population, it is claimed, but those Muslims who are selected
by the parties and do sit in the legislatures are not true representatives of Muslim sentiment.

Although it has been claimed frequently that Muslims are under-
represented in the legislatures and that those Muslims who do get
into the legislatures and into government do not effectively represent
Muslim causes, Muslims have not gone unrepresented either in
government or in the political parties in north India during the past
twenty years. On the whole, during the first twenty years of Congress rule, Muslims were better represented in the Bihar than in the
Uttar Pradesh government, which may help to explain the more
liberal policy of the Bihar government towards facilities for Urdu-
speakers. Of 57 ministers, deputy ministers, and ministers of state in

[1] A. J. Faridi, *Communal Riots and National Integration*, p. 3.
[2] *Radiance*, 4 December 1966.
[3] *Ibid.*, 13 November 1966.

Bihar from 1949 to 1966, 11 or 19.3% were Muslims, whereas only 9 out of 67 ministers in U.P. (from 1947 to 1966) or 13.4% were Muslims.[1]

While it may be true that Muslim ministers have not represented Muslim causes as effectively as they could have, several of the Muslim Congress ministers in both states were men of considerable power and influence in Congress factional politics. While it cannot be said, therefore, that Muslims have been seriously under-represented in government in north India or that they have lacked power, it is important to note that the crucial education portfolio has never been given to a Muslim in either state in the past twenty years. This is surely not a coincidence, but must represent a conscious design on the part of the predominant Hindu leadership of the Congress in both states.

In the legislatures of the two states, Muslims have been under-represented. The number and percentage of Muslims elected to the Bihar Legislative Assembly from 1952 to 1972 are as follows: 1952, 24 (7.27%); 1957, 25 (7.86%); 1962, 21 (6.60%); 1967, 18 (5.67%); 1969, 18 (5.67%); 1972, 24 (7.55%). The corresponding figures for Uttar Pradesh are: 1952, 44 (10.23%); 1957, 39 (9.07%); 1962, 28 (6.59%); 1967, 26 (6.12%); 1969, 33 (7.76%).[2]

It is frequently charged by the more militant spokesmen for the cause of Urdu and the Muslims that even those few Muslims who do get elected and do get positions in government do not represent effectively the Muslim community or are Marxists and secularists opposed to Muslim minority causes. Some evidence to support this charge has been provided by Theodore Wright, who argues that 'the nomination and election processes work to put into the legislatures Muslims who are inclined to be docile and not to raise embarrassing issues too persistently lest they either not "get the ticket" next election

---

[1] The information on U.P. and Bihar ministers and their portfolios was compiled for me from various reference volumes by my research assistant, Frances Svensson.

[2] Figures for 1952 to 1969 were compiled from the official reports of the Election Commission of the Government of India. The 1972 figure for Bihar was compiled from unofficial result sheets provided by the Press Information Bureau of the Government of India. My figures for 1952 and 1957 agree with those in Sisir K. Gupta, 'Moslems in Indian Politics, 1947–60', *India Quarterly*, XVIII (1962), 373–4, but disagree slightly with those for 1962 and 1967 in Zaheer Masood Quraishi, 'Electoral strategy of a Minority Pressure Group: The Muslim Majlis-e-Mushawarat', *Asian Survey*, VIII, No. 12 (December 1968), 984.

Dispersed minorities tend to be under-represented in electoral systems without proportional representation. Blacks, for example, are much less well represented in the United States Congress (14 out of 535 or 2.62% in 1970, and 17 out of 535 or 3.18% in 1972, compared to their proportion of 11% in the population) than Muslims in Uttar Pradesh and Bihar; *Ebony* (January 1973).

or get shifted to less safe constituencies'.[1] Wright also reports a rumor that it was Congress Muslim MPs of modernist and secularist views 'who initiated the movement for reform of Muslim personal law in 1963'.[2] It is clear at any rate that the Union education minister, Mohammad Ali Chagla,[3] took decisive measures during the Aligarh Muslim University agitation of 1965 'to purge the faculty and administration, once and for all, of "communalists and reactionaries"',[4] measures which were interpreted by the leaders of most Muslim interest associations as designed to destroy the minority character of the university.

Thus, the general picture of Muslim representation in north India presents three features. First, Muslims have been generally underrepresented as MLAs in both states. Second, Muslims have been well represented in the Bihar government and not seriously underrepresented in the U.P. government over the past two decades, but they have been denied control over the key education portfolio. Finally, most of the Muslims elected to the legislatures and selected to government positions in both the states and at the center have not raised their voices on behalf of Muslim minority causes and some have taken actions which have been interpreted by the Muslim interest associations as opposed to Muslim minority rights.

Muslims in government service

Muslim leaders have charged that the prospects for Muslims in government employment in post-independence India have been bleak. It is alleged that Muslims have been victims of discrimination in government appointments, particularly in security departments such as the police, where no Muslims are permitted to attain high office. A series of articles published in *Radiance* in October through December 1968 have demonstrated that Muslims are seriously underrepresented in all-India services – in central government departments, councils, and boards; in the IAS; and in the army.[5]

An examination of the civil lists for U.P. and Bihar yields similar results. Table 4.6 demonstrates starkly the decline of Muslim representation in government and in government service in U.P. in

[1] Theodore P. Wright, Jr., 'The Effectiveness of Muslim Representation in India', in Donald E. Smith (ed.), *South Asian Politics and Religion* (Princeton: Princeton University Press, 1966), p. 110.

[2] *Ibid.*, pp. 116–17.

[3] In contrast to the situation in the states, the education portfolio at the center has been held often by Muslims.

[4] Theodore P. Wright, Jr., 'Muslim Education in India at the Crossroads: The Case of Aligarh', *Pacific Affairs*, xxxix, Nos. 1 and 2 (Spring–Summer 1966), p. 55.

[5] *Radiance*, 13, 20, 27 October, 3 and 10 November, and 15 and 29 December 1968.

TABLE 4.6 *Representation of Muslims in government and administration in Uttar Pradesh, 1 July 1964*

Category[a]	Total No.	Muslims[b] No.	Muslims[b] %	Remarks
1. Government	538	43	8.0	
(a) Ministers of cabinet rank	16	2	12.5	
(b) Legislative Council	108	13	12.0	
(c) Legislative Assembly	430	30	7.0	
2. Indian administrative service cadre of U.P.	256	25	9.8	
3. General secretariat	149	18	12.1	
(a) Superintendents	67	12	17.9	
(b) Superintendents (temporary and officiating)	82	6	7.3	
4. U.P. civil service	679	59	8.7	
(a) Deputy collectors in selection grade	56	12	21.4	10 of 12 Muslims appointed before 15 August 1947
(b) All deputy collectors	516	38	7.4	
(c) Officiating deputy collectors	163	21	12.9	
5. Judicial officers service	260	12	4.6	
(a) Judicial officers	214	10	4.7	
(b) Judicial officers (temporary)	46	2	4.4	
6. Judicial department	467	25	5.4	
(a) Justices in the Allahabad High Court	35	2	5.7	
(b) District and sessions judges	33	3	9.1	
(c) Civil and sessions judges	31	4	12.9	
(d) U.P. civil service (judicial branch)	254	15	5.9	
(e) Temporary munsifs	114	1	0.9	
7. Police department	530	40	7.6	
(a) Indian police service cadre of U.P.	161	6	3.7	
(b) Deputy superintendents of police	201	11	5.5	
(c) Officiating deputy superintendents of police	168	23	13.7	
8. Grand total	2,879	222	7.7	

[a] Some of the sub-categories are overlapping, e.g. 1(a) with 1(b) and 1(c) and 4(a) with 4(b). Main category totals and grand total have been calculated to avoid overlapping. Some minor offices have been eliminated from the table, though included in the *Civil List*, so that category totals are somewhat below the actual strength of the government departments of U.P.

[b] Identified by name.

SOURCE. Uttar Pradesh Civil Secretariat, Appointment (A) Department, *The Civil List, Part I for Uttar Pradesh* (Allahabad, Superintendent, Printing and Stationery, 1965).

the post-independence period. In none of the major departments of government in 1964 did Muslim representation equal the proportion of Muslims in the population of the state. In the general secretariat, Muslim over-representation among permanent superintendents was more than balanced by their under-representation among temporary and officiating superintendents, so that, in the general secretariat as a whole, Muslim representation came to only 12.1%. Among the 56 deputy collectors in the selection grade, Muslim representation was far above the Muslim proportion in the population, but this fact in itself emphasizes the precipitous Muslim decline in the U.P. services because 10 of the 12 Muslims in the selection grade were appointed before independence. Among all deputy collectors (including the selection grade), Muslim representation was about half the Muslim proportion in the population. Most striking of all, in comparison to the position of Muslims in the pre-independence period, was the representation of Muslims in the police department where, from a position of dominance, Muslim representation declined to 7.6%. In the judicial services, Muslim representation was the lowest of all government departments, ranging from a low representation of 1 Muslim out of 114 temporary munsifs to a high of 4 out of 31 civil and sessions judges. The extent of the decline of Muslim representation in the post-independence period is revealed clearly when it is considered that the absolute number of Muslims employed in all elected and appointed offices listed in table 4.6 was smaller than the number of Muslims employed in the executive and judicial branches of the uncovenanted service alone in U.P. in 1886–7.

In Bihar, where figures are available for all government departments for 1960, the position of Muslims has been similar to that in U.P. Muslim representation ranged from zero in the political and welfare departments to highs of 12% in the Bihar Public Service Commission and in the excise department. The Muslim share of all gazetted posts in Bihar in 1960 was 541 out of 9,773 or 5.53%.[1] An examination of a less comprehensive list of gazetted officers in Bihar for 1968 revealed 117 Muslim names in a list of 1,691 officers, or 6.92%.[2]

The dramatic decline in Muslim representation cannot be attributed only to the failure of the U.P. and Bihar governments to recruit Muslims, but has much to do with the emigration of Muslim

[1] *Ibid.*, 14 February 1965.
[2] Compiled from Government of India, Ministry of Home Affairs, *All-India Civil List* (Delhi: Manager of Publications, 1970), pp. 389–410.

elites to Pakistan after 1947. Figures on the numbers of Muslims in government service who left the country at that time are not available to the writer, but it must be remembered that the Muslim population in U.P. cities declined by 10% between 1941 and 1951 (see table 3.1, p. 143, above). At the same time, the figures leave no doubt that there has been disproportionate under-recruitment of Muslims into government departments in both states since 1947.

CONCLUSION

Muslim separatist leaders argued before independence that, in a free and democratic India, the dominant Hindu majority would attempt to absorb Muslim culture and that Muslims would become a permanent minority without significant influence in the representative system. Those Muslim political leaders and government servants who left north India for Pakistan after partition have made this prophecy partly a self-fulfilling one. Moreover, even in the best of circumstances, a proportionate decline of Muslim representation in desirable positions in the public and political life of the northern states was to be expected in view of the advantaged position of the Muslim elites before independence. At the same time, there is no doubt that the decline in the cultural and political status of the Muslim community in the north since 1947 has been precipitous and that it has been fostered by specific policies of the state governments.

Urdu, once the dominant language of north India and the official and court language of both U.P. and Bihar, has been practically eliminated as a language of administration in both states. Large numbers of Urdu-speakers have been denied their constitutional right to receive primary education through the medium of their mother tongue. The state governments have attempted to integrate and assimilate the unmobilized Muslim populations into a homogeneous culture through an educational system based upon Sanskritized Hindi and infused with symbols of Hinduism. Although the central government has been supportive of the rights of Urdu-speakers in the schools, it has not been able to compel the state governments to take the desired corrective actions. Moreover, the non-secularist, non-Marxist Muslim leaders have not been satisfied with the educational policies of the Government of India. The status of Muslim minority institutions, such as the Aligarh Muslim University, has seemed threatened by the secularizing policies and trends of the central government and by the hostility of Hindu leaders and organizations. In politics and government service, the Muslims of north India have been reduced from their previous position of political privilege to one of under-representation in nearly all elected and appointed offices of government. Finally, the threats to the personal security and property of Muslims through communal riots have increased in recent years.

Yet it is doubtful that state government policies of integration and assimilation of the Muslim and Urdu-speaking minority can continue to succeed in the long run. Although educational policies have probably directed large numbers of Muslims from a path of education which would reinforce their sense of separateness, the sense of Muslim separateness cannot be eliminated. Consciousness among Muslims of Urdu as their mother tongue has increased and is nearly universal among urban Muslims. The central government has not so far dared to touch the Muslim Personal Law. Islam, Islamic ideology, and Islamic law continue to regulate the lives of all but a small number of secularist and Marxist Muslims among the educated classes.

Moreover, since 1964 in north India, serious efforts have been made to revive Muslim politics and political organizations and to mobilize Muslim sentiment on the issues of Muslim grievances, particularly on the question of Urdu. Those efforts are the subject of the following chapter.

5

CONTEMPORARY MUSLIM POLITICS AND POLITICAL ORGANIZATION IN NORTH INDIA

Three great changes took place in Muslim leadership and organization after 1947 in the north. One was the dissolution of the Muslim League, the only inclusive Muslim political organization in north India. The second was the disappearance of the previous League leadership and the disintegration of its political and economic bases of organization. As has been noted above, many of the most prominent League leaders migrated to Pakistan. Moreover, even for those who remained, the conditions for separatist Muslim political action were radically altered. The bitterness of Hindu feeling after partition would have made untenable in the north the continuance of the Muslim League as an effective political organization in the immediate post-independence period. Moreover, the elimination of the system of separate electorates made the Muslim electorate no longer easily accessible and easily organized. Third, the abolition of the zamindari system substantially reduced the rural influence of the former Muslim landlords, even more than that of their Hindu counterparts, because of the smaller numbers of Muslim peasants in the north and the greater number of urban rentiers among the Muslim landlords. Finally, the introduction of universal suffrage brought the lower classes of Muslims, who had not been organized electorally before, into the system of electoral politics.

In the post-independence period, leadership of the Muslim community passed to three identifiable groups of leaders, divided into various parties and associations. First, there was the small group of middle-class lawyers, doctors, teachers, and journalists of secular and frequently Marxist persuasion who tended initially to work within the Congress and later to join other leftist, secular parties as well. Second, there were Muslims from among the same class who remained less concerned with secularism than with the interests of the Muslim community and who tended to be politically conservative, some of them concentrated in the Aligarh Muslim University and others scattered in the cities and towns of north India. Some of these people remained politically inactive for many years after independence until opportunities arose in the 1960s for new forms of political action on behalf of the Muslim community. Others, like Dr A. J. Faridi of Lucknow, attempted unsuccessfully to work for Muslim causes through the secular political parties, again only until the opportunity arose for separate Muslim political action. Third, there were the ulama, who for a time after independence represented the only group who could speak openly and relatively fearlessly for Muslim causes. However, the interests of the ulama were narrow and confined primarily to the protection of the religious rights of Muslims and the preservation, untouched by secular legislation, of the Muslim Personal Law. Moreover, the ulama were themselves increasingly sharply divided between the orthodox ulama of the Deoband school, who had political respectability in the Congress, and the fundamentalist ulama and their allies in the Jamaat-e-Islami. Finally, a third group of Muslims in politics, who acquired greater importance after independence, were the 'backward' Muslims or Momins, concentrated primarily in Bihar.

This chapter will be concerned with the attempts of these sets of Muslim leaders to organize effectively in the post-independence political arena in north India to promote Muslim interests and with the interaction between Muslim leaders and organizations and the established political parties in contemporary politics in U.P. and Bihar. The chapter will describe, first, the major Muslim political associations in north India; second, the attitudes of the prominent political parties towards Muslim demands; and, third, the effectiveness of Muslim political action on the major issue of concern to Muslims in contemporary north Indian politics, the preservation and protection of Urdu.

MUSLIM ASSOCIATIONS AND LEADERSHIP AND THE CAUSE OF URDU

It has become conventional to distinguish four distinct strands of Muslim religio-political ideology in contemporary India and Pakistan – traditional orthodoxy, fundamentalist revivalism, modernism, and secularism.[1] Traditional orthodoxy is represented by the conservative ulama and their adherents who follow the inherited paths of religious observance among Muslims in the subcontinent. Fundamentalist revivalism has been articulated most clearly by Maulana

---

[1] The classification was originally used by Leonard Binder, *Religion and Politics in Pakistan* (Berkeley: University of California Press, 1961), esp. pp. 3–9.

Maududi and the Jamaat-e-Islami and is characterized by a desire to recapture the pristine values and the glory of Islam in its classical period. Modernism has been best represented in India by Syed Ahmad Khan and the Aligarh Muslim University, which was founded by Syed Ahmad both to provide modern, Western education to Indian Muslims and to re-orient Islamic thinking to make it compatible with modern, scientific knowledge. Secularism among Muslims has taken many forms, but has usually involved a primary concern for either the Muslim community or Indian or Pakistan nationalism rather than for Islamic ideology and religion.

These categories are useful and their political expressions will be discussed below. However, they only begin to suggest the extent of internal differentiation amongst Muslims in contemporary India. For the purposes of this analysis, which is concerned exclusively with the political and associational expressions of Muslim interests, a different kind of fourfold division will be made which cuts across the traditionalist, fundamentalist, modernist, secularist distinctions and introduces other differentia.

For present purposes, four types of Muslim associational interests will be distinguished – religio-political associations, non-economic interest associations, occupational and class associations, and inclusive political organizations. In a subcontinent-wide survey of Muslim associations, it would be necessary also to distinguish between all-India or all-Pakistan associations and regional associations. Since the present analysis is concerned only with north India and only with those Muslim associations which have had an impact upon north Indian politics, it will be sufficient to distinguish between those groups which have an all-India focus and those which are practically confined to or have their greatest impact in the north. It will also be shown that even those associations which are all-India in organization tend to act very differently in the two states of U.P. and Bihar.

Religio-political associations

Jamiyyat-ul-Ulama-e-Hind

The Jamiyyat-ul-Ulama is the leading political organization in north India of Muslim traditional orthodoxy. It is the political arm of the orthodox ulama, centered in the traditionalist Muslim university at Deoband in the Saharanpur district of U.P.[1] It was founded in 1919

---

[1] On the relationship between the Jamiyyat-ul-Ulama and the Deoband institution, see Ziya-ul-Hasan Faruqi, *The Deoband School and the Demand for Pakistan* (Bombay: Asia Publishing House, 1963), ch. 3.

and joined in political alliance with the Indian National Congress from its inception.[1] Its political ideology has been marked by three features – traditional orthodoxy, pan-Islamism, and a belief in composite Indian nationalism. Traditional orthodoxy has been expressed politically in its consistent and persistent defense of the Muslim Personal Law and in its opposition to any attempts by the state to change or interfere with it through either specific laws or through the enactment of a uniform civil code.[2] Pan-Islamism was the original motive which brought the Jamiyyat into an alliance with the Congress during the Khilafat and non-cooperation movements of 1920 and 1921.[3] Its belief in what Aziz Ahmad has called the 'covenantal theory of composite nationalism' (involving an implied covenant between Hindus and Muslims against the British and for an independent, secular Indian state)[4] led it to join forces with the Indian National Congress in a political alliance which was maintained throughout the independence movement and continues in important respects up to the present.

Although the Jamiyyat has been primarily concerned with protecting and preserving Islam and Islamic law in nationalist and independent India, it has also worked for the political advancement of the Muslims as a community. The Jamiyyat opposed the Muslim League and the Pakistan movement, but it supported the retention of separate electorates for Muslims in 1928 when the Nehru Report recommended their abolition.[5] Jamiyyat leaders have occupied prominent positions in parliament and in the central government. With other Muslim organizations in north India, the Jamiyyat has supported the cause of Urdu and the demand to declare Urdu the second official language in the states of north India.[6] Despite its historic opposition to the modernist wing of the Muslim community in India represented by the Aligarh Muslim University and to the

[1] Aziz Ahmad, *Islamic Modernism in India and Pakistan, 1857–1964* (London: Oxford University Press, 1967), p. 135.

[2] Ziya-ul-Hasan Faruqi notes that the Jamiyyat 'was organized with the exclusive purpose of safeguarding the *Shari'ah* and giving the Muslim community religious and political guidance according to Islamic principles and commandments' (*Deoband School*, p. 68). See also Faruqi's chapter, 'Indian Muslims and the Ideology of the Secular State', in Donald E. Smith (ed.), *South Asian Politics and Religion* (Princeton: Princeton University Press, 1966), pp. 145–6.

[3] See Ram Gopal, *Indian Muslims: A Political History (1858–1947)* (Bombay: Asia Publishing House, 1959), p. 147.

[4] Aziz Ahmad, *Islamic Modernism*, p. 190; see also Wilfred Cantwell Smith, *Islam in Modern History* (New York: New American Library, 1959), p. 285, and Faruqi, 'Indian Muslims', p. 140.

[5] Faruqi, *The Deoband School*, p. 80; Ram Gopal, *Indian Muslims*, p. 212.

[6] See the *Leader*, 11 December 1960, and the *Express*, 13 December 1960.

fundamentalist Jamaat-e-Islami, the Jamiyyat-ul-Ulama joined the movement in 1965 to preserve the minority status of the Aligarh Muslim University and participated – if briefly – with the Jamaat-e-Islami in the Muslim Majlis-e-Mushawarat formed in 1964.[1]

There is no doubt that the Jamiyyat-ul-Ulama represents an important segment of Muslim opinion in contemporary India. Moreover, the Jamiyyat has organized Muslim political opinion during elections and at other times through the ulama in the towns and in the countryside. The Jamiyyat also publishes a daily Urdu newspaper from Delhi which has a circulation of nearly 4,500.[2] However, during major upsurges of Muslim political sentiment, the Jamiyyat leadership has been isolated from dominant trends of Muslim political opinion. This has occurred twice in its political history – first when the Muslim League succeeded in mobilizing the Muslim masses behind the Pakistan demand and more recently when the predominant Jamiyyat leadership withdrew from the Muslim Majlis-e-Mushawarat after a brief flirtation with that organization. Its refusal to participate in major Muslim political movements in opposition to the Indian National Congress caused it to feel the wrath of both Jinnah[3] and more recently Dr Faridi. Dr Faridi has argued that 'the bogus and selfish claims of Congress Muslims and those of the Jamaitul Ulama' to represent Muslim political opinion prevented reconcilation between the Congress and the League in the pre-independence period and led to the partition of India. It is Dr Faridi's contention that 'the Jamiatul Ulama-e-Hind is the Muslim wing of the Congress party' and that it and other 'Congress Muslims are immensely disliked by the Muslim masses of India'.[4]

The Jamiyyat has played a possibly decisive role, as an ally of the

[1] Theodore P. Wright, Jr., 'Muslim Education in India at the Crossroads: The Case of Aligarh', *Pacific Affairs*, xxxix, Nos. 1 and 2 (Spring–Summer 1966), 50–63. Wright overly stresses the incongruity of the Jamiyyat-ul-Ulama support of the Aligarh Muslim University agitation. The agitation essentially defended, in fact wished to restore, traditionalist forces and aspects in the institution against the onslaught of modernist forces and trends both inside and outside the university. Hence, the support of the Jamiyyat-ul-Ulama for the agitation is consistent with its broad ideological position.

[2] Government of India, Ministry of Information and Broadcasting, *Press in India, 1965* (Delhi: Manager of Publications, 1965), vol. II, p. 630.

[3] Jinnah is reported to have said in 1937, in a reference to the Jamiyyat: 'What the League has done is to set you free from the reactionary elements of Muslims and to create the opinion that those who play their selfish game are traitors. It has certainly freed you from that undesirable element of Maulvis and Maulanas. I am not speaking of Maulvis as a whole class. There are some of them who are as patriotic and sincere as any other; but there is a section of them which is undesirable.' Cited in Faruqi, *The Deoband School*, p. 79.

[4] A. J. Faridi, *Tashkent Declaration and the Problem of Indo-Pak Minorities* (Lucknow, 1966), p. 39.

Congress, in preventing any serious moves by the Congress leadership to interfere with the Muslim Personal Law,[1] a matter of concern to Dr Faridi and other Muslim leaders. Yet, it is true that its orthodoxy has isolated the Jamiyyat from modernist Muslim sentiment,[2] its pan-Islamism has distracted Indian Muslims from their political goals in India, and its alliance with the Congress has isolated it from the great movements of Muslim political sentiment and has sometimes reinforced the refusal of the Congress leaders to accommodate Muslim political demands.

Jamaat-e-Islami

The Jamaat-e-Islami, like the Jamiyyat-ul-Ulama, belongs to the category of all-India Muslim religio-political associations. In fact, it arose out of and in reaction to the religio-political ideology of the Jamiyyat-ul-Ulama through the efforts of Maulana Abul-Ala Maududi. Maududi began his public career as the editor of the Jamiyyat-ul-Ulama organ, the *Aljamiat*, but later founded his own journal in 1932 and broke with the Jamiyyat. In his own writings and through the Jamaat-e-Islami, which he founded in 1941, he developed a religio-political ideology which is quite different from that of the Jamiyyat-ul-Ulama.[3]

The Jamaat-e-Islami opposed both the composite nationalism of the Jamiyyat-ul-Ulama and the separatist nationalism of the Muslim League, the former because it seemed to threaten the absorption of Muslims into a predominantly Hindu society and the latter because it was secular and not based upon the religious law and ideology of Islam.[4] The ideology of the Jamaat-e-Islami has been described as fundamentalist and revivalist. Its orientation is towards the revival of pristine Islamic principles, purged of features taken from other religions, and their adoption by temporal rulers in Muslim countries as the bases for Islamic states. Essentially, this means accepting 'the validity of Islamic canon law as unalterable and immutable for all time to come'[5] and the adoption of the *shari'a* rather than a modern constitution as the fundamental law of the state.

Little is known about the actual functioning of the Jamaat-e-Islami as an organization. In principle, it has adopted a cell-like organization 'highly centralized, pyramidally converging on a single amīr [leader], obedience to whom [is] binding upon Muslims'.[6]

---

[1] Aziz Ahmad, *Islamic Modernism*, p. 259, also makes this point.
[2] Smith, *South Asian Politics and Religion*, p. 286.
[3] Aziz Ahmad, *Islamic Modernism*, ch. 12.
[4] *Ibid.*, pp. 208, 213.   [5] *Ibid.*, p. 212.   [6] *Ibid.*, p. 215.

The Jamaat claimed in 1959 to have 183 local units and a member-ship of 1,318.[1] Its pattern of organization and its militancy have caused it to be characterized as a communal and fascist organization in contemporary Indian politics. Congress leaders tend to equate it with the RSS when condemning Hindu and Muslim communal forces.[2] In theory, the Jamaat-e-Islami eschews party and electoral politics. In practice, it adopts a militant stance on all issues affect-ing the Muslim community and has had a great impact in the phrasing of Muslim demands in connection with the Aligarh Muslim University agitation of 1965[3] and in supporting through its English press organ, *Radiance*, the militant posture of Dr Faridi and the U.P. unit of the Muslim Majlis-e-Mushawarat.[4]

Although its defense of the *shari'a* gives it a common ground with the Jamiyyat-ul-Ulama, the Jamaat-e-Islami considers the former organization its primary enemy within the Muslim community in India.[5] Not only is its underlying religio-political ideology different, but its political orientation has been historically anti-Congress, in contrast to the Jamiyyat-ul-Ulama. Although the Jamiyyat has been historically the more influential of the two associations because of its close relationship with the Congress, the Jamaat-e-Islami is pres-ently more in tune with the sentiment of the Muslim elites in north India in its defense of the rights of the Muslim minority. The Jamaat-e-Islami also has a larger audience than the Jamiyyat-ul-Ulama through both its official Urdu organ, the *Dawat*, which has a claimed circulation of 5,920 compared to 4,459 for the *Aljamiat*, and through its unofficial English-language organ, *Radiance*, which claims a circulation of 10,660 and is read by the English-educated Muslim elite of all political persuasions.[6]

[1] *Introducing the Jamaat-e-Islami Hind* (Delhi: Jamaat-e-Islami Hind, 1959), p. 22.
[2] The publications of the Sampradayikta Virodhi Committee of Mrs Subhadra Joshi, a dedicated secularist Congress M.P., especially take this view. See, for example, Inayat Ullah, *The Real Face of Jamaat-e-Islami* (Delhi: Sampradayikta Virodhi Committee, n. d.).
[3] Wright, 'Muslim Education in India at the Crossroads', p. 60.
[4] The Inayat Ullah pamphlet claims that 'the leadership of the Majlis fell into the hands of leaders like Dr Faridi who were fully under the dominance of Jamaat-e-Islami' (p. 13). Although there has been a coincidence of posture and some direct influence of Jamaat-e-Islami ideas in the demands of the Majlis, Dr Faridi has been critical of the Jamaat in his *Communal Riots and National Integration* (Lucknow, 1962), p. 53.
[5] For example, see *Radiance*, 2 April 1972, p. 4.
[6] Circulation figures from *Press in India, 1965*, vol. II, pp. 630, 635. *Radiance* denies that it is an organ of the Jamaat-e-Islami, but its editor, M. Yousuf Siddiqi, is a prominent member of the Jamaat and the line of the paper is unequivocally a Jamaat line. On the importance of *Radiance* for the educated Muslim elites, see Wright, 'The Effectiveness of Muslim Representation in India', in Smith, *South Asian Politics and Religion*, p. 114. The Jamaat also sponsors the publication of a weekly periodical in Malayalam from Kerala;

Non-economic interest associations

Anjuman Taraqqi-e-Urdu (Hind)

The Anjuman Taraqqi Urdu is the leading organization in India, and in the states of U.P. and Bihar, supporting the cause of Urdu.[1] It was formed in 1903 as an all-India organization, but was reorganized after the partition of India into separate Pakistan and India organizations. Its primary purpose has been to promote and encourage both Urdu and popular Hindustani. The Anjuman has stressed the links between Hindi and Urdu, while demanding special protection for Urdu. Its central leadership has come from both Hindus and Muslims. Dr Zakir Husain, the late President of India, was president of the Anjuman from 1948 to 1956. Another president was a Hindu, Pandit H. N. Kunzru, a Liberal politician of an earlier generation in Indian politics. The general secretary has been a Muslim, Ali Ahmad Saroor, dean of the faculty of arts of the Aligarh Muslim University.

There are significant differences in the leadership and manner of operation of the U.P. and Bihar units of the Anjuman. The leadership of the U.P. unit has often been identical with the leadership of the all-India organization and consists of eminent 'nationalist' Muslims and liberal Hindus of an older generation. The U.P. Anjuman and its district branches have filed complaints with the Commissioner for Linguistic Minorities and the U.P. Language Committee over the status of Urdu in the schools and in administration in the state,[2] delegations of the leadership have met with the chief ministers of U.P. to present demands on behalf of Urdu, and memoranda were submitted and representations were made to the President of India in 1953 and 1958 and to the prime minister in 1963 and 1965 (by both the state and national units of the Anjuman)[3] on the status of

a weekly, *Margdeep*, in Marathi dealing with literary and cultural affairs, with a circulation of 1875; a Telugu monthly, *Vigyan Chandrika*, with a circulation of 820; and two monthlies from Rampur in U.P., dealing with religion and philosophy, of which the Urdu periodical, *Zindagi*, had a circulation of 2,082 and the Hindi monthly, *Kanti*, had a circulation of 737 in 1964; *Introducing the Jamaat-e-Islami Hindi*, p. 22, and *Press in India, 1965*, vol. II, pp. 26, 246, 500, 520.

[1] See Jyotirindra Das Gupta, *Language Conflict and National Development: Group Politics and National Language Policy in India* (Berkeley: University of California Press, 1970), pp. 209–13.

[2] *Kripalani Committee Report*, p. 5, and app. iii; *CLM* v, pp. 70–2.

[3] The history of these demands, representations, and memoranda from U.P. is given in Das Gupta, *Language Conflict and National Development*, pp. 142ff; see also the *Memorandum* submitted by H. N. Kunzru, president, Anjuman Taraqqi Urdu (Hind), to Lal Bahadur Shastri, prime minister of India, on 7 April 1965, and the report of a delegation of the Anjuman to chief minister Gupta in U.P. in the *Statesman*, 19 August 1961.

Urdu in U.P. However, the U.P. Anjuman has not engaged in an organized way in party and electoral politics and has not adopted a militant stance. Muslim militancy in U.P. has been associated more with the Muslim Majlis-e-Mushawarat under the leadership of Dr Faridi.

In Bihar, the roles of the two organizations have been reversed, the Anjuman being the more militant organization and the Majlis the more moderate. The Bihar branch of the Anjuman was founded in 1951 and it claims to have 180 branches in the state. Its organization appears to be more formalized than in U.P. Three elections of office bearers of the Anjuman in Bihar have been held in 1951, 1957, and 1960. The membership of the organization has been above 10,000. The activities of the Bihar Anjuman in the past have included a two-year signature campaign during which more than 900,000 signatures were collected for an Urdu petition; a census campaign which attempted to reach every Urdu-speaking household in Bihar; deputations from time to time to state and central ministers and to the president of India to achieve recognition for Urdu in schools and colleges, in state administration, and on the Patna station of the All-India Radio; deputations to the Commissioner for Linguistic Minorities and to numerous commissions and official bodies at the local, state, and national levels; the calling of Urdu conventions of 'representatives of all educational, literary, social, cultural, and political societies' concerned with Urdu; and celebrations of Ghalib, Iqbal, and Prem Chand days.[1]

The Anjuman appears to have acquired much of its energy from the activities of Ghulam Sarwar, the first general secretary of the state branch and also its president for some time. Ghulam Sarwar is an Urdu journalist who occupies a similar position in Bihar to Dr Faridi in U.P. He and his Urdu paper, the *Sangam*, have been prosecuted several times by the state government for allegedly publishing inflammatory communal propaganda. During the 1967 elections, the Anjuman released a list of candidates to whom it gave its support. In contrast to the Majlis in Bihar, but like the Majlis in U.P., the Bihar Anjuman adopted an anti-Congress position and refused to support any Congress candidates. In the prestige constituency of Patna West, where the Bihar Majlis supported the Congress chief minister, K. B. Sahay, the Anjuman worked for his main opponent, Mahamaya Prasad Sinha.[2] The Anjuman in Bihar under

---

[1] *Two Words with Well-Wishers of Urdu*, translated from Urdu, and interview, L4:4–7, 31–48, 65–6.
[2] Interview, L4:31–48.

the leadership of Ghulam Sarwar has been the primary organization of Muslim political militancy. In the 1969 mid-term elections in Bihar, Ghulam Sarwar supported the Communist party, whereas the Majlis did not participate in the elections at all.

Urdu Muhafiz Dasta

The Urdu Muhafiz Dasta (Urdu Protective Society) is a minor Muslim organization founded in April 1964 in Uttar Pradesh by a wealthy contractor of Lucknow. It has achieved some notice in the press because it is the only Muslim or Urdu organization which has adopted agitational tactics in recent years. These have included throwing leaflets into the U.P. assembly demanding the declaration of Urdu as second official language in the state[1] and hunger-strikes and demonstrations before parliament, the All-India Congress Committee office in New Delhi, and opposite the council house in Lucknow.[2] The Dasta erected *shamianas* opposite both the AICC office in New Delhi and the council house in Lucknow, which remained in these places for years.[3] However, the Muhafiz Dasta does not have the importance either for Muslims or for government of the Anjuman Taraqqi Urdu.

Deeni Talimi Council

The Deeni Talimi Council was formed in 1959 ostensibly for two purposes – to establish primary schools to impart 'religious and moral education' along with primary education and to keep watch over the textbooks prescribed in government schools in Uttar Pradesh to see that they do not impart Hindu religious education.[4] Not much information is available on the organization and membership of the Council, but the prominent Muslim leaders associated with it have been Dr A. J. Faridi, Zafar Ahmad Siddiqi, Hazrat Maulana Abul Hasan Ali, Qazi Adeel Abbasi, and Maulana Afzal Hussain. The Council has acquired some prominence through the publication of a pamphlet, *Brief Scrutiny of Prescribed Books in U.P.*, which consists of some 123 translations and references to passages in U.P. school textbooks which allegedly contain 'matter contrary to the basic tenets of Islam', items propagating 'Hindu religion and mythology' and 'Hindu culture', and material inciting 'hatred

[1] *Radiance*, 14 August 1966.
[2] *Ibid.*, 6 December 1966, and personal observation.
[3] Personal observation.
[4] Deeni Talimi Council, *Brief Scrutiny of Prescribed Books in U.P.* (Lucknow: Deeni Taleemi Council, 1966), p. ii; and *Presidential Address* of Dr A. J. Faridi, delivered at the district conference Deeni Talimi Council held on 21 March 1965 at Shahjahanpur, p. 1.

against Muslims'.[1] Through various deputations and memoranda to officers and ministers of the U.P. and central governments since 1960, the Council has sought to have the textbooks or their offending passages removed from the schools. In September 1966 the Council achieved a measure of success when the central education minister agreed to appoint a committee of inquiry to examine the allegedly offending passages in the U.P. textbooks.[2] The Council has also contributed to the cause of Urdu by filing complaints to the CLM against the U.P. government policies towards providing instruction in Urdu.[3]

Aligarh Muslim University Old Boys' Association

Another non-economic interest association of some importance in U.P. and Bihar is the AMU Old Boys' Association. In normal times, the Old Boys perform the functions customary for alumni associations all over the world. In times of crisis, the Old Boys can mobilize the educated Muslim elite of north India in defense of the university, as they did in August 1965, in connection with the AMU agitation of that year, when they joined forces with other Muslim organizations in north India to protect the minority character of the university.

Occupational and class associations

Momins and handloom weavers in Bihar

In both Uttar Pradesh and Bihar, the Congress has had allies in the Muslim community throughout the nationalist movement and up to the present. In Uttar Pradesh, the chief ally of the Congress was the religio-political organization, the Jamiyyat-ul-Ulama. In Bihar, support for the Congress from the Muslims came from the so-called backward Muslims or Momins, who are primarily handloom weavers, constitute more than 20% of the Muslim population of Bihar, and live overwhelmingly in the rural areas of the state.[4]

The Momin movement, which began during the second decade of the twentieth century, reflected a class and caste division in the Muslim community.[5] In a sense, it is a Muslim counterpart to the non-Brahman movements and the backward castes movements which

---

[1] *Brief Scrutiny.*
[2] *Radiance,* 2 October 1966.
[3] *CLM* v, pp. 12, 15.
[4] The Momin movement seems to have drawn most of its support from the caste known in the old census reports as Julahas.
[5] The material in this section is drawn from three interviews in Patna on 5 and 10 April 1967, and 12 February 1969.

have developed at different times in different parts of India amongst Hindus. The Momin movement rebelled against the dominance of higher-caste Muslims – Syed, Shaikh, and Pathan – in education and public service. The Muslim League, dominated by elite Muslim leaders, had no appeal to the Momins, whereas the Congress, with its Gandhian symbol of the spinning wheel and its pledges of support to indigenous handicrafts, appealed to the economic interests of the Muslim handloom weavers.

The pre-eminent leader of the Momins in Bihar during the nationalist period was Abdul Quayyum Ansari, who became a minister in the Bihar Congress government after independence until 1951 and then again from 1962 to 1966. Ansari has been the leader of a Momin organization known as the Bihar Momin Conference. Under his leadership and during his ministership in 1948, an economic organization of the handloom weavers was established with the patronage of the Congress government. This organization, the Bihar State Handloom Weavers' Cooperative Union, claims to have a membership of 142,205, mostly Momins, organized into 1,062 Weavers' Cooperative Societies.[1]

The Bihar Momin Conference under Abdul Quayyum Ansari has maintained its alliance with the Congress and has criticized other Muslim organizations in Bihar which have opposed the Congress. Ansari has personally attacked the Jamaat-e-Islami and the Muslim Majlis-e-Mushawarat as communal bodies similar to the Jan Sangh, RSS, and other Hindu communal organizations.[2] During the 1967 elections in Bihar, some Momins joined with other Muslim leaders in opposing the Congress. The general secretary of the Handloom Weavers Union also reported, in April 1967, that the Union and the weavers were dissatisfied with the patronage of the Congress government during the previous twenty years and that the Momins had voted against the Congress in the 1967 elections.[3] In March 1967, a new Momin organization was formed, the Bihar State Momin Advisory Committee, to negotiate with the non-Congress government for aid to the weavers and for the inclusion of Momins in the government.

---

[1] *Report on the Working of the Bihar State Hand-loom Weavers' Co-operative Union Ltd. and Weavers' Co-operative Societies of Bihar* (Patna: Bihar State Hand-loom Weavers' Co-operative Union Ltd., 1963(?)), p. 1.

[2] See his remarks quoted in *Radiance*, 14 August and 23 October 1966.

[3] Dissatisfaction with state government support for the hand-loom weaving industry was expressed in the secretary's *Report on the Working of the Bihar State Hand-loom Weavers' Co-operative*. The secretary gave me the information on Momin voting behavior, as he saw it, in an interview.

Other occupational associations

Although the Momins are the major organized force among the non-elite Muslim castes, there are other occupational associations among the backward Muslims. These include associations of the Rains (vegetable sellers), of the Duniyas (workers in cotton and thread), of the Hawaris (washermen), and of the Rangrez (dyers). In the early post-independence period, A. Q. Ansari also established a federated caste organization of the backward Muslim castes, called the Bihar State Backward Muslim Federation, but this organization is no longer active. Finally, it should be noted that the president of the Anjuman Taraqqi Urdu, Ghulam Sarwar, the most prominent Muslim political activist in Patna, is a Rain. Thus, not only is there significant economic and class differentiation within the Muslim community, but there is also political differentiation among the backward Muslims, whose prominent leaders belong to different Muslim organizations, some of whom support the Congress while others oppose it.

Inclusive political organizations and Muslim political action in Uttar Pradesh and Bihar: the Muslim Majlis-e-Mushawarat

The accumulation of Muslim grievances in India and the ineffectiveness of the various Muslim and Urdu organizations, working separately, to achieve significant concessions from government had begun to affect the thinking of Muslim leaders of all political and ideological persuasions by the early 1960s. The terrible communal riots in eastern India in 1964, in which hundreds of Muslims were slaughtered, provided the necessary catalyst for the formation of a new, broadly based confederation of Muslim organizations to articulate the grievances of Muslims and to seek ways of alleviating them through the processes of party and electoral politics. To this end, preparations were made in the spring of 1964, under the leadership of Dr Syed Mahmud, the most senior member of the Congress party in India, for a meeting of Muslim leaders from all the leading Muslim organizations in India, which was held in Lucknow on 8 and 9 August 1964.[1] This meeting, which included representatives of every segment

[1] The factors leading to this meeting and the preparations made for it and for the formation of the Majlis-e-Mushawarat are given by Dr Faridi in *Radiance*, 9 October 1966; in my interviews, L1:8–9 and L2:2; in a typescript document in my possession, titled 'The Birth of Muslim Majlis-e-Mushawarat and What it is'; in a pamphlet by Sundar Lal, *India's National Integration – A New and Welcome Phase* (New Delhi: All-India Muslim Majlis-e-Mushawarat, 1965); and in an undated pamphlet with no title on the 8 and 9 August 1964 meetings in my possession.

of Muslim opinion except the radical left, passed a series of resolutions which emphasized the Muslim concern for their very existence in India in the wake of the terrible riots of that year. The resolutions deplored the deaths of those killed, condemned the proposals for and the actual incidents of forced exchange of populations between India and Pakistan in the east, blamed both the governments of India and Pakistan for not taking necessary measures to provide security for their minorities, and chastised members of the legislatures in India – particularly the Muslim members – for not raising their voices to protest these atrocities and for not voicing 'the problems and grievances of Muslims'. The conference simultaneously deplored the failure of the majority community and of government in India to promote true national integration in the country after seventeen years of independence and rededicated Muslims to this task. For this purpose, the conference agreed to establish a permanent organization, to be called the Muslim Majlis-e-Mushawarat (Muslim Consultative Committee (MMM)) and elected Dr Syed Mahmud as its president.

The conference and the decision to establish the MMM had a dual significance, recognized by most participants, which went beyond the resolutions of the moment. First, it was agreed that, because of the failures of the political process and of government in India to protect Muslims and promote national integration, the time had come for Muslims as Muslims to act on their own behalf and on behalf of the general interests of the country. Second, it was felt that the time had come for Muslims of different opinions to ignore their differences and work together to protect the broad interests of the Muslim community in India.

The formation of the MMM had its greatest impact in the north Indian states, particularly in the two states of U.P. and Bihar,[1] which have the largest concentrations of Muslim population in India and where Muslim political activity had been largely dormant since the partition of India. In Uttar Pradesh, Dr Abdul Jalil Faridi, a prominent physician-cum-politician of Lucknow, who had been active in Muslim causes for many years, immediately became the dominant and driving force in the state branch of the MMM.

[1] State units of the Majlis were also formed in Andhra Pradesh, Madhya Pradesh, Maharashtra, Mysore, Rajasthan, and West Bengal. The Muslim League in Madras and Kerala participated in the formation of the All-India Majlis, but the League retained its separate identity in those states. Zaheer Masood Quraishi, 'Electoral Stategy of a Minority Pressure Group: The Muslim Majlis-e-Mushāwarat', *Asian Survey*, VIII No. 12 (December 1968), 978.

Branches of the Majlis were formed in 40 districts of U.P.[1] In September 1966 Dr Faridi established an Urdu daily paper specifically to air the platform and policies of the MMM and to articulate Muslim grievances and demands.[2] The Bihar branch of the MMM was not established until 1 June 1966.[3] The primary organizer of the MMM in Bihar was Mohammed Yakub Younis, a hotel-owner in Patna, a less dynamic personality than Dr Faridi. Yakub Younis toured most of the districts of Bihar throughout the latter part of 1966 and assisted in the formation of district units of the Majlis throughout Bihar.[4] The two state units eventually followed different political strategies in their respective states, which will be examined presently.

Although the new-found unity among Muslims provided new vigor to Muslim political activity in the north, which carried through the 1967 elections and after, the unity itself proved to be illusory. Differences on purposes and political strategy developed almost immediately. Broadly speaking, there were three main elements comprising the MMM – individual Muslim politicians like Dr Faridi who had unsuccessfully tried to voice the grievances of Muslims through the non-Congress political parties; the militant, 'fundamentalist' Jamaat-e-Islami; and 'nationalist' Muslims like Dr Syed Mahmud, who were members either of the Congress or of the Congress-oriented Jamiyyat-ul-Ulama.[5] The main burden of political activity ultimately fell upon those in the first category because the Jamaat-e-Islami leaders are in principle opposed to participation in party and electoral activity,[6] whereas the 'nationalist' and Congress Muslims soon became uncomfortable with the militance and anti-Congress attitudes of men like Dr Faridi. The Jamaat-e-Islami leaders were torn between their desire for Islamic unity and their admiration for Dr Faridi's militance, but they continued to support the Majlis through their press organs. A section of the Jamiyyat-ul-

[1] Interview, L1:21.
[2] *Radiance*, 25 September 1966.
[3] *Radiance*, 6 November 1966.
[4] Interview, L3:22. See also *Radiance*, 18 September 1966, for reports of district and town meetings of the Majlis in Sitamarhi and Champaran.
[5] For two somewhat different formulations of the nature of the Muslim coalition in the Majlis, see Quraishi, 'Electoral Strategy of a Minority Pressure Group', pp. 976–7, and Theodore P. Wright, Jr., 'Muslims as Candidates and Voters in 1967 General Election', *Political Science Review*, VIII, No. 1 (January–March 1969), 24–5. Wright and Quraishi disagree on the extent to which ex-Muslim Leaguers in the north formed a significant element in the coalition. My information is that ex-Muslim Leaguers were not in prominent leadership positions at the state level in U.P. and Bihar.
[6] *Radiance*, 25 December 1966.

Ulama, soon withdrew,[1] and the Congress Muslims who remained became embroiled in controversy with Dr Faridi over strategy and tactics.

It was clear from the beginning that there were differences among the various Muslim leaders over even the general purposes of the MMM. All were gratified by the initial unity of Muslim groups, but some, like Dr Mahmud, saw the MMM primarily as a vehicle by which the Muslims of India could express their love for their Indian homeland and their devotion to Hindu–Muslim unity,[2] whereas the Jamaat-e-Islami saw the MMM as a vehicle for Muslims 'to preserve their identity'.[3] A third orientation was that of Dr Faridi, who saw the MMM as primarily a vehicle for political action, to press home the political demands of Muslims. Those who saw the MMM as an instrument to preserve Muslim identity won an initial victory in selecting the name of the organization by prefixing the word 'Muslim' to it, whereas Dr Mahmud preferred simply the name Majlis-e-Mushawarat, without a specific Muslim identification.[4] Those who saw the MMM as an organization to promote Hindu–Muslim unity succeeded in orienting the first activity of the MMM towards that task by organizing a joint Hindu–Muslim goodwill tour to riot-affected areas of the country. During the year 1965, the Majlis also took part in the agitation against the Government of India's policies toward the Aligarh Muslim University and for the preservation of the minority character of the university.[5] However, as the 1967 elections approached, the MMM increasingly turned itself into a political instrument to bargain with the political parties and individual candidates to support the demands of the MMM in return for the backing of the MMM in the elections.

Although the MMM decided not to contest the elections directly, it prepared a *People's Manifesto*, containing nine points, which effectively summarized the main grievances and demands of Muslims – including, specifically, revision of textbooks, the demand for a system of proportional representation in elections, protection of the Muslim Personal Law, the demand to declare Urdu a second official

[1] *Radiance*, 28 August, 11 and 18 September, and 23 October 1966; interview, L2:6.
[2] See, e.g., Dr Mahmud's article in the *Radiance*, 18 September 1966. This sentiment has a practical side also, which was written into the *People's Manifesto* (New Delhi: All-India Muslim Majlis-e-Mushawarat, 1966), namely, that 'no step can be successful unless it finds response in the preponderant section of the majority community'; citation from p. 7.
[3] *Radiance*, 28 August 1966.
[4] Interview, L2:13.
[5] Article by Dr Faridi in *Radiance*, 9 October 1966, and resolution on AMU passed by the All-India Muslim Majlis-e-Mushawarat on 19 and 20 June 1965, a typescript document in my possession.

language in the north Indian states, and an insistence on preserving 'the minority character and traditions' of the Aligarh Muslim University.[1] The most controversial aspects of the manifesto within the Majlis were two portions of the introduction which expressly blamed the government and the Congress party for failing to protect Muslims and to alleviate the sources of Muslim discontent.[2] Disagreement on the attitude to be taken towards the Congress in the coming elections within the Majlis soon became open when Dr Faridi made it clear that he intended to follow through on the logic of the manifesto by refusing to support any Congress candidates, agreeing to support only non-Congress candidates, and by generally adopting an explicit anti-Congress posture. Although the differences were papered over,[3] the U.P. Majlis in the end supported only one Congress candidate in the 1967 elections, Mrs Subhadra Joshi, who has devoted her political life to combating Hindu communalism and who was contesting her parliamentary seat against one of the most prominent leaders of the Jan Sangh. The Bihar unit did not go along with Dr Faridi's nearly pure anti-Congressism and supported 53 Congress candidates for the Bihar assembly.[4] However, it is worth nothing that, even in Bihar, the MMM supported more non-Congress than Congress candidates and that, if the proportion of party candidates supported by the Majlis to the number of seats contested by each party is considered, then the Bihar MMM gave greater proportionate support to the JKD and to the CPI than to the Congress. Moreover, important and influential Muslim leaders in Bihar, such as Ghulam Sarwar, editor of the Patna Urdu daily, the *Sangam*, and a leader of the Bihar Anjuman Taraqqi Urdu, adopted the same anti-Congress stand as Dr Faridi in Uttar Pradesh, which neutralized the Majlis support for the Congress, particularly in the key constituency of Patna West.[5]

[1] *People's Manifesto.*
[2] Referring to the communal riots of 1964, the Manifesto declares: 'The Government on whose shoulders lay squarely the responsibility to control the situation had unfortunately pleaded the philosophy of reaction. The support of this theory of reaction by those who had the greatest responsibility to maintain law and order, has rendered the situation even more hopeless.' And, on the Congress: 'It is generally felt among the Muslims that the party which has been continuously in power for the last 19 years has failed to abide by its lofty principles and has not proved itself earnest particularly in the amelioration of Muslim grievances'; *People's Manifesto*, pp. 3, 5. Dr Mahmud, particularly, was unhappy with this section of the manifesto; interview, L2:8.
[3] *Radiance*, 8 January 1967.
[4] For the figures on candidates supported by the MMM, see Quraishi, 'Electoral Strategy of a Minority Pressure Group', p. 979.
[5] *Radiance*, 11 December 1966; interview, L4:7–15, 36–47. In Patna West, the Majlis bowed to the personal wishes of Dr Syed Mahmud and supported Congress chief

The electoral strategy adopted by the Majlis was one of considerable political sophistication. Three mimeographed sheets were prepared and sent or given to candidates, containing a résumé of the nine points in the *People's Manifesto* and two duplicate pledge forms to be signed and returned to the president of the state unit of the MMM and to the all-India general secretary. The pledge forms committed those candidates who signed them to support the nine points 'and work for their adoption by the Legislature and the Government' if elected in return for the support of the Majlis in the election. Sixty-nine candidates in Bihar signed and returned the pledge forms. The state units supported these candidates as well as others who were considered generally sympathetic to the Muslim cause. Implicit in this pledge was a commitment on the part of the Majlis to attempt to deliver a solid bloc of Muslim votes to sympathetic candidates.

Although the Majlis supported both Hindu and Muslim candidates and, especially in U.P., made it a point to work against Muslim candidates who had not supported Muslim causes in the past,[1] a large percentage of the candidates supported by the Majlis were Muslims. In Bihar, 38 out of 161 assembly candidates supported or 23.6% were Muslims. The figure for U.P. is 29 out of 134 or 21.6%.[2]

There has been considerable speculation and some scholarly analysis of the impact of the MMM and of Muslim discontent generally upon the 1967 elections and particularly upon the Congress electoral decline in those elections. Both Theodore Wright and Zaheer Masood Quraishi have demonstrated that the Majlis itself played at most a marginal role in the election results in the states and constituencies where it attempted to influence the outcome.[3] As an electoral organization, the Majlis was not particularly effective in either state. However, there is some ground for believing that the Majlis contributed to a heightening of Muslim discontent, to its expression through the political process, and to 'detouring' Muslims 'from their usual solid support for the Congress'.[4]

In their own assessments of the election results in 1967 the pro-

minister K. B. Sahay, but most Muslim leaders and voters supported Mahamaya Prasad Sinha (who signed the Majlis pledge) and who became chief minister of the first united front government in Bihar.
[1] In the words of Dr Faridi, 'The MMM would prefer to support an honest non-Muslim to the existing stock of Muslim legislators.' *Radiance*, 9 October 1966; also my interview, L1:28.
[2] Quraishi, 'Electoral Strategy of a Minority Pressure Group', p. 979.
[3] Wright, 'Muslims as Candidates and Voters', p. 5, and Quraishi, 'Electoral Strategy of a Minority Pressure Group', p. 985.
[4] Quraishi, 'Electoral Strategy of a Minority Pressure Group', p. 987.

vincial Congress organizations in U.P. and Bihar conceded that they had lost Muslim votes. The Bihar PCC reported to the AICC that 'Muslims generally voted against the Congress'. In an indirect reference to the Majlis, the report went on to say that 'some kind of secret [*sic*] organization was at work among them which aimed at defeating the Congress candidates irrespective of whether the opponents were Communists or Jan Sangh candidates'. There is a somewhat petulant suggestion in this statement that the Majlis was so blinded by anti-Congressism that it was willing to support or permit the victory of parties whose ideological principles were opposed to Islam (in the Communist case) and the Muslims (in the Jan Sangh case). The U.P. organization attributed its electoral decline in part to both Hindu and Muslim communalism, but did not mention the Majlis even indirectly. However, the U.P. report remarked that 'the Congress base hitherto was mostly minorities, Muslims, Harijans, backward classes and the peasantry. This time opposition succeeded in making a dent in this Congress stronghold.'[1] The available electoral evidence and these admissions of the provincial Congress committees do indicate that the Majlis and the Muslims in the north succeeded in achieving a primary objective of the MMM, namely, demonstrating that the Congress could no longer take the Muslim vote for granted.[2]

The political strategy of the MMM for the 1967 elections included the extraction of commitments from those candidates who signed the Majlis pledge form to support the demands in the *People's Manifesto* in the legislature and before government if they were elected. The general feeling even of the Majlis leaders was that this aspect of their strategy was not at all effective. After the 1967 elections in Bihar and U.P., the political context in those states changed from party systems in which the Congress was dominant to a fluid system of coalition politics. The new patterns of coalition politics presented both new opportunities and new dangers for non-party interest groups and required a re-evaluation of previous political strategies. In principle, in a fluid system of coalition politics in which the support even of individuals and independent MLAs is courted by competing coalitions, minority interests ought to be able to enhance their importance. In fact, however, as will be shown below, the period of coalition politics in U.P. and Bihar did not benefit Muslim political interests

---

[1] Citations from 'Preliminary Reports on Election Results from Some Pradesh Congress Committees', provided by the courtesy of the All-India Congress Committee, New Delhi.

[2] E.g., see *People's Manifesto*, pp. 5–6, and *Radiance*, 2 October 1966.

for two reasons. First, some individuals elected with the support of the Majlis did not pursue the interests of Muslims or Urdu, but only their own personal ambitions. Second, although some of the political parties attempted to make good on their campaign pledges to the Majlis, when they did, the issue of Urdu became a basis for inter-party struggle which disrupted the stability of coalitions.

The failure of the initial Majlis strategy to achieve concrete benefits for Muslims or for Urdu in U.P. and Bihar had different consequences in the two states. In Bihar, the Majlis became defunct. In September 1970 a new organization was formed in Bihar, called the Awami Tanzeem,[1] which became a constituent of the all-India MMM, but it has been even less effective than the original unit of the MMM in that state. In U.P., the Majlis took a different course. Continuing under the leadership of Dr Faridi, the U.P. unit transformed itself in June 1968 into a political party,[2] called the U.P. Muslim Majlis and affiliated to the all-India MMM. The U.P. Muslim Majlis contested the 1969 mid-term elections to the legislative assembly and formed alliances with other minority candidates in some constituencies. Dr Faridi claimed that the Majlis ran seventeen candidates, of whom five were successful,[3] but the official returns show only two Majlis candidates, both of whom forfeited their security deposits.

Since its transformation into a political party, the U.P. Muslim Majlis has faced two major problems. The first has been the continuing problem of finding the most productive political strategy to achieve concrete benefits for Muslims and Urdu. In pursuit of a viable political strategy, the U.P. Majlis ultimately came full circle from its total opposition to Congress in 1967 to an explicit alliance with the Congress (R) under the leadership of Mrs Gandhi in the 1971 parliamentary elections.[4] However, the alliance with Congress (R) in U.P. also has not been productive of concrete benefits for Urdu or for Muslims. The Congress (R) leader in U.P. and the man who became chief minister with the support of Mrs Gandhi has been Kamalapati Tripathi, long considered by Muslims to be an inveterate enemy of Urdu and of Muslim interests.[5] A second problem for the U.P. Majlis has been to establish itself as the major political party representing Muslim interests in the north. In this respect, it

[1] *Radiance*, 27 September 1970.
[2] A. J. Faridi, 'Judge Us by Our Policies', *Radiance*, 7 March 1971, p. 9.
[3] Interview in Lucknow on 5 March 1969.
[4] See *Radiance*, 14 and 21 February, 7 March, and 18 April 1971.
[5] *Ibid.*, 22 August 1971 and 9 April 1972.

has recently faced competition from the Muslim League, which has extended its organization into northern India.[1]

Although the Majlis in U.P. has, therefore, not achieved major success either in pursuit of Muslim interests or in establishing itself as a serious political party representing Muslims, it continues to play an important role in articulating Muslim grievances and demands. In a letter to chief minister Tripathi in May 1971, Dr Faridi reiterated the major demands of the Majlis: increased facilities for teaching Urdu in the schools, the right to use Urdu and have Urdu speeches recorded in Persian script in the legislative assembly, the granting to Urdu of status as second official language, the creation of an Urdu university at Rampur, removal of objectionable materials from school textbooks, the appointment of a committee to inquire into 'the socio-economic and the educational backwardness of the Muslim minority', recruitment of Muslims to public services in proportion to their percentage in the population of the state, punishment of police officers who behave improperly during communal riots, and the establishment of a minorities council in the state with the chief minister as chairman.[2] In the absence of a viable Muslim political strategy, however, the fulfillment of such demands depends upon the good wishes of the leaders of the predominant political parties in the state, who have so far not found the support of the Muslim Majlis to be critical to their political futures.

MUSLIMS, URDU, AND PARTY POLITICS IN UTTAR PRADESH AND BIHAR

Political party attitudes towards Urdu and Muslim minority rights

The public attitudes of the major political parties in India towards Urdu and the Muslim minority differ sharply and reflect several distinct underlying ideological positions. They cover a complete spectrum from the refusal of the Jan Sangh, on the one side, to recognize the existence of a Muslim minority in India to the nearly complete identification of the two Communist parties with Muslim demands on Urdu and other matters, on the other side.

As with most issues, the public position of the Congress before the split was squarely in the center. The Congress manifesto for the 1967 elections made no specific mention of either Urdu or Muslims, but declared its continued adherence to 'full equality and no discrimina-

---

[1] *Ibid.*, 19 July 1970; 10 and 31 January, 21 February, 7 March, 6 and 13 June 1971.
[2] *Ibid.*, 16 May 1971.

tion as between one citizen and another', 'equal respect for all religions', and 'strengthening secular forces so that even the smallest minority in India enjoys a honoured place in the new social order'. The Congress promised in its manifesto 'to see that any impediment to the enjoyment of equal rights and obligations with other citizens of India is suitably dealt with' and looked forward to the creation of 'an atmosphere of unity and national integration in which caste or communal distinctions cease to have any importance or relevance'.[1] Although these statements were pious and vague, they did reflect a distinct Congress ideology which may be summed up as a belief in the integration of India through the practice of secularism, equality, non-discrimination, and opposition to all communal forces. Although the ideology of the Congress (R) under Mrs Gandhi's leadership has not changed, references to linguistic minority and to Urdu and Muslim interests were more specific and more favorable in the 1971 election manifesto, which promised implementation of constitutional provisions concerning the use of the mother tongue for linguistic minorities in primary schools and concerning the right of minorities 'to establish, manage and run educational and other institutions'; the granting to Urdu of 'its due place which has been denied to it so far'; prevention of 'discrimination against minorities' in recruitment to the public services; and 'urgent attention . . . to the socio-economic problems faced by Muslims'.[2]

On one extreme from the Congress stands the Jan Sangh, which claims also to believe in equal rights for all the people of India, but considers both discrimination and 'separatist demands claiming special privileges and protection on the basis of province, religion, caste or language' as contradictory to the principle of equality.[3] Moreover, the Jan Sangh, unlike the Congress, does not recognize the existence of minorities in India. There is one Indian nation, to which Muslims ought to belong, but do not because they identify themselves with a foreign power, have sought 'to build up a communal entity distinct from [Indian] society', and have cut themselves away from all 'the customs and traditions, modes and manners, which bind the people here to this land itself'.[4] The Jan Sangh favors

---

[1] The 1967 election manifestos of the major parties have been collected in R. Chandidas *et al.* (eds.), *India Votes: A Source Book on Indian Elections* (New York: Humanities Press, 1968). The citations here are from p. 10.

[2] *Handbook of Election Manifestos, 1971* (Bombay: Commerce Ltd., 1971), pp. 21–2.

[3] Chandidas, *India Votes*, pp. 22, 24.

[4] A. B. Vajpayee, *National Integration* (note submitted by A. B. Vajpayee, leader of the Jan Sangh group in parliament, at the National Integration Conference held at New Delhi, on 28, 29 and 30 September 1961), p. 3.

the adoption of Sanskrit as the national language for ceremonial occasions, replacement of English by Hindi at the center within ten years, the use of regional languages as media of instruction 'up to the highest class', and a three-language formula at the secondary stage comprising the mother tongue, Hindi, and Sanskrit, eliminating English. The 1971 Jan Sangh manifesto promised to provide to the Urdu language the 'facilities due to it under the law', but specifically opposed granting Urdu status as second official language in any state.[1] Moreover, the Jan Sangh leaders have on other occasions made it clear that they consider Urdu merely a style of Hindi written in a foreign script.[2] Finally, the Jan Sangh has pledged itself to enact a uniform civil code, anathema to most Muslim elites.[3] The Jan Sangh position on language and on the Muslims may best be described as militant nationalist, with the emphasis on Hindu culture, Sanskrit, and Hindi as the basic elements in all-India nationality.

At the other extreme has been the position of the CPI, which was especially favorable to Muslim interests in its 1967 manifesto:

Muslims, who constitute the second biggest community in India and occupy a distinctive place in our national life, have to be guaranteed full protection in regard to their specific cultural, social and religious rights. The real test of a secular democracy lies in its attitude to minorities. It is an unfortunate fact that in India today there are certain reactionary, orthodox and revivalist elements belonging to the majority community who are seeking to reduce Muslims to the position of second-rate citizens. Such elements should be vigorously fought out and isolated. It is the duty of the majority Hindu community to ensure that the secular character of our State is not endangered, and that the Muslim minority as all other religious minorities are given full protection in matters relating to their culture, language and religious beliefs. Security of their life and property has to be guaranteed not merely in law but in actual life. Every form of discrimination against the minorities, whether in recruitment to government services, in trade and commerce and administration or in the sphere of educational and cultural development should be put an end to. Such textbooks or educational courses which create in the minds of youth, hatred or prejudice against any minority community should be eliminated and the whole educational system should be thoroughly secularised.

In the realm of language, Urdu, which is spoken by a very large number of Muslims, particularly in the north, should be given its due place in States like U.P., Bihar, Madhya Pradesh, Delhi, etc. All facilities should be provided to Urdu-speaking children to get education in their own mother-tongue up to the higher stage. Besides, Urdu should be allowed to be used for official purposes as the second language . . . in all such states or regions.

All specific and legitimate grievances of religious minorities should be speedily

[1] *Handbook of Election Manifestos, 1971*, p. 67.
[2] *National Herald*, 8 May 1961.
[3] Chandidas, *India Votes*, p. 51.

examined and redressed by the government and to facilitate this special committees or minority boards should be set up at the state level.

Communalism in India is a serious danger to our democracy, freedom and progress and as such must be ruthlessly fought out and conditions created to give both the majority and minority communities equal rights and opportunities to grow and flourish together as inseparable, integral parts of one Indian nation.[1]

The CPI statement is noteworthy from the Muslim point of view in three respects. It singles out the Muslims and Urdu for special protection. It chastises the communalism of the majority community, but makes no mention of Muslim communal groups. It wholly identifies with every grievance of the Muslims in India. The statement is, in fact, a rewording of nearly all the demands in the *People's Manifesto* of the Muslim Majlis-e-Mushawarat. When to this statement is added the CPI position that Hindi should be introduced as the official language of the Union only gradually and with the consent of the non-Hindi speaking states,[2] a consistent ideological position is manifest. The CPI position is pluralistic, recognizing not only individual but distinct group minority rights, including religious rights. The CPM position on Muslims and Urdu in 1967 was substantially the same.[3] However, both Communist party manifestos in 1971 made less specific reference to Muslim grievances and the 1971 CPM manifesto emphasized the need for the Muslim masses to be brought into the class struggle against Congress rule, rather than moving in a separatist direction.[4]

Closest to the Communist position among the major parties, interestingly enough, is that of Swatantra, which adopts a similar posture of pluralism, but does not identify explicitly with specific Muslim demands.[5] Among the smaller parties, the Republican party in 1967 adopted a clear pluralistic position and also specifically supported the demand to recognize Urdu 'as a regional language in Uttar Pradesh and Bihar'.[6]

The fourth distinct ideological position which deserves special notice is that of the SSP, which viewed the problem of language and minorities from a class perspective, as opposed to the individual, group, and national perspectives of the Congress, the CPI, and the Jan Sangh respectively. The SSP position has been widely misinterpreted as respresenting Hindi chauvinism and fanaticism. Although some SSP members in the Hindi-speaking areas were as dedicated to Hindi as the Jan Sanghis, the ideological position of the party and the party leadership was quite different. The SSP, like

---

[1] *Ibid.*, p. 51.   [2] *Ibid.*   [3] *Ibid.*, p. 69.
[4] *Handbook of Election Manifestos, 1971*, p. 143.   [5] Chandidas, *India Votes*, p. 18.
[6] *Ibid.*, p. 91.

the Jan Sangh, wished to get rid of English, but where the Jan Sangh position is based primarily upon militant nationalism, the SSP position was based upon a combination of nationalist and class sentiment. The SSP wanted to end the domination of English not only because it is an alien language, but because it is the language of a narrow bureaucratic and professional class, which continues to dominate Indian public life. Moreover, the SSP emphasis was more on the mother tongues and the regional languages as replacements for English, rather than Sanskrit and Sanskritized Hindi. In the words of the 1967 SSP manifesto, it is 'peoples' dress, peoples' language, peoples' housing, and peoples' food [which] have to be built up' and 'feudal language, food, housing and dress [which] have to be destroyed'.[1]

The SSP manifestos did not speak of minorities and minority languages primarily, but rather of backward and suppressed peoples. For such peoples, which include 'harijans, adivasis, shudras and backward sections of the religious minority and more particularly for backward sections of the Muslim community like weavers', the party pledged to reserve 60% of important positions in public offices. However, the SSP manifestos do not refer to the Muslim community as a whole and the 1971 manifesto specifically warns the Muslims not to 'fall prey to the Communal forces in the country'.[2] Although SSP policy has sometimes been favorable to the Muslim masses and to Urdu, the Muslim elite, which tends to come from high-caste Muslim families, does not find SSP policy attractive. Because the SSP has frequently joined with the Jan Sangh in supporting Hindi and abolition of English and in political alliances generally, some Muslims fear the SSP as much as the Jan Sangh. However, the party policy is quite distinct from that of the Jan Sangh in principle and in practice.

Although it cannot be taken for granted that all members of the Congress, the Jan Sangh, the CPI, and the SSP understand and support fully their party positions on language, minorities, and Indian nationality and although some members of the Congress and the SSP especially believe and act differently in practice, the party positions have been important in recent patterns of coalition politics in northern India. In both U.P. and Bihar, party policies had a considerable impact upon the attitudes of the parties toward the demand to declare Urdu the second official language in those states after the 1967 elections, which will be examined in the next two sections.

[1] *Ibid.*, p. 35.　　[2] *Handbook of Election Manifestos, 1971*, pp. 80–1.

The Urdu issue and coalition politics in Bihar and Uttar Pradesh

The Urdu issue and coalition politics in Bihar

Although no single Muslim organization can take sole credit for it, there is no doubt that the rising tide of Muslim discontent had become sufficiently clear to the leaders of all political parties in north India before the 1967 elections to force them to take a stand at least on the most prominent issue raised by the Muslims, that is, the demand for recognition of Urdu as the second official language in U.P. and Bihar. On the eve of the 1967 elections in both states, the Urdu issue had achieved a position of significant political saliency. It proved after the elections to be the most bitter and divisive issue in the non-Congress governmental coalitions, particularly in Bihar, where it became intertwined with a ghastly communal riot in the city and suburbs of Ranchi and with the complexities of coalition politics.

Divisions within the Congress in both Bihar and U.P. and at the center effectively prevented the Congress from taking a firm position one way or another on the demand. In December 1966, the Congress chief minister of Bihar in effect passed the buck on the Urdu demand to the center, which sat on it until after the elections and then passed it back to the non-Congress government. According to article 347 of the Constitution, the President of India 'may, if he is satisfied that a substantial proportion of the population of a State desire the use of any language spoken by them to be recognised by the State, direct that such language shall also be officially recognised throughout that State or any part thereof for such purposes as he may specify'. This article, clearly designed as a protective resort for linguistic minorities in the states, in no way detracts from the powers of the states, according to article 345, to 'adopt any one or more of the languages in use in the State or Hindi as the language or languages to be used for all or any of the official purposes of that State'. In other words, it was clearly within the powers of the state governments of Bihar and U.P. to declare Urdu the second official language of those states if they so desired. Instead, the chief ministers of both states chose to interpret article 347 as giving the President sole authority to take the necessary action. Most likely in order to avoid divisions within the Congress in Bihar and to avoid providing the Jan Sangh with a campaign issue against the Congress,[1] the Bihar

---

[1] This was not made explicit at the time, but Dr Ram Subhagh Singh, a central minister from Bihar, later indicated that he opposed conceding the demand to give Urdu the

government asked the Government of India, in December 1966, for directions under article 347 to declare Urdu the second official language of the state.[1] Presumably, the Bihar Congress government would then be able to satisfy the Muslims, while pleading to militant Hindu opponents of Urdu that it had no choice but to implement an order of the President. The central Congress leaders, themselves divided on the issue,[2] did not provide this painless solution for the Bihar Congress. In August 1967, when the non-Congress government seemed to be endangered by the divisive impact of the Urdu issue, the central home ministry, which had previously indicated that it did not consider it necessary to make use of article 347, announced that it was in the process of sending a communication to both the U.P. and Bihar governments urging them to 'implement fully the policy decisions on Urdu spelt out by the Union Government' in its statement of 14 July 1958.[3] In effect, the Urdu issue became a political football in the new context of center–state relations in a situation where different political parties controlled the central and state governments.

The united front government in Bihar in turn, as the center well knew, was immobilized and threatened by the Urdu issue. The left parties in the coalition, particularly the SSP and the CPI, had committed themselves in their election campaigns to the satisfaction of the demand to make Urdu the second official language of Bihar and they had succeeded in including a point to that effect in the 33-point program of the coalition government over the opposition of the Jan Sangh, which submitted a note of dissent on the point and reiterated its dissenting view from time to time thereafter.[4] As a direct consequence of this impasse in center–state relations and immobilism in the united front government, a chain of events was launched in August 1967, which ended in the catastrophe of a week of violence, bloodshed, and murder in the city and suburbs of Ranchi, which left at the minimum, according to official figures, 184 people dead and 173 injured.[5]

Both the events leading up to the riot and the course of the riot itself were directly linked (or thus used by politicians at the state level and in the district of Ranchi) to the complex manoeuverings by the

status of second official language because that would mean 'playing into the hands of the Jan Sangh'; *Searchlight*, 2 August 1967.
[1] *Ibid.*, 5 August 1967.
[2] The divisions in the central Congress leadership on the issue became known later. See *ibid.*, 2 August 1967.
[3] *Ibid.*, 5 August 1967.   [4] *Indian Nation*, 24 March 1967.
[5] *Raghubar Dayal Commission Report*, pp. 46–8.

Congress and disaffected elements within the non-Congress government to bring the government down and by opposed parties in the coalition government to embarrass and discredit each other. The first overt link in the chain leading to disaster was provided by a Congress Muslim member of the Bihar Assembly. The Congress leadership, still unwilling or unable to support wholeheartedly the Urdu demand, nevertheless permitted a Muslim member of the party to introduce a private member's bill in the Bihar Assembly to declare Urdu in Persian script the second official language of Bihar.[1] The introduction of the bill forced the members of the government to face up to their commitments and to their disagreements over Urdu.

The first response to the bill came from the president of the Bihar Jan Sangh, who held a press conference on 17 July 1968, and announced that his party would vigorously oppose the bill, which he reportedly viewed as an instrument 'of the communal elements of Bihar'. The Jan Sangh president called upon all political parties and social and educational institutions in the state to oppose the bill.[2] On the same day, however, the SSP deputy chief minister of the united front government announced in the assembly that the government was inclined to give Urdu the status of second official language and that orders to that effect would soon be passed.[3] In the meantime, the Bihar branch of the Hindi Sahitya Sammelan joined the Jan Sangh in bitter opposition to the bill, describing it as 'anti-national, anti-social and against the interest of the people of Bihar', and formed a committee to oppose the bill and any government efforts to make Urdu the second official language.[4] Jan Sangh ministers in the government began to declare openly in public meetings their opposition to any move to give Urdu the place of second official language.[5]

The public controversy over the status of Urdu threatened to harm the rights and privileges which Urdu-speakers had already achieved and were likely to achieve even without a symbolic declaration giving official status to Urdu. In fact, the actual demand of the

[1] *Ibid.*, 31 July 1967.
[2] *Ibid.*, 18 July 1967.
[3] *Searchlight*, 18 July 1967. Apparently, however, even the deputy chief minister had no intention of supporting an official declaration of Urdu as second official language, but only conceding the substance of the demand. He was reported in the *Searchlight* of 24 August 1967 as sharing the view of the previous Bihar Congress government that the state government did not have the power to make Urdu a second official language, but that only the president could do so.
[4] *Indian Nation*, 21 July 1967. The opposition of the Bihar Hindi Sahitya Sammelan to any proposal to give Urdu the status of second official language had been known for some time; e.g., see *Indian Nation*, 18 March 1967.
[5] *Ibid.*, 22 July 1967, and *Searchlight*, 8 August 1967.

Bihar Anjuman Taraqqi Urdu was for a declaration making Urdu the second official language only for specified purposes in education, in the courts, and in administration. Any or all of the specific demands, which have been discussed in detail above, could have been implemented and some had been implemented without a formal declaration of Urdu as second official language. Such a declaration would have facilitated implementation of the specific rights of Urdu-speakers, but nothing more was asked for by such a declaration than the rights accorded to minority language speakers by the Constitution and by the decisions of the Government of India and of the conferences of chief ministers. Militant Hindu opponents of Urdu, however, interpreted the demand for a formal declaration as a demand for equality with Hindi for all purposes, which would transform Bihar into a bilingual state in all respects.[1]

The SSP deputy chief minister had already issued orders before the controversy broke in July for implementing decisions reached by the Bihar cabinet to make arrangements for instruction in Urdu in the schools, for government officers to give replies in Urdu to applications presented in Urdu, and for the printing of government publications in Urdu.[2] When the controversy intensified in July, the Jan Sangh demanded the deferment of these decisions and began threatening to resign from the government if its views were not respected.[3] The cabinet, in a meeting on 27 July, agreed to defer any action on behalf of Urdu.[4]

Despite the decision to defer further action, the anti-Urdu forces

---

[1] The CPI made it clear that it supported the right of Urdu-speakers to use Urdu in dealing with government offices and the duty of the government to publish important government notices in Urdu, but that the internal work of government should continue to be carried on solely in Hindi; *Searchlight*, 3 August 1967. The Jan Sangh leaders, however, claimed to be in favor of granting certain privileges to Urdu-speakers, but interpreted the Urdu demands as attempts to make Urdu 'the language of Bihar from Secretariat to the gram panchayat level' and opposed them on this ground; *ibid.*, 2 August 1967.

Ghulam Sarwar issued a press release on 19 August in which he stressed that the demand for declaring Urdu second official language was only for specific purposes. He also stated: 'The Bihar State Anjuman Taraqqi Urdu recognises Hindi as the link language of the country and the official language of the State of Bihar. The demands put forth by the Anjuman in no way hamper the growth of Hindi. Equal status with Hindi is not wanted for Urdu. It is not a demand for a bilingual state for Bihar. By no implication all the non-Urdu students and officers would be required to read and work in Urdu.' (The citation is from the original press release, only portions of which were published in the *Searchlight*, 22 August 1967.) See also an earlier statement of Abdul Moghni, a member of the executive of the Bihar State Anjuman Taraqqi Urdu, published in the *Indian Nation*, 16 April 1967.

[2] *Indian Nation*, 29 July 1967.

[3] *Searchlight*, 2, 6, 8, and 9 August 1967.

[4] *Indian Nation*, 29 and 30 July 1967.

gathered strength. These forces now included the RSS and the Jan Sangh; the Bihar Hindi Sahitya Sammelan; a group of Congressmen led by the former speaker of the assembly, Dr Lakshmi Narayan Sudhanshu; the spokesmen for Maithili, who considered any concessions to Urdu a slight to Maithili; individual MLAs and members from among other parties in the government, particularly the PSP and the BKD; and students.[1] At a meeting on 27 July in the Hindi Sahitya Sammelan building in Patna, comprising some of these elements, it was decided to launch a two-week statewide anti-second state language agitation, beginning 12 August.[2]

The forces supporting the Urdu demand comprised the Anjuman Taraqqi Urdu, the SSP, and the two Communist parties.[3] All other parties and groups were divided on the issue. The Congress party leadership took no position.[4] Although it was a Muslim Congressman who introduced the bill, individual Congressmen openly opposed giving Urdu the status of a second official language, and a small group of Hindu Congress leaders joined the agitation against the bill and against the SSP–CPI policy. The PSP was divided on the issue, with the result that individual PSP members and legislators participated on both sides of the controversy.[5] The chief minister, Mahamaya Prasad Sinha, took an equivocal position, stating only that he thought that steps should be taken to give Urdu recognition according to the Constitution.[6]

The anti-second state language fortnight began on 12 August with a rally in Patna, followed by smaller meetings, processions, and demonstrations from day to day in other cities and towns in Bihar.[7] On 22 August, however, all attention shifted to the city of Ranchi where violence broke out on a massive scale and the army was called in to restore order.

[1] *Searchlight*, 30 March, 29 and 30 July, 2, 7, 11, 18, 21, and 23 August 1967. On the opposition of Maithili spokesmen, see also *MM*, 28 August and 20 November 1966.
[2] *Searchlight*, 30 July and 6 August 1967.
[3] *Ibid.*, 3, 4, 19, and 22 August 1967.
[4] Mahesh Prasad Sinha, leader of the Congress legislative party, made it clear that the bill sponsored by a member of his party was a non-official bill which the party had not discussed. Asked what the position of the Congress was on Urdu, he was reported as responding that the party position 'was known to all since the last 30 years'; *Indian Nation*, 31 July 1967.
[5] *Searchlight*, 6 August 1967.
[6] It was charged at the time that the chief minister had not been entirely honest in the matter and that he had assured Dr Sudhanshu that the proposal to make Urdu a second official language would remain on paper only. The chief minister denied having made such a statement. *Ibid.*, 14 August 1967.
[7] *Searchlight*, 12, 15, 19, and 24 August 1967, notes some of these activities and the prominent role of the Jan Sangh in them.

Interpretations of the causes of the riots in Ranchi, of the responsibility of various groups and parties in promoting them, and of the extent to which, if at all, the riots were pre-planned and organized, vary greatly. However, the sequence of events in Ranchi has been established and it demonstrates an indisputable connection between the politics of language and the politics of the parties opposed on the issue, on the one hand, and the massacres which took place in the last week of August 1967.[1] Communal riots in India have been in the past and were in Ranchi a continuation and extension of communal politics by other means.[2] The murderers, arsonists, looters, and rapists who roamed the streets and ransacked the houses mostly of Muslims in Ranchi were not political people. It is also true, in Ranchi as elsewhere in India, that communal riots feed on preexisting communal antagonisms, which surface when an emotional issue is presented which divides Hindus and Muslims. However, the specific occasion for the Ranchi riots was the Urdu isue, in which the politicians were directly involved, and the riot was used by the political parties to discredit one another. In effect, there is a continuum from political rivalry leading to communal riots to political rivalry feeding on communal riots.

The riot, occasioned by the language controversy, now became an inter-party issue and was used by elements disaffected with the united front government in an attempt to topple it. Four political versions of the causes of the riot were promoted. One, sponsored particularly by the CPI, was that the riot was a pre-planned and organized affair on the part of a faction of the Congress, the RSS–Jan Sangh, and the Anand Marg, aided and abetted by agents of these forces among the administrative officials, the police, and the army, and was staged in order to bring the government down.[3] The Jan Sangh shared the CPI view that the riot was organized in part by a faction of the

---

[1] My information on the Ranchi riots is based upon both the official *Raghubar Dayal Commission Report* cited previously and a collection of typewritten documents in my possession, including statements prepared for the Commission of Inquiry on Communal Disturbances at Ranchi by Muslim organizations, individual Muslims, the two Communist parties, and members of the Congress and other political parties in Bihar and in Ranchi district.

[2] See also the description of the relationship between the Aligarh riots of 1961 and the politics of Aligarh district in Paul R. Brass, *Factional Politics in an Indian State: The Congress Party in Uttar Pradesh* (Berkeley: University of California Press, 1965), pp. 98–111.

[3] The Anand Marg is a Hindu religious sect, which also has a fringe political wing in the politics of Bihar, known as the Proutist movement. The Anand Margis seem to be hated equally, for reasons which are not entirely clear to me, by tribals, Muslims, and some Hindus with whom I have discussed them.

The CPI interpretation of the riots noted here comes from a letter of Jagannath Sarkar, general secretary of the Bihar CPI, to Mahamaya Prasad Sinha, chief minister

Congress and that it was aimed at the non-Congress government, but the party attributed the chief role in the riots to an alliance of Communists and pro-Pakistani and pro-China elements.[1] The Congress version combined portions of both interpretations and blamed equally the Communists, Muslim communalists, and the RSS–Jan Sangh, but denied that any prominent Congressmen had anything to do with it.[2] The version of the chief minister and the SSP, mediating between the CPI and the Jan Sangh, blamed the entire riot on the Congress faction.[3]

The importance of the Urdu controversy and the Ranchi riots with respect to the Muslim role in the new coalition politics in Bihar is that the course of events outlined above limited the leverage available to the Muslim and Urdu interest associations. The strategy of the Muslim leadership before the 1967 elections had been to demonstrate to the major political parties, most especially to the Congress, that the Muslim vote could no longer be taken for granted and to force the political parties to bargain for Muslim support by promising concessions to Muslim demands in exchange for Muslim votes. Exactly the opposite happened, however, after the elections. The Muslim and Urdu associations found instead that they had antagonized the Congress leadership; that they had contributed to a situation in which their worst political enemy, the Jan Sangh, was brought to power; that those parties whose leaders were sympathetic to the cause of Urdu either could not unite their parties behind the Muslim cause or were ineffective against the opposition of the Jan Sangh; and that only the CPI was willing to support the Muslim demands and the Muslim interpretation of events fully. Only the CPI interpretation of the events leading up to and through the

of Bihar, dated 3 September 1967, and from a memorandum submitted by a delegation on behalf of the Ranchi CPI to the prime minister, dated 6 September 1967.

The secretary of the Ranchi district CPM gave a similar interpretation in his memorandum to the Commission of Inquiry: 'The Jan Sangh, the RSS and a section of the Congress are the only political and communal parties which tried to spread communalism and organised the communal riots at Ranchi between 22nd till 29th of August 1967.'

[1] See *Searchlight*, 25 August 1967, and *Organiser*, 19 September 1967, which says: 'The evidence is quite clear that pro-Pakistani and communist elements combined to create the riot with the active support of local Congress leaders . . . to discredit the Coalition Ministry of Bihar.' The article praises the army and the police for their work during the riot.

[2] See *Searchlight*, 26 and 27 August 1967. A memorandum prepared by Congress members of Ranchi district blames the Muslim Majlis, Ghulam Sarwar and the Anjuman Taraqqi Urdu, ministers of the united front government, the Jan Sangh, and the Bihar Hindi Sahitya Sammelan equally for creating a communal atmosphere in connection with the demand to make Urdu second official language. It is argued that this communal atmosphere led up to the riots, but that there was no pre-planning or organization.

[3] See *Searchlight*, 25 August 1967.

Ranchi riots corresponded to the predominant Muslim view. The Jan Sangh blamed the riots on the Muslims and the Communists; the SSP refused to condemn the Jan Sangh for its alleged role in precipitating the riots; the Congress condemned both Hindu and Muslim communalists equally. Only the CPI condemned the Hindu communalists, while avoiding criticism of the Muslim interest associations. Moreover, the Muslim political leadership had to face the fact that neither under a Congress regime nor under a coalition regime in which the Jan Sangh was a partner could their demands be achieved. Finally, the conservative Muslim leaders oriented to the religious ideology of Islam could not but be uncomfortable in finding the Communists their only possible allies.

In this situation, and when political instability in Bihar precipitated mid-term elections for February 1969, Muslim leaders could see three possible strategies open to them. One strategy would be to ignore the longer-term incompatibility between Communist and Islamic ideology and ally primarily with the CPI. The second would be to form a Muslim political party and enter the electoral arena and the coalition system directly. The third would be to withdraw from the party-electoral arena.

In Bihar, both the first and the third strategies were adopted by different Muslim leaders. Ghulam Sarwar, the most important leader of the Anjuman Taraqqi Urdu, campaigned during the 1969 elections with the CPI candidates.[1] The Majlis-e-Mushawarat, however, withdrew from the electoral arena entirely. In a press statement issued by the general secretary of the Majlis, it was noted that Muslims had generally wanted to defeat the Congress in 1967, but the result had been that a worse party, the Jan Sangh, had been brought to power and the Muslims had consequently been disillusioned by the united front government also. The Majlis general secretary remarked that the trend of Muslim opinion was to defeat the Jan Sangh and support the Communists. He also noted that none of the 110 candidates who had signed the 1967 pledge of the MMM had done anything for the Muslim cause. Consequently, the Majlis saw no point in repeating the previous effort and saw only danger in allying with one side in a political situation which was perceived as moving towards political polarization. In this context, the Majlis saw no profit in participating in the elections at all and urged Muslims to look to their own ideology and try as best they could to serve the country.[2]

[1] Personal observation.
[2] 'Press statement issued by Sohail Ahmad, General Secretary, Muslim Majlis-e-

In general, the interests of Bihar Muslims and of Urdu were not advanced significantly during the period of coalition politics between 1967 and 1972. The 1969 elections were as inconclusive as the 1967 elections and were followed by a series of unstable coalition governments. Several of the ministries which came and went during this period adopted a sympathetic stance toward Urdu and other Muslim grievances. The SVD ministry of Karpuri Thakur took one step which may benefit Muslim interest in the long run, namely, the establishment of a minority commission to 'look after the interest of the religious and linguistic minorities and suggest measures for their educational, social, political and economic well-being'.[1] However, few concrete measures were taken to respond to specific Muslim demands and, in April 1970, another communal riot occurred in Chaibasa, which once again aroused the resentment of Muslim political leaders.

Muslim demands remained politically salient in this period and continued to win some support from the political parties. For example, in July 1970, the Jamiyyat-ul-Ulama sponsored a protest demonstration in reaction to alleged police misbehavior during the Chaibasa riots. The demonstration was supported by the SSP and other minor parties.[2] The SSP also took a sympathetic attitude toward the concerns expressed by some Muslim leaders in Bihar over the treatment of Bihari Muslims in Bangladesh during the secessionist movement and after the India–Pakistan war.

In balance, however, during the period of coalition politics in Bihar, the strategies of the Muslim interest associations failed to advance the interests of Muslims and to enhance the status of Urdu. A more general conclusion relating to the role of interest associations in a context of multi-party coalition politics is that the power of such associations does not necessarily increase as political patterns become more fluid. The major political parties may sometimes find the demands of such associations useful in promoting their own interests, but they are not likely to be willing to limit their own prospects by identifying too closely with a single interest. The Jan Sangh threatened to resign from the first united front government if concessions were granted to Urdu and forced the government to defer such concessions. The SSP and the CPI continued to support the Urdu de-

Mushawarat, Bihar' (typescript, n.d.). The then secretary was a young man with no stature in the Muslim community. He replaced Yakub Younis, the original secretary, who was reported to be ill. Sohail Ahmad indicated to me, in an interview on 14 January 1969, that the Majlis would contest the next general elections as a political party in Bihar, but the organization has become defunct since then.

[1] *Indian Nation*, 2 June 1971.　　　　　[2] *Ibid.*, 1, 2, and 3 July 1970.

mand, but not even the CPI was willing to jeopardize its own position in the government or the stability of the coalition over the Urdu issue. The conclusion reached by some Muslim minority leaders in Bihar was that they did not have the power to operate effectively in the political arena *indirectly*, as a bargaining interest association. Consequently, at the end of this period, moves were being made to establish Muslim political parties in Bihar, which have included efforts to revive the Muslim League and the establishment of the Awami Tanzeem.[1] Without the unlikely event of a change in the electoral system, however, it is doubtful that Muslim demands can be pressed any more effectively through political parties than through voluntary associations.

The Urdu issue and coalition politics in Uttar Pradesh

It is somewhat ironic that the Urdu issue and communal politics in Bihar took such a bitter and violent turn in comparison to U.P., where the coalition government was never seriously threatened by the issue and no violence occurred. On the basis of the historical antagonisms between Hindus and Muslims, the comparative strength of the Jan Sangh in U.P., and the greater grievances of Muslims in U.P. on both the Urdu issue and the Aligarh Muslim University controversy, it would have been reasonable to expect greater bitterness and violence, if it were to occur at all, to occur in U.P, rather than in Bihar. In fact, the opposite took place, for reasons which seem to relate most importantly to differences in political leadership and coalition patterns in the two states.

Four aspects of the politics of the two states contrast sharply in their impact upon the politics of Urdu. The first was a difference in the leadership and in the basic strategy of the Congress towards the united front governments in the two states. In Bihar, the Congress was completely fractionalized, the leader of the party had been elected by a majority of one vote, and the strategy of the Congress was to adopt any means to embarrass and overthrow the first united front government. The Urdu issue provided one such opportunity and Congress members were free to embarrass the government by agitating either for or against Urdu. In U.P., after the defection of Charan Singh in April 1967, C. B. Gupta was the undisputed leader of the Congress party; he had been elected leader unanimously; and his strategy was to criticize and embarrass the government whenever possible, but to wait for it to fall from the weight of its own internal

[1] *Searchlight*, 11, 18, and 25 September 1970; *Indian Nation*, 20 October, 14 and 28 December 1970, and 6, 11, and 12 January 1971.

divisions. In July 1967, the chief whip of the legislative party, Banarsi Das, demanded that the united front government live up to its promise to declare Urdu the second state language of U.P.,[1] but no Congress bill, non-official or otherwise, was placed before the assembly.

The second major difference between Bihar and U.P. was the strength of the Jan Sangh in the U.P. coalition and the importance of the portfolios which it held. The Jan Sangh in U.P. was the largest party in the coalition and it controlled the deputy chief ministership and the portfolios of education and local self-government. In Bihar, it was the SSP which held all three of these positions, which include the key portfolios relating to the demands of Urdu-speakers. In Bihar, decisions and orders relating to Urdu made by the SSP deputy chief minister, who also held the education portfolio, were opposed by the Jan Sangh. In U.P., similar orders were issued by the Jan Sangh deputy chief minister-cum-education minister himself.[2] In both states, the Jan Sangh claimed to be willing to accord to Urdu-speakers the educational facilities they desired, and even to increase them, but the party refused to entertain any proposal to declare Urdu the second official language.[3] In Bihar, the Jan Sangh chose to interpret the actions of the SSP minister as giving effect to the latter proposal. In U.P., the Jan Sangh itself issued the orders and did not have to fear that more would be granted than its ministers wished to grant.

A third difference between Bihar and U.P. was in the nature of the leadership of the united front government. Mahamaya Prasad Sinha exercised no leadership in Bihar on the Urdu issue and permitted the constituent parties in his government to quarrel openly amongst themselves over it. Charan Singh, a strong and effective leader, insisted that his ministers adhere to cabinet decisions and respect the collective responsibility of the cabinet on issues decided by it. Moreover, he declared his own position, namely that he personally and his government were not bound by the 33-point program of the United Legislative Party, which was formulated before he took over the leadership on the basis of his own program, which did not include recognition of Urdu as second language. He declared his opposition to such recognition, but also announced that his government would implement all previous government decisions to

---

[1] *National Herald*, 27 July 1967.

[2] *Ibid.*, 29 May 1967.

[3] *Ibid.*, 12 and 29 May 1967. In U.P., as in Bihar, the Jan Sangh threatened to resign from the government if the demand was accepted. *Statesman*, 29 July 1967; *National Herald*, 31 July 1967.

accord facilities to Urdu-speakers. Moreover, he ensured against the disaffection of the Jan Sangh on the issue by appointing a committee to supervise the implementation of those decisions, with Ram Prakash, the Jan Sangh deputy chief minister, as chairman.[1]

Finally, the fourth major difference between Bihar and U.P. was that the Jan Sangh did not need to take the initiative in agitating against the second state language proposal, over which it held an effective veto. The agitational initiative was forced upon the supporters of Urdu, who were unwilling or unable to mobilize mass opinion behind the demand. Demonstrations opposite the council house in Lucknow were held from time to time by a minor Muslim organization, the Muhafiz Dasta, which maintained a *shamiana* (tent) there for more than two years.[2] However, the Muslim Majlis under Dr Faridi's leadership did not adopt agitational tactics. Dr Faridi continued to demand official status for Urdu and rejected as 'eye-wash' the appointment of the implementation committee under Ram Prakash. He called upon the legislators and cabinet ministers who had signed the Majlis pledge form to resign from the government on the issue,[3] but none did so. Only the CPI, the SSP, and a few independent MLAs and MPs consistently supported the Urdu demands,[4] but the CPI at no point threatened to resign over this issue and the SSP was more concerned with promoting Hindi and getting rid of English than with making Urdu second official language.[5]

Thus, although the circumstances in U.P. and Bihar were entirely different, the consequences for the Muslim and Urdu minority interest associations were the same. None of the parties felt that the issue was of sufficient importance to their own interests to insist upon the satisfaction of the demands of Urdu-speakers and most legislators who were elected with the support of the Majlis did not feel that Majlis support was so crucial to their future prospects as to warrant strict adherence to their pledges. Consequently, as mentioned above, the Majlis before the 1969 elections transformed itself into a political party.

Thus, neither in U.P. nor in Bihar have Muslim minority interest associations been able to achieve their maximum demands. After the

[1] *Ibid.*, 27 July 1967.
[2] Personal observation. See also the *National Herald*, 20 June, 1, 4, 21, 26, and 31 July 1967.
[3] *Ibid.*, 24 and 27 July 1967.
[4] *Ibid.*, 7, 10, and 13 May and 28 July 1967.
[5] *Ibid.*, 7 June 1967. In this respect, SSP and Jan Sangh policies on language are similar. Dr Faridi lumped together 'the RSS and the SSP' in the SVD government and criticized them 'for their fanatic language policy'; *ibid.*, 27 May 1967.

1969 elections, it appeared that the U.P. strategy of forming a separate political party and then bargaining with the government had been more successful than the Bihar strategies. However, the situation of the Muslims and of Urdu-speakers has not changed significantly in either state, where the satisfaction of the grievances of the Urdu-speaking minority continues to depend upon the effective implementation of administrative orders. Moreover, most political parties and political leaders in both states have had their fingers burned over the official language demand and will not easily take up the issue again. It would appear unlikely that this demand will ever be conceded in either state through the efforts of the Muslim minority spokesman alone, no matter what political strategy is adopted.

CONCLUSION

The history of Muslim politics and of the Urdu movement in north India throws into sharp relief the relationships between processes of social mobilization and political leadership in the development of nationalism. A comparison of the Muslim and the Maithili movements supports the argument of Deutsch and others that the processes of nationality-formation cannot gather strength in the absence of the prerequisite of national consciousness, that is, a socially mobilized population. However, it is important to recognize that political differentiation does not follow automatically from the social mobilization of an objectively dissimilar group. Muslim politics could have taken an entirely different turn in north India and, in fact, it did not follow a uniform path. There were periods of Hindu–Muslim cooperation during the nationalist movement in north India and there were different nationalist ideologies among Muslims throughout that period. Political differentiation was, for separatist Muslim leaders, a conscious choice which did not have to follow from the religious and linguistic differences between Hindus and Muslims. Rather, the political choices were made first and linguistic and cultural differences were exploited in order to build mass support for a political course which proved disastrous to the protection of the language and culture of north Indian Muslims, but served the political interests of the Muslim political elite. In fact, the predominant Muslim elites never provided the Muslim masses of north India with political choices which were relevant to their own circumstances. They demanded political privileges for themselves rather than the integration of the Muslim masses into the political life of the provinces. When they were denied political power in 1937, they formulated the Pakistan demand, which brought them to power in another country on the backs of the Muslim masses of north India, who were left to fend for themselves. On the only two occasions when mass Muslim opinion was mobilized in north India, it was for interests *unrelated* to the condition of Muslims in the north – for the preservation of the Turkish khalifa in 1920–1 and for the creation of Pakistan between 1940 and 1946. In the post-independence period the Muslims of north India have reaped the consequences of the political opportunism of their pre-independence leaders.

It has been only in the post-independence period that most Muslim political leaders have resigned themselves to the fact that India is their homeland and that the political choices of responsible leadership are limited to the formulation of specific demands relating to the protection and preservation of minority rights within India. But the political context and the rules of the game have been changed. The Muslim minority is a minority nearly everywhere in independent India and certain kinds of demands are no longer acceptable. Muslims can legitimately demand proportionate representation, but not weightage. They can make linguistic demands, but the informal rules of Indian political behavior now prohibit the association of linguistic with religious or communal demands. Finally, Muslim political leaders are now on the defensive, forced to defend not only their rights but their loyalties, which are called into question by Hindu communalist leaders whenever Muslim demands become assertive. Once again politics are the primary variable in determining the choices available to Muslims, but now it is political realities which are determinant and not the political ambitions of a narrow elite.

The Muslim elites of northern India in the post-independence period have been removed from their previous position of political privilege to one of under-representation in many respects, including in political and administrative positions and in educational facilities for Urdu-speakers. During the two decades when the privileges of Muslims and Urdu-speakers were being removed and a sense of grievance was developing among Muslims, there was no effective Muslim leadership available to protect and defend the rights of Muslims. Muslims did not go unrepresented in government in U.P. and Bihar, but those in government did not effectively represent Muslims. What the fate of Muslims in the north would have been if Muslim League leaders like Nawabzada Liaquat Ali Khan or Chaudhury Khaliquzzaman had not gone to Pakistan is impossible to guess. There is no doubt, however, that their removal to Pakistan created a gap in Muslim political leadership. Dr Faridi in U.P. is the first Muslim in that state to speak as boldly for Muslim community rights as his Muslim League predecessors did in the pre-independence period. It is much more difficult, however, for an organization like the Majlis to demonstrate that it represents Muslim sentiment or to persuade party leaders that Muslim sentiment matters in the absence of separate electorates. Yet it is certain that no change in the Indian representative system, and certainly not a revival of separate electorates, is likely to materialize which would automatically increase the influence of the Muslim community. The Muslim minority in north India, unless it allies with other groups, is doomed to marginality and ineffectiveness. Alliance with other groups is also no guarantee of effectiveness, for the Muslims were, in fact, allied with the ruling party for twenty years. The choices available to Muslims are considerably restricted not only in comparison to the pre-independence period but in comparison to those available to other, more compact and concentrated linguistic-cultural groups in contemporary India. This is the dilemma of north Indian Muslims in contemporary Indian politics. Mobilized in the pre-independence period on the theory that they constituted a separate nation, not a minority, they helped to create a nation where Muslims were in a majority, but reduced themselves to a small and scattered minority in a Hindu state. It is as one minority among many in India that they must now find a political place for themselves – some on an individual basis, some for the community as a whole. The political future of the Muslims is, therefore, bound up inescapably with the kind of nationalist ideology and the kinds of policies towards minorities which become dominant in the center and the states. As long as the center follows a policy of pluralism, the Muslims need not fear the elimination of their language and culture, although it is clear that both may suffer at the hands of state governments following policies of integration. The future political role of the Muslims as a community in India will likely be no more than one minority among many pushing the central and the state governments towards pluralism in theory and practice.

PART IV

THE POLITICS OF LANGUAGE
AND RELIGION IN THE PUNJAB:
SIKHS, HINDUS, AND THE PUNJABI
LANGUAGE

JAMMU and KASHMIR

HIMACHAL
PRADESH

CHINA

LAHAUL and SPITI

PAKISTAN

GURDASPUR

KANGRA

KULU

AMRITSAR

KAPUR-
THALA

HOSHIARPUR

JULLUNDUR

AMBALA

SIMLA

HIMACHAL
PRADESH

LUDHIANA

Chandigarh

PATIALA

UTTAR
PRADESH

FEROZEPUR

SANGRUR

AMBALA

BHATINDA

KARNAL

SANGRUR

HISSAR

RAJASTHAN

ROHTAK

Delhi
New Delhi

MOHINDERGARH

GURGAON

Hindi speaking

Punjabi speaking

Bilingual

Fig. 7   Political divisions of the Punjab, 1956–66

SOURCE. Redrawn after map 'Punjab', facing p. 435 of Baldev Raj Nayar, 'Political Divisions of the Punjab, 1956–1966', in Myron Weiner, *State Politics in India* (copyright © 1968 by Princeton University Press). Reprinted by permission of Princeton University Press.

6

SIKHS AND HINDUS IN THE PUNJAB: THE DEVELOPMENT OF SOCIAL AND POLITICAL DIFFERENTIATION

Of the three movements which are considered in this book, that of the Sikhs for a separate Punjabi-speaking state within the Indian Union has been the most powerful and the most successful in contemporary politics in north India. It represents in fact the only political movement based on either language or religion in north India (excluding Bengal) which has succeeded in differentiating politically a group of people off from the Hindi-speaking fold. Only the Punjabi-speaking Sikhs in the north have been able to withstand the trend toward linguistic assimilation in north India to the extent of achieving dominance for themselves and for the Punjabi language in a territorially demarcated political unit. Moreover, of all the ethnic groups and peoples of the north, the Sikhs come closest to satisfying the definition of a nationality or nation. The Punjabi-speaking Sikhs are a people objectively distinct in religion, though not in language, from other ethnic groups in the north; who have succeeded in acquiring a high degree of internal social and political cohesion and subjective self-awareness; and who have achieved political significance as a group within the Indian Union.

The acquisition of a cohesive Sikh identity and of a significant political status for the Sikh community has sometimes had the appearance of the advance of an invincible, solidary, national force. Yet the Sikhs have suffered many political setbacks and their social and political successes have sometimes been ambiguous. Socially, boundary definition between Sikhs and other religious groups is only superficially clear and sharp. In fact, though there is a strong solidary core to the contemporary Sikh nationality, the boundaries of the Sikh people remain flexible and uncertain. Politically, the Sikhs did achieve a state in which they are politically dominant in fact; but in theory they were awarded not a Sikh state but a Punjabi-speaking state in which they must share power with both Punjabi-speaking and Hindi-speaking Hindus.

The successful Sikh political movement for a separate Punjabi-speaking state demonstrates unequivocally that there is no such thing as a 'natural' movement of an objectively distinct ethnic group to subjective self-consciousness and political status. Ambiguity, arbitrariness and uncertainty in ethnic identification, and the need for political compromise and accommodation with other groups and forces have been marked features of the Sikh movement. Moreover, the Sikh political movement demonstrates that when an ethnic group turns to politics to achieve group demands, the political movement takes on a life of its own to such an extent that political organizations may shape communal identities as well as be shaped by them.

SIKH COMMUNAL CONSCIOUSNESS

The underlying basis for Sikh political aspirations has been a widespread sense of group identity, which has acquired increased strength and definition during the past century. Three sets of symbols have been especially prominent in the development of communal consciousness among the Sikhs – historical symbols derived from the history of the Sikh kingdoms before the British conquest of the Punjab; religious symbols which have been used to define the boundaries between Sikhs and Hindus in the Punjab in modern times; and linguistic symbols which have associated the Sikhs with a particular form of the Punjabi language written in the Gurumukhi script.

Sikh identity and the Sikh kingdoms

The history of the growth and consolidation of Sikh power in the Punjab under Maharaja Ranjit Singh has provided Sikh leaders in modern times with a vast pool of symbols to draw upon to feed the modern sense of Sikh identity. Not all the historic facts of Sikh rule can be accommodated with pride into modern Sikh self-consciousness, but there is sufficient glory from the past to counterbalance the historic evidence of internal divisions and betrayal of the Sikh cause by the traitors to, and campfollowers of, the British imperial power. From the history of the growth of Sikh power in the late eighteenth century and its consolidation under Ranjit Singh between 1799 and 1839, promoters of a modern Sikh identity have devised symbols of great emotional appeal: symbols of the Sikh people as an incredibly courageous fighting force, who, at great cost, unflinchingly fought the tyranny of the Mughal power and destroyed it in the Punjab; of the Sikhs as a ruling race who once held sway over a vast province;

and of the Sikhs as a power strong enough to fight the advancing British imperial power and to come close to defeating it.

Moreover, both British and Sikh historians have infused these historic symbols with modern ideas and a modern sense of self-consciousness. Thus, the Sikh historian, Ganda Singh, has commented upon the short-lived victories of the martyr, Banda Singh, in his struggles against the Mughals in the early eighteenth century in the following way:

Although the successes of Banda Singh were but temporary, there was a revolution effected in the minds of people of which history often fails to take notice. A will was created in the ordinary masses to resist tyranny and to live and die for the national cause. The example set by Banda Singh and his companions in this respect was to serve as a beacon-light in the darker days to come. The idea of a national State, long dead, once again became a living aspiration, and, although suppressed for the time being by relentless persecution, it went on working underground like a smouldering fire, and came out forty years later with a fuller effulgence never to be suppressed again.[1]

Although he put it somewhat more reservedly, Cunningham too described the growth of Sikh power in the 1760s as arising not only out of the ambitions of particular leaders but also out of the fact that 'a vague feeling that they were a people had arisen' among the Sikhs, who 'were bent on revenge' for past defeats and persecutions.[2] In fact, Cunningham's classic account of the warfare and intrigue through which Sikh power was established in the Punjab is permeated with the recurring theme of the development of the Sikhs from 'a sect into a people' under Guru Gobind and from a people to a 'nation' under Ranjit Singh.[3]

Cunningham, whose account was contemporaneous with many of the events in Sikh history of the time and who was himself a witness to many events, was clearly impressed by the corporate spirit of the Sikh army and people[4] which underlay the power of the Sikh kingdoms, especially that of Ranjit Singh. Whether that corporate spirit constituted a modern sense of nationality is another question, which contemporary Sikh historians and politicians answer readily in the affirmative. Khushwant Singh, for example, writes of the struggles of the Sikh forces against the British in 1848 as of a nation rising in

[1] Ganda Singh, *A Brief Account of the Sikhs* (Amritsar: Shiromani Gurudwara Parbandhak Committee (SGPC), n.d.), p. 26.
[2] Joseph D. Cunningham, *A History of the Sikhs from the Origin of the Nation to the Battles of the Sutlej* (Delhi: S. Chand & Co., 1966), p. 92.
[3] *Ibid.*, pp. 120, 200, and *passim*.
[4] *Ibid.*, pp. 153 and 215–16.

arms and of the second Anglo-Sikh War of 1848 as 'a national war of independence'.[1]

It must be stressed, however, that Sikh historians and politicians have been engaged in a process of symbol selection from the events of the past, adapting those which would best support contemporary Sikh self-consciousness and rejecting those which would not. The corporate spirit of the Sikhs, the masterly figure of Ranjit Singh, and the idea of the Sikhs as the ruling race of the Punjab serve the purpose well. The factional divisions in the Sikh state which destroyed it after the death of Ranjit Singh; the traitorous actions of Sikh commanders in the field in the battles against the British forces;[2] and the fact that the Sikh kingdoms were always more or less divided against each other, even under Ranjit Singh, provide less satisfying and less unifying symbols. The latter symbols suggest, in fact, a characteristic lack of congruence in pre-modern times between the corporate spirit of the people and the factional divisions of their leaders; between the loyalties of fighting forces and the treachery of commanders; and between the distribution of the Sikh people and the extent of the Sikh kingdoms. In modern nations, political leaders may disagree over goals and over the best way to advance the national cause, but a modern nation cannot exist where leaders and people pursue fundamentally different goals. Traitors exist in modern nations, but they are more likely to be found in laboratories and government offices than in command of forces in the field. Modern nations seek to make political unity and social unity congruent, whereas pre-modern states seek territorial aggrandizement for its own sake.

If the symbols of Sikh rule in the Punjab are not entirely free from ambiguity, the symbols of Sikh resistance to British imperialism are not less so. It feeds modern Sikh self-consciousness well to learn that 'the quality of resistance experienced from the Sikhs was higher than the British had ever met in India before, *even from the Gurkhas*';[3] to know that, to break Sikh power, the British in 1845 concentrated the largest invasion force 'ever assembled' by them in India;[4] and to read that, in 1849, Punjabi soldiers administered 'the worst defeat suffered by the British since their occupation of India'.[5] It is less satisfying to recall that the cis-Sutlej Sikh kingdoms were allied with

[1] Khushwant Singh, *The Fall of the Kingdom of the Punjab* (Bombay: Orient Longmans, 1962), p. 147.
[2] See, for example, Khushwant Singh, *A History of the Sikhs*, vol. II: *1839–1964* (Princeton, N.J.: Princeton University Press, 1966), p. 50.
[3] Landen Sarsfield, *Betrayal of the Sikhs* (Lahore: Lahore Book Shop, 1946), p. 18; italics in original.
[4] Khushwant Singh, *The Sikhs*, vol. II, p. 43.   [5] *Ibid.*, p. 79.

the British from 1809 and that several of these states 'gave unstinted support to the enemy' in 1846 against the trans-Sutlej Sikh powers and that they turned the tide in favor of British rule during the Mutiny of 1857, thereby securing British imperialism in India for another century.[1]

Moreover, the roles played by the surviving cis-Sutlej or Phulkian states in modern times in Punjab politics serve to demonstrate again the proposition that it is the symbolic memory of rule which is most important in the growth of a modern sense of community and not necessarily the visible embodiment of such rule in the present, which may in fact be inconvenient. The traditions of loyalty to British rule were rigorously maintained by the leading surviving Sikh state of Patiala and by most other of the surviving Sikh states during the nationalist period. Throughout the crucial years of the late nineteenth and early twentieth centuries when a modern Sikh national identity was being built in the Punjab, the dominant patterns in the Sikh kingdoms were loyalty to the British Raj, opposition to the main Sikh nationalist organizations, and internecine conflict.[2] Thus, the historic Sikh kingdoms have provided to modern Sikh nationalism diverse symbols of national identity to choose from, but not much of substance in the recent past. Modern nations are anyway built more upon the selection and manipulation of symbols from the past than the persistence of real political structures into the present.

Religious differentiation and boundary definition between Sikhs and Hindus in Punjab

The growth of internal solidarity among Sikhs has been accompanied by processes of boundary definition and boundary maintenance and selective adoption of aspects of Sikh history, culture, and religion as special marks of the true Sikh community. It has not been possible to eliminate all indefiniteness in the boundaries between Sikhs and other communities nor to overcome entirely significant elements of internal differentiation amongst Sikhs, but it seems evident that the Sikh community has passed a threshold in the development of a self-conscious group identity which sets the community apart as one of the more distinct peoples of India and the world.

[1] Sarsfield, *Betrayal of the Sikhs*, p. 36. See also the comments by P. C. Joshi, 'Triumph of a Just Cause', in *Punjabi Suba: A Symposium* (New Delhi: National Book Club, n.d.), p. 61.
[2] The evidence on these points is overwhelming in both Ganda Singh (ed.), *Some Confidential Papers of the Akali Movement* (Amritsar: SGPC, 1965) and Ruchi Ram Sahni, *Struggle for Reform in Sikh Shrines* (Amritsar: SGPC, n.d.).

The character of inter-ethnic relations between Sikhs and Hindus in the Punjab has been influenced by the common and indigenous origin of Hindu and Sikh religious practices and beliefs and by the conflict between Hindu efforts to re-absorb Sikhs into the Hindu fold and Sikh efforts to establish definitively a separate identity. In origin, the Sikh community and its religion are, no doubt, outgrowths from Hindus and Hinduism. In fact, it has been pointed out that up through the 1880s and beyond, 'the Sikhs regarded themselves and were regarded by everybody else as an integral part of the Hindus'.[1] Moreover, it is generally agreed that, until the late nineteenth century, intermarriage between Hindus and Sikhs was common and that different members of a single family could be either Hindu or Sikh in their religious inclinations.[2] Yet, in his classic *History of the Sikhs*, written in 1849, Joseph Cunningham was more impressed by the differences than by the similarities between Sikhs and Hindus, when he remarked that 'it has been usual to regard the Sikhs as essentially Hindu, and they doubtless are so in language and everyday customs . . . yet in religious faith and worldly aspirations, they are wholly different from other Indians, and they are bound together by a community of inward sentiment and of outward object unknown elsewhere'.[3] The historic tendencies toward differentiation between Hindus and Sikhs received powerful support in the religious reform movements of the late nineteenth and early twentieth centuries, which emphasized doctrinal and religious differences between the religious practices of the two communities.[4] Sikh religious and social tracts of the time and later sought to emphasize that Guru Nanak was not to be seen as merely another Hindu reformer, but as the self-conscious founder of a new religion, meant to be distinct from Hinduism in fundamental ways.[5] Such statements have had more than doctrinal import. They have been meant to impress upon Sikhs their separateness from Hindus and to prevent them from 'retreating back into the Hindu ranks'.[6]

[1] Sahni, *Sikh Shrines*, p. 12.
[2] Baldev Raj Nayar, *Minority Politics in the Punjab* (Princeton, N.J.: Princeton University Press, 1966), pp. 61–2. A classic case is that of the family of Lajpat Rai, the Arya Samaj leader and Hindu nationalist, whose father was inclined more to Islam than Hinduism and whose mother came from a family oriented to Sikhism, but who herself followed orthodox Hindu rituals; Vijaya Chandra Joshi (ed.), *Lajpat Rai Autobiographical Writings* (Delhi: University Publishers, 1965), pp. 12, 15, 77–8.
[3] Cunningham, *History of the Sikhs*, pp. 75–6.
[4] Nayar, *Minority Politics*, pp. 62–3.
[5] See, e.g., Teja Singh, *Guru Nanak and His Mission* (Amritsar: SGPC, 1963), pp. 1–2.
[6] *Ibid.*, p. 9. The fear of re-absorption into Hinduism is a common theme in both Sikh religious and political tracts. In fact, Baldev Nayar has argued that Sikh fears of assimil-

Although the building of a widespread sense of group consciousness is a modern phenomenon among the Sikhs as among any people,
the movement towards increased differentiation acquired considerable force as early as the 1880s and 1890s[1] so that 'by 1900 Sikhs
were less and less willing to class themselves automatically with the
Hindu community'.[2] Moreover, by the turn of the century, 'the
gradual institutionalization of communal identity' in the Punjab had
penetrated into political life in the form of communally oriented all-
Punjab political organizations – the Punjab Hindu Sabha; the Punjab Muslim League; and the Chief Khalsa Diwan, the first modern
political instrument of the Sikh community, founded in 1902.[3]

The decisive period in the growth of a modern, militant Sikh
identity and in the institutionalization of Sikh consciousness came in
the early 1920s, during the gurudwara reform movement. In the
period between 1920 and 1925, Sikh leaders launched a series of
militant agitations at the sites of important Sikh shrines in order to
remove them from the control of allegedly corrupt and Hinduized
mahants, who were accused of mismanaging their affairs and funds.
The agitations of the 1920s,[4] which culminated in the passage of the
Sikh Gurudwara Act of 1925, had profound consequences for the
development of Sikh consciousness and Sikh political action. Out of
the gurudwara reform movement emerged the Shiromani Gurudwara Prabandhak Committee (SGPC) to manage the Sikh gurudwaras[5] and the Akali Dal, its agitational and political arm. These
two organizations, discussed in detail below, continue to be the
primary institutional expressions of Sikh communal and political

ation into Hinduism provided one of the main driving forces of the Punjabi Suba movement. Master Tara Singh particularly saw a separate political status for Sikhs as
essential to preserve their religious separateness. See Baldev Raj Nayar, 'Sikh Separatism in the Punjab', in Donald Eugene Smith (ed.), *South Asian Politics and Religion*
(Princeton, N.J.: Princeton University Press, 1966), pp. 164–7.

[1] N. Gerald Barrier, 'The Punjab Government and Communal Politics, 1870–1908',
Journal of Asian Studies, XXVII, No. 3 (May 1968), 527–8.
[2] Kenneth W. Jones, 'Communalism in the Punjab: The Arya Samaj Contribution',
Journal of Asian Studies, XXVIII, No. 1 (November 1968), 50.
[3] N. Gerald Barrier, 'Mass Politics and the Punjab Congress in the pre-Gandhi Period',
mimeo (April 1970), pp. 3–4, and Khushwant Singh, *The Sikhs*, vol. II, p. 145.
[4] Accounts of the agitational movements of this period may be found in Ganda Singh,
The Akali Movement; Sahni, *Sikh Shrines*, and Khushwant Singh, *The Sikhs*, vol. II, ch. 13.
[5] The SGPC was formed in October–November 1920 to head the gurudwara reform
movement. The Gurudwara Act, passed on 7 July 1925, formally placed 'all Historical
Gurudwaras' under the control of the SGPC and established procedures for its election.
Ganda Singh, *A Brief Account*, p. 61; Khushwant Singh, *The Sikhs*, vol. II, p. 198;
Patrick Fagan, 'Minority Communities, I. The Sikhs', in John Comming (ed.), *Political
India, 1832–1932: A Co-operative Survey of a Century* (Delhi: S. Chand and Co., 1968),
pp. 129–31; and Azim Husain, *Fazl-I-Husain: A Political Biography* (Bombay: Long-
mans, Green, 1946), pp. 144–6.

consciousness and identity. Both the gurudwara reform movement and the formation of the SGPC and the Akali Dal also served to sharpen the line of demarcation between Sikhs and Hindus in the Punjab. The SGPC became not only a temple-managing committee, but an elected, representative organization of the Sikh community, in which only Sikhs could participate. The Akali Dal also limited its membership to Sikhs. The reform of the gurudwaras frequently meant removal of Hinduized priests and Hindu influences, including Hindu idols, from the precincts of Sikh shrines. Some Hindus in the Punjab naturally resented these aspects of the reform movement. In fact, Khushwant Singh has argued that 'the most significant outcome of the four years of intense agitation, in which the Hindus supported the Udasi *mahants* against the Akalis, was to widen further the gulf between the two communities'.[1]

The development of an increasing sense of Sikh consciousness and separateness had political consequences in the Punjab in the 1920s and 1930s when Sikh political groups began to demand communal representation and weightage for the Sikhs in Punjab political bodies. Moreover, in presenting their demands, Sikh political spokesmen were quick to resent any suggestion that 'the Sikhs were not a distinct community'. In response to that suggestion before the Indian Statutory Commission in 1928, Sardar Sundar Singh Majithia, speaking on behalf of the Chief Khalsa Diwan, remarked:

Sikhs have been a distinct community. From the time of the Gurus they have been a distinct community, and I cannot accept the statement from a rival community that we are not a distinct community; I cannot accept it at all . . . Religiously and socially we are a distinct community, and as such our interests are not identical with those of any other community at all.[2]

In modern times, the emphasis on Sikh separateness has been carried still further. Sikhs are not to be seen, it is argued, merely as a group of individuals with distinctive traits, but as an indivisible social and political community with an historic 'theo-political status', whose loyalties to any secular state are qualified and contingent upon that state's adherence to truth and morality and upon its recogni-

---

[1] Khushwant Singh, *The Sikhs*, vol. II, p. 213.

[2] 'Deputation from the Chief Khalsa Diwan, Amritsar', in *Indian Statutory Commission (ISC)*, vol. XVI, *Selections from Memoranda and Oral Evidence by Non-Officials (Part I)* (London: His Majesty's Stationery Office, 1930), p. 138. For details on the demands made by Sikh organizations for communal representation in the Punjab in the 1920s and 1930s, see *ibid.*, pp. 138–47; Sewaram Singh, *Report of the Working of the Sikh Deputation to England, Indian Reforms Scheme* (Lahore: Sewaram Singh, 1920); and Khushwant Singh, *The Sikhs*, vol. II, pp. 223, 230–2.

tion of the 'collective group' character of the Sikh community.[1] This doctrine, one of whose propounders was the first chief minister in the Punjabi Suba, implies 'that the state must deal with [the Sikhs] as one people, and not by atomising them into individual citizens'.[2] This emphasis on the indivisible character of the Sikhs as 'a civic group'[3] is the political counterpart of Sikh religious fears of reabsorption into Hinduism. Just as Hindu religious reformers have tried to bring Sikhs back into the Hindu fold, it is argued that governments in independent India have been determined 'to atomise and absorb' the Sikhs politically as well.[4]

There is no doubt that the sense of Sikh separateness is strongest among a particular social class of Sikhs – that is, the Jat Sikh peasantry – and particularly among the *keshadhari* Sikhs, distinguished by their attachment to the five symbols of Sikhism (unshaven hair, short drawers, iron bangle, steel dagger, and comb). The sense of separateness is less strong among Scheduled Caste Sikhs and *sahajdari* Sikhs, who do not display the five symbols.[5] Moreover, the boundaries between these groups and Hindu groups are less definite. The presence of considerable internal differentiation among Sikhs and of continual lack of sharpness in some aspects of boundary maintenance does not, however, mean that the existence of a cohesive Sikh community can be denied. Rather, these features emphasize the point that the creation of a cohesive community includes a process of symbol and myth selection which includes some groups, excludes others, and treats still others as marginal. In this process among the Sikhs, the *sahajdari* Sikhs, while not formally excluded, are considered less 'genuine'.[6] Religious sects such as the Nirankaris and Radha Soamis are difficult to classify as clearly Hindu or clearly Sikh.[7]

The attitudes of Sikh religious and political leaders towards the Scheduled Castes are different. With regard to these groups, Sikh and Hindu movements have been engaged in a process of competition for the mobilization of the low castes into Sikhism and Hinduism.

---

[1] Gurnam Singh, *A Unilingual Punjabi State and the Sikh Unrest* (New Delhi: Gurnam Singh, 1960), pp. 10–11.

[2] *Ibid.*, p. 17.   [3] *Ibid.*, p. 24.   [4] *Ibid.*, p. 41.

[5] This point has been particularly emphasized by Nayar, *Minority Politics*, esp. pp. 59–63 and 196–7. Moreover, Nayar argues that British policies, especially in census operations, sharpened lines of demarcation between Hindus and Sikhs in areas where the lines were indefinite; Nayar, 'Sikh Separatism', pp. 159–60. For an example of the difficulties encountered by census enumerators in classifying Sahajdaris as Sikhs or Hindus, see *Census of India, 1931*, vol. 1: *India*, pt. 1: *Report*, by J. H. Hutton (Delhi: Manager of Publications, 1933), p. 388.

[6] Nayar, *Minority Politics*, p. 60.

[7] Khushwant Singh, *The Sikhs*, vol. II, pp. 121, 123–5.

Since the late nineteenth century, the Arya Samaj has especially sought to 'reclaim' these low caste groups for Hinduism and has earned the resentment of Sikh leaders thereby. This process of competition for the allegiance of low caste groups has been especially important in contemporary Punjab politics because the cleavage between the dominant Jat Sikhs and the Sikh Scheduled Castes was used as an argument against conceding the Punjabi Suba, to which the low castes were reputed to be opposed. Sikh political leaders attempted to counteract this argument by insisting that the Sikh Scheduled Castes would support the Punjabi Suba if they were not 'officially designated as depressed classes' and given special privileges by the Congress regime[1] and by proclaiming their determination to work for an end to Scheduled Caste disabilities.[2] Whatever the intentions of Sikh political leaders and the wishes of Hindu political leaders and religious reformers, the large Scheduled Caste population in the Punjab has constituted an area where the boundaries between Hindus and Sikhs remain unclear.

Thus, while the existence of a self-conscious group identity among certain categories of Sikhs is no longer open to serious doubt, it is important to keep in view that the formation of a separate Sikh identity is still in progress, that there has been and continues to be competition with Hindus for the allegiance of particular sects and castes, and that boundaries in some respects remain indefinite. In recent times, the primary symbols of Sikh and Hindu competition over group allegiances have been linguistic. Increasingly in the Punjab, the competition for the allegiance of particular groups has been in the arena of linguistic conflict and the politically important marks of group identification have been language and script.

The Punjabi language in relation to Hindi

During the British period, in the vast multi-communal and multi-lingual province of the Punjab, the predominant vernacular languages or mother tongues of the people were Lahnda in the western, Muslim-majority districts; Punjabi in the central districts occupied by Hindus and Sikhs; and Hindi in the Hindu-dominated districts in the east. The official languages of the province were English and Urdu. In no district of the old Punjab province, however, was Urdu the predominant mother tongue of the people. No elite group in the Punjab developed any fondness for Lahnda and no language move-

---

[1] Gurnam Singh, *A Unilingual Punjabi State*, p. 47.
[2] Jagjit Singh Anand, 'Sant Fateh Singh on the Suba', in *Punjabi Suba*, p. 13.

ments promoting Lahnda have appeared in modern times. Lahnda has, consequently, disappeared from the records and been merged into Punjabi in Pakistan. The language movements of modern times in the Punjab have evolved in two stages. There has been first the movement of the vernacular mother tongues to displace Urdu and English in the schools and courts of the province. Second, there has been competition between the two primary mother tongues, Punjabi and Hindi, for supremacy. In the pre-independence period, these two conflicts frequently were occurring simultaneously. In the post-independence period, of course, the language cleavage has been exclusively between Hindi and Punjabi, which crystallized in the Punjabi Suba movement.

The Hindi movement in the nineteenth century in the Punjab was led both by Hindi-speaking and Punjabi-speaking urban Hindus, whose higher education had been in Urdu and English. In its origins, it was clearly a religio-political or communal movement promoted by the Arya Samaj to displace Urdu in Persian script as the official vernacular language of the province because Urdu was associated with Muslim dominance and Hindi with Hindu religious reform and political aspirations. The Hindi–Urdu controversy in the Punjab arose for the first time in 1882, a year after the decision to substitute Hindi in the Devanagari script for Urdu in Persian script in Bihar. The demand in the Punjab by urban Hindus was the same and it was seen by both sides as an aspect of Hindu–Muslim communal conflict. The Anjuman-i-Islamya of Lahore protested against the movement which it saw as aiming 'a death-blow to the prospects of the Muhammadans'.[1] The famous Arya Samaj leader and Punjab politician, Lala Lajpat Rai, who 'actually did not know the Hindi alphabet' entered political life in this controversy because he came to believe that Hindi could 'be the foundation for the edifice of Indian nationality'. From the Hindi–Urdu controversy, Lajpat Rai learnt his 'first lesson in Hindu nationalism' and 'became convinced that political solidarity demanded the spread of Hindi and Devanagri'.[2]

In contrast to the situation in Bihar and U.P., however, Muslims retained political dominance and Urdu official status in the Punjab right up to independence. Demands were made before the Simon Commission for replacing Urdu as medium of instruction in primary

---

[1] Selections from the Records of the Government of India, Home Department, No. ccv, Home Department Serial No. 2, *Correspondence on the Subject of the Education of the Muhammadan Community in British India and Their Employment in the Public Service Generally* (Calcutta: Superintendent of Government Printing, India, 1886), p. 317.

[2] Joshi, *Lajpat Rai*, pp. 25-7 and 79.

schools with Punjabi and Hindi but without success.[1] The spread of the vernacular languages, Hindi and Punjabi, was done largely by private agencies through the educational and publishing efforts of such organizations as the Arya Samaj for Hindi and the Chief Khalsa Diwan for Punjabi.[2] The political conflict took place primarily in the census operations.

What began as a movement to replace Urdu by Hindi soon developed into a three-way conflict among Urdu, Hindi, and Punjabi. In this conflict, Punjabi was the primary loser as Punjabi-speaking Muslims opted for Urdu and Punjabi-speaking Hindus for Hindi. By 1947, when, because of the emigration of the Muslim population, the status of Urdu was no longer a major issue in the Punjab, many Punjabi-speaking Hindus had already become accustomed to what has been characterized as 'disowning' their mother tongue for Hindi.

Contemporary conflict over the status of the Punjabi language has focused upon three chief issues, each of which has also been relevant in the Maithili and Urdu cases, namely, the status of Punjabi as a distinct language or a dialect; the region in which the language is spoken as the mother tongue of the people; and the script used to write the language.[3] Grierson's views on the status of Punjabi are fairly unambiguous.[4] He considered Punjabi a distinct language, with both a standard form and with its own dialectal and sub-dialectal variations. Although he believed that modern Punjabi was a composite language based upon an earlier fusion of Lahnda or Western Punjabi with Western Hindi, he was clear that the pronunciation, grammar, and vocabulary of modern Punjabi were sufficiently distinct to classify it as a separate language. Moreover, though he recognized that Punjabi literature was not extensive, he argued that this did not reflect upon the literary capabilities of the language, which he clearly considered to be more than adequate.[5] Finally, although he considered it impossible to draw a sharp geographic

---

[1] 'Memorandum Submitted by Pandit Nanak Chand', *ISC*, vol. xvi, p. 93.

[2] These efforts, though significant, never challenged seriously the dominance of Urdu as the pre-eminent medium of education and publication in the province. See Satya M. Rai, *Partition of the Punjab: A Study of Its Effects on the Politics and Administration of the Punjab (I) 1947–56* (Bombay: Asia Publishing House, 1965), pp. 218–9.

[3] For a discussion by a linguist of these three issues, see Kali Charan Bahl, 'Panjabi', in Thomas A. Sebeok (ed.), *Current Trends in Linguistics*, vol. v: *Linguistics in South Asia* (The Hague: Mouton, 1969), pp. 153–200.

[4] G. A. Grierson (ed.), *Linguistic Survey of India*, vol. ix: *Indo-Aryan Family, Central Group*, pt. i: *Specimens of Western Hindī and Panjābī* (Delhi: Motilal Banarsidass, 1968), pp. 607–618 and 624.

[5] See also Suniti Kumar Chatterji, *Languages and Literatures of Modern India* (Calcutta: Prakash Bhavan, 1962), pp. 34–5 and 247–55.

dividing line between Lahnda and Punjabi in the west, he was clear that the boundary line between Punjabi and Western Hindi or Hindustani was 'very fairly defined'.[1] Grierson was sufficiently confident of his views on these points to take a stand on what was already a controversial issue between Punjabi and Hindi protagonists. He concluded his general discussion of the distinctive features of Punjabi with the following remarks:

> Even at the present day there is too great a tendency to look down upon [Punjabi] as a mere dialect of Hindōstānī (which it is not), and to deny its status as an independent language. Its claim mainly rests upon its phonetic system and on its store of words not found in Hindī, both of which characteristics are due to its old Lahnda foundation. Some of the most common Pañjabi words do not occur in Hindōstānī.[2]

Modern linguists are more reluctant than Grierson was to distinguish between languages and dialects and are inclined to speak of relative language distances between 'linguistic codes'. John Gumperz has shown that an educated person from a Punjabi-speaking family in Delhi may control three such 'codes', each of which will be used in different social contexts.[3] One 'code', Hindi, would be used in speaking to a Hindi-speaker; a second code, which Gumperz calls 'code-switching' Punjabi, would be used with another educated Punjabi-speaker in Delhi; a third code, Punjabi, would be the 'native idiom' or 'regional dialect' of the speaker. The distance between the first two codes is slight, so that 'it almost seems as if the two languages were gradually merging'.[4] However, language distance increases substantially between the first and third codes. Gumperz's study was carried on in Delhi, but it may be broadly relevant to the urban environment of the Punjab generally and may help to understand some of the disputed points in contemporary controversies concerning the status and functions of Hindi and Punjabi in the Punjab.

Although Grierson's and Gumperz's discussions of Hindi and Punjabi leave considerable room for controversy, they do enable an objective observer to dismiss certain arguments as clearly prejudiced or incorrect. Thus, the extreme pro-Hindi view that Punjabi 'is nothing more than a spoken language, or a mere dialect'[5] is as much

---

[1] Grierson, *Linguistic Survey*, vol. IX, pt. I, p. 607.
[2] *Ibid.*, p. 617. Contemporary linguistic studies of Punjabi have emphasized also its distinctive tonal features; see Bahl, 'Panjabi', p. 160.
[3] John J. Gumperz, 'Hindi–Punjabi Code-Switching in Delhi', in Anwar S. Dil (ed.), *Language in Social Groups: Essays by John J. Gumperz* (Stanford, California: Stanford University Press, 1971), pp. 205–19.   [4] *Ibid.*, p. 217.
[5] Government of India, Home Department, *Report of the Punjab Commission* (Delhi: Manager of Publications, 1962), p. 15.

contrary to the known linguistic facts as is the extreme pro-Punjabi view that Punjabi has 'a written literature that in antiquity, volume and variety compares well with that of any other vernacular of India'.[1] On the other hand, the ability of an educated Punjabi-speaker to control three codes makes it at least understandable how Punjabi-speaking Hindus may choose to relegate Punjabi to the status of a spoken language of the home only and use Hindi for social interaction and written correspondence. It is less clear, however, whether the following argument of the States Reorganization Commission was valid for the pre-reorganization Punjab:

> . . . there is no real language problem in the State of Punjab as at present consti-tuted. This is so because the Punjabi and Hindi languages as spoken in the Punjab are akin to each other and are both well-understood by all sections of the people of the State. Nobody has seriously argued before us that the present set-up presents any serious difficulty so far as the communicational needs of the people are concerned.[2]

On the basis of Gumperz's analysis of code-switching in Delhi, it might well be argued that urban, educated people in the Punjab are likely to be able to communicate effectively in several codes, but there is no linguistic evidence to suggest or disprove that such a code-switching capability applied to 'all sections of the people' of the pre-reorganization Punjab.

This question is related to the second issue concerning the char-acteristics of the Punjabi language, namely, its regional distribution. Grierson argued that Punjabi was the mother tongue of the people in the eastern Punjab districts. Although he did not believe that a line could be drawn separating Punjabi from Lahnda in the west, he was more confident about the existence of a reasonably distinct regional boundary between Punjabi and Hindi in the east. The great demographic changes in Punjab which took place during the mass migrations of 1946–7 would, if anything, have reinforced the Pun-jabi-speaking character of the eastern Punjab districts, since Hindu-stani- and Urdu-speaking Muslims emigrated while Lahnda-speaking and Punjabi-speaking Hindus and Sikhs migrated into the eastern Punjab districts.[3] The important policy decisions on language in the post-independence period, such as the Sachar Formula and the

---

[1] Gurnam Singh, *A Unilingual Pubjabi State*, p. 84.

[2] Government of India, Home Department, *Report of the States Reorganisation Commission, 1955* (New Delhi: Government of India Press, 1955), p. 141. (Hereafter referred to as SRC, *Report*.)

[3] It is sometimes further argued that some of the districts in which Hindi-speakers were previously predominant have, since partition, acquired a Punjabi-speaking majority. See, e.g., *Punjabi Suba*, p. 171.

Regional Formula, were based upon the assumption that district Hindi-speaking and Punjabi-speaking zones existed.[1]

Proponents of Hindi in the Punjab were sometimes willing to accept the argument that a line could be drawn separating the Hindi-speaking region from the rest of the Punjab, but they argued that the so-called Punjabi-speaking region was actually bilingual. The pro-Punjabi reply to these arguments was simply that they contradicted the facts. It was argued rather that the mother tongue of all people of all creeds in city, town, and villages was Punjabi. The issue, on which linguistic evidence is not adequate, is whether the so-called Punjabi-speaking region is inhabited by people of different religions speaking the same mother tongue or by people of different religions *and* different mother tongues.

There is finally the question of script. On this issue, it is easier to distinguish fact from emotion. Gurumukhi and Devanagari both have been and can be used to write either Hindi or Punjabi. Since the Sikh scriptures are written in Gurumukhi, Sikhs favor the use of that script to write Punjabi. For the same reason, even those Hindus who acknowledge Punjabi as their mother tongue refuse to acknowledge Gurumukhi as its proper script and prefer to use Devanagari instead. Sikhs take the position that the refusal of Hindus to accept Gurumukhi demonstrates the communal, anti-Sikh character of their views on language, whereas Hindus argue that it is improper for Sikhs to impose their religious script upon them.[2]

Thus, the evidence concerning the status of the Punjabi language may be summarized as follows. Punjabi in the Punjabi region is a grammatically and lexically distinct language from Hindi, but an intermediate form of Punjabi also exists, which is closer to Hindi. Most people in the 'Punjabi-speaking region' probably speak Punjabi as their mother tongue, but some Hindus may not do so in fact and many more Hindus have learned to deny it in practice. Sikhs in the Punjab identify with Punjabi both as their mother tongue and

---

[1] See below, ch. 7.

[2] For the various views on the issue of script, see Grierson, *Linguistic Survey*, vol. IX, pt. I, p. 624; SRC, *Report*, p. 143; Punjab Commission, *Report*, p. 15; Government of India, Parliamentary Committee on the Demand for Punjabi Suba, *Report* (New Delhi: Lok Sabha Secretariat, 1966), p. 41; Om Prakasha Kahol, *Hindus and the Punjabi State: A Psycho-Political Discussion on the Conception & Rationale of Punjabi State* (Ambala Cantt.: Hindu Prachara Sabha, 1955), pp. 3–5, 8–11, and 22–3; *Tribune*, 17 May 1960. The preferences of different religious groups in the Punjab for different scripts are not new developments. British educational records show that 'popular education' in the Punjab when the British annexed the province was transmitted in Hindu schools 'in the Hindee character' whereas, in the Sikh schools, the Granth was taught in Gurumukhi. J. A. Richey, *Selections from Educational Records*, pt. II: *1840–1859* (Calcutta: Superintendent of Government Printing, India, 1922), p. 278.

as their language of public discourse and correspondence, but educated Sikhs may well command Gumperz's three 'codes'. Many Hindus in Punjab speak Punjabi as their mother tongue, but fewer use it outside the house or for correspondence, and fewer still will use the Gurumukhi script to write it.

The questions concerning the relative status of the Hindi and Punjabi languages can be better understood once it is recognized that the standing of a language in relation to particular social groups is not something fixed, but may evolve and change over time and may be subject to deliberate direction. Such has been the case at least with regard to language in the Punjab in modern times.

Punjabi, Hindi, and the census

The struggle for the achievement of the Punjabi Suba has taken place in the political arena of the Punjab in the post-independence period. The competition between the Hindi movement and the other languages of the Punjab, including Punjabi, has taken place in the census and has been in progress for nearly a century. In this competition in the Punjab, as elsewhere in north India, Hindi has been the gainer, Punjabi the chief loser.

The earliest efforts of the census authorities in the Punjab in 1881 and 1891 to count the number of speakers of the various mother tongues of the people encountered difficulties similar to those experienced elsewhere in north India. It was found that the people spoke a wide variety of regional dialects which frequently shaded off imperceptibly into one another from place to place and that large numbers of people, if not most rural residents, had no conception of the name to call their language. On the other hand, census officials and enumerators frequently had very definite ideas on the subject. Even where the census officers had no intent to predetermine the outcome, the desire for uniformity and precision in an area of variability and uncertainty meant that the census superintendents, supervisors, and enumerators could not avoid influencing the results in the way they defined, grouped, and classified the returns. Finally, in a situation of such variability and indefiniteness, there was considerable opportunity for organized efforts to influence the results.

Organized efforts by private interest associations and individuals to influence the census returns in favor of Urdu, Hindi, and Punjabi were noted as early as 1911. The main line of conflict in the censuses of 1911, 1921, and 1931 was between educated Muslims, who were urging their religious brethren to declare their mother tongue as

Urdu, and Arya Samajists, who worked among Hindus to urge them to declare for Hindi. In this conflict, both Hindustani – the favorite term of the census superintendents for both Hindi and Urdu – and Punjabi lost strength as Hindus and Muslims alike avoided the term 'Hindustani' and opted for Hindi or Urdu, while some Punjabi-speaking Hindus declared Hindi and Punjabi-speaking Muslims Urdu to be their mother tongue. Similar results were noted by the census superintendent in 1931.[1] By 1941, conflict over the language issue had become so severe and deception so widespread that the results of the mother tongue returns were not tabulated.[2] In 1951, again, efforts to influence the results, this time primarily in favor of Hindi and Punjabi, were so intense and so widespread that the census authorities ultimately lumped all the major dialects and languages of the Punjab together in one group, described as Hindi, Urdu, Punjabi, and Pahari.[3] In 1961, Arya Samajists launched a major campaign, including the publication of 'articles in newspapers exhorting the Hindus to declare Hindi as their mother-tongue'. Because of the intense feelings aroused by the language agitations in 1961, census enumerators were instructed to record whatever language respondents gave as their mother tongue without attempting to verify the response.[4] There is good reason to believe, therefore, that the 1961 census accurately reflects the language preferences of the people of the Punjab, although certainly not the actual mother tongues spoken.[5]

The publication of the results of the 1961 census was disastrous for the cause of the Punjabi language. It showed that, despite the influx of millions of Lahnda- and Punjabi-speaking Hindus and Sikhs from West Pakistan into east Punjab, the partition of the province and the Hindi movement had reduced declared Punjabi-speakers to a minority in the province for the first time in the history of the census.

---

[1] See *Census of India, 1911*, vol. XIV, pt. I, *Report*, pp. 345–6; *Census of India, 1921*, vol. XV: *Punjab & Delhi*, pt. I, pp. 310–12; *Census of India, 1931*, vol. XVII: *Punjab*, pt. I, *Report*, pp. 271–2; Hukam Singh, *The Punjab Problem: An Elucidation* (Amritsar: Shiromani Akali Dal, n.d.), p. 1.

[2] *Census of India, 1941*, vol. I, pt. I, *Tables*, pp. 8–9 (Delhi: Manager of Publications, 1946), p. 9.

[3] On the conflicts surrounding the 1951 census in the Punjab, see *Census of India, 1961*, vol. XIII: *Punjab*, pt. I-A (i): *General Report*, by R. L. Anand (Delhi: Manager of Publications, 1969), p. 399; Nayar, *Minority Politics*, pp. 49–51; Government of India, Home Department, Punjab Boundary Commission, *Report* (Delhi: Manager of Publications, 1966), p. 19; SRC, *Report*, p. 141; Khushwant Singh, *The Sikhs*, vol. II, p. 293; letter of C. S. Khanna to the *Hindustan Times*, 14 June 1960; *Spokesman*, 24 May 1965.

[4] Punjab Boundary Commission, *Report*, p. 12.

[5] The views of the Punjab census superintendent on the accuracy and reliability of the 1961 mother tongue returns are given in the *1961 Census*, vol. XIII, pt. I-A (i), 400–1.

The figures in table 6.1 (which have been adjusted for boundary changes) show how declared Hindi-speakers were transformed from a small minority to a majority in the Punjab, while Punjabi-speakers, who never constituted less than 60% of the total population of the pre-partition province, constituted only 41% of the post-partition Punjab state. In fact, the adjusted figures show that Punjabi suffered an absolute, as well as a relative, decline between 1931 and 1961.

A comparison of the ratios of Hindi-speakers to Hindus in 1921[1] and 1961 with the ratios for Punjabi-speakers to Sikhs in the same years (table 6.2) demonstrates the extent to which language identifications have become congruent with religious identifications in the Punjab during the past four decades. In 1921, the ratio of Hindi-speakers to Hindus in the Punjab was only 0.26. That is, assuming that, for the most part, only Hindus declared themselves as Hindi-speakers in 1921, nearly three-quarters of the Hindu population of the time were recorded as declaring Punjabi, Hindustani, or some other language to be their mother tongue. In contrast, in 1961, the ratio of Hindi-speakers to Hindus was 0.87. That is, in 1961, assuming that only Hindus declared Hindi as their mother tongue, only 13% of the Hindu population of the Punjab did not do so. For most Hindus in the Punjab, their language and religion have become congruent. The evidence, moreover, suggests that they have become congruent by choice, in consequence of political action and ethnic conflict.[2]

The other side of the coin of language change is that Punjabi which, in 1921, was the language of Hindus, Muslims, and Sikhs alike has increasingly become identified with the Sikhs alone. In the state as a whole, Hindus increased by 14%, Sikhs by 15%, and Hindi-speakers by 43%, while Punjabi-speakers declined by 23%. Assuming that nearly all Sikhs declared themselves as Punjabi-speakers in both 1921 and 1961, there were five non-Sikh Punjabi-speakers for every two Sikh Punjabi-speakers in 1921, but only one non-Sikh Punjabi-speaker for every five Sikh Punjabi-speakers in 1961. Thus, in effect, language and religion have become increasingly congruent for Sikhs in the Punjab, as well as for Hindus, as Punjabi has become primarily the language of the Sikhs.

Once again, therefore, in the Punjab as elsewhere in north India,

---

[1] 1921 has been selected as the comparison year because this was the most recent census in which Hindi was recorded separately.

[2] See Nayar, *Minority Politics*, also on this point, especially pp. 49–51, where he discusses the language choices of Hindus and Harijans in the 1951 census.

TABLE 6.1 *Speakers of most important languages in the Punjab, 1911–61*[a]

Language	1961[b]		1951[c]		1931[d]		1921[e]		1911[f]	
	No.	%	No.	%	No.	%	No.	%	No.	%
1. Hindi	11,298,855	55.64	N.A.	N.A.	N.A.	N.A.	1,641,268	13.16	1,670,022	13.94
2. Punjabi	8,343,264	41.09	N.A.	N.A.	8,418,240	61.56	7,990,683	64.08	7,682,186	64.13
3. Urdu	255,660	1.26	N.A.	N.A.	N.A.	N.A.	1,221,885	9.80	322,495	2.69
4. Pahari	248,176	1.22	N.A.	N.A.	836,720	6.12	423,905	3.40	228,150	1.90
5. Hindustani	47	0.00	N.A.	N.A.	3,783,704	27.67	496,247	3.98	1,348,448	11.26
Total	20,146,002	99.21	15,858,835	99.95	13,038,664	95.36	11,773,988	94.42	11,251,301	93.93

[a] Bases of enumeration between 1911 and 1961 varied as follows: 1911: 'language ordinarily spoken in the household'; 1921: 'language ordinarily used'; 1931–61: 'mother tongue'.

[b] The following comments appear in the *General Report* volume, pt. 1-A (i), p. 400: 'Long before the enumeration was due to commence, uneasiness among certain sections about the recording of mother tongue became apparent. The topic began to be discussed in families, social groups and public meetings. Articles appeared in press, formal resolutions were passed, slogans were shouted, and posters were exhibited. . . .

. . .

'On his part, the Superintendent of Census Operations contacted local leaders at various places and delivered talks on the radio, explaining that the question on mother tongue . . . was very specific, relating to the early life of the individual and that it did not ask for any choice while recording the reply. The enumerators were instructed to record faithfully the replies as given by the respondents and they were strongly cautioned against cross-examining or using their discretion in recording information on this topic.'

'In view of the language controversy that raged in Punjab until a few weeks before the enumeration commenced it would be presumptuous to claim that the answers given on mother tongue are entirely free from bias. Some persons must have intimated their mother tongue with ulterior motives, and the possibility of a very few enumerators having influenced the returns can also not be altogether ruled out. However, since all enumerators were drawn from Government servants who were strictly instructed to keep aloof from the language controversy and a very close watch was exercised over them by the supervisors, charge officers and District officers, the information presented for the 1961-census is fairly dependable.'

[c] The following remarks on the results of the 1951 mother-tongue census are found in *ibid.*, p. 399: 'The language controversy fanned communal passions to the extent that it was eventually decided to sort slips showing the mother tongues Hindi, Urdu, Punjabi, Pahari and their dialects, as one group. As a result, the 1951-Census Report does not show the Hindi and Punjabi-speaking people separately.'

[d] The instructions to enumerators were 'the same as those issued in 1921 except that they were supplemented by a direction that Urdu

and Hindi should be recorded as Hindustani'. The report also notes that circulars were distributed asking people to declare themselves Hindi speakers and that Punjabi suffered because of this action and because some Punjabi speakers declared their mother tongue as Urdu. *Census of India, 1931*, vol. XVII: *Punjab*, pt. I: *Report*, pp. 271–2. The following comments appear in *Census of India, 1921*, vol. XV: *Punjab and Delhi*, pt. I, pp. 310–12: 'The decrease in the number of Hindustani speakers has occurred on account of the large number of persons having given their language as Urdu . . .

'. . . The increase in the strength of the Urdu-speaking population has been more or less general throughout the provinces . . . The general increase has resulted chiefly from the distinguishing line becoming indeterminate in the course of years . . . The other cause of this increase is found in the Urdu–Hindi–Punjabi controversy observed in 1911 which resulted in all [*sic*] Musalmans returning their language as Urdu, instead of Hindostani, as distinguished from Hindi, a word adopted by Hindus for denoting Hindostani spoken by them . . . One may conclude that the strength of partisan sentiment, and the small linguistic difference between Urdu and Hindostani are largely responsible for the violent fluctuations from census to census of the recorded numbers of Urdu speaking persons.'

The following comments appear in *Census of India, 1911*, vol. XIV

pt. I: *Report*, pp. 345–6: 'The enumeration books were to show for each person, the language or the dialect in which he talked at home. The enumerators were requested to put down the dialect exactly as the person enumerated described it, but, at the same time, they were instructed, in each unit, to call a particular dialect by the same name. Had it not been for the Urdu–Hindi–Punjabi controversy, which has been going on for a considerable time in the Province, the figures should, with the precautions taken, have been almost thoroughly reliable. Unfortunately, however, the leaders of different sections issued open or confidential instructions to their adherents asking them to advocate the cause of their favored language or dialect . . . Party feeling [influenced] the accuracy of the returns.

'The agitation was, however, confined mainly to towns and the figures of the cities of Delhi and Lahore, where it was at its worst, show that, although both Hindi and Urdu gained in the measure of the numerical strength of their supporters, at the expense of Hindustani and Punjabi (the supporters of the former – mainly Arya Samajists being far more limited than those of Urdu, viz., the educated (Muhammadans), yet the extent of the error was insignificant on the whole.'

SOURCE. *Census of India, 1961*, vol. XIII: *Punjab*, pt. II–C (i), *Social and Cultural Tables* (Delhi: Manager of Publications, 1965), pp. 229–36.

TABLE 6.2 *Changes in the proportions of Hindus, Hindi-speakers, Sikhs and Punjabi-speakers in the Punjab,*[a] *1921 and 1961*

Religion/language	1921	1961
1. Hindus (%)	49.78	63.67
2. Hindi-speakers (%)	13.16	55.64
3. Ratio Hindi/Hindu	0.26	0.87
4. Sikhs (%)	17.98	33.34
5. Punjabi-speakers (%)	64.08	41.09
6. Ratio Punjabi/Sikhs	3.56	1.23

[a] The figures are based on adjusted boundaries, except that adjustments could not be made in some cases for 'transfers of isolated villages or groups of small villages'.

SOURCES. Adapted from *Census of India, 1961*, vol. XIII: *Punjab*, pt. I–A (i), *General Report* (Delhi: Manager of Publications, 1969), pp. 427 and 430, and *ibid.*, pt. II–C (i), *Social and Cultural Tables* (Delhi: Manager of Publications, 1965), pp. 224–36.

it is clear that the long-term process of language change has been favorable to the Hindi movement. The Hindi movement over time has succeeded in absorbing millions of speakers not only of mother tongues generally considered to be regional dialects of Hindi, but of mother tongues generally considered to constitute grammatically distinct languages. Although the movements of the minority religions and language groups for recognition and political status in north India have received the greater attention and have achieved some important concessions, the achievements of the Hindi movement, which have been more quiet, have been equally impressive, if not more so. The regional languages of the north have been able to survive against the inroads of Hindi only where they have been useful as symbols in the struggles of minority peoples, such as Muslims and Sikhs, whose demands have not been primarily linguistic. In the absence of intense attachment on the part of such minority groups to these regional languages, it is likely that Hindi would eventually become the only major, standardized language throughout the whole of north India.

HINDUS AND SIKHS IN THE PUNJAB: SOCIAL MOBILIZATION AND COMMUNICATIONS

The analyses of the processes of assimilation and differentiation in the relationships between different language and religious groups in Bihar and U.P. have identified in north India three classic processes of change which have occurred in other parts of the world as well.

The first process, exemplified in the Maithili case, is one in which the less advanced (socially mobilized) speakers of a minority language have adopted the dominant Hindi language and culture of north India. The second process, exemplified by the relations between Hindus and Muslims in the United Provinces before independence, is one in which a backward majority of Hindus developed too rapidly to be assimilated by a more privileged Muslim minority and achieved social, cultural, and political dominance. The third process, exemplified by the Urdu movement in north India in the post-independence period, is one in which a cultural minority of Urdu-speaking Muslims has sought to acquire protection for its language and religion in a society dominated by an overwhelming majority of Hindi-speaking Hindus in which Hindu political leaders have pursued a political strategy of assimilating the language and culture of the minority group. In the Punjab, yet other processes have been occurring. Before independence, two mobilizing minorities of Hindus and Sikhs sought protection for their language and culture and political power against a less advanced, but politically dominant majority of Muslims. The displacement of the Muslims in the Punjab after independence and the consequent demographic changes transformed the communal situation into one in which a socially and politically mobilizing minority of Sikhs struggled for cultural and political advancement against a socially and politically mobilizing Hindu majority. The dominant Hindu majority, unable to assimilate the Sikhs, adopted the tactic of avoiding their own assimilation by disowning the Punjabi language so that the Sikhs, a minority people by religion, might become a minority by language as well. In this section, the quantitative dimensions of the changes which have taken place in the relations between Hindus and Sikhs in the Punjab during the past half century will be presented.

Urbanization

In the pre-partition Punjab province, Muslims comprised slightly more than half, Hindus somewhat less than a third, and the Sikhs approximately one-eighth of the total population. The population ratio between Muslims and Hindus in the cities was not much different from their relative ratio in the total population of the province (table 6.3). Nevertheless, the percentage of Hindus living in towns was always higher than that for Muslims or Sikhs. For their part, the Sikhs were a significantly smaller minority in the cities than they were in the province as a whole. In the pre-partition Punjab,

TABLE 6.3   *Total and urban population by religion in the undivided Punjab,*ᵃ *1881–1941 (in percentages)*

Year	Total population			Urban population			Living in towns			
	Hindu	Muslim	Sikh	Hindu	Muslim	Sikh	Total	Hindu	Muslim	Sikh
1941	(29.79)	(52.88)	(14.62)	(37.64)	(51.37)	(8.36)	(14.44)	(18.09)	(14.05)	(8.28)
1931	30.18	52.40	14.29	37.65	51.90	7.26	12.36	(15.41)	(12.24)	(6.28)
1921	35.06	51.05	12.38	40.21	50.60	6.28	10.34	(11.87)	(10.25)	(5.25)
1911	35.79	51.07	12.11	39.23	51.21	6.61	9.81 (10.61)	(11.83)	(10.57)	(5.42)
1901	41.27	49.61	8.63	43.33	49.06	4.57	10.59 (11.27)	(11.92)	(11.31)	(5.62)
1891	44.08	47.39	8.09	44.61	48.51	4.69	10.71 (11.42)	(11.92)	(11.07)	(5.62)
1881	43.84	47.56	8.22	45.26	48.05	4.88	11.90 (12.65)	(13.75)	(12.17)	(7.29)

ᵃ All figures in the table are for the undivided Punjab, including the Punjab states, but excluding the North-West Frontier Province.

SOURCES. All figures, except those in parentheses, have been taken or compiled from retroactive tables in the 1931 census volumes. The figures in parentheses have been taken or compiled from census volumes for the years indicated in the table without retroactive adjustments. The citations are *Census of India, 1941*, vol. I, pt. I, pp. 56, 88–9, 92–3, 98–100; *1931*, vol. I, pt. I, pp. 422–3; vol. XVII, pt. I, pp. 96 and 100, pt. II, pp. 6 and 16; *1921*, vol. I, pt. II, pp. 6, 32–3, 36–7; *1911*, vol. I, pt. I, pp. 30–1, 34–5, 38–9, 41; *1901*, vol. XVII-A, pt. II, pp. I–ii, v–ii, iii; and VI–ii, iii; *1891*, vol. XX, pt. II, pp. 2, 12–15; *1881*, vol. I, pp. 17, 20, 106. The 1931 and the retroactive figures are based upon 222 towns. The number of places classified as towns in the Punjab in 1941 was 283; in 1921, 186; in 1911, 174; in 1901, 228; in 1891, n.a.; in 1881, 302.

the Sikhs were predominantly a dispersed rural minority dependent on separate electorates and weightage in the representative system of government under the British for their political influence. With these two colonial political devices, however, the Sikhs did maintain political importance as a balancing force between Hindus and Muslims in the political life of the province.

Some of the vast demographic changes which took place in the Punjab after 1947 and their impact upon the relationship between Hindus and Sikhs in town and country can be seen in table 6.4, which compares the total and urban and rural population distribution of the three main communities in the Punjab between 1901 and 1961, with the boundaries of Punjab retroactively adjusted to conform to those of 1961. In the total population of the 1961 Punjab districts, the Muslims were practically completely displaced, the Hindus increased their majority, and the Sikhs were transformed from a small minority group in a multi-communal province to a substantial minority in a dual-community province. Moreover, the Sikhs also became a compact minority with majority concentrations in a large number of contiguous districts in the divisions of Jullundur and Patiala particularly (table 6.5). Although the urban Sikh population of the Punjab more than doubled, the urban Hindu population also increased tremendously as a consequence of the post-partition population transfers. Moreover, proportionate to their population, more than twice as many Hindus lived in towns in 1961 as did Sikhs. Even in the Sikh-majority districts, all the major cities of the post-partition Punjab contained Hindu majorities. Thus, the post-independence urban–rural demography of the Punjab may be summarized as follows. In the province as a whole, Hindus constituted a majority in urban and rural areas alike, but in a compact geographical region, the Sikhs constituted a rural hinterland surrounding the major Hindu-dominated cities. Out of this demographic pattern, there emerged the characteristic three-way political division in the Punjab of the 1950s and the 1960s among the Hindi-speaking Hindus concentrated in the districts of Ambala division or Haryana; the Sikhs, concentrated in the districts of Jullundur and Patiala divisions; and the Punjabi-speaking Hindus of the Jullundur and Patiala divisions, led politically by an urban Hindu elite concentrated in the leading towns of Jullundur, Ludhiana, and Amritsar.

Literacy and communications

Although the Muslims in pre-partition Punjab constituted a majority

TABLE 6.4 *Urban and rural populations in the Punjab (post-partition boundaries)*[a] *by religion, 1901–61 (in percentages)*

Year	Total population			Urban population			Rural population			Living in towns[b]			
	Hindu	Muslim	Sikh	Hindu	Muslim	Sikh	Hindu	Muslim	Sikh	Total	Hindu	Muslim	Sikh
1961	63.67	1.94	33.34	76.23	1.11	20.91	60.51	2.15	36.47	20.13	24.10	11.50	12.63
1951	62.28	1.80	35.00	70.35	1.05	27.13	60.48	1.96	36.76		Not available →		
1941	43.59	33.09	22.25	42.75	45.92	9.42	43.74	30.86	24.48				
1931	45.46	32.42	21.12	43.03	46.81	7.96	45.81	30.30	23.06				
1921	49.78	31.23	17.98	45.17	45.20	7.17	50.35	29.49	19.33				
1911	50.71	31.27	17.26	44.14	45.84	7.22	51.50	29.50	18.47				
1901	55.51	31.75	12.24	47.34	45.41	5.12	56.52	30.06	13.12				

[a] All figures, except those in parentheses, have been adjusted by the census authorities to be comparable with 1961 territorial boundaries.

[b] Retroactive figures for persons living in towns are not available. See table 6.3 for the figures for the undivided Punjab.

SOURCES. Compiled from *Census of India, 1961,* vol. XIII, pt. I–A (i), pp. 427, 429–30, and pt. II–C (i), pp. 350–1; *1951, Paper No. 1, 1957,* pp. 157 and 238.

TABLE 6.5   *Urban and rural populations of Hindus and Sikhs in the Punjab by division, 1961 census (in percentages)*

	Total population		Urban population		Rural population	
Division	Hindu	Sikh	Hindu	Sikh	Hindu	Sikh
1. Ambala	85.9	9.6	88.1	9.6	85.4	9.6
2. Jullundur	52.1	45.7	72.4	25.3	46.6	51.2
3. Patiala	50.2	47.6	64.6	30.3	46.9	51.7

SOURCE. Government of India, Home Department, *Report of the Punjab Boundary Commission* (Delhi: Manager of Publications, 1966), pp. 103–4.

in urban and rural areas alike and were a more urbanized community than the Sikhs, in other aspects of social mobilization they failed to keep pace with Hindus and Sikhs. The available figures on literacy in the early decades of the twentieth century show clearly that the Hindus and the Sikhs were the mobilizing communities of the Punjab and that they left the Muslims far behind. Tables 6.6 and 6.7 show that rates of both general literacy and English literacy were highest between 1901 and 1931 among Hindus, followed by Sikhs, but were consistently lowest among Muslims.

TABLE 6.6   *Male literacy by religion in the Punjab,[a] 1901–31 (in percentages)*

	1931	1921	1911	1901
1. Total population	9.5	7.4	6.3	6.5
2. Hindus	14.7	11.3	9.5	9.8
3. Muslims	5.5	3.7	2.7	2.6
4. Sikhs	12.6	9.3	9.4	8.5

[a] Figures for the Punjab include the Punjab States.

SOURCES. Compiled from *Census of India, 1931*, vol. XVII, pt. I, pp. 252 and 263; pt. II, p. 230; *1921*, vol. XV, pt. I, p. 292; *1901*, vol. XVII, pt. I, p. 276; vol. XVII–A, pt. II, pp. VIII–ii, VIII–vi.

The figures on general literacy and English literacy among the three main communities in the Punjab are valuable as indices of social mobilization. The Punjab census documents from 1891 to 1931 also provide figures on literacy by religion in the vernacular languages (by script) of the province, which provide information on

TABLE 6.7   *Male English literacy by religion in the Punjab, 1901–31 (in percentages)*

	1931	1921[a]	1911[a]	1901[a]
1. Total population	1.60	1.03	0.67	0.68
2. Hindus	2.30	1.42	0.96	0.69
3. Muslims	0.99	0.51	0.37	0.26
4. Sikhs	1.89	0.99	0.56	0.46

[a] Figures for the Punjab including the Native States.

SOURCES. *Census of India, 1901*, vol. XVII, pt. I, p. 277; vol. XVII–A, pt. II, pp. VIII–ii, iii, vi; *1911*, vol. I, pt. II, pp. 76 and 80; *1921*, vol. I, pt. II, pp. 78 and 82; *1931*, vol. XVII, pt. II, p. 230.

inter-communal communication. Those figures can be broken up in two ways. Table 6.8 shows the percentage of literates in each vernacular language from each religious community in 1901 and 1931. Table 6.9 shows the number and percentage of literates in the main vernacular languages of the Punjab as a proportion of the total literates in each religious group in 1901 and 1931. Since the number of languages enumerated and the precise classification of each language and religion changed from census to census, the figures should not be used carelessly to show changes over time. They do, however, provide valuable information at two points in time concerning the ability of literate male members of each religious group to use the major vernacular languages, with their characteristic scripts, and concerning the degree of identification between language and religion in the Punjab.

In the Punjab before independence, English and Urdu were both official languages. Consequently, it is not surprising that the 'Urdu' or Persian script was by far the most important script for the *literate* population of the state, although, as was shown above, Punjabi was the predominant *spoken* language of the province. It is also not surprising that all three communities contained considerable proportions of 'Urdu'-literates in both 1901 and 1931. The figures on literacy in the 'Urdu' or Persian script also point up again the fact that Hindus were the most advanced community in the Punjab for, even in 'Urdu', the characteristic literary language of the Muslims, Hindus had more literates than the Muslims did in 1901 and nearly as many in 1931. Hindus were also the most eclectic and pervasive community in the Punjab, for they provided large proportions of literates in both 1901 and 1931 in all the major vernacular scripts.

TABLE 6.8 *Male literacy in the most important vernaculars (scripts) of Punjab*[a] *by religion, 1901 and 1931*

Vernacular		1931				1901			
		All religions	Muslim	Hindu	Sikh	All religions	Muslim	Hindu	Sikh
1. 'Urdu'[b]	No.	840,529	368,914	346,391	108,252	333,154	145,003	152,758	28,947
	%		43.89	41.21	12.88		43.52	45.85	8.69
2. 'Hindi'[b]	No.	176,044	2,022	161,384	9,573	133,368	3,021	122,028	4,980
	%		1.15	91.67	5.44		2.27	91.50	3.73
3. Gurumukhi	No.	148,157	1,649	36,196	107,017	137,450	2,378	66,060	68,702
	%		1.11	24.43	72.23		1.73	48.06	49.98
4. Lande	No.	← Not available →				233,466	5,577	207,726	11,928
	%						2.39	88.97	5.12

[a] Including the Punjab States, excluding the North-West Frontier Province.

[b] In the Punjab census tables, the terms 'Urdu' and 'Hindi' were used to refer to the scripts, which presumably were Persian-Arabic for Urdu and Devanagari for Hindi.

SOURCES. *Census of India, 1931*, vol. XVII, *Punjab*, pt. I, p. 260, and *1901*, vol. XVII-A, *Punjab*, pt. II, pp. VIII-x and xi.

TABLE 6.9 *Number and percentage of male literates in important vernaculars of the Punjab as a proportion of the total literates of the major religious groups, 1901 and 1931*

Religion		1931				1901				
		All literates	Literate in 'Urdu'a	'Hindi'a	Gurumukhi	All literates	Literate in 'Urdu'a	'Hindi'a	Gurumukhi	Lande
1. Hindu	No.	594,363	346,391	161,384	36,196	551,980	152,758	122,028	66,060	207,726
	%		58.28	27.15	6.09		27.67	22.11	11.97	37.63
2. Sikh	No.	246,203	108,252	9,573	107,017	100,859	28,947	4,980	68,702	11,928
	%		43.97	3.89	43.47		28.70	4.94	68.12	11.83
3. Muslim	No.	378,742	368,914	2,022	1,649	171,583	145,003	3,021	2,378	5,577
	%		97.41	0.53	0.44		84.51	1.76	1.39	3.25

a See table 6.8, n.b., above.

SOURCES. Same as for table 6.8.

Nevertheless, some suggestion of the developing communication barriers between Hindus and Sikhs in the Punjab is evident in the figures for literacy in 'Hindi' (i.e. Devanagari) and Gurumukhi. Practically speaking, Hindi in the Devanagari script, as a literary language, both in 1901 and 1931, was the language of Hindus only. Gurumukhi, however, was not yet the exclusive script of the Sikhs. In 1901, when the census authorities were still uncertain and indecisive about classifying persons as either Sikh or Hindu, nearly as many Hindus as Sikhs were recorded as literate in Gurumukhi. Even in 1931, nearly 25% of Gurumukhi literates were Hindu. Still, by 1931 – and partly because of the way the census itself was conducted – Gurumukhi was becoming classified and identified primarily as the literary script of the Sikhs.

The identification of each of the three major literary languages with one of the three main communities in the Punjab appears stronger when the literates in each language are viewed in proportion to the total literates in each religion (table 6.9). Thus, although Muslims, Hindus and Sikhs all had high proportions of literates in 'Urdu' in the Persian script, Muslims were literate primarily in 'Urdu' in both 1901 and 1931. The leading scripts among Hindus were 'Urdu' and Lande in 1901 (with 'Hindi' a strong third) and 'Urdu' and 'Hindi' in 1931, when Lande was not recorded. However, although Hindu literates in Gurumukhi constituted nearly 25% of the total Gurumukhi literates in 1931 (table 6.8), they were only 6% of the total Hindu literates in the Punjab (table 6.9). As for male Sikh literates, they too had a high proportion of 'Urdu'-literates, with Gurumukhi a close second, but 'Hindi' was very far behind.

Consequently, the bases for the post-independence conflict between Hindus and Sikhs existed in 1931 and earlier. They consisted, first, in the general feature of the discontinuity between spoken and literary languages in the Punjab. The major spoken languages of the Punjab before independence were Punjabi, Lahnda, Hindi, and Urdu. At the literary level, however, Urdu, the least common spoken language, was dominant in the Persian script whereas Punjabi, the predominant spoken language of the province, became, in its written Gurumukhi style, a distinctly minority language. The particular basis for the developing language conflict between Hindus and Sikhs was the fact that Hindi in Devanagari script was overwhelmingly the language of Hindus and Punjabi, in its written Gurumukhi style, primarily the language of Sikhs. When British rule ended and the partition displaced the Muslims from the Punjab, the backing for the two official languages of English and Urdu was withdrawn and the literate Hindu and Sikh elites were left in political and linguistic dominance in the Punjab. While the mass of the people, Hindus and Sikhs alike, continued to communicate with each other in the spoken languages of the province, the Hindu and Sikh literate elites took up the battle of scripts, the symbolic superstructure of a contest for political power in post-independence Punjab.

TABLE 6.10 *Newspapers and periodicals published in the Punjab by script, 1891–1931*

Year	Total No.	English		'Urdu'[a]		Gurumukhi		'Hindi'[a]		Mixed	
		No.	%	No.	%	No.	%	No.	%	No.	%
1931	579	81	13.99	375	64.77	56	9.67	24	4.15	42	7.25
1921	270	45	16.67	181	67.04	27	10.00	13	4.81	4	1.48
1911	229	25	10.92	177	77.29	17	7.42	9	3.93	1	0.44
1901	166	17	10.24	135	81.33	5	3.01	7	4.22	2	1.20
1891	74	4	5.41	64	86.49	1	1.35	3	4.05	2	2.70

[a] See table 6.8 n.b., above.

SOURCE. *Census of India, 1931*, vol. XVII, pt. I, p. 280.

TABLE 6.11 *Newspapers and periodicals published in the Punjab (pre- and post-reorganization) by language*

Year	Total No.	English		Urdu		Punjabi		Hindi		Others and mixed	
		No.	%	No.	%	No.	%	No.	%	No.	%
1967	395	45	11.39	143	36.20	120	30.38	43	10.89	44	11.14
1964	595	71	11.93	216	36.30	153	25.71	98	16.47	57	9.58
1960	584	65	11.13	177	30.31	104	17.81	66	11.30	172	29.45

SOURCES. Government of India, Ministry of Information and Broadcasting, *Press in India, 1968* (Delhi: Manager of Publications, 1968), pt. I, p. 263; *ibid., 1965*, p. 209; *ibid., 1961*, pp. 296–7.

The developing competition between Devanagari and Gurumukhi was fought, among other arenas, in the Punjab press, where Hindi/ Devanagari and Gurumukhi newspapers slowly, but perceptibly, over the decades began to compete with Urdu and English for the attention of the literate classes of the Punjab (table 6.10). The

Gurumukhi press was the slowest in the province to develop. The census records only one Gurumukhi paper in 1891 and only five a decade later, but a more considerable development after the turn of the century. By 1911, there were more Gurumukhi than Hindi/ Devanagari newspapers published in the province. It was not until after independence, however, that the Gurumukhi/Punjabi and Hindi/Devanagari press surpassed the English press in numbers. Moreover, even in post-partition Punjab and even in the truncated Punjab after the 1966 reorganization, the Urdu press continued to have the largest number of newspapers (table 6.11). However, table 6.11 shows that the Punjabi press (including Gurumukhi and other scripts) maintained its lead over the Hindi/Devanagari press after independence, with 25% of the newspapers in the Punjab of 1964 before reorganization and 30% in the Punjab of 1967 after reorganization, compared to 16% and 11% for Hindi, respectively.

Although Gurumukhi as a script was slow to develop in the Punjab press because of its identification as the script of the Sikh religion, the Punjabi language had a more rapid literary development in the several scripts of the province. Census records on books published in the Punjab by language rather than script (table 6.12) show that Punjabi was far ahead of either English or Hindi even before the turn of the century and that, by 1921, it bid fare to replace Urdu as the dominant literary as well as spoken language of the province.

TABLE 6.12   *Books published in the Punjab by language, 1891–1931*

Language	1922–31		1911–21		1901–10		1891–1900	
	No.	%	No.	%	No.	%	No.	%
1. Urdu	9,169	39.87	6,282	39.98	5,934	42.02	5,924	47.61
2. Punjabi	7,248	31.52	6,162	39.22	3,981	28.19	2,479	19.93
3. English	2,235	9.72	1,826	11.62	992	7.03	768	6.17
4. Hindi	1,557	6.77	748	4.76	885	6.27	785	6.31
5. Other	2,787	12.12	695	4.42	2,330	16.50	2,486	19.98
Total	22,996	100.00	15,713	100.00	14,122	100.01	12,442	100.00

SOURCES. Compiled from *Census of India, 1931*, vol. XVII: *Punjab*, pt. I, p. 281; *1921*, vol. XV: *Punjab and Delhi*, pt. I, p. 321; *1911*, vol. XIV: *Punjab*, pt. I, p. 344; *1901*, vol. XVII: *Punjab*, pt. I, p. 292.

On the whole, the pre-independence census data on urbanization, literacy, and communications suggest the following conclusions concerning processes of social mobilization, assimilation, and differentiation among the three religious groups in the Punjab. Muslims were numerically and politically the dominant community in the Punjab and Urdu, the characteristic literary language of the Muslims, was the dominant official vernacular language. The chief mobilizing communities in the Punjab, however, were the Hindus and Sikhs, of whom the Hindus were the most advanced in urbanization and literacy. Whereas the Hindu, Sikh, and Muslim elites communicated with each other in either of the two official languages of the Punjab, English or Urdu, a dual process of language change was occurring which would later affect profoundly the relations between Hindus and Sikhs. First, a gap developed between the literary languages of the Hindu and Sikh elites and the popular language of the masses. Second, a symbolic communications barrier was created between Hindu and Sikh literate elites, with Hindus preferring the use of the Hindi language in the Devanagari script and Sikhs the Punjabi language in the Gurumukhi script. The next step, which we have seen was already being taken in the pre-independence period and which became a major political issue in post-independence Punjab, was for the Hindu and Sikh literate elites to persuade the Punjabi-speaking masses that, if they were Hindu, they spoke Hindi and ought to learn to write Devanagari, and that, if they were Sikh, they ought to learn to write Punjabi exclusively in the Gurumukhi script.

HINDUS AND SIKHS IN THE PUNJAB:
POLITICAL DIFFERENTIATION

Sikh political organizations

Early organizations

In the late nineteenth and early twentieth centuries in the Punjab, a modern sense of self-consciousness and identity was promoted among the Sikhs by the Singh Sabha movement and the Chief Khalsa Diwan. The Singh Sabha movement began in the early 1870s to spread literacy, education, and religious awareness among the Sikhs.[1] The Chief Khalsa Diwan, formed in 1902, acted as a coordinating body for the Singh Sabha movement,[2] which by then had developed a broad network of voluntary associations throughout the province. The Chief Khalsa Diwan also took on specifically political functions on behalf of the Sikh community.

[1] On the origin of the Singh Sabhas, see Jones, 'Communalism in the Punjab', p. 49, and Khushwant Singh, *The Sikhs*, vol. II, ch. 9.
[2] On the formation of the Chief Khalsa Diwan, see Ganda Singh, *The Akali Movement*, p. xxv, and Sahni, *Sikh Shrines*, pp. 14ff.

Although a full history of the Singh Sabha movement and the Chief Khalsa Diwan has yet to be written, enough information on their activities is available to identify the functions which they performed in developing the modern Sikh community. The first important role played by the Singh Sabhas was to introduce an associational form into Sikhism instead of the traditional sectarian pattern of organization. Along with this associational form went a deliberate effort to consolidate Sikhs into a single community in contrast to the previously predominant pattern of proliferation of sects. The consolidating impact of the Singh Sabha movement was noted by the Punjab census superintendent in 1901:

In the recent Census 731,198 Sikhs, or 40 per cent returned no sect. This is far in excess of the numbers shown as returning no sect in 1891, . . . It is . . . to be attributed, I think, to a tendency to abandon the sects and join the religious associations, the Sabhas and so on. The Singh Sabha, the chief Sikh association, has not been returned as a sect.[1]

The second major role played by both the Singh Sabhas and the Chief Khalsa Diwan was to promote the social mobilization of the Sikh community and to strengthen internal communication. A literacy drive was launched, educational institutions were established, religious tracts were published, and newspapers were founded.[2] Moreover, most of these educational and communication activities either promoted or used the Punjabi language written in the Gurumukhi script.[3] Barrier has reported that the Singh Sabhas issued thousands of publications in Punjabi in the late nineteenth and early twentieth centuries.[4] Between 1891 and 1905, these associated Sikh organizations published ten newspapers.[5] A Khalsa college was formed in 1892 and many high schools and other educational institutions were also formed from year to year. By 1928, 275 educational institutions and 100 Singh Sabhas were associated with the Chief Khalsa Diwan.[6]

A third set of functions performed by these early Sikh organizations involved boundary definition and differentiation from other groups in the Punjab. Although the Singh Sabha movement was founded by the 'rich, landed gentry and the orthodox',[7] it opted for an inclusive definition of the Sikh community by supporting the right of untouch-

[1] *Census of India, 1901*, vol. XVII, pt. I, p. 124.
[2] Khushwant Singh, *The Sikhs*, vol. II, pp. 122 and 144–5.
[3] *Ibid.*
[4] Barrier, 'Mass Politics', p. 5.
[5] N. Gerald Barrier and Paul Wallace, *The Punjab Press, 1880–1905* (East Lansing, Mich.: Asian Studies Center, Michigan State University, 1970), p. 166.
[6] 'Deputation from the Chief Khalsa Diwan, Amritsar', in *ISC*, XVI, p. 143.
[7] Khushwant Singh, *The Sikhs*, vol. II, p. 141.

ables to worship in the gurudwaras.[1] At the same time, the Singh Sabha movement emphasized the distinctness of the Sikhs as a community, particularly their separateness from Hindus.[2] Much of the energy of the movement in the late nineteenth century was spent in defending Sikhism and Sikh identity from the inroads of Christian missionaries and of Hindu proselytizers from the Arya Samaj.[3]

Finally, the Chief Khalsa Diwan performed a fourth set of functions for the Sikh community in this period, that of political representation. In this respect, the Chief Khalsa Diwan acted for the Sikh community in the Punjab in a manner similar to and partly patterned after the role played by the Aligarh movement and the early Muslim League for the Muslim community of north India. Using a similar myth of backwardness, the Chief Khalsa Diwan, like the Aligarh movement, adopted a loyalist political strategy of seeking political patronage from the British rulers for an allegedly backward Sikh community to help it catch up with the more advanced and more favored Hindus and Muslims.[4] To this end, the Chief Khalsa Diwan demanded separate representation, weightage in representation, 'special privileges and safeguards in services, and facilities for developing their language and preserving their way of life'.[5]

Thus, in the fifty-year period in which they dominated Sikh public life in the Punjab, the Singh Sabha movement and the Chief Khalsa Diwan performed several critical functions for, and established the foundations of several requisites for, a modern Sikh nationality. Although the leadership of the Sikh organizations in this period was highly elitist, the functions of consolidation, social mobilization, differentiation, and political representation which they performed for the Sikh community laid the basis for the mass political movements of the 1920s, when the SGPC and the Akali Dal took up the religious and political leadership of the Sikh community.

The SGPC

The SGPC is the largest and most important non-governmental bureaucratic organization in the Punjab and the pre-eminent institution in the Sikh community. It was founded in October and November 1920, during the gurudwara reform movement, as a com-

[1] This was not achieved without an internal struggle, however; *ibid.*, pp. 143 and 196.
[2] *Ibid.*, pp. 122 and 196, and Nayar, 'Sikh Separatism', p. 158.
[3] Khushwant Singh, *The Sikhs*, vol. II, pp. 143–4, and Ganda Singh, *A Brief Account*, p. 53.
[4] Ganda Singh, *The Akali Movement*, pp. xxv–xxvi.
[5] Khushwant Singh, *The Sikhs*, vol. II, p. 217.

mittee to manage the affairs of the gurudwaras.[1] The circumstances surrounding its formation and early activities and the strategic position which it has come to occupy in the Sikh community have given the SGPC power and authority among the Sikhs, which have been used to mount and support agitational movements for Sikh rights and to provide both an arena and a base for Sikh political activity. In the period between its formation in 1920 and the passage of the Sikh Gurudwara Act of 1925, by which SGPC control over Sikh shrines was formalized, the SGPC and its action arm, the Akali Dal, sponsored a number of agitational movements connected with gurudwara reform at various places in the Punjab. Several of these agitations, which brought the SGPC into conflict with British authority, the Punjab government, and the princely states, ended in violent confrontations in which many Sikh volunteers lost their lives.[2] From these struggles, the SGPC and the Akali Dal emerged as battle-tested and successful organizations. Moreover, both institutions became highly politicized. It was not only that many of the confrontations ostensibly concerned with gurudwara management had political implications as well, but that the SGPC participated directly in the political process by supporting Sikh candidates for public office.[3]

The SGPC also emerged from these early struggles with control over most of the Sikh gurudwaras, including the center of Sikh religious authority, the Golden Temple at Amritsar. It is estimated that some 700 gurudwaras have been brought under the control of the SGPC since the passage of the Sikh Gurudwara Act of 1925.[4] Control over the gurudwaras has meant control over the distribution of gurudwara resources (which nowadays amount to an annual budget of more than twelve million rupees)[5] and over the 'vast powers of patronage' in the staffing of the gurudwaras and their affiliated and associated institutions.[6] Since the Akali Dal has been in control of the SGPC from the beginning, the resources and patronage of the SGPC have been available to it for its political activities.[7]

[1] *Ibid.*, p. 198, and Sahni, *Sikh Shrines*, p. 63.
[2] For information on some of these early agitations, see Ganda Singh, *The Akali Movement*; Sahni, *Sikh Shrines*; and Barbara N. Ramusack, 'Incident at Nabha: Interaction between Indian States and British Indian Politics', *Journal of Asian Studies*, xxviii, No. 3 (May 1969), 563–77.
[3] Ganda Singh, *The Akali Movement*, p. 214.
[4] Balbir Singh Mann, *The Punjabi Suba Morcha: A Plea for Sympathy* (Fatehgarh Sahib, Distt. Patiala: Balbir Singh Mann, n.d.), p. 11.
[5] *Spokesman*, 26 February 1968.
[6] Nayar, *Minority Politics*, p. 179.
[7] *Ibid.*, pp. 178–9.

The SGPC has been described as 'a government within the government' of the Punjab[1] and as an alternative to the formal government as a source of legitimacy and authority for the Sikh community. It has been argued, in effect, that the Punjab has a dual political system and a dual political arena, one secular and multi-communal, the other religious and confined to Sikhs. In this last political arena, the Akali Dal has been pre-eminent and has successfully warded off attempts by other political parties to acquire control of the SGPC.[2] However, power has sometimes been transferred from one set of Akali leaders to another within the SGPC.

Elections are held every five years for positions on the governing board of the SGPC. Those elections frequently center upon great issues affecting the future of the Sikh community[3] and they often determine which groups in the Akali Dal will have control over the resources of the SGPC and a mandate from the Sikh community to carry forward its political struggles. Thus, in the 1960 gurudwara elections, the Akali Dal under Master Tara Singh's leadership overwhelmingly defeated an attempt by a Congress-dominated group to gain control over the SGPC by winning 136 out of 140 seats.[4] From these elections, Master Tara Singh also secured his mandate to launch a new agitation for Punjabi Suba.[5] After the failure of the Punjabi Suba agitations of 1960–1, the development of differences over strategy and tactics between Master Tara Singh and Sant Fateh Singh, and the formation of two rival Akali Dals, the 1965 gurudwara elections were fought to determine which leadership had the confidence of the Sikh community. The annual presidential elections also may become important tests of leadership and control within the SGPC between competing groups in the Akali Dal.[6] In fact, the SGPC is often the ultimate arbiter within the Sikh community of conflicts which develop in the secular or parliamentary arena between different factions of the Akali Dal. For example, in November 1967, Sardar Lachman Singh Gill, a leader in the Sant Akali Dal and a cabinet minister in the Akali-dominated united front govern-

---

[1] Khushwant Singh, *The Sikhs*, vol. II, 215.
[2] Paul Wallace, 'The Political Party System of Punjab State (India): A Study of Factionalism', unpublished Ph.D. dissertation, University of California, Berkeley, 1966, pp. 46, 268–9, 335, 348.
[3] Nayar, *Minority Politics*, p. 180.
[4] *Ibid.*, p. 182; Wallace, 'The Political Party System', p. 269; Balbir Singh Mann, *The Punjabi Suba Morcha*, p. 11.
[5] Nayar, *Minority Politics*, pp. 182–3; Punjab Commission, *Report*, p. 3.
[6] See, for example, Master Tara Singh's comments on the SGPC presidential elections of 1953 and 1958 in his pamphlet, *To All Men of Good Conscience* (New Delhi: Shiromani Akali Dal, 1959), pp. 2–3 and 607.

ment, defected from the government with his followers and brought it down, against the wishes of Sant Fateh Singh. Sardar Gill, though he was general secretary of the SGPC, did not have sufficient support in the SGPC to legitimize his action in the arena of Sikh politics. Although his defection enabled him to become chief minister of the secular government of the Punjab for a time, it lost him and his followers the support of the Sikh community as represented in the SGPC. At a crucial meeting of the SGPC in February 1968, Sant Fateh Singh demonstrated that his own group continued to command overwhelming support among its members.[1] The Sant's supporters then acted to remove Sardar Gill from positions of influence in the SGPC.[2] Without support in the SGPC, Sardar Gill was unable to build political strength in the secular arena. His government was brought down in August 1968. All of Sardar Gill's followers were defeated in the Punjab mid-term elections of 1969, whereas the Sant Akali Dal emerged with new strength to form a government once again.

Thus, the SGPC constitutes the primary political arena for Sikh politics in the Punjab. The results of important political contests in this arena determine both the political direction which Sikh politics will take and which leadership commands the confidence of the Sikh community. Success in this arena provides the winning group with the necessary resources to win support in the electoral and parliamentary arena. In the new Punjabi Suba, the struggles within the SGPC are sometimes as important in determining who shall exercise power in the Punjab government as the results in electoral and parliamentary contests.

The Akali Dal

The Akali Dal is one of the oldest and most successful regionally based political organizations in India. It has been the spearhead of all political demands made on behalf of the Sikhs for the last half-century. In the period since its formation in the 1920s, it moved from a position as a religious reform organization concerned with the reform of Sikh shrines to a political party using both agitational and electoral tactics to its present position as a leading political party in the Punjab and an alternative governing party in that state. Its role was critical in the attainment of Punjabi Suba. Without the Akali Dal, the winning of Punjabi Suba would have been unthinkable in the face of the persistent opposition of government in the post-independence period.

[1] *Spokesman*, 19 February 1968.　　[2] *Ibid.*, 26 February, 1968.

The contemporary Akali Dal has its origins in the Akali movement of the early 1920s when the religious reform movement in Sikhism culminated in a dramatic and successful drive to gain control over Sikh gurudwaras. In this movement, the Akalis, though they ostensibly existed separately from the SGPC, acted on its behalf as its agitational spearhead.[1] During the gurudwara reform movement, the Akali Dal came into being as an institutionalized political force in the Sikh community under the leadership of Master Tara Singh. It moved immediately from religious reform to political action, because the gurudwara reform movement itself involved a direct confrontation with British authority and, hence, brought the Akali Dal into alliance with the Congress in the non-cooperation movement of 1920–1. Although the Akali Dal continued to cooperate with the Congress through most of the nationalist period, it always retained a separate organizational existence and increasingly attempted to act as the political spokesman for the Sikh community.

In fact, from its beginning, the basic principles of the party, which presume the inseparability of religion and politics, have been opposed to the secular principles of the Congress.[2] Its specific demands for a special status for the Sikh community in India also brought it into conflict with the Congress. In the 1940s, the Akali Dal made explicit its demand for a special political position for the Sikhs by proposing the reorganization of the then boundaries of the Punjab and the creation of a new province of Azad Punjab, in which the Muslim population would be reduced and the Sikh population increased to the point where the Sikhs would constitute a balancing force between the larger Muslim and Hindu communities.[3] When the proposal for the partition of the Punjab into Muslim-majority and Hindu-majority areas was made, the Akali Dal opposed the plan which would have divided the Sikh community between the two sectors, and demanded a separate state for the Sikhs.[4] Akali leaders have since contended that they were only persuaded to give up this demand at the time upon the assurances of Congress leaders that the Sikhs would be granted a special status in independent India. It was the failure of Congress leaders in independent India to fulfill their promises to the Sikhs which, it is charged, compelled the Akali Dal to launch the post-independence movement for a Punjabi Suba.

Over the years of its development, the Akali Dal has not only attempted to establish itself as the sole legitimate representative of

[1] Sahni, *Sikh Shrines*, pp. 61, 91, 239, 245–7; Nayar, 'Sikh Separatism', p. 169; *Spokesman*, 28 June 1965.
[2] Cf. Nayar, *Minority Politics*, pp. 27, 74.   [3] *Ibid.*, p. 83.
[4] *Ibid.*, p. 86, and Punjab Commission, *Report*, p. 2.

the Sikh community or Panth, but its leaders have attempted to identify the party with the Panth.[1] This attempt has been so successful that an election tribunal in 1953 was compelled to concede that the terms 'Panth' and 'Panthic' had become synonymous with the Akali Dal.[2] The successful identification of the Akali Dal with the Sikh Panth is a measure of the strong roots which the organization has developed in the Sikh community.

The strength and success of the Akali Dal have been based upon the quality of its leadership, upon its clever use of a variety of tactics while maintaining its sights on a relatively fixed goal, and, most important, upon its resources in Sikh religious institutions and in the Sikh community. From its early period up to the present, the Akali Dal has had a dual leadership and a dual set of tactics – agitational and parliamentary. Until recently, the agitational leadership has been dominant in the Akali Dal and has largely directed the course of Akali politics. In the pre-independence period and afterward until the 1960s, the pre-eminent leader of the Akali Dal was Master Tara Singh, who maintained nearly dictatorial control both over the SGPC and the Akali Dal.[3] Master Tara Singh's leadership of the organization and of the agitational side of Akali politics did not eliminate either factionalism or opportunism in the movement, but it did maintain organizational continuity and persistence in the drive toward the goal of Punjabi Suba. In the meantime, many individual leaders and groups in the parliamentary wing of the party pursued both Akali goals and their own interests in the electoral and legislative arenas in Punjab.[4] Throughout, however, Master Tara Singh remained in control of the SGPC, the Akali Dal, and the entire dynamic of Sikh politics.

When a successful challenge finally came to Master Tara Singh's leadership, it came from an agitational leader with strength in the SGPC who challenged him in his own organizational stronghold. The challenge arose after the most signal humiliation in the career and leadership of Master Tara Singh when, in October 1961, he gave up a fast-unto-death for the Punjabi Suba without any significant concession from government.[5] Moreover, it was during this fast that the central government under Pandit Nehru made it clear that, whatever support Master Tara Singh had in the Sikh community

---

[1] Nayar, *Minority Politics*, pp. 170, 175, 209–10.
[2] Government of India, Law Department, *Election Law Reports*, vi, edited by A. N. Aiyar (Delhi: Manager of Publications, n.d.), 316.
[3] See the biography of Master Tara Singh in Nayar, *Minority Politics*, pp. 142–9.
[4] *Ibid.*, pp. 81 and 127–8.
[5] *Ibid.*, p. 262, and P. C. Joshi, 'Triumph of a Just Cause', in *Punjabi Suba*, pp. 72–3.

and in the Akali Dal, he was not an acceptable leader with whom government would negotiate because of the openly communal character of his appeal for Punjabi Suba. In the aftermath of Master Tara Singh's humiliation, one of his lieutenants, Sant Fateh Singh, mounted a challenge to Tara Singh's leadership in the SGPC and founded a separate Akali Dal in 1962.[1] An agitational leader himself, with a following among the Jat Sikh peasantry and a base in the gurudwaras in the Malwa region of Punjab, Sant Fateh Singh succeeded in winning control over the SGPC from Master Tara Singh in 1965. The new Akali Dal, under his leadership, made a final, successful drive for a Punjabi Suba while separating the demand as far as possible from its previous communal associations. In the 1967 elections, the Sant Akali Dal extended its hold over Sikh politics in the Punjab by contesting the election as a separate organized force from the Master Akali Dal and by returning enough candidates to the Punjab legislative assembly to emerge after the elections as the dominant partner in the first non-Congress government in the reorganized Punjab.

Although the Akali Dal has undergone considerable internal conflict for leadership and organizational control, there is no doubt that the quality of its leadership has been a decisive factor in its success. Though they were different kinds of personalities, both Master Tara Singh and Sant Fateh Singh were dynamic, aggressive, single-minded, and immensely popular leaders who demonstrated a capacity to bring large masses of Sikh volunteers into public demonstrations and to win popular support in the electorate. It is also clear, however, that, however great their personal popularity, the success of both men depended upon their ability to gain control over the main organizational and financial resources of the Sikh community, the SGPC.

The Akali Dal has also benefited from its ability to pursue a variety of agitational and parliamentary tactics in the pursuit of its goal. Two of the agitational movements launched in the Punjab on behalf of the Punjabi Suba were especially important in the post-independence period – the Punjabi Suba Slogan Agitation of 1955, in which an estimated 12,000 Sikhs were arrested, and the massive Punjabi Suba Agitations of 1960–1, in which an estimated 26,000 volunteers were arrested and which was marked by two epic fasts, first by Sant Fateh Singh and then by Master Tara Singh.[2] Upon achieving control over the Akali movement in the 1960s, Sant Fateh Singh favored the more personal and individual method of fasting, with the added

[1] Nayar, *Minority Politics*, p. 262.   [2] Nayar, 'Sikh Separatism', pp. 173–4.

317

threat of self-immolation at the end of a specified time-period if his demands were not met. The Sant adopted this technique on two occasions – in September 1965 for the Punjabi Suba and in December 1966 for the inclusion of Chandigarh in the Punjabi Suba. Although both fasts ended inconclusively, both demands were ultimately accepted by the Government of India.

Throughout most of its history, the Akali Dal has also used negotiation in the parliamentary arena as a means of achieving its ends. The Akali Dal worked both through the Congress and through representation to the British government in the 1920s and 1930s to achieve special concessions for Sikh interests. On other occasions in the pre-independence period, the Akali Dal negotiated with the Unionist Party and the Muslim League to gain a favorable position for Sikh interests.[1] And, in the post-independence period, the parliamentary wing of the Akali Dal alternated between electoral opposition to Congress and merger with it, as in 1957. Even during the more frequent times when the party has opposed the Congress, there have always been prominent former Akali leaders in the Congress who were able to act as intermediaries between the Akali Dal and the Congress to win new concessions for the Sikhs. However, the Akali movement never lost its dynamic thereby and never completely lost the momentum of its drive toward the Punjabi Suba, which was relentlessly pursued by the extra-parliamentary leadership of the party, first under Master Tara Singh, then under Sant Fateh Singh, until it was finally achieved in 1966.

In the aftermath of the achievement of the Punjabi Suba, the Akali Dal has entered a new phase and a new role as an alternative governing party. This position obviously favors the strengthening of the parliamentary wing of the party, but the continued dependence of the party on the resources of the SGPC and the gurudwaras for its strength means that the extra-parliamentary wing of the party remains the dominant wing of the party.

The demand for a Punjabi Suba

A brief history of the demand

The history of the Punjabi Suba demand contrasts sharply with the history of the Maithili movement. The Maithili movement, basing itself on objective distinguishing characteristics of the Maithili language and the Mithila region, failed to generate the subjective

[1] Nayar, *Minority Politics*, pp. 76–81.

regional consciousness necessary for success. In contrast, the Punjabi Suba movement demonstrates how a subjectively conscious
group of people may create the objective conditions necessary for the
success of a regional movement. The Punjabi Suba movement also
illustrates clearly the ways in which the formal and informal rules
governing center–state relations on matters of regionalism may
affect the course of a regional movement. Finally, the Punjabi Suba
movement demonstrates the importance of political leadership, in
promoting and opposing regionalism, as a factor in the success of a
regional movement.

A widespread sense of Sikh identity and its expression in explicitly
political demands already existed before the formal demand for a
Sikh-dominated state was made. The dispersal of the Sikh community in pre-independence Punjab, however, meant that Sikh political demands had to be confined primarily to questions of representation rather than to territorial dominance. Under the Montagu–
Chelmsford reforms introduced in 1921, the Sikhs were granted communal representation through separate electorates in the Punjab
legislature and were awarded twelve of the seventy-one elective
seats or 17%. Sikh representatives before the Simon Commission in
1928 demanded an increase in Sikh representation to 30%, but the
Communal Award of 1932 granted only 18% representation to Sikhs
in the Punjab legislature.[1] Still, the Sikh community was propor-
tionally over-represented in the legislatures in the pre-1947 Punjab
and was often able to act effectively as a decisive swing force in the
communal political balance between the larger Muslim and Hindu
communities.

When it became clear in 1946 that the Punjab was to be parti-
tioned into Muslim-majority and Hindu-majority areas, Sikh political leaders demanded the establishment of an independent and
sovereign Sikh state.[2] Moreover, it has been argued by British
observers and admitted by some Sikh leaders, that Sikh political
leaders set about self-consciously to force the Muslims out of the east
Punjab to make way for a total migration of the Sikh people from
the Muslim-majority areas to east Punjab.[3] In this way, the Sikh

---

[1] *ISC*, xvi, 137, and Fagan, 'Minority Communities, 1. The Sikhs', pp. 131–2.
[2] Punjab Commission, *Report*, p. 2.
[3] See Nayar, 'Sikh Separatism', pp. 152–3. Master Tara Singh claimed, in an interview
   with the author in February 1967, that the Akali leaders took the deliberate decision at
   the time of partition to 'turn the Muslims out' of the east Punjab, that they provided
   Sikh policemen in uniform with bombs and weapons for the purpose, that a Sikh
   deputy commissioner collaborated with them in their actions, and that there was not
   much secrecy about it at the time.

community established itself as the numerically dominant community in six districts of east Punjab and as a very large minority in five other districts in the region.

It was not long before Sikh political leaders raised the demand for the conversion of their numerical dominance in a territorial area into a separate political status for the area. In fact, Sikh leaders argued that they were promised the right to determine their own status by the British and by Congress leaders in 1946 and that they were to be considered a sovereign community in independent India and in the Constituent Assembly of India.[1] By October 1949, the demand was explicitly made for a Sikh-majority Punjabi Suba.[2] In August 1950 the Akali Dal launched its first major agitational movement for the demand.[3]

In the aftermath of the partition of India on a religious basis, Congress leaders were unwilling to consider seriously a proposal based explicitly on religious and communal grounds. Consequently, in the presentation of their demands before the States Reorganisation Commission in 1953, the Akali Dal emphasized the linguistic basis of the demand, proposing the creation of a Punjabi-speaking state rather than a Sikh-majority state. The Commission, however, found itself unable to ignore the communal component of the Akali Dal demand and 'the inflammation of Communal passions' in the Punjab, which it attributed to the agitation on behalf of a Punjabi Suba.[4] In rejecting the demand, however, the Commission based its opposition on two grounds primarily – that the Punjabi language was not sufficiently distinct either grammatically or spatially from Hindi and that the movement lacked 'the general support of the people inhabiting the area'.[5] The lack of general support referred particularly to the opposition of the Punjabi-speaking Hindus who, the Commission noted, had gone to the extent of denying that Punjabi was their mother tongue.[6] The dismissal by the Commission not only of the demand but of the separate status of the Punjabi language prompted Sardar Hukam Singh, then associated with the Akali Dal, to remark: 'While others got States for their languages, we lost even our language.'[7]

In response to the rejection of their demand by the States Reorganisation Commission, the Akali Dal launched its Punjabi Suba Slogan Agitation of 1955, which was terminated by negotiations

---

[1] See, for example, *Punjabi Suba*, p. 147, and Gurnam Singh, *A Unilingual Punjabi State*, pp. 28–9, 38–9, 55–6.
[2] Wallace, 'The Political Party System', p. 199.   [3] *Ibid.*, p. 200.
[4] SRC, *Report*, pp. 140–1.   [5] *Ibid.*, p. 146.
[6] *Ibid.*, p. 141.   [7] Hukam Singh, *The Punjabi Problem*, p. 3.

with the Congress in Punjab. As a result of these negotiations, a Regional Formula was adopted in the Punjab by which the work of the state legislature was assigned to separate regional committees organized according to language. The Akali Dal agreed to work the formula and to merge with the Congress party in contesting the 1957 elections and in the Punjab legislature.[1]

Dissatisfaction with the working of the Regional Formula and with the unwillingness of the Punjab government under the leadership of Pratap Singh Kairon to enhance the status of the Punjabi language led to the split of the Akali Dal from the Congress, a renewal of its demands for a Punjabi Suba, and finally the launching of a prolonged movement beginning in May 1960. The launching of the movement was heralded by a convention in Amritsar on 22 May 1960,[2] which was followed by processions and demonstrations during which the government acknowledges that 26,000 people were arrested.[3] When it became clear that government was not going to be coerced by the demonstrations, Sant Fateh Singh, then a lieutenant of Master Tara Singh, began a fast-unto-death for the demand. On the advice of Master Tara Singh, the Sant broke his fast on 9 January 1961, to enter negotiations with Nehru. During these negotiations, Sant Fateh Singh emphasized the linguistic basis of the demand, rather than its communal basis, which made Pandit Nehru more sympathetic than he had been before, but apparently did not satisfy Master Tara Singh, who now launched his own fast-unto-death for the Punjabi Suba.[4] However, neither Pratap Singh Kairon, the Punjab chief minister, nor Pandit Nehru were willing to make any concessions to Master Tara Singh, who broke his fast after forty-eight days merely with the agreement of the government to appoint a commission not to inquire into the Punjabi Suba demand, but only to consider the charge that there was discrimination against the Sikhs in the Punjab.[5]

In retrospect, it is clear that the fasts of Sant Fateh Singh and Master Tara Singh, their different approaches to the Punjabi Suba demand, and their differential treatment by government marked a turning point in the history of the movement and its leadership. In the aftermath of the failure of both fasts, the two leaders were forced to perform religious penance, but the humiliation of Master Tara

[1] Nayar, 'Sikh Separatism', p. 173.
[2] Gurnam Singh, *A Unilingual Punjabi State*, p. 33.
[3] Nayar, 'Sikh Separatism', p. 173.
[4] Nayar, *Minority Politics*, pp. 252–4.
[5] Baldev Raj Nayar, 'Punjab', in Myron Weiner (ed.), *State Politics in India* (Princeton, N.J.: Princeton University Press, 1968), p. 452.

Singh was the greater. Sant Fateh Singh now launched a direct challenge to the leadership of Master Tara Singh. The Sant formed a separate Akali Dal in 1962. In 1965, he and his followers succeeded in gaining control over the SGPC from Master Tara Singh. In August 1965 the Sant held two conversations with Lal Bahadur Shastri in which he argued forcefully on behalf of a Punjabi Suba.[1] Upon the failure of these conversations, Sant Fateh Singh announced that he would embark upon a ten-day fast on 10 September 1965, at the end of which he would burn himself alive if the Punjabi Suba demand were not conceded.

In the meantime, significant changes had taken place in the leadership of the Congress in Punjab and at the center. Pratap Singh Kairon, who had dominated the Punjab Congress and government between 1956 and 1964, had been removed from office and then assassinated in 1964. After his death, the Punjab Congress split into a number of factions and lacked the will or the leadership to oppose the Punjabi Suba demand with vigor. On 31 August 1965 a meeting of fifteen Sikh Congress legislators announced their support for some form of Punjabi Suba.[2] At the center, the death of Nehru had brought new leaders to power, who were more receptive to regional demands. On 7 September, talks began again between central leaders and Sant Fateh Singh, which ended with an agreement by the central government to appoint a cabinet subcommittee to resolve the Punjabi Suba issue and by Sant Fateh Singh to postpone his fast. As the center began to give way, political leaders from Haryana and the hill areas became more outspoken and joined in the demand for the reorganization of the Punjab.[3] In the meantime, the war with Pakistan in September 1965 provided the Government of India with an additional incentive to solve the political unrest in the Punjab and an opportunity to acknowledge the contribution of the Sikh people to the defense of India by conceding the Punjabi Suba demand. In March 1966, the central parliament and the cabinet accepted the demand and appointed a boundary commission to propose an appropriate reorganization of the Punjab. The report of the boundary commission was submitted in May. In June, the central government announced that the Punjab would be trifurcated in such a way that the Hindi-speaking plains districts would go to the new state of Haryana, the hill districts to Himachal Pradesh, and the remaining Punjabi-speaking areas to the new Punjabi Suba (cf.

[1] *Two Talks between Sant Fateh Singh Ji and Shri Lal Bahadur Shastri, the Prime Minister of India on 7th and 8th August 1965* (Amritsar: Shiromani Akali Dal, 1965).

[2] Wallace, 'The Political Party System', pp. 304–5.

[3] *Ibid.*, pp. 305–6.

322

figs. 7 and 8).[1] For the time being, the state capital of Chandigarh was given the status of a Union Territory; but, after further agitation by the Akali Dal and prolonged negotiations with Akali and Haryana political leaders, the central government awarded Chandigarh to the new state of Punjab in February 1970.

Language, religion, and the Punjabi Suba demand

The history of the Punjabi Suba movement throws further light on the variable importance and functions of language in the development of subjective group identities. It has been shown that, in the Maithili movement, the mere existence of a distinct language with a distinguished literary heritage has not been sufficient, in the absence of other preconditions, for the development of a sense of language consciousness or group identity among Maithili-speakers. In the case of Urdu, an already self-conscious elite, supported by the socially mobilized segment of the Muslim community, has sought to differentiate Urdu from Hindi and to use the language as a basis for transmitting a sense of separateness to the remaining unmobilized, largely rural Muslim population. Muslim leaders seek to reinforce the separate status of the Muslim community by making Urdu-consciousness coextensive with Muslim-consciousness. Among the Sikh political leaders in the Punjab, the role of language has been similar, but somewhat more ambiguous. Sikh political leaders value Punjabi in the Gurumukhi script as a means for transmitting a sense of separateness to Sikhs, but they reject Punjabi written in the Devanagari script because the Punjabi language would then be too inclusive for their purposes, which have been the promotion of a Sikh, not a Punjabi identity. The ambiguity surrounding the language issue in the Punjab, however, has arisen because the rules of the game in India do not permit the Sikhs any more than the Muslims to make a demand based on religion, but only on language. The consequences of this ambiguity have been the infusion of religious meaning into language identification in the Punjab. Thus, a Sikh could not say that he wanted a Punjabi Suba because he is a Sikh and this would be a Sikh-majority state, but because he is a Punjabi-speaker and wanted to live in a Punjabi-speaking state. Similarly, a Punjabi-speaking Hindu could not oppose a Punjabi Suba because he is a Hindu and did not want to live in a Sikh-majority state, but had to say that he is a Hindi-speaker and did not want to live in a Punjabi-speaking state.

That the Punjabi Suba movement was, in origin, no more than a

---

[1] *Ibid.*, pp. 307–8.

— District boundary
········ Tahsil boundary
● District headquarters town
○ Tahsil headquarters town

Fig. 8   Punjabi Suba, 1966

tactic to acquire by means considered legitimate in Indian politics a goal considered illegitimate has been forcefully argued by Baldev Nayar. Nayar argues, in effect, that the Punjabi Suba movement was a demand for a state in which Sikhs would be dominant camouflaged as a demand for a Punjabi-speaking state.[1] During the period when the movement was dominated by the leadership of Master Tara Singh, that camouflage was too thin for the demand to be

[1] Nayar, *Minority Politics*, pp. 35–42 and 101–2, and 'Sikh Separatism', p. 150.

seriously considered by the Government of India, whose leaders refused to negotiate with him.

It was only when Sant Fateh Singh took over the leadership of the
Akali Dal and when he adopted a consistent position that the demand for Punjabi Suba be treated as a language demand[1] that the
Government of India became willing to negotiate. The adherence to
the linguistic basis for the demand did not mean that religious
arguments could not be used, but rather that such arguments could
now be more effective because it could now be argued that the refusal
to concede the demand represented discrimination against the Sikhs.
Thus, Sant Fateh Singh could make the statement on one occasion
that the demand for a Punjabi Suba 'is not on the basis of religion.
Ours is only this just demand that when other states in India have
been formed on the basis of language, not to do so in regard to the
Punjabi language is a discrimination against the people of Punjab.'[2]
However, at the same time, Sant Fateh Singh would argue that the
Sikhs and their religion were being discriminated against.[3] And, on
another occasion, he would make it clear that the discrimination in
not conceding a Punjabi Suba is not 'against the people of Punjab'
as a whole, but against the Sikhs: 'No status is given to the Punjabi
language, because Sikhs speak it. If non-Sikhs had owned Punjabi as
mother tongue then the rulers of India would have seen no objec-

---

[1] The most outspoken distinction between the positions of Sant Fateh Singh and Master
Tara Singh was made by Sant Fateh Singh in an interview:

Q. Why is it that when our linguistic states were agreed to, the formation of a
Punjabi-speaking state was denied?
A. Initially, I thought the motive behind the opposition was purely communal . . .
Then I found that there were lots of misconceptions among the people. Master
Tara Singh was talking of Punjabi Suba and '56 per cent majority for the Sikhs' in
the Suba, in the same breath . . .
I squarely posed the issue before Master Tara Singh: Do you want a Sikh-majority
Suba, or a Punjabi Suba? If you want Sikh-majority Suba, don't bring in the
language as its basis. If you base the demand on language, don't talk of Sikh majority.
This duplicity does not help.

. . . . .

His reply was: 'For the present, we will talk of the language as the basis, later on
things will get crystallized by themselves.'
To me his stand was obviously fraudulent. I could not reconcile myself to that
position.

. . . . .

. . . My simple and straight-forward demand was for a Punjabi Suba based purely
on language.
Jogjit Singh Anand, 'Sant Fateh Singh on the Suba', in *Punjabi Suba*, pp. 4–5. See also
Sant Fateh Singh, *Our Stand on Punjabi Suba* (Amritsar: Shiromani Akali Dal, 1963).
[2] *Two Talks*, p. 11. See also the long statement of Gurnam Singh, p. 3, which argues that
the association of the Sikhs with the Punjabi demand is merely 'accidental'.
[3] *Two Talks, passim.*

tion in establishing a Punjabi State.'[1] In this way, Sant Fateh Singh proved a skilled tactician in moving toward the achievement of the Akali goal – by stressing the linguistic basis of the demand and by arguing not that the demand should be conceded because the Sikh religious community should have a state of its own but because failure to concede the demand for a Punjabi-speaking state would constitute discrimination against a religious group which spoke a distinct language.

That Punjabi has played a secondary role to religion in the development of Sikh consciousness, however, is clear. Punjabi in the nineteenth century was no more developed and no more or less distinct grammatically from Hindi than Maithili. Moreover, Punjabi was not even the predominant language of the Sikh scriptures, which are written primarily in old Hindi, though in the Gurumukhi script.[2] Yet, over the last century, Punjabi-speaking Sikhs have increasingly come to attach importance to Punjabi written in Gurumukhi script 'as symbolic of the separateness of the Sikh community'.[3] As a consequence of the more or less simultaneous growth of Hindu and Sikh religious revival movements and the literature associated with them, Sikhs in the Punjab came to attach increasing significance to Punjabi in Gurumukhi script as the language of the Sikhs and of the Sikh religion and Hindus developed a similar attachment to Hindi in the Devanagari script.[4] There remained a fundamental difference in this respect, however, between Sikhs and Hindus in that the mother tongue of most Sikhs was, in fact, Punjabi, whereas the mother tongue of many Hindus in the Punjab was not Hindi, but was also Punjabi. Over the years, many Punjabi-speaking Hindus developed the practice of confining Punjabi to the language of the home and the street, while using Hindi for correspondence and preferring it as a medium for secondary and higher education for their children. Thus, Hindus in the Punjab began to adopt a position on Hindi similar to that of Muslims in Uttar Pradesh on Urdu.

The final stage in the linguistic differentiation of Hindus and Sikhs on religious grounds came in the post-independence period, during the Punjabi Suba movement, when Punjabi-speaking Hindus went to the extent of declaring their mother tongue as Hindi to the census

[1] 'The Sikhs are Slaves', a signed article of Sant Fateh Singh dated 27 August 1965 and published in *Two Talks*, p. 46.
[2] G. A. Grierson (ed.), *Linguistic Survey of India*, vol. 1, pt. 1: *Introductory* (Delhi: Motilal Banarsidass, 1967), p. 170.
[3] Nayar, *Minority Politics*, p. 48.
[4] See, for example, the Punjab Boundary Commission, *Report*, pp. 2–3.

enumerators in 1951 and 1961. In this way, two groups of people from the same racial stock (many of whom continue to intermarry) and speaking the same language, but holding different religious beliefs and an attachment to separate scripts, have, as a consequence of political action on the basis of religion, chosen to differentiate themselves further by changing their language identification. Although Punjabi-speaking Hindus have been accused of 'disowning' their mother tongue in 1951 and 1961, it must be stressed that the process of linguistic differentiation on the basis of religion has been at work among both Sikhs and Hindus during the past century, with the Sikhs shifting from Urdu and Hindi to Punjabi in Gurumukhi script and many Hindus shifting from Urdu and Punjabi to Hindi in Devanagari script. The shift of Punjabi-speaking Hindus in 1951 and 1961 was, however, more dramatic than any previous shift because it was an overt and deliberate political act designed to undercut the linguistic basis of the Punjabi Suba demand.

Hindu political organizations

The Arya Samaj

The fountainhead of modernized Hindu cultural aspirations in the Punjab and of opposition to Sikh communal and Punjabi language demands has been the Arya Samaj. The Arya Samaj was founded in 1875 in Gujarat as a movement of modernizing religious reform within Hinduism. Introduced into the Punjab in 1877–8, it soon became a powerful religious, educational, cultural, and political force within the Hindu community of the province.[1] The Arya Samaj founded a network of high schools and colleges promoting both Sanskrit and Western studies.[2] Its presses issued a stream of books, pamphlets, and periodicals promoting Hindu religious and communal consciousness.[3] Its propaganda promoted the use of Hindi in the Devanagari script as a medium of education in the schools.[4]

The primary thrust of Arya Samaj activities in the Punjab in the 1880s was in education and in religious reform and proselytization. Its proselytizing activities, particularly among low caste groups whose religious loyalties were indefinite, brought the Arya Samaj into conflict with the religious ideologies and organizations of the

---

[1] See Jones, 'Communalism in the Punjab', pp. 39–54.
[2] *Ibid.*, p. 45. See also Charles H. Heimsath, *Indian Nationalism and Hindu Social Reform* (Princeton, N.J.: Princeton University Press, 1964), pp. 295–7.
[3] Jones, 'Communalism in the Punjab', p. 47.
[4] *Ibid.*, pp. 45–6.

Sikhs and Muslims. Although Arya Samaj and Singh Sabha leaders sometimes cooperated in the Punjab in the 1880s, the ultimate consequence of Arya Samaj activities was to instill in Sikh religious leaders a fear of absorption by the Hindu community and to promote a sharp and antagonistic differentiation between Hindus and Muslims in the Punjab. As inter-communal rivalry intensified, solidarity among Hindus increased and Arya Samajis and orthodox Hindus in the province came closer together.[1] Thus, the Arya Samaj activities promoted, in the long run, internal Hindu solidarity and external differentiation in relations with other communities, despite its efforts to convert or otherwise absorb Sikhs into its fold.

The primary bases of support for the Arya Samaj in the Punjab were among urban Hindu business castes.[2] During the pre-independence period, the political activities of Arya Samaj leaders in Hindu communal politics were oriented primarily toward protection and promotion of urban Hindu interests against the dominant rural Muslim interests in the province. Political alliances between Hindus and Sikhs in this period were not uncommon. However, there remained a latent antagonism between Arya Hindu and Sikh political leaders in the province on religious, educational, and linguistic matters, which became the dominant cleavage in post-independence Punjab politics.

Communally oriented Sikhs in the Punjab harbor considerable resentment against the Arya Samaj, both for its religious activities in the late nineteenth and early twentieth centuries and for its pro-Hindi, anti-Punjabi activities in more recent times.[3] In contemporary politics, it has been the language issue which has ostensibly aroused the most bitterness between the Arya Samaj and Sikh political leaders, but this issue itself is partly an expression of the more fundamental religious cleavage. Throughout the post-independence period, the Arya Samaj has taken a more consistent pro-Hindi position on the language issue than any other organization in the Punjab. It insisted throughout that there should be no compulsion upon Hindus, whatever their mother tongue, to be educated through the medium of Punjabi and that Hindus should have the right to choose Hindi in the Devanagari script as medium of instruction in the schools.[4] The Arya Samaj never deviated from this position.

[1] *Ibid.*, p. 53.
[2] Norman G. Barrier, 'The Arya Samaj and Congress Politics in the Punjab, 1894–1908', *Journal of Asian Studies*, xxvi, No. 3 (May 1967), 364.
[3] E.g., see Ganda Singh, *A Brief Account*, p. 53. See also Sahni, *Sikh Shrines*, pp. 16–17, and Hukam Singh, *The Punjabi Problem*, pp. 9, 11, 15.
[4] See, for example, *Tribune*, 12 and 19 April 1960.

The Hindi movement

The Arya Samaj has been the leading force for the cause of Hindi in the Hindu community in the Punjab and Haryana in organization, resources, and mass support. During the height of the Punjabi Suba movement, the Arya Samaj formed alliances with other Hindu organizations and also spawned inter-organizational fronts to fight for the protection of Hindi in the Punjab. In the years immediately following the adoption of the Regional Formula in the Punjab, by which the state was formally divided into Punjabi-speaking and Hindi-speaking zones, cooperation among the Arya Samaj, the Sanatan Dharam Pratinidhi Sabha (SDPS), the Hindu Mahasabha, and the Jan Sangh was common. These groups were united in their opposition particularly to the adoption of Punjabi as the sole official language in the Punjabi-speaking region. Their common line was that the entire Punjab was bilingual; that the state could not be divided into discrete Punjabi-speaking and Hindi-speaking regions; and that, therefore, parents should have the right to choose the medium of instruction for their children. They differed, however, in their attitudes towards Punjabi and their emphasis on Hindi. The more orthodox Hindu groups, such as the SDPS and the Hindu Mahasabha, were willing to consider the Punjab a bilingual state in which both languages in both scripts were used for official and educational purposes. They opposed imposition of Punjabi and favored freedom of choice. The more radical groups, associated with the Arya Samaj, took the position that the Punjab was primarily a Hindi-speaking state in which Hindi should be the sole official language and in which Punjabi should be recognized only as a minority language. Moreover, their posture was one of aggressive promotion of Hindi.[1]

The high watermark of cooperation among Hindu and Hindi organizations in the Punjab was achieved in 1957, during the 'Save Hindi' agitation, when all the major Hindu groups in both regions of the state joined together in a mass agitation to protest against the Regional Formula and against compulsion in the use and teaching of Punjabi.[2] A Hindi Raksha Samiti was formed, which carried on the movement from April through December 1957. The movement was unsuccessful in achieving any of its main demands. Moreover, in the

---

[1] For the views of various Hindu and Hindi organizations, see *Tribune*, 18 April and 22 August 1960; *Times of India*, 10 April 1961; *Express*, 24 April 1961; *Tribune*, 13 June 1961. See also Kahol, *Hindus and the Punjabi State*, pp. 33–5, 44–5.

[2] See Wallace, 'The Political Party System', pp. 255–8; Nayar, 'Punjab', p. 473; *Election Law Reports*, xxiv, 388–90; Balbir Singh Mann, *The Punjabi Suba Morcha*, p. 5.

course of the movement, it became evident that the interests of Haryana Hindus and Punjabi Hindus were quite different. The former saw the division of the Punjab as a possible solution to their demands,[1] whereas Punjabi Hindus feared a division of the state which would leave them an isolated minority in a Sikh-dominated, Punjabi-speaking state. A second attempt to forge a united front of Hindu organizations was made in 1961 in opposition to the Punjab Official Languages Act, passed in October 1960, which declared Punjabi and Hindi as official languages in their respective regions. A Hindi Raksha Sammelan was formed in April 1961, but the component groups resolved to bring the issues to the electorate in the forthcoming elections rather than to launch a mass movement.[2]

The most important observation to be made about Hindi cooperation in the Hindi movement is that it did not overcome the fundamental cleavage between the interests of rural Hindi-speaking Hindus from Haryana and urban Hindus from the Punjabi-speaking districts. Consequently, the leaders of the Punjabi Suba movement had another advantage not available to minority groups in Bihar and Uttar Pradesh, namely, a division in the majority group favorable to the interests of the minority.

The Haryana movement

It has been argued above that one of the rules conditioning the attitude of the central government toward regional demands is that they must have support in both parts of the region to be divided if the center is to yield. The development of regional sentiment and organizations in the Haryana region of the Punjab in the 1950s and 1960s supports this proposition. The Haryana movement for the creation of a separate Haryana Prant or State was never more than a weak sister, in terms of popular support and organizational strength, to the Punjabi Suba movement. Nevertheless, the Haryana movement was important in creating the necessary conditions for the division of the Punjab.

Although the demand for the creation of a separate Haryana Prant was made before the States Reorganisation Commission and was supported by certain Haryana politicians in 1954 and 1955,[3] the Commission was not at all impressed by the movement. The demand was dismissed in three paragraphs of the SRC *Report*.[4]

---

[1] Wallace, 'The Political Party System', p. 258.
[2] *Express*, 24 April 1961, and *Tribune*, 13 June 1961.
[3] Satya Rai, *Partition of the Punjab*, pp. 234–5.
[4] SRC, *Report*, p. 147; see also Wallace, 'The Political Party System', pp. 15–16.

Two important political and policy changes occurred in Haryana in the decade after the publication of the SRC *Report*, which increased the strength of the demand for a separate Haryana state. One was the attempt of Pratap Singh Kairon to consolidate his power in the district Congress organizations in the Haryana region, which, though successful, led to the defection of some important politicians from the Congress, especially in the Hissar, Gurgaon, and Rohtak districts.[1] In Rohtak, the traditional center of Haryana regional sentiment, an organization called the Haryana Lok Samiti (HLS) was formed in April 1961 to contest the general elections. Associated with the Arya Samaj, its election campaign emphasized opposition to the imposition of Punjabi in the schools in Haryana, promotion of Hindi, and opposition to the alleged discrimination against the Haryana region by the Punjab government in the allocation of economic resources.[2] The HLS contested eight seats in Rohtak and won three of them, polling 24.4% of the popular vote in the district.[3]

The second important change was the growth of opposition in the Haryana region to the compulsory teaching of Punjabi in the schools.[4] The consequence of this development was to emphasize the difference between the interests of Punjabi-speaking Hindus in Jullundur division, who feared Sikh domination in a Punjabi Suba, and Hindi-speaking Hindus in Haryana, who were in a majority in their region and did not fear Sikh domination, but rather saw that they could achieve greater political and economic prominence in a smaller and more homogeneous state. By 1965, at any rate, the sentiment for separation was widespread among political leaders and even Arya Samajists in Haryana, so that the Parliamentary Committee on the Demand for Punjabi Suba could report that the sentiment of the people had changed since the SRC *Report* and that 'an overwhelming majority of the people in the State now supports its reorganisation on linguistic basis'. The *Report* especially noted the difference between the sentiment of representatives from Haryana and those of the Hindus of Jullundur division, when it remarked:

The representatives of Haryana have opposed the formation of one unilingual State with Punjabi language and they have unanimously expressed their strong resentment against Punjabi in Gurmukhi Script being imposed on them even as

---

[1] *Ibid.*, pp. 272–4.
[2] *Election Law Reports*, xxiv, 378–84, 391–4, 396–7, 404–14, 416.
[3] Craig Baxter, *District Voting Trends in India: A Research Tool* (New York: Columbia University, 1969), p. 88.
[4] See, for example, the reports in *Statesman*, 30 June 1960, and *Tribune*, 14 January 1961; also the Punjabi Suba Committee, *Report*, pp. 7, 17, 43.

a second language as envisaged in the Regional Formula. The spokesmen of the Haryana Arya Samajists categorically stated before the Committee that the Hindi-speaking people from Jullundur Division who opposed the demand for a Punjabi-speaking State did not represent the views of the people of Haryana on this issue.

As has emerged from the evidence given before the Committee, . . . the active opposition to the creation of a Punjabi-speaking State now proceeds from a section of the population in the Punjabi region. How large the section is, is a matter of judgement. There is also a difference in the degree of opposition. A part of this section opposes a separate Suba with vigour and determination but another sizeable section while not welcoming it would submit to the inevitable.[1]

In this way, by 1965–6, the central leadership of the country was convinced that there was sufficient popular support in both regions of Punjab and that the determined opposition was sufficiently isolated to justify the division of the state.

RSS and Jan Sangh

The Hindu counterpart of the Sikh Akali Dal in the political arena of the Punjab has been the Jan Sangh and its organizational cadres of RSS workers. However, the Jan Sangh was not as effective in mobilizing the Hindu community in opposition to the Punjabi Suba movement as the Akali Dal was in mobilizing the Sikh community on behalf of the Punjabi Suba. Both Sikh and Hindu protagonists were internally divided in their attitudes toward the Punjabi Suba issue, but the divisions among Hindus were more serious. The Sikh supporters of the Punjabi Suba were divided only on tactics – whether to work through the Akali Dal or the Congress and whether to emphasize the religious or the linguistic basis of the demand. In attempting to consolidate and unify Hindu opinion, however, the RSS and Jan Sangh faced more serious divisions – between Haryana Hindus and urban Punjabi Hindus; between those concerned primarily with Hindu cultural interests and those concerned with political power; and between those with only a local perspective and those with a broader perspective on Hindu interests.

Until 1966, the Jan Sangh and RSS, along with the Arya Samaj, consistently opposed the division of the Punjab. However, the effectiveness of both the Jan Sangh and the Arya Samaj in opposing the Punjabi Suba was increasingly limited by the rise of sentiment in the Haryana region for the creation of a separate Haryana province. Both the RSS–Jan Sangh and the Arya Samaj have been organized primarily from among urban Punjabi-speaking Hindus in the leading cities of the Punjabi-speaking area, especially in the post-independence period in Amritsar, Jullundur, and Ludhiana. How-

[1] *Ibid.*, p. 7.

ever, both organizations have also had support in the towns and even in the rural areas of Haryana. In fact, Jan Sangh popular vote percentages were consistently higher in all elections after 1952 in Haryana than in the Punjabi region.[1] Consequently, as the Haryana movement began to acquire strength, Arya Samajists began to oppose each other in Haryana and Jan Sangh candidates found that they could poll better in the Haryana region by relating to the positive sentiment in favor of a Haryana province than by opposing the Punjabi Suba.[2]

A second line of division between Hindu cultural and political interests tended to divide many Arya Samajists from the RSS–Jan Sangh party men. Whereas many Arya Samajists were concerned primarily with educating Hindus in Hindu values through the medium of Hindi and, therefore, in protecting Hindi in Devanagari script at all costs, the RSS and Jan Sangh party leaders were more concerned with maintaining Hindu political dominance in the Punjab. For the sake of Hindu political power, RSS and Jan Sangh people were prepared to compromise the standing of Hindi *vis-à-vis* Punjabi. They were even willing to go so far as to admit that their own language was Punjabi. Arya Samajists, up to the reorganization of the Punjab, denied that there was any linguistic justification for the division of the Punjab. The Jan Sangh, however, finally accepted the reorganization of the Punjab on the argument that it was based on a linguistic and not a communal division.[3]

Finally, when it became clear that a reorganization of the Punjab was unavoidable, the Jan Sangh leadership moved quickly to an accommodating stance which would maximize Hindu opportunities to achieve a share of power in all portions of the reorganized Punjab. In his presidential address to the Jan Sangh in 1966, Balraj Madhok called for his party's acceptance of the division of the Punjab on a linguistic basis and made clear his opposition to 'extremist elements among the Akalis and the Arya Samajists', who were dissatisfied with the reorganization.[4] Both Madhok and the RSS leader, Golwalkar, who toured the Punjab in April 1966, urged the Hindus of the Punjab to acknowledge Punjabi as a legitimate language and Gurumukhi as a proper script for Hindus to accept. In fact, Madhok said, 'The Jana Sangh regards the Sikhs as part and parcel of the Hindu Society.'[5]

---

[1] See the figures in Craig Baxter, *The Jana Sangh: A Biography of an Indian Political Party* (Philadelphia: University of Pennsylvania Press, 1969), app. ii.
[2] *Ibid.*, p. 225.   [3] *Ibid.*, p. 255.   [4] Cited in *ibid.*
[5] *Hindustan Times*, 4 April 1966, cited in *ibid.*, p. 256.

Having lost the war over the Punjabi Suba, the Jan Sangh chose to cut its losses and to avoid losing any further battles. On the post-reorganization controversy over the status of the city of Chandigarh, the Jan Sangh units in the Punjabi Suba, in Haryana, and in Chandigarh all accommodated themselves to local sentiment on the issue. In the Punjabi Suba, much to the chagrin of many Arya Samajists, the Jan Sangh agreed to accept Punjabi as the sole official language of the province, while Hindi was reserved a compulsory place in the schools by virtue of its status as a national language.[1]

The behavior of the Jan Sangh on the Punjabi Suba and Punjabi language issues suggests two conclusions concerning the politics of language and religion. First, it demonstrates the ability of a political party to be accommodating and flexible on cultural issues for the sake of political power. Second, it demonstrates the extent of variability in the manipulation of cultural symbols. When necessary, the Jan Sangh fought against Punjabi and for Hindi, against Sikh Akali politicans alongside Arya Samajists. When a shift of tactics became desirable, the issues could become not just Hindi but Hindu political interests.

CONCLUSION

During the past century, the Sikhs of the Punjab have developed from a distinctive religious sect, a dispersed minority intermixed among the much larger Hindu and Muslim communities, into a subjectively self-conscious nationality, occupying a position of political dominance in a compact territorial unit created by their own political efforts. In their development from a religious sect to a political nation, Sikh religious and political elites were able to draw upon a vast storehouse of historical, religious, and linguistic symbols. In the process of symbol selection, certain elements of Sikh history and religion and of the Punjabi language have been emphasized while others have been ignored or downplayed. The process of symbol selection among the Sikhs demonstrates that when an ethnic group seeks political status, one symbol or set of symbols tends to be central, and that the end result is to achieve multi-symbol congruence with the central symbol. Thus, it was *keshadhari* Sikhs, who displayed the five symbols of Sikhism, who formed the central core of the Sikh nationality movement. The historical symbols with which

---

[1] On Arya Samaj disappointment over the Jan Sangh stand on the language issue in the Punjabi Suba, see also Veena Dua, 'Arya Samaj and Punjab Politics', *Economic and Political Weekly*, v, Nos. 43 and 44 (24 October 1970), 1790.

they identified emphasized Sikh political dominance in pre-British times and the valor of the Sikhs as a fighting people. The religious symbols chosen were those which most distinctively marked off the Sikhs as separate from the Hindus. The form of the Punjabi language which was preferred was one written in a script, the Gurumukhi, associated with the Sikh scriptures. In this way, membership in the Sikh nation has come to refer primarily to *keshadhari* Sikhs who speak Punjabi and write it in the Gurumukhi script and who identify with the martial traditions of the Sikh people. Those Sikhs who do not display the five symbols of Sikhism, who value the more quietist aspects of Sikh religious and political history, and who view the Punjabi language as a vehicle of communication between Sikhs and Hindus and not as a symbol of difference between the two communities have been marginal to and, in some cases, have even been defined out of the Sikh nation.

Although many people have argued that the Sikhs constituted a nation even in pre-modern times, the development of the modern Sikh nation as defined above has been associated with processes of social mobilization and political organization which have occurred only during the past century. In the pre-independence Punjab, Sikhs and Hindus were mobilizing communities, both seeking to assert themselves, their languages, and their cultures in a society in which Muslims were a less advanced, but politically dominant community. In the process of social mobilization, Sikh elites identified their cultural language as Punjabi in Gurumukhi script whereas Hindu elites identified with Hindi in the Devanagari script. In the post-independence period, when the Sikh population became concentrated in a compact geographical area and a demand for territorial autonomy became feasible, the linguistic division which had begun to develop in the pre-independence period between Sikhs and Hindus began to be used as a basis for the demand to create a separate Punjabi-speaking province in which Sikhs would be the politically dominant force.

In the development of Sikh communal consciousness and in the successful achievement of a Punjabi Suba, political associations and organizations played decisive roles. The Singh Sabha movement and the Chief Khalsa Diwan in the late nineteenth and early twentieth centuries were instrumental in defining and building Sikh communal identity and in introducing processes of change affecting literacy, education, and communications. The formation of the SGPC in 1920 provided the Sikh community with a solid institutional foundation in the Punjab from which its political action arm, the Akali Dal, could move toward the articulation and achievement of political advantages for the Sikh community.

The achievement of the demand for the Punjabi Suba was the culmination of Sikh political aspirations in the Punjab. It was not achieved without setbacks and political compromise. Sikh political leaders were required by the rules of Indian politics, enforced by the central government, to present their demands in linguistic, rather than in religious terms. The refusal of the central government to consider demands made in the name of religious communalism was an important factor in the shift of political leadership in the Akali Dal from Master Tara Singh to Sant Fateh Singh.

The success of the Sikh political movement owes as much to the weakness and internal divisions among its opponents as it does to its own internal strength. Sikh social and political mobilization was paralleled by social and political mobilization among Hindus in the Punjab. However, Hindu political organization in the Punjab was limited by the fact that there were two sets of conflicting interests in the pre-1966 Punjab, those of the Hindi-speaking Hindus of Haryana and those of the Punjabi-speaking Hindus in the Punjabi region. Moreover, Hindus in the Punjab were more divided than the Sikhs into social and political organizations with conflicting purposes – particularly the Arya Samaj, which was rigidly pro-Hindi, and the Jan Sangh, which was prepared to compromise on the issue of the relative status of Hindi and Punjabi. Moreover, neither of these two organizations have ever commanded support in the Hindu community comparable to that held by the Akali Dal among the Sikhs.

7

GOVERNMENT POLICY AND
PARTY POLITICS

The process of social and political differentiation between Sikhs and Hindus in the Punjab which preceded the formation of the Punjabi Suba in 1966 has been examined in the previous chapter. It is clear from that account that politics in the Punjab, both before and since 1947, have frequently been dominated by communal considerations and antagonisms. Communal differences have twice in the past quarter century been made the bases for successful political demands for partition (in 1947) or reorganization (in 1966) of the state to conform to patterns of communal and linguistic concentrations of populations. The partition of 1947 was turned into a communal holocaust. The reorganization of 1966 passed peacefully, but the threat of violence was a consideration in the final decision to divide the state. It will probably not be disputed that the Punjab, of all the Indian regions, has been the scene of the most intense, bitter, and prolonged communal cleavages in modern Indian history.

From the point of view of the study of political integration in regimes of competitive political parties, the theoretical questions which are most important in such a situation concern the relationships among the communal cleavages of the society, the policies pursued by governments, and the appeals of and bases of support for the political parties. To what extent do political parties reflect or shape communal cleavages and to what extent do they moderate or exacerbate them? Under what conditions, if at all, is governance possible in communally divided societies in a regime of competitive political parties? To what extent can political leadership overcome communal differences when they take organized form in politics? Can linguistic and religion-based demands be accommodated and the conflicting claims of rival communal groups be reconciled by democratically-elected political leaders and parties?

These questions will be considered in this and the following chapter. This chapter will be concerned with the language policies formulated by the Punjab government before and after the creation of the Punjabi Suba, the attitudes of the various political parties on the language issue and the question of the Punjabi Suba, the actual

337

appeals of the parties to the electorate, and the patterns of political coalition-building and accommodation of ethnic group demands which were evolved by the parties and by the Punjab and the central governments. In the following chapter, the bases of communal support for the political parties in the electorate will be analyzed.

GOVERNMENT AND PARTY POLICIES ON THE
LANGUAGE ISSUES BEFORE AND AFTER THE
PUNJABI SUBA

Hindi, Punjabi, and the Punjab government

The language policies pursued by the Punjab government in the period between 1947 and 1966 deserve detailed consideration because, during that period, the full variety of policies and policy options open to any bilingual society were discussed and several were tried. Problems similar to those faced in the Punjab during that period continue to exist in such diverse environments as Malaya, Sri Lanka, Belgium, and Canada.

The first point that deserves stressing about the attempts to formulate a viable language policy in the Punjab during this period is that they revealed the wide variety of policy choices available in such a situation. Language policies are not simply consequences of conflicts between linguistic groups, but they influence the terms of controversy. Political leaders have many options available to them to shape such controversies. They need not simply react to them.

During the period 1949 to 1966, three 'formulae' were implemented in the Punjab to deal with the language disputes – the Sachar and PEPSU Formulae, which were concerned with educational policy, and the Regional Formula, which was meant to solve the political and administrative issues. The Sachar Formula was, in origin, an agreement between two Hindu and two Sikh politicans, reached on 1 October 1949, to solve the question of the medium of instruction in the Punjab schools, excluding the princely states. The formula replaced a pre-independence order of the Punjab government education department which had provided that:

All education in the schools of the East Punjab shall be given in the mother-tongue of the children and either Devanagari or Gurmukhi script can be used in the 1st and 2nd class, provided arrangements be made to teach Gurmukhi in the third class in schools where initially Hindi is taught. The same rule is required to be observed in such schools where the initial education was in Gurmukhi.[1]

---

[1] Government of India, Home Department, Punjab Boundary Commission, *Report* (Delhi: Manager of Publications, 1966), p. 3.

The basic underlying principles of the order are two, namely, that education should be through the medium of the mother tongue, but that bilingualism should be enforced. The order, however, was vague on three points. First, it did not specify how the decisions would be made and who would make them on the selection of the mother tongue medium in the schools. Secondly, the term 'Punjabi' is not used in the order, only the term Gurumukhi. Third, it is not clear whether, in Hindi-medium schools, the Punjabi language was to be taught from the third class or only the Gurumukhi script.

The Sachar Formula retained the two basic principles of mother tongue education and enforced bilingualism, but eliminated the vagueness of the previous order.[1] The formula clearly differentiated two main languages or mother tongues in the Punjab, namely, Punjabi in the Gurumukhi script and Hindi in the Devanagari script. It also assumed that areas where one of the two languages was predominant could be demarcated[2] and it anticipated that the Punjab government would so demarcate the Hindi-speaking and Punjabi-speaking areas of the state. The formula also specified the method of selecting the medium of instruction. Hindi in the Hindi-speaking areas and Punjabi in the Punjabi-speaking areas, as demarcated, were to be the media of instruction in their regions, but the parents or guardians of the pupils were to have the right to opt for Hindi in the Punjabi region or Punjabi in the Hindi region provided there was sufficient demand for such options in the class or school.[3] Hindi was to be taught as a compulsory language from the last class of the primary stage in the Punjabi-speaking areas and Punjabi was to be similarly required as a second language in the Hindi-speaking areas.

The Sachar Formula is an ideal model for enforced bilingualism in a bilingual society, which retains also the principles of the mother tongue as the medium of education and freedom of choice to the parents to decide the medium of education of their children. The formula is ideal in the sense that it solves the technical problems without restricting the freedom of the parents to choose the medium of education for their children, but it does assume the desirability of

[1] The text of the formula is in Government of India, Parliamentary Committee on the Demand for Punjabi Suba, *Report* (New Delhi: Lok Sabha Secretariat, 1966), pp. 79–81. (Hereafter referred to as Punjabi Suba Committee, *Report.*)

[2] Baldev Raj Nayar, *Minority Politics in the Punjab* (Princeton, N.J.: Princeton University Press, 1966), p. 218.

[3] In 1958, the restriction limiting the implementation of this option to schools or classes where a specified number of students requested it was removed. In principle, instruction through the medium of Hindi in the Punjab region and Punjabi in the Hindi region was to be available to any student whose parents requested it. *Hindustan Times*, 4 March 1960.

enforced bilingualism. In other words, no better a pluralistic model can be devised for a bilingual society in which the two main language groups are nearly equal in size and wish to maintain social and political communications within a common political framework. The formula ran into difficulties because this was not in fact the case. In the Punjabi region, Akali Sikhs resented the option given to Hindus to have their children educated through the medium of Hindi. In the Hindi region, most Hindus objected to the compulsion of learning Punjabi.

The PEPSU Formula, which was applied in the former princely states areas of the Punjab, was similar to the Sachar Formula in that it divided the area into Hindi-speaking and Punjabi-speaking zones in which the respective languages would be media of instruction, but in which the other language would be taught compulsorily from the third class.[1] However, unlike the Sachar Formula, it did not provide freedom of choice for the parents.[2]

The Regional Formula was introduced with the integration of PEPSU into the Punjab in 1956.[3] It was primarily a political-administrative formula rather than an education formula. In education, it simply maintained the Sachar and PEPSU Formulae in the areas where they had been in force before the merger.[4] The chief importance of the Regional Formula was in its extension of the principle of linguistic demarcation of the Punjab into two language zones, which was now to be applied to the governance of the state through the establishment of two regional committees in the legislature, consisting of the elected members from the Hindi- and Punjabi-speaking regions. The regional committees were to have large powers in the legislation for their regions.[5] Finally, the Regional Formula declared Punjab to be a bilingual state, but provided that the regional languages would be the official languages in their respective regions at the district level and below.[6]

---

[1] Punjabi Suba Committee, *Report*, p. 82.

[2] In this respect, the PEPSU formula was in violation of article 350A of the Constitution, a matter pointed out by the Commissioner for Linguistic Minorities in *CLM* v, 69; *CLM* vi, 5; and *CLM* vii, 6, 91–2.

[3] Punjabi Suba Committee, *Report*, pp. 8, 63, 67, 72, and Punjab Boundary Commission, *Report*, pp. 5–6.

[4] Nayar, *Minority Politics*, p. 223.

[5] In fact, the extent of their powers remained a matter of dispute between Sikh leaders and the Punjab government. See the *Tribune*, 19 April and 7 May 1960; *Spokesman*, 26 July and 30 August 1965; Punjabi Suba Committee, *Report*, pp. 10–14.

[6] The Punjab government attempted to implement this provision with effect from October 1962 under the terms of the Official Language Act, 1960; *CLM* v, 101; *Statesman*, 11 August 1960; *Hindustan Times*, 11 August 1960; *Tribune*, 29 September 1960 and 12 September 1962; *Hindu*, 21 September 1962; *Times of India*, 2 October 1962. The Pun-

If the various language formulae implemented in the Punjab suggest the variety of solutions available to policy-makers in a bilingual
society, the course of Hindu–Sikh political conflict in the Punjab on
the language issue suggests that no formula, no matter how in-
genious, will work if the basic issues are not really linguistic, but
communal, and if there exists a determined political organization
with significant support whose purpose is to exploit linguistic divisions for political advantage. The various formulae ultimately failed
to promote integration in the Punjab for three reasons, which reflected the communal basis of politics in that state. First, the Akali
Dal never considered the formulae as solutions to the language or
educational issues, but only as temporary compromises on the way to
the ultimate goal of a Sikh-dominated political unit.[1] Second, large
numbers of Hindus in the Punjabi region took advantage of the freedom of choice option in the Sachar Formula to opt for Hindi,[2] which
the Sikhs interpreted as a denial by the Punjabi-speaking Hindus of
their mother tongue for communal reasons.[3] Finally, Hindus in the
Haryana region decided that it was not in their interests that their
children should be required to learn Punjabi compulsorily.[4] That
is, the Hindi-speaking Hindus of Haryana rejected the idea of the

jab High Court did the same with effect from 2 January 1962; *Tribune*, 23 December
1960; *Express*, 2 August 1962.
   The implementation of the provision was opposed by several Hindu-dominated
municipal committees in the Punjabi region; *Tribune*, 11 October 1962. It was reported
as late as 1965 that implementation had been only nominal and that English and Urdu
continued to be used in government offices; Attar Singh, 'State of Regional Languages
in Punjab', *Spokesman*, 23 August 1965.

[1] Nayar, *Minority Politics*, pp. 264–5.
[2] *Hindustan Times*, 4 March 1960. It is not known precisely how widespread this exercise
of the freedom of choice option was because the Punjab government never provided any
statistics on the question during this period; *CLM* v, 71; *CLM* vi, 39; *CLM* vii, 20.
[3] In 1960, a two-man (one Hindu, one Sikh) Good Relations Committee recommended
the removal of this option because, according to the press report, the committee was
'afraid that if this option continues it will divide Hindus and Sikhs into two different
nations, both claiming to have different languages, different religions, and different
cultures'. *Tribune*, 9 March 1960. The committee's recommendations were not implemented. See also the *Tribune*, 19 April 1960; *Statesman*, 30 June 1960.
[4] An agitation against the Sachar Formula was launched by Hindi supporters on 30 May
1957; *Hindustan Times*, 4 March 1960. As noted on p. 347 below, the Good Relations
Committee recommended the removal of the compulsion on the teaching of Punjabi in
the Hindi region in a report made public in March 1960; *Tribune*, 9 March 1960.
Another, larger committee came to a similar agreement at the same time; *Statesman*, 25
March 1960; *Tribune*, 12 April 1960. The Sikh political groups were willing to have the
compulsion removed provided Punjabi had the same status in the Punjabi region as
Hindi had in the Hindi region; *ibid*. The Hindi regional committee of the Punjab Vidhan Sabha recommended removal of compulsory instruction in Punjabi in the Hindi
region in May 1960; *Statesman*, 18 May 1960. However, no agreement could be reached
among all concerned parties in the Punjab and the Sachar and PEPSU Formulae remained in force; *Hindustan Times*, 20 May 1960; *Tribune*, 11 June and 2 and 25 July

equal distribution of linguistic burdens for the sake of emotional integration and realized that they could get along both in India and in the Punjab with Hindi alone, as long as the Punjabi-speakers were required to learn Hindi and as long as Hindi was an official language of the state.[1]

The creation of the Punjabi Suba by no means resolved the language controversy. It only reversed the relative positions of the two leading protagonist groups. Hindus in the Punjabi Suba were now the minority group and Hindi-speakers a still smaller minority. Conflict soon developed both between and within the Hindu and Sikh communities on the status to be given to the two languages in the Punjab. Within the Hindu community, the Arya Samaj demanded that Hindi be recognized as a distinct minority group language in the Punjabi Suba. The Jan Sangh, which formed a coalition with the Akali Dal in the first government formed after the creation of the Punjabi Suba, initially took a position that Punjabi should be recognized as the official language of the state but that Hindi should be given special status in the Punjab as the 'national language' of the country.[2] Consequently, the Jan Sangh acquiesced in the passage on 19 December 1967 of the Punjab Language Act, which gave Punjabi status as the only official language of the Punjab. However, the Punjab government announced simultaneously that Hindi would be taught as a compulsory language in all schools and colleges in the state and would be used as the medium of communication with the central government.[3]

These decisions left all the old questions unresolved. Was Hindi the mother tongue of a minority group in the state? Should Hindi be a medium of instruction in the schools or only a language for study? Should government-aided private schools be permitted to select their own medium of instruction? From what class should Hindi be introduced in the schools? The Arya Samaj kept to a consistent line on these questions, insisting that Hindi-speakers were a distinct minority group in the state, constitutionally entitled to receive their education through the medium of their mother tongue from the first class in both public and privately managed schools.[4] Ultimately, the Jan Sangh also came round to a similar position, demanding that the Sachar Formula should be retained in the Punjabi Suba.[5] However,

1960; *Statesman*, 17 and 19 July 1960; *Hindustan Standard*, 20 July 1960; *Times of India*, 26 July 1960.
[1] See, e.g., *Hindustan Times*, 4 March 1960.
[2] *Spokesman*, January 1968 (Guru Gobind Singh number).
[3] *Ibid.*, 22 January 1968 and 29 April 1968.
[4] *Ibid.*, January 1968 (Guru Gobind Singh number) and 16 December 1968.
[5] *Ibid.*, 5 May 1969.

the Akali Dal took the position that the Punjabi Suba was a uni-lingual state, that Hindi was not a mother tongue of the Punjab but only a second language to be taught in the schools from the third or sixth class, that the Sachar Formula should be done away with and Punjabi be introduced as the sole medium of instruction in both government and privately managed schools.[1]

In July 1969, the Punjab government introduced a three-language formula for the government schools and announced a decision on the medium of instruction for the private schools. According to the three-language formula, Punjabi would be the sole medium of instruction in government schools, but Hindi would be a compulsory subject of study from the fourth class and English a compulsory subject from the sixth class. Students would have to pass in all three languages for matriculation. Private schools would be left free to choose their medium of instruction from the first class.[2] Left unsatisfied still were those who continued to insist that Hindi-speakers in the Punjabi Suba were a linguistic minority, constitutionally entitled to receive instruction in the government schools through the medium of Hindi from the first class.

Political party attitudes on the language issues in the Punjab

During the twenty-five years of agitation on the communal-linguistic issues in post-independence Punjab, the political parties have articulated every important segment of opinion on the language issues. The main non-Congress parties have held distinctive and frequently mutually incompatible positions, which were related either to the interests of their constituencies or to their ideologies. The Congress has had no fixed position, but has contained within it, in the manner of a dominant party, nearly all relevant opinions.

On one end of the political spectrum, the Akali Dal, despite numerous shifts in strategy, tactics, and leadership, adhered single-mindedly to the ultimate goal of a separate Punjabi-speaking political unit. Short of a Punjabi Suba, its demands on the language issue were for the recognition of Punjabi in Gurumukhi script as the official and court language and the medium of instruction in the schools in the Punjabi-speaking region of the state.[3] The Akali Dal was

---

[1] *Ibid.*, 2 June 1969.
[2] *Ibid.*, 14 July, 25 August, and 22 September 1969, and 10 May 1971.
[3] These demands were formulated as early as 8 May 1949. See Paul Wallace, 'The Political Party System of Punjab State (India): A Study of Factionalism', unpublished Ph.D. dissertation, University of California, Berkeley, 1966, p. 192.

sometimes willing to make concessions concerning the use of Punjabi in Haryana, but it believed that the Punjabi-speaking areas could be demarcated, that Punjabi in Gurumukhi script was the proper language of the people in those areas, and that it should be compulsorily taught in the schools and should be used by the state for all official purposes. In the Punjabi Suba, the Akali Dal has adhered to the position that the sole official language of the state must be Punjabi in Gurumukhi script, with Hindi occupying a position as link language for communication between the state and the center. The Akali Dal has kept open for bargaining with other parties the extent to which Hindi, as link language, may be taught from the lower grades in the public schools.

On the other side has been the Jan Sangh which, throughout the period up to reorganization of the state, articulated the interests of the urban, Punjabi-speaking Hindus in opposing the Punjabi Suba and demanding not only the maintenance of a multi-communal state, but the enlargement of the Hindu majority in that state through the inclusion of Himachal Pradesh in it.[1] On the language issue, Jan Sangh leaders did not usually explicitly deny that Punjabi was the mother tongue of most Punjabi Hindus,[2] but they argued that it was 'nothing more than a spoken language, or a mere dialect' of Hindi.[3] Moreover, they objected to the imposition of Gurumukhi, which they considered merely a religious script of the Sikhs, on the Hindus.[4] Their public argument was that the Punjabi issue was a front to impose Sikh domination and the religious script of the Sikhs upon Punjabi Hindus, that it was in fact a communally motivated demand.[5] What they did not say publicly was that they themselves considered Hindi in the Devanagari script the only proper language for a Hindu outside his home.[6]

The identification of the Jan Sangh with the interests of Punjabi Hindus threatened by absorption in a Sikh-dominated state was sufficiently great for the party to oppose the increasingly popular

[1] Nayar, *Minority Politics*, p. 42; *Tribune*, 27 September 1960.
[2] Such views were frequently attributed to them, however, and Jan Sangh leaders were supposed to have been 'taken aback' in November 1960 when the RSS leader, M. S. Golwalkar, visited the Punjab and urged Hindus to 'accept Punjabi as their mother tongue'. See the reports on this incident in *Times of India*, 4 November 1960; *Hindustan Times*, 10 November 1960; and *Express*, 10 November 1960.
[3] Punjab Commission, *Report*, p. 15.
[4] *Ibid.*; see also *Tribune*, 26 May 1961.
[5] Punjabi Suba Committee, *Report*, pp. 41–2.
[6] Nayar attributes this view to Hindus generally in the Punjab; *Minority Politics*, p. 44. See also the claim attributed to the Jan Sangh and Arya Samaj 'that 45% of the Hindus in the Punjab region use Hindi for writing purposes'. *Express*, 18 November 1960.

demand of Haryana Hindus for a Haryana Prant.[1] (In principle, of course, the Jan Sangh is opposed to all linguistic states in any case.) The position of the Jan Sangh on the language issue was that Punjab was a bilingual state which could not be demarcated into Hindi-speaking and Punjabi-speaking areas and that, consequently, Hindi and Punjabi in both scripts should be the official languages of the entire state.[2] In education, the Jan Sangh favored enforced bilingualism with freedom of choice for the parents to select the medium of instruction for their children, but with an important difference from the Sachar Formula in that the party favored the teaching of Punjabi in both the Devanagari and Gurumukhi scripts.[3] The Jan Sangh position on the language issue in Punjab was thus consistent with its position elsewhere in north India, namely, that all languages of the north are nothing more than dialects of Hindi, which are suitable for use in the home and as media of primary education only (if at all), but are not to be considered separate languages equal in status to Hindi. Consequently, the enforced identification of any of the north Indian 'dialects' with a script different from Devanagari has been opposed consistently by Jan Sangh leaders. Minority language leaders among both the Urdu-speaking and Punjabi-speaking communities have demanded equally consistently the badge of separateness of a different script to prevent the absorption of their languages into Hindi by means of the Devanagari script. After the formation of the Punjabi Suba, the Jan Sangh modified its position significantly. As mentioned above, the party acquiesced in the passage of the Punjab Official Language Act, 1967, and in the adoption of the three-language formula to replace the Sachar Formula. It insisted only that freedom of choice of medium of instruction be allowed to the private schools. In its 1972 election manifesto, the Jan Sangh recognized 'Punjabi as a spoken language of Punjab with Hindi as the language of usage of a very large section of the people in the state'.[4] The phrase, 'language of usage', to refer to Hindi in the Punjab, is a significant one. In the context of the history of the language conflict in the state, it may be interpreted as a more accurate statement than many others which have been made concerning the reality of the linguistic situation, namely, that many Punjabi-speaking Hindus in the Punjab prefer the use of Hindi for many, or most public purposes. It is a different kind of statement from some previous

[1] See the dissenting note by A. B. Vajpayee in the Punjabi Suba Committee, *Report*, p. 43.
[2] *Tribune*, 4 October and 25 November 1960, and *Express*, 10 November 1960.
[3] *Tribune*, 27 September and 25 November 1960.
[4] Cited in the *Spokesman*, 10 January 1972.

claims by Hindu groups that Punjabi is not their mother tongue at all. In any event, the Jan Sangh has demanded on behalf of Hindi-users that official government notices be published in Hindi as well as Punjabi.

The Communist parties in the Punjab have followed a consistent policy on the language issue of support for the use of the regional languages in both education and administration, while opposing the linking of the linguistic and religious issues. The CPI supported the creation of two new states in the Punjab on a strict linguistic basis, but opposed the formulation of the Punjabi Suba issue by Master Tara Singh in the form of a Sikh communal demand.[1] After Sant Fateh Singh took over the leadership of the Akali movement and began to emphasize the linguistic character of the demand and to build mass Sikh sentiment behind it, the Communist party joined forces on the issue with the Akali Dal.[2] Short of a linguistic reorganization of the state, the party position was that the regional languages should be encouraged for all purposes in their respective regions, including as compulsory media of instruction.[3] However, the party opposed the compulsory teaching of Punjabi in Haryana.[4] Since the formation of the Punjabi Suba, the Communist parties have adhered to the position that Punjabi is the regional language of the new state and that there is no linguistic minority in it.

The Congress party, true to its image as an aggregative, pragmatic, dominant center party, contained within its fold before 1966 representatives of the three main viewpoints – communalist Sikhs who wished to enforce Punjabi as the sole medium of instruction in the Punjabi region; communalist Hindus who wished to turn Punjabi into a language of the minority Sikh community; and secularists who proposed formula after formula to satisfy all opposed interests and to attempt to maintain the communal, linguistic, and territorial unity of the Punjab. The Sachar Formula served the Congress purpose well until the Hindus of Haryana began to oppose the compulsory learning of Punjabi in the Hindi-speaking region. The Sachar Formula might have been optimal for unity if the Punjab were a separate, sovereign state. In the Indian context, it served rather as a means of convincing both Haryana Hindus and Punjabi Sikhs that it was not in their interests to continue in the same political unit.

Until it became clear to both the principal parties, Punjabi Sikhs

[1] *Express*, 18 November 1960. *Punjabi Suba: A Symposium* (New Delhi: National Book Club, n.d.), pp. 149–56.
[2] Baldev Raj Nayar, 'Punjab', in Myron Weiner (ed.), *State Politics in India* (Princeton, N.J.: Princeton University Press, 1968), p. 482.
[3] *Statesman*, 20 July 1960.   [4] *Tribune*, 5 March 1960.

and Haryana Hindus, that separation would benefit both sides, the Congress acted as the primary arena for political bargaining on the language and communal issues and as the main cohering force in the multi-communal Punjab. The Congress performed this role with some success, especially during the period 1956 to 1964, which was marked by the predominant leadership of Pratap Singh Kairon and the unity of the central and state Congress leadership. During this period, Congress policy was oriented towards the maintenance of the unity of the Punjab state and the adoption of a language policy minimally satisfactory to all three communal forces in the Punjab – Punjabi-speaking Sikhs, Hindi-speaking Haryana Hindus, and Punjabi Hindus.

In the spring of 1960, the discontent of Haryana Hindus with the Sachar Formula and of Punjabi Sikhs with the working of both the Sachar and the Regional Formulae led Congress leaders to a reconsideration of the language issues in the Punjab and to an attempt to formulate a new proposal to replace the Sachar Formula. The Sachar Formula was entirely satisfactory only to Punjabi-speaking Hindus, who wished to have the option of educating their children through the medium of Hindi, but had no objection to learning Punjabi in addition as a compulsory language. Haryana Hindus, however, objected to the compulsion of learning Punjabi,[1] while Punjabi Sikhs objected to the absence of compulsion in the use of the Punjabi medium in the Punjabi-speaking region.

After the agitation by Haryana Hindus in 1957–8 on the language issue, a two-man committee, comprised of one Hindu and one Sikh,[2] had been appointed to reconsider the language issue. It presented its report to the Punjab Vidhan Sabha in March 1960. The Good Relations Committee, as it was called, recommended unanimously the removal of compulsion in the learning of Punjabi in the Hindi-speaking region, but could not agree on a single formula for the Punjabi-speaking region. Instead, two alternative formulae for the Punjabi-speaking region were presented.[3] The first proposal was that Punjabi should be the compulsory medium of instruction, but that students should have the option of writing it in Devanagari or Gurumukhi. At a later stage, those who opted for Devanagari would also learn Gurumukhi and those who opted for Gurumukhi would also learn Hindi. This proposal, as expected, was opposed strongly

[1] *Tribune*, 26 and 27 July 1960.
[2] *Tribune*, 1 March 1960. The members of the committee were Jai Chand Vidyalankar (Hindu) and Bhai Jodh Singh (Sikh).
[3] *Tribune*, 9 March 1960.

by the leading Sikh political groups. The second proposed formula provided for instruction in both languages in both scripts at the primary stage, with Punjabi as the medium for all. This proposal came close to satisfying all groups, but was finally opposed by both Punjabi Hindus, who found it less satisfactory than the Sachar Formula, and the Akali Dal, which claimed by then to be uninterested in any proposal except a Punjabi Suba.

All lines of conflict were reflected within the Punjab Congress, which contained sub-groups whose leaders articulated the major viewpoints expressed outside the Congress. One sub-group, led by the former Akali leaders, Giani Kartar Singh and Gian Singh Rarewala, argued for the introduction of Punjabi in Gurumukhi script as the medium of instruction, to be followed only in later classes by instruction in Hindi as well.[1] A second sub-group, led by a Hindu, Harbans Lal, supported the second alternative proposal of the Good Relations Committee. A third sub-group, led by both a Sikh, Sardar Darbara Singh, and a Hindu, Yash, and supported by Dr Gopichand Bhargava, favored the retention of the Sachar Formula.[2]

The chief minister, Pratap Singh Kairon, favored the second proposal of the Good Relations Committee, but was unable to convince the Sikh leaders, Giani Kartar Singh and Gian Singh Rarewala.[3] After weeks of negotiation among the various sub-groups, the chief minister developed still another formula, called a Unity Formula, by which Punjabi in Gurumukhi script and Hindi in Devanagari script would be compulsory media of instruction at the primary stages in their respective regions and the second language would be taught compulsorily in the secondary stage.[4] This proposal satisfied the demands of Punjabi Sikhs, but did not satisfy either Haryana or Punjabi Hindus, the central Congress leadership, or the Constitution of India.[5] The Kairon formula was, consequently, attacked by both Hindu and Hindi parties and groups outside the Congress and by the Darbara Singh-Yash-Bhargava sub-group within the Congress.[6] Ultimately, it proved impossible to win acceptance for any alternative formula acceptable to the three principal ethnic-linguistic communities in the Punjab.[7]

The negotiations in 1960 represented a significant turning point

---

[1] *Statesman*, 18 and 19 May 1960; *Tribune*, 19 May 1960.
[2] *Tribune*, 19 and 21 May, and 2 and 16 July 1960; *Statesman*, 19 May, 17, 19, 26, and 27 July 1960.
[3] *Statesman*, 19 May 1960.
[4] *Times of India*, 6 July 1960; *Statesman*, 17 and 19 July 1960.
[5] *Statesman*, 17 July 1960; *Tribune*, 23 July 1960; *Times of India*, 26 July 1960.
[6] *Hindustan Standard*, 20 July 1960.
[7] *Times of India*, 26 July 1960.

in the Punjabi Suba controversy because they laid bare a fundamental rift between the interests of Haryana and Punjabi Hindus.
In principle, there was no conflict of interest because both groups
favored maximum freedom of choice.[1] In practice, Haryana Hindus
were being held hostage for the sake of the Punjabi Hindus. Punjabi
was imposed on Haryana so that Punjabi Hindus could maintain a
special status for Hindi as a compulsory language in the Punjabi-
speaking region.[2] Punjabi Sikhs were not willing to alter the Sachar
Formula to remove the compulsory teaching of Punjabi in the Hindi
region unless the position of Punjabi in the Punjabi region was
strengthened. Punjabi Hindus, however, were opposed to any such
further strengthening of Punjabi in their region. This was surely a
major tactical error on the part of the Punjabi Hindus because it left
Haryana Hindus with only one option to remove compulsory Punjabi instruction, namely, separation of the Hindi-speaking regions
from the Punjab entirely. From this point on, it was increasingly
clear to both Haryana Hindus and Punjabi Sikhs that a Punjabi
Suba was in their mutual interest.

While the Congress, therefore, ultimately was not able to formulate a proposal capable of satisfying all groups in Punjab politics, this
was more because the possibility of political separation always existed
as a real and non-catastrophic alternative, which undercut efforts at
compromise. It has been argued that the kind of conflict which
occurred in the Punjab would have made difficult the maintenance
of 'political stability and democracy' if the Punjab had been a
separate sovereign state.[3] However, the evidence suggests as equally
plausible that one of the many alternatives proposed by political
leaders in the Punjab would have been accepted by all groups with
less difficulty in those circumstances, if the alternative were a catastrophic disintegration. Although the Akali Dal and the Jan Sangh
adopted incompatible positions which reflected the communal concerns of their constituencies, the Communist party and the Congress
consistently sought to separate the communal and linguistic issues
and to moderate communal attitudes and the potential for communal conflict in the Punjab. The potential for a political polarization of communal attitudes was also moderated by the persistent
efforts of party leaders, especially in the Congress, to find a language
formula acceptable to all groups in the Punjab. Their inability to do
so reflected less a failure of the parties to adjust competing communal
interests than the availability to the two most important political
communities of other, more attractive political alternatives.

---

[1] *Tribune*, 24 July 1960.   [2] *Statesman*, 5 May 1960.   [3] Nayar, 'Punjab', p. 496.

In the aftermath of the creation of the Punjabi Suba, the Congress has interposed itself once again between the two leading competing communal parties, the Akali Dal and the Jan Sangh. The Punjab Pradesh Congress Committee president Giani Zail Singh, a Sikh, criticized the Punjab government in June 1969 for not providing a proper status for Hindi in the state.[1] A group of the most important Punjab Congress leaders, including both Sikhs and Hindus, released a statement the following month in favor of the teaching of both Punjabi and Hindi from the first class and in favor of leaving to the parents the choice of which of the two languages should be the medium of instruction in the public schools.[2]

Clearly, the creation of the Punjabi Suba has not solved the language issue in the state, but has only altered the relative positions of the main communal groups. The large Hindi-speaking Hindu population of Haryana has been removed and the Punjabi Hindus have been reduced to a minority position. Most of the Punjabi Hindus actually speak Punjabi as their mother tongue, but there is a minority of actual Hindi-speakers as well as a group of Punjabi-speakers who prefer, for whatever reasons, that their children be instructed through the medium of Hindi. The Constitution of India is clear on the rights to which minority language speakers are entitled, but it will probably take some time before all political parties in the Punjab reach a mutually satisfactory compromise which is true both to the linguistic situation of the Punjab and to the Constitution of the country.

COMMUNAL CLEAVAGE AND COMMUNAL COALITION-BUILDING

The process of policy-making on the language issues in the Punjab has taken place in a political context marked by opposing tendencies among the leading political groups and by discontinuity in the nature of politics at the local and state levels. At the local level, in the electoral arena, the communal parties and groups, particularly the Akali Dal and the Arya Samaj, have attempted to appeal to the religious sentiments of the people in order to build communal solidarity behind their linguistic and political demands. The secular parties, particularly the Congress, have adopted a distinctly different approach, attempting to build inter-communal alliances in the electorate. In the post-independence period, neither the Akali Dal nor any of the Hindu communal groups have succeeded in monopolizing

---

[1] *Spokesman*, 2 June 1969.   [2] *Ibid.*, 14 July 1969.

the electoral arena. The only party which has been able to achieve a majority alone in both the pre-reorganization Punjab and in the post-1966 Punjabi Suba has been the inter-communal Congress. For the Congress, therefore, there has been no discontinuity between its electoral appeals and its behavior in the legislature and in government. The communal parties, however, have had to operate differently in the electoral arena and in the legislative arena. In the electorate, they appeal to religious sentiment and solidarity for support. Once the elections are over, however, they must form inter-communal alliances with each other to achieve power in the legislative arena.

Electoral appeals and communal solidarity and conflict in the Punjab

The Akali Dal in the pre-reorganization Punjab deliberately used the electoral arena to strengthen Sikh solidarity behind its demands. The party and its candidates openly attempted to identify the party with the interests of the Sikh community and appealed directly to the religious sentiments of the Sikhs in doing so. In response, some Hindu politicians made similar appeals to the sentiment and feelings of solidarity of the Hindu community, particularly in Haryana. Considerable evidence is available from court cases concerned with election petitions in the Punjab to demonstrate the kinds of appeals made by Akali Dal candidates to Sikh voters, particularly during the 1952 and 1962 elections.

Three clauses in section 123 of the Representation of the People Act, 1951, define as corrupt practices in elections the following kinds of references to 'religion, race, caste, community, or language': any appeal by a candidate or his agents to vote for him or against an opponent on those grounds and any use of or appeal to religious symbols for the purpose; any attempt to exercise 'undue influence' by threatening either 'social ostracism' or 'divine displeasure or spiritual censure'; and, 'any attempt to promote feelings of enmity or hatred between different classes of the citizens of India' on those grounds.[1] The original act was milder than in its later, amended form. Originally, religious appeals had to be systematic before a candidate using them could be found guilty of a corrupt practice and, even if the appeal was proven to have been systematic, the election

[1] Government of India, Ministry of Law, *The Representation of the People Act, 1951 (43 of 1951), As modified up to the 1st August 1967* (Delhi: Manager of Publications, 1967), pp. 50–1.

result was not necessarily to be set aside unless it was proven that the result had been materially affected by the use of a corrupt practice. Under the later terms of the act, the mere proof of violation of any one of the three provisions was sufficient grounds for setting aside the election result.

These provisions were enforced in the Punjab, as in other states, through the filing of election petitions, usually by defeated candidates. Considerable information is available from seven election cases concerned with alleged violations of these provisions in the Punjab, of which six involved organized political groups and will, consequently, be discussed here – four from the 1952 and two from the 1962 elections.[1] Five cases concerned candidates of the Akali Dal and one, in 1962, involved a candidate of the Haryana Lok Samiti. In four cases, charges of corrupt practices were sustained and, in two cases (in 1962), the election results were overturned on grounds related to the provisions mentioned above.[2]

It is obviously not possible from six election cases to estimate in any quantifiable way the extent to which the parties used religious or other communal appeals in the general elections. However, the cases do reveal the kinds of appeals that were made in certain constituencies during two general elections. Moreover, there is considerable evidence in the reported judgments in these cases and from scholarly research that the kinds of appeals referred to in those cases were very widespread in the Punjab.

The earliest case reported is *Sardul Singh Caveeshar v. Hukam Singh and Others*. This case is of considerable interest because the first respondent, Hukam Singh, was at the time the president of the Akali Dal, and because the charges against him referred to the kinds of appeals made primarily through the newspapers owned, controlled by, or sympathetic to Hukam Singh and the Akali Dal. The basic charge of the petitioner was that these newspapers had made systematic appeals on behalf of the Akali Dal candidates to vote for them and against their opponents on the grounds of religion and community, first, by identifying the Akali Dal with the Sikh 'Panth' or community and urging voters to vote for the 'Panthic' party and 'Panthic' candidates; second, by identifying the party symbols with the symbols of the Sikh religion; and, third, by accusing the Congress of interfering with the Sikh religion. The election tribunal was satis-

---

[1] The seventh case concerned an independent candidate in the 1957 elections and the support of the Satguru of the Namdhari sect on his behalf. *Ram Dial v. Sant Lal and Another*, in Government of India, Law Department, *Election Law Reports*, xix (Delhi: Manager of Publications, 1959), 430.

[2] The results were overturned in two of the other cases also, but on other grounds.

fied that all three charges were correct and the judgment provides ample documentation of them. The election was not set aside, however, because the first charge was not considered by the tribunal as constituting an infringement of the law and because it could not be proved that the clear religious appeal made constituted 'undue influence' under the terms of the act, but only a corrupt practice, which did not then constitute unambiguous legal grounds for setting aside the election.[1]

On the first charge, the court decided that the words 'Panth' and 'Panthic' had been in such common use by the Akali Dal for so long that they constituted permissible synonyms for the Akali Dal and its candidates. With regard to the other two charges, the tribunal decided that the Akali Dal agents had committed corrupt practices by attempting to identify the party symbols with the symbols of the Sikh religion, by appealing to voters on the grounds of religion in this way, and by urging voters not to vote for the Congress candidate because he had interfered with the Sikh religion. Although the tribunal did not set aside the election result, its judgment was clear that there had 'been an attempt throughout in these papers to rouse the religious sentiments of the Sikh community to a high pitch and to tell the Sikh people that they gain spiritual advantage and become defenders of the faith by voting for the Akali party candidates and by refraining from voting for the Congress candidates'.[2]

Three other cases against Akali candidates in the 1952 elections raised similar issues. In *Rattan Singh v. Devinder Singh and Others*, more subtle uses of religious symbols and appeals were not considered either corrupt practices or exercise of undue influence. In this case, religious symbols were merely prominently associated with the Akali candidate in election posters. Such a use of religious symbols was not considered a 'systematic appeal on the grounds of religion'.[3] Moreover, the court found no legal objection to 'a general exhortation to the voters of the constituency and particularly to the members of the Sikh community to vote solidly for the nominees of the Akali party so as to make it clear even to the Congress party that they are solidly behind the Panthik party'.[4] In the other two cases, less subtle religious appeals in the form of posters carrying statements to the effect that 'a vote cast for the Akali Party candidate was a vote in favour of the Guru', asking 'the Sikhs to get the blessings of the Gurus by sup-

---

[1] *Sardul Singh Caveeshar v. Hukam Singh and Others, Election Law Reports*, VI, 316–17.
[2] *Ibid.*, 329.
[3] *Rattan Singh v. Devinder Singh and Others, Election Law Reports*, VII, 258.
[4] *Ibid.*, 259.

porting the Akali Party candidate', and suggesting that voters should not vote for the Congress because that party was a threat to the Sikh religion, were considered corrupt practices, although not exercises of undue influence.[1]

Ten years later, under an amended Representation of the People Act (which permitted the courts to set aside elections in which corrupt practices had been committed without requiring evidence that the election result had been materially affected by such practices), the Punjab High Court overturned the election of an Akali candidate from the Dharamkot constituency in 1962. The grounds for setting aside the election in this case were speeches and posters distributed on behalf of the Akali candidate suggesting 'that every Sikh vote should go to the Akali Dal', that Sikhs should vote for the Akali candidate in the constituency because he 'was the proper representative of the Sikh Panth', whereas the Congress candidate 'represented the Hindu-ridden party'.[2] The court also objected to speeches made on behalf of the Akali candidate in which he promised to protect the language and religion of the Sikhs. The court found that the import of the speeches and posters on behalf of the Akali candidate was to communicate the message: 'You must all vote for me, because I alone am the true representative of the Sikh religion while my opponent, being a non-Akali candidate, is an enemy of the Sikh faith.'[3] The judgment of the court also mentioned a poster which sought to identify Jawaharlal Nehru and Pratap Singh Kairon with Aurangzeb and Wazida, Nawab of Sirhind, whom most Sikhs identify as the most notorious historical oppressors of the Sikh religion. While the import of this message did not escape the high court justices either, the court found that the poster was somewhat ambiguous in that it seemed to attack in a direct way only tyrannical rule.[4]

Evidence that such appeals to Sikh voters on behalf of Akali candidates on the basis of religion were not confined to the case before the court is available from a study of the 1962 election campaign in the Sidhwan Bet constituency, written by Baldev Raj Nayar. Nayar states unequivocally that the significant campaigning for the Akali candidate in this constituency was done in the gurudwaras where the candidate or his agent or the priest of the gurudwara appealed to the voters 'frankly and openly in the name of religion'.[5] Nayar refers

[1] *Faqir Chand v. Pritam Singh and Others, Election Law Reports,* VII, 119, and *Gurnam Singh and Another v. Partap Singh and Others, ibid.,* 359–60.
[2] *S. Kultar Singh v. S. Mukhtiar Singh, Election Law Reports,* XXIV, 419.
[3] *Ibid.,* 429.
[4] *Ibid.,* 426–7.
[5] Baldev Raj Nayar, 'Religion and Caste in the Punjab: Sidhwan Bet Constituency', in

here especially to the open identification of the Akali Dal with the Sikh Panth (which the election tribunal in 1952 considered permissible). Among the posters distributed in this constituency was the one referred to in the Dharamkot constituency case, identifying Nehru and Kairon with Aurangzeb and the Nawab of Sirhind.

Nor was the Akali Dal the only political group whose candidates and agents were found guilty of such corrupt practices in 1962. Evidence of the increased communal polarization in Punjab politics at the time of the 1962 election is available from a successful case prosecuted against the winning candidate of the Haryana Lok Samiti in the Jhajjar parliamentary constituency. The Haryana Lok Samiti was the political arm of the Gurukul section of the Arya Samaj in the 1962 election. It was formed in 1961 under the leadership of the dissident Congressman and Arya Samaj leader of Haryana, Sher Singh, and was largely an expression of the movement to protect the Hindi language in Haryana and Punjab, which had begun to gather force since the 1957 'Save Hindi' agitation. The Samiti opposed especially the compulsory teaching of Punjabi in the Haryana region.[1]

The petitioner in this case accused the candidate and his agents not only of appeals on the basis of caste, language, religion, and community, but also of promoting feelings of hatred between Hindus and Sikhs in the Punjab. It is of some interest to note that there is no case reported where such a charge was seriously pressed against a candidate of the Akali Dal. The court did not, however, find that there was sufficient evidence to substantiate the charge made in this case that 'in the speeches delivered at the election meetings it was brought out prominently that the Congress party had entered into an unholy alliance with the Akalis who were a communal organisation and the interests of the Hindus had been placed in [grave] peril and that the people of the Hariana region should resist the imposition of a language foreign to their culture and traditions, namely, Punjabi, and thus a great deal of bitterness and hatred had been created between the Hindus and the Sikhs residing in the Punjab State'.[2] The court did, however, find sufficient evidence to substantiate the charges that the candidate of the Haryana Lok Samiti or his agents had made systematic use of an 'Om Flag', which is a religious symbol of the Arya Samaj and of Hindus generally, to support the candidate's prospects and that they had made systematic appeals on the

Myron Weiner and Rajni Kothari (eds.), *Indian Voting Behaviour: Studies of the 1962 General Elections* (Calcutta: Firma K. L. Mukhopadhyay, 1965), p. 126.
[1] *Pratap Singh Daulta v. Jagdev Singh Sidhanti, Election Law Reports*, xxiv, 381–2, 389–91, 409.
[2] *Ibid.*, 416.

basis of language by claiming that if the Congress candidate were to be elected, the 'Punjabi language would be forced on the Hariana people' because he was an opponent of Hindi, whereas the Haryana Lok Samiti candidate, who had taken a prominent part in the Hindi agitation of 1957, could be counted upon to protect and promote the interests of Hindi-speakers.[1]

The court judgments summarized above provide clear evidence that candidates of the Akali Dal, newspapers supporting the party, and posters distributed from the party offices did appeal directly to the religious sentiments of the Sikhs and to their feelings of communal solidarity in both the 1952 and 1962 elections. Moreover, the Akali Dal has been doing so, successfully, for so long that an election tribunal in 1952 felt compelled to recognize that the Akali Dal had succeeded in identifying its name and its interests with the name and interests of the Sikh community.

It also deserves notice that none of the four cases involving Akali Dal candidates mentioned prominently efforts to appeal to voters in the name of the Punjabi language. At the elite level and in the public statements of prominent leaders, the issues were usually framed in terms of language, but the actual appeals of the Akali candidates (in these cases) stressed religious rather than linguistic themes. In the case involving the Haryana Lok Samiti, appeals both to the interests of Hindus and Hindi-speakers were equally prominent. This contrast suggests that the really salient issue for Sikhs was religion and language was secondary, whereas Hindus in Haryana may have attached at least equal significance to the language issue itself.

A third point which can be suggested on the basis of these election cases is that, at least as far as the Akali Dal candidates were concerned, their appeals were oriented more towards invoking and promoting Sikh solidarity than towards arousing Sikh antagonism towards Hindus. Charges were sometimes reported in the cases that Akali candidates and newspapers referred to the Congress as a Hindu-dominated body or that the Congress was attempting to interfere with the Sikh religion. However, it was usually the Congress which was criticized and not the Hindu community as such. At least no charge was successfully prosecuted in any of the six cases that a candidate or his agents promoted feelings of enmity or hatred between Hindus and Sikhs or Hindi-speakers and Punjabi-speakers.

Finally, it should be noted that there are no election cases available to the author in which similar charges to those made in these six cases were made against candidates of any of the other established

[1] *Ibid.*, 379.

parties in the Punjab, including the Jan Sangh. Either the other party candidates did not make such appeals to language or religion or they were more subtle in doing so or, for some reason, their opponents did not file election petitions against them on these grounds.

Party politics, communal cleavage, and communal coalition-building in the Punjab

Although the Punjab, with its long history of communal conflict and violence and with the existence of political parties appealing directly to the religious sentiments of the people, would seem *prima facie* to support the fears of those concerned about the disintegrative effects of competitive politics in multi-ethnic societies, political patterns in the region since 1947 have not had uniformly catastrophic consequences. In fact, at different times since 1946–7, Punjab politics have moved in three distinctly different directions. In 1946 and 1947, just before the partition, the organization of the political parties reflected the communal organization of society at the time, with catastrophic results. For most of the period between 1947 and the reorganization of the Punjab in 1966, the second pattern prevailed in which a single, large, dominant, secular, broad-based political party, the Congress, performed the tasks of communal political coalition-building and provided stable and, some would say, effective government. In the reorganized and much-diminished Punjab after the general elections of 1967, communal differences were reflected in the organization of the political parties and were prominent in the electoral arena, but they were accommodated after the elections in inter-party coalitions to govern the state. After the general elections of 1972, the second pattern of governance by the Congress was restored.

The three different patterns of Punjab politics have, of course, been influenced by the different communal composition of the Punjab in the three periods in which they were prominent. The tri-communal cleavage of the Punjab just before partition, when Muslims comprised more than half the population, Hindus somewhat less than a third, and Sikhs approximately 14%, was transmitted into the 1946 Punjab legislature in which most Muslim members identified with the Muslim League, most Hindus with the Congress, and most Sikhs with the Akali Dal. The Muslim League party in the assembly comprised seventy-five of the ninety-one Muslim legislators; the Congress comprised forty of the forty-four Hindus; and the Akali Dal had twenty-two of the thirty-two Sikhs (see table 7.1, below). The League had only Muslim members and the Akali Dal only Sikhs. The

Unionist party continued to comprise some Hindus as well as Muslims and the Congress some Sikhs as well as Hindus, but neither party was large enough to play the role of a dominant, inter-communal center party. In post-partition Punjab, after the migration of nearly all Muslims and after the unification of east Punjab in 1954, the population was predominantly either Hindu (64% in 1961) or Sikh (33%). The system of Congress dominance in this period was based on the ability of the Congress to combine both Hindu and Sikh support. Up through the 1962 election, the Congress succeeded in preventing severe erosion of its Hindu base by the Jan Sangh and succeeded also in electing more Sikh legislators than the Akali Dal in both 1952 and 1962.

TABLE 7.1   *Punjab Legislative Assembly election results by party and community, 1946*

Party	Muslims	Hindus	Sikhs	Christians	Not known	Total
Muslim League	75	0	0	0	0	75
Congress	1	40	10	0	0	51
Akali Dal	0	0	22	0	0	22
Unionist Party	15[a]	4	0	1	0	20
Independents	0	0	0	0	7	7
Total	91	44	32	1	7	175

[a] Includes three seats won by one man, Khizr Hyat Khan.

SOURCE. Paul Wallace, 'The Political Party System of Punjab State (India): A Study of Factionalism', unpublished Ph.D. dissertation, Berkeley, University of California, 1966, p. 168.

The Congress was able to maintain both Hindu and Sikh support largely for three reasons – because it was able to evolve a minimally satisfactory compromise on the language issues; because it adhered faithfully to a parity formula by which Sikh representation in all cabinets was 50%; and because the predominant leader of the Congress between 1956 and 1964 was himself a Sikh. The Congress demonstrated its inter-communal character in the 1952 elections, when it elected sixty-nine Hindus, twenty-four Sikhs, and three Muslims.[1] In that election, the Jan Sangh had no victories and the Akali Dal won only thirteen seats.[2] The Congress policy was sufficiently successful for a time to make possible a temporary alliance and merger of the Akali Dal into the Congress during the 1957 elections, as a

[1] Wallace, 'The Political Party System', p. 211.   [2] *Ibid.*, p. 210.

consequence of which Sikh representation in the Congress assembly party nearly equalled that of Hindus (fifty-eight Sikhs, fifty-nine Hindus).[1] When the Congress had to confront the Akali Dal directly again in 1962, it again succeeded in electing more Sikh legislators than its rival. Table 7.2 shows the balance in the 1962 legislature between the Congress and other parties with respect to their communal composition. In that legislature, all non-Congress parties, whether communal parties like the Akali Dal and the Jan Sangh or secular parties such as the CPI and the Socialists, had members exclusively or nearly exclusively from one community. The Congress, however,

TABLE 7.2 *Composition of the Punjab Legislative Assembly by party and community, 1962–7*[a]

Party	Hindu	Sikh	Muslim	Not known	Total
Congress	57	35	4	1	97
Akali Dal	1	17	..	..	18
CPI	..	8	..	1	9
Jan Sangh	7	1	..	..	8
Socialist	4	..	..	..	4
Swatantra	2	..	..	1	3
Independents and others	16	2	..	..	18
Total	87	63	4	3	157[a]

[a] The total number of seats in the table and the totals for the Congress, the Akali Dal, and independents differ from the election results for 1962 because the figures in the table include some members elected after 1962 to replace previous members whose elections were set aside and because they reflect changes of party allegiance of some members after their election. For example, some members elected as independents are included in the table with the Congress.

SOURCE. Compiled from Punjab Vidhan Sabha, *Who's Who, 1962–67* (Chandigarh: Controller, Printing and Stationery, 1964).

had nearly 66% of the Hindu MLAs in its fold; nearly 56% of the Sikh MLAs; and more than twice as many Sikh MLAs as the Akali Dal. Unlike the Unionist party, therefore, the Congress did not lose either its dominant position or its inter-communal character before the reorganization of the state. Thus, the evidence from the Punjab on legislative representation suggests that there is no clear relationship of dependency between communal and political conflict in a regime of competitive political parties. In 1946, before partition, the parties did reflect the communal organization of society. In 1962, before reorganization, they did not because the Congress succeeded in maintaining an inter-communal coalition.

[1] *Ibid.*, p. 248.

In the first general elections in the Punjabi Suba, the Congress, though it failed to win a majority of seats in the assembly, emerged once again as the only large party able to recruit successful candidates from the two major religious communities (see table 7.3). Moreover, the Congress demonstrated its ability to adjust to the new communal balance in the population of the state by electing more Sikhs than Hindus for the first time in its history. As in 1962, the Congress also succeeded in electing more Sikh candidates than the Akali Dal. The

TABLE 7.3 *Composition of the Punjab Legislative Assembly by party and community, 1967 general elections*

Party	Hindu	Sikh	Muslim	Total
Congress	16	31	1	48
Akali Dal (Sant)	1	23	..	24
Akali Dal (Master)	..	2	..	2
Jan Sangh	9	..	..	9
CPI	1	4	..	5
CPM	..	3	..	3
RPI	1	2	..	3
SSP	1	..	..	1
Independents	4	5	..	9
Total	33	70	1	104

SOURCE. Adapted from J. C. Anand, 'General Elections in Punjab', *Political Science Review*, VI, Nos. 3 and 4 and VII, Nos. 1 and 2 (July–September and October–December 1967 and January–March and April–June 1968), 438.

other major parties in the Punjabi Suba Legislative Assembly recruited successful candidates overwhelmingly or exclusively from only one of the two leading communities. The communal composition of the parties in the legislative assembly elected in 1969 (table 7.4) was broadly similar, though there were some important differences. The Congress again succeeded in winning a large number of seats with both Hindu and Sikh candidates, of whom more than twice as many successful candidates were Sikh. However, the Akali Dal this time succeeded in electing more Sikh MLAs than the Congress. All other parties except the CPI again drew their successful candidates exclusively or nearly exclusively from one or the other of the two main religious communities in the Punjab.

The possibilities for political solutions to communal conflicts are not limited to inter-communal parties. Possibilities also exist for direct negotiation and compromise between communal or communally based parties, which occurred in Punjab in 1946 before partition and in the reorganized Punjab after 1967. Although all political parties in 1946 were predominantly based in a single community and two were explicitly communal in orientation, a coalition government was formed consisting of the Congress, the Akali Dal, and the Unionist party, essentially an inter-communal coalition of members from the three main communities.[1] However, the intransigent adherence of Jinnah and the Muslim League to the goal of partition and the persistent demand for total Muslim solidarity to achieve that goal finally destroyed the Unionist party completely. Its Muslim members deserted to the Muslim League as communal tensions increased and as Muslims, Hindus, and Sikhs prepared themselves for civil war.[2]

TABLE 7.4 *Composition of the Punjab Legislative Assembly by party and community, 1969 mid-term elections*

Party	Hindu	Sikh	Muslim	Total
Congress	12	26	..	38
Akali Dal	..	42	1	43
Jan Sangh	7	1	..	8
CPI	2	2	..	4
CPM	..	2	..	2
SSP	2	..	..	2
PSP	..	1	..	1
Swatantra	..	1	..	1
Janata	..	1	..	1
Independents	..	4	..	4
Total	23	80	1	104

SOURCE. Adapted from J. C. Anand, 'Mid-Term Poll in Pubjab', *Political Science Review* x, Nos. 1 and 2 (January–June 1971), 21.

Another deliberate effort to overcome communal conflict through inter-party coalition of communal parties occurred in 1967, when the desire for communal harmony and the political interests of the Akali Dal and the Jan Sangh in capturing political power from the Congress combined in the reorganized Punjab. After the reorganization in 1966, the communal balance was altered in favor of the Sikhs, who now comprised approximately 54 or 55% of the total population compared to the Hindu population of approximately 44 or 45%. The creation of a narrow Sikh majority in the reorganized Punjab provided the conditions for greater inter-party competitiveness,

[1] *Ibid.*, p. 169.
[2] The ministry lasted until 5 March 1947 when governor's rule was promulgated in the state; *ibid.*, pp. 170–1.

which was reflected in the results of the 1967 elections in which the Congress, although it successfully maintained its inter-communal character, failed to win a majority of seats (table 7.3, above). After the 1967 elections, when the non-Congress parties saw an opportunity to gain power and popular sentiment seemed to favor it, the Akali Dal and the Jan Sangh joined in a coalition with the Communist party to form a united front government in the Punjab.[1] Although the coalition government proved to be unstable and some dissident Akali leaders split from the Akali Dal partly on the pretext of the slow pace of enforcing Punjabi as the sole official language of the state, the alliance between the two communal parties was maintained until 22 November 1967 (table 7.5, below). The Akali Dal and the Jan Sangh formed an electoral alliance to fight the 1969 mid-term elections and returned to power in a coalition government thereafter. The alliance between the two communal parties came to an end on 30 June 1970 when the Jan Sangh withdrew from the government, giving as its chief reasons for doing so issues concerning the jurisdiction of a new Punjabi-medium university over Hindi-medium colleges.[2]

Although Punjab political history, therefore, provides evidence to support contradictory viewpoints, namely, that political parties sometimes reflect communal antagonisms and sometimes moderate them, the predominating tendency in Punjab legislative politics has been towards political communal coalition-building, whether this is done by a single broadly aggregative party or by inter-party alliance and coalition. The tension in Punjab politics and the potential for violence have arisen when one party lays claim to the exclusive support of a single community and that claim is contested by other parties. This was the situation produced by the Muslim League in its final drive towards Pakistan. The conflict between the Akali Dal and the Congress has sometimes taken on this character, but the Congress has always had sufficient Sikh representation in its leadership to make it a legitimate contender for the support of the Sikhs in the political arena. The Akali Dal, for its part, has been sufficiently secure in its base within the SGPC that it has not had to fear elimination as a major political force in the Punjab through the party-electoral process. In this way, Punjab politics have in the past two decades displayed tendencies both toward the cross-cutting of social cleavages by the inter-communal Congress and towards the political

[1] Paul R. Brass, 'Coalition Politics in North India', *American Political Science Review*, LXII, No. 4 (December 1968), 1174–91.
[2] *Patriot*, 30 June 1970; see also *Spokesman*, 27 April 1970.

compartmentalization of those cleavages in single-community parties, which then transcend their differences through inter-party coalition.

TABLE 7.5   *Party constituents of Punjab ministries, 1967–71*

	People's United Front Ministry of Gurnam Singh, 8 March 1967– 22 Nov. 1967	Ministry of Lachman Singh Gill, 25 November 1967– 24 August 1968	Coalition Ministry of Gurnam Singh, 17 February 1969– 27 March 1970	Coalition Ministry of Prakash Singh Badal, 27 March– 1970 13 June 1971
Akali Dal (Sant)	x		x	x
Jan Sangh	x		x	x[a]
CPI	x			
Janata Party		x		
RPI		x		

[a] The Jan Sangh ministers resigned from this ministry on 30 June 1970, before its termination.

NOTE. The dates given for each ministry are for the date of formation and termination, but the parties included in each ministry were not all necessarily included from beginning to end.

The two patterns of politics depend for their success on the quality of available political leadership. The Congress system of secular, inter-communal politics worked best under the forceful leadership of Pratap Singh Kairon, who implemented a policy of communal bargaining but challenged the legitimacy of the strictly communal parties. The alternative system of inter-party coalition between communal parties requires accommodative leadership which explicitly recognizes the existence of significant social cleavages but works to accommodate them.[1] In neither case do the politicians and the parties merely reflect social antagonisms.

The difficulty with a political game of this sort, in which some political parties strive to arouse communal sentiments and to organize a solidary communal group, while others seek inter-communal alliances and all parties attempt to avoid violent communal confrontation, is not that political separation may ultimately prove mutually desirable, but that intense opposition to political separation may remain among one or more groups and that the separation may,

[1] See Arend Lijphart, *The Politics of Accommodation: Pluralism and Democracy in the Netherlands* (Berkeley: University of California Press, 1968).

therefore, be catastrophic. Such was the situation in the Punjab in 1946 when the Muslim League was determined upon separation. Hindus were at best reluctantly willing to accept the inevitable, while the Sikhs were intensely opposed to a partition which left them a divided people. In 1966, of course, the situation was quite different in several key respects. First, the leaders of the two most important communities in the Punjab – Punjabi Sikhs and Haryana Hindus – positively favored reorganization. Second, the Punjabi Hindus were consequently isolated in their opposition, deserted by their religious brethren in Haryana. Third, party politics did not reflect precisely the communal organization of the society. Finally, the reorganization was obviously not a division into separate sovereign states.

THE PUNJABI SUBA AND THE GOVERNMENT OF INDIA

One conventional view of the role played by the central government in the settlement of regional issues is that the government of India, too weak and indecisive to act in a positive manner, procrastinates as long as possible when faced with regional demands and comes to a decision only when forced to, frequently succumbing to threats of violence. This view of central government policy is often presented by those who have been opposed to the government's concessions to regional demands and by others who have supported particular regional demands, but have been disaffected by long delays on the part of the center in conceding them.[1]

The history of central government decision and action during the Punjabi Suba movement, and later on the resolution of the conflict over the disposition of the city of Chandigarh, is frequently cited as evidence in support of this view.[2] Closer examination, however, suggests that central government procrastination follows from the underlying rules governing center–state relations in India and that the Government of India often delays for good reason. Moreover, the history of the Government of India's responses to the coercive fasts and threats of self-immolation by Sikh leaders in the Punjab shows that the central government has, more often than not, called the bluff and that when it has made concessions during a fast, either they are meant to save the faster's honor by providing him a face-saving concession or they are concessions which would have been made anyway.

Rather than indicating a procrastination based on vacillation and

---

[1] See, e.g., Punjabi Suba Committee, *Report*, p. 34.
[2] E.g., see *Hindu*, 16 January 1967.

weakness, the central government's initial resistance to the Punjabi Suba demand and the manner in which it ultimately acceded to the demand suggests that the center succeeded, in a long and protracted struggle, in imposing its rules upon Punjab politics. The Government of India, through its own policy statements and through the reports of its commissions, refused to concede the demand or to negotiate seriously with leaders of the movement as long as the demand was presented as based upon religion and as long as it lacked the support of significant groups in both the Punjabi- and Hindi-speaking regions. The resistance of the central government was instrumental in promoting a change in the leadership of the Punjabi Suba movement and in the manner in which its demands were presented. Moreover, between the publication of the States Reorganisation Commission report in 1955 and the *Report of the Parliamentary Committee on the Demand for Punjabi Suba* in 1966, sentiment in Haryana had undergone a shift which made a division of the Punjab acceptable to the important groups in both major regions of the state. The committee itself was careful to point out the changes which had taken place during that time.[1]

Moreover, the central government refused to be coerced by the fasts of both Sant Fateh Singh and Master Tara Singh in 1961, which ended in their humiliation, not that of the government. It refused to make an open concession to Sant Fateh Singh in December 1966, granting the city of Chandigarh to Punjab when the Sant threatened to immolate himself. It took no action to prevent the death by fasting of Sardar Darshan Singh Pheruman in connection with the Chandigarh issue in October 1969.[2] Nor is it clear whether the fast and threat of self-immolation by Sant Fatch Singh on the issue of Chandigarh in January–February 1970 influenced the final decision of the Government of India to award Chandigarh to Punjab or whether the Sant merely anticipated and capitalized upon that decision to enhance his own leadership and prestige.[3]

The evidence suggests, in fact, that the central government has refused to be coerced into the position of imposing a decision on evenly balanced contending forces. The center will support a position acceptable to a majority (e.g. Punjabi Sikhs and Haryana Hindus

[1] Punjabi Suba Committee, *Report*, pp. 5 and 7.
[2] Sardar Darshan Singh Pheruman, an 84-year-old Sikh leader, a former Akali, but in 1969 the Punjab Swatantra Party chairman, began a fast-unto-death for the inclusion of Chandigarh in the Punjab in August 1969. He died on 27 October. See the issues of *Spokesman* for August, September, and October for accounts of this fast and its complicated political implications.
[3] On this fast, see *Spokesman*, 19 and 26 January and 9 February 1970.

on the Punjabi Suba), but opposed by a minority (Punjabi Hindus in this case). It will also play the role of mediator on such issues as the disposition of Chandigarh and other areas in dispute between the new states of Haryana, Punjab, and Himachal Pradesh. However, the center will not impose a decision unless the balance of sentiment among important groups favors it. Its mediation also always provides concessions to both sides in a dispute. For example, although the center awarded Chandigarh to Punjab in February 1970, it simultaneously awarded most of the Hindu-majority tahsil of Fazilka to Haryana.[1] Thus, far from demonstrating central weakness, vacillation, and submission to force, the history of the Punjabi Suba demand demonstrates that the center follows consistent rules in making policy; that it has considerable staying power in doing so, which ought not to be confused with procrastination based on weakness; and that its policy-makers seek a role of mediator or arbiter, appropriate to a diverse and pluralized federal system.

[1] *Ibid.*, 19 February 1970; *India News*, 13 February 1970.

8

ELECTORAL POLITICS AND
COMMUNAL CLEAVAGE IN THE
PUNJABI SUBA

It often has been argued in the literature on political development that competitive political parties in developing multi-ethnic societies are likely at best to reflect and at worst to exacerbate ethnic antagonisms. The argument has been based upon three simplifying assumptions. One assumption, that linguistic and religious attachments are 'givens', involves an underestimation of the ambiguities which often exist in the relations among ethnic groups as processes of ethnic mobilization and differentiation proceed. The second assumption is that the capacities of less-than-charismatic political leaders to mediate ethnic group conflicts are highly limited. It has been suggested in the previous chapter that these mediating skills have, in fact, been more widespread in the Punjab. The third assumption is that political organizations tend to be shaped by their social and ethnic environments. This assumption underestimates the extent to which political organizations in fact shape their environments and the identities of group members. That these assumptions do, in fact, oversimplify the interrelationships among ethnic groups and political organizations is demonstrated by the complexity of the interactions between social and political structures in the Punjab during the past century.

Historically, it has been demonstrated in chapter 6 that there has been a long-term tendency towards increased differentiation between and segmentation of the Hindu and Sikh communities in the Punjabi-speaking region. However, the process of differentiation has not led to a complete separation of the two communities in either social structure or culture. Moreover, whereas some political organizations have fostered separatist tendencies, others have worked towards inter-communal communication.

It was shown in chapter 6 that tendencies toward separation of the Sikh community from Hindus in the Punjab and towards strengthening of internal communications among Sikhs developed in the Singh

Sabha movement in the nineteenth century, which attempted to consolidate the different Sikh sects into a single, cohesive religious community; in the development of a network of schools under the Chief Khalsa Diwan to impart both religious and secular instruction to Sikh students; in the formation in the 1920s of the Shiromani Gurudwara Prabhandak Committee (SGPC) to administer the Sikh gurudwaras and to provide a mechanism of representation for the governance of the religious affairs of the Sikhs; in the formation of the Akali Dal at the same time to articulate Sikh political demands; in the increasing identification of Sikhs with the Punjabi language written in the Gurumukhi script; and in the publication of books and newspapers in Punjabi reflecting Sikh social, religious, and political aspirations. Similar tendencies developed among Hindus in the Punjab, though with less force. The Arya Samaj attempted to unify Hindus in the Punjab as the Singh Sabha movement attempted to unify Sikhs. The Arya Samaj also developed a network of schools, imparting religious and secular instruction to Hindu students. Moreover, these schools have prompted the use of Hindi in Devanagari script among Hindus, which has encouraged the development of modern Hindi literature and a Hindi press in the Punjab. Both the Arya Samaj and the Jan Sangh, a Hindu communal party, have been important political forces mobilizing Hindus in the politics of post-1947 Punjab. There is, however, no counterpart in the Hindu community to the SGPC, which is the pre-eminent institution and consolidating force in the Sikh community in the Punjab.

Tendencies toward segmentation of the two communities in the Punjab have been modified in important respects both socially and politically. Although the boundaries between Hindus and Sikhs have become more sharply defined during the past century, there remain Hindu and Sikh sects and individuals in both religions who do not consider the differences between the two creeds to be substantial. In addition, the allegiances of many of the low caste or Scheduled Caste groups in the Punjab, who comprise more than 20% of the population of the state, are by no means clear. Moreover, the language division between Hindus and Sikhs in the Punjab is more symbolic than real. Hindus and Sikhs alike in the Punjab can communicate effectively in both rural and urban areas in Punjabi, though many Hindus prefer to use Hindi and the Devanagari script for certain purposes. Politically, the ideology of secularism and composite nationalism is important even in the Punjab, where the Congress and the Communist parties, particularly, adhere to it and seek to make it effective by appealing to both Hindus and Sikhs. Finally, factional politics and personal political opportunism have often cut across both communal and ideological differences among the parties and have provided a basis for movement, communication, and alliances of individuals and groups across party lines.

These contradictory tendencies towards segmentation and inter-communal communication have been expressed in Punjab politics in the drive by some parties, particularly the Akali Dal and the Jan Sangh, either to lay claim to the exclusive support of a single community or to base themselves on the support of only one community; in the contrary attempts of the secular parties to combine support from both communities; and in the failure of both types of parties to maintain internal cohesion, particularly in their legislative groups. In the process of interaction among these three types of political forces, both the communal composition of the population and the aspirations of political parties and individuals to acquire political power propel the system toward a variant of the 'politics of accom-modation' in which a premium is placed on political communal coalition-building. The differences between the communal and secular parties then become differences not over whether to construct communal coalitions but over when and how. The Congress follows the strategy of the aggregative party in its organizational structure and maintains an inter-communal character in both the electoral and legislative arenas. The communal parties base their organizations and electoral appeals on one community but form electoral alliances with each other during the elections and governing coalitions after-wards. In this process, the political parties do not merely reflect the pre-existing cleavages of the society, but they shape, deflect, and accommodate them.

I propose to demonstrate this general argument in the remainder of this chapter by analyzing the relationship between the bases of electoral support for political parties in the Punjab and patterns of communal cleavage. The remainder of this chapter is divided into two parts. In the first part, data on state electoral returns are used to outline the structure of the party system in the Punjab. Although data are analyzed for 1952 through 1969, they are organized to con-form to post-1966 Punjab boundaries. In the second part of the chapter, an ecological analysis of the religious, language, and caste bases of political party support in the Punjab is presented, which is based upon correlations between electoral returns and census data for groups of constituencies and corresponding tahsils and groups of tahsils.

ELECTORAL SUPPORT FOR POLITICAL PARTIES
AND COMMUNAL CLEAVAGE IN THE PUNJAB

State patterns

Tables 8.1 and 8.2 show the percentage of votes polled and the number of seats won by all political parties which have won seats in the Punjab Legislative Assembly since 1952.[1] The tables show the results of all general and mid-term elections held in the Punjab since independence except for the mid-term election in PEPSU in 1954. The data are for elections held only in those areas which fall within the present boundaries of the Punjab.

It is possible from these two tables to identify the main political forces in Punjab politics, the persistent features of patterns of inter-party competition, and the long-term tendencies in the party system. Twenty-six political groups have contested elections in the Punjab since 1952, of which fifteen have won at least one seat in one election. Even the latter figure, however, exaggerates the number of significant political contestants in the Punjab electoral arena both over time and at any one time. The number of significant contestants over time would be reduced to eleven if those political groups which have won only one seat in one election (PSP, Forward Bloc, Janata, and Swatantra) were eliminated. Moreover, the maximum number of political groups which have won at least one seat in the Punjab in any single election is nine, in 1969. That figure has twice been as low as four in both 1957 and 1962. The figures for the number of groups which have won seats in each election are as follows: 1952, 6; 1957, 4; 1962, 4; 1967, 8; 1969, 9; 1972, 4.

Tables 8.1 and 8.2 have been arranged in a way which is designed to order the varying degrees of fragmentation and complexity in Punjab politics into five major groupings of parties, which have persisted over time.[2] These five groupings reflect five distinct, reasonably discrete sets of political forces. The first group consists of the Congress, its splinters, and the non-Communist left.

What is most significant about the first group of parties is the overwhelming predominance of the Congress within it, in marked con-

---

[1] The figures are for only those constituencies which fall within the post-1966 reorganized boundaries of the Punjab. The tables have been set up to be comparable with the tables on the West Bengal elections in Marcus F. Franda, 'Electoral Politics in West Bengal: The Growth of the United Front', *Pacific Affairs*, XLII, No. 3 (Fall 1969), 279–93.

[2] Cf. *ibid.*, pp. 282–3.

TABLE 8.1   *Percentage of votes polled by political parties in the Punjab,[a] 1952–72[b]*

Political party	1952	1957	1962	1967	1969	1972
Congress	31.3	48.6	45.7	35.7	39.2	42.8
SSP (founded in 1964)				0.7	0.8⎱	
PSP	3.4[c]	0.9	0.7	0.5	0.5⎰	0.9[e]
Forward Bloc (FB)	2.2	..	..	..	..	..
	36.9	49.5	46.4	38.7	40.5	43.7
Akali Dal	24.0	..	20.7	..	29.5	..
Akali Dal (Sant)	..	..	..	20.5	..	27.7
Akali Dal (Master)	..	..	..	4.2	..	..
Janata (founded in 1969)					1.7	..
	24.0	..	20.7	24.7	31.2	27.7
Jan Sangh	4.0	7.2	7.6	9.8	9.0	5.0
Swatantra (founded in 1959)			2.4	0.5	0.9	0.0
	4.0	7.2	10.0	10.3	9.9	5.0
Scheduled Caste Federation (SCF)	3.8	6.2	..	..	..	..
RPI	..	..	2.8	1.8	1.1	0.2
CPI	6.1	17.7	9.8	5.2	5.0	6.5
CP(L)	2.1	..	..	..	..	..
CPM (founded in 1964)				3.3	2.9	3.3
	8.2	17.7	9.8	8.5	7.9	9.8
Unsuccessful parties and independents	23.1	19.4	10.3	16.0	9.4	13.6
Total	100.0	100.0	100.0	100.0	100.0	100.0
F_e[d]	0.836	0.723	0.732	0.802	0.747	0.732

[a] Baxter's data are arranged according to 1969 state boundaries.

[b] The data include all general and mid-term elections in post-independence Punjab, except the mid-term elections in PEPSU in 1954.

[c] This figure represents the combined proportion of votes won by the old SP and KMPP.

[d] F_e is Douglas Rae's index of electoral party system fractionalization. The formula for computation is:

$$F_e = 1 - \left(\sum_{i=1}^{} T_i^2 \right)$$

'where T_i = any party's decimal share of the vote'. The index, on a scale of 0 to 1, measures 'the probability that any two randomly selected voters will have chosen different parties in any given election'. A value of 0.0 would apply only to one-party systems; a value of 1.0 could not be achieved in practice since it would mean that every voter chose a different party. See Douglas Rae, *The Political Consequences of Electoral Laws* (New Haven: Yale University Press, 1967), pp. 53–8.

[e] This figure is the percentage share of the popular vote won by the Socialist Party, formed after the merger of the SSP and the PSP in 1971.

SOURCE. Compiled from Baxter, *District Voting Trends in India*, pp. 235–6; 1972 figures provided by courtesy of Election Commission of India.

TABLE 8.2 *Number and percentage of seats won by political parties in Punjab Legislative Assembly elections, 1952–72*

Political party	1952 No.	1952 %	1957 No.	1957 %	1962 No.	1962 %	1967 No.	1967 %	1969 No.	1969 %	1972 No.	1972 %
Congress	60	54.54	71	82.56	49	56.98	48	46.15	38	36.54	66	63.46
SSP (founded in 1964)							1	0.96	2	1.92	..	..
PSP	..	..	..	..	..	..	..	..	1	0.96	..	..
Forward Bloc (FB)	1	0.91	..	..	..	..	..	..	..	..	..	..
	61	55.45	71	82.56	49	56.98	49	47.12	41	39.42	66	63.46
Akali Dal	31	28.18	..	..	19	22.09	..	..	43	41.35	..	..
Akali Dal (Sant)	..	..	..	..	..	..	24	23.08	..	..	24	23.08
Akali Dal (Master)	..	..	..	..	..	..	2	1.92	..	..	..	..
Janata (founded in 1969)									1	0.96	..	..
	31	28.18	..	..	19	22.09	26	25.00	44	42.31	24	23.08
Jan Sangh	..	..	5	5.81	4	4.65	9	8.65	8	7.69	..	..
Swatantra (founded in 1959)			..	..	..	..	..	..	1	0.96	..	..
	..	..	5	5.81	4	4.65	9	8.65	9	8.65	..	..
Scheduled Caste Federation (SCF)	1	0.91	1	1.16	..	..	..	..	..	..	..	..
RPI	..	..	..	..	..	..	3	2.88	..	..	..	..
	1	0.91	1	1.16	..	..	3	2.88	..	..	..	..
CPI	6	5.46	3	3.49	9	10.47	5	4.81	4	3.85	10	9.61
CP(L)	2	1.81	..	..	..	..	..	..	..	..	..	..
CPM (founded in 1964)							3	2.88	2	1.92	1	0.96
	8	7.27	3	3.49	9	10.47	8	7.69	6	5.77	11	10.58
Unsuccessful parties and independents	9	8.19	6	6.98	5	5.81	9	8.65	4	3.85	3	2.89
Total	110	100.00	86	100.00	86	100.00	104	99.98	104	100.00	104	100.00
$F_p{}^a$		0.620		0.315		0.613		0.721		0.687		0.534

[a] F_p is Rae's index of parliamentary party system fractionalization. It is computed according to the same formula described in table 8.1, n.d., except that seat shares are substituted for vote shares; Rae, *The Political Consequences of Electoral Laws*, p. 62.

SOURCE. Same as for table 8.1.

trast to the situation in U.P., Bihar, and Bengal.[1] In the Punjab, the Congress has always been for all practical purposes the *only* major secular party of the non-Communist left. It is in fact the only Punjab

[1] On Bengal, see *ibid.* On U.P. and Bihar, see Paul R. Brass, 'Coalition Politics in North India', *The American Political Science Review*, LXII, No. 4 (December 1968), 1176–8.

party which is both multi-communal in theory and practice and moderate socialist in ideology. The Congress alone occupies the center position in the party system in both communal and ideological respects.

There are two important features of Congress electoral strength and seat-winning capacity to be noted. One is that the Congress has been from the beginning and remained as of 1972 by a considerable margin the strongest political party in the Punjab in terms of electoral support. The second feature to note, however, is that Congress fortunes in the electoral arena have varied greatly over time in the Punjab. The Congress emerged after independence in the Punjab as the weakest Congress organization in any of the major Indian regions. Its proportion of the popular vote in 1952, 31.3%, is the lowest proportion of votes won by any Congress organization in any of the fifteen major states since independence.[1] The Congress found itself in this position first because it had not been the main political force in the pre-independence Punjab; second, because it was divided into two bitterly opposed factional groups; and third, because it lacked an authoritative leader who transcended factional divisions in the party.[2] In the period between 1952 and 1957, however, the situation of the Punjab Congress was radically transformed in two respects. A single, dynamic leader, Pratap Singh Kairon, took control of both the party organization and the government, transforming bi-factional cleavage into single-group dominance.[3] Second, the Congress succeeded under his leadership in forging an inter-communal alliance of Hindus and Sikhs, including the merger of the Akali Dal into the Congress in the 1957 elections. The consequence was a dramatic increase in the electoral strength of the Congress in 1957, which was largely maintained through 1962 despite the withdrawal of the Akali Dal from the Congress before the 1962 election. In the period between 1957 and 1969, however, the Congress suffered a decline, first, because of the pressure for Punjabi Suba, with the consequent growth of communal-linguistic politics; and second, and even

---

[1] This statement is based on an examination of the figures compiled by Craig Baxter, *District Voting Trends in India: A Research Tool* (New York: Columbia University Press, 1969).

[2] For a comparison of the post-independence Punjab Congress organizational development with that of the U.P. and Bihar Congress, see Paul R. Brass, 'Political Participation, Institutionalization and Stability in India', *Government and Opposition*, IV, No. 1 (Winter 1969), 29–31.

[3] *Ibid.* For more detailed analyses of the history of Punjab factional politics, see Baldev Raj Nayar, 'Punjab', in Myron Weiner (ed.), *State Politics in India* (Princeton, N.J.: Princeton University Press, 1968), pp. 458–80, and Paul Wallace, 'The Political Party System of Punjab State (India): A Study of Factionalism', unpublished Ph.D. dissertation, University of California, Berkeley, 1966.

more important, because of the removal of Pratap Singh Kairon from the leadership of the Congress, his assassination in 1964, and the consequent fragmentation of the Congress into a multiplicity of factional groups without an authoritative leader once again. After the Congress split in 1969, the Congress under Mrs Gandhi's leadership restored its strength in 1972 to a position considerably better in popular support than in either 1967 or 1969, though below its peak strength in 1957 and 1962.

The fluctuations in the seat-winning capacity of the Congress have been even more dramatic than its shifts in popular support. The Congress won only a slight majority of seats in 1952. It then moved to its peak strength of 82.6% of the seats in 1957, but declined steadily in every election thereafter through the 1969 mid-term elections. In 1969, for the first time, the Congress won fewer seats than its leading rival, the Akali Dal. Then, in 1972, the Congress position of dominance in seats won was restored to a peak higher than that of any election except 1957.

The second group of parties consists of the Akali Dal and its splinters. There are three features of this grouping which deserve attention. First, despite the splintering of the Akali Dal into two in the period between 1962 and 1967 and despite the existence of a new splinter group in the post-1967 period, there has been a tendency for one entity to be dominant in vote-winning and even more in seat-winning capacity. Divisions in the leadership of the Akali movement have not so far been carried down successfully into its Jat Sikh electoral base, which persists as the single largest and relatively most cohesive electoral base in the Punjab.[1]

The second prominent feature of this party grouping is its persistent strength. If the Congress has been always the strongest party in the Punjab, the Akali Dal or one of its splinters has been always the second strongest party by a wide margin, in all elections it has contested. In fact, the distance between the Akali Dal and the third largest party has always been greater than the distance between it and the Congress. Nor has the strength of the Akali Dal, unlike that of the Congress, fluctuated very much. The Akali Dal polled 24.0% of the popular vote in 1952. In 1962, despite the fact that it left some of its former leaders and members behind in the Congress and despite the fact that the Congress itself was led by a Sikh, the Akali Dal polled 20.7% of the vote. In 1967, the combined vote of the two Akali parties just passed the previous peak of Akali strength in 1952. In 1969, the Akali Dal made a significant gain in both inner

---

[1] See pp. 384–6, below.

cohesion after the death of Master Tara Singh and in popular support, despite the existence of a splinter group. In 1972, the Akali Dal (Sant) held most of its percentage vote share despite a dramatic loss in its percentage seat share.

The third important feature of this grouping or, rather, of its leading party, the Akali Dal, is that there is a top on both its electoral strength and its seat-winning capacity. The Akali Dal has never passed the 30% barrier in electoral support and it does not have the capacity to win a majority of seats by itself. In 1962, the Akali Dal won 22.1% of the seats; in 1967, the two Dals won 25.0% of the seats, still less than the proportion of seats won in 1952; in 1969, the united Akali Dal, aided by an electoral alliance with the Jan Sangh, surpassed the Congress and won 41.4% of the seats in the Punjab assembly. After the 1967 and 1969 elections, the Akali Dal played the role of the leader of a non-Congress governing coalition of parties (table 7.5), in which it was the dominant partner in a precariously balanced coalition with a precarious majority in the assembly.[1] However, the Akali Dal in 1972 was set back to its 1967 position in seats won.

The third grouping of parties is a somewhat arbitrary one in that it includes a Hindu communal party based primarily in the cities and towns of the Punjab and a right-wing secular party based among rich peasants and landlords. It is customary, however, to place these two parties close together in a left–right spectrum.[2] Nothing is lost here in doing so. Rather, it serves to emphasize the dominance of communal forces among the non-Congress political parties in the Punjab. Swatantra lacks a base in the state because the Akali Dal takes the vote of the rich Sikh peasants and because Hindu conservatism finds an outlet in the Jan Sangh. Consequently, the third grouping is like the other two in the dominance within it of a single party. The Jan Sangh polled 4.0% of the popular vote in 1952, but won no seats in the Punjab region. It achieved major party status in 1957 by winning 7.2% of the popular vote and five seats. Its electoral strength and its seat-winning capacity increased somewhat in 1967 and 1969 when it benefited from its governing and electoral alliances with the Akali Dal. However, in 1972, the Jan Sangh was reduced to minor party status once again, polling only 5.0% of the vote and winning no seats in the legislative assembly.

[1] On post-1967 coalition politics in the Punjab, U.P., and Bihar, see Brass, 'Coalition Politics'.

[2] For example, Franda does so in the article previously cited. For an analysis of the similarities, differences, and relations between the two parties in U.P., see Paul R. Brass, 'Uttar Pradesh', in Myron Weiner (ed.), *State Politics*, pp. 88–94.

The fourth grouping consists of only one party, the Scheduled Caste Federation and its descendant, the Republican Party of India (RPI). Before the 1969 elections, the RPI split into two wings, but the splinter RPI(A) polled only 0.5% of the vote and won no seats. This grouping is significant in two respects – in its persistence and in the decline of its popular support. A party of the low castes has contested every election in post-independence Punjab. However, only in 1967 did the Scheduled Caste party win more than one seat. In three elections, in 1962, 1969, and 1972, it won none. Since 1957, there has been a steady decline in electoral support for the party representing the political interests of the Scheduled Castes.

The fifth group of parties consists of the Communist parties, of which there have been three in the post-independence Punjab. The Lal Communist Party (CP(L)), founded in 1948, was a splinter from the CPI. It fought the 1952 elections separately, but disintegrated thereafter. Its leaders returned to the CPI between 1952 and 1954.[1] The current split into the CPI and CPM occurred in the Punjab in 1964. Two features of this grouping of parties are important. One is that, with the exception of 1957 when the CPI gained considerable new support among Sikh voters in the absence of an Akali opposition party, the level of electoral support for the Communist parties has been relatively stable, ranging from 7.9% to 9.8%. The second distinctive feature of this grouping, in contrast to the others, is its persistent fragmentation. In all other groupings, one party has always been dominant in every election. In the Communist grouping, in three of the six post-independence elections, there have been two major contenders for both electoral support and seats. However, the CPI did much better than the CPM in number of seats won in 1972 because of its electoral alliance with the Congress.

The final grouping includes those tiny parties which have never won seats in the Punjab and independents. This grouping provides a measure of the extent to which the institutionalized parties have succeeded in establishing their dominance in the electoral arena. There has been an over-all decline in the proportion of the popular vote won by these scattered groups and individuals and, of course, a corresponding increase in the proportion of votes won by the established parties, when the first two elections are compared with the last four. Although the 1967 vote in this grouping did increase significantly from 1962, it did not go as high as the corresponding vote of either 1952 or 1957. In 1969, the proportion of both votes and

[1] See Selig S. Harrison, *India: The Most Dangerous Decades* (Princeton, N.J.: Princeton University Press, 1960), p. 203.

seats won by unsuccessful parties and independents was lower than it had ever been since independence. However, even at that, the proportion of votes won in this grouping was higher than that for every other political party in the state except the Congress and the Akali Dal and the number of seats won here was greater than the number won by any other political party except the Congress, the Akali Dal, and the Jan Sangh.

The five groupings reveal both persistent features and some significant changes over time. The persistent features include the very existence of the five groups over six elections, with only one group showing tendencies toward disintegration; the dominance of one party in four of the groupings; the dominance of communal parties in the opposition to the Congress and either the extreme weakness (on the right) or the fragmentation (on the left) of non-communal opposition to the Congress. The significant changes over time include the near-elimination of the Scheduled Caste parties from the electoral arena as serious contestants and the decline of the independent share of votes and seats.

It is easier to pinpoint particular features of persistence and change than to characterize the structure of the system as a whole and its central tendencies. A major difficulty in doing so arises from the sometimes striking differences between patterns of electoral support and party strength in the legislature. An application of Douglas Rae's index of party system fractionalization to the vote shares (F_e) of the parties shows a high degree of fractionalization in the Punjab party system in all elections.[1] Electoral fractionalization has never been lower than 0.723 (in 1957) and has been above 0.80 twice (in 1952 and 1967). The electoral party system, therefore, can be characterized as a fragmented extreme multi-party system. However, the index of party system fractionalization in the legislature (F_p) has shown greater variation over time. Legislative fractionalization has been high in 1952, 1962, 1967, and 1969, but it has always been lower than the lowest measure of electoral fractionalization. Still, in four of the six elections, extreme multi-partism has existed in the legislature as well as in the popular vote. However, in 1957, the distribution of seat shares produced, unequivocally, a one-party dominant system in the Punjabi region, whereas the distribution in 1972 produced moderate multi-partism with only three major parties, of which two were clearly dominant.

[1] Compare the figures for F_e in Punjab with the mean value of 0.69 for ninety-eight elections in twenty European and English-speaking countries. Douglas Rae, *The Political Consequences of Electoral Laws* (New Haven: Yale University Press, 1967), p. 127.

Behind the fractionalization in the electoral system and the variability in the structure of the legislative party system, there is one underlying structural principle in the system in the opposition between the Congress and the Akali Dal, which has only once been eliminated in 1957 when the two parties merged.

If trends over the six elections are considered, then it appears that there has been a persistent tendency, except in 1957, toward dualism in the system in the opposition between the Congress and the Akali Dal and in the proportion of votes and seats won by these two leading contenders. Over the six elections, the Congress and the Akali Dal have persistently been the two strongest parties. Their combined proportion of the popular vote has ranged from approximately 55 to 70% and their combined proportion of seats in the assembly has ranged from approximately 70 to somewhat over 85%. However, it is apparent that this dualistic pattern deviates significantly from a classic two-party system because one of the two main parties, the Congress, has always been electorally stronger than the other; because, consequently, the smaller of the two parties must form either electoral or parliamentary alliances (or both) with other parties to achieve power in the system; and because, for the same reason, the two main parties do not control enough of the electorate and the distribution of seats in the assembly to monopolize power. The chief obstacles to the development of a classic two-party system have been the deliberate limitation by the Akali Dal of the scope of its constituency to the Sikh community; the strong tendencies toward the institutionalization of Jan Sangh and Communist strength in the electorate; and the persistent importance of the independent vote.

The existence of five distinct party groupings in the Punjab over time and the tendencies for at least four of the groupings to become institutionalized suggests also a comparison with the Dutch system described by Lijphart, in which five parties, reflecting the religious and class cleavages of the society, dominated the electoral and parliamentary arena but did not permit their fundamental differences to interfere with the formation of governing coalitions.[1] In such a system, all the leading parties have relatively discrete and secure electoral bases, no single party can achieve a governing majority by itself, but all the major parties are willing to form alliances and enter coalitions with each other. Clearly, for this kind of pattern to develop in the Punjab, a reduction in the strength of the Congress and in its ability to achieve a legislative majority by itself would be required.

[1] Arend Lijphart, *The Politics of Accommodation: Pluralism and Democracy in the Netherlands* (Berkeley: University of California Press, 1968).

In order to assess the long-term likelihood of the two possibilities – dualism or multiple segmentation – it is necessary to consider the electoral bases of support for the parties.

RELIGIOUS, LANGUAGE, AND CASTE BASES OF PARTY SUPPORT IN THE PUNJAB

Religion, language, and caste have been the predominant symbols in Punjab politics in the post-independence era. They are also the most important explanatory variables in analyzing the bases of party support in the electorate for most Punjab parties. The parties do differ, however, in the extent to which their electoral support bases are confined to one community over time or combine support from different communities.

In the remainder of this chapter, the analysis will be focused upon fifteen 'cultural' variables pertaining to religion, language, and caste, which are broken up into rural and urban dimensions and, in the case of Scheduled Castes, into a literacy dimension as well. The statistics used are simple correlation coefficients (Pearson's r). The units of analysis are groups of constituencies and tahsils arranged into geographically discrete and exactly comparable units.[1]

Congress

There are two predominant hypotheses about the nature of Congress electoral support in the Punjab over time, both of which have been elaborated by Baldev Raj Nayar. The first is the hypothesis of changing coalitions. The argument here is that the Congress, as a broadly aggregative and secular political party, has deliberately attempted both to accommodate different religious, language, and caste groups in the Punjab and to avoid accommodating one group at the expense of another. Since this is by nature a difficult process and since different groups are likely to become disaffected by Congress policies or to make unacceptable demands at different times, the political coalitions constructed by the Congress do not last, but change from election to election. Thus, Nayar has argued specifically that the religious and ethnic bases of Congress electoral support

[1] The electoral and census data were grouped into geographically discrete and comparable units in which the legislative assembly constituency and the tahsil formed the building blocks. In the reorganized Punjab, there were thirty-seven tahsils. The process of matching tahsils with constituencies from the 1956 constituency delimitation yielded fourteen groups and from the 1966 constituency delimitation yielded nineteen groups, of which two were discarded because they could not be matched exactly.

changed fundamentally from 1952 to 1957 and from 1957 to 1962 as follows:

During the 1952 general elections the Congress party firmly opposed the demand for Punjabi Suba and was able to win considerable Hindu and Harijan support. Prior to the 1957 general elections, the Congress party conceded the regional formula to the Akali Dal and allowed the Dal to merge politically into the Congress party; in this manner it was able to secure larger support from that part of the Sikh community which was under the influence of the Akali Dal, but in the process it also lost a large part of the Hindu vote. Before the 1962 general elections the Congress party firmly opposed the Akali demand for Punjabi Suba and refused to be intimidated by Akali agitations, and consequently was able to count on Hindu and Harijan votes to a greater extent than would have been possible if it had made further concessions to the Akali Dal.[1]

Table 8.3 shows the correlations between the Congress share of the popular vote and the percentage of Hindus, Sikhs, Scheduled Castes, Hindi-speakers, and Punjabi-speakers in the Punjab for all elections since 1957 and for Hindus and Sikhs since 1952. The correlations support fully Nayar's hypothesis and his specific descriptions of the changing bases of Congress electoral support between 1952 and 1962. The correlation in 1952 between the Congress vote and the proportion of Hindus in the population was positive; that between the Congress vote and the proportion of Sikhs was negative. In 1957, there was a dramatic reversal, such that the correlations with Hindus, Hindi-speakers, and Scheduled Castes were all negative, but with Sikhs and Punjabi-speakers (except urban) were all positive. Moreover, seven of the correlations with cultural variables in 1957 were significant at the 0.05 level or higher. In 1962, the areas of Congress support again shifted. In this election, the correlations between the Congress vote and percent Hindus (except urban Hindus), Hindi-speakers (except urban), and Scheduled Castes were all positive; those between the Congress vote share and percentage of Sikhs and Punjabi-speakers were all negative. Although only two of the correlations with cultural variables in 1962 were significant at the 0.05 level, the swing data, showing the relationship between shifts in the Congress vote and percent of the religious and ethnic groups, show ten such correlations. All correlations between the Congress swing, 1957 to 1962, and percent of Hindus, Hindi-speakers, and Scheduled Castes were positive; those for total Hindus and rural Hindus, total and rural Hindi-speakers, and for total Scheduled Castes and rural male literates among Scheduled Castes were significant at the 0.05 level or lower. Conversely, all correlations between Congress swing

[1] Baldev Raj Nayar, *Minority Politics in the Punjab* (Princeton, N.J.: Princeton University Press, 1966), pp. 300–1.

and percent Sikh and percent Punjabi-speakers were negative – those for total and rural Sikh and total and rural Punjabi-speakers being significant at the 0.05 level or lower. In other words, the evidence is considerable that there was a significant shift in voting patterns between 1957 and 1962 in Sikh and Punjabi-speaking areas away from the Congress and in Hindu, Hindi-speaking, and Scheduled Caste areas to the Congress.

TABLE 8.3   *Correlation matrix of cultural variables and Congress vote shares for Punjab grouped constituencies, 1952–69*

Variable	1952[a]	1957	1962	1957–62 swing	1967	1969	1967–9 swing
	N=8	N=14	N=14	N=14	N=17	N=17	N=17
1. Total Hindu	0.39	−0.54[b]	0.40	0.64[c]	−0.38	0.15	0.33
2. Rural Hindu		−0.42	0.47[b]	0.57[b]	−0.27	0.13	0.25
3. Urban Hindu		−0.29	−0.07	0.22	−0.28	0.08	0.22
4. Total Sikh	−0.37	0.60[c]	−0.41	−0.69[c]	0.37	−0.06	−0.25
5. Rural Sikh		0.58[b]	−0.29	−0.63[c]	0.43[b]	−0.12	−0.34
6. Urban Sikh		−0.07	−0.42	−0.12	−0.23	0.23	0.31
7. Total Scheduled Caste		−0.33	0.43	0.47[b]	0.03	0.51[b]	0.38
8. Rural Scheduled Caste		−0.20	0.40	0.35	0.10	0.34	0.21
9. Rural male literate Scheduled Caste		−0.43	0.46[b]	0.57[b]	−0.02	0.22	0.18
10. Total Hindi-speakers		−0.62[c]	0.27	0.65[c]	−0.27	0.12	0.25
11. Rural Hindi-speakers		−0.49[b]	0.34	0.57[b]	−0.17	0.12	0.19
12. Urban Hindi-speakers		−0.33	−0.07	0.25	−0.25	0.03	0.17
13. Total Punjabi-speakers		0.64[c]	−0.27	−0.67[c]	0.26	−0.11	−0.23
14. Rural Punjabi-speakers		0.60[c]	−0.15	−0.58[b]	0.36	−0.14	−0.31
15. Urban Punjabi-speakers		−0.06	−0.31	−0.09	−0.44[b]	0.13	0.35

[a] 1952 correlations are based on district units.
[b] Significant at the 0.05 level.
[c] Significant at the 0.01 level.

How was the Congress electoral base affected in the 1967 and 1969 elections by the reorganization of the Punjab and by the emergence of an alternative non-Congress governing coalition of parties dominated by the Akali Dal and the Jan Sangh? For the 1967 elections, it is necessary to look for hypotheses in interviews and in newspaper accounts of the impact on group attitudes toward the Congress of the reorganization and Congress responsibility for it. However, accounts of popular sentiment before the 1967 elections are conflicting. It was reported from some constituencies that Hindu and Harijan votes would remain with the Congress,[1] from others that Hindus were turning to the Jan Sangh in resentment at the Congress concession of the Punjabi Suba demand and that Scheduled Castes were also discontented.[2] Other reports suggested that Congress would lose both Hindu and Sikh votes – Hindus in the towns especially because of the creation of the Punjabi Suba, Sikhs in the rural areas because Chandigarh and other areas had not been included in it.[3] While there were conflicting reports about how Hindus and Harijans would vote in 1967, the consensus before and after the elections was that rural Sikhs would vote against the Congress because of Congress procrastination on the Punjabi Suba demand and because of the failure to include Chandigarh in it.[4]

The correlations for 1967 and 1969 between electoral and census data are based on a different delimitation of constituencies and a different grouping of census units than those for 1957 and 1962. Consequently, it is not possible to correlate the Congress swing from 1962 to 1967 with cultural variables, only to compare the 1967 correlations with those for 1962. It is clear that the correlations for 1967 are once again different, from 1962 and from 1957 as well. They are negative for Hindus and Hindi-speakers, positive for Sikhs and Punjabi-speakers (except urban) and for Scheduled Castes (except rural male literate). The expectation that rural Sikh areas would shift against the Congress in 1967 is not supported by the data here, which show a positive correlation of 0.43 with the Congress vote share, which is the highest positive correlation for any cultural variable with the Congress vote in 1967. The most that can be said about the impact of reorganization on group attitudes towards the Congress is that the Congress polled less well in 1967 than in 1962 in areas of Hindu and Scheduled Caste concentrations, but polled better in Sikh areas.

Although the Congress share of seats won declined still further in the 1969 mid-term elections, its share of the popular vote increased somewhat (see tables 8.1 and 8.2). One hypothesis to explain the increased support for the Congress at a time when the Akali vote

[1] *Tribune*, 12, 15, and 17 February 1967; personal interview documents PG 10 and 23.
[2] *Tribune*, 2, 8, 9, 12, and 26 February 1967.
[3] Personal interview documents PG 22 and 23.　　　　　[4] *Ibid.*

share also increased was that Hindus, especially urban Hindus, discontented with the Jan Sangh alliance with the Akali Dal, had now turned back once again to the Congress. Sikhs, however, had no strong reasons to feel discontented with the first Akali-dominated government in the Punjab, but rather now saw the Akalis as a real alternative to the Congress. Consequently, Congress had gained support among Hindus, but lost support among Sikhs.[1] The correlations for 1969 do reflect such a shift in the areas of Congress support and opposition, back to the 1962 pattern of strength in Hindu and Scheduled Caste areas and weakness in areas of Sikh concentration. However, with the exception of the correlation with total Scheduled Castes in 1969, none of the correlations in 1969 or for the 1967–9 swing are high or statistically significant.

Thus, the hypothesis of changing coalitions is fully supported by the correlations in table 8.3. If Nayar's descriptions and the data in the table are combined, then the following picture of the shifting pattern of Congress electoral coalitions among the three main communities in the Punjab emerges: in 1952, Hindus and Scheduled Castes; in 1957, rural Sikhs; in 1962, rural Hindus and Scheduled Castes; in 1967, rural Sikhs and Scheduled Castes; in 1969, all Hindus and Scheduled Castes. At the same time, it should be stressed that support for the Congress in each election year has never been confined solely to the communities mentioned. Although the correlations in 1957 and for the swing between 1957 and 1962 are rather high, considering the variability of Punjab politics, the highest positive correlations in any single election between the Congress vote share and the percent population of any of the three main communities and the two language groups in the Punjab were the correlations of 0.60 with percent total Sikh, and 0.64 with percent total Punjabi-speakers in 1957, which, in principle, explain no more than 36% and 41%, respectively, of the variation in Congress support in that year.

By the same token, a negative correlation with a particular community obviously does not mean that the Congress got no support from members of that community. A second hypothesis of Nayar's provides some assistance here and qualifies the first hypothesis of shifting support somewhat. This hypothesis, which can be called the hypothesis of minority support, suggests that the Congress gets:

the votes of all those groups which fear domination by an opposing group. Thus, in a Sikh-majority constituency, it is likely to get the votes of Hindus and Harijans who would not like to see an Akali or Communist Sikh candidate elected. On the

[1] Interview in Chandigarh on 18 March 1969.

other hand, in a Hindu-majority constituency in the Punjabi-speaking region, the Congress party is likely to get the votes of Sikhs and Harijans who would not like to see a Jan Sangh candidate elected. Thus, the Congress party may turn out to be the beneficiary of a situation in which groups do not like the Congress party so much as distrust the other political parties and the groups they represent.[1]

It is not possible to test this hypothesis directly since it is one which emphasizes the group composition of particular constituencies for which census data are not available. However, it is useful to remember that this hypothesis is not incompatible with the hypothesis of shifting support and that it may help to explain the absence of high correlations between the Congress vote and percent population of the three main communities in all elections except 1957, when the merger of the Akali Dal into the Congress altered significantly the bases of Congress support, and 1969, when the correlation between the Congress vote and percent total Scheduled Castes was unusually high.

Does the Congress have any stable areas of support or opposition in the Punjab? If we look at each cultural variable over the entire post-independence electoral history of the Punjab, there are none for which the correlation signs have been the same in all elections. For all groups, the sign has changed at least once and usually twice. The Congress vote has correlated positively with percent Scheduled Castes in all elections except 1957 and negatively with percent urban Hindus in all elections except 1969. The correlations between the Congress vote and percent total Hindus have been positive three times and negative twice; those with total Sikhs positive twice, negative three times. Thus, the picture which emerges of Congress electoral support in the Punjab confirms the view of it as a broadly based, aggregative party which builds inter-communal coalitions which shift over time and territory, but which has relatively consistent opposition in areas where urban Hindus are concentrated and relatively consistent support in areas where there are large numbers of Scheduled Castes.

Akali Dal

Patterns of electoral support for and opposition to the Akali Dal, the second main party in the Punjab, have been entirely different. The Akali Dal is an avowedly Sikh party, whose membership is confined to Sikhs, and which only on the rarest occasions has given its party symbol to non-Sikh candidates in an election.[2] It is widely believed

[1] Nayar, 'Punjab', p. 460.
[2] One such occasion, and the reasons for it, has been fully reported in Baldev Raj Nayar,

TABLE 8.4 *Correlation matrix of cultural variables and Akali votes for Punjab grouped constituencies, 1952–69*

Variable	1952[a] N=8	1962 N=14	1967 ADS N=17	ADM N=17	ADS & ADM N=17	1969 N=17	1967–9 swing[b] N=17
1. Total Hindu	−0.24	−0.60^d	−0.77^e	0.00	−0.80^e	−0.76^e	−0.12
2. Rural Hindu		−0.59^d	−0.73^e	0.05	−0.73^e	−0.59^d	0.07
3. Urban Hindu		−0.10	−0.31	−0.07	−0.35	−0.50^c	−0.32
4. Total Sikh	0.21	0.57^c	0.65^d	−0.01	0.67^d	0.73^e	0.24
5. Rural Sikh		0.55^c	0.70^e	0.01	0.73^e	0.75^e	0.18
6. Urban Sikh		−0.01	−0.21	−0.07	−0.25	−0.09	0.20
7. Total Scheduled Caste		−0.46^c	−0.07	−0.28	−0.22	−0.17	0.04
8. Rural Scheduled Caste		−0.41	0.01	−0.18	−0.08	−0.01	0.10
9. Rural male literate Scheduled Caste		−0.54^c	−0.26	−0.15	−0.34	−0.40	−0.17
10. Total Hindi-speakers		−0.56^c	−0.66^d	−0.12	−0.74^e	−0.78^e	−0.22
11. Rural Hindi-speakers		−0.55^c	−0.62^d	−0.08	−0.68^d	−0.62^d	−0.04
12. Urban Hindi-speakers		−0.11	−0.27	−0.10	−0.33	−0.49^c	−0.33
13. Total Punjabi-speakers		0.55^c	0.64^d	0.14	0.74^e	0.78^e	0.22
14. Rural Punjabi-speakers		0.51^c	0.62^d	0.10	0.70^e	0.76^e	0.26
15. Urban Punjabi-speakers		−0.02	−0.22	0.06	−0.19	−0.30	−0.21

[a] 1952 correlations are based on district units.
[b] ADS and ADM to AD.
[c] Significant at the 0.05 level.
[d] Significant at the 0.01 level.
[e] Significant at the 0.001 level.

that the main base of Akali support in the Punjab is among the Jat Sikh peasantry.[1] Hindus are naturally disinclined to vote for such a party. It has also been frequently said that Scheduled Castes – both Hindu and Sikh – do not find the Akali Dal appealing because of its base among the Jat Sikhs, who are the rural overlords of the lower castes.[2] As one respondent put it in 1966, 'No sensible Hindu will vote for an Akali, nor will the Harijans.'[3]

The correlations in table 8.4 between the Akali Dal vote and the same cultural variables used for the Congress fully support these expectations (though the census data do not distinguish 'sensible' from non-sensible Hindus or Harijans!). Although there is nothing surprising in the correlations in table 8.4, their strength and their

'Religion and Caste in the Punjab: Sidhwan Bet Constituency', in Myron Weiner and Rajni Kothari (eds.), *Indian Voting Behaviour: Studies of the 1962 General Elections* (Calcutta: Firma K. L. Mukhopadhyay, 1965), pp. 123–40. See also *Statesman*, 21 January 1962 and 3 February 1962.
[1] E.g., see Nayar, 'Religion and Caste', pp. 134–7; personal interview documents PG 6, 19, and 27; *Tribune*, 12 Feburary 1967.
[2] Nayar, 'Religion and Caste', pp. 134–7.   [3] Personal interview document PG 10.

consistency over time deserve to be discussed. All correlations for all elections between the Akali Dal (excluding the ADM) vote and per- cent total Sikh are positive. Moreover, all correlations between the Akali Dal (excluding the ADM) and percent total and rural Sikh and percent total and rural Punjabi-speakers for the 1962, 1967, and 1969 elections are positive; all are significant at the 0.05 level or better; several are above 0.7 (which is rare for social science data); and all show an increase at each election. All correlations between the Akali Dal vote (excluding the ADM) and percent total Hindu, rural Hindu, and total and rural Hindi-speakers for 1962, 1967, and 1969 are negative; all are significant at the 0.05 level or lower, and many of these are also unusually high for data of this sort. (The correlation of −0.77 between the Akali Dal (Sant) vote share and percent total Hindu in 1967 in principle accounts for 59% of the variation in the Sant group's vote.) Although the coefficients are lower, all correlations between the Akali Dal vote and percent urban Hindus, total Scheduled Castes, and rural male literates among Scheduled Castes are negative for all elections.

There can be no doubt about the main bases of electoral support for and opposition to the Akali Dal, which are clear and sharp. The Akali Dal is a party primarily of the rural Sikh peasantry, for whom indeed it is highly unlikely that 'sensible' Hindus vote. Moreover, its strength in rural Sikh areas has increased at every election it has contested since 1952. However, the declining strength of the negative correlations since 1962 between the Akali Dal vote and the percent of the several categories of Scheduled Caste population suggest greater variability in the relationship of this group of voters to the party.[1]

Jan Sangh

Although the Jan Sangh does not restrict its membership to Hindus as the Akali Dal does to Sikhs, the Jan Sangh appeal has been directed explicitly to Hindu and Hindi sentiment in the Punjab. It is rare for the Jan Sangh to give the party nomination to a Sikh candidate in an election. The party took the lead in launching or supporting counter- agitations opposing the Akali Dal demand for Punjabi Suba during

[1] In fact, the second- and third-order partial correlations for percent total Scheduled Caste, controlling first for total Hindus and then adding total Sikhs in 1967, turn positive to 0.06 in the second-order and 0.23 in the third-order correlation. In 1969, however, the second-order correlations, controlling for total Punjabi-speakers, become more strongly negative for both total and rural Scheduled Castes (−0.31 and −0.26 respectively). However, none of these correlations is statistically significant.

the twenty years of agitation in the Punjab over this demand. It opposed concessions to the Punjabi language at the expense of Hindi before reorganization and it has sought to protect the status of Hindi in the reorganized Punjab. (After the reorganization, however, the Jan Sangh in Punjab accepted the fact of it and did not oppose the inclusion of Chandigarh in the Punjabi Suba.[1]) The Jan Sangh has been considered the polar opposite of the Akali Dal, with its electoral base almost entirely among Hindus, particularly Hindus living in the cities and towns. It is generally believed that the Jan Sangh draws Hindu support from the Congress at times of Hindu resentment over Congress concessions to Akali demands, but that the party has a relatively stable base among urban Hindus, especially businessmen.[2]

There is no question that the Jan Sangh has been stronger in the cities than in the rural areas. In the eight wholly urban Punjab constituencies, the party polled 43.0% of the vote in 1967 and 40.75% in 1969, compared to its state-wide poll of only 9.8% in 1967 and 9.0% in 1969. The data in table 8.5 reveal that the Jan Sangh vote has been correlated positively in all elections with percent urban Hindus. All correlations with percent urban Hindus were significant at the 0.05 level or lower. In 1962, the correlation was a very high 0.72. The correlations with percent rural Hindu, however, have not been consistently positive (-0.01 in 1962) and only one of the positive correlations (in 1969) was significant at the 0.05 level. In fact, percent Hindi-speakers seems to be a more powerful explanatory variable than percent Hindus, both in urban and rural areas. Since many, if not most, Hindus in the Punjab actually speak Punjabi as their mother tongue, the percentage of Hindi-speakers in a particular area is to a considerable extent a measure of Hindu solidarity as much as it is a count of Hindi-speakers. It identifies the population of Hindi-speakers plus Punjabi-speaking Hindus who have consciously chosen to declare Hindi their mother tongue. In areas where urban Hindi-speakers are concentrated, the Jan Sangh has been even stronger than it has been among urban Hindus. All correlations for all elections since 1957 have been positive and significant at the 0.01 level or above (including a high 0.75 correlation in 1962) and all, except that for 1969, have been higher than the correlations for urban Hindus. Moreover, the negative correlation with rural Hindus in 1962 turns positive for rural Hindi-speakers. All correlations for rural Hindi-speakers are equal to or higher than those for rural Hindus.

[1] On this point, see Brass, 'Coalition Politics', p. 1181.
[2] Nayar, 'Punjab', p. 483; *Statesman*, 8 January 1962; *Hindu*, 24 January 1967; *Tribune*, 6, 10, 12, 14, and 15 February 1967; personal interview documents PG 19 and 27.

TABLE 8.5 *Correlation matrix of cultural variables and Jan Sangh votes for Punjab grouped constituencies, 1952–69*

Variable	1952[a] N=8	1957 N=14	1962 N=14	1957–62 swing N=14	1967 N=17	1969 N=17	1967–9 swing N=17
1. Total Hindu	0.18	0.45	0.38	−0.12	0.55[c]	0.71[d]	0.35
2. Rural Hindu		0.12	−0.01	−0.19	0.31	0.46[b]	0.31
3. Urban Hindu		0.62[c]	0.72[c]	0.09	0.53[b]	0.60[c]	0.17
4. Total Sikh	−0.17	−0.50[b]	−0.43	0.13	−0.55[c]	−0.68[c]	−0.31
5. Rural Sikh		−0.55[b]	−0.55[b]	0.04	−0.58[c]	−0.72[d]	−0.33
6. Urban Sikh		0.34	0.60[c]	0.34	0.15	0.18	0.09
7. Total Scheduled Caste		0.07	−0.41	−0.65[c]	−0.36	0.02	0.42[b]
8. Rural Scheduled Caste		−0.13	−0.59[c]	−0.61[c]	−0.48[b]	−0.16	0.34
9. Rural male literate Schedule Caste		0.19	−0.27	−0.63[c]	−0.15	0.28	0.48[b]
10. Total Hindi-speakers		0.60[c]	0.58[b]	−0.07	0.66[c]	0.69[c]	0.19
11. Rural Hindi-speakers		0.28	0.21	−0.11	0.41[b]	0.46[b]	0.17
12. Urban Hindi-speakers		0.66[c]	0.75[c]	0.07	0.59[c]	0.57[c]	0.09
13. Total Punjabi-speakers		−0.60[c]	−0.58[b]	0.07	−0.65[c]	−0.68[c]	−0.19
14. Rural Punjabi-speakers		−0.64[c]	−0.70[c]	−0.03	−0.66[c]	−0.73[d]	−0.25
15. Urban Punjabi-speakers		0.32	0.57[b]	0.31	0.31	0.47[b]	0.26

[a] 1952 correlations are based on district units.
[b] Significant at the 0.05 level.
[c] Significant at the 0.01 level.
[d] Significant at the 0.001 level.

Language appears to be a more powerful variable also in explaining opposition to the Jan Sangh. All correlations for total and rural Sikh and total and rural Punjabi-speakers and the Jan Sangh vote share are negative, but all those for total and rural Punjabi-speakers are more strongly so (except for 1969 where both total Sikh and total Punjabi-speakers are − 0.68) and all are significant at the 0.05 level or above. (The high positive correlations between the Jan Sangh vote and urban Sikh and urban Punjabi-speakers do not hold up in partial correlations. For example, the partial correlation for urban Sikhs in 1962 reduces to 0.11 when percent urban Hindus is controlled.)

The correlations for the Jan Sangh vote and percent Scheduled Castes are much less consistent than those for percent Hindus and Sikhs. The correlations with percent total Scheduled Castes were slightly positive in 1957 and in 1969, but were negative in 1962 and 1967. The correlations with rural Scheduled Castes have been consistently negative in all elections, with a strongly negative coefficient in 1962. However, with rural male literate Scheduled Castes, the correlations are similar to those for the total Scheduled Caste population – positive in 1957 and in 1969, negative in 1962 and in 1967. The strongest correlations are the negative correlations, all significant at the 0.05 level or higher, between the swing vote for the Jan Sangh in 1962 and all categories of Scheduled Castes, suggesting a movement of the Scheduled Caste areas away from the Jan Sangh between 1957 and 1962.

Thus, the correlations between the Jan Sangh vote and cultural variables provide support for the hypotheses that the party has a consistent electoral basis of support among urban Hindus and among Hindi-speakers in both urban and rural areas and that the party polls poorly in areas where Sikhs and Punjabi-speakers are concentrated. There is, however, no evidence of consistent support for or opposition to the party in Scheduled Caste areas.

The Communist parties

Like the other major non-Congress parties in the Punjab, the Communist parties have consistent bases of support and opposition among sections of the electorate. It is well-known that the leadership of the Communist movement in the Punjab has been predominantly Sikh and it is generally believed that the party's electoral base has also been among the Sikhs.[1] The Communist vote increased sharply in 1957 in areas of Akali strength. Moreover, the strongholds of both the CPI and the Akali Dal have been traditionally in Bhatinda and Sangrur districts. It has also been reported that the Communist parties have been supported by the Jat Sikh peasants rather than by Scheduled Castes and that both Hindus and Harijans have tended to oppose the Communists. It has been reported that Hindus were hostile to the CPI because of its support for the Punjabi Suba and because of its alliance with the Akali Dal in 1962.[2]

The correlations between the CPI vote and percent total and rural Sikhs and Punjabi-speakers have been consistently positive in all

[1] Nayar, *Minority Politics*, p. 28, and 'Punjab', p. 482; *Statesman*, 10 January 1962.
[2] *Statesman*, 10 January 1962.

elections (table 8.6), but the highest correlation of 0.48 in 1957 with percent rural Sikhs is lower than the lowest correlation of the Akali Dal vote with the same categories of Sikhs and Punjabi-speakers. Thus, the evidence does support the view that the two parties are competing for the same electoral base, but that the Akali Dal is much more strong and secure in its Sikh support base. (As between the two Communist parties, the very low and changing correlations between the percent CPM vote and percent total and rural Sikhs and Punjabi-speakers suggest that it is the CPI which has retained the main electoral base of the Communist movement in areas of rural Sikh population concentration.)

Evidence for the reported Hindu opposition to the Communist parties in the Punjab is also provided by the correlations in table 8.6. All correlations for all elections between the CPI vote and percent of all categories of the Hindu population as well as total and urban Hindi-speakers are negative. There is one weak positive correlation between the CPI vote and rural Hindi-speakers and again there are generally low and some positive correlations between the CPM vote and percent Hindus and Hindi-speakers, but the general picture is one of Communist weakness in areas where Hindus and Hindi-speakers are concentrated. However, partial correlation of the data for percent Hindus and the CPI vote, with percent total Sikhs controlled, gives quite different results. In both 1967 and 1969, the partial correlations with percent total Hindu turn positive – to 0.39 in 1967 and to a strong correlation of 0.60 (significant at the 0.05 level) in 1969. The partial correlations suggest that the CPI has had some areas of electoral support where Hindus are concentrated. The CPI, then, is different both from the Congress and from the Akali Dal and the Jan Sangh in its configuration of electoral support areas over time. Like the Akali Dal and the Jan Sangh, the CPI has consistent bases of support (primarily in Sikh areas), but unlike these two parties, the CPI has succeeded in combining support in both Sikh and Hindu areas.

Finally, the correlations between the votes for the Communist parties and the several categories of Scheduled Castes are rather low and, for the CPI, inconsistent. All correlations between the CPI vote and percent total and rural Scheduled Castes are positive, but all those for rural male literate Scheduled Castes are negative. All correlations between the CPM vote and all categories of Scheduled Castes are negative, but all are also low. The evidence, therefore, is that the Communist parties do not have strong and consistent bases of support or opposition in areas of Scheduled Caste concentrations,

TABLE 8.6 *Correlation matrix of cultural variables and Communist votes for Punjab grouped constituencies, 1952–69*

Variable	1952[a] N=8	1957 N=14	1962 N=14	1957–1962 swing N=14	1967 CPI N=17	1967 CPM N=17	1967 CPI & CPM N=17	1969 CPI N=17	1969 CPM N=17	1969 CPI & CPM N=17	1967–1969 swing CPI N=17	1967–1969 swing CPM N=17	1967–1969 swing CPI & CPM N=17
1. Total Hindu	−0.53	−0.42	−0.19	0.24	−0.20	−0.02	−0.18	−0.22	−0.13	−0.28	−0.11	−0.43[b]	−0.20
2. Rural Hindu		−0.16	−0.11	0.03	−0.07	−0.08	−0.11	−0.03	−0.12	−0.11	0.01	−0.16	−0.02
3. Urban Hindu		−0.52[b]	−0.16	0.38	−0.26	0.07	−0.15	−0.36	−0.07	−0.34	−0.22	−0.52[b]	−0.33
4. Total Sikh	0.48	0.42	0.19	−0.23	0.31	−0.14	0.14	0.39	−0.02	0.30	0.25	0.41[b]	0.34
5. Rural Sikh		0.48[b]	0.20	−0.29	0.29	−0.09	0.16	0.27	0.05	0.26	0.10	0.51[b]	0.21
6. Urban Sikh		−0.37	−0.07	0.32	0.07	−0.17	−0.08	0.38	−0.26	0.11	0.53[c]	−0.37	0.43[b]
7. Total Scheduled Caste		0.21	0.01	−0.22	0.02	−0.22	−0.15	0.10	−0.14	−0.03	0.12	0.25	0.17
8. Rural Scheduled Caste		0.33	0.05	−0.30	0.00	−0.20	−0.15	0.17	−0.10	0.07	0.22	0.37	0.29
9. Rural male literate Scheduled Caste		−0.03	−0.13	−0.14	−0.35	−0.06	−0.33	−0.19	−0.02	−0.18	0.05	0.14	0.08
10. Total Hindi-speakers		−0.33	−0.19	0.14	−0.09	0.04	−0.04	−0.20	−0.05	−0.20	−0.18	−0.35	−0.25
11. Rural Hindi-speakers		−0.08	−0.13	−0.07	0.05	−0.04	0.01	−0.00	−0.06	−0.05	−0.07	−0.08	−0.09
12. Urban Hindi-speakers		−0.49	−0.13	0.39	−0.24	0.14	−0.09	−0.35	−0.00	−0.29	−0.23	−0.51[b]	−0.33
13. Total Punjabi-speakers		0.31	0.17	−0.14	0.12	−0.12	−0.00	0.21	−0.02	0.16	0.18	0.37	0.26
14. Rural Punjabi-speakers		0.42	0.20	−0.23	0.20	−0.08	0.10	0.27	0.04	0.25	0.17	0.48[b]	0.27
15. Urban Punjabi-speakers		−0.46[b]	−0.13	0.35	−0.32	−0.08	−0.31	−0.26	−0.20	−0.36	−0.03	−0.49[b]	−0.13

[a] 1952 correlations are based on district units.
[b] Significant at the 0.05 level.
[c] Significant at the 0.01 level.

although the CPI vote has tended to correlate positively with per-cent Scheduled Castes more often than not.

The Scheduled Caste Federation (SCF) and the Republican Party (RPI)

The party of the Scheduled Castes contested the 1952 and 1957 elections as the Scheduled Caste Federation and subsequent elections as the Republican Party. It is, of course, generally assumed that the SCF and RPI have won their small proportions of Punjab votes primarily from the Scheduled Caste population.[1] The party opposed both the Akali Dal and the Punjabi Suba movement[2] and, consequently, should be expected to have done poorly among Sikh voters.

TABLE 8.7 *Correlation matrix of cultural variables and votes for the SCF and RPI for Punjab grouped constituencies, 1952–69*

Variable	1952[a] N=8	1957 N=14	1962 N=14	1967 N=17	1969 N=17
1. Total Hindu	0.73[b]	0.58[b]	0.64[c]	0.29	0.52[c]
2. Rural Hindu		0.57[b]	0.53[b]	0.35	0.65[c]
3. Urban Hindu		0.09	0.28	0.01	−0.03
4. Total Sikh	−0.67[b]	−0.52	−0.60[c]	−0.26	−0.49[b]
5. Rural Sikh		−0.45	−0.54[b]	−0.22	−0.39
6. Urban Sikh		−0.18	−0.12	−0.14	−0.32
7. Total Scheduled Caste		0.80[d]	0.59[c]	0.63[c]	0.60[c]
8. Rural Scheduled Caste		0.73[c]	0.42	0.57[c]	0.59[c]
9. Rural male literate Scheduled Caste		0.91[d]	0.73[c]	0.69[c]	0.74[d]
10. Total Hindi-speakers		0.34	0.55[b]	0.11	0.48[b]
11. Rural Hindi-speakers		0.33	0.45	0.16	0.60[c]
12. Urban Hindi-speakers		0.07	0.27	−0.03	−0.02
13. Total Punjabi-speakers		−0.31	−0.54[b]	−0.09	−0.47[b]
14. Rural Punjabi-speakers		−0.26	−0.48[b]	−0.09	−0.33
15. Urban Punjabi-speakers		−0.08	−0.02	0.02	−0.26

[a] 1952 correlations are based on district units.
[b] Significant at the 0.05 level.
[c] Significant at the 0.01 level.
[d] Significant at the 0.001 level.

As expected, the correlations between the SCF and RPI vote and all categories of Scheduled Castes are positive for all elections (table 8.7). Moreover, all but one are significant at the 0.05 level or lower

[1] *Statesman*, 18 February 1967; *Tribune*, 20 February 1967.
[2] Nayar, *Minority Politics*, p. 263; *Statesman*, 6 January 1962.

and the correlations in 1957 are extraordinarily high. In all elections, the rural male literate category of Scheduled Castes has been correlated more strongly with the SCF and RPI vote than the other two categories of Scheduled Caste population. It is also clear from the correlations that the SCF and RPI have done much better in Hindu areas than in Sikh areas. All correlations between the SCF and RPI vote shares and all categories of Hindu population, except urban Hindu in 1969, are positive and many are significant at the 0.05 level or lower. In contrast, all correlations with all categories of Sikh population for all elections are negative, some significantly so. The correlations with Hindi-speakers are similar to, but tend to be lower than those with the corresponding categories of Hindus; whereas those for Punjabi-speakers are similar to but somewhat less strongly negative than those with the corresponding categories of Sikhs, suggesting that religion and caste rather than language are more powerful explanatory variables in relation to the SCF and RPI.

Independents

It is risky to attempt to assess the meaning of the vote for independent candidates, which one might think would have an unpredictable variability. However, since the main interest above has been in assessing the broad tendencies in the relationship between the leading established political parties and religious, caste, and language sections of the population, the independent vote may be seen as the opposite, that is, as reflecting the extent to which particular sections of the population are *not* tied to any of the organized parties. The independent vote may, of course, reflect many other things as well, but it seems reasonable to interpret positive correlations between percent vote and percent of the population of a particular community as a possible measure of the *dissatisfaction* with established parties and negative correlations as a measure of *satisfaction* with established parties. The assumption here is simply that if members of a religious or other group identify strongly with one or more parties, they will not be voting consistently for non-party candidates and *vice versa*. A closely related consideration here is the extent to which the party of preference is available in all areas. For example, if Hindus generally identify with the Jan Sangh, but the Jan Sangh contests only where there are very large concentrations of Hindus, one might expect a consistent vote of minority Hindu groups for independent Hindu candidates in areas where the Jan Sangh does not contest. Consequently, a positive correlation may be, more accurately, a measure of dissatisfaction with *available* political parties and not with the policies of all parties operating in the state.

TABLE 8.8 *Correlation matrix of cultural variables and independent votes for Punjab grouped constituencies, 1952–69*

Variable	1952[a] N=8	1957 N=14	1962 N=14	1957–62 swing N=14	1967 N=17	1969 N=17	1967–9 swing N=17
1. Total Hindu	−0.47	0.14	0.22	0.04	0.69[c]	0.20	−0.53[b]
2. Rural Hindu		0.01	0.47[b]	0.26	0.58[c]	0.05	−0.51[b]
3. Urban Hindu		0.25	−0.40	−0.36	0.38	0.29	−0.20
4. Total Sikh	0.45	−0.21	−0.18	0.01	−0.63[c]	−0.27	0.44[b]
5. Rural Sikh		−0.27	−0.09	0.10	−0.67[c]	−0.23	0.49[b]
6. Urban Sikh		0.34	−0.35	−0.38	0.16	−0.15	−0.23
7. Total Scheduled Caste		−0.68[c]	0.71[c]	0.77[d]	0.18	−0.20	−0.28
8. Rural Scheduled Caste		−0.70[c]	0.79[d]	0.83[d]	0.06	−0.22	−0.17
9. Rural male literate Scheduled Caste		−0.53[b]	0.73[c]	0.71[c]	0.34	−0.04	−0.34
10. Total Hindi-speakers		0.22	0.13	−0.05	0.55[c]	0.19	−0.41[b]
11. Rural Hindi-speakers		0.10	0.37	0.16	0.47[b]	0.03	−0.41[b]
12. Urban Hindi-speakers		0.25	−0.40	−0.36	0.32	0.30	−0.13
13. Total Punjabi-speakers		−0.24	−0.11	0.07	−0.54[c]	−0.19	0.40
14. Rural Punjabi-speakers		−0.32	0.00	0.18	−0.59[c]	−0.21	0.43[b]
15. Urban Punjabi-speakers		0.34	−0.36	−0.39	0.39	0.15	−0.28

[a] 1952 correlations are based on district units.
[b] Significant at the 0.05 level.
[c] Significant at the 0.01 level.
[d] Significant at the 0.001 level.

The correlation matrix in table 8.8 reveals positive correlations eleven out of thirteen times (excluding swing correlations) between the independent vote and percent total, rural, and urban Hindus and eleven out of twelve times for the corresponding categories of Hindi-speakers. Moreover, two of the correlations with Hindus in 1967 are significant at the 0.01 level. Keeping in mind the fact that Hindus tended to oppose the Congress in 1967 because of their resentment against the Congress acceptance of the Punjabi Suba demand and the positive, but low, correlations in table 8.5 between percent rural Hindus and the Jan Sangh vote, it seems likely that Hindu resentment was expressed only partly through the Jan Sangh and partly through independent candidates. In contrast, the Sikh areas have been more contented with the parties which are based upon them and which speak in their name. Ten out of thirteen correlations (excluding swing) between percent Sikhs and the independent vote are negative, two in 1967 significantly so. (The correlations with

Punjabi-speakers are roughly similar, with eight out of twelve negative.) Finally, there is no consistency over time in the correlations between the independent vote and percent Scheduled Caste population. Six coefficients have been positive, six negative. In 1957 and 1962, however, there was a sharp swing from strongly negative to strongly positive correlations, perhaps reflecting the decline in support for the RPI as compared to its predecessor, the SCF, in Scheduled Caste areas.

Summary

Table 8.9 summarizes the positive and negative correlations between the three main communal variables and the votes for the six leading parties and for independents in the Punjab for all Punjabwide elections since 1952. The table brings out clearly the communal bases of Punjab politics. All four of the leading non-Congress parties have their primary electoral bases either in Hindu areas (Jan Sangh and the Scheduled Caste party) or in Sikh areas (Akali Dal and the CPI). Two of these parties (the CPI and the SCF/RPI) also have consistent bases of support in areas of Scheduled Caste concentrations. Only the CPM has had no positive correlations with any of the three main communal groups in the Punjab, which suggests that, of the two Communist parties, it is the CPI which has the stronger electoral base. Independent candidates find support in Hindu areas, but not in areas of Sikh concentrations. Only the Congress has had positive correlations with percent members of all three main social groups in the Punjab.

Thus, the parties can be distinguished according to their ability to draw support from areas where each of the three main groups are concentrated, as follows. The Congress only once, in 1957, had negative correlations with both Hindus and Scheduled Castes. In alliance with the Akali Dal in that year, the Congress won overwhelming support in areas dominated by the Sikh community and the highest proportion of the popular vote that it has achieved since independence, but it lost support in areas of Hindu and Scheduled Caste concentrations. Since then, the Congress has never been dependent on support from areas dominated by one community, but has combined support from areas where one of the two religious groups are concentrated with support in Scheduled Caste areas as well. The Congress' main rival, the Akali Dal, though it is the second largest party in the state, is the only party which has never had much support either in Hindu or Scheduled Caste areas. From this point

TABLE 8.9 *Summary of positive and negative correlations for communal variables and party votes for Punjab grouped constituencies, 1952–69*

Party	Total Hindu					Total Sikh					Total Scheduled Caste			
	1952	1957	1962	1967	1969	1952	1957	1962	1967	1969	1957	1962	1967	1969
1. Congress	+	−	+	−	+	−	+	−	+	−	−	+	+	+
2. Akali Dal	−	NC	−	−	−	+	NC	+	+	+	NC	−	−	−
3. Jan Sangh	+	+	+	+	+	−	−	+	−	+	+	−	−	+
4. CPI	−	−	NC	−	−	+	+	+	−	+	+	+	+	+
5. CPM	NC	NC	NC	−	−	NC	NC	NC	−	−	NC	NC	−	−
6. SCF/RPI	+	+	+	+	+	−	−	−	−	−	+	+	+	+
7. Independents	−	+	+	+	+	+	−	−	−	−	−	+	+	−

NC = No contest.

of view, though its base in Sikh areas is very strong, it is the most narrowly based of the four leading parties in the Punjab. The Jan Sangh, though it is a smaller party, is more broadly based from a communal point of view in that it has sometimes combined support in Hindu and Scheduled Caste areas. The CPI has consistently combined some support in Sikh and Scheduled Caste areas in every election, the SCF/RPI some support in Hindu and Scheduled Caste areas.

The underlying duality of Punjab politics between the two main parties is revealed once again in the fact that, with the exception of the 1967 election, the signs for the Congress and the Akali Dal are opposite. A complete polarization of parties is, however, prevented in the Punjab by two features of society and politics. One is that the Scheduled Castes constitute a large and relatively non-attached third force, for whose support all parties compete. The second is that no party has succeeded in monopolizing the support of any single community. Hindus divide among the Congress, the Jan Sangh, the SCF/RPI, and Independents; Sikhs among the Congress, the Akali Dal, and the CPI; Scheduled Castes among all parties except the Akali Dal.

In other words, the parties in Punjab do not simply reflect basic religious and caste antagonisms, but they divide and deflect them. The system is not completely fragmented and compartmentalized into congruent cultural-political segments. Communal coalition-building is the strategy of most parties and internal political differentiation within each community the result of this process. In fact, internal division within the three main social groups in Punjab is sufficient to prevent not only polarization but the emergence of stable political majorities based upon a temporary or permanent combination of any one of the two religious groups with the Scheduled Castes.

The consequence of such a system is some discontinuity between the electoral bases of the parties and the necessities of coalition-building in the state, which once again suggests the independence of political leadership from social forces. It is difficult for a major party to combine Hindu and Sikh votes in the electoral arena, for identification of a party with the interests or the good of one community antagonizes the other. However, the Congress has succeeded in avoiding identification over time with any one community in the Punjab. Moreover, it always combines support from at least two of the three social groups in the Punjab in each election and it has continued to elect both Hindu and Sikh candidates. When the Congress fails to win a majority of seats in the assembly, Hindu- and

Sikh-based parties may combine in the parliamentary arena to
govern the State. In this way, between 1967 and 1970, Punjab
politics constituted another variant of the 'politics of accommodation' in which parties divided potentially antagonistic social groups
in the process of competing for their support and then combined
with each other for purposes of government. That accommodation,
however, broke up on a language-related issue in June 1970, after
which the Jan Sangh resigned from the government (see table 7.5)
and the Akali Dal governed alone until June 1971. In the 1972
election (although data are not available at this writing to demonstrate the point), a reinvigorated Congress succeeded in combining
enough support from the main social groups in the Punjab to win a
majority of seats in the assembly and form a government by itself.
In both cases, of coalition politics and single-party dominance, it
has been necessary to combine support from both Hindus and Sikhs
in order to construct a governing majority in the Punjab.

CONCLUSION

The preceding description of the structure of the Punjab party system
over time and its relationship to the communal cleavages in the
population suggests the following conclusions.

The basic structure of the Punjab party system is dualistic.
Dualistic competition between the Congress and the Akali Dal has
persisted over time and has provided the primary dynamic of the
system. However, the dualism has been partial. It has been qualified
in two important respects, which have prevented its development
into a classic two-party system. First, one of the two main parties, the
Congress, has been much stronger electorally than its chief rival, the
Akali Dal, which has meant that the Akali Dal has required both
pre- and post-electoral alliances with other parties to compete
successfully against the Congress. Second, two of the minor parties or
groups of parties in Punjab politics (the Jan Sangh and the Communist parties) have acquired a regional concentration of strength
and a stable support base in the electorate, which has so far resisted
the inroads of the two major competitors. Thus, the dualistic pattern
is precarious and unstable.

The Punjab party system both expresses communal cleavages and
prevents a complete polarization of communal forces in state politics.
Communal cleavages are expressed principally through the activities
of the Akali Dal and the Jan Sangh, whose appeals are made explicitly or implicitly only to the Sikh and Hindu communities, respec-

tively. These parties build upon, reinforce, and shape the segmental tendencies in Punjab society. They do not, however, merely reflect pre-existing cleavages. The Akali Dal particularly has done much to create and consolidate Sikh communal solidarity in the Punjab during the past half-century.

A thoroughgoing polarization of Punjab politics has been prevented partly by the presence of a large Scheduled Caste population, of uncertain religious allegiance, to whom all parties must appeal. Second, the leading secular parties in Punjab, particularly Congress and the CPI, have successfully appealed to both Hindus and Sikhs in the past. Here too the parties have not been simply reflecting social tendencies, but they have been actively promoting an ideology of secularism and inter-communal political cooperation. The dynamic of the entire system and its dualism has consisted in the drives of the communal parties, particularly the Akali Dal, to monopolize support from one community, and the contrary efforts of the Congress to build inter-communal support.

Where does the Punjab party system fit in the comparative study of party systems? It is highly fractionalized, but not atomized because two parties, Congress and Akali Dal, have become strong, highly institutionalized political forces. It is dualistic, but falls considerably short of meeting the requirements of a two-party system. It has shown tendencies in the past towards one-party dominance, but that designation no longer seems appropriate for a system in which alternation in power has occurred. It contains some of the features of Sartori's model of 'polarized pluralism'[1] – more than five parties; a large center party; multi-polarity (left–right; communalism–secularism); in theory, anti-system opposition in the Communist parties; and governmental instability. However, there is no authentic anti-system opposition of either the right or the left; ideological differences among the parties do not present insurmountable barriers to coalition formation; and genuine alternation in power has taken place. Finally, the system contains features which are similar to the model of 'segmented pluralism' and 'consociational democracy', particularly in the congruent patterning of political and religious cleavages, in their articulation in the electoral arena, and in the pattern of inter-party coalition formation after the elections. However, segmentation is not complete. Large sections of the population have uncertain allegiances to the parties and only the

[1] Giovanni Sartori, 'European Political Parties: The Case of Polarized Pluralism', in Joseph La Palombara and Myron Weiner (eds.), *Political Parties and Political Development* (Princeton, N.J.: Princeton University Press, 1966), pp. 137–76.

two leading parties can be considered fully institutionalized political forces in the Punjab politics.

That the Punjab party system does not fit neatly any one of the institutionalized models described above should not be surprising because the Punjab is a developing society and its party system has been unstable. The comparison does suggest alternative paths of development and institutionalization for the Punjab party system, however, of which two long-term tendencies seem most likely. The first would be a reinforcing of the dualist tendencies through either a broadening of the Akali Dal or an institutionalization of its alliance relationships. The second would be the institutionalization of a four-party segmented system through the increased institutionalization of both the Jan Sangh and the CPI and the reduction of the non-party, independent proportion of votes and seats won. In the short run, a revitalized Congress may be able to reestablish a dominant position in Punjab politics, but the tendencies toward both dualism and segmentation are structural ones, with strong social and institutional support in the Punjab, and they are likely to continue to assert themselves over time.

The analysis in chapter 7 of patterns of communal coalition formation in the legislature and in this chapter of patterns of communal support for political parties in the Punjabi Suba suggest two general conclusions concerning the relationship between ethnic conflict and party politics in a developing society. First, the consequences of ethnic politics in a regime of competitive parties may be, but are not necessarily, catastrophic. The possibilities for political solutions to ethnic-linguistic conflicts and for inter-communal collaboration for political advantage are very great and are the rule, rather than the exception. Second, political parties and political leaders do not simply reflect pre-existing ethnic cleavages. In the process of political competition, they shape them and moderate them as well. In a word, ethnic politics are as much subject to the manipulative abilities of party politicians as they are influenced by them.

PART V
CONCLUSION

9

THE PROCESS
OF NATIONALITY-FORMATION IN
NORTH INDIA

Nationality-formation has been defined as the process by which objectively distinct groups of people or ethnic groups acquire subjective self-consciousness and political significance either within an existing state or within a separate state. Four sets of variables have been identified as critical in determining whether, when, and how the unfolding of this process will take place – the nature and variability of the objective distinguishing features of the group; the character of internal values and internal processes of change taking place within the group; the nature of the group's relations with other groups; and the form of political organization of the group's members and its relationship to state policies toward the political rights of the group. Three north Indian cases have been examined to illustrate the process and the critical variables involved in it. The cases were chosen to represent ethnic groups which have achieved differing degrees of subjective self-awareness and political success. At one extreme are the Maithili-speaking people, an objectively distinct group of people which has not acquired a sense of internal solidarity, has not achieved significant political strength or success by its own efforts, and whose members have been assimilating to the Hindi speech community. The second case, that of the Muslim minority in north India, provides examples of two types of situations over time. The history of the Muslim minority in the United Provinces before partition provides an example of a narrow political elite which mobilized a minority community in order to protect its political privileges against the rise to self-consciousness of new elites from the Hindu majority community. The history of the Muslim minority in Uttar Pradesh and Bihar since 1947 shows how the position of a community may change over time when the political and social environment changes. After 1947, the Muslim minority was transformed into a relatively self-conscious but leaderless community, subjected to demands for it to accept the language and to work within the political boundaries set by a now dominant set of elites from the Hindu majority community. The final case, at the other extreme from the Maithili movement, is the example of the Sikhs, an objectively distinct people that has achieved a high degree of subjective consciousness and political unity, culminating in the creation of a political unit in which it is culturally and politically the dominant group. In this concluding chapter, the three cases will be considered comparatively and generalizations will be drawn from them concerning the process of nationality-formation and its consequences for political integration in multi-ethnic societies.

OBJECTIVE DIFFERENCES BETWEEN PEOPLES

A comparison of the cases suggests the following conclusions and generalizations concerning the importance of objective differences between peoples as a factor in the process of nationality-formation.

The fact that an impartial observer – a linguist, a student of comparative religion, or a geographer – may be able to identify at a particular point in time those ethnic groups which have distinctve differences from other groups in a multi-ethnic society does not provide the student of nationalism with any basis for predicting the group's development. At the turn of the century, George Grierson, arguing on the basis of grammatical and literary evidence, unequivocally identified both Punjabi and Maithili as distinct languages of north India, grammatically and lexically distinguishable from Hindi and other languages of the north. Yet, during the past century, neither Maithili-speakers nor Punjabi-speakers have developed into self-conscious communal groups and many millions of speakers of both languages have been assimilated into the Hindi speech community. Punjabi has fared better than Maithili over time in maintaining its separateness from Hindi, not because it is linguistically more distinct, but because it became an important secondary symbol in the struggle of the Sikhs to preserve their separate religious identity and to acquire a territorial unit in which they would be dominant. Similarly, Urdu, in its spoken form generally considered by linguists to be no more than a variant of the common language of north India, synonymous in fact with Hindi and Hindustani, has preserved its separateness only because Muslim political and religious elites value it and find it useful as a symbol to demand special rights for Muslims.

In fact, language in north India has generally played a secondary role to religion as a source of social and political differentiation. Yet it would not be correct to conclude from these cases that religion is inherently a more powerful motive force in identity formation than language because elsewhere in the world, and in India itself, the roles of these two forces have been reversed. In south India, in Europe, and in Africa, it has been more common for language to provide a basis for nationalism in religiously diverse societies whereas, in north India, religion has united linguistically distinct peoples, particularly the Muslims. Moreover, there is also very recent evidence from the South Asian subcontinent, in the case of Bangladesh, that language which at one time may play a secondary role to religion, may at another time become primary. It is not inconceivable that language differences may yet become more significant in north India as well.

Objective differences between peoples are not only insufficient as bases for nationality formation, but they are themselves highly variable. Especially in traditional societies in the early stages of social mobilization, it is misleading to think of gross differences in the religious or linguistic composition of populations as 'givens' or as immutably fixed. This is so for several reasons. First, in traditional societies, the differences between elite and mass speakers of a particular language or communicants of a particular religion may be as great or greater than the differences between ordinary people who are presumed to speak different languages or practice different religions. Processes of social change may work in such a way as either to close the elite–mass gap and consolidate particular linguistic or religious communities or to widen the elite–mass gap so that some languages or religions may lose their mass followings and become preserves only of isolated elites. Thus, in the Maithili-speaking region, the distance between the language of Maithil Brahman elite speakers of Maithili and non-elite Maithili-speakers has appeared to many of the latter to be greater than the distance between spoken Maithili and spoken Hindi. Processes of social change have brought Maithili- and Hindi-speakers even closer, but have not reduced the elite–mass distance among Maithili-speakers.

Among Hindi-Urdu speakers the contrast between elite and popular versions of the languages are even clearer. The differences between Persianized Urdu and Sanskritized Hindi are great at the elite and literary levels, but the spoken language of Hindus and Muslims alike in north India is more or less the same. In fact, ordinary Hindus and Muslims can communicate more easily with each other than they can with elite speakers of the language of their own religious group. In this case, the competing Hindu and Muslim elites have been attempting to persuade their followers that, if they are Hindus, they speak Hindi, and if they are Muslims, they speak Urdu, and have also been attempting to create two competing standards of the same language.

Among Punjabi-speakers, the problem of elite–mass differences has been less important. The regional standard of Punjabi which is taught in the schools is, of course, different from many of the regional Punjabi dialects, but there is not among Punjabi-speakers anything comparable to the caste distinctions which exist among Maithili-speakers. Nor should the conflict between Punjabi and Hindi be seen as one concerning the establishment of competing standards for the same spoken language. It is, rather, a conflict for supremacy between two regional standard languages which are distinct in both their spoken and written forms.

Elite–mass differences have also been important in religious behavior in north India. The Sanskritized Vedic rituals of learned Brahman pandits are quite different forms of religious behavior from the devotional worship of low castes, yet both types of worshippers are conventionally described as Hindus. Similarly, Muslim ulama and educated Muslims are likely to confine their forms of worship to either the prescribed individual worship in the home or the routinized congregational worship in the mosque, but ordinary, uneducated Muslim believers may visit the tombs and shrines of local saints and sing devotional prayers, often in the company of Hindus doing the same. Similarly, educated *keshadhari* Sikhs are likely to conform closely nowadays to only the prescribed rituals of Sikhism whereas a Scheduled Caste Sikh in the Punjab may, literally with a flick of his turban, find Hindu devotional worship more to his taste. In all three cases, political elites who have attempted to build political support on the basis of religious solidarity have had to take such differences into account. They have not been able to take as given the religious loyalties of ordinary people. Rather, in the process of building political support, they have had to develop ways of closing the elite–mass gap in religious practices and to create the religious solidarity of the communities for whom they claim to speak. And, in the process of creating such religio-political solidarity, some communicants may remain marginal or be lost to other religious communities.

Elite–mass differences are only one type of variation in the objective marks of an ethnic group, which may affect the process of nationality-formation. In the early stages of language development, dialect variation on a geographical rather than on a class or caste basis is also commonly very great. The choice of one dialect as a standard for a language may alienate speakers of other dialects. Thus, in the case of Maithili, the dialect which Grierson identified as 'Standard Maithili' was spoken primarily in four districts (Darbhanga, Monghyr, Bhagalpur, and Purnea), in the portions of those districts north of the Ganges. Although Grierson classed other dialects south of the Ganges, on the eastern and western fringes, and that spoken by Muslims as also part of Maithili, the historic tendencies during the past half century have moved towards either separation of the fringe dialects from Maithili or towards their absorption by other languages – Bhojpuri, Hindi, Urdu, and Bengali.

Dialect differences also exist among Punjabi-speakers. Although Grierson identified eight dialects and 'sub-dialects' of Punjabi, he considered the differences among them to be slight, with the exception of the Dogra dialect spoken in Jammu. Moreover, dialect differences have been less critical to the processes of linguistic assimilation and differentiation in the Punjab than religion and script. Religion has been the principal basis for differentiation in the Punjab, followed by script, so that the historic movement has been towards the congruence of Muslims, Urdu, and the Persian script; Hindus, Hindi, and the Devanagari script; Sikhs, Punjabi, and the Gurumukhi script.

In the so-called Hindi-speaking area in the rest of north India between the Punjab and Bengal, the range of dialect variation is enormous. On grammatical grounds alone, many of the *bhāshās* or speeches of north India, such as Awadhi, Braj Bhasha, or Bhojpuri have as good a claim as Punjabi or Maithili to a separate status from Hindi. In some cases, political claims have been staked by local voluntary associations and by Marxist intellectuals for the encouragement of these languages. In the face of this enormous dialectal diversity, however, the process of assimilation to one or the other standards, Hindi or Urdu, has gone on apace. The development of future political movements based on the regional dialects cannot be dismissed, but so far no movements other than those for Punjabi or Urdu have been successful in achieving a significant political status for any of the regional dialects. The reason, clearly, is that something other than a claim to grammatical distinctiveness is necessary.

Corresponding to the phenomenon of dialect variation in language groups is the existence of sectarian differentiation in religious groups. It is customary to comment loosely on 'Hindu–Muslim' or 'Hindu–Sikh' political conflicts in modern Indian history and politics and to think of Hindus, Muslims, and Sikhs as undifferentiated religious communities. Of course, this is not true now and was even less true before religious and political elites began to use the symbols of religious distinctiveness as bases for social and political mobilization in India. Sectarian differences within religious groups are relevant to the process of nationality-formation in three respects particularly. First, when religious symbols begin to be used for political purposes, the elites who begin the process often come from particular sub-groups within the religious group – *keshadhari* Sikhs, Arya Samaj Hindus, or Sunni Muslims. If one wants to be able to predict the course a movement of political-religious mobilization will take, it is clearly important to know which sub-groups are taking the lead and whether they occupy central positions in their religious traditions. Second, to the extent that elites from particular sects are successful in mobilizing their religious communities for political ends, they may have a profound impact on the nature of religious identity in their religious group and on defining the membership of the group as a whole. This process is exemplified best by the history of religio-political mobilization among the Sikhs, where *keshadhari* Sikhs have taken the lead in forming the Akali Dal, have gone a long way in convincing themselves and external observers that they represent the Sikh community or Panth as a whole, have institutionalized their dominance in the Sikh religion through their control of the gurudwaras, and have defined non-*keshadhari* Sikhs as either excluded from or marginal to the Sikh religion. This kind of success has not been achieved by any other sub-group within the other two religions of north India. Internal differentiation has been less great, though not completely absent, in Islam than in either Sikhism or Hinduism to start with. In Hinduism, both caste and sectarian differentiation have been too great for any single sub-group to succeed in defining membership in the community in any way comparable to what the *keshadhari* Sikhs have achieved. Finally, the extent of sectarian differentiation within a religious group and the intensity of divisions between sects will influence profoundly the abilities of particular elites to mobilize the religious groups for political purposes. For example, Sunni-Shi'a divisions in Islam are intense and have occasionally developed into violent conflicts. In certain parts of India, particularly in Lucknow, they have presented serious obstacles to political unity. However, Shi'as are a tiny minority in the Islamic community of north India as a whole, so that Sunni-Shi'a differences have not seriously impeded the development of communal solidarity among Muslims. Among Hindus, it has been the enormous range of caste and sectarian differences and the social barriers between groups which have prevented religio-political consolidation. Among

Sikhs, however, a very definite process of religious consolidation has taken place, whose origins can be traced to the efforts of the Singh Sabha movement in the nineteenth century.

Another reason why objective differences between peoples cannot be taken as 'givens' is that there is frequently a range of choice in selecting symbols of group difference and identity. Some symbols may facilitate communication with other groups while others may impede it. The most striking examples of symbol selections which have been made specifically for purposes of linguistic group differentiation in north India are in the choice of scripts. Ordinary Muslims and Hindus in north India can communicate perfectly well in spoken Hindi–Urdu. Consequently, those elites who have wanted to emphasize the differences between Muslims and Hindus in language as well as in religion have insisted that Urdu must be written in the Persian–Arabic script while Hindus similarly have insisted that Hindi can be written properly only in the Devanagari script. In this way, during the past several decades, symbolic barriers to effective communication between the literate populations of Hindus and Muslims have been erected. The same process has been at work in the Punjab in the insistence of Sikhs that Punjabi can be written properly only in Gurumukhi script, while Hindus prefer the Devanagari. In contrast, Maithili has, for the most part, been written in the Devanagari script, which has made it easier for Hindi spokesmen to continue to refer to Maithili as only a dialect of Hindi and more difficult for Maithili-speakers to assert their claim of distinctiveness.

Whereas it has been commonly argued that ethnic group cohesion and conflict between ethnic groups are most likely to arise and to be most intense when several objective differences reinforce each other, this proposition too overemphasizes the importance of the merely objective dissimilarities between peoples. It also ignores the fact that even approximately exact correspondences rarely occur when more than one attribute of an ethnic group is taken into account. In fact, the selection of more than one attribute to define a group may be detrimental to the development of the desired group solidarity, may actually provide opponents with a basis for splitting the group. In fact, it can be assumed that, even if the aspirant group does *not* lay claim to more than one attribute, its opponents will point to contradictions in its claims which occur when more than one attribute is taken into account.

Thus, it is difficult enough to define what it is to be a Maithil or a Maithili-speaker, using the one attribute of language. If, however, one adds other attributes to language in this case, contradictions immediately arise. Is a Maithil to be defined also by residence or ancestry in Mithila defined in terms of the boundaries of the mountains and the three rivers? If so, some Maithili-speakers will be lost. Is the Muslim community of north India to be defined by religion alone or by language as well, as the Urdu-speaking Muslim community? If so, its opponents will quickly point out that not all Muslims in the north identify themselves as Urdu-speakers and only a small proportion can read the script. Similarly, with regard to the Sikhs and the Punjabi language, although most Sikhs in the Punjab are also Punjabi-speakers, not all Punjabi-speakers are Sikhs.

The importance given to the mutually reinforcing character of certain kinds of cultural cleavages in the literature of political science and political sociology is, therefore, largely misplaced insofar (and for the same reasons) as it considers them as objective phenomena. In fact, the development of mutually reinforcing cleavages usually arises after a process of ethnic nationality-formation and ethnic group conflict has run its course, not before. In the process, it usually becomes clear at some point that one attribute or symbol is central to a group's self-definition. The process of nationality-formation itself then becomes one in which other symbols are brought into congruence with the leading symbol either by choice or out of conflict with competing or antagonistic groups. Nationalism, then, is the striving to achieve multi-symbol congruence among a group of people defined initially in terms of a single criterion.

In north India, the development of multi-symbol congruence has been advanced both by choice and by conflict among Sikhs and Hindus in the Punjab and Muslims and Hindus in Uttar Pradesh and Bihar. Furthest advanced in this regard is the Sikh nationality, which a hundred years ago was an internally differentiated religious group containing a variety of sects, some of them hardly distinguishable from similar Hindu sects; using in speech and writing several languages – Punjabi, Hindi, Urdu, and English; and dispersed and intermingled in a large territory among Hindus and Muslims. Today, although many of these characteristics continue to apply to adherents of the Sikh faith, the Sikh nationality can be defined as *keshadhari* Sikhs, who speak Punjabi and write it in the Gurumukhi script, and who occupy a compact geographical area, the Punjabi Suba. The central symbol has been identification as a *keshadhari* Sikh. The other symbols have been made congruent with it over time. Thus, an Akali Dal leader might include *keshadhari* Sikhs in California and Malaya in the Sikh nationality, but would probably exclude a Hindi-speaking *sahajdari* Sikh living in the Punjabi Suba.

Similarly, some Muslim elites in north India have sought to include in the concept of Muslim identity and separateness not only belief in the principles of Islam, but identification with the Urdu language. Here again, religious identity has been the central symbol. During the past century, Muslim political and cultural elites have tried to persuade all Muslims in north India to identify their language in the census returns as Urdu, not Hindi or Hindustani, and they have insisted on the right of all Muslims who go to school to be instructed through the medium of Urdu in the Persian-Arabic script. Perfect congruence between religion and language among Muslims has not yet been achieved in north India. Nearly all urban Muslims do in fact identify their mother tongue as Urdu and most rural Muslims do so now also, but the struggle for the right of all Muslims to learn Urdu in the schools has not yet been won.

In both the cases of Sikhs and Muslims, the movement toward multi-symbol congruence has taken place as much by conflict with Hindus as by self-definition. Sikhism and the Punjabi language, Islam and Urdu have become more congruent over time not only because these two minority groups have chosen to make religion and language congruent, but also because some elites in the Hindu majority group have identified Hinduism with Hindi in the Devanagari script and with Sanskrit culture and have attempted to absorb the minority groups into the language and culture of the majority. In order more effectively to resist assimilation, therefore, minority groups seek to reinforce their differences from the majority by adding other attributes to their self-definition. Here, however, the minority group may then face the problem of contradiction between two attributes. Thus, the Sikhs added Punjabi in Gurumukhi script to their self-definition and then made their political claims for a Punjabi Suba on the basis of language, whereupon many Punjabi-speaking Hindus decided that they did not speak Punjabi after all and that, therefore, the demand for a Punjabi Suba was not a legitimate one.

In the case of the Maithili movement, the contradictions have been so great to begin with that they have contributed to the failure of the movement. The central symbol of the movement has been the Maithili language. Its supporters, however, have faced critical problems of self-definition from the start. Is Maithili the language as spoken by the Maithil Brahman elite of Darbhanga or is it the language as spoken by the mass of the people in most of north Bihar? If the movement is to be based upon the pure Maithili of Darbhanga, its scope will be severely limited. If it is to be the spoken language of the

411

mass of the people, then how will the language be standardized in a form acceptable to as wide a group as possible and usable as a medium of instruction and examination in the schools? Clearly, the Maithili movement stands at an earlier stage of development, from which it may or may not move forward, in which basic agreement is lacking even on the definition and scope of the central symbol.

INTERNAL VALUES AND PROCESSES OF CHANGE

Internal values

The process of nationality-formation begins not in the mere existence of objective differences between peoples or in the availability of symbols of group differentiation, but in the attachment of value to those differences or symbols. Maithili spokesmen, of course, emphasize that Maithili is grammatically distinct from both Hindi and Bengali; but, even more important, they stress that the language has a glorious literary heritage of centuries and that it has produced one of the world's greatest poets and literary geniuses, Vidyapati Thakur. The literary excellence of Maithili is such, it is argued, that it must be preserved and further encouraged to develop along modern lines. Similar claims have been made on behalf of Urdu literature. Punjabi has a less persuasive claim as a vehicle of a long and glorious literary heritage, but the language has been praised for its rustic expressiveness and for its modern literary development.

Both Urdu and Punjabi, particularly through their associations with the Persian-Arabic and Gurumukhi scripts, respectively, are also valued because they are the languages and scripts in which the religious scriptures and other religiously oriented works of Islam and Sikhism are written. The religions themselves, it goes without saying, are also valued in themselves. In addition to the attachment of value to symbols of language and religion, other associated symbols have been brought into prominence by both Muslims and Sikhs. Spokesmen for the Muslim community look for inspiration from the past in the history of Muslim empires; those for the Sikh community find their glory in the history of the Sikh kingdoms and in the valor of the Sikh warriors of the past. In this process of symbol selection from the past, it is often necessary to ignore inconvenient aspects of a community's history. The process involves deliberate selectivity in search of myth, not truth.

As symbols of language, religion, history, and cultural traits are added, a full-blown and coherent myth may ultimately develop. The process of myth construction has not developed strongly in the Maithili movement, but it was fully evident in the self-image of the Muslim elites in the United Provinces before partition and among Punjabi Sikhs in contemporary times. In its final development, such a myth tends not only to attach value to symbols of group identity but to provide an explanation of the unfortunate condition of the community in the present and a remedy for its condition in the future. Thus, both the Muslim and Sikh myths contained within them the argument that their communities had been displaced from positions of rulership and dominance by British rule and that previously subordinate groups had risen to eminence and economic and political advantage as a consequence of British rule. Muslim elites in the United Provinces before partition, though they themselves came from privileged classes, made use of W. W. Hunter's famous description of the ruin of the Bengali Muslim aristocracy and applied it to their own condition. This myth, in U.P., as in Bengal, also included the element that the Hindus had risen to eminence as a consequence of British rule and were acting in ways which further threatened the position of the Muslim community. Consequently, it became necessary to adopt educational and political measures to advance the position of the Muslim community, particularly in relation to the majority Hindu community. It has been shown that the Muslim elites in the United Provinces also had in their armory another myth, closer to the facts, which argued that the Muslims were entitled to a special place in public life because of their past and current political and economic importance. This myth, however, had the disadvantage of revealing the true nature of the relations between Muslims and Hindus in the United Provinces at the time, namely, of a narrow, privileged Muslim elite struggling to maintain its political privileges against the rising tide of socially and politically mobilizing groups from within the majority Hindu community.

Leaders of the Sikh political movement in the Punjab in the post-independence period also attempted to cultivate a sense of grievance concerning their political subordination in contemporary India. At times, the oppressors were identified as 'fanatic' Hindus of the Arya Samaj variety, at other times as 'political Hindus' of the Congress variety. Charges of discrimination against the Sikhs were made and became increasingly strident during the 1960s. However, when a commission was appointed by the Government of India to inquire into the nature of the discrimination practiced against the Sikhs, no evidence was presented which provided any substance to the charges.

The two cases of the Muslim elite in the United Provinces before independence and of Sikhs in the Punjab after independence bring out sharply, by the very absence of an objective basis for the charges of discrimination, the political importance of identifying oppressors and cultivating a sense of grievance against them. Often enough, as in the case of Muslims in post-independence Uttar Pradesh and Bihar, there is an objective basis for such charges. However, even when there is not, the charges are likely anyway to be made because communalism and nationalism generally have both positive and negative features and nearly always arise in contexts of competition with other ethnic groups.

Elites

The particular symbols of group identity which are selected and the character of the myth which is constructed depend greatly upon the elite groups which do the selecting and myth construction. The Westernized elite which led the independence struggle in India through the Indian National Congress sought to build a sense of identification which would unite all peoples, languages, and religions in the entire subcontinent. Their choice of symbols was influenced partly by their class position and elite status, partly by the nature of the political entity which they wanted to construct. Educated in English and emancipated from traditional religious and caste restrictions, they tried to communicate across linguistic, caste, and religious barriers, often effectively. The languages they selected for inter-provincial communication were English and Hindustani. To overcome religious distinctions, they argued on behalf of secularism and toleration. To provide unifying symbols from the past, they selected the imperial consolidators and syncretistically oriented rulers, Ashoka and Akbar.

In the provincial and local arenas, there were other elite groups manipulating other kinds of symbols to achieve or maintain political power in their arenas. While the Westernized and English-educated, secular, and all-India-oriented elites struggled against British imperial power and for the assertion of an all-India nationalism, other elites and counter-elites in the provinces and municipalities used the symbols of the vernacular languages, of religious identity, and of regional history in struggles with their opponents. In some cases, the opponents of these regional and local elites were the all-India-oriented nationalists themselves; in other cases, the opponents were other regionally and locally oriented elite groups. Sometimes, regional and local conflicts spilled over into and had great consequences for the political course of events in the all-India arena.

In the United Provinces before partition, privileged Muslim elite groups found that the best way to maintain their positions of dominance in political and public life in the municipalities and in the provincial arena as a whole was to mobilize the Muslim community on a basis separate from the Hindus, to cooperate with the British against the rising Hindu elites, and to argue against the introduction of democratic reforms which would provide a majority to the Hindus. Islam, the Urdu language, the myth of Muslim backwardness, and the special historical position of the Muslims in the U.P. were the symbols called upon in this political struggle. The strategy succeeded for a time in winning important political concessions for Muslims and in slowing down the political advance of Hindu politicians, but the entire strategy collapsed with the overwhelming victory of the Congress in the U.P. in the 1937 elections. The Muslim elites, defeated in the provincial arena, now turned to the all-India arena and led the struggle to develop an all-India force against the Congress in the Muslim League and the Pakistan movement.

In the Punjab, Sikh religious and political leaders struggled to achieve as much political weight as possible before partition when the Sikh community formed a small minority in a multi-communal province. Unable to achieve a position of dominance in the public life of the provinces in a situation in which Muslims controlled the political arena and Hindus dominated the economic life of the cities, Sikh religious and political leaders made the most of their rural economic strength in the political arena and built a separate institutional base for their activities in politics through their control of the gurudwaras. Naturally, in such a situation, religion became the most powerful symbol in the Sikh movement.

In contrast to the Muslim elites in the United Provinces, who switched the focus of their attention to the national arena, the Sikh political leaders in the Punjab had no such option and concentrated their efforts on making the most of their position in the Punjab itself. The consequences for these two minorities in the post-independence period of their different strategies in the pre-independence period were dramatically different. The Muslim minority in the U.P. found itself still a minority after independence, now without leaders and without the support of the majority Muslim populations of pre-independence Punjab and Bengal. The Sikh leaders, however, deliberately set out to take advantage of the partition holocaust by turning the Muslims out of the East Punjab and moving the Sikh population in. After partition, the Sikh leaders found themselves in a better position than before, with their community concentrated geographically. It only remained to turn their new-found geographical advantage into a demand for a separate political status for the Sikhs. Since religion was not an acceptable symbol in post-independence India, the Sikh political leadership turned to the symbol of the Punjabi language in order to achieve its goals. In this way, it is clear, the symbols of group identity which are used to advance the cause of a community come to depend upon the political strategies pursued by its elites and leaders.

Not only do the symbols used and the myth constructed depend upon the composition of the elites which take the lead, but the success of the movement as a whole depends upon the ability of an elite group to communicate effectively with its potential followers and to prevent the growth of counter-elites who would take the ethnic group members along a different course. The importance of elites in this regard is brought out by the contrast between the Maithili movement and the more successful Muslim and Sikh separatist movements. The Maithil Brahman elite is a narrow, upper caste, socially exclusive, and culturally and linguistically distinctive group which has been unable to provide effective leadership to middle and lower caste groups in Mithila. Moreover, counter-elites have developed in the region along caste lines, who have found that they could achieve political power for themselves and economic advantages for their caste fellows by participating in the arena of Bihar politics rather than in attempting to build a separatist power base in Mithila.

The early Muslim elite groups in the United Provinces also constituted a relatively narrow group, but they were by no means as narrow and exclusive as the Maithil Brahman elite. In the early stages of Muslim separatism, it was government servants and Muslim aristocrats and landlords who took the lead. However, these early elite groups created the means for broadening their own leadership element through the education and ideology of the Aligarh movement, which trained young Muslims to enter the modern professions and provided them with a belief in the value of Muslim solidarity. Counter-elites did develop in the Muslim community, particularly among the ulama, but they did not seek different goals from those sought by the Aligarh leadership, only different means and political paths. Both elite groups promoted the ideology of Muslim separatism. In the later stages of the movement, lawyers and other members of the professional middle and upper classes began to occupy positions of leadership in the Muslim League. In the post-independence period, the old aristocratic elite has been completely removed or displaced and leadership has passed back to, on the one side, the ulama and, on the other side, the professional people – doctors, professors, lawyers, and journalists. However, the contemporary Muslim middle class has been divided between separatist leaders and secular, often Marxist, leaders, who are oriented towards the Congress and the Communist parties. Thus, Muslim politics in the post-independence period have come to be divided on basic goals, in contrast to the situation before independence.

The leadership of Sikh separatism has been the most cohesive of all in terms of consistency of goals, though the elite composition of the Sikh community has changed over time. The early leadership of the Singh Sabhas came from 'the rich, landed gentry and the orthodox'.[1] The most prominent leader of the Chief Khalsa Diwan was Sir Sunder Singh Majithia, who was descended from a family which had served under Maharaja Ranjit Singh.[2] During the Akali movement in the 1920s, the leadership was broadened to include middle-class professionals such as Master Tara Singh himself. The middle-class leadership of teachers and lawyers became increasingly prominent in later years, particularly after partition when urban Sikh refugees became prominent in the Akali Dal. Ex-servicemen and contractors have also been of some consequence in recent years. However, the backbone of Sikh leadership through the Punjabi Suba movement continued to comprise a combination of Sikh religious leaders, represented particularly by Sant Fateh Singh, and the rich Sikh farmers who dominate the SGPC. Divisions have existed within the Akali movement, particularly between the urban, refugee, predominantly middle-class groups and the rural leadership elements. There has also been division between the Sikh separatist and Marxist secularist leadership, which has expressed itself in the electoral arena. However, the rural, religiously oriented Jat Sikh leadership has maintained its nearly complete dominance of the SGPC, which has enabled it both to control the Akali Dal and to prevail over the Communist parties in the electoral arena.

Social change and social mobilization

Nationalist and communalist movements may have narrow beginnings among particular elite groups and may even achieve significant

---

[1] Khushwant Singh, *A History of the Sikhs*, vol. II: 1839–1964 (Princeton, N.J.: Princeton University Press, 1966), p. 141.
[2] *Ibid.*, p. 145.

political successes either against weak opposition or by means of alliances with other powerful forces. However, a self-conscious communal group or nation does not come into being until there is a socially mobilized population to whom the myth of group solidarity can be communicated. Elites relate in two ways to processes of social change and social mobilization affecting the groups they wish to lead. On the one hand, they must develop means of communication with the already mobilized and the newly mobilizing population. At the same time, they must be prepared to compete with other elites manipulating other symbols to capture the allegiance of the newly mobilizing and unmobilized groups.

The Maithil Brahman elite has so far failed in both respects. Social change and social mobilization have been slower in north Bihar than almost anywhere else in India, but the leadership of the Maithili movement has failed even to develop adequate means of communicating with the relatively small population of urban, newspaper reading, Maithili-speakers. In fact, the Maithili leadership has not been able to compete successfully even in its cultural heartland in Darbhanga in developing Maithili as a medium of communication among the literate public, who prefer Hindi, English, and Urdu newspapers to the few Maithili papers which do exist.

Muslim separatism in the United Provinces began with a decided advantage in contrast with the Maithili movement. The Muslim population of the U.P. was traditionally more concentrated in urban centers than the Hindu and Urdu was the dominant literary language in those provinces in the nineteenth century. Competition developed between rival Hindu and Muslim elites for the allegiance of the newly mobilizing populations. This competition took the form of a struggle between Hindi in Devanagari script and Urdu in Persian-Arabic script for supremacy as the official and court language and the medium of instruction in the primary schools of the provinces. The struggle was essentially a political and economic struggle between a privileged Muslim upper-class elite and rising Hindu middle-class groups, in which the symbols of language and religion were brought in partly to gain political and economic advantage and partly as bases for the mobilization of communal solidarity. Gradually, the rising Hindu elite groups succeeded in displacing Urdu as the predominant language of public and official life in the U.P. and in displacing Muslims from their predominant positions in government and administration. In the post-independence period in north India, the struggle has continued, with the significant difference that the Muslims have been relegated to secondary positions in

the public life of the provinces and have been subjected to a deliberate policy of linguistic assimilation, including efforts to minimize the
use of the Urdu language in the public schools.

In the Punjab before independence, the social context of political
competition was somewhat different. In the pre-partition tri-communal province, the Muslims, though they were educationally and
economically less advantaged than either the Hindus or the Sikhs,
were politically dominant. The Hindu and Sikh minority communities were both engaged in rapid processes of internal social change
and communication, which were moving both communities toward
more intensive internal communication and sharper external boundary definition. Segmentation of the two communities was increasing,
as was competition between them; but the major confrontation between Sikh and Hindu communal forces did not occur until after
partition when the Muslim population was removed and the Sikh
population was concentrated in East Punjab. The social context of
Sikh–Hindu political competition now became, in the Punjabi region, the classic case of a rapidly mobilizing, predominantly rural
Sikh community confronting a more urbanized Hindu community.
As in the U.P., language became the symbol of a political-economic
conflict in which the underlying solidarities were based on religious
identification.

INTER-GROUP RELATIONS

The basic condition for group conflict based on ethnic differences is
the perception of the existence of unevenness in development between two or more groups. It does not matter, as the Maithili case
shows, that one can point to objective facts which demonstrate an
imbalance between two peoples if the peoples themselves do not per-
ceive it. Objectively, the Maithili-speaking region of north Bihar is
economically less developed than other parts of Bihar and charges
have been made that there has been discrimination against the region on such matters as the absence of a university and a radio station. However, this evidence of regional imbalance has either not
been perceived as significant by most Maithili-speakers or other
kinds of discriminations, particularly those based on caste, have been
perceived as more important and have, therefore, provided more
powerful bases for political mobilization.

If subjective perception of unevenness does not flow automatically
where objective imbalances exist, it is also the case that a subjective
perception of discrimination may be politically useful even where,

objectively speaking, discrimination does not exist. This point has already been made in connection with the discussion of the myth of Muslim backwardness in the pre-independence period and the charges of discrimination against the Sikhs made in post-independence Punjab.

Unevenness between social groups is practically a universal fact of human existence. The chances that any two defined human populations will be equally well placed with regard to the allocation of all important values in any society are nearly zero. The fact of unevenness can, for all practical purposes, be assumed in any plural society. The significant questions then become how the inequalities are distributed between groups and along different measures and how they are perceived.

On a spectrum of uneven inter-group relations, there are two polar situations – a more advanced or dominant minority set against a mobilizing majority and the opposite case of a more advanced or dominant majority set against a mobilizing minority. The closest approximation to the former situation in the north Indian cases was that of the Muslim minority in the United Provinces before partition. However, it must always be kept in mind, especially in societies where the processes of social mobilization are at early stages, that the real conflicts are between particular sub-groups within each community who attempt to manipulate symbols of communal identity for purposes of mobilizing communities, the overwhelming majority of whose members are in a pre-mobilized state. In other words, the vast majority of both Muslims and Hindus in the U.P. were illiterate and powerless. The conflict between Muslims and Hindus can be described as dominant minority against a mobilizing majority only in a gross and relative sense.

At the other end of the spectrum of inter-group relations in north India is the relationship between the majority Hindu community in Uttar Pradesh and Bihar and the Muslim minority. The props of Muslim advantage in the pre-independence period arose out of the access which Muslim elites had to political power, out of their control over land revenue resources from the big Muslim estates, out of their ability to mobilize a heavily urban Muslim population, and out of the relatively slow pace of social mobilization among Hindus. In the post-independence period, all these props have been removed. The Muslims of north India now constitute a relatively disadvantaged minority in a society and political order in which Hindus are an overwhelming majority. Moreover, many of the politically important sub-groups among Hindus harbor resentment over previous

Muslim advantages and political activities and are, therefore, reluctant to make political, economic, or cultural concessions to Muslim minority demands.

The relationships between Maithili- and non-Maithili-speakers in Bihar and between Sikhs and Hindus in the Punjab have been more ambiguous. In Bihar as a whole, Maithili-speakers are a backward minority in a region which is culturally and ethnically heterogeneous and in which other linguistic groups are more advanced and identify with Hindi. In the Maithili region alone, Maithili-speakers are a backward majority in a situation where Hindi- and Urdu-speakers control the political and economic centers in the towns and where Hindi and Urdu are the chief media of education and communication. The critical factor in either description of the position of Maithili-speakers is the extraordinarily slow pace of social change among them.

The relationship between Sikhs and Hindus in the Punjab has also been less sharply defined than the two polar situations defined above. In the pre-independence period, Sikhs and Hindus both constituted socially mobilizing communities competing with each other, but also with the less advanced but politically dominant Muslim community. In the post-independence period, in the pre-reorganized Punjab, Sikhs were a mobilizing minority in the state as a whole, competing against an also rapidly mobilizing Hindu majority. In the Punjabi region alone, however, it was more a case of two numerically nearly equal communities, both mobilizing rapidly, but with the Sikhs dominant in the rural areas and the Hindus in the cities.

It has already been stressed that a great simplification is involved in speaking of whole communities set against each other in this way because of the fact that particular sub-groups usually take the lead within each community. Moreover, in comparing the relative advantages possessed by different communities taken as wholes, the various measures of political, economic, and educational advancement do not always coincide. Thus, as was just noted, Sikhs and Hindus were economically and educationally more advanced than Muslims in pre-independence Punjab, but the Muslims had numerical preponderance in the cities and were politically dominant. Similarly, in referring to the relations between Hindus and Sikhs in Punjab, one cannot speak at any time of one community being more advantaged than the other community in all respects, but only of specific measures in which in one respect Sikhs, in another respect Hindus have the edge.

The critical question in discussing the relationship between two communities, of course, is the precise sets of relationships which are likely to engender communally-based political differentiation and conflict. The central hypothesis on this point, which has been discussed at length in this book, is that the conditions for political differentiation are created when social mobilization outpaces assimilation and, conversely, that assimilation will occur when social change in a cultural group is slow enough for its members to be absorbed gradually into another, dominant cultural group. The first situation characterizes best the gradual social mobilization of the Hindus in north India which, though it occurred slowly, could not be contained by the Muslim elites within the confines of an Indo-Muslim culture in which Urdu in Persian-Arabic script was the language of education and administration. Hindu revivalist leaders and rising Hindu politicians demanded that their social and economic progress should be accompanied by cultural changes as well, that Hindi in Devanagari script should become the medium of instruction in the public schools and that the official language of courts and government offices should be changed accordingly so that Hindus educated in Devanagari Hindi would not suffer in the competition for jobs.

The contrasting situation in north India is that of the Maithili-speakers where an elite has made cultural demands which have not been met because the people have not been mobilized rapidly enough to provide a constituency which would support them. Consequently, Hindi continues to be the predominant medium both for educational advancement and for access to the public service. The slow pace of change in Mithila and the consequently slow pace of entry of Maithili-speakers into the modern sectors of the society and polity makes it relatively easy for the dominant pro-Hindi cultural elements to absorb and assimilate educated and otherwise socially mobilized Maithili-speakers.

There are three critical qualifications of the basic Deutschian hypothesis, however, which were partly suggested in *Nationalism and Social Communication* itself. First, it must not be assumed that the underlying pre-mobilized rural population lacks social and political consciousness. In fact, the rural population may develop an identification with a particular language or culture which will make its assimilation into another culture more difficult, even if the rate of social mobilization is relatively slow and the capacity of the dominant culture to absorb new socially mobilized elements from the different culture is very high. In other words, political consciousness of cultural difference may precede social mobilization and prevent assimilation. The evidence for this proposition comes most clearly from the politics of the census operations in India where elite protagonists of the demands of particular languages have attempted to instill in the unmobilized rural populations a knowledge of the 'correct' name of their mother tongue. The purpose is primarily to provide large census figures to back up demands for educational and other facilities, but it also means that when a Muslim Hindustani-speaker who has been instructed that the name of his mother tongue is Urdu goes to register his children in the local school, he may demand that the medium of instruction be Urdu in Persian script even though the local school is fully equipped to instruct him in the dominant language, Hindi in Devanagari script. Thus, the unmobilized population may be primed for social differentiation even before social mobilization takes place.

A second important distinction involved in the relationships between processes of assimilation and social mobilization is that between capacity to communicate and willingness to communicate in particular languages. It has been amply demonstrated throughout this book that assimilation is a subjective more than an objective process. Muslims and Hindus have the capacity to communicate in ordinary Hindustani, Sikhs and Hindus in Punjabi. However, both Muslims and Sikhs, in order to enhance their sense of separateness from Hindi-speaking Hindus, have set up symbolic barriers to communication, particularly in their choice of script for the Urdu and Punjabi languages.

The third and most important qualification concerns the centrality of politics and political action in the entire process. The grand processes of social mobilization and assimilation do not take place in a political vacuum. Nor do they determine the course of political development in multi-ethnic societies. Political leadership, political organization, and political choice are involved in the development and interrelationship of these processes. The most striking example of the impact of political choice on linguistic differentiation in north India is the case of the shift of millions of Punjabi-speaking Hindus to Hindi as their language of preference. However, the influence of political considerations has been present in all the movements described above. The processes of social mobilization and assimilation in north India have been occurring in a political context in which particular elites have been interested in and have attempted to determine the outcome by competing for the cultural-political allegiances of both the mobilizing and pre-mobilized populations.

POLITICAL ACTION

Political organization

The impact of political organization on nationality-formation is two-fold. First, political organization is essential to complete the process. Second, political organizations play important roles in defining the nationality and shaping its identity.

Nations are defined in political terms and they require political organization to acquire their status. There is a considerable range in the type of organization which may provide the driving force for national organizations and in their strength and impact. A major reason for the failure of the Maithili movement has been the small scale and relative weakness and narrowness of the political organizations which speak in its name. The organizations concerned with the advancement of the Maithili cause have been voluntary associations, principally caste associations such as the Maithil Mahasabha and literary-cultural associations such as the Maithili Sahitya Parishad. Their leadership has come from a small elite group, primarily Maithil Brahmans; their membership has been tiny; their activities minimal; and their finances dismal. The leading political organizations in the Maithili-speaking region have not been oriented primarily or even at all to the interests of the Maithili movement. Mithila is an area whose politics have been dominated by the leading political parties in Bihar – the Congress, the CPI, and the Socialist Party particularly. These parties, oriented toward achieving power in Bihar as a whole, have been willing to consider and support specific demands for the advancement of the Maithili-speaking region and its people, but none of them has been interested in making the Maithili cause its own.

At the other extreme from the Maithili voluntary associations are the political organizations of the Sikh community, which illustrate both the importance of political organization to the success of a nationality movement and the capacity of strong political organizations to shape the process of identity formation. Sikh political aspirations were initially expressed through voluntary associations, such as the Singh Sabhas and the Chief Khalsa Diwan. However, the institutional basis for Sikh political activities was radically transformed with the formation of both the SGPC and the Akali Dal in the 1920s. The Akali Dal, as the chief political instrument for Sikh nationalist aspirations in the Punjab, has been characterized by a number of features which have made it eminently successful in its role. First, it has had the organizational and financial support of the SGPC, which has provided it with an unshakeable institutional basis and a vast source of finance for its activities. Second, it has not only defined itself exclusively as the political arm of the Sikh community and, accordingly, restricted its membership to Sikhs, but it has succeeded in identifying itself with the Panth or Sikh community in the Punjab. Third, it has been instrumental in defining Sikh identity itself, emphasizing particularly values associated with religion, with the five outward symbols of *keshadhari* Sikhism, with the Punjabi language, with militancy, and with the merging of religion and politics. Fourth, it has provided continuity of political leaderhip, first under Master Tara Singh, then under Sant Fateh Singh. Fifth, however, the Akali Dal has shown itself able to withstand changes of leadership, such as that which occurred when Sant Fateh Singh defeated Master Tara Singh in a struggle for control of both the Akali Dal and the SGPC. Finally, despite changes in leadership and persistent factionalism, one wing of the Akali Dal – that in control of the SGPC – has always been overwhelmingly dominant whenever the movement has split or has undergone struggles for leadership.

Intermediate between the Maithili voluntary associations and the Akali Dal in effectiveness have been the political organizations in north India which have expressed Muslim political and cultural aspirations. Muslim politics in north India have spawned a wide variety of religious, economic, educational, and political associations, which have been described above. Two of these organizations have aspired to represent the Muslim community as a whole – the Muslim League and the Muslim Majlis-e-Mushawarat. Neither of these two organizations has had as strong an institutional or financial base as the Akali Dal, although the League proved to be an effective mobilizer of Muslim political opinion in the north in 1946. More important, both organizations had narrower aims than did the Akali Dal. The Akali Dal considers itself integral with the Sikh Panth, as a political arm of the Sikh religious body. The Muslim League in north India before independence sought to achieve recognition as the sole legitimate political spokesman of the Muslim community, but it did not seek to identify itself with the Muslim community as such. Nor did it play the role of shaping Islamic identity in the same way that the Akali Dal did for the Sikhs. In a sense, the task of the Muslim League was much simpler than that of the Akali Dal. It was presented, simply by the asking, with the political gift of separate electorates in 1909. Separate electorates provided Muslim political leaders with a separate political arena in which they could achieve a dominant position without competition from political elites in other communities. It only remained for the Muslim League to mobilize the Muslim community into a cohesive political bloc to achieve its political and cultural goals. However, the political context of the first two decades of the twentieth century did not bring sufficient threat to the privileges of the Muslim political elites to provide the necessary catalyst for them to complete the task of Muslim political mobilization. When the threat came in the 1930s, the mechanism of separate electorates was available, but it required a massive effort and two elections, in 1936 and 1946, before the Muslim League could achieve its goal of complete dominance in the Muslim political arena.

Since independence, neither the political mechanism of separate electorates nor the political cohesion of 1946 has been available to Muslim political leaders in U.P. and Bihar. The Muslim community of north India is highly differentiated politically. This is a different kind of situation from that of both the Maithili-speakers and the Sikhs. In the former case, there is neither strong political organization nor political differentiation. Among the Sikhs, there is strong political organization and, though it has competitors, the Akali Dal has occupied a position of pre-eminence among Sikh political organizations. Muslim political organizations are stronger than the Maithili organizations, but there is no single Muslim political organization which can claim to speak for the interests of the Muslim community as a whole. What is not clear is whether the high degree of political differentiation within the Muslim community in north India is a result primarily of the constraints of the contemporary political context and rules of the game in India, which make it difficult for Muslim politicians to mobilize Muslims in the manner of the pre-independence Muslim League, or whether this differentiation represents a stage in the modernization of Muslims on the way to their ultimate integration into Indian political life on a new basis. In the latter case, symbols of language and religion would become less important for Muslims and economic issues more important in the long term. In recent years, however, it is clear that language and religion have maintained a high degree of salience in north Indian Muslim politics.

Government policies

The preceding discussion of the role of separate electorates in the pre-independence political mobilization of the Muslim community suggests both the importance and the limitations of institutional mechanisms and government policies in promoting the process of nationality-formation in an ethnic group. Such mechanisms and policies may provide arenas and opportunities for political mobilization. They may also provide constraints on the kinds of political demands that are permissible that in turn affect the course of political movements. However, institutional mechanisms and government policies alone cannot provide the generative force to transform ethnic groups into nations. On the other hand, institutions and policies designed to discourage such transformations may be more effective, especially in relation to ethnic groups whose self-awareness has not proceeded very far.

Examples of the encouraging and limiting effects of institutions and policies in India are abundant in the three movements discussed in this book. A good contrast with the role of separate electorates for Muslims is the role of the Sikh Gurudwara Reform Act for the Sikhs. Separate electorates were won initially without a major struggle and provided an arena for the ultimate political mobilization of Muslims. The Gurudwara Reform Act, in contrast, was won out of struggle in which a large segment of the Sikh community was involved. The passage of the Gurudwara Act provided a testimony to the strong sense of self-assertion which already existed among Sikhs. The act also established an institutional arena for Sikh politics which made it possible for Sikhs to preserve not only their religious but their political identity in the face of catastrophic changes in their environment and total transformations in the official political arenas. Once again, however, the institution of the SGPC did not promote Sikh mobilization, but only provided a critical arena for it.

The history of government language policies in north India provides further examples of the interrelationship between government decisions and processes of nationality-formation. A comparison of British policy towards Urdu in Bihar, the United Provinces, and Punjab is especially instructive. In Bihar, in 1881, Urdu was completely displaced as an official language of the province by Hindi. In the United Provinces, Urdu retained a position of equality with Hindi after 1900. In the Punjab, Urdu remained the sole official vernacular language until independence. What were the consequences of these three different decisions for the development of the various language movements in north India? The 1881 decision in Bihar did not eliminate Urdu as a symbol of Muslim identity in Bihar. It was more important for the Hindi movement which was presented with the linguistically heterogeneous province of Bihar as a field in which to extend the hold of Hindi among the various dialect speakers. The 1900 decision in the United Provinces also was more helpful to the Hindi movement than it was harmful to Urdu as a symbol of Muslim identity, since it put a brake on the process of assimilation of newly educated Hindus to Indo-Persian culture and introduced an alternative linguistic-cultural model for Hindus. In both cases, Urdu lost status as a medium of written communication between members of different religions and was relegated increasingly to a position as the language of a particular minority group. However, the example of the Punjab suggests that, even if Urdu had been retained as the dominant language of inter-communal communication, it would not have prevented the increasing identification of Hindus with Hindi in Devanagari script. For, in the Punjab, where Urdu retained official status as court language and medium of primary education up to independence, the promoters of Hindu and Sikh cultural identity established large networks of private schools imparting instruction to Hindus in Hindi in the Devanagari script and to Sikhs in Punjabi in Gurumukhi script. In other words, the language movements of north India were influenced by, but did not receive their motive force from government decisions.

It is also instructive to compare the language demands made by minority language groups and the language policies and policy alternatives considered in the post-independence period in the Punjab with those in U.P. and Bihar. Although there are numerous variations of detail in policy choices available on questions of medium of education and official language, there are two basic issues which determine the limits of minority language group rights in a bilingual society. One is the issue of whether the speakers of the minority language are to be recognized and granted rights according to group criteria or individual choice. In the three north Indian states, the relevant group criteria have not been philological, but territorial and religious. In these three states, the issue has been whether all persons occupying a particular territory or belonging to a particular religious group should be presumed to be speakers of a minority language and to be entitled to protection on that basis or whether they should be required to express their identity individually through conscious choice and specific request to the local authorities. In most cases, the adoption of group criteria works to the advantage of the minority group. Only in the initial stages of a minority language movement are its leaders likely to be satisfied with the minimal concession that those who declare themselves speakers of a minority language will be entitled to receive education through the medium of their mother tongue. The Maithili-speaking minority has achieved only this minimal recognition, but even here some spokesmen for the movement have demanded that Maithili be recognized as the regional language of north Bihar. At the other extreme is the PEPSU Formula in the Punjab, which required all inhabitants of the region demarcated as Punjabi-speaking to be educated through the medium of Punjabi. A compromise between the two positions is represented by the Sachar Formula which demarcated the areas where both the minority and majority languages are spoken and where the regional language was to be the medium, but permitted parents to opt out.

Although a vigorous minority language movement is likely to seek an objective basis of differentiation, some criteria may be excluded in particular political systems as illegitimate. For example, it would be to the advantage of the Muslim Urdu-speakers to win the concession that all Muslims are to be presumed to be Urdu-speakers and to be entitled to be educated through the medium of Urdu, but it is not possible under the present political rules of the game in India to make such a demand. Unfortunately for Urdu-speakers, their territorial dispersion limits their effective political demand to the exercise of the parent choice preference. In the Punjab, both religion and territory were available criteria to distinguish Punjabi-speakers. Nearly all Sikhs claim to be Punjabi-speakers, but the Punjabi-speaking region included both Sikhs and Hindus and it was the territorial principle that was invariably adopted by policy-makers.

The second major issue is one of equality or minority rights, whether the minority language is to have equal status for official purposes with the majority language or is to be used only for specified purposes or in certain areas, whether bilingualism is to be enforced for all or only for the minority, whether or not both languages are to be media of examination for entry into the public services, and the like. In Bihar, the Maithili movement is very far from being in a position to demand full equality, but even there the demand has occasionally been made to permit the use of Maithili as medium of examination for the public service. In U.P. before independence, enforced bilingualism was the policy both for official and educational purposes, but the post-independence government changed to an attempt at assimilation of the minority language speakers combined with enforced bilingualism for those who refuse to be assimilated. In the Punjab before reorganization, the minority language movement succeeded in winning full equality for Punjabi, including enforced bilingualism for all. Enforced bilingualism for all, however, is a viable strategy only for a large and cohesive minority group. In the

Punjab, it proved to be an effective strategy to make political separation not only acceptable but desirable for the Hindi-speaking Hindus of Haryana.[1]

This discussion of language policy alternatives indicates that there is a very broad range of policy options open to decision makers and competing ethnic-linguistic groups in multi-lingual societies. The choice of particular policies, however, is likely to depend upon the broad strategy which policy-makers wish to implement. While, on balance, government policies in India have been pluralistic and have provided an environment which encourages ethnic groups to achieve self-consciousness and to articulate their demands, there have been some limitations imposed upon minority groups and some contradictions in government policies. It was noted in the introductory chapter and it has been confirmed in the case studies that the Government of India has applied four rules in its treatment of ethnic group demands, namely, that no secessionist demands or demands based upon religion will be entertained, that concessions will not be made to minority groups that do not demonstrate their ability to mobilize politically for their demands, and that concessions made to one ethnic group must be acceptable to rival groups. Thus, Sikh demands in the early post-independence period seemed to central government leaders to have the odor of both secession and religious communalism, but the Punjabi Suba demand could be entertained under the rules of the game. Even the Punjabi Suba demand, however, was not conceded until the fourth rule of mutual acceptance by opposed ethnic groups could be applied. Similarly, Muslim Urdu-speakers may demand that Urdu be protected so long as Urdu is not identified as the language of Muslims only. The third rule concerning the need to demonstrate popular support has been most in evidence in the Maithili case, where the central government has refused to grant Maithili a place in the eighth schedule of the Constitution. In all these examples, again, government policy has influenced the form in which demands are made and their consequences for political stability. It has not, however, prevented ethnic groups from mobilizing under the rules of the game.

There has, however, been a contradiction in Government of India policy and some differences between central and state government policies toward linguistic group demands. The contradiction in Government of India policy is in its strivings to promote an all-India

---

[1] *Statesman*, 30 June 1960 remarked that the attempts to impose Punjabi in Haryana 'promoted not the linguistic unity of Punjab which was intended but a separatist demand for Haryana Prant'.

nationality on a territorial basis while simultaneously granting rights on a group basis to linguistic minorities. If the Government of India succeeds in the long run in promoting symbols of all-India nationality and in maintaining the political cohesion of the Indian Union, the contradiction may be resolved in the creation of dual nationalities whose members see themselves as Sikhs, Hindus, and Muslims or as Bengalis and Tamils in relation to one another but as loyal and devoted Indians in relation to the rest of the world.

The ultimate development of such a politically integrated and plural society in India also depends upon how the states resolve their relations with ethnic minorities. Muslims in Uttar Pradesh and Bihar acquire some solace from the pluralistic policies of the Government of India, but they feel threatened by the policies of the state governments. They are not likely to feel that sense of a dual identification with their own community and with India as a whole until their cultural demands are achieved in the north Indian states. For their part, many of the Hindu political leaders who dominate all political parties and governments in U.P. and Bihar have felt that the Muslims of their states, because of the prominence of the Pakistan movement there before independence, have been more loyal to Pakistan than to India. Thus, the consequences of earlier Hindu–Muslim conflicts have yet to work themselves out in north India into a situation where governments will be willing to look at Muslim demands solely on the merits, without reference to past resentments.

Party politics, ethnic cleavage, and political integration

The primary purpose of this book has been to elaborate and apply a concept of nationality-formation. A secondary purpose has been to demonstrate that the process of nationality-formation in multi-ethnic societies is not necessarily incompatible with political integration, even in regimes of competitive political parties where the parties are permitted to articulate the demands of ethnic groups. In order to demonstrate this argument, it has been necessary to come to grips with three widely accepted propositions in the literature of political development and political sociology which seem to contradict it. The first is that mutually reinforcing cleavages in culturally fragmented societies are inherently more destabilizing than cross-cutting cleavages. The second is that political parties, especially in developing societies, are dependent forces, which at best reflect and at worst exacerbate existing cleavages. The third is that ethnic cleavages are inherently more dangerous than other forms of cleavage, that there is a conflict in multi-ethnic societies between 'primordial' loyalties and behavior and civil loyalties and behavior.

The first proposition stands in direct contradiction of the argument. For, if it is true that mutually reinforcing or congruent social cleavages are more detrimental to integrative processes than cross-cutting cleavages and if one accepts the view of the process of nationality-formation presented in this book as a striving by ethnic groups to achieve multi-symbol congruence, then there is an inevitable contradiction between political integration and nationality-formation in multi-ethnic societies. This apparent contradiction dissolves, however, when two implicit assumptions are removed from it, namely, that political integration must involve national integration or assimilation and that the nation is a 'terminal community', constituting 'the effective end of the road for man as a social animal, the end point of working solidarity between men'.[1] If, however, one views political integration as a process analytically separate from national integration,[2] and begins to think in terms of pluralist solutions to state–nation relationships, then the necessary contradiction begins to dissolve. It dissolves even more rapidly when one substitutes for the idea of the nation as a terminal loyalty the recognition that human beings usually have a hierarchy of values[3] which may incorporate multi-level national conceptions as well. Men may operate effectively with each other for specific purposes in an all-India nation while still considering themselves members of a Sikh or Bengali nation.

Moreover, there is no reason to consider membership in a nation or other congruent group as a permanent loyalty. Men's loyalties may change, sometimes within a single generation, sometimes over several generations. Loyalties which are congruent at one point in time may be cross-cut by other loyalties later. Nations are not fixed entities, but groups whose boundaries are continually in flux.

The second proposition, that political parties are dependent upon social cleavages, has already been challenged by other scholars. The analysis of party politics in the Punjab in this book throws further light on this question. It is clear, first of all, that political parties in

---

[1] Rupert Emerson, *From Empire to Nation: The Rise to Self-Assertion of Asian and African Peoples* (Boston: Beacon Press, 1962), p. 96.

[2] On this point, see Jyotirindra Das Gupta, 'Language Diversity and National Development', in Joshua A. Fishman *et al.* (eds.), *Language Problems of Developing Nations* (New York: John Wiley, 1968), pp. 17–26, and Myron Weiner, 'Political Integration and Political Development', in Jason L. Finkle and Richard W. Gable (eds.), *Political Development and Social Change* (New York: John Wiley, 1966), 551–62.

[3] Cf. M. N. Srinivas, *Caste in Modern India and Other Essays* (Bombay: Asia Publishing House, 1962), pp. 110–11.

the Punjab have played independent roles both in creating or shaping and in moderating ethnic group loyalties and antagonisms. The Akali Dal has not been simply a political expression of pre-existing Sikh aspirations, but it has played a critical role in creating a modern Sikh nation. At the same time, the Congress, the leading governing party in the Punjab, has also played an independent role in state politics, consistently bringing together Hindus and Sikhs on a common political platform and at the same time presenting an alternative conception of the political life in which religion is relegated to the private sphere.

Moreover, the history of party politics in the Punjab suggests that the striving for power in multi-ethnic societies with parliamentary systems tends to promote inter-communal collaboration. Such collaboration or coalition-building may be done in the electoral arena itself by parties such as the Congress which strive to appeal to all or most ethnic groups in the society, or it may be done in the legislative arena after the elections are over by parties such as the Jan Sangh or the Akali Dal that appeal to only one community during the election, but combine to achieve power thereafter. The danger in parliamentary systems arises when a major political force sees no route to power in the existing political arena or sees an alternative political arena which would provide easier access to power. This was the position in which the Muslim League found itself in the United Provinces after the 1937 elections and in which the Akali Dal found itself in the Punjab after 1947. After 1937, the Muslim League saw its future in the U.P. as one of a permanent minority. Its leaders, therefore, shifted their attention to the all-India political arena where the Muslim community might have greater weight. Similarly, the Akali Dal could not hope to achieve power alone in the united Punjab and, therefore, sought to create a new political arena in which Sikh and Akali aspirations could be more easily achieved. Such decisions are not always productive of the results sought even when the goal of creating a new arena is achieved. The Muslim League shift to the all-India arena led to the creation of Pakistan, but did not bring power to most U.P. Muslim League politicians who remained in U.P. Nor has the creation of a Punjabi Suba guaranteed power to the Akali Dal, which continues to be a minority party even in a Sikh-majority political unit. The Akali Dal now has two alternative paths before it. It can escalate Sikh demands even further and demand still another kind of political unit or it can once and for all adjust its political goals to the realities of political life in the Punjabi Suba and seek power by broadening its own social and ethnic base or by coalescing with other political groups. Either choice will certainly have consequences not only for Punjab political stability but for Sikh ethnic identity.

The third and final proposition which has been questioned in this book is the contradiction between ethnicity and civility, between primordial and civil politics. It can hardly be denied that ethnic politics have sometimes led to catastrophe, even to genocide. This has been true in the South Asian sub-continent as well as in Europe. It is also true, however, that economic conflicts have sometimes led to revolutionary warfare and to the extermination of whole classes of people. Violent results are, therefore, not confined to ethnic political interactions. Nor does it seem to be the case that ethnic conflicts are any less subject to compromise or adjustment than economic conflicts. The range of policy options open to governments and the forms of political accommodation available to political leaders when ethnic and nationality issues are at stake are very great. Moreover, over time, ethnicity may give way to class and *vice versa*. Ultimately, it is a matter of ideological preference which category of issues one considers more suitable to civil society, but there is no evidence to demonstrate that one is more conducive than the other to civil order.

BIBLIOGRAPHY

PUBLIC DOCUMENTS

Bihar. Vidhan Sabha, *Bihar Vidhan-Sabha ke SadasyoN ka Sankshipt Jivan-Parichay*. Patna: Bihar Vidhan-Sabha Press, 1966.

Great Britain. Indian Statutory Commission, vol. xvi: *Selections from Memoranda and Oral Evidence by Non-Officials (Part I)*. London: His Majesty's Stationery Office, 1930.

India. The Aligarh Muslim University (Amendment) Ordinance, 1965, *Gazette of India Extraordinary*, pt. ii, 20 May 1965.

Census of India, 1872. Census of N.-W. Provinces, 1872, vol. i: *General Report*, by W. C. Plowden. Allahabad: North-Western Provinces' Government Press, 1873.

Census of India, 1881. Report on the Census of Bengal, vol. i, by J. A. Bourdillon. Calcutta: Bengal Secretariat Press, 1883.

Census of India, 1881. Report on the Census of the Punjab, vol. i: *Text; and Appendices C and D*, by Denzil Charles Jelf Ibbetson. Calcutta: Superintendent of Government Printing, India, 1883.

Census of India, 1881. Report on the Census of the N.-W.P. and Oudh and of the Native States of Rampur and Native Garhwal, by Edmund White. Allahabad: North-Western Provinces and Oudh Government Press, 1882.

Census of India, 1891, vol. iii: *The Lower Provinces of Bengal and Their Feudatories*, by C. J. O'Donnell. Calcutta: Bengal Secretariat Press, 1893.

Census of India, 1891, vol. xvi: *The North-Western Provinces and Oudh*, pt. i: *Report and Provincial Tables*, by D. C. Baillie. Allahabad: North-Western Provinces and Oudh Government Press, 1894.

Census of India, 1891, vol. xvii: *The North-Western Provinces and Oudh*, pt. ii: *Imperial Tables*, by D. C. Baillie. Allahabad: North-Western Provinces and Oudh Government Press, 1894.

Census of India, 1891, vol. xx: *The Punjab and Its Feudatories*, pt. ii: *Imperial Tables and Supplementary Returns for the British Territory*, by E. D. Maclagan. Calcutta: Superintendent of Government Printing, India, 1892.

Census of India, 1901, vol. vi: *The Lower Provinces of Bengal and Their Feudatories*, pt. i: *The Report*, by E. A. Gait. Calcutta: Bengal Secretariat Press, 1902.

Census of India, 1901, vol. vi–a: *The Lower Provinces of Bengal and Their Feudatories*, pt. ii: *Imperial Tables*. Calcutta: Bengal Secretariat Press, 1902.

Census of India, 1901, vol. xvi: *N.-W. Provinces and Oudh*, pt. i: *Report*, by R. Burn. Allahabad: Superintendent, Government Press, 1902.

Census of India, 1901, vol. xvi–a: *N.-W. Provinces and Oudh*, pt. ii: *Imperial Tables*, by R. Burn. Allahabad: Superintendent, Government Press, 1902.

Census of India, 1901, vol. xvii: *The Punjab, Its Feudatories, and the North-West Frontier Province*, pt. i: *The Report on the Census*, by H. A. Rose. Simla: Government Central Printing Office, 1902.

Bibliography

Census of India, 1901, vol. XVII–A: *Punjab (British Territory and Native States) and North-West Frontier Province*, pt. II: *Tables*, by H. A. Rose. Lahore: 'Civil and Military Gazette' Press, 1902.

Census of India, 1911, vol. I: *India*, pt. I: *Report*, by E. A. Gait. Calcutta: Superintendent, Government Printing, India, 1913.

Census of India, 1911, vol. I: *India*, pt. II: *Tables*, by E. A. Gait. Calcutta: Superintendent, Government Printing, India, 1913.

Census of India, 1911, vol. V: *Bengal, Bihar and Orissa and Sikkim*, pt. I: *Report*, by L. S. S. O'Malley. Calcutta: Bengal Secretariat Book Dept, 1913.

Census of India, 1911, vol. V: *Bihar and Orissa*, pt. III: *Tables*, by L. S. S. O'Malley. Calcutta: The Bengal Secretariat Book Depot, 1913.

Census of India, 1911, vol. XIV: *Punjab*, pt. I: *Report*, by Pandit Harikishan Kaul. Lahore: 'Civil and Military Gazette' Press, 1912.

Census of India, 1911, vol. XV: *United Provinces of Agra and Oudh*, pt. I: *Report*, by E. A. H. Blunt. Allahabad: Superintendent, Government Press, 1912.

Census of India, 1911, vol. XV: *United Provinces of Agra and Oudh*, pt. II: *Imperial Tables*, by E. A. H. Blunt. Allahabad: Superintendent, Government Press, 1912.

Census of India, 1921, vol. I: *India*, pt. II: *Tables*, by J. T. Marten. Calcutta: Superintendent, Government Printing, India, 1923.

Census of India, 1921, vol. VII: *Bihar and Orissa*, pt. I: *Report*, by P. C. Tallents. Patna: Superintendent, Government Printing, Bihar and Orissa, 1923.

Census of India, 1921, vol. VII: *Bihar and Orissa*, pt. II: *Tables*, by P. C. Tallents. Patna: Superintendent, Government Printing, Bihar and Orissa, 1923.

Census of India, 1921, vol. XV: *Punjab and Delhi*, pt. I: *Report*, by L. Middleton. Lahore: 'Civil and Military Gazette' Press, 1923.

Census of India, 1921, vol. XVI: *United Provinces of Agra and Oudh*, pt. I: *Report*, by E. H. H. Edye. Allahabad: Superintendent, Government Press, United Provinces, 1923.

Census of India, 1921, vol. XVI: *United Provinces of Agra and Oudh*, pt. II: *Imperial Tables*, by E. H. H. Edye and W. R. Tennant. Allahabad: Superintendent, Government Press, United Provinces, 1923.

Census of India, 1931, vol. I: *India*, pt. I: *Report*, by J. H. Hutton. Delhi: Manager of Publications, 1933.

Census of India, 1931, vol. I: *India*, pt. II: *Imperial Tables*, by J. H. Hutton. Delhi: Manager of Publications, 1933.

Census of India, 1931, vol. VII: *Bihar and Orissa*, pt. I: *Report*, by W. G. Lacey. Patna: Superintendent, Government Printing, Bihar and Orissa, 1933.

Census of India, 1931, vol. VII: *Bihar and Orissa*, pt. II: *Tables*, by W. G. Lacey. Patna: Superintendent, Government Printing, Bihar and Orissa, 1932.

Census of India, 1931, vol. XVII: *Punjab*, pt. I: *Report*, by Khan Ahmad Hasan Khan. Lahore: 'Civil and Military Gazette' Press, 1933.

Census of India, 1931, vol. XVII: *Punjab*, pt. II: *Tables*, by Khan Ahmad Hasan Khan. Lahore: 'Civil and Military Gazette' Press, 1933.

Census of India, 1931, vol. XVIII: *United Provinces of Agra and Oudh*, pt. I: *Report*, by A. C. Turner. Allahabad: Superintendent, Printing and Stationery, United Provinces, 1933.

Census of India, 1931, vol. XVIII: *United Provinces of Agra and Oudh*, pt. II: *Imperial and Provincial Tables*, by A. C. Turner. Allahabad: Superintendent, Printing and Stationery, United Provinces, 1933.

Census of India, 1941, vol. I: *India*, pt. I: *Tables*, by M. W. M. Yeatts. Delhi: Manager of Publications, 1946.

Census of India, 1941, vol. V: *United Provinces, Tables*, by B. Sahay. Delhi: Manager of Publications, 1942.

Census of India, 1951, Paper No. 1, 1957: General Population Tables and Summary Figures by Districts of Reorganised States. Delhi: Manager of Publications, 1957.

Census of India, 1951, vol. II: *Uttar Pradesh*, pt. I–A: *Report*, by Rajeshwari Prasad. Allahabad: Superintendent, Printing and Stationery, Uttar Pradesh, 1953.

Census of India, 1951, vol. II: *Uttar Pradesh*, pt. II–C: *Age and Social Tables*, by Rajeshwari Prasad. Allahabad: Superintendent, Printing and Stationery, Uttar Pradesh, 1953.

Census of India, 1951, vol. V: *Bihar*, pt. II–A: *Tables*, by Ranchor Prasad. Patna: Superintendent, Government Printing, Bihar, 1953.

Census of India, 1961, Paper No. 1 of 1962: Final Population Totals. New Delhi: Government of India Press, 1962.

Census of India, 1961, A Guide to the 1961 Census Publication Programme. Delhi: Manager of Publications, 1965.

Census of India, 1961, vol. I: *India*, pt. I–A (ii): *Tables*, by A. Mitra. Delhi: Manager of Publications, 1966.

Census of India, 1961, vol. IV: *Bihar*, pt. I–A (i): *General Report on the Census*, by S. D. Prasad. Delhi: Manager of Publications, 1968.

Census of India, 1961, vol. IV: *Bihar*, pt. II–A: *General Population Tables*, by S. D. Prasad. Delhi: Manager of Publications, 1963.

Census of India, 1961, vol. IV: *Bihar*, pt. I–C: *Subsidiary Tables*, by S. D. Prasad. Delhi: Manager of Publications, 1965.

Census of India, 1961, vol. IV: *Bihar*, pt. II–C: *Social and Cultural Tables*, by S. D. Prasad. Delhi: Manager of Publications, 1965.

Census of India, 1961, Bihar. District Census Handbooks, by S. D. Prasad. Patna: Government of Bihar, 1965–8. 1: *Patna*; 2: *Gaya*; 3: *Shahabad*; 4: *Saran*; 5: *Champaran*; 6: *Muzaffarpur*; 7: *Darbhanga*; 8: *Monghyr*; 9: *Bhagalpur*; 10: *Saharsa*; 11: *Purnea*.

Census of India, 1961, vol. XIII: *Punjab*, pt I–A (i): *General Report*, by R. L. Anand. Delhi: Manager of Publications, 1969.

Census of India, 1961, vol. XIII: *Punjab*, pt. II–C (i): *Social and Cultural Tables*, by R. L. Anand. Delhi: Manager of Publications, 1965.

Census of India, 1961, vol. XV: *Uttar Pradesh*, pt. I–A (ii): *General Report on the Census*, by P. P. Bhatnagar. Delhi: Manager of Publications, 1967.

Census of India, 1961, vol. XV: *Uttar Pradesh*, pt. I–C (iii): *Subsidiary Tables*, by P. P. Bhatnagar. Delhi: Manager of Publications, 1967.

Census of India, 1961, vol. XV: *Uttar Pradesh*, pt. II–C (ii): *Cultural and Migration Tables*, by P. P. Bhatnagar. Delhi: Manager of Publications, 1965.

Constituent Assembly of India, *Report of the Linguistic Provinces Commission.* New Delhi: Government of India Press, 1949. Portions reprinted in Myron Weiner (ed.), *Introduction to the Civilization of India: Developing India.* Chicago: University of Chicago Press, 1961.

Ministry of Education, *Education in India, 1957–58*, vol. I: *Report.* Delhi: Manager of Publications, 1962.

Ministry of Education, *Education in India, 1958–59*, vol. I: *Report.* Delhi: Manager of Publications, 1962.

Ministry of Education, *Education in India, 1960–61*, vol. 1: *Report*. Delhi: Manager of Publications, 1966.

Ministry of Education, *Education in India*, vol. 1: *Report, 1961–62*. Delhi: Manager of Publications, 1968.

Ministry of Education, *Education in India, 1962–63*, vol. 1: *Report*. Delhi: Manager of Publications, 1966.

Ministry of Education, *Education in India, 1963–64*, vol. 1: *Report*. Delhi: Manager of Publications, 1968.

Ministry of Education, *Education in India, 1964–65*, vol. 1: *Report*. Delhi: Manager of Publications, 1969.

Ministry of Education, *Report of the Education Commission, 1964–66: Education and National Development*. Delhi: Manager of Publications, 1966.

Bureau of Education, *Selections from Educational Records*, pt. II: *1840–1859*, compiled by J. A. Richey. Calcutta: Superintendent, Government Printing, India, 1922.

Ministry of Home Affairs, *All India Civil List*. Delhi: Manager of Publications, 1970.

Home Department, Selections from the Records, *Correspondence on the Subject of the Education of the Muhammadan Community in British India and Their Employment in the Public Service Generally*. Calcutta: Superintendent of Government Printing, India, 1886.

Ministry of Home Affairs, *Report, 1966–67*. Delhi: Manager of Publications, 1967.

Ministry of Home Affairs, *Report, 1967–68*. Delhi: Manager of Publications, 1968.

Home Department, *Report of the Commission of Inquiry on Communal Disturbances, Ranchi-Hatia (August 22–29, 1967)*. Delhi: Manager of Publications, 1968.

Ministry of Home Affairs, *Report of the Commissioner for Linguistic Minorities (Fourth Report)*, Delhi: Manager of Publications, 1962.

Ministry of Home Affairs, *Report of the Commissioner for Linguistic Minorities (Fifth Report)*, Delhi: Manager of Publications, 1963.

Ministry of Home Affairs, *Report of the Commissioner for Linguistic Minorities (Sixth Report)*, Delhi: Manager of Publications, 1965.

Ministry of Home Affairs, *Report of the Commissioner for Linguistic Minorities (Seventh Report)*. Delhi: Manager of Publications, 1965.

Ministry of Home Affairs, *Report of the Commissioner for Lingustic Minorities (Eighth Report)*. Delhi: Manager of Publications, 1967.

Ministry of Home Affairs, *Report of the Commissioner for Linguistic Minorities (Ninth Report)*. Delhi: Manager of Publications, 1968.

Ministry of Home Affairs, *Report of the Commissioner for Linguistic Minorities (Tenth Report)*. Delhi: Manager of Publications, 1969.

Ministry of Home Affairs, *The Eleventh Report of the Commissioner for Linguistic Minorities in India for the Period, July 1968 to June 1969*. Delhi: Manager of Publications, 1970.

Home Department, *Report of the Punjab Boundary Commission*. Delhi: Manager of Publications, 1966.

Home Department, *Report of the Punjab Commission*. Delhi: Manager of Publications, 1962.

Home Department, *Report of the States Reorganisation Commission, 1955*. New Delhi: Government of India Press, 1955.

438

Bibliography

Ministry of Information and Broadcasting, *Annual Report of the Registrar of Newspapers for India, 1961*, pt. I: Delhi: Manager of Publications, 1961.

Ministry of Information and Broadcasting, *Press in India 1965*, pts. I and II. Delhi: Manager of Publications, 1965.

Ministry of Information and Broadcasting, *Press in India 1968*, pt. I. Delhi: Manager of Publications, 1968.

Ministry of Information and Broadcasting, *Press in India 1969*, pt. II. Delhi: Manager of Publications, 1970.

Ministry of Information and Broadcasting, *Press in India 1970*, pt. I. Delhi: Manager of Publications, 1970.

Ministry of Information and Broadcasting, *Press in India 1971*, pt. I. Delhi: Manager of Publications, 1971.

Ministry of Law, *The Constitution of India (As Modified up to the 1st April, 1966)*. Delhi: Manager of Publications, 1966.

Law Department, *Election Law Reports*, vol. VI, edited by A. N. Aiyar. Delhi: Manager of Publications, n.d.

Law Department, *Election Law Reports*, vol. VII, edited by A. N. Aiyar. Delhi: Manager of Publications, n.d.

Law Department, *Election Law Reports*, vol. XIX, edited by A. N. Aiyar. Delhi: Manager of Publications, 1959.

Law Department, *Election Law Reports*, vol. XXIV, edited by R. K. P. Shankardass. Delhi: Manager of Publications, 1968.

Ministry of Law, *The Representation of the People Act, 1951 (43 of 1951), As Modified up to the 1st August 1967*. Delhi: Manager of Publications, 1967.

Lok Sabha, *Estimates Committee (1965–66) Hundred and First Report (Third Lok Sabha): Ministry of Education, Aligarh Muslim University*. New Delhi: Lok Sabha Secretariat, 1966.

Parliamentary Committee on the Demand for Punjabi Suba, *Report*. New Delhi: Lok Sabha Secretariat, 1966.

Punjab. Punjab Vidhan Sabha, *Who's Who, 1962–67*. Chandigarh: Controller, Printing and Stationery, 1964.

Uttar Pradesh. Civil Secretariat, Appointment (A) Department, *The Civil List, Part III for Uttar Pradesh*, corrected up to 1 January 1961 (Allahabad: Superintendent, Printing and Stationery, 1961).

Civil Secretariat, Appointment (A) Department, *The Civil List, Part I for Uttar Pradesh*. Allahabad: Superintendent, Printing and Stationery, 1965.

Report of the Uttar Pradesh Language Committee. Lucknow: Superintendent, Printing and Stationery, U.P., 1963.

BOOKS, ARTICLES, AND DISSERTATIONS

Ahmad, Aziz, *Islamic Modernism in India and Pakistan, 1857–1964*. London: Oxford University Press, 1967.

Ake, Claude, *A Theory of Political Integration*. Homewood, Ill.: The Dorsey Press, 1967.

Akzin, Benjamin, *State and Nation*. London: Hutchinson University Library, 1964.

Almond, Gabriel A., 'Comparative Political Systems', *Journal of Politics*, XVIII, No. 3 (August 1956), 391–409.

439

'Introduction: A Functional Approach to Comparative Politics', in Gabriel A. Almond and James S. Coleman (eds.), *The Politics of the Developing Areas*. Princeton, N.J.: Princeton University Press, 1960.

Almond, Gabriel A. and Powell, G. Bingham, *Comparative Politics: A Developmental Approach*. Boston: Little, Brown, 1966.

Anand, J. C., 'General Elections in Punjab', *Political Science Review*, VI, Nos. 3 and 4, and VII, Nos. 1 and 2 (July–September and October–December 1967 and January–March and April–June 1968), Special Number on Fourth General Elections in India, 412–46.

'Mid-Term Poll in Punjab', *Political Science Review*, x, Nos. 1 and 2 (January–June 1971), 1–29.

Azad, Maulana Abul Kalam, *India Wins Freedom: An Autobiographical Narrative*. Bombay: Orient Longmans, 1959.

Bahl, Kali Charan, 'Panjabi', in Thomas A. Sebeok (ed.), *Current Trends in Linguistics*, vol. V: *Linguistics in South Asia*, pp. 153–200. The Hague: Mouton, 1969.

Barrier, N. G., 'The Arya Samaj and Congress Politics in the Punjab, 1894–1908', *Journal of Asian Studies*, XXVI, No. 3 (May 1967), 363–79.

'The Punjab Government and Communal Politics, 1870–1907', *Journal of Asian Studies*, XXVII, No. 3 (May 1968), 523–39.

Barrier, N. Gerald and Wallace, Paul, *The Punjab Press, 1880–1905*. East Lansing, Michigan: Asian Studies Center, Michigan State University, 1970.

Baxter, Craig, *District Voting Trends in India: A Research Tool*. New York: Columbia University Press, 1969.

The Jana Sangh: A Biography of an Indian Political Party. Philadelphia: University of Pennsylvania Press, 1969.

Beni Prasad, *India's Hindu–Muslim Questions*. London: George Allen and Unwin, 1946.

Bentley, Arthur, F., *The Process of Government: A Study of Social Pressures*, 4th ed. Evanston, Ill.: The Principia Press, 1955.

Binder, Leonard, *Religion and Politics in Pakistan*. Berkeley: University of California Press, 1961.

Blair, Harry, 'Caste, Politics and Democracy in Bihar State, India: The Elections of 1967', unpublished Ph.D. dissertation. Duke University, 1969.

Bolitho, Hector, *Jinnah: Creator of Pakistan*. London: John Murray, 1954.

Brass, Paul R., 'Coalition Politics in North India', *American Political Science Review*, LXII, No. 4 (December 1968), 1174–91.

Factional Politics in an Indian State: The Congress Party in Uttar Pradesh. Berkeley: University of California Press, 1965.

'Political Participation, Institutionalization and Stability in India', *Government and Opposition*, IV, No. 1 (Winter 1969), 23–53.

'Radical Parties of the Left in Bihar: A Comparison of the SSP and CPI', in Paul R. Brass and Marcus F. Franda (eds.), *Radical Politics in South Asia*. Cambridge: M.I.T. Press, 1973.

'Uttar Pradesh', in Myron Weiner (ed.), *State Politics in India*, pp. 61–124. Princeton, N.J.: Princeton University Press, 1968.

Brecher, Michael, *Nehru's Mantle: The Politics of Succession in India*. New York: Frederick A. Praeger, 1966.

Broomfield, J. H., *Elite Conflict in a Plural Society: Twentieth-Century Bengal*. Berkeley: University of California Press, 1968.

Bibliography

'The Non-Cooperation Decision of 1920: A Crisis in Bengal Politics', in D. A. Low (ed.), *Soundings in Modern South Asian History*. Berkeley: University of California Press, 1968.

Cassinelli, C. W., 'The National Community', *Polity*, II, No. 1 (September 1969), 15–31.

Chatterji, Suniti Kumar, *Indo-Aryan & Hindi*, 2nd ed. Calcutta: Firma K. L. Mukhopadhyay, 1960.

Languages and Literatures of Modern India. Calcutta: Prakash Bhavan, 1962.

Cohn, Bernard S., 'Recruitment of Elites in India Under British Rule', in Leonard Plotnicov and Arthur Tuden (eds.), *Essays in Comparative Social Stratification*. Pittsburgh: University of Pittsburgh Press, 1970. The University of Chicago Committee on Southern Asian Studies Reprint Series No. 44.

'Regions Subjective and Objective: Their Relation to the Study of Modern Indian History and Society', in Robert L. Crane (ed.), *Regions and Regionalism in South Asian Studies: An Exploratory Study*. Duke University: Program in Comparative Studies on Southern Asia, 1967.

Connor, Walker, 'Nation-Building or Nation-Destroying?' *World Politics*, XXIV, No. 3 (April 1972), 319–55.

Coupland, R., *Indian Politics, 1936–1942*. London: Oxford University Press, 1943.

Cunningham, Joseph Davey, *A History of the Sikhs from the Origin of the Nation to the Battles of the Sutlej*. Delhi: S. Chand and Co., 1966.

Das Gupta, Jyotirindra, *Language Conflict and National Development: Group Politics and National Language Policy in India*. Berkeley: University of California Press, 1970.

'Language Diversity and National Development', in Joshua A. Fishman, Charles A. Ferguson, and Jyotirindra Das Gupta (eds.), *Language Problems of Developing Nations*, pp. 17–26. New York: John Wiley, 1968.

Das Gupta, Jyotirindra and Gumperz, John J., 'Language, Communication and Control in North India', in Joshua A. Fishman, Charles A. Ferguson, and Jyotirindra Das Gupta (eds.), *Language Problems of Developing Nations*. New York: John Wiley, 1968.

de Bary, Wm. Theodore, *et al.* (eds.), *Sources of Indian Tradition*. New York: Columbia University Press, 1960.

Deutsch, Karl, *Nationalism and Social Communication: An Inquiry into the Foundations of Nationality*, 2nd ed. Cambridge, Mass.: M.I.T. Press, 1966.

Dua, Veena, 'Arya Samaj and Punjab Politics', *Economic and Political Weekly*, V, Nos. 43 and 44 (24 October 1970), 1787–91.

Dumont, Louis. 'Nationalism and Communalism', *Contributions to Indian Sociology*, VII (March 1964), 30–70.

Elkins, David J., 'Regional Contexts of Political Participation: Some Illustrations from South India', *Canadian Journal of Political Science*, V, No. 2 (June 1972), 167–89.

Emerson, Rupert, *From Empire to Nation: The Rise to Self-Assertion of Asian and African Peoples*. Boston: Beacon Press, 1962.

'Parties and National Integration in Africa', in Joseph La Palombara and Myron Weiner (eds.), *Political Parties and Political Development*, pp. 267–301. Princeton, N.J.: Princeton University Press, 1966.

Erdman, Howard L. *The Swatantra Party and Indian Conservatism*. Cambridge: Cambridge University Press, 1967.

Fagan, Patrick, 'Minority Communities, I. The Sikhs', in John Comming (ed.), *Political India, 1832–1932: A Co-operative Survey of a Century*, pp. 124–32. Delhi: S. Chand and Co., 1968.

Faruqui, Ziya-ul-Hasan, *The Deoband School and the Demand for Pakistan*. Bombay: Asia Publishing House, 1963.

'Indian Muslims and the Ideology of the Secular State', in Donald E. Smith (ed.), *South Asian Politics and Religion*, pp. 138–49. Princeton, N.J.: Princeton University Press, 1966.

Ferguson, Charles A., 'Language Development', in Joshua A. Fishman, Charles A. Ferguson, and Jyotirindra Das Gupta (eds.), *Language Problems of Developing Nations*, pp. 27–35. New York: John Wiley, 1968.

Fishman, Joshua A., 'Nationality-Nationalism and Nation-Nationism', in Joshua A. Fishman, Charles A. Ferguson, and Jyotirindra Das Gupta (eds.), *Language Problems of Developing Nations*, pp. 39–51. New York: John Wiley, 1968.

'Sociolinguistics and the Language Problems of the Developing Countries', in Joshua A. Fishman, Charles A. Ferguson, and Jyotirindra Das Gupta (eds.), *Language Problems of Developing Nations*, pp. 3–16. New York: John Wiley, 1968.

Ford, Henry Jones, *The Rise and Growth of American Politics: A Sketch of Constitutional Development*. New York: The Macmillan Co., 1911.

Franda, Marcus F., 'Electoral Politics in West Bengal: The Growth of the United Front', *Pacific Affairs*, XLII, No. 3 (Fall 1969), 279–93.

West Bengal and the Federalizing Process in India. Princeton, N.J.: Princeton University Press, 1968.

Gandhi, M. K., *Our Language Problem*. Bombay: Bharatiya Vidya Bhavan, 1965.

Geertz, Clifford, 'The Integrative Revolution: Primordial Sentiments and Civil Politics in the New States', in Clifford Geertz (ed.), *Old Societies and New States: The Quest for Modernity in Asia and Africa*, pp. 105–57. New York: The Free Press, 1967.

Gorekar, N. S., *Glimpses of Urdu Literature*. Bombay: Jaico Publishing House. 1961.

Grierson, G. A., *An Introduction to the Maithili Dialect of the Bihari Language as Spoken in North Bihar*, 2nd ed., pt. 1: *Grammar*. Calcutta: Asiatic Society, 1909.

(ed.), *Linguistic Survey of India*, vol. I, pt. 1: *Introductory*. Delhi: Motilal Banarsidass, 1967.

(ed.), *Linguistic Survey of India*, vol. V, *Indo-Aryan Family, Eastern Group*, pt. II: *Specimens of the Bihari and Oriya Languages*. Delhi: Motilal Banarsidass, 1968.

(ed.), *Linguistic Survey of India*, vol. IX, *Indo-Aryan Family, Central Group*, pt. 1: *Specimens of Western Hindi and Panjābī*. Delhi: Motilal Banarsidass, 1968.

Grodzins, Morton, 'Political Parties and the Crisis of Succession in the United States: the Case of 1800', in Joseph La Palombara and Myron Weiner (eds.), *Political Parties and Political Development*, pp. 303–27. Princeton, N.J.: Princeton University Press, 1966.

Gumperz, John J., 'Hindi–Punjabi Code-Switching in Delhi', in Anwar S. Dil (ed.), *Language in Social Groups: Essays by John J. Gumperz*, pp. 205–19. Stanford, California: Stanford University Press, 1971.

'Language Problems in the Rural Development of North India', in University of Chicago, The College, *Introduction to the Civilization of India: Changing Dimensions of Indian Society and Culture*, pp. 39–47. Chicago: University of Chicago Press, 1957.

'Some Remarks on Regional and Social Language Differences in India', in University of Chicago, The College, *Introduction to the Civilization of India: Changing Dimensions of Indian Society and Culture*, pp. 31–8. Chicago: University of Chicago Press, 1957.

Gupta, Sisir K., 'Moslems in Indian Politics, 1947–60', *India Quarterly*, XVII (1962), 355–81.

Hardy, P., *The Muslims of British India*. Cambridge: University Press, 1972.

Partners in Freedom – and True Muslims: The Political Thought of Some Muslim Scholars in British India (1912–1946). Lund: Studentlitteratur, 1971.

Harrison, Selig S., 'Hindu Society and the State: The Indian Union', in K. H. Silvert (ed.), *Expectant Peoples: Nationalism and Development*, pp. 267–99. New York: Random House, 1963.

India: The Most Dangerous Decades. Princeton, N.J.: Princeton University Press, 1960.

Heimsath, Charles H., *Indian Nationalism and Hindu Social Reform*. Princeton, N.J.: Princeton University Press, 1964.

Herring, Pendleton, *The Politics of Democracy: American Parties in Action*. New York: W. W. Norton, 1965.

Hoernle, A. F. Rudolf, *Centenary Review of the Asiatic Society of Bengal from 1784–1883*, pt. II: *Archaeology, History, Literature, etc.* Calcutta: Published by the Society and printed by Thacker, Spink, 1885.

Horowitz, Donald L., 'Three Dimensions of Ethnic Politics', *World Politics*, XXIII, No. 2 (January 1971), 232–44.

Hunter, W. W., *The Indian Mussalmans*, 2nd ed. London: Trübner and Co., 1872.

Husain, Azim, *Fazl-I-Husain: A Political Biography*. Bombay: Longmans, Green, 1946.

Husain, Mahmud *et al.*, *A History of the Freedom Movement*, vol. II: *1831–1905*, pt. II. Karachi: Pakistan Historical Society, 1961.

Irschick, Eugene F., *Politics and Social Conflict in South India: The Non-Brahman Movement and Tamil Separatism, 1916–1929*. Berkeley: University of California Press, 1969.

Jain, M. S., *The Aligarh Movement: Its Origin and Development, 1858–1906*. Agra: Sri Ram Mehra, 1965.

Jaszi, Oscar, *The Dissolution of the Habsburg Monarchy*. Chicago: University of Chicago Press, 1966.

Jones, Kenneth W., 'Communalism in the Punjab: The Arya Samaj Contribution', *Journal of Asian Studies*, XXVIII, No. 1 (November 1968), 39–54.

Joshi, Vijaya Chandra (ed.), *Lajpat Rai Autobiographical Writings*. Delhi: University Publishers, 1965.

Kearney, Robert N., *Communalism and Language in the Politics of Ceylon*. Durham, N.C.: Duke University Press, 1967.

Kellogg, S. H., *A Grammar of the Hindi Language*, 3rd ed. London: Routledge and Kegan Paul, 1938.

Khaliquzzaman, Choudhry, *Pathway to Pakistan*. Lahore: Longmans, 1961.

Khushwant Singh, *The Fall of the Kingdom of the Punjab*. Bombay: Orient Longmans, 1962.

A History of the Sikhs, vol. II: *1839–1964*. Princeton, N.J.: Princeton University Press, 1966.

Kloss, Heinz, 'Notes Concerning a Language–Nation Typology', in Joshua A. Fishman, Charles A. Ferguson, and Jyotirindra Das Gupta (eds.), *Language Problems of Developing Nations*, pp. 69–85. New York: John Wiley, 1968.

443

Kumar, Jnanendra Nath, *The Genealogical History of India*, pt. II. Calcutta: Jnanendra Nath Kumar, 1933 (?).

Leonard, John G., 'Politics and Social Change in South India: A Study of the Andhra Movement', *Journal of Commonwealth Political Studies*, v, No. 1 (March 1967), 60–77.

Lewis, Martin Deming (ed.), *Gandhi: Maker of Modern India?* Boston: D. C. Heath, 1968.

Lijphart, Arend, *The Politics of Accommodation: Pluralism and Democracy in the Netherlands*. Berkeley: University of California Press, 1968.

Lipset, Seymour Martin, *Political Man: The Social Bases of Politics*. New York: Anchor Books, 1963.

Lipset, Seymour Martin and Rokkan, Stein, 'Cleavage Structures, Party Systems, and Voter Alignments: An Introduction', in Seymour M. Lipset and Stein Rokkan (eds.), *Party Systems and Voter Alignments: Cross-National Perspectives*. New York: The Free Press, 1967.

Low, D. A., 'Introduction', in D. A. Low (ed.), *Soundings in Modern South Asian History*, pp. 1–24. Berkeley: University of California Press, 1968.

Lowell, A. Lawrence, *The Government of England*, new ed., vol. I. New York: The Macmillan Co., 1931.

Lütt, Von Jürgen, *Hindu-Nationalismus in Uttar Prades*. Stuttgart: Ernst Klett Verlag, 1970.

Lynch, Owen M., *The Politics of Untouchability: Social Mobility and Social Change in a City of India*. New York: Columbia University Press, 1969.

McCully, Bruce Tiebout, *English Education and the Origins of Indian Nationalism*. Gloucester, Mass.: Peter Smith, 1966

Malik, Hafeez, *Moslem Nationalism in India and Pakistan*. Washington, D.C.: Public Affairs Press, 1963.

Melson, Robert and Wolpe, Howard, 'Modernization and the Politics of Communalism: A Theoretical Perspective', *American Political Science Review*, LXIV, No. 4 (December 1970), 1112–30.

Nayar, Baldev Raj, *Minority Politics in the Punjab*. Princeton, N.J.: Princeton University Press, 1966.

National Communication and Language Policy in India. New York: Frederick A. Praeger, 1969.

'Punjab', in Myron Weiner (ed.), *State Politics in India*. Princeton, N.J.: Princeton University Press, 1968.

'Religion and Caste in the Punjab: Sidhwan Bet Constituency', in Myron Weiner and Rajni Kothari (eds.), *Indian Voting Behaviour: Studies of the 1962 General Elections*, pp. 123–40. Calcutta: Firma K. L. Mukhopadhyay, 1965.

'Sikh Separatism in the Punjab', in Donald E. Smith (ed.), *South Asian Politics and Religion*, pp. 150–75. Princeton, N.J.: Princeton University Press, 1966.

Pathak, Devavrat N., 'State Politics in Gujarat: Some Determinants', in Iqbal Narain (ed.), *State Politics in India*. Meerut: Meenakshi Prakashan, 1967.

Quraishi, Zaheer Masood, 'Electoral Strategy of a Minority Pressure Group: The Muslim Majlis-e-Mushawarat', *Asian Survey*, VIII, No. 12 (December 1968), 976–87.

Rae, Douglas, *The Political Consequences of Electoral Laws*. New Haven: Yale University Press, 1967.

Rai, Satya M., *Partition of the Punjab: A Study of Its Effects on the Politics and Administration of the Punjab (I) 1947–56*. Bombay: Asia Publishing House, 1965.

Bibliography

Ram Gopal, *Indian Muslims: A Political History (1858–1947)*. Bombay: Asia Publishing House, 1959.

Ramusack, Barbara N., 'Incident at Nabha: Interaction between Indian States and British Indian Politics', *Journal of Asian Studies*, xxviii, No. 3 (May 1969), 563–77.

Reeves, P. D., 'Changing Patterns of Political Alignment in the General Elections to the United Provinces Legislative Assembly, 1937 and 1946', *Modern Asian Studies*, v, No. 2 (April 1971), 111–42.

'Landlords and Party Politics in the United Provinces, 1934–7', in D. A. Low (ed.), *Soundings in Modern South Asian History*, pp. 261–93. Berkeley: University of California Press, 1968.

Roy, Ramashray, 'Dynamics of One-Party Dominance in an Indian State', *Asian Survey*, vii, No. 7 (July 1968), 553–75.

Rudolph, Lloyd I. and Rudolph, Susanne Hoeber, *The Modernity of Tradition: Political Development in India*. Chicago: University of Chicago Press, 1967.

Rustow, Dankwart, A., *A World of Nations: Problems of Political Modernization*. Washington, D.C.: Brookings Institution, 1967.

Sahni, Ruchi Ram, *Struggle for Reform in Sikh Shrines*. Amritsar: SGPC, n.d.

Sajun Lal, K., *A Short History of Urdu Newspapers*. Hyderabad, A. P.: Institute of Indo-Middle East Cultural Studies, 1964.

Saksena, Ram Babu, *A History of Urdu Literature*. Allahabad: Ram Narain Lal, 1927.

Sarsfield, Landen, *Betrayal of the Sikhs*. Lahore: Lahore Book Shop, 1946.

Sartori, Giovanni, 'European Politican Parties: The Case of Polarized Pluralism', in Joseph La Palombara and Myron Weiner (eds.), *Political Parties and Political Development*, pp. 137–76. Princeton, N.J.: Princeton University Press, 1966.

Sayeed, Khalid B., *The Political System of Pakistan*. Boston: Houghton Mifflin, 1967.

Schwartzberg, Joseph E., 'The Distribution of Selected Castes in the North Indian Plain', *Geographical Review*, lv, No. 4 (1965), 447–95.

Seal, Anil, *The Emergence of Indian Nationalism: Competition and Collaboration in the Later Nineteenth Century*. Cambridge: Cambridge University Press, 1968.

Shoup, Paul, *Communism and the Yugoslav National Question*. New York: Columbia University Press, 1968.

Smith, Wilfred C., *Islam in Modern History*. New York: New American Library, 1959.

Modern Islam in India. London: Victor Gollancz, 1946.

Srinivas, M. N., *Caste in Modern India and Other Essays*. Bombay: Asia Publishing House, 1962.

Titus, Murray T., *Islam in India and Pakistan*. Calcutta: Y.M.C.A. Publishing House, 1959.

Truman, David B., *The Governmental Process: Political Interests and Public Opinion*, 2nd ed. New York: Alfred A. Knopf, 1971.

Wallace, Paul, 'The Political Party System of Punjab State (India): A Study of Factionalism', unpublished Ph.D. dissertation. University of California, Berkeley, 1966.

Wallbank, T. Walter (ed.), *The Partition of India: Causes and Responsibilities*. Boston: D. C. Heath and Co., 1966.

Weiner, Myron, *Party Building in a New Nation: The Indian National Congress*. Chicago: University of Chicago Press, 1967.

'Political Development in the Indian States', in Myron Weiner (ed.), *State Politics in India*. Princeton, N.J.: Princeton University Press, 1968.

'Political Integration and Political Development', in Jason L. Finkle and Richard W. Gable (eds.), *Political Development and Social Change*, pp. 551–62. New York: John Wiley, 1966.

Weiner, Myron and La Palombara, Joseph, 'The Impact of Parties on Political Development', in Joseph La Palombara and Myron Weiner (eds.), *Political Parties and Political Development*. Princeton, N.J.: Princeton University Press, 1966.

Wright, Theodore P., Jr., 'The Effectiveness of Muslim Representation in India', in Donald E. Smith (ed.), *South Asian Politics and Religion*, pp. 102–37. Princeton University Press, 1966.

'Muslim Education in India at the Crossroads: The Case of Aligarh', *Pacific Affairs*, XXXIX, Nos. 1 and 2 (Spring–Summer 1966), 50–63.

'Muslims as Candidates and Voters in 1967 General Election', *Political Science Review*, VIII, No. 1 (January–March 1969), 23–40.

'The Muslim Personal Law Issue in India: An Outsider's View', *Indian Journal of Politics*, IV (1970), 69–77.

Zakaria, Rafiq, *Rise of Muslims in Indian Politics: An Analysis of Developments from 1885 to 1906*. Bombay: Somaiya Publications, 1970.

PAMPHLETS, PAMPHLET COLLECTIONS, AND OTHER PRIMARY SOURCES

Ali Alvi, Md. Ehtram, *Address of Welcome*. Lucknow: All-India Aligarh University Old Boys' Convention, 1965.

Aligarh Muslim University Old Boys' Convention, *The Aligarh Muslim University: Its Past, Present and Future*. Lucknow: All-India Aligarh Muslim University Old Boys' Convention, 1965.

Resolution Passed by the All India Aligarh Muslim University Old Boys' Convention, Lucknow, Held on 7th & 8th August 1965. Lucknow, 1965.

Ali Khan, Hamid, *The Vernacular Controversy: An Account and Criticism of the Equalisation of Nagri and Urdu, as the Character for the Court of the North-West Provinces and Oudh, Under the Resolution No. 5885 of Sir A. P. Macdonnell, The Lieutenant-Governor, N.-W.P., and Chief Commissioner, Oudh, Dated 18th April 1900*. No publication details, but apparently published in 1900.

Ali Nadwi, Maulana Syed Abul Hasan, *Welcome Address*. Lucknow: All-India Muslim Consultative Convention, 1964.

Anjuman Taraqqi Urdu, *Memorandum Submitted by Dr H. N. Kunzru, President, Anjuman Taraqqi Urdu (Hind), to Shri Lal Bahadur Shastri, Prime Minister of India, on 7th April, 1965*. No publication details.

Memorandum Submitted to the Chief Minister of Bihar by Bihar Urdu Deputation on Behalf of Bihar Reyasati Anjuman Taraqqui-e-Urdu, Patna for Recognition of Urdu as Regional Language of Bihar on 14 June 1966. Patna: Bihar Reyasati Anjuman Taraqqui-e-Urdu, 1966.

Two Words with Well-Wishers of Urdu, pt. II. Patna: Bihar State Anjuman Taraqqi Urdu, n.d. Originally in Urdu.

Bihar State Hand-loom Weavers' Co-operative Union, *Report on the Working of the Bihar State Hand-loom Weavers' Co-operative Union Ltd. and Weavers' Co-operative Societies of Bihar*. Patna: Bihar State Hand-loom Weavers' Cooperative Union Ltd., 1963.

Bibliography

Chandidas, R. *et al.* (eds.), *India Votes: A Source Book on Indian Elections.* New York: Humanities Press, 1968.

Chetana Samiti, *Maithili: What It Is and What It Claims.* Patna: Chetana Samiti, 1964.

Deeni Talimi Council, *Brief Scrutiny of Prescribed Books in U.P.* Lucknow: Deeni Taleemi Council, 1966.

A Defense of the Urdu Language and Character (being a reply to the pamphlet called 'Court Character and Primary Education in N.-W.P. and Oudh'). Allahabad: Liddell's N.-W.P. Printing Works, 1900.

Faridi, A. J., *Communalism: Its Causes and Cure.* Lucknow, 1961.

Communal Riots and National Integration. Lucknow, 1962.

Presidential Address of Dr A. J. Faridi Delivered at the District Conference, Dini Talimi Council, Held on 21 March 1965 at Shahjahanpur. No publication details.

Tashkent Declaration and the Problem of Indo-Pak Minorities. Lucknow: publisher not listed, 1966.

Fateh Singh, Sant, *Our Stand on Punjabi Suba.* Amritsar: Shiromani Akali Dal, 1963.

Ganda Singh, *A Brief Account of the Sikhs.* Amritsar: SGPC, n.d.

(ed.), *Some Confidential Papers of the Akali Movement.* Amritsar: SGPC, 1965.

Gurnam Singh, *A Unilingual Punjabi State and the Sikh Unrest.* New Delhi: Gurnam Singh, 1960.

Handbook of Election Manifestos, 1971. Bombay: Commerce Ltd., 1971.

Hukam Singh, *The Punjab Problem: An Elucidation.* Amritsar: Shiromani Akali Dal, n.d.

Inayat Ullah, *The Real Face of Jamaat-e-Islami.* Delhi: Sampradayikta Virodhi Committee, n.d.

Jamaat-e-Islami, *Introducing the Jamaat-e-Islami Hind.* Delhi: Jamaat-e-Islami Hind, 1959.

Jha, J. C., 'Language Controversy in Bihar', *Indian Nation,* 11 and 18 August 1968.

Jha, Laksman, *Mithila: A Union Republic.* Darbhanga: Mithila Mandal, 1952.

Mithila in India. Laheriasarai, Darbhanga: Mithila Mandal, 1953.

Mithila Will Rise. Darbhanga: Mithila Mandal, 1955.

The Northern Border. Darbhanga: Mithila Mandal, 1955.

Jha, Ramanath, 'Maithili: Needs Popular Patronage', reprint of article, publication details not known.

'The Panjis of Mithila', *Indian Nation,* 11 April 1971.

Kahol, Om Prakasha, *Hindus and the Punjabi State: A Psycho-Political Discussion on the Conception & Rationale of Punjabi State.* Ambala Cantt.: Hindu Prachara Sabha, 1955.

Kripalani, J. B., *Minorities in India.* Calcutta: Vigil Office, n.d.

Maharajadhiraja of Darbhanga, *Inaugural Address by the Maharajadhiraja of Darbhanga at the XIV All-India Oriental Conference, Darbhanga, 1948.* No publication details.

Maithil Mahasabha, *Address by the Chairman, Reception Committee, Pandit Sri Amar Choudhry, B.A., LL.B., at the 27th Conference of the Maithil Mahasabha at Sitamarhi.* No publication details. Originally in Maithili.

Address by the Chairman, Reception Committee, Babu Sri Jagdish Nandan Singh, at the 37th Conference of the All India Maithil Mahasabha, 8 August 1948. No publication details. Originally in Maithili.

447

Presidential Addresses of His Highness, the Maharajadhiraja of Darbhanga, at the 37th Conference of the Maithil Mahasabha. No publication details. Originally in Maithili.

Presidential Address of His Highness, the Maharajadhiraja of Darbhanga, at the 38th Conference of the Maithil Mahasabha Held at Madhubani on the 7th May 1949. No publication details. Originally in Maithili.

Address by His Highness, the Maharajadhiraja of Darbhanga, at the 40th Conference of the Maithil Mahasabha, 20 January 1951. No publication details. Originally in Maithili.

Presidential Address of His Highness, the Maharajadhiraja of Darbhanga, Dr Sir Kameshwar Singh, D.Litt., LL.D, K.C.I.E., at the 44th Conference of the Maithil Mahasabha, 5 November 1955. No publication details. Originally in Maithili.

Maithili Sahitya Samiti, *What They Say About Maithili.* Allahabad: All-India Maithili Sahitya Samiti, 1963.

Malaviya, Madan Mohan, *Court Character and Primary Education in the N.-W. Provinces and Oudh.* Allahabad: The Indian Press, 1897.

Manifesto on the Position of Urdu in India. New Delhi, 1966. No other publication details.

Mann, Balbir Singh, *The Punjabi Suba Morcha: A Plea for Sympathy.* Fatehgarh Sahib, Distt. Patiala: Balbir Singh Mann, n.d.

Memorandum of Members of the U.P. Legislative Assembly (Western Districts) to the Indian Central Commission for Reorganisation of States. Saharanpur: Malhipur Branch Press, 1954.

Memorandum, Submitted to the President of India by Bihar Urdu Deputation on Behalf of Urdu Speaking People of Bihar for Recognition of Urdu as a Regional Language of Bihar, on 24 February 1956. Patna: Ghulam Sarwar, 1956.

Mishra, Jayakanta, *A Case for a Radio Station in the Maithili Area at Darbhanga.* Allahabad: Tirabhukti Publications, 1956.

Misra, Raghunath Prasad, 'Touchstone of a Maithil or the Criterion of Being a Maithil', *Mithila Bandhu*, XVII, Nos. 1 and 2 (January–February 1956). Originally in Maithili.

Muslim Majlis-e-Mushawarat, *People's Manifesto.* New Delhi: All-India Muslim Majlis-e-Mushawarat, 1966.

Nuri, M. Y., *Presidental Address.* Lucknow: All-India Aligarh Muslim University Old Boys' Convention, 1965.

Punjabi Suba: A Symposium. New Delhi: National Book Club, n.d.

Ray, Aswini K. and Chakravarti, Subhash, *Meerut Riots: A Case Study.* New Delhi: Sampradayikta Virodhi Committee [1968 or 1969].

Representation of the Muslims of the United Provinces (India) to the Indian Statutory Commission (July 1928). No publication details.

Sewaram Singh, *Report of the Working of the Sikh Deputation to England. Indian Reforms Scheme.* Lahore: Sewaram Singh, 1920.

Shiromani Akali Dal, *Two Talks between Sant Fateh Singh Ji and Shri Lal Bahadur Shastri, the Prime Minister of India on 7th & 8th August 1965.* Amritsar: Shiromani Akali Dal, 1965.

Singh, Jankinandan, *Memorandum for the Formation of the Mithila State.* Darbhanga: Jankinandan Singh, 1954.

Sinha, Jayadhari, 'Claims of Maithili as Language and Literature', *Searchlight*, 5 April 1970.

Bibliography

Sinha, Shiva Prasad, *Presidential Address by Mr Shiva Prasad Sinha, Senior Advocate, Supreme Court, Delhi, at the Bihar Urdu Convention. Held at Patna, on 10 and 11 September 1966*. No publication details. Originally in Urdu.

Sundar Lal, *India's National Integration – A New and Welcome Phase*. New Delhi: All-India Muslim Majlis-e-Mushawarat, 1965.

Tara Singh, Master, *To All Men of Good Conscience*. New Delhi: Shiromani Akali Dal, 1959.

Teja Singh, *Guru Nanak and His Mission*. Amritsar: SGPC, 1963.

Vajpayee, A. B., *National Integration* (Note submitted by A. B. Vajpayee, leader of the Jan Sangh group in parliament, at the National Integration Conference held at New Delhi, on 28, 29, and 30 September 1961.) No publication details.

NEWSPAPERS AND PERIODICALS

Several of the newspapers were consulted through the clipping file maintained by the Press Information Department of the All-India Congress Committee, New Delhi, by courtesy of the general secretary, AICC, and with the kind assistance of Mr C. L. Sharma, head of the Press Information Department, and his staff.

Ebony, January 1973
Hindu
Hindustan Standard
Hindustan Times
Indian Affairs Record
Indian Express
Indian Nation
India News
Leader
Mithila Mihir (in Maithili)

National Herald
Organiser
Patriot
Radiance
Searchlight
Spokesman
Statesman
Times of India
Tribune

UNPUBLISHED PAPERS AND DOCUMENTS

Bahl, Kali C., 'On the Present State of Modern Rajasthani Grammar'. Mimeo, University of Chicago, Department of South Asian Languages and Civilizations, December 1971.

Barrier, N. Gerald, 'Mass Politics and the Punjab Congress in the pre-Gandhi Period'. Mimeo, April 1970.

Indian National Congress, All-India Congress Committee, 'Preliminary Reports on Election Results from Some Pradesh Congress Committees'. Mimeo. New Delhi: All-India Congress Committee, 1967.

Muslim Majlis-e-Mushawarat, 'The Birth of Muslim Majlis-e-Mushawarat and What It is'. Typescript.

Press Statement issued by Sohail Ahmad, General Secretary, Muslim Majlis-e-Mushawarat, Bihar. Typescript, 1966 or 1967.

Resolution Passed by the All-India Muslim Majlis-e-Mushawarat at Its Meetings in Delhi on 19 and 20 June 1965. Typescript.

Reeves, P. D., '"Class or the Communal Platform?": Muslim Political Strategy in the United Provinces, 1936'.

Bibliography

Statements prepared for the Commission of Enquiry in the Communal Disturbances at Ranchi by Muslim organizations, individual Muslims, the two
Communist parties, and members of the Congress and other political parties
in Bihar and in Ranchi district. A collection of typewritten documents.

Weiner, Myron and Field, John Osgood, 'India's Urban Constituencies', presented at the Seminar on Electoral Patterns in the Indian States. Boston,
1972.

OTHER SOURCES

Personal interviews in the north Indian states, conducted from August 1966 to
August 1967 and from January 1969 to March 1969. The interviews are cited
in the footnotes anonymously for the sake of discretion, but references in most
footnotes are to pages and paragraphs in typewritten transcripts of the interviews, some of which were from notes, others from tape recordings.

INDEX

Abbasi, Qazi Adeel, 244
Abdullah, Sheikh, 219
Abu'l Fazl, 123
Abul Hasan Ali, Hazrat Maulana, 244
Abul Kalam Azad, Maulana, 162, 175, 176
adivasis, 259
Africa, elites in, 30–1; multi-tribal states in,
 13; nationalism and national integration
 in, 5–7, 405
Afzal Husain, Maulana, 244
Aga Khan, the, 161
Agra, city, 142; province, 173
Ahirs, 56n; *see also* Yadavs
Ahmad, Aziz, 238
Ahmad, Kalimuddin, 212n
Ahmad, Sohail, 268n
Ahmad Khan, Syed, 137, 141, 160, 165–7,
 171, 179, 224, 237
Ahmad of Sirhind, Shaikh, 123
Akali Dal, 20, 37, 105, 332, 335, 350, 400;
 electoral appeals, 351–6; electoral support, 369, 371–2, 374–5, 377, 380, 382–6,
 389–90, 395–7; gurudwara reform movement and, 283–4, 311–12; history, 314–
 318; language policy in Punjab and,
 340–1, 343–4, 346, 348, 349; leadership,
 17, 317, 336, 417, 425; (Master), 317,
 360, 371–2; partition of India and, 319n;
 in Punjab government, 314, 362, 381,
 398; in Punjab Legislative Assembly,
 357–9; Punjabi Suba demand and,
 320–5; as a regional political organization, 115; relations with other parties:
 Communist party, 346, Congress, 373,
 378, 397, Jan Sangh, 333–4, 342, 387,
 Scheduled Caste Federation and Republican Party of India, 392; (Sant),
 313–14, 317, 322, 360, 363, 371–2, 375,
 386; Sikh community and, 368, 399, 408,
 426, 433
Akbar, 123, 125; established dynasty in
 Mithila, 58; as unifying symbol, 139, 414
Akzin, Benjamin, 215
al-Biruni, 123
Ali brothers, 167
Aligarh, district, 265; movement, 120–1,
 136, 158, 160, 163, 165–9, 179, 311, 416;

riots in, 219–20, 265n; town, 225n
Aligarh Muslim University, grievances of
 Muslims concerning, 223–7, 230, 233,
 239, 250, 251, 269; history, 167, 237; and
 Muslim leadership, 235, 238, 242;
 student politics in, 219
Aligarh Muslim University (Amendment)
 Act, 1972, 227
Aligarh Muslim University Old Boys'
 Association, 225n, 226, 245
Aljamiat, 240–1
Allahabad city, 113, 131n, 136
Allahabad University, 70, 166
All-India Congress Committee (AICC),
 54, 244, 253
All-India Maithil Mahasabha, *see* Maithil
 Mahasabha
All-India Maithili Mahasangh, *see* Maithili
 Mahasangh
All-India Muslim League, *see* Muslim
 League
All-India Muslim Majlis-e-Mushawarat,
 see Muslim Majlis-e-Mushawarat
All-India Radio, 243
All-India Sahitya Akademi, *see* Sahitya
 Akademi
Almond, Gabriel A., 38, 40
Ambala division, 300, 302
Amritsar, 300, 312, 321, 332
Anand Marg, 102, 265
Andhra Pradesh, 248n
Angika, 66, 102
Anglo-Saxon Protestants, 28
Anglo-Sikh War of 1848, 280
Anjuman-i-Islamya, 287
Anjuman Taraqqi-e-Urdu (Hind), 136,
 187n, 199, 242–4, 247, 262–4, 266n, 267
Ansari, Abdul Quayyum, 246–7
Arabia, 140
Arabic, 157; as a source language for Urdu
 and Hindustani, 123, 128, 130–1, 132n,
 157
Aristotle, 222
Arjun, 222
Arya Samaj, 282n, 286–8, 293, 296n, 311,
 327–9, 331–4, 336, 342, 344n, 350, 355,
 368, 408, 413

Arya Varta, 100
Asansol railway station, 54
Ashoka, 139, 222–3, 414
Asia, elites in, 30–1; nationalism, national integration, and nation-states in, 5–7, 9
Assam, 16–17, 23, 146
Assamese, 78n, 81
assimilation, ethnic, 9, 22–3, 34–6, 44, 46, 411; and Government of India policies, 42; Hindi–Urdu, 158; Hindu–Muslim, 123, 125, 223; Hindu–Sikh, 282–3n, 298; of Hindus to Indo-Persian culture, 428; linguistic, xv, 12, 22, 297, 407; of minority languages and dialects to Hindi, xiv, 51, 61–3, 72, 74–5, 78, 82–96, 277, 419; and national integration, 10–11, 432; religious, 297, 308; and social mobilization, 422–3; and state government policies, 42–3, 116, 202, 234, 429
Aurangzeb, 139, 222–3, 354–5
Austro-Hungarian empire, 29
Awadhi, 70, 407
Awami League, 38
Awami Tanzeem, 254, 269
Azad Punjab, 315

backward caste, attitude towards Maithili, 71; in 1967 elections, 253; movements, 79–80, 245
Badal, Prakash Singh, *see* Prakash Singh Badal
Bajika, 66
Ballia district, Bhojpuri spoken in, 66n
Banaras (Benares), district of Bhojpuri-speakers, 66n; Hindi movement centered in, 61, 67, 108, 129–30, 136; Maithil Mandal in, 53n
Banaras Hindu University, recognition of Maithili in, 91, 102
Banarsi Das, 270
Banda Singh, 279
Bangladesh, 38, 405
Barrier, N. Gerald, 310
Behari, *see* Bihari
Belgium, 7, 338
Bengal, 66n, 277, 407; *bhadra lok* in, 31, 114; conquest by British, 59; Muslim condition and Muslim politics in, 121, 137, 140–1, 146, 150, 165, 176, 178, 180, 183, 413, 415; party system in, 372; social reform organizations in, 97
Bengali, and Bengali-speakers in relation to Maithili cause and Maithili language, 18, 62, 77, 92, 101, 407, 412; complaints concerning, 110; language, 73, 198n;

medium of education in Bihar, 104, 212; nationalism, 127; and Vidyapati, 63
Bentley, Arthur, 40, 83
bhadra lok, *see* Bengal
Bhagalpur district, Bihar ministers from, 95; Darbhanga Raj estates in, 59, 66n; Maithili-speakers in, 55, 64, 85, 93n, 110, 407
Bhagalpur University, 111
Bhargava, Dr Gopichand, 348
Bhatinda district, as a CPI stronghold, 389
Bhim, 222
Bhojpuri, in census, 65, 73–4, 76, 87, 92; characteristics of districts where spoken, 89; characteristics of people, 79n; as a dialect of Bihari language, 62, 68–9; language spoken in Bihar and U.P., 55, 66, 71, 85, 93n, 108; literature, 70; Muslim speakers of, 106; newspapers in language, 84; in relation to Maithili, 407; role of speakers in Bihar politics, 58; support for language, 102
Bihar, 22, 297, 330; facilities for Urdu in, 209ff.; government expenditures on Mithila, 57; government language policies, 52, 55, 73–4, 76, 95–114, 116, 199, 203, 211–15, 228, 260–1, 262n, 428–9; Hindi and Urdu in, 26; Hindi sentiment in, 16; Maithili language area in, xiv, 18, 411, 419, 421; Maithili movement in, 47, 51–116; major languages of, 192ff.; Muslim associations and leadership in, 243ff.; Muslims in political parties and in government service in, 228–33; Muslim politics and political attitudes in, 177–8, 181, 255–68, 403, 410, 420, 426, 431; official language of, 130, 198, 287, 427; political parties and politics in, 372, 373n, 375n, 416, 424; political research on, xv, 21; social mobilization in, 88ff., 418
Bihar Anjuman Taraqqi Urdu, *see* Anjuman Taraqqi-e-Urdu (Hind)
Bihar Hindi Sahitya Sammelan, *see* Hindi Sahitya Sammelan
Bihar Legislative Assembly, Muslims elected to, 229
Bihar Momin Conference, 246
Bihar PCC, *see* Indian National Congress
Bihar Public Service, 104
Bihar Rashtrabhasha Parishad, 74n
Bihar State Backward Muslim Federation, 247
Bihar State Handloom Weavers' Cooperative Union, 246

Bihar State Momin Advisory Committee, 246

Bihar University, 111; Vidyapati chair in, 102

Bihari, in census, 65, 75–6, 92, 193n; language and dialects, 62–3, 68, 69n, 86, 194

Bihari Muslims in Bangladesh, 268

bilingualism, 429; in Bihar, 92; in Punjab, 339–40, 345

BKD, 264

Blacks, representation in U.S. Congress, 229n

Blunt, E. A. H., 190n, 191n

Bombay, city, Maithils in, 91; city, Muhammadan Educational Conference held in, 168n; city, Muslim lawyers in, 162; presidency, 21, 33; presidency, Muslim education in, 146; state, division of, 18–20

Brahmans, 29, 406; in U.P., 153; *see also* Maithil Brahmans and Tamil Brahmans

Brahmo Samaj, 98

Braj Bhasha, 407

Brief Scrutiny of Prescribed Books in U.P., pamphlet, 244

British, administration, Muslims in, 160, 165; and Aligarh movement, 166–7; annexation of territory in India by, 54, 59, 127, 278; census authorities, 27; culture and society of, 35, 51; governors in U.P., 172; and the Gurkhas, 55; and Hindi–Urdu controversy, 131n; imperialism, 30; India, Muslim education in, 145; and Indian nationalists, 29, 176, 414; language policy, 62n, 129, 427; and partition of India, 124; rule in India, effect on language and religious groups of, 42, 120, 123, 140–1, 179, 413; rule in India, leading groups during, 31, 60; and the Sikhs, 279–81, 311–12, 315, 318, 320

Budden, J. H., 62

Buddha, 222–3

Buddhism, conversion of Chamars to, 13n

Bundeli, 70

Calcutta, AICC meeting in, 54

Calcutta University, Maithili in, 91, 102

California, Sikhs in, 410

Canada, 7, 13, 338

caste and castes, 13, 42, 45, 256, 408, 414; antagonisms, 397; associations, 6; in elections, 351, 355, 379–98; elites, regional, 32; federation, 197; groups, 12–14; Hindus, 170; low, 29, 37, 124–5;

286, 327; in Mithila, 56, 61, 67, 71, 79–81, 114–15, 406, 419; Muslim, 259; upper, 31

Census of India, 33; attempts to affect results of, 243, 423; data correlated with election returns in Punjab, 369–98; language figures for Bihar, 85–8, 90, 92, 107–8, 110; literacy figures in Punjab, 302–6; literacy figures in U.P., 147; Maithili and the, 73–8, 81; occupational distribution by religion in U.P., 152–6; in Punjab, 27, 285n, 288; Punjabi, Hindi, and the, 292–7, 326–7; Sikhs in, 310; urban and rural population in Punjab, 299–302; urban and rural population in U.P., 143; Urdu and the, 188–97, 207, 212, 411

Chagla, Mohammad Ali, 225, 230

Chaibasa, communal riot in, 268

Chamars, 13n, 219

Champaran district, Bhojpuri-speakers in, 55; Muslim Majlis-e-Mushawarat meeting in, 249n; *satyagraha* in, 93

Chandigarh, dispute concerning status of, 318, 323, 334, 364–5, 382, 387

Charan Singh, 269, 270

Chatterjee, Bankim Chandra, 126–7

Chetna Samiti, 99, 113

Chhatari, Nawab of, 172–4, 177n

Chief Khalsa Diwan, 283–4, 288, 309–11, 335, 368, 417, 424

Chikka-Chikki, dialect in Bihar, 66–76

China, 222

Chinese, in Malaysia, 13

Chitpavans, 31

Chota Nagpur, 55, 193n; levels of modernization in, 62; Maithili in, 62; male literacy in English in, 93

Christ, 222

Christian and Christians, church organization, 26; in Cyprus, 13; missionaries, 311; mythology, 222; in Punjab Legislative Assembly, 358; use of English, 189

cleavages, communal, and electoral politics in Punjab, 367–400; congruent and cross-cutting, 22, 27–8, 38–40, 42; ethnic bases of, 12, 41; and party politics, 38–41, 431–4; religious and communal, 22, 47

C.M. College, at Darbhanga, 98

Cohn, Bernard S., 138

Commissioner for Linguistic Minorities (CLM), 43, 109–10, 198, 201–2, 206, 210, 215, 217, 242–3, 245

Commissioner for Scheduled Castes and Scheduled Tribes, 43

Committee for the Demands of U.P. Muslims, 161

communal, antagonisms between Hindus and Muslims, 116, 136; antagonisms and political parties, 360, 362–3; appeal of Akali Dal, 356; appeal of Muslim League, 176; cleavages in Punjab party system, 398; coalition-building in Punjab legislature, 362; consciousness and identity within ethnic groups, 13, 37, 45, 178, 404; demands, 273; forces, Hindu and Muslim, 241; forces and political parties, 256, 259, 262, 375, 398; groups, political organization of, 46, 363; identifications and solidarity among Hindus and Muslims, 125, 408, 418; issues and Muslims in U.P., 176; minority, Muslims as a, 186; parties, 363, 377; polarization between Hindus and Muslims in U.P., 172–7, 180; polarization in Punjab politics, 355; political representation, 9; politics in Bihar, 269; propaganda in Bihar, 243; riots and violence in north India, 22, 183, 218–20, 226, 228, 234, 255, 260, 265–8

Communal Award, 172, 319

communalism, CPI attitude towards, 258; defined, 9; Hindu and Muslim, 253; and the Sikhs, 336, 430

communications, barriers to, 28; and language, 22, 25–6; and nationalism, 31; in Punjab, 302–9, 335; and social mobilization, 28, 32–3; in U.P., 156–9; in Urdu, 197

Communist parties, in Bihar, 244; and Muslim middle class, 417; in Punjab, 346, 368, 376, 389–92, 398; support for Urdu, 255, 264

Communist Party (Lal) (CP(L)), 371–2, 376

Communist Party of India (CPI), attitudes of members towards Maithili, 71, 101; attitudes towards Muslims, 257–8; in Bihar, 95, 251, 261, 424; position on minorities generally, 259; in Punjab, 346, 349, 359–63, 371–2, 376, 389–92, 395–7, 399–400; and Ranchi riots, 265–7; support for Urdu, 263n, 264, 268–9, 271

Communist Party of India (Marxist) (CPM), attitudes of members towards Maithili, 101; position on Muslims and Urdu, 258; in Punjab, 360, 371–2, 376, 390–1, 395–6; and Ranchi riots, 266n

Communists, absence of communalism among, 228; in Aligarh Muslim University, 225; candidates in 1967 elections

in Bihar, 253; and Ranchi riots, 267

community and communities, boundaries between Sikh and others, 281; defined, 8, 9n; forces of, attitude of central government towards, 42; Hindu and Muslim, 125–6; and language among Maithils, 78–81, 115; transformation from ethnic group to, 33; Urdu-speaking, 204

Congress, *see* Indian National Congress

Constituent Assembly of India, Sikh role in, 320

Constitution of India, articles concerning minority rights in, 43, 188n, 200–2, 205–7, 215, 226, 260, 263–4, 348, 350; article 44 on uniform civil code, 220; languages included and not included in eighth schedule of, 72–3, 105–6, 108, 198, 214, 430

court languages, *see* official language

Cunningham, Joseph D.: *History of the Sikhs*, 279, 282

Cyprus, 13

Czechs, 35

Dacca, Muslim League founded in, 168

Dara, 222

Dara Shikoh, 123

Darbara Singh, Sardar, 348

Darbhanga, demand for Mithila university in, 111–12; district included in Darbhanga Raj, 58–9; Hindi printing press established in, 60; language newspapers published in, 84, 418; Maithili in, xiv–xv, 64, 66n, 85–6, 90, 93n, 109–10, 407, 411; meetings of Maithili organizations in, 53–4, 100n; ministers from, 95; MP from district introduces Bill concerning Maithili in Lok Sabha, 106; party leaders interviewed in, 101

Darbhanga, Maharaja of, Kameshwar Singh, 60, 97; and Maithili movement, 53–4, 59–60, 84, 100

Darbhanga Raj, family provided leadership for Maithil Mahasabha, 99; regional identity and the, 58–61

Darshan Singh Pheruman, Sardar, 365

Das Gupta, Jyotirindra, 134–5, 137

Dawat, 241

Deeni Talimi Council, 210n, 221, 244–5

Delhi, enthusiasm for Maithili movement in, 91; language agitations in, 296n; languages of, 128, 184n, 257, 289; Maithili book exhibition in, 83

Deoband school, 163, 236, 237

depressed classes, 170, 171n

Deutsch, Karl, 33, 35, 36, 86, 272, 422
Devanagari script, 26, 129; and Gurumukhi, 291, 307–8, 338, 345, 347; and
Hindi, 67, 130–2, 185, 194, 287, 304,
306, 309, 326, 328, 333, 335, 339, 348,
368, 409, 418; and Hindi as medium of
instruction, 422; and Hindi as official
language of the Union, 178, 198;
Hindus, Hindi, and the, 133, 186n, 407,
411, 428; and Punjabi, 323; and Urdu,
134, 186
Dharamkot constituency, election case in,
354–5
dialect and dialects, absorbed by Hindi,
51, 90, 134, 297; of Bihar, 52, 63, 68,
73–5, 77n, 108; of Bihari, 62, 76, 86, 92,
193n; in census, 78, 192n; in Hindi-
speaking states, 22; Jan Sangh position
on north Indian, 345; Magahi as a, 91;
of Maithili, 64, 66, 80, 90, 115, 407;
Maithili considered as a, 70–2, 101, 103,
113, 409; in north India, 25; in Punjab,
292–3, 295–6; of Punjabi, 406; Punjabi
considered as a, 288–9, 344; in U.P.,
193–4; Urdu and local, 128, 133
differentiation, and assimilation, 34–6; of
ethnic groups and communities, 9, 12,
23, 367, 412, 422–3; as a widespread
process in north India, 46, 404; linguistic, 71, 78, 84–6, 297, 407; in Maithili
community, 81; political, absence of
among Maithili-speakers, 426; political,
among Muslims, 165–78, 272; political,
between Sikhs and Hindus, 337;
religious, xv, 12, 27, 124–7, 281–6, 308
District Boards Act, Muslim attitude towards, 171
Dogra, dialect, 407
Dravida Munnetra Kazagham (DMK),
17, 20, 38, 115
Dravidian, regional nationalism, 31
Dube, Yadavendra Dutt, 189
Duniyas, 247
Dutch democracy, 41, 378

Education Commission, 130–1
Egypt, 222
elections, in Bihar, 60, 94–6, 101–2; and
Muslims, 226–7, 244, 249, 251–6, 259–
260, 266–8, 271–2; in Punjab, 314, 321,
345, 351–62, 369–98; in U.P., 173–5,
177, 180, 219, 415, 433
elites, communication between, 86; educated, 26, 157; languages of, 131, 133,
184, 194, 405; in Mithila, 52, 60–1, 78,
95, 114–15; Muslim, 121, 124, 127, 156,

159–65, 173, 179–80, 187, 228, 232–3,
241, 245–7, 259, 272, 323, 404, 411, 413,
420, 422, 426; and nationalism and
nationality-formation, 4, 10, 37, 44–5,
125, 138, 178, 408, 414–18; political, 22,
28, 406; in Punjab, 307, 309; religious,
27, 119, 126, 135, 137; Sikh, 334–5;
Westernized, role in nationalism in
developing countries, 5–6, 30, 30n, 32,
45
elite-mass gap, 6, 26–7, 405–6
employment, of Muslims and Hindus in
U.P., 150–6
English, as an all-India language, 138–9;
in Canada, 13; in census, 77; and
Christians, 189; culture and society, 35;
and Indian nationalism, 156; as language of Westernized elites, 32, 83, 414;
literacy and English education, 91–3, 98,
115, 120, 141, 148–50, 161, 302–3; as
official language of India and its
provinces, 25, 73, 129, 257, 286–7, 306,
309, 341n; political party attitudes towards, 259, 271; publications in, 84,
307–8, 418; and three-language formula,
213–15; used by Sikhs, 410
English-speaking countries, 15
Etah, 207
ethnic group and ethnic groups, boundaries, 14; cleavages and political
integration, 39, 431–4; cleavages and
political parties, 41; conflict between,
36, 294, 367, 400, 409–10, 414, 419, 434;
consciousness within, 11, 38, 91, 93;
definition of, 9; demands in Punjab, 338;
differences in Bihar, 78n; identification,
27, 38, 278; Indian government policies
towards, 430; and language, 69; and
nationality-formation, 4, 7–8, 24, 28, 30,
33–4, 37, 114, 277–8, 403–4, 406, 416,
427; and the nation-state, 9; origin and
equality, 215; relationships between, 29,
44, 52, 115–16; and symbols, 334
ethnicity, 8
Europe, 7, 29–30, 434

factions, in Punjab Congress, 322
Fakhruddin, Maulana Syed, 186n
Faridi, Dr Abdul Jalil, 185n, 187n, 189,
198n, 199, 216, 221–3, 236, 239–41,
243–4, 248–51, 254–5, 271, 274
Fateh Singh, Sant, 365, 417, 425; and
Akali Dal, 17, 313–14, 317, 318, 321–2,
325–6, 336, 346
Fazilka tahsil, awarded to Haryana, 366
Fazlul Haq, 176

Fishman, Joshua, 25
Forward Bloc, in Punjab, 370–2
Ford, Henry Jones, 40–1
France, 7
French, in Canada, 13, 35; imperialism, 30
Fyzabad district, Bhojpuri spoken in, 66n

Gait, E. A., 66, 74, 193n
Ganda Singh, 279
Gandak river, western boundary of Mithila, 55
Gandhi, Mrs Indira, and Congress, 227, 254, 256, 374; visited by Mithila MPs, 106
Gandhi, M. K., and the Hindi–Urdu controversy, 135–6; and Hindu revivalism, 127
Ganges river, mythological origin, 222; southern boundary of Maithili-speaking region, 55, 407
Gautam, 222
Gaya district, Magahi spoken in, 66n
Geertz, Clifford, 11
Germans, 35
Germany, 7
Ghalib, 243
Ghazipur district, Bhojpuri spoken in, 66n
Ghaznavi, Mahmood, 222
Ghulam Sarwar, 243–4, 247, 251, 263n, 266n, 267
Gian Singh Rarewala, 348
Gill, Sardar Lachman Singh, *see* Lachman Singh Gill, Sardar
Gita, 127
Gokhale, G. K., 162
Golden Temple, 312
Golwarkar, M. S., 333, 344n
Good Relations Committee, 341n, 347–8
Gorakhpur, district, Muslim Schools in, 207; division, Bhojpuri spoken in, 66n
Government of India, 103, 144, 151, 219; Education Ministry, 112; Information and Broadcasting Ministry, 113; policies concerning language, religions, and regional groups, 17, 18, 42–3, 105, 116, 188, 207, 215–16, 330, 430–1; policy concerning Aligarh Muslim University, 223–6, 233, 250; policy concerning Muslim Personal Law, 234; policy concerning Punjabi Suba and Sikhs, 318, 322, 325, 336, 364–6, 413; policy concerning Urdu, 200–3, 233, 261, 263; three-language policy, 214–15
Government of India Act of 1935, 162
Granth, 291
Great Britain, 7

Greek, Christians in Cyprus, 13; philosophers, 222
Grierson, G. A., on the languages of Bihar, 50, 61–4, 66–7, 69, 74–6, 80, 85, 90, 107, 194, 404, 407; on the languages of U.P., 194; on Maithil Brahmans, 56; on Punjabi, 288–90, 404
Gujarat, 19; Arya Samaj founded in, 327
Gujaratis, and division of Bombay state, 18–20
Gumperz, John, 25, 134, 289–90, 292
Gupta, C. B., 187n, 204n, 206n, 269
Gurgaon district, Congress in, 331
Gurkhas, 54, 280
Gurnam Singh, 363
Guru Gobind, 279
Guru Nanak, 123, 282
Gurus, Sikh, 284, 353
gurudwara reform movement, 283; SGPC and Akali Dal founded during, 311, 315
gurudwaras, as base for Akali Dal, 317–18, 354, 408, 415; managed by SGPC, 312, 368; untouchable entry into, 311
Gurumukhi script, 26, 67, 278, 291–2, 304–10, 323, 326–7, 331, 333, 335, 338–9, 343–5, 347–8, 368, 407, 409–12, 428
Guyana, 7

Haj, 125
Harbans Lal, 348
Harijans, language choices in Punjab of, 294n; and political parties, 253, 259, 380, 382, 384, 389; *see also* Scheduled Castes
Harsh Vardhan, 222–3
Haryana, 16, 18–20, 300, 322–3, 329–30, 332–4, 336, 341, 344, 346–7, 349, 351, 355, 364–6, 430; movement, 330–2; Prant, 330, 345
Haryana Lok Samiti, 331, 352, 355–6
Hasan, Dr Nurul, 227
Hawaris, 247
Hazaribagh district, Magahi spoken in, 66n
Herring, Pendleton, 40–1
Himachal Pradesh, 322, 344, 366
Himalayas, 55
Hindi, assimilation to and differentiation from other languages, xiv, 46, 51, 61, 69, 75, 83, 197, 297; in Bihar, 65–6, 76–7, 84, 107–9, 260, 427; and Devanagari, 67, 422–3; as official language of Bihar, 68; as official language of India, 16–17, 24–5, 186, 257; policies of political parties towards, 258–9, 271, 343–50, 355; promoted by Arya Samaj, 287, 327–8, 333, 368; publications in, 100,

159, 307–8; in Punjab and Haryana, 292–3, 305–6, 322, 327, 329–31, 334–6, 356, 410, 430; in relation to Maithili, 18, 47, 52, 60, 62–3, 69–73, 85–92, 101, 103, 112–13, 115, 403–5, 407, 409, 412, 418, 421; in relation to Punjabi, 277, 286–97, 320, 326, 338–43, 404; in relation to Urdu and Muslims, 25–6, 75, 116, 123, 128–38, 156–9, 168, 182, 184–5, 187–95, 197–9, 204–6, 210–13, 233, 242, 263, 287, 323, 406, 411, 428; -speakers as percent of population in Punjab correlated with party votes, 379–94; -speaking region, 15, 21–3; in three-language formula, 214–15; Western, 288–9

Hindi Raksha Samiti, 329
Hindi Raksha Sammelan, 330
Hindi Sahitya Sammelan, 70, 74, 136, 262, 264, 266
Hindu and Hindus, backward caste movements among, 246; castes, 170, 171n; communal forces, groups, and sentiment, 219, 224–6, 228, 246, 251, 267, 350; dialects of, 62, 80; and elections and party politics in Punjab, 351–64, 367–400; in Haryana, 20, 430; and Hindu–Punjabi question, 286–96, 337–343, 347–50, 407, 423; and Hindu–Urdu question, 131–3, 135–6, 184, 188–9, 192n, 194, 196, 211–12, 242, 261, 263, 409, 423, 428; kingdoms, 140; and Maithil Mahasabha, 97–8; –Muslim relations, 12, 17, 22, 27, 29, 31, 41–2, 46, 52, 119–29, 132, 134–5, 137–8, 141,144, 169, 171, 178–9, 182, 184, 186–8, 218, 224, 233, 235, 238, 240, 250, 257, 265, 272, 274, 287, 403, 410–11, 413, 415, 418–19, 431; nation and nationalism, 15–16, 287; political leadership among, 47, 172, 174, 229, 264; political organizations in Punjab, 327–8; refugees, 144; revivalism and revivalists, 15, 204n, 220, 228; –Sikh relations, 31, 41, 46, 277, 281–6, 309–27, 329–37, 410–11, 421, 433; social mobilization, 142–63, 165–6, 297–309, 420, 422; stories in schools, 221–3, 244
Hinduism, 26–7, 408; and Arya Samaj, 327; elite-mass differences in, 406; and Hindi, 411; in Mithila, 57, 97, 114; in relation to Islam and Muslims, 122, 125, 127, 178, 233; in relation to Sikhs and Sikh religion, 282, 283n, 285–6; shift of Chamars from, 13n
Hindustani, 25, 63, 75, 128–9, 132n, 135,

188, 190–5, 242, 289–90, 293, 295–6, 404, 411, 414, 423
Hindustani Prachar Sabha, 136
Hissar district, Congress in, 331
Ho, 110
Hoernle, A. F. R., 61–3, 69
Horowitz, Donald L., 11
Hukam Singh, Sardar, 320, 352
Hunter, W. W.: *The Indian Mussalmans*, 140–1, 145, 150, 413
Hyderabad state, 160

Ibrahim, Hafiz Mohammad, 175
identity and identities, formation of group, 4, 6, 8–10, 29, 31; language and religion as symbols of group, 3, 22, 27; of regional groups in India, 19, 21
Independents, in Punjab elections and Legislative Assembly, 358–60, 371–2, 393–7
independence movement, Congress–Jamiyyat cooperation in, 238
India, elites in, 31–2; languages of, 24–5; as a multi-ethnic and multi-national state, 7, 11–20, 23; problem of unity of, 21; *see also* nationalism
India–Pakistan war, 268
Indian Administrative Service (IAS), Muslims in, 230
Indian Council of Hindi, 70
Indian Nation, 100
Indian National Congress, as an aggregative party, 41; in Aligarh district, 219; and Arya Samaj, 127; in Bihar, 95–6, 424; in Darbhanga district, 53n; in Gujarat, 19; and Hindu–Muslim relations, 135–6, 160–3, 167, 171–7, 180, 228; and linguistic reorganization of states, 20; and Muslims and Muslim organizations, 182, 227, 229, 235–6, 238–41, 243, 245–7, 250–1, 253–6, 258–259, 415, 417; nationalist ideology of, 215, 256; and nationalist movement, 32, 37, 414; in Punjab, 286, 315, 318, 320–2, 331–2, 343, 346–54, 356–63, 368–74, 376–84, 390, 395–400, 433; (R), 254, 256; supported by Maharajas of Darbhanga, 60; and Urdu issue in Bihar and U.P., 187, 260–2, 264–7, 269–70; views of leaders on Maithili, 101
Indian Statutory Commission, 284
Indo-Muslim culture, 422
industrialization, levels in Bihar, 89, 115
integration, Congress ideology of, 256; cultural, 205, 211, 221; policies of, 36, 42–3, 202, 234, 274; political, 7, 10, 14,

integration, political—*contd.*
337, 431–4; problems of, 215; processes of, 51; *see also* national integration
Iqbal, 243
Iran, 222
Irish national movement, 51
Islam, 26–7; and Communism, 253, 267; divisions in, 408; and Islamic unity, 249; and Jamiyyat-ul-Ulama, 238; in Muhammadan Anglo-Oriental College and Aligarh Muslim University, 166, 224; and Muslim League, 176, 180, 240, 425; in Pakistan, 3; in relation to Hindus and Hinduism, 119, 122–5, 127, 178, 220–2, 244, 282n, 415; revivalist movements in, 126, 236–7; and sense of Muslim separateness, 234, 411; and ulama, 163; and Urdu, 136, 187n, 188, 412
Ismail Khan, Nawab, 161

Jain, M. S., 137, 165–6, 168
Jamaat-e-Islami, 163, 187n, 220, 236–7, 239–41, 246, 249–50
Jamiyyat-ul-Ulama-e-Hind, 163–4, 172, 182, 186n, 219, 237–41, 245, 249–50, 268
Jammu, Dogri spoken in, 407
Jamshedpur, communal riot in, 219
Jan Congress, 53n
Jan Sangh, attitudes towards Maithili, 101, 106n; in Bihar, 95, 253; as a Hindu communal organization, 246; policy towards Hindi and English, 258–9; policy towards Hindi and Punjabi, 329, 336, 342, 344–6, 349–50; policy towards Urdu and Muslims, 186n, 187n, 189n, 206n, 255–7, 260–71; in Punjab, 332–4, 357–60, 362–3, 368–9, 371–2, 375, 377–8, 381–4, 386–90, 393, 395–8, 400, 433; in U.P., 251
Janata Party, 363, 370–2
Japan, 9, 15
Jaszi, Oscar, 29
Jats, Hindu, in U.P., 153; Sikh, 285–6, 317 374, 385, 389, 417
Jaunpur district, Bhojpuri spoken in, 66n
Jewish people, 28
Jha, Adya Charan, 77, 81, 91
Jha, Amarnath, 70
Jha, Laksman, 53, 53n, 61n
Jhajjar parliamentary constituency, 355
Jharkhand, forces, 107; state, demand for, 53n
Jinnah, Muhammad Ali, 122–3, 139, 141, 162–3, 167, 173, 176, 239; and fourteen points, 168
JKD, 251

Jodh Singh, Bhai, 347n
Joshi, Mrs Subhadra, 241n, 251
Julahas, 125, 245n
Jullundur, division, 302, 331–2; town, 300, 332

Kabir, 123
Kaikhusro, 222
Kairon, Pratap Singh, *see* Pratap Singh Kairon
Kaithi script, 67
Kannada (Kannari), 73, 198n
Kanti, 242
Karna Kayasthas, 68; *see also* Kayasthas
Kartar Singh, Giani, 348
Kashmir, 16–17
Kauravas, 61n, 139
Kayasthas, in Mithila, 56–7, 59, 79–80, 97–9, 114; in U.P., 131, 132n, 153
Kellogg, S. H., 63
Kerala, 23; Muslim League in, 248n
khalifa, 127, 273; *see also* Khilafat movement
Khaliquzzaman, Chaudhury, 162, 173, 175–6, 182, 273
Khalsa college, 310
Khari Boli, 128
Khushwant Singh, 279, 284
Kidwai, Rafi Ahmad, 167, 173, 175
Khilafat movement, 173, 238
Kosi river, eastern boundary of Mithila, 55
Kripalani, Acharya J. B., chairman of Uttar Pradesh Language Committee, 185, 187n, 204–7
Krishna, 222
K. S. Darbhanga Sanskrit Vishvavidyalaya, 111
Kunzru, Pandit H. N., 242
Kurukshetra, 139

Lachman Singh Gill, Sardar, 313–14, 363
Lahnda, 286–90, 293, 306
Lahore, Anjuman-i-Islamya in, 287; language agitation in, 296n; Muhammadan Educational conference in, 167; session of Muslim League, 122, 169, 176, 177n
Lajpat Rai, Lala, 127, 282n, 287
Lande script, 304, 306
language, and community among Maithils, 78–81; as an ethnic characteristic, 8, 24, 28; groups and political demands, 4; modernization, 25–6; and Muslim separatism, 127–37; and party support in Punjab, 379–98; problems, groups, and demands in India, 13–14, 16–18,

20–3; and religion in India, 27; and religion and the Punjabi Suba demand, 323–7; as a symbol of group identity, 3, 6, 12; variation, 26

language policy, 428–31; of Bihar government, 102–11, 211–15; of Government of India, 200–3; of Punjab government, 338–43; of Uttar Pradesh government, 203–11, 213–15

leadership, 41, 44, 337, 397; in Akali Dal and Punjabi Suba movement, 316–17, 319; in Maithili movement, 52

Liaquat Ali Khan, Nawabzada, 161, 182, 273

Lijphart, Arend, 40, 378

lingua franca, Urdu as a, 123, 127, 133, 188, 197

linguistic minority and minorities, complaints of and government policies towards, 107, 110, 207, 211, 216; Congress policy towards, 256; and Constitution, 200–1, 206, 260; pupils, statistics on, 202; and three-language formula, 213–214; Urdu-speakers as a, 187n, 188

linguistic reorganization of states, 16, 19–20, 23, 42

Lipset, Seymour Martin, 38, 40

literacy, in Bihar, 89, 93; and social mobilization, 28, 33; in Mithila, 83, 90, 115; in Punjab, 300, 302–6, 335; in U.P., 141–50

Lok Sabha, 219–20, 227

Loktantric Congress, 101

Lowell, A. Lawrence, 38

Lucknow, 142, 176, 244, 247–8, 271, 408

Lucknow Pact, 162, 171

Ludhiana, 300, 332

MacDonnell, Sir A. P., 156; circular of, 168

Madhok, Balraj, 333

Madhya Pradesh, 16, 248n, 257

Madras, city, 167; province, 20–1, 31, 33, 146, 162; state, 16, 248n

Magadh University, 111

Magahi (Magadhi), bilinguals, 92; language, 62–3, 68–9, 91, 93, 102, 108; newspapers in, 84; -speaking people and region, 52, 55, 58, 65–6, 71, 73–4, 76, 79n, 85, 87, 89, 115–16; spoken by Muslims, 106

Mahabharata, 61n, 139, 222

Maha Gujarat Parishad, 19

mahants, 283–4

Maharashtra, 31, 56, 58, 127, 139, 223, 248n

Mahmud, Dr Syed, 247–50, 251n

Mahmudabad, Raja of, 160–1, 174

Mahrattas, 140

Maithils, 56, 79–80, 91, 93, 97–9, 104, 105n, 115, 409–10

Maithil Brahmans, 56–7, 59, 61, 67–8, 71, 77, 79–80, 97–101, 114, 405, 411, 416, 418, 424

Maithil Mahasabha, 53, 59, 79, 82, 96–100, 424

Maithil Mandal, 53n

Maithili, in the census, 73–8; characteristics of, 25, 55–6, 61–73, 318, 326, 404–5, 407, 409; demands for recognition of, xiv, 197, 212; policy of Bihar government towards, 107–11, 215; publications in, 82–5; in relation to Hindi, 85–91, 298; script, 67; -speakers, 47, 323, 404, 406, 418, 421–2, 426; -speaking people, 403, 429; -speaking region, 18, 405, 419; status of, 102–7, 288; and Urdu, 264; voluntary associations, 95–100, 425

Maithili Mahasangh, 100n

Maithili movement, xv; compared with other movements, 119, 184, 188, 272, 318, 404, 411–13, 416; demands of, 111–14; weakness of, xiv, 47, 78–82, 91–5, 100–2, 323, 418–19, 424, 429–30; *see also* Mithila

Maithili Prachar Sena, 82

Maithili Sahitya Parishad, 53n, 79, 81, 98–100, 424

Maithili Sahitya Samiti, 92, 113

Majithia, Sardar Sundar Singh, 284, 417

Majlis-e-Mushawarat, *see* Muslim Majlis-e-Mushawarat

Malaviya, Madan Mohan: *Court Character and Primary Education in the N.-W. Provinces and Oudh,* 131, 157

Malaya, 338; Sikhs in, 410

Malays, 13

Malaysia, 7, 13

Malda district, Maithili spoken in, 66n

Malto, 65n

Malwa, 317

Manifesto on the Position of Urdu in India, 189

MAO College Magazine, 169

Marathi, 242n; -speakers and division of Bombay state, 18–19

Margdeep, 242n

Marwari, 70

Marxists, 234–5, 407, 417

Master Akali Dal, *see* Akali Dal

Maududi, Maulana Abul-Ala, 236–7, 240

Mecca, 125

medium of education, in Bihar, languages recognized as, 62n, 69n, 72, 75, 78, 109, 212; in bilingual societies, problem of, 428; Hindustani as, 135; Maithili as, 81–3, 103–5, 110–11, 412; in Punjab, 287–8, 327–9, 338–50, 428; in U.P. and Bihar, status of Hindi and Urdu as, 157, 199, 206–12, 287, 288n, 418, 422–3

Meerut, communal riots in, 219–20

Methodist, 123

minority and minorities, linguistic, religious, and cultural, 23, 109–10, 116, 210, 215, 263; Muslims as a, 172, 182, 186; Urdu as language of a, 204

Minto, Lord, 161

Mirzapur district, Bhojpuri spoken in, 66n

Mishra, Dr Umesh, 70, 113

Misra, Harinath, 77

Mithila, demand for separate state of, 18, 52–8; Maithili in, 66–8; regional identity in, 58–61, 79–80, 91, 95, 115, 318–19, 416, 422, 424

Mithila Mihir, 53, 70, 76–7, 81, 84, 91, 100, 103, 110

Mithila university, demand for a, 111–12

Mittal, Gopal, 188

MLAs, and Maithili, 71, 99, 101, 103

modernization, in Bihar, levels of, 51, 89, 93; and the nation-state, 5, 7; and social change, 34

Mohammad Ali Chagla, *see* Chagla, Mohammad Ali

Mohsin-ul-Mulk, Nawab, 160, 167n, 168

Momins, 236, 245–7

Monghyr district, Darbhanga Raj estates in, 59; Maithili-speakers in, 55, 64, 66n, 86, 110, 407; ministers from, 95

Montagu–Chelmsford reforms, 319

Morley–Minto reforms, 168

mother tongue and mother tongues, in Bihar, relations among and conflicts concerning status as medium of education, 52, 61, 69, 71, 74, 76, 82, 85–7, 92, 101, 103–5, 108–10, 116, 212; in census, 190n, 191n, 192n, 193, 295n, 423; in Constitution, 201, 206, 215–16; defined, 72n; political party positions on, 256, 259, 344; in Punjab, relations among and conflicts concerning status as medium of education, 286–8, 290–5, 297, 320, 325–6, 328, 338–9, 341–3, 346, 387; Urdu as a, 185n, 202–4, 233–4, 411; in U.P., 195, 206–7, 211; in three-language formula, 214–15, 257

MPs, and Maithili, 99, 101, 103, 106

Mughal and Mughals, court, 160; emperors, 123; and Sikhs, 278–9

Mughal Empire, 139

Mughul, caste of Muslims, 125

Muhafiz Dasta, *see* Urdu Muhafiz Dasta

Muhammad Ali, 171

Muhammadan Anglo-Oriental College, 165–7, 170, 224; *see also* Aligarh Muslim University

Muhammadan Anglo-Oriental Defence Association, 168

Muir, Sir William, 130

Munda, 65n

Muslims, backwardness of, 138–41, 420; elites among, 159–65, 414–17; employment of, 150–6, 230–3; grievances of, 182–3, 217–28, 233–4, 431; and Hindi-Urdu controversy, 127–38; leadership of, 179–80, 235–6; literacy and English education among, 144–50, 298, 300, 302–6; and Maithili, 66, 69n; and party politics, 228–30, 255–72; political organizations and voluntary associations of, 175, 236–55, 311, 425–6; political strategy of, 169–78; in Punjab Legislative Assembly, 358; relations with Hindus, 12, 16, 22, 27, 29, 31–2, 41–2, 46, 185, 420–3; relations with Sikhs and Hindus in Punjab, 315, 319, 328, 335, 357, 419; revivalism among, 122–7; and separate electorates, 427; separatism and communal identity of, 32, 47, 51, 78, 119–22, 167, 173, 178–81, 183, 187, 272–4, 403, 412–14, 416, 418; urbanization of, 142–4, 298–9, 301–2; and Urdu, xv, 47, 52, 80, 84, 106, 156–9, 183–217, 293, 297, 308–9, 323, 326, 405–7, 409–412, 418, 428–30

Muslim League, and Aligarh movement, 161, 167, 224; in Bihar, 249n, 269; compared to Chief Khalsa Diwan, 311; dissolution of in north India, 235; as an ethnic political organization, 37; foundation of, 168; and Jinnah, 122, 141; leadership of, 416–17; and Momins, 246; and Muslim separatism, 136, 426; and other Muslim organizations, 238–40, 425; and Pakistan movement, 22, 42, 124, 415; in Punjab, 318, 357–8, 362, 364; in U.P., 144, 162–5, 169, 171–82, 212, 249n, 255, 273–4, 433

Muslim Majlis-e-Mushawarat, defends Aligarh Muslim University, 226; founded, 239; and Jamaat-i-Islami, 241; as representative of Muslim community,

425; in U.P. and Bihar, 189, 198n, 243, 246–55, 266n, 267, 271, 274
Muslim Unity Board, 161
Mutiny of 1857, British blamed Muslims for, 120; Sikh role in, 281
Muzaffarpur district, Bihar University at, 111; and Darbhanga Raj, 58–9; languages spoken in, 55, 64, 66n, 85–6, 93n, 110; ministers from, 95
Mysore, 248n
myth, role in nationalist ideology, 28–9, 122, 412–13

Nagaland, 16, 17, 51
Nagari, *see* Devanagari
Nagari Pracharini Sabha, 136, 186n
Namdhari sect, 352
nation and nations, defined, 8–9, 9n, 125, 280, 424, 432; development of, 122, 418; and ethnic groups, 24, 28, 114, 427; Hindus and Muslims as separate, 119, 124, 165; Indian, 256, 258; Sikhs as a, 277, 279, 334–5; *see also* nationality
nation-building, 15
nation-state, 5, 7, 15; defined, 9, 9n; Indian, 138, 223; Muslim, 123
National Agriculturalist Party (NAP), 162, 172–4, 177, 179–80
national integration, 4–15, 21, 39, 432; of India, 42, 60, 204, 215–17, 223, 248; *see also* national unity
national language, Hindi as a, 70, 72, 334; usage of term in India, 73n
National Muhammadan Association, 141, 145, 150
national unity, and central government policies, 216; and competitive political parties, 41; in India, problems of, 14–20; in South Asian states, threats to, 3; *see also* national integration
nationalism, defined, 9–10, 37; importance of India to theories of, 21, 23, 121, 124–5; in India, 21, 29, 32, 34, 123, 127, 156, 160, 217, 238, 259, 368, 414; language as basis for, 3, 405; and Muslims, 237, 240; and myth construction, 29; national integration, nationality-formation and, 4–20, 24; and religious symbols, 3, 27; Sikh, 281; theories of and literature on, 35, 51, 272; and Westernized elites, 30, 30n
nationalist and nationalists, elites, 33, 45; ideology, 122, 274; Indian, 119
nationalist movement, Indian, 32, 138, 162, 245, 272; Muslim separatism as, 121, 178

'nationalist' Muslims, 162, 177, 182, 242, 249
nationality and nationalities, Bihar language groups as, 78n; defined, 8–9, 9n; development of, 43–4; and ethnic groups, 24n, 114; Indian, 16, 31–2, 46, 119, 122, 124, 125n, 126, 136n, 139, 223, 257, 259, 287, 431; movements, 61; in multi-ethnic states, 15; Sikhs as a, 277, 279, 311, 334; Syed Ahmad's conception of, 137; *see also* nation
nationality-formation, elites and, 30–2, 414–17; government policies and, 41–3; 426–31; inter-group relations and, 33–6, 419–24; internal values and, 28–9, 412–14; nationalism, national integration and, 4–14, 21; objective differences between peoples and, 24–8, 404–12; party politics and, 38–41, 431–4; political organization and, 36–7, 424–6; process of, xv, 23–4, 43–5, 114, 272, 403–4; social mobilization and, 32–3, 417–19
nationism, 10
Nau Muslim, 125
Nausherwan, 222
Nayar, Baldev Raj, 324, 354, 379–80, 383
Negro, slavery, 11
Nehru, Pandit Jawaharlal, chairman of Sahitya Akademi, 103; death of, 322; inaugurates Maithili book exhibition, 83; and Muslims, 176; relations with Akali Dal, 316–17, 321, 354–5
Nehru Report, 238
Nepal, Maithili-speaking areas in, 50, 55, 64; wars with British of, 54
Nepalese, 104
Nigeria, 7
Nirankaris, 285
non-Brahman, castes in Mithila, 61; movements of in India, 31, 38, 80, 245
non-Congress governments, and Mithila university issue in Bihar, 112; and Momins in Bihar, 246; and Urdu issue in Bihar and U.P., 260–72; in Punjab, 363
non-cooperation movement, 238, 315
North America, 30
North-West Frontier Province, 299n, 304n
North-Western Provinces and Oudh, 119n; controversy over official language in, 129–31, 134, 156–8; Muslim education in, 145–6, 166; Muslim employment in government of, 150–1; *see also* United Provinces

official language, of India, issue of, 16–17, 20–1, 42, 70, 72–3, 178, 186, 198, 204, 258; in N.-W. Provinces and Oudh, U.P., and Bihar, issue of, 68–9, 108, 110, 168, 184, 193n, 200, 204, 206, 213, 233, 238, 244, 250–1, 255, 257, 259–64, 270, 428; of Punjab, issue of, 286, 306, 309, 329, 334, 340, 342–5, 362, 422, 427–8
Old Boys, *see* Aligarh Muslim University Old Boys' Association
Oraon, 65n
Orissa, 23, 53n, 55
Oriya, 55, 81, 110, 212
Oudh, talukdars of, 160–1, 173–4; *see also* North-Western Provinces and Oudh

Pahari, 293, 295
Pakistan, and Aligarh Muslim University, 167; Anjuman Taraqqi-e-Urdu in, 242; demand and movement for creation of, 3, 22, 121n, 123, 163, 169, 176, 178, 180, 182, 238–9, 273, 362, 415, 433; migration of Indian Muslims to, 144, 181, 232–3, 235; Muslims in contemporary India and, 228, 248, 431; Sindhi refugees from, 106; war between India and, 17, 322
Palamau district, Magahi spoken in, 66n
Pandavas, 61n, 139
pan-Islamism, 126–7, 238
Panth, identification of Akali Dal and Sikh, 316, 352–5, 408, 425
paracommunity, Maithil Mahasabha as a, 97
Parliamentary Committee on the Demand for Punjabi Suba, 331
Parsis, 222
partition of India, 12, 16, 42, 120, 124, 198, 224, 239, 337, 357, 360; consequences of for Muslims of U.P. and Bihar, 178, 235, 248; effect of on Congress policies towards communal demands, 320; and the Sikhs, 364, 415
Pathan, caste of Muslims, 125, 246
Patiala division, 300, 302
Patna city, 101; anti-Urdu meeting in, 264; Maithili political activities in, xiv, 99–100, 103; Muslim politics in, 247, 249
Patna district, Darbhanga Raj estates in, 59; Magahi spoken in, 66n
Patna Radio Station, demand for Maithili programs on, 112–14
Patna University, founded, 111; Maithili in, 59, 99, 102
patriotism, 10, 15

PEN, recognizes Maithili, 69, 102
people, and ethnic group, 8
People's Manifesto of Muslim Majlis-e-Mushawarat, 250, 252–3, 258
People's United Front Ministry, *see* non-Congress governments
PEPSU Formula, 338, 340, 429
Permanent Settlement, effect on Raja of Darbhanga, 59
Persian, as an all-India language, 138; as official language in British-ruled provinces, 129; in schools in N.-W. P. and Oudh, 157; script used for Urdu (and Hindi), 26, 129–32, 134–5, 185–6, 188, 194, 255, 262, 287, 303–4, 306, 407, 409, 411, 412, 418, 422–3; as a source language for Urdu, 123, 128, 129n, 131, 132n, 134–5, 179, 188, 193n, 194, 405
Persian-Arabic script, *see* Persian
Personal Law (*shari'a*), attitude of Jamaat-e-Islami towards, 240–1; attitude of Muslim League towards, 165; issue of reform of, 220, 230, 234, 236, 238, 240, 250; and ulama, 163, 164, 180, 238n
Pheruman, Sardar Darshan Singh, *see* Darshan Singh Pheruman, Sardar
Phulkian states, 281
Pioneer, 214
Pirpur Report, 176n, 178
pirs, 125
Plato, 222
pluralism, and British policy, 42; and Government of India policy, 43, 116, 202, 215–17, 274; policies of, 7, 10–11, 37; and political party policies, 258
political development, and national integration, literature on, 5
political mobilization, language and religion as bases for, 3, 18
political modernization, 14–15
political parties, attitudes of on the language issues in the Punjab, 343–50; attitudes of towards Urdu and Muslim minority rights, 255–9; and social and ethnic cleavage, 36, 38–41, 367–400, 432
Prakash Singh Badal, 363
Pratap Singh Kairon, 321–2, 331, 347–8, 354–5, 363, 373–4
Prem Chand, 243
President of India, and Aligarh Muslim University, 227; role in language policies, 201, 260; and Urdu demands, 200, 261; Dr Zakir Husain as, 242
primordial loyalties, 5
princely states, in Punjab, 312, 338; in U.P., 143n, 147n

Proutist Bloc of India, 102
PSP, in Bihar, 95, 101, 264; in Punjab, 370–2
Punjab, xv, 18, 22, 47, 223, 407; bases of party support in, 379–400; division of, 19–20; electoral turnout in, 33n; government and SGPC, 312; language problems and policies in, 26, 286–96, 337–50, 409–10, 427–30; Muslims in, 146, 151, 176, 178, 180, 183; political parties and leaders in, 115, 127, 370–9, 424–5, 433–4; religious groups and communal cleavage in, 17, 27, 41, 350–64, 413–15, 419–21; reorganization of, 357, 364, 381–2, 387; Sikh communal consciousness in, 278–96; Sikhs and Hindus in, political differentiation of, 309–36; Sikhs and Hindus in, social mobilization and communications among, 297–309
Punjab High Court, 354
Punjab Hindu Sabha, 283
Punjab Language Act, 1967, 342
Punjab Legislative Assembly, 341n, 347, 358–60, 370
Punjab Muslim League, 283; *see also* Muslim League
Punjab Official Languages Act, 1960, 330
Punjab Pradesh Congress Committee, *see* Indian National Congress
Punjab Unionist Party, 176
Punjab Vidhan Sabha, *see* Punjab Legislative Assembly
Punjabi, attitudes of Hindus and Hindu groups towards, 328, 331, 333–4, 336, 356, 387, 423; attitudes of political parties in Punjab towards, 343–50; in Bihar, 110; characteristics of, 25, 288–92, 404, 406–7, 412; language movement, 51–2, 67, 116; publications in, 307–8; and Punjab government policies, 321, 330, 338–43, 429; in relation to Hindi, 22, 26, 67, 72, 184, 197, 286–97, 306–10, 404, 406; and the Sikhs, xv, 78, 277–8, 294–7, 323, 326–7, 334–5, 368, 409–11, 416, 423, 425, 428; -speaking region, 19, 198n, 322, 329, 367; -speakers, percent of correlated with party votes in Punjab, 380–95
Punjabi-speaking Hindus, interests different from Hindi-speaking Hindus, 330–2, 336, 347–9, 364–6; and Jan Sangh, 344; shift from Punjabi to Hindi, 327, 345, 350, 387, 411, 423
Punjabi-speaking state, *see* Punjabi Suba
Punjabi Suba, Akali Dal in, 433; and

Congress, 360, 373, 380, 382, 394; and the Government of India, 364–7, 430; language conflict in, 342–5, 350; movement, 17, 20, 47, 105, 283n, 287, 292, 313–27, 330, 336–7, 348–9, 351, 410–11, 417; opposition to, 286, 329, 331–3, 386, 392; and status of Chandigarh, 387
Punjabi Suba Agitations of 1960–1, 317
Punjabi Suba Slogan Agitation of 1955, 317, 320
Purbia, 192n
Purnea district, 93n; Darbhanga Raj estates in, 59; Maithili spoken in, 55, 64, 66n, 85–6, 110, 407; ministers from, 95; Yadavs in, 56

Quebec, 35
Quraishi, Yaheer Masood, 252

Radha Soamis, 285
Radiance, 230, 241
Rae, Douglas, 371n, 377
Raghubar Dayal Commission Report, 218–19
Rains, 247
Rajasthan, 62n, 248n
Rajendra Prasad, 69n
Rajput, 125
Ram Prakash, 271
Ram Rajya, 127
Rama, 222
Ramayana, 61n, 139, 222
Rampur, 143, 242n, 255
Rana Pratap, 223
Ranchi, Bhojpuri spoken in, 66n; communal riot of 1967 in, 219–20, 260–1, 264–7; university in, 111
Ranchi-Hatia, *see* Ranchi
Rangrez, 247
Ranjit Singh, Maharaja, 278–80, 417
Rarewala, Gian Singh, *see* Gian Singh Rarewala
Rashtriya Swayamsevak Sangh (RSS), 241, 246, 271n; in Punjab, 332–4; role in anti-Urdu agitation and Ranchi riots in Bihar, 264–6
Ravanna, 61n
Reeves, Peter, 172
Regional Formula, 291, 321, 329, 332, 338, 340, 347, 380
regional languages, 17, 25, 72–3n
regional movements, 61
regionalism, 51, 80, 115n, 319; and national unity in India, 14–21
religion, as an ethnic, group, and communal symbol, 3, 6, 24, 26, 28; and language in India, 26–7; and language

religion, and language—*contd.*
and the Punjabi Suba demand, 323–7; and party support in the Punjab, 379–398; and religious differentiation in the Punjab, 281–6; and religious groups and demands in India, 13–14, 16–17, 20–3; and revivalism in India, 122–27
Representation of the People Act, 1951, 351, 354
Republican party (RPI), in Aligarh, 219; policy towards Urdu and Muslims, 258; in Punjab, 360, 363, 371–2, 376, 392–3, 395–7; and RPI(A), 376
revivalism and revivalist movements, 29; Hindu, Muslim, and Sikh, 126–7, 136, 140, 163, 236, 240, 326
Ripon, 141
Rohtak district, Congress in, 331
Roman Catholic, 123
Rustam, 222

Sachar Formula, 290, 338–49, 429
sahajdari, 285
Saharanpur district, 237
Saharsa district, Maithili spoken in, 85–6, 90, 93n
Sahay, K. B., 252n
Sahitya Akademi, and recognition of Maithili, 69, 71, 82, 100, 102–3
Saiyid, 125, 153
Salempur, Raja of, 161, 172, 174
Sami'ullah Khan, 160
Sampradayikta Virodhi Committee, 218, 241n
Sampurna Maharashtra Samiti, 20
Sampurnanand, Dr, 187n, 204n, 206n, 221–2
Sanatan Dharam Pratinidhi Sabha (SDPS), 329
Sangam, 243, 251
Sangrur district, as a CPI stronghold, 389
Sanskrit, as an all-India language, 138–9; and Arya Samaj, 327; attitudes of political parties towards, 257, 259; devotion of Maithils to, 57, 59, 80n, 91–2, 98, 114; and Hinduism, 411; in schools in Oudh, 157; as source language for Hindi, 129, 135, 194, 215; and three-language formula, 210–11, 214–15
Sanskrit University, at Darbhanga, 112
Sanskritization of Hindi, 129, 134, 215, 259, 405
Sant Akali Dal, *see* Akali Dal
Santal Parganas district, Maithili in, 64, 66n, 85–6, 110

Santali, as medium of education in Bihar, 104, 212; publications in, 84
Saran district, 93n
Sarkar, Jagannath, 265n
Sarkar of Tirhut, 58
Saroor, Ali Ahmad, 242
Sartori, Giovanni, 399
satyagraha, in Champaran, 93
'Save Hindi' agitation, 329, 355
Sayeed, Khalid B., 140, 162
Scheduled Caste Federation (SCF), 371–2, 376, 392–3, 395–7
Scheduled Castes, and bases of party support in Punjab, 379–99; Hindu and Sikh in Punjab, 285–6, 368, 406; parties of, 377
Scotland, 51
Scotsmen, 35
script and scripts, as an aspect of language variation, 26; for Hindi and Urdu, 133–4, 136, 158, 184, 187, 206n, 257, 409, 410; and language in Punjab, 286, 288, 291, 302–3, 327, 407; for Maithili, 67, 113, 200; right to preserve protected by Indian Constitution, 43, 188n, 204; *see also* Devanagari, Gurumukhi, and Persian
Searchlight, 100
secession, 7, 11n; Government of India policy towards, 17, 18, 21
secularism, among Muslims, 237; and political parties, 256, 368; and Westernized elite, 414
separate electorates, abolished in India after independence, 178, 182, 183, 235, 274; and communal conflict, 46; and minority representation during British rule, 42; for Muslims, 159, 163, 168, 170, 171, 179, 238, 425–7; for Sikhs, 300, 319
separatism, cultural, 44; defined, 9; in Nagaland, 51; religious, 46; Sikh, 32, 417; *see also* Muslims
Shaikhs, Muslim caste, 125, 153, 246
Shankaracharya, 222
Shareef report, 176n
shari'a, *see* Personal Law
Shastri, Lal Bahadur, conversations with Sant Fateh Singh, 322
Sher Singh, 355
Shi'a, 125, 408
Shiromani Gurudwara Prabandhak Committee (SGPC), 283–4, 311–14, 335, 368, 417, 424; and Akali Dal, 315–18, 322, 425
Shivaji, 58, 139, 223
Shiva Prasad, Babu, 130

Shoup, Paul, 15
shudras, 259
Siddiqi, M. Yousuf, 241n
Siddiqi, Zafar Ahmad, 244
Sidhwan Bet constituency, 354
Sikhs, communal consciousness, identity, and separatism among, 32, 277ff., 334–6, 413–15, 417, 420, 431–4; in Congress, 374; demand for separate state, 17, 47, 318–27, 430; electoral appeals to, 351–7; and electoral support for political parties in Punjab, 376, 380–99; *keshadhari*, 285, 334, 406, 408, 410, 425; literacy and communications among, 300, 302–9; organizations among, 309–318, 378, 424; and Punjab government language policy, 338–49; and Punjabi, xv, 52, 67, 72, 78, 286–97, 404, 407, 409–11, 416, 423, 428; relations with Hindus, 27, 31, 41, 281–6, 309–18, 327–328, 367–8, 373, 421, 423; and religious cleavage in Punjab, 19, 22, 46, 357–64, 419; *sahajdari*, 285, 410; scriptures of, 326, 335; and Sikh kingdoms, 140, 278–81, 412; urbanization of, 298–301
Sikh Gurudwara Reform Act of 1925, 283, 312, 427
Sikhism, 26–7, 282n; elite–mass differences in practice of, 406; and low castes, 285; internal differentiation in, 408; and Punjabi, 411–12; and Singh Sabha movement, 310–11; symbols of, 285, 335
Simon Commission, 161, 168, 178, 287, 319
Sindh, 106
Sindhi, 105, 107
Singh, Jankinandan, 53, 53n, 54
Singh, Maharaja Kameshwar, *see* Darbhanga, Maharaja of
Singh, Dr Ram Subhagh, 260n
Singh Sabha, 309–11, 328, 335, 367–8, 409, 417, 424
Sinha, Mahamaya Prasad, 243, 252n, 264, 265n, 270
Sinha, Mahesh Prasad, 264n
Sinha, Satya Narain, 114n
Sinhalese Buddhists, in Sri Lanka, 13
Sita, 222
Sitamarhi, 249n
Smith, Wilfred Cantwell, 169, 183–4
social mobilization, 24, 28, 32–6, 43–4, 178, 272, 405, 417–20, 422–3; in Bihar, 61; among Hindus and Muslims in north India, 135, 142–59, 179–80; among Hindus and Sikhs in the Punjab, 297–311, 335; among Maithili-speaking people, 51, 66–7, 72, 85–93, 115

Socialist Party, in Bihar, 424; in Punjab, 359, 371n
Socrates, 222
South Africa, 7; Gandhi's return from, 93
South Asia, 3, 26–7, 29, 405, 434
south India, 405
Soviet Union, 7, 15
Sri Lanka, 3, 7, 13, 38, 338
Sri Lanka Freedom Party, 37–8
SSP, in Bihar and U.P., 95, 101, 106, 261–264, 266–7, 270–1; position on language and minorities, 258–9; in Punjab, 360, 371–2
standardization, of Hindi, 69
state, and nation, 14–15, 24; and theories of nationalism and national integration, 4–8, 10
States Reorganisation Commission, and demands for division of Punjab, 290, 320, 330–1, 365; and division of Bombay state, 19; and Mithila state demand, 52–4
Sudetenland, 35
Sudhanshu, Dr Lakshmi Narayan, 74n, 264
Sugauli, treaty of, 54
Sunni (Muslims), 125, 408
Supreme Court of India, decision on Aligarh Muslim University, 226
SVD government, in Bihar, 268; in U.P., 271n; *see also* non-Congress governments *and* united front governments
Swatantra Party, in Bihar, 53n; position on minority rights, 258; in Punjab, 359, 365n, 370–2, 375
Switzerland, 7, 15
Syed, Muslim caste, 246
symbols, all-India, 32, 221, 223; of group identity and national movements, 3, 10, 13, 23, 26, 28–30, 178, 281, 412; in the Maithili movement, 60–1, 61n, 79–80; of Muslim separatism, 122–41, 180, 404, 411, 426; religious, 27, 408; of Sikh separateness, 286, 334–5, 415, 419

talukdars, 160–1, 172–4, 182
Tamil and Tamils, 138, 431; Hindus in Sri Lanka, 13; language, 73n, 198n; -speaking people, opposition to Hindi of, 72
Tamil Brahmans, 31
Tamil Nadu, 223; DMK in, 17, 38; Ramayana reinterpreted in, 61n, 139
Tara Singh, Master, 17, 283n, 313, 315–18, 319n, 321–2, 324, 325n, 336, 346, 365, 375, 417, 425

Teli, Muslim caste, 125
Telugu, 198n, 242n
Thakur, Karpuri, 268
three-language formula, Jan Sangh policy
 on, 257; in Punjab, 343, 345; in U.P.
 and Bihar, 210, 213–15
Tilak, 56, 127
Tirhut, Raja of, 59
Tirhuti, script for Maithili, 67
Titus, Murray T., 124
tribal, languages and population in Bihar,
 65, 71, 89, 107–8, 265
tribe, 6, 13, 45
Tripathi, Kamalapati, 254–5
Truman, David B., 38, 40
Turkey, 127
Turkish Muslims, in Cyprus, 13
two-nation theory, 124, 168

ulama, 406; alliance of with Congress in
 U.P., 173, 175–7; opposed Aligarh
 leadership, 416; opposed modern secular
 education, 120; opposed Pakistan demand, 163–5, 179–80; role in post-
 independence politics in India, 236,
 417
uniform civil code, opposed by Jamiyyat-
 ul-Ulama, 238; supported by Jan Sangh,
 257
Unionist Party, 41, 318, 358
united front governments, in Bihar, 106,
 109, 252n, 261–2, 265, 267–9; in
 Punjab, 313–14, 362; in U.P., 269–70;
 see also non-Congress governments *and*
 SVD governments
United Kingdom, 35
United Legislative Party, in U.P., 270
United Provinces, Aligarh movement in,
 165–9; British policy towards Hindi and
 Urdu in, 427–8; Muslim elites in, 159–
 165; Muslim League in, 172–81, 433;
 Muslim separatism in, 47, 119–22,
 169–81, 413–16, 418; relations between
 Hindus and Muslims in, 298, 403, 420;
 social mobilization and communications
 among Hindus and Muslims in, 142–59;
 see also North-Western Provinces and
 Oudh
United States, 7, 28, 35, 40
United States Congress, blacks in, 229n
Unity Formula, 348
University Grants Commission, 112
untouchables, in the Sikh community,
 310–11; *see also* Scheduled Castes
urbanization, 33, 33n, 44; in Bihar, 89;
 among Hindus and Muslims in the

United Provinces, 141–4, 148, 156;
 among Hindus, Sikhs, and Muslims in
 the Punjab, 299–302; among Maithili-
 speakers, 115
Urdu, characteristics, development, and
 use of, 63, 123, 127–9, 131, 404; competition with and divergences from
 Hindi, 22, 25–6, 129–38, 157–9, 167–8,
 170, 345, 405, 409; in the census of
 Punjab, 292–3, 295–6, 304–6; in the
 census of U.P. and Bihar, 65, 86, 92,
 188–97; Government of India policy
 towards, 200–3, 215–17; 429–30, and
 Muslim cultural identity, 78, 184–8, 407,
 410–12, 415; Muslim movement on
 behalf of, xv, 47, 52, 80, 116, 176, 180,
 298, 323, 326, 404–6; publications in, 84,
 307–8; in Punjab, status of, 286–8, 290,
 303, 309, 327, 341n, 427; U.P. and
 Bihar government policies towards,
 203–17, 260–9, 419, 423; in U.P. and
 Bihar, status of, 101, 104, 106–7, 110,
 183–4, 197–200, 418, 421–2, 427
Urdu Muhafiz Dasta, 244, 271
Uttar Pradesh, xv, 21, 47, 55, 68, 297, 372,
 373n, 375n; government language policies, 107, 186n, 199, 203–17, 261; Hindu
 nationalism and Hindi sentiment in, 16;
 Muslim politics and political organization in, 235–45, 247–59, 269–74, 403,
 426; Muslim representation in government of, 228–33; religious cleavage in,
 22, 41, 410, 419; Urdu and Muslim
 grievances in, 182–200, 203–11, 213–34,
 287, 326, 330, 414, 431
Uttar Pradesh Language Committee, 185,
 186n, 187, 204–5, 242
Uttar Pradesh (and United Provinces)
 Legislative Assembly, 18, 172, 186n, 187
Uttar Pradesh Muslim Majlis, 254; *see also*
 Muslim Majlis-e-Mushawarat
Uttar Pradesh Official Language Act,
 1951, 198

Vaidehi, 84
Vajpayee, A. B., 345n
Varanasi, facilities for Urdu in, 206; *see
 also* Banaras
varna, 27
Vashishtha, 222
Vedic, orthodoxy in Mithila, 57
Vidyalankar, Jai Chand, 347
Vidyapati, 56, 63, 412; celebrations, 56n,
 99, 100; chair at Bihar University, 412
Vigyan, Chandrika, 242
Viqar-ul-Mulk, Nawab, 168

466

Vishnu, Lord, 222
Vyas, 222

Wales, 51
Wali-Ullah, Shah, 123
Wazida, Nawab of Sirhind, 354–5
weightage, in representation of minorities during British rule, 42, 169–71, 175, 179
Weiner, Myron, 11
Welshmen, 35
West, Negro slavery in, 11
West Bengal, 53n, 248n, 370n
West Pakistan, migration of Hindus and Sikhs from, 293
Western, education and Western-educated elites in India, 79, 93, 141, 166, 237; ethnocentrism in theories of national integration, 5, 8; ideas, 127; religious organization, 26–7
Western Europe, 5, 9, 15
Westernized elites, *see* elites
Wright, Theodore P., Jr, 229–30, 252

Yadavs, 56, 56n
Yash, 348
Younis, Mohammed Yakub, 249, 268n
Yugoslavia, 7, 15

Zail Singh, Giani, 350
Zakir Husain, Dr, 167, 242
zamindari system, 235
zamindars, 59, 160, 163; Muslim, 167, 172–3, 182
Zindagi, 242

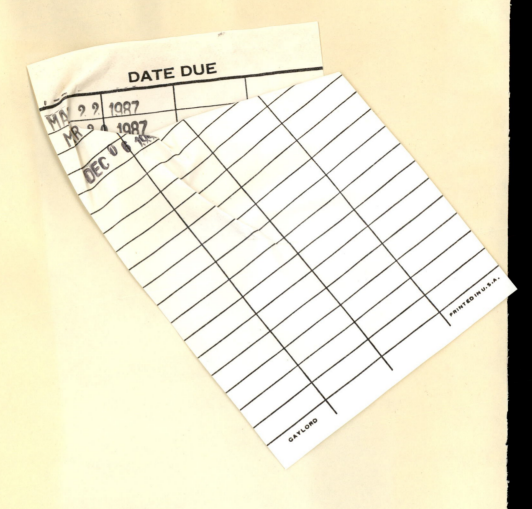

DATE DUE

MA 2 2 1987
MR 2 0 1987
DEC 0 6 198

PRINTED IN U.S.A.

GAYLORD